ACCOUNTING AND FINANCE

FOR NON-SPECIALISTS

Pearson

At Pearson, we have a simple mission: to help people make more of their lives through learning.

We combine innovative learning technology with trusted content and educational expertise to provide engaging and effective learning experiences that serve people wherever and whenever they are learning.

From classroom to boardroom, our curriculum materials, digital learning tools and testing programmes help to educate millions of people worldwide – more than any other private enterprise.

Every day our work helps learning flourish, and wherever learning flourishes, so do people.

To learn more, please visit us at **www.pearson.com/uk**

TENTH EDITION

ACCOUNTING AND FINANCE FOR NON-SPECIALISTS

Peter Atrill
Eddie McLaney

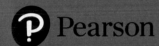

Harlow, England • London • New York • Boston • San Francisco • Toronto • Sydney
Dubai • Singapore • Hong Kong • Tokyo • Seoul • Taipei • New Delhi
Cape Town • São Paulo • Mexico City • Madrid • Amsterdam • Munich • Paris • Milan

PEARSON EDUCATION LIMITED
Edinburgh Gate
Harlow CM20 2JE
United Kingdom
Tel: +44 (0)1279 623623
Web: www.pearson.com/uk

First published 1995 by Prentice Hall Europe (print)
Second edition published 1997 (print)
Third edition published 2001 by Pearson Education Ltd (print)
Fourth edition published 2004 (print)
Fifth edition published 2006 (print)
Sixth edition published 2008 (print)
Seventh edition published 2011 (print)
Eighth edition published 2013 (print and electronic)
Ninth edition published 2015 (print and electronic)
Tenth edition published 2017 (print and electronic)

The Financial Times. With a worldwide network of highly respected journalists, The Financial Times provides global business news, insightful opinion and expert analysis of business, finance and politics. With over 500 journalists reporting from 50 countries worldwide, our in-depth coverage of international news is objectively reported and analysed from an independent, global perspective. To find out more, visit www.ft.com/pearsonoffer.

ISBN: 978-1-292-13560-1 (print)
      978-1-292-13561-8 (PDF)
      978-1-292-13565-6 (ePub)

British Library Cataloguing-in-Publication Data
A catalogue record for the print edition is available from the British Library

Library of Congress Cataloging-in-Publication Data
A catalog record for the print edition is available from the Library of Congress

10 9 8 7 6 5 4 3 2 1
20 19 18 17 16

Front cover image © Getty Images

Print edition typeset in 9/12.5 Helvetica Neue LT W1G by Spi Global
Printed in Slovakia by Neografia

NOTE THAT ANY PAGE CROSS REFERENCES REFER TO THE PRINT EDITION

Brief contents

Contents

3 Measuring and reporting financial performance   71

4 Accounting for limited companies   115

Preface

This book provides an introduction to accounting and finance. It is aimed at:

- Students who are not majoring in accounting or finance but who are, nevertheless, studying introductory-level accounting and finance as part of their course. The course may be in business, economics, hospitality management, tourism, engineering, or some other area. For these students, the book provides an overview of the role and usefulness of accounting and finance within a business.
- Students who are majoring in either accounting or finance. These students should find the book a helpful introduction to the main principles, which can serve as a foundation for further study.

The book does not focus on the technical aspects, but rather considers principles and underlying concepts. It also examines the ways in which financial statements and other financial information may improve the quality of decision making. To reinforce the practical emphasis of the book, there are illustrative extracts from company reports, survey data and other sources throughout.

In this tenth edition, we have made improvements suggested by students and lecturers who used the previous edition. We have also increased the number of diagrams in order to aid learning. Examples from real life have been updated and their number has been increased. Finally, we have improved the range and quality of self-assessment material.

The book is written in an 'open-learning' style. This means that there are numerous integrated activities, worked examples and questions throughout the book to help you to understand the subject fully. You are encouraged to interact with the material and to check your progress continually. Irrespective of whether you are using the book as part of a taught course or for personal study, we have found that this approach is more 'user-friendly' and makes it easier for you to learn.

We recognise that most of you will not have studied accounting or finance before, and we have therefore tried to write in a concise and accessible style, minimising the use of technical jargon. We have also tried to introduce topics gradually, explaining everything as we go. Where technical terminology is unavoidable we try to provide clear explanations. You will find all of the key terms highlighted in the book, and then listed at the end of each chapter with a page reference. All of these key terms are also listed alphabetically, with a concise definition, in the glossary towards the end of the book. This should provide a convenient point of reference from which to revise.

A further important consideration in helping you to understand and absorb the topics covered is the design of the book itself. The page layout and colour scheme have been carefully considered to allow for the easy navigation and digestion of material. The layout features a large page format, an open design, and clear signposting of the various features and assessment material.

We hope that you find the book both readable and helpful.

Peter Atrill
Eddie McLaney

Acknowledgements

We are grateful to the following for permission to reproduce copyright material:

Figures

Figure 3.9 from European Payment Index 2014, www.intrum.com, Intrum Justitia; Figure 4.8 from Guidance on the strategic report p20, https://www.frc.org.uk/Our-Work/Publications/Accounting-and-Reporting-Policy/Guidance-on-the-Strategic-Report.pdf, Financial Reporting Council, © Financial Reporting Council (FRC). All rights reserved. For further information, please visit www.frc.org.uk or call +44 (0)20 7492 2300; Figure 5.6 from BP plc Annual Report 2014 P.18 www.bp.com BP plc; Figure 6.2 adapted from Office of National Statistics, 'Profitability of UK companies Q1 2015, www.statistics.gov.uk 8 July 2015, Crown copyright, © Crown copyright. Contains public sector information licensed under the Open Government Licence (OGL) v3.0. http://www.nationalarchives.gov.uk/doc/open-government-licence/version/3/; Figure 8.11 adapted from *Activity Based Costing: A Review with Case Studies* CIMA Publishing (Innes J. and Mitchell F. 1990) CIMA Reproduced with permission of The Chartered Institute of Management Accountants; Figure 8.12 from A survey of factors influencing the choice of product costing systems in UK organisations *Management Accounting Research* December (Al-Omiri, M. and Drury, C. 2007), Reproduced with permission of The Chartered Institute of Management Accounts; Figure 8.13 adapted from *Management accounting tools for today and tomorrow*, CIMA (2009) 12, Reproduced with permission of The Chartered Institute of Management Accounts; Figure 9.9 adapted from *Management Accounting Tools for Today and Tomorrow CIMA* CIMA (2009) 12, Reproduced with permission of The Chartered Institute of Management Accountants; Figure 11.10 from Office for National Statistics (2015), Ownership of quoted shares for UK domiciled companies 2014, 2 September, Contains public sector information licensed under the Open Government Licence v3.0 http://www.nationalarchives.gov.uk/doc/open-government-licence/version/3/; Figure 12.9 adapted from Table 2 p6 in All Tied Up: Working Capital Management Report 2014, Ernst and Young, p. 7, www.ey.com., Ernst and Young

Text

Real World 1.1 from K. Inagaki Sony seeks delay in releasing full results in wake of cyber attack, 23 January 2015, ft.com, Financial Times, © The Financial Times Limited 2015. All Rights Reserved; Real World 1.2 from www.standardlife.com, accessed 24 October 2015, Standard Life Employee Services Ltd, © 2015 Standard Life reproduced with permission of Standard Life; Real World 1.3 from adapted from Waters, R. Apple has incentive to worry about worker' rights 25 February 2012, ft.com, Financial Times, © The Financial

Times Limited 2012. All Rights Reserved.; Real World 1.4 from Goyder, M. (2009) How we've poisoned the well of wealth, Financial Times, 15 February., ft.com, Financial Times, © The Financial Times Limited 2009. All Rights Reserved; Real World 2.4 from J.Kay Playing dice with your money 4 September 2015, ft.com, Financial Times, © The Financial Times Limited 2015. All Rights Reserved; Real World 2.5 from J. Wilson Anglo American to write down value of mining assets by up to $4bn July 16, 2015 ft.com, Financial Times, © The Financial Times Limited 2015. All Rights Reserved; Real World 2.7 adapted from Balance sheets: the basics accessed 14 April 2010 www.businesslink.gov.uk, Crown Copyright, © Crown copyright. Contains public sector information licensed under the Open Government Licence (OGL) v3.0. http://www.nationalarchives.gov.uk/doc/open-government-licence/version/3/; Real World 3.5 from British Airways Annual Report and Accounts 2008/09 Note 15, www.britishairways.com, British Airways; Real World 4.1 from Urquhart, Lisa (2003) Monotub Industries in a spin as founder gets Titan for £1, Financial Times, 23 January, © The Financial Times Limited 2003. All Rights Reserved; Real World 4.4 adapted from UK Corporate Governance Code, Financial Reporting Council, September 2014, pages 5 and 6, www.frc.org.uk, Financial Reporting Council, © Financial Reporting Council (FRC). All rights reserved. For further information, please visit www.frc. org.uk or call +44 (0)20 7492 2300; Real World 4.5 from Ryanair Holdings plc, Annual Report 2015, p. 156, Ryanair; Real World 4.7 from H. Mance, Betfair admits to £80m pay-outs mistake, 3 August 2014, ft.com, Financial Times, © The Financial Times Limited 2014. All Rights Reserved; Real World 4.8 from Powley T., WS Atkins signals confidence by proposing 8.1% dividend rise, 11 June 2015, ft.com, Financial Times, © The Financial Times Limited 2015. All Rights Reserved; Real World 5.1 from Johnson L., The most dangerous unforced errors 9 July 2013, ft.com, Financial Times, © The Financial Times Limited 2013. All Rights Reserved; Real World 5.2 from John Timpson, The management column, The Daily Telegraph Business, 14 June 2010. copyright © Telegraph Media Group Limited; Real World 5.3 adapted from Tesco plc, Annual Report and Financial Statements 2015, P.87 www.tescoplc.com, Tesco plc; Real World 5.5 from Ryanair Holdings plc Annual Report 2015 Pages 161, 108 and 109; Real World 6.4 adapted from Wild, J. 'Ryanair sees sharp fall in profits due to higher fuel costs', 29 July 2013., ft.com, Financial Times, © The Financial Times Limited 2013. All Rights Reserved; Real World 6.5 from S. Gordon UK small businesses spend £11bn chasing payments 16 July 2015, ft.com, Financial Times, © The Financial Times Limited 2015. All Rights Reserved; Real World 6.6 from Smith,. T (2014) 'How investors ignored the warning signs at Tesco' 5 September, ft. com, Financial Times; Real World 7.1 adapted from Foley, S. Is a university degree a good investment? 7 September 2014, ft.com, Financial Times, © The Financial Times Limited 2014. All Rights Reserved; Real World 8.2 from A survey of factors influencing the choice of product costing systems in UK organisations, *Management Accounting Research,* December, 399–424 (Al-Omiri, M. and Drury, C. 2007), Reprinted with permission of Elsevier; General Displayed Text on page 329 from 2015 annual report, BSkyB Group plc, Sky News; Real World 9.1 from Greene King plc Annual Report 2015, page 40; Real World 10.3 from *RECKONING WITH RISK: LEARNING TO LIVE WITH UNCERTAINTY* (Penguin Press 2003) (Gigerenzer G. 2002) Copyright © Gerd Gigerenzer, 2003. Reproduced by permission of Penguin Books Ltd and CALCULATED RISKS: How to know when numbers Deceive by Gerd Gigerenzer. Copyright © 2002 by Gerd Gigerenzer.

Chapter 1

INTRODUCTION TO ACCOUNTING AND FINANCE

INTRODUCTION

Welcome to the world of accounting and finance! In this opening chapter, we provide a broad outline of these subjects. We begin by considering the roles of accounting and finance and then go on to identify the main users of financial information. We shall see how both accounting and finance can be valuable tools in helping users improve the quality of their decisions. In subsequent chapters, we develop this decision-making theme by examining in some detail the kinds of financial reports and methods used to aid decision making.

For many of you, accounting and finance are not the main focus of your studies and you may well be asking, 'Why do I need to study these subjects?' So, after we have considered the key features of accounting and finance, we shall go on to discuss why some understanding of them is likely to be important to you.

Learning outcomes

When you have completed this chapter, you should be able to:

- explain the nature and roles of accounting and finance;
- identify the main users of financial information and discuss their needs;
- distinguish between financial accounting and management accounting;
- explain why an understanding of accounting and finance is likely to be relevant to your needs.

WHAT ARE ACCOUNTING AND FINANCE?

Let us begin by trying to understand the purpose of each. **Accounting** is concerned with *collecting, analysing* and *communicating* financial information. The ultimate aim is to help those using this information to make more informed decisions. Unless the financial information being communicated can lead to better decisions being made, there really is no point in producing it.

Sometimes the impression is given that the purpose of accounting is simply to prepare financial (accounting) reports on a regular basis. While it is true that accountants undertake this kind of work, it does not represent an end in itself. As already mentioned, the ultimate aim of the accountant's work is to give users financial information to improve the quality of their decisions. This decision-making perspective of accounting provides the theme for this book and shapes the way in which we deal with each topic.

Finance (or **financial management**), like accounting, exists to help decision makers. It is concerned with the ways in which funds for a business are raised and invested. This lies at the very heart of what business is about. In essence, a business exists to raise funds from investors (owners and lenders) and then to use those funds to make investments (in equipment, premises, inventories and so on) in order to create wealth. As businesses often raise and invest large amounts over long periods, the quality of the financing and investment decisions can have a profound impact on their fortunes.

Funds raised may take various forms and the particular forms chosen should fit with the needs of the business. An understanding of finance should help in identifying:

- the main forms of finance available;
- the costs and benefits of each form of finance;
- the risks associated with each form of finance; and
- the role of financial markets in supplying finance.

Once funds have been raised, they must be invested in a suitable way. When deciding between the investment opportunities available, an understanding of finance can help in evaluating the risks and returns associated with each opportunity.

There is little point in trying to make a sharp distinction between accounting and finance; we have seen that both are concerned with the financial aspects of decision making. Furthermore, there are many overlaps and interconnections between the two areas. Financial (accounting) reports, for example, are a major source of information when making financing and investment decisions.

WHO ARE THE USERS OF ACCOUNTING INFORMATION?

For accounting information to be useful, the accountant must be clear *for whom* the information is being prepared and *for what purpose* it will be used. There are likely to be various groups of people (usually known as 'user groups') with an interest in a particular organisation, in the sense of needing to make decisions about it. For the typical private sector business, the more important of these groups are shown in Figure 1.1. Take a look at this figure and then try Activity 1.1.

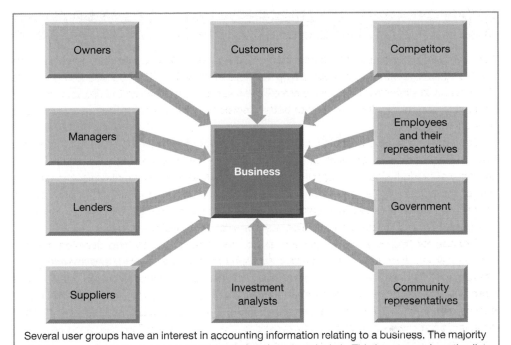

Several user groups have an interest in accounting information relating to a business. The majority of these are outside the business but nevertheless have a stake in it. This is not an exhaustive list of potential users; however, those groups identified are normally the most important.

Figure 1.1 Main users of financial information relating to a business

Activity 1.1

Ptarmigan Insurance plc (PI) is a large motor insurance business. Taking the user groups identified in Figure 1.1, suggest, for each group, the sorts of decisions likely to be made about PI and the factors to be taken into account when making these decisions.

Your answer may be along the following lines:

User group	Decision
Customers	Whether to take further motor policies with PI. This might involve an assessment of PI's ability to continue in business and to meet customers' needs, particularly in respect of any insurance claims made.
Competitors	How best to compete against PI or, perhaps, whether to leave the market on the grounds that it is not possible to compete profitably with PI. This may involve competitors using various aspects of PI's performance as a 'benchmark' when evaluating their own performance. They may also try to assess PI's financial strength and to identify changes that may signal PI's future intentions (for example, raising funds as a prelude to market expansion).

→

User group	Decision
Employees	Whether to continue working for PI and, if so, whether to demand higher rewards for doing so. The future plans, profits and financial strength of the business are likely to be of particular interest when making these decisions.
Government	Whether PI should pay tax and, if so, how much, whether it complies with agreed pricing policies, whether financial support is needed and so on. In making these decisions an assessment of PI's profits, sales revenues and financial strength would be made.
Community representatives	Whether to allow PI to expand its premises and/or whether to provide economic support for the business. When making these decisions, PI's ability to provide employment for the community, its use of community resources and its willingness to fund environmental improvements are likely to be important considerations.
Investment analysts	Whether to advise clients to invest in PI. This would involve an evaluation of the likely risks and future returns associated with PI.
Suppliers	Whether to continue to supply PI and, if so, whether to supply on credit. This would require an assessment of PI's ability to pay for goods and services supplied at the due dates.
Lenders	Whether to lend money to PI and/or whether to demand repayment of any existing loans. PI's ability to pay the interest due and to repay the principal sum on time would be important factors in such decisions.
Managers	Whether the performance of the business needs to be improved. Performance to date would be compared with earlier plans or some other 'benchmark' to decide whether action needs to be taken. Managers may also wish to consider a change in PI's future direction. This may involve determining whether it has the financial flexibility and resources to take on new challenges.
Owners	Whether to invest more in PI or to sell all, or part, of the investment currently held. As with investment analysts (see above) this would involve an evaluation of the likely risks and returns associated with PI. Owners may also have to decide on the rewards offered to senior managers. When doing so, the financial performance and position of the business would normally be considered.

Although this answer covers many of the key points, you may have identified other decisions and/or other factors to be taken into account by each group.

PROVIDING A SERVICE

One way of viewing accounting is as a form of service. The user groups identified in Figure 1.1 can be seen as the 'clients' and the accounting (financial) information produced can be seen as the service provided. The value of this service to the various 'clients' can be judged according to whether the accounting information meets their needs.

To be useful to users, the information provided must possess certain qualities. In particular, it must be relevant and it must faithfully represent what it is supposed to represent. These two qualities, **relevance** and **faithful representation**, are regarded as fundamental qualities and are explained in more detail below:

- **Relevance**. Accounting information should make a difference. That is, it should be capable of influencing user decisions. To do this, it must help to *predict future events* (such as predicting next year's profit), or help to *confirm past events* (such as establishing last year's profit), or do both. By confirming past events, users can check on the accuracy of their earlier predictions. This can, in turn, help them to improve the ways in which they make predictions in the future.

To be relevant, accounting information must cross a threshold of **materiality**. An item of information should be considered material, or significant, if its omission or misstatement could alter the decisions that users make.

Activity 1.2

Do you think that what is material for one business will also be material for all other businesses?

No, it will normally vary from one business to the next. What is material will depend on factors such as the size of the business, the nature of the information and the amounts involved.

Ultimately, what is considered material is a matter of judgement. In making this judgement, managers should consider how the information is likely to be used by the various user groups.

Where a piece of information is not considered to be material, it should not be included within the accounting reports. It will merely clutter them up and, perhaps, interfere with the users' ability to interpret them.

- **Faithful representation**. Accounting information should represent what it is supposed to represent. To do this, the information should be *complete.* In other words, it should reflect all of the information needed to understand what is being portrayed. It should also be *neutral,* which means that the information should be presented and selected without bias. Finally, it should be *free from error.* This is not the same as saying that it must always be perfectly accurate; this is not really possible. Estimates may have to be made that eventually turn out to be inaccurate. It does mean, however, that there should be no errors in the way in which the estimates are prepared and described.

Accounting information must contain both of these fundamental qualities if it is to be useful. There is little point in producing information that is relevant but lacks faithful representation, or producing information that is irrelevant, even if it is faithfully represented.

Further qualities

Where accounting information is both relevant and faithfully represented, there are other qualities that, if present, can enhance its usefulness. These are **comparability**, **verifiability**, **timeliness** and **understandability**. Each of these qualities is now considered.

- **Comparability**. Users of accounting information often want to make comparisons. They may want to compare performance of the business over time (such as profit this year compared with last year). They may also want to compare certain aspects of business performance with those of similar businesses (such as the level of sales achieved during the year). Better comparisons can be made where the accounting system treats items that are basically the same in the same way and where policies for measuring and presenting accounting information are made clear.
- **Verifiability**. This quality provides assurance to users that the accounting information provided faithfully represents what it is supposed to represent. Accounting information is verifiable where different, independent experts would be able to agree that it provides a faithful portrayal. Verifiable information tends to be supported by evidence.
- **Timeliness**. Accounting information should be produced in time for users to make their decisions. A lack of timeliness will undermine the usefulness of the information. Normally, the later accounting information is produced, the less useful it becomes.
- **Understandability**. Accounting information should be set out as clearly and concisely as possible. It should also be understood by those for whom the information is provided.

It is probably best that we regard accounting reports in the same way that we regard a report written in a foreign language. To understand either of these, we need to have had some preparation. When producing accounting reports, it is normally assumed that the user not only has a reasonable knowledge of business and accounting but is also prepared to invest some time in studying the reports. Nevertheless, the onus is clearly on accountants to provide information in a way that makes it as understandable as possible to non-accountants.

It is worth emphasising that the four qualities just discussed cannot make accounting information useful; they can only enhance the usefulness of information that is already relevant and faithfully represented.

WEIGHING UP THE COSTS AND BENEFITS

Even when a piece of accounting information may have all the qualities described, it does not automatically mean that it should be collected and reported to users. There is still one more hurdle to jump. Consider Activity 1.5.

Activity 1.5

Suppose an item of information is capable of being provided. It is relevant to a particular decision and can be faithfully represented. It is also comparable, verifiable, timely and could be understood by the decision maker.

Can you think of a good reason why, in practice, you might decide not to produce the information?

You may judge the cost of doing so to be greater than the potential benefit of having the information. This cost–benefit issue will limit the amount of accounting information provided.

In theory, a particular item of accounting information should be produced only if the costs of providing it are less than the benefits, or value, to be derived from its use. In practice, however, these costs and benefits are difficult to assess.

To illustrate the practical problems of establishing the value of information, let us assume that we accidentally reversed our car into a wall in a car park. This resulted in a dented boot and scraped paintwork. We would like the dent taken out and the paintwork re-sprayed at a local garage. We know that the nearest garage would charge £350 but we believe that other local garages may offer to do the job for a lower price. The only way of finding out the prices at other garages is to visit them, so that they can see the extent of the damage. Visiting the garages will involve using some fuel and will take up some of our time. Is it worth the cost of finding out the price for the job at the various local garages? The answer, as we have seen, is that if the cost of discovering the price is less than the potential benefit, it is worth having that information.

To identify the various prices for the job, there are several points to be considered, including:

- How many garages shall we visit?
- What is the cost of fuel to visit each garage?
- How long will it take to make all the garage visits?
- At what price do we value our time?

The economic benefit of having the information on the price of the job is probably even harder to assess in advance. The following points need to be considered:

- What is the cheapest price that we might be quoted for the job?
- How likely is it that we shall be quoted a price cheaper than £350?

As we can imagine, the answers to these questions may be far from clear – remember that we have only contacted the nearest garage so far. When assessing the value of accounting information we are confronted with similar problems.

Producing accounting information can be very costly. The costs, however, are often difficult to quantify. Direct, out-of-pocket costs, such as salaries of accounting staff, are not usually a problem, but these are only part of the total costs involved. There are other costs such as the cost of users' time spent on analysing and interpreting the information provided.

Activity 1.6

What about the economic benefits of producing accounting information? Do you think it is easier, or harder, to assess the economic benefits of accounting information than to assess the costs of producing it?

It is normally much harder to assess the economic benefits. We must bear in mind that accounting information will be only one factor influencing a decision; other factors will also be taken into account. Furthermore, the precise weight attached to each factor when making the decision cannot normally be established.

There are no easy answers to the problem of weighing costs and benefits. Although it is possible to apply some 'science' to the problem, a lot of subjective judgement is normally involved.

The qualities, or characteristics, influencing the usefulness of accounting information, discussed above are summarised in Figure 1.2.

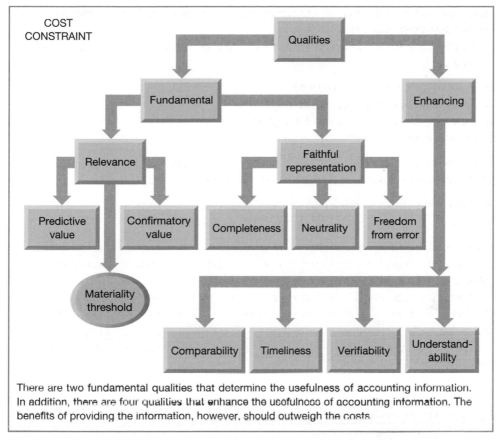

There are two fundamental qualities that determine the usefulness of accounting information. In addition, there are four qualities that enhance the usefulness of accounting information. The benefits of providing the information, however, should outweigh the costs.

Figure 1.2 The qualities that influence the usefulness of accounting information

ACCOUNTING AS AN INFORMATION SYSTEM

We have already seen that accounting can be viewed as the provision of a service to 'clients'. Another way of viewing accounting is as a part of the business's total information system. Users, both inside and outside the business, make decisions concerning the allocation of scarce resources. For these resources to be efficiently allocated, they often need financial (accounting) information on which to base decisions. It is the role of the accounting system to provide this information.

The **accounting information system** should have certain features that are common to all information systems within a business. These are:

- identifying and capturing relevant information (in this case financial information);
- recording, in a systematic way, the information collected;
- analysing and interpreting the information collected; and
- reporting the information in a manner that suits users' needs.

The relationship between these features is set out in Figure 1.3.

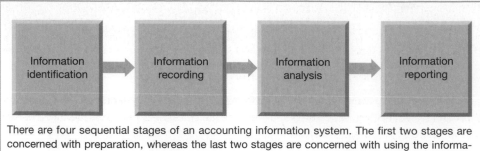

There are four sequential stages of an accounting information system. The first two stages are concerned with preparation, whereas the last two stages are concerned with using the information collected.

Figure 1.3 The accounting information system

Given the decision-making emphasis of this book, we shall be concerned primarily with the final two elements of the process: the analysis and reporting of financial information. We shall focus on the way in which information is used by, and is useful to, users rather than the way in which it is identified and recorded.

Most businesses rely on computerised systems to process financial information. When these systems fail, it can be both costly and disruptive. **Real World 1.1** describes the problems experienced by Sony Corporation, the electronics and entertainments business, following a cyber attack from an outside source.

REAL WORLD 1.1

Hacked off

The fallout of the November 2014 cyber attack on Sony continued, as the Japanese group said it expects to delay the release of its full financial results due to continuing system disruptions at its movie studio. In a statement on Friday, the company said the financial and accounting systems of Sony Pictures will not be fully restored until early next month after they were damaged by the attack, which the US government has blamed on North Korea. It added that the studio was taking care to avoid further damage by prematurely restarting its systems.

Pyongyang has denied responsibility of the hacking which came as Sony was preparing to release *The Interview*, a comedy about an assassination attempt on Kim Jong Un, North Korea's leader.

Sony asked Japanese financial regulators to extend the deadline for submitting its third-quarter earnings to the end of March from mid-February, citing 'the amount of destruction and disruption that occurred'.

FT

Source: Extract from Inagaki, K. (2015) 'Sony seeks delay in releasing full results in wake of cyber attack', ft.com, 23 January.
© The Financial Times Limited 2015. All Rights Reserved.

MANAGEMENT ACCOUNTING AND FINANCIAL ACCOUNTING

Accounting is usually seen as having two distinct strands. These are:

- **management accounting**, which seeks to meet the accounting needs of managers; and
- **financial accounting**, which seeks to meet the needs of the other users identified earlier in the chapter (see Figure 1.1).

The difference in their targeted user groups has led each strand of accounting to develop along different lines. The main areas of difference are as follows:

- *Nature of the reports produced.* Financial accounting reports tend to be general-purpose. Although they are aimed primarily at providers of finance such as owners and lenders, they contain financial information that will be useful for a broad range of users and decisions. Management accounting reports, meanwhile, are often specific-purpose reports. They are designed with a particular decision in mind and/or for a particular manager.
- *Level of detail.* Financial accounting reports provide users with a broad overview of the performance and position of the business for a period. As a result, information is aggregated (that is, added together) and detail is often lost. Management accounting reports, however, often provide managers with considerable detail to help them with a particular operational decision.
- *Regulations.* The financial accounting reports of many businesses are subject to regulations imposed by the law and by accounting rule makers. These regulations often require a standard content and, perhaps, a standard format to be adopted. Management accounting reports, on the other hand, are not subject to regulation and can be designed to meet the needs of particular managers.

Activity 1.7

Why do you think management accounting reports are not subject to the same regulations imposed on financial accounting reports?

Management accounting reports are produced exclusively for managers and are for internal use only. Financial accounting reports, on the other hand, are for external publication. To protect external users, who depend on the quality of information provided by the business, they are subject to regulation.

- *Reporting interval.* For most businesses, financial accounting reports are produced on an annual basis, though some large businesses produce half-yearly reports and a few produce quarterly ones. Management accounting reports will be produced as frequently as needed by managers. A sales manager, for example, may need routine sales reports on a daily, weekly or monthly basis so as to monitor performance closely. Special-purpose reports can also be prepared when the occasion demands: for example, where an evaluation is required of a proposed investment in new equipment.

- *Time orientation.* Financial accounting reports reveal the performance and position of a business for the past period. In essence, they are backward-looking. Management accounting reports, on the other hand, often provide information concerning future performance as well as past performance. It is an oversimplification, however, to suggest that financial accounting reports never incorporate expectations concerning the future. Occasionally, businesses will release forward-looking information to other users in an attempt to raise finance or to fight off unwanted takeover bids. Even preparation of financial accounting reports for the past period typically requires making some judgements about the future, as we shall see in Chapter 3.

- *Range and quality of information.* Two key points are worth mentioning. First, financial accounting reports concentrate on information that can be quantified in monetary terms. Management accounting also produces such reports, but is also more likely to produce reports that contain information of a non-financial nature, such as physical volume of inventories, number of sales orders received, number of new products launched, physical output per employee and so on. Second, financial accounting places greater emphasis on the use of objective, verifiable evidence when preparing reports. Management accounting reports may use information that is less objective and verifiable, but nevertheless provide managers with the information they need.

We can see from this that management accounting is less constrained than financial accounting. It may draw from a variety of sources and use information that has varying degrees of reliability. The only real test to be applied when assessing the value of the information produced for managers is whether or not it improves the quality of the decisions made.

The main differences between financial accounting and management accounting are summarised in Figure 1.4.

The differences between management accounting and financial accounting suggest differences in the information needs of managers and those of other users. While differences undoubtedly exist, there is also a good deal of overlap between the information needs of both.

Activity 1.8

Can you think of any areas of overlap between the information needs of managers and those of other users? (*Hint*: Think about the time orientation and the level of detail of accounting information.)

Two points that spring to mind are:

- Managers will, at times, be interested in receiving a historical overview of business operations of the sort provided to other users.
- Other users would be interested in receiving detailed information relating to the future, such as the planned level of profits, and non-financial information, such as the state of the sales order book and the extent of product innovations.

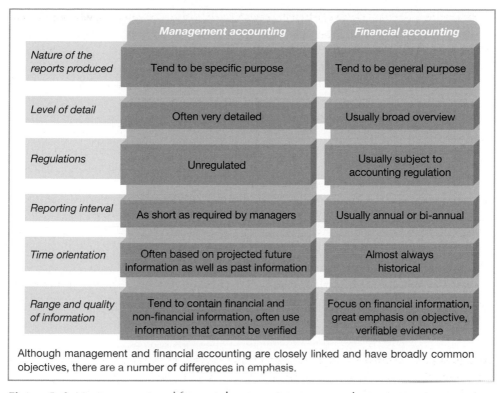

	Management accounting	Financial accounting
Nature of the reports produced	Tend to be specific purpose	Tend to be general purpose
Level of detail	Often very detailed	Usually broad overview
Regulations	Unregulated	Usually subject to accounting regulation
Reporting interval	As short as required by managers	Usually annual or bi-annual
Time orientation	Often based on projected future information as well as past information	Almost always historical
Range and quality of information	Tend to contain financial and non-financial information, often use information that cannot be verified	Focus on financial information, great emphasis on objective, verifiable evidence

Although management and financial accounting are closely linked and have broadly common objectives, there are a number of differences in emphasis.

Figure 1.4 Management and financial accounting compared

To some extent, differences between the two strands of accounting reflect differences in access to financial information. Managers have much more control over the form and content of the information that they receive. Other users have to rely on what managers are prepared to provide or what financial reporting regulations insist must be provided. Although the scope of financial accounting reports has increased over time, fears concerning loss of competitive advantage and user ignorance about the reliability of forecast data have meant that other users do not receive the same detailed and wide-ranging information as that available to managers.

SCOPE OF THIS BOOK

This book covers both financial accounting and management accounting topics. The next five chapters (Part 1, Chapters 2 to 6) are broadly concerned with financial accounting, and the following three (Part 2, Chapters 7 to 9) with management accounting. The final part of the book (Part 3, Chapters 10 to 12) is concerned with the financial management of the business, that is, with issues relating to the financing and investing activities of the business.

THE CHANGING FACE OF ACCOUNTING

Over the past four decades, the business environment has become increasingly turbulent and competitive. Various reasons have been put forward to explain these changes, including:

- the increasing sophistication of customers;
- the development of a global economy where national frontiers become less important;
- rapid changes in technology;
- the deregulation of domestic markets (for example, electricity, water and gas);
- increasing pressure from owners (shareholders) for competitive economic returns; and
- the increasing volatility of financial markets.

This new, more complex environment has brought fresh challenges for managers and other users of accounting information. Their needs have changed and both financial accounting and management accounting have had to respond. This has led to a radical review of the kind of information to be reported.

The changing business environment has given added impetus to the search for a clear conceptual framework, or framework of principles, upon which to base financial accounting reports. Various attempts have been made to clarify their purpose and to provide a more solid foundation for the development of accounting rules. The conceptual frameworks that have been developed try to address fundamental questions such as:

- Who are the users of financial accounting information?
- What kinds of financial accounting reports should be prepared and what should they contain?
- How should items such as profit and asset values be measured?

The internationalisation of businesses has created a need for accounting rules to have an international reach. It can no longer be assumed that users of accounting information are based in the country in which the particular business operates or are familiar with the accounting rules of that country. Thus, there has been increasing harmonisation of accounting rules across national frontiers.

Activity 1.9

How should the harmonisation of accounting rules benefit:
(a) An international investor?
(b) An international business?

An international investor should benefit because accounting terms and policies used in preparing financial accounting reports will not vary across countries. This should make the comparison of performance between businesses operating in different countries much easier.

An international business should benefit because the cost of producing accounting reports in order to comply with the rules of different countries can be expensive. Harmonisation can, therefore, lead to significant cost savings. It may also broaden the appeal of the business among international investors. Where there are common accounting rules, they may have greater confidence to invest.

In response to criticisms that the financial reports of some businesses are opaque and difficult for users to interpret, great efforts have been made to improve reporting rules. Accounting rule makers have tried to ensure that the accounting policies of businesses are more comparable and more transparent and that the financial reports portray economic reality more faithfully.

Management accounting has also changed by becoming more outward-looking in its focus. In the past, information provided to managers has been largely restricted to that collected within the business. However, the attitude and behaviour of customers and rival businesses have now become the object of much information-gathering. Increasingly, successful businesses are those that are able to secure and maintain competitive advantage over their rivals.

To obtain this advantage, businesses have become more 'customer driven' (that is, concerned with satisfying customer needs). This has led to the production of management accounting information that provides details of customers and the market, such as customer evaluation of services provided and market share. In addition, information about the costs and profits of rival businesses, which can be used as 'benchmarks' by which to gauge competitiveness, is gathered and reported.

To compete successfully, businesses must also find ways of managing costs. The cost base of modern businesses is under continual review and this, in turn, has led to the development of more sophisticated methods of measuring and controlling costs.

WHY DO I NEED TO KNOW ANYTHING ABOUT ACCOUNTING AND FINANCE?

At this point you may well be asking yourself, 'Why do I need to study accounting and finance? I don't intend to become an accountant!' Well, from the explanation of what accounting and finance is about, which has broadly been the subject of this chapter so far, it should be clear that the accounting/finance function within a business is a central part of its management information system. On the basis of information provided by the system, managers make decisions concerning the allocation of resources. These decisions may concern whether to:

- continue with certain business operations;
- invest in particular projects; or
- sell particular products.

These decisions can have a profound effect on all those connected with the business.

It is important, therefore, that *all* those who intend to work in a business should have a fairly clear idea of certain important aspects of accounting and finance. These aspects include:

- how financial reports should be read and interpreted;
- how financial plans are made;

- how investment decisions are made;
- how businesses are financed; and
- how costs are managed.

Many, perhaps most, students have a career goal of being a manager within a business – perhaps a human resources manager, production manager, marketing manager or IT manager. If you are one of these students, an understanding of accounting and finance is very important. When you become a manager, even a junior one, it is almost certain that you will have to use financial reports to help you to carry out your role. It is equally certain that it is partly, perhaps largely, on the basis of financial information and reports that your performance as a manager will be judged.

As part of your management role, it is likely that you will be expected to help in plotting the future path of the business. This will often involve the preparation of forward-looking financial reports and setting financial targets. If you do not understand what the financial reports really mean and the extent to which the financial information is reliable, you will find yourself at a distinct disadvantage to those who do. Along with other managers, you will also be expected to help decide how the limited resources available to the business should be allocated between competing options. This will require an ability to evaluate the costs and benefits of the different options available. Once again, an understanding of accounting and finance is important to carrying out this task.

This is not to say that you cannot be an effective and successful human resources production, marketing or IT manager unless you are also a qualified accountant. It does mean, however, that you need to become a bit 'streetwise' in accounting and finance if you are to succeed. This book aims to give you that street wisdom.

THE QUEST FOR WEALTH CREATION

A business is normally formed to enhance the wealth of its owners. Throughout this book we shall assume that this is its main objective. This may come as a surprise, as other objectives might be pursued that would fulfil the needs of others with a stake in the business. A business may, for example, seek to provide good working conditions for its employees, or it may seek to conserve the environment for the local community. While it may pursue these objectives, it is normally set up primarily with a view to increasing the wealth of its owners. In practice, the behaviour of businesses over time appears to be consistent with this objective.

Within a market economy there are strong competitive forces at work that ensure that failure to enhance owners' wealth will not be tolerated for long. Competition for the funds provided by the owners and competition for managers' jobs will normally mean that the owners' interests will prevail. If the managers do not provide the expected increase in ownership wealth, the owners have the power to replace the existing management team with a new team that is more responsive to the owners' needs.

MEETING THE NEEDS OF OTHER STAKEHOLDERS

The points made above do not mean that the needs of other groups with a stake in a business, such as employees, customers, suppliers, the community and so on, are unimportant. In fact, the opposite is true, if the business wishes to survive and prosper over the longer term. For example, a business with disaffected customers may well find that they turn to another supplier, resulting in a loss of owners' wealth. **Real World 1.2** provides examples of businesses that acknowledge the vital link between satisfying customers' needs and creating wealth for their owners (shareholders).

REAL WORLD 1.2

Standard practice

Standard Life, a leading long-term savings and investment business, states its approach as follows:

> We have a clear strategy. We will continue to drive shareholder value through being a leading, customer-centric business, focused on long-term savings and investment propositions. This means finding, acquiring and retaining valuable customers for mutual and sustained financial benefit.

Cheers!

Mitchells and Butlers plc is a leading restaurant and pub owner. It states:

> Our vision is to run businesses that guests (customers) love to eat and drink in, and as a result grow shareholder value.

Sources: Standard Life plc, www.standardlife.com, accessed 24 October 2015; and Mitchells and Butlers plc, www.mbplc.com, accessed 25 October 2015.

Other stakeholders that contribute towards the wealth-creation process must also be considered. A dissatisfied workforce can lead to low productivity and strikes while dissatisfied suppliers can withhold vital supplies, or give lower priority to orders received. A discontented community can withdraw access to community resources. In each case, the owners' wealth will suffer.

Real World 1.3 describes how one well-known business became concerned with how labour 'sweatshop' practices could damage its brand and lead to a reduction in owners' wealth.

Upsetting the Apple cart

Imagine a company generating an extra $1.5 billion in sales every week compared to what it earned only a year ago – and nearly all of that coming from products that it had dreamt up from scratch within the last half decade. These were things the world didn't know until recently that it needed. This gives some idea of the enormity of Apple's recent success on the back of the iPhone and iPad.

This surge in demand, however, has consequences. In late 2010, it was shipping 1.8 million shiny new iPhones and iPads a week. A year later, it had upped that weekly quota by nearly 1.5 million – and still couldn't satisfy demand. This has created one of the great historic challenges of manufacturing. The supply chain of the electronics industry, with its hub in south China, was already one of the most impressive manifestations of the forces that have brought a new, globally distributed workforce into play. But this system is now being tested in the extreme.

Apple's handling of the supply chain labour problems are a central concern, not just for its own future but for the industry at large. Its scale and conspicuous brand have brought it unwelcome attention. But it is already ahead of its main rivals in trying to grapple with the underage labour, excessive forced overtime and inadequate safety standards that continue to be alleged against it – and the new standards it is helping to set will be felt across the industry.

Transparency appears to be one problem. Apple executives argue strenuously that they audit suppliers thoroughly and have identified any problems. Tim Cook, chief executive, says that he gets weekly data on the working hours put in by 500,000 workers around the world. Yet independent investigations – most recently one by the New York Times – continue to point to significant shortcomings.

Apple's leaders certainly have plenty of incentive to get to the root of this problem. The consequences of failing to deal with it would be significant. As Nike and Reebok found a decade ago, customers can rebel against brands associated with sweatshop practices. For Apple's brand to thrive as it moves into its new phase of global manufacturing superpower it will have to show that their company is dedicated to the betterment of a large slice of the world's working population.

It is clear from the above that creating wealth for the owners is not the same as trying to maximise the current year's profit. Wealth creation is concerned with the longer term; it relates not only to this year's profit but to that of future years as well. In the short term, corners can be cut and risks taken that improve current profit at the expense of future profit.

Real World 1.4 provides some examples of how the focus on short-term profit, without any consideration of the long-term consequences, can be very damaging.

Short-term gains, long-term problems

For many years, under the guise of defending capitalism, we have been allowing ourselves to degrade it. We have been poisoning the well from which we have drawn wealth. We have misunderstood the importance of values to capitalism. We have surrendered to the idea that success is pursued by making as much money as the law allowed without regard to how it was made.

Thirty years ago, retailers would be quite content to source the shoes they wanted to sell as cheaply as possible. The working conditions of those who produced them was not their concern. Then headlines and protests developed. Society started to hold them responsible for previously invisible working conditions. Companies like Nike went through a transformation. They realised they were polluting their brand. Global sourcing became visible. It was no longer viable to define success simply in terms of buying at the lowest price and selling at the highest.

Financial services and investment are today where footwear was thirty years ago. Public anger at the crisis will make visible what was previously hidden. Take the building up of huge portfolios of loans to poor people on US trailer parks. These loans were authorised without proper scrutiny of the circumstances of the borrowers. Somebody else then deemed them fit to be securitised and so on through credit default swaps and the rest without anyone seeing the transaction in terms of its ultimate human origin.

Each of the decision makers thought it okay to act like the thoughtless footwear buyer of the 1970s. The price was attractive. There was money to make on the deal. Was it responsible? Irrelevant. It was legal, and others were making money that way. And the consequences for the banking system if everybody did it? Not our problem.

The consumer has had a profound shock. Surely we could have expected the clever and wise people who invested our money to be better at risk management than they have shown themselves to be in the present crisis? How could they have been so gullible in not challenging the bankers whose lending proved so flaky? How could they have believed that the levels of bonuses that were, at least in part, coming out of their savings could have been justified in 'incentivising' a better performance? How could they have believed that a 'better' performance would be one that is achieved for one bank without regard to its effect on the whole banking system? Where was the stewardship from those exercising investment on their behalf?

The answer has been that very few of them do exercise that stewardship. Most have stood back and said it doesn't really pay them to do so. The failure of stewardship comes from the same mindset that created the irresponsible lending in the first place. We are back to the mindset that has allowed us to poison the well: never mind the health of the system as a whole, I'm making money out of it at the moment. Responsibility means awareness for the system consequences of our actions. It is not a luxury. It is the cornerstone of prudence.

 Source: Extract from Goyder, M. (2009) 'How we've poisoned the well of wealth', *Financial Times*, 15 February.
© The Financial Times Limited 2009. All Rights Reserved.

BALANCING RISK AND RETURN

All decision making involves the future and financial decision making is no exception. The only thing certain about the future, however, is that we cannot be sure what will happen. Things may not turn out as planned and this risk must be carefully considered when making financial decisions.

As in other aspects of life, risk and return tend to be related. Evidence shows that returns relate to risk in something like the way shown in Figure 1.5.

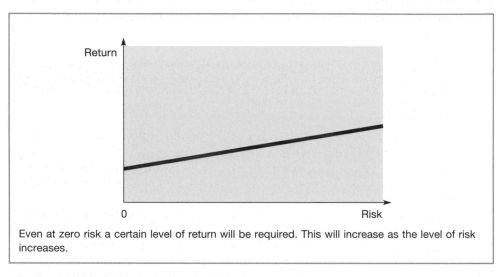

Even at zero risk a certain level of return will be required. This will increase as the level of risk increases.

Figure 1.5 Relationship between risk and return

Activity 1.10

Look at Figure 1.5 and state, in broad terms, where an investment in:

(a) a UK government savings account, and
(b) a lottery ticket

should be placed on the risk–return line.

A UK government savings account is normally a very safe investment. Even if the government were in financial difficulties, it may well be able to print more money to repay investors. Returns from this form of investment, however, are normally very low. Investing in a lottery ticket runs a high risk of losing the whole amount invested. This is because the probability of winning is normally very low. However, a winning ticket can produce enormous returns. Thus, the government savings account should be placed towards the far left of the risk–return line and the lottery ticket towards the far right.

This relationship between risk and return has important implications for setting financial objectives for a business. The owners will require a minimum return to induce them to invest at all, but will require an additional return to compensate for taking risks; the higher the risk, the higher the required return. Managers must be aware of this and must strike the appropriate balance between risk and return when setting objectives and pursuing particular courses of action.

The turmoil in the banking sector has shown, however, that the right balance is not always struck. Some banks have taken excessive risks in pursuit of higher returns and, as a consequence, have incurred massive losses. They are now being kept afloat with taxpayers' money. **Real World 1.5** discusses the collapse of one leading bank, in which the UK government took a majority stake, and argues that the risk appetite of banks must now change.

REAL WORLD 1.5

Banking on change

The taxpayer has become the majority shareholder in the Royal Bank of Scotland (RBS). This change in ownership, resulting from the huge losses sustained by the bank, will shape the future decisions made by its managers. This does not simply mean that it will affect the amount that the bank lends to homeowners and businesses. Rather it is about the amount of risk that it will be prepared to take in pursuit of higher returns.

In the past, those managing banks such as RBS saw themselves as producers of financial products that enabled banks to grow faster than the economy as a whole. They did not want to be seen as simply part of the infrastructure of the economy. It was too dull. It was far more exciting to be seen as creators of financial products that created huge profits and, at the same time, benefited us all through unlimited credit at low rates of interest. These financial products, with exotic names such as 'collateralised debt obligations' and 'credit default swaps', ultimately led to huge losses that taxpayers had to absorb in order to prevent the banks collapsing.

Now that many banks throughout the world are in taxpayers' hands, they are destined to lead a much quieter life. They will have to focus more on the basics such as taking deposits, transferring funds and making simple loans to customers. Is that such a bad thing?

The history of banking has reflected a tension between carrying out banks' core functions and the quest for high returns through high-risk strategies. It seems, however, that for some time to come banks will have to concentrate on the former and will be unable to speculate with depositors' cash.

Source: Based on information in 'We own Royal Bank', Robert Peston, 28 November 2008, BBC News, www.bbc.co.uk.

NOT-FOR-PROFIT ORGANISATIONS

Although the focus of this book is accounting as it relates to private sector businesses, there are many organisations that do not exist mainly for the pursuit of profit.

Can you think of at least four types of organisation that are not primarily concerned with making profits?

We thought of the following:

- charities;
- clubs and associations;
- universities;
- local government authorities;
- national government departments;
- churches; and
- trade unions.

You may have thought of others.

All of these organisations need to produce accounting information for decision-making purposes. Once again, various user groups need this information to help them to make decisions. These user groups are often the same as, or similar to, those identified for private sector businesses. They may have a stake in the future viability of the organisation and may use accounting information to check that the wealth of the organisation is being properly controlled and used in a way that is consistent with its objectives.

Real World 1.6 provides an example of the importance of accounting to relief agencies, which are, of course, not-for-profit organisations.

REAL WORLD 1.6

Accounting for disasters

In the aftermath of the Asian tsunami more than £400 million was raised from charitable donations. It was important that this huge amount of money for aid and reconstruction was used as efficiently and effectively as possible. That did not just mean medical staff and engineers. It also meant accountants.

The charity that exerts financial control over aid donations is Mango: Management Accounting for Non-Governmental Organisations (NGOs). It provides accountants in the field and it provides the back-up, such as financial training and all the other services that should result in really robust financial management in a disaster area.

The world of aid has changed completely as a result of the tsunami. According to Mango's director, Alex Jacobs, 'Accounting is just as important as blankets. Agencies have been aware of this for years. But when you move on to a bigger scale there is more pressure to show the donations are being used appropriately.'

More recently, the earthquake in Haiti led to a call from Mango for French-speaking accountants to help support the relief programme and to help in the longer-term rebuilding of Haiti.

Sources: Adapted from Bruce, R. (2005) 'Tsunami: finding the right figures for disaster relief', ft.com, 7 March; Bruce, R. (2006) 'The work of Mango: coping with generous donations', ft.com, 27 February; and Grant, P. (2010) 'Accountants needed in Haiti', *Accountancy Age*, 5 February.

SUMMARY

The main points of this chapter may be summarised as follows.

What are accounting and finance?

- Accounting provides financial information to help various user groups make more informed judgements and decisions.

- Finance also helps users to improve the quality of their decisions and is concerned with the financing and investing activities of the business.

Accounting and user needs

- For accounting to be useful, it must be clear *for whom* and *for what purpose* the information will be used.

- Owners, managers and lenders are important user groups but there are several others.

Providing a service

- Accounting can be viewed as a form of service as it involves providing financial information to various users.

- To provide a useful service, accounting must possess certain qualities, or characteristics. The fundamental qualities are relevance and faithful representation. Other qualities that enhance the usefulness of accounting information are comparability, verifiability, timeliness and understandability.

- Providing a service to users can be costly and financial information should be produced only if the cost of providing the information is less than the benefits gained.

Accounting information

- Accounting is part of the total information system within a business. It shares features common to all information systems within a business, which are the identification, recording, analysis and reporting of information.

Management accounting and financial accounting

- Accounting has two main strands – management accounting and financial accounting.

- Management accounting seeks to meet the needs of the business's managers. Financial accounting is primarily concerned with meeting the needs of owners and lenders but will also be useful to other external user groups.

- These two strands of accounting differ in terms of the types of reports produced, the level of reporting detail, the time orientation, the degree of regulation and the range and quality of information provided.

The changing face of accounting

- Changes in the economic environment have led to changes in the nature and scope of accounting.

- Financial accounting has improved its framework of rules and there has been greater international harmonisation of accounting rules.

- Management accounting has become more outward-looking and new methods for managing costs have been developed to help a business gain competitive advantage.

Why study accounting?

- Everyone connected with business should be a little 'streetwise' about accounting and finance because they exert an enormous influence over the ways in which a business operates.

The quest for wealth creation

- The key financial objective of a business is to enhance the wealth of its owners.

- To achieve this objective, the needs of other groups connected with the business, such as customers, employees and the community, cannot be ignored.

- When setting financial objectives, the right balance must be struck between risk and return.

Not-for-profit organisations

- Produce accounting information for decision-making purposes.

- They have user groups that are similar to, or the same as, those of private-sector businesses.

KEY TERMS

For definitions of these terms, see Appendix A.

accounting p. 2	**verifiability** p. 6
finance p. 2	**timeliness** p. 6
financial management p. 2	**understandability** p. 6
relevance p. 5	**accounting information**
faithful representation p. 5	**system** p. 9
materiality p. 5	**management accounting** p. 11
comparability p. 6	**financial accounting** p. 11

FURTHER READING

If you would like to explore the topics covered in this chapter in more depth, we recommend the following books:

Atrill, P. (2014) *Financial Management for Decision Makers,* 7th edn, Pearson, Chapter 1.

Drury, C. (2015) *Management and Cost Accounting,* 9th edn, Cengage Learning EMEA, Chapter 1.

Elliott, B. and Elliott, J. (2015) *Financial Accounting and Reporting,* 17th edn, Pearson, Chapter 9.

McLaney, E. (2014) *Business Finance: Theory and Practice,* 10th edn, Pearson, Chapters 1 and 2.

? REVIEW QUESTIONS

Solutions to these questions can be found at the back of the book on pages 538–539.

1.1 What is the purpose of producing accounting information?

1.2 Identify the main users of accounting information for a university. For what purposes would different user groups need information? Is there a major difference in the ways in which accounting information for a university would be used compared with that of a private sector business?

1.3 Management accounting has been described as 'the eyes and ears of management'. What do you think this expression means?

1.4 Financial accounting statements tend to reflect past events. In view of this, how can they be of any assistance to a user in making a decision when decisions, by their very nature, can only be made about future actions?

PART ONE

FINANCIAL ACCOUNTING

Chapter 2

MEASURING AND REPORTING FINANCIAL POSITION

INTRODUCTION

We saw in Chapter 1 that accounting has two distinct strands: financial accounting and management accounting. This chapter, along with Chapters 3, 4 and 5, examines the three major financial statements that form the core of financial accounting. We start by taking an overview of these statements to see how each one contributes towards an assessment of the overall financial position and performance of a business.

Following this overview, we begin a more detailed examination by turning our attention towards one of these financial statements: the statement of financial position. We shall see how it is prepared and examine the principles underpinning it. We shall also consider its value for decision-making purposes.

Learning outcomes

When you have completed this chapter, you should be able to:

- explain the nature and purpose of the three major financial statements;

- prepare a simple statement of financial position and interpret the information that it contains;

- discuss the accounting conventions underpinning the statement of financial position;

- discuss the uses and limitations of the statement of financial position for decision-making purposes.

THE MAJOR FINANCIAL STATEMENTS – AN OVERVIEW

The major financial accounting statements aim to provide a picture of the financial position and performance of a business. To achieve this, a business's accounting system will normally produce three separate financial statements on a regular, recurring basis. These three statements are concerned with answering the following questions relating to a particular period:

- What cash movements took place?
- How much wealth was generated?
- What is the accumulated wealth of the business at the end of the period and what form does it take?

To address each of the above questions, there is a separate financial statement. The financial statements are:

- the **statement of cash flows;**
- the **income statement** (also known as the profit and loss account);
- the **statement of financial position** (also known as the balance sheet).

Together they provide an overall picture of the financial health of the business.

Perhaps the best way to introduce these financial statements is to look at an example of a very simple business. From this we shall be able to see the sort of information that each of the statements can usefully provide. It is, however, worth pointing out that, while a simple business is our starting point, the principles for preparing the financial statements apply equally to the largest and most complex businesses. This means that we shall frequently encounter these principles again in later chapters.

Example 2.1

Paul was unemployed and unable to find a job. He therefore decided to embark on a business venture. With Christmas approaching, he decided to buy gift wrapping paper from a local supplier and to sell it on the corner of his local high street. He felt that the price of wrapping paper in the high street shops was unreasonably high. This provided him with a useful business opportunity.

He began the venture with £40 of his own money, in cash. On Monday, Paul's first day of trading, he bought wrapping paper for £40 and sold three-quarters of it for £45 cash.

What cash movements took place in Paul's business during Monday?
For Monday, a *statement of cash flows* showing the cash movements (that is, cash in and cash out) for the day can be prepared as follows:

Statement of cash flows for Monday

	£
Cash introduced (by Paul)	40
Cash from sales of wrapping paper	45
Cash paid to buy wrapping paper	(40)
Closing balance of cash	45

→

The statement shows that Paul placed £40 cash into the business. The business received £45 cash from customers, but paid £40 cash to buy the wrapping paper. This left £45 of cash by Monday evening. Note that we are taking the standard approach found in the financial statements of showing figures to be deducted (in this case the £40 paid out) in brackets. We shall take this approach consistently throughout the chapters dealing with financial statements.

How much wealth (that is, profit) was generated by the business during Monday?

An *income statement* can be prepared to show the wealth generated (profit) on Monday. The wealth generated arises from trading and will be the difference between the value of the sales made and the cost of the goods (that is, wrapping paper) sold:

Income statement for Monday

	£
Sales revenue	45
Cost of goods sold ($^3/_4$ of £40)	(30)
Profit	15

Note that it is only the cost of the wrapping paper *sold* that is matched against (and deducted from) the sales revenue to find the profit, not the whole of the cost of wrapping paper acquired. Any unsold inventories (also known as *stock*) will be charged against the future sales revenue that it generates. In this case the cost of the unsold inventories is $^1/_4$ of £40 = £10.

What is the accumulated wealth on Monday evening and what form does it take?

To establish the accumulated wealth at the end of Monday's trading, we can draw up a *statement of financial position* for Paul's business. This statement will also list the forms of wealth held at the end of that day:

Statement of financial position as at Monday evening

	£
Cash (closing balance)	45
Inventories of goods for resale ($^1/_4$ of £40)	10
Total assets	55
Equity	55

Note the terms 'assets' and 'equity' that appear in this statement. 'Assets' are business resources (things of value to the business) and include cash and inventories. 'Equity' is the word used in accounting to describe the investment, or stake, of the owner(s) – in this case Paul – in the business. Both of these terms will be discussed in some detail a little later in this chapter. Note that the equity on Monday evening was £55. This represented the £40 that Paul put in to start the business, plus Monday's profit (£15) – profits belong to the owner(s).

We can see from the financial statements in Example 2.1 that each statement provides part of a picture of the financial performance and position of the business. We begin by showing the cash movements. Cash is a vital resource that is necessary for any business to function effectively. It is required to meet debts that become due and to acquire other resources (such as inventories). Cash has been described as the 'lifeblood' of a business.

Reporting cash movements alone, however, is not enough to portray the financial health of the business. To find out how much profit was generated, we need an income statement. It is important to recognise that cash and profits rarely move in unison. During Monday, for example, the cash balance increased by £5, but the profit generated, as shown in the income statement, was £15. The cash balance did not increase in line with profit because part of the wealth generated (£10) was held in the form of inventories.

Let us now continue with our example.

Example 2.1 (continued)

On Tuesday, Paul bought more wrapping paper for £20 cash. He managed to sell all of the new inventories and all of the earlier inventories, for a total of £48.

The statement of cash flows for Tuesday will be as follows:

Statement of cash flows for Tuesday

	£
Opening balance (from Monday evening)	45
Cash from sales of wrapping paper	48
Cash paid to buy wrapping paper	(20)
Closing balance	73

The income statement for Tuesday will be as follows:

Income statement for Tuesday

	£
Sales revenue	48
Cost of goods sold £20 + £10	(30)
Profit	18

The statement of financial position as at Tuesday evening will be:

Statement of financial position as at Tuesday evening

	£
Cash (closing balance)	73
Inventories	–
Total assets	73
Equity	73

The statement of financial position reveals that total business wealth had increased to £73 by Tuesday evening. This represents an increase of £18 (that is, £73 – £55) over Monday's figure – which, of course, is the amount of profit made during Tuesday as shown on the income statement.

The statement of financial position that was drawn up as at the end of Monday's trading provides information on the total wealth of the business. This wealth can be held in various forms. For Paul's business, wealth is held in the form of cash and inventories. This means that, when drawing up the statement of financial position, both forms will be listed. For a large business, many other forms of wealth may be held, such as property, equipment, motor vehicles and so on.

Activity 2.1

On Wednesday, Paul bought more wrapping paper for £46 cash. However, it was raining hard for much of the day and sales were slow. After Paul had sold half of his total inventories for £32, he decided to stop trading until Thursday morning.
Try drawing up the three financial statements for Paul's business for Wednesday.

The financial statements should look like this:

Statement of cash flows for Wednesday

	£
Opening balance (from the Tuesday evening)	73
Cash from sales of wrapping paper	32
Cash paid to buy wrapping paper	(46)
Closing balance	59

Income statement for Wednesday

	£
Sales revenue	32
Cost of goods sold ($\frac{1}{2}$ of £46)	(23)
Profit	9

Statement of financial position as at Wednesday evening

	£
Cash (closing balance)	59
Inventories ($\frac{1}{2}$ of £46)	23
Total assets	82
Equity	82

Note that the total business wealth has increased by £9 (that is, the amount of Wednesday's profit) even though the cash balance has declined. This is because the business is holding more of its wealth in the form of inventories rather than cash, compared with the position on Tuesday evening.

By Wednesday evening, the equity stood at £82. This arose from Paul's initial investment of £40, plus his profits for Monday (£15), Tuesday (£18) and Wednesday (£9). This represents Paul's total investment in his business at that time. The equity of most businesses will similarly be made up of injections of funds by the owner plus any accumulated profits.

We can see that the income statement and statement of cash flows are both concerned with measuring flows (of wealth and cash respectively) during a particular period. The statement of financial position, however, is concerned with the financial position at a particular moment in time. Figure 2.1 illustrates this point.

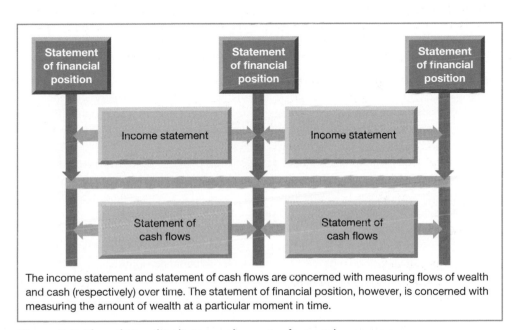

The income statement and statement of cash flows are concerned with measuring flows of wealth and cash (respectively) over time. The statement of financial position, however, is concerned with measuring the amount of wealth at a particular moment in time.

Figure 2.1 The relationship between the major financial statements

The three financial statements discussed are often referred to as the **final accounts** of the business.

For external users (that is virtually all users except the managers of the business concerned), these statements are normally backward-looking because they are based on information concerning past events and transactions. This can be useful in providing feedback on past performance and in identifying trends that provide clues to future performance. However, the statements can also be prepared using forward-looking data to help assess likely future profits, cash flows and so on. Normally, this is done only for management decision-making purposes and is not made publicly available.

Now that we have an overview of the financial statements, we shall consider each one in detail. The remainder of this chapter is devoted to the statement of financial position.

THE STATEMENT OF FINANCIAL POSITION

We saw a little earlier that this statement shows the forms in which the wealth of a business is held and how much wealth is held in each form. We can, however, be more precise about the nature of this statement by saying that it sets out the **assets** of a business, on the one hand, and the **claims** against the business, on the other. Before looking at the statement of financial position in more detail, we need to be clear about what these terms mean.

Assets

An asset is essentially a resource held by a business. For a particular item to be treated as an asset, for accounting purposes, it should have the following characteristics:

- *A probable future economic benefit must exist.* An economic benefit is one that will have some monetary value. This value may arise either through the item's future use within the business or through its future hire or sale. Thus an obsolete piece of equipment that can be sold for scrap would be considered an asset, whereas something that has no scrap value would not be regarded as one.
- *The benefit must arise from some past transaction or event.* In other words, the transaction (or other event), giving rise to a business's right to the benefit, must have already occurred and will not arise at some future date. For example, an agreement by a business to buy a piece of equipment at some future date would not mean the item is currently an asset of the business.
- *The business must have the right to control the resource.* Unless the business controls the resource, it cannot be regarded as an asset for accounting purposes. To a business offering holidays on barges, for example, the canal system may be a valuable resource but, as the business will not be able to control the access of others to the canal system, it cannot be regarded as an asset of the business. (However, any barges owned by the business would be regarded as assets.)
- *The asset must be capable of measurement in monetary terms.* Unless the item can be measured in monetary terms, with a reasonable degree of reliability, it will not be regarded as an asset for inclusion on the statement of financial position. For instance, the title of a magazine (for example *Hello!* or *Vogue*) that was created by its publisher may be extremely valuable to that publishing business, but this value is difficult to quantify. It will not, therefore, be treated as an asset.

Note that all four of these conditions must apply. If one of them is missing, the item will not be treated as an asset for accounting purposes and will not, therefore, appear on the statement of financial position. Figure 2.2 summarises the above discussion in the form of a decision chart.

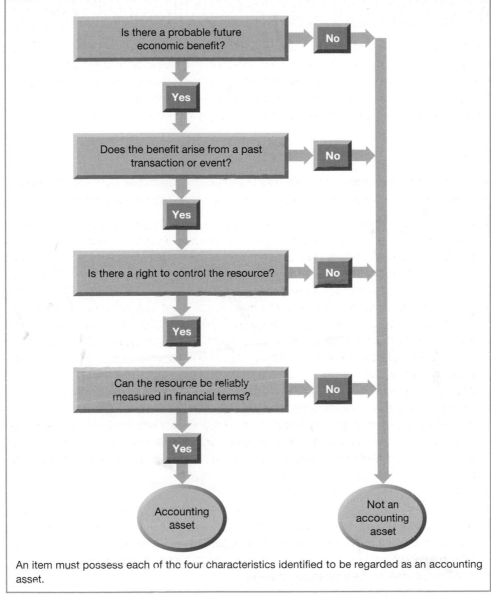

An item must possess each of the four characteristics identified to be regarded as an accounting asset.

Figure 2.2 Decision chart for identifying an accounting asset

We can see that these conditions will strictly limit the kind of resources that may be referred to as 'assets' in the statement of financial position. Some resources, like the canal system or the magazine title *Hello!,* may well be assets in a broader sense, but not for accounting purposes. Once an asset has been acquired by a business, it will continue to be considered an asset until the benefits are exhausted or the business disposes of it.

Activity 2.2

Indicate which of the following items could appear as an asset on the statement of financial position of a business. Explain your reasoning in each case.

1 £1,000 owed to the business by a credit customer who is unable to pay.
2 A patent, bought from an inventor, which gives the business the right to produce a new product. Production of the new product is expected to increase profits over the period during which the patent is held.
3 A recently hired marketing director who is confidently expected to increase profits by more than 30 per cent during the next three years.
4 A recently purchased machine that will save the business £10,000 each year. It is already being used by the business but it has been acquired on credit and is not yet paid for.

Your answer should be along the following lines.

1 Under normal circumstances, a business would expect a customer to pay the amount owed. Such an amount is therefore typically shown as an asset under the heading 'trade receivables' (or 'debtors'). In this particular case, however, the customer is unable to pay. As a result, the item is incapable of providing future economic benefits and the £1,000 owing would not be regarded as an asset. Debts that are not paid are referred to as 'bad debts'.
2 The patent would meet all of the conditions set out above and would therefore be regarded as an asset.
3 The new marketing director would not be considered to be an asset. One argument for this is that the business does not have exclusive rights of control over the director. (It may have an exclusive right to the services that the director provides, however.) Perhaps a stronger argument is that the value of the director cannot be measured in monetary terms with any degree of reliability.
4 The machine would be considered an asset even though it is not yet paid for. Once the business has agreed to buy the machine, and has accepted it, the machine represents an asset even though payment is still outstanding. (The amount outstanding would be shown as a claim, as we shall see shortly.)

The sorts of items that often appear as assets in the statement of financial position of a business include:

- property;
- plant and equipment;
- fixtures and fittings;
- patents and trademarks;
- trade receivables (debtors); and
- investments outside the business.

Can you think of two additional items that might appear as assets in the statement of financial position of a typical business?

You may be able to think of a number of other items. Two that we have mentioned so far are inventories and cash, as they were held by Paul's wrapping paper business (in Example 2.1).

Note that an asset does not have to be a physical item – it may be a non-physical one that gives a right to certain benefits. Assets that have a physical substance and can be touched (such as inventories) are referred to as **tangible assets**. Assets that have no physical substance but which, nevertheless, provide expected future benefits (such as patents) are referred to as **intangible assets**.

Claims

A claim is an obligation of the business to provide cash, or some other form of benefit, to an outside party. It will normally arise as a result of the outside party providing assets for use by the business. There are essentially two types of claim against a business:

- **Equity**. This represents the claim of the owner(s) against the business. This claim is sometimes referred to as the *owner's capital*. Some find it hard to understand how the owner can have a claim against the business, particularly when we consider the example of a sole proprietor-type business, like Paul's, where the owner is, in effect, the business. For accounting purposes, however, a clear distinction is made between the business and the owner(s). The business is viewed as being quite separate from the owner. It is seen as a separate entity with its own separate existence. This means that, when financial statements are prepared, they relate to the business rather than to the owner(s). Viewed from this perspective, any funds contributed by the owner will be seen as coming from outside the business and will appear as a claim against the business in its statement of financial position.
- **Liabilities**. Liabilities represent the claims of all individuals and organisations, apart from the owner(s). They arise from past transactions or events such as supplying goods or lending money to the business. A liability will be settled through an outflow of assets (usually cash).

Once a claim from the owners or outsiders has been incurred by a business, it will remain as an obligation until it is settled.

Now that the meanings of the terms *assets, equity* and *liabilities* have been established, we can consider the relationship between them. This relationship is quite straightforward. If a business wishes to acquire assets, it must raise the necessary funds from somewhere. It may raise these funds from the owner(s), or from other outside parties, or from both. Example 2.2 illustrates this relationship.

Example 2.2

Jerry and Company is a new business that was created by depositing £20,000 in a bank account on 1 March. This amount was raised partly from the owner (£6,000) and partly from borrowing (£14,000). Raising funds in this way will give rise to a claim on the business by both the owner (equity) and the lender (liability). If a statement of financial position of Jerry and Company is prepared following the above transactions, it will appear as follows:

Jerry and Company
Statement of financial position as at 1 March

	£
ASSETS	
Cash at bank	20,000
Total assets	20,000
EQUITY AND LIABILITIES	
Equity	6,000
Liabilities – borrowing	14,000
Total equity and liabilities	20,000

We can see from the statement of financial position that the total claims (equity and liabilities) are the same as the total assets. Thus:

Assets = Equity + Liabilities

This equation – which we shall refer to as the *accounting equation* – will always hold true. Whatever changes may occur to the assets of the business or the claims against it, there will be compensating changes elsewhere that will ensure that the statement of financial position always 'balances'. By way of illustration, consider the following transactions for Jerry and Company:

2 March	Bought a motor van for £5,000, paying by cheque.
3 March	Bought inventories (that is, goods to be sold) on one month's credit for £3,000. (This means that the inventories were bought on 3 March, but payment will not be made to the supplier until 3 April.)
4 March	Repaid £2,000 of the amount borrowed to the lender, by cheque.
6 March	Owner introduced another £4,000 into the business bank account.

A statement of financial position may be drawn up after each day in which transactions have taken place. In this way, we can see the effect of each transaction on the assets and claims of the business. The statement of financial position as at 2 March will be:

Jerry and Company
Statement of financial position as at 2 March

	£
ASSETS	
Cash at bank (20,000 − 5,000)	15,000
Motor van	5,000
Total assets	20,000
EQUITY AND LIABILITIES	
Equity	6,000
Liabilities – borrowing	14,000
Total equity and liabilities	20,000

As we can see, the effect of buying the motor van is to decrease the balance at the bank by £5,000 and to introduce a new asset – a motor van – to the statement of financial position. The total assets remain unchanged; it is only the 'mix' of assets that has changed. The claims against the business remain the same because there has been no change in the way in which the business has been funded.

The statement of financial position as at 3 March, following the purchase of inventories, will be:

Jerry and Company
Statement of financial position as at 3 March

	£
ASSETS	
Cash at bank	15,000
Motor van	5,000
Inventories	3,000
Total assets	23,000
EQUITY AND LIABILITIES	
Equity	6,000
Liabilities – borrowing	14,000
Liabilities – trade payable	3,000
Total equity and liabilities	23,000

The effect of buying inventories has been to introduce another new asset (inventories) to the statement of financial position. Furthermore, the fact that the goods have not yet been paid for means that the claims against the business will be increased by the £3,000 owed to the supplier, who is referred to as a **trade payable** (or trade creditor) on the statement of financial position.

Have a go at drawing up a statement of financial position for Jerry and Company as at 4 March.

The statement of financial position as at 4 March, following the repayment of part of the borrowing, will be:

Jerry and Company
Statement of financial position as at 4 March

	£
ASSETS	
Cash at bank (15,000 − 2,000)	13,000
Motor van	5,000
Inventories	3,000
Total assets	21,000
EQUITY AND LIABILITIES	
Equity	6,000
Liabilities − borrowing (14,000 − 2,000)	12,000
Liabilities − trade payable	3,000
Total equity and liabilities	21,000

The repayment of £2,000 of the borrowing will result in a decrease in the balance at the bank of £2,000 and a decrease in the lender's claim against the business by the same amount.

Try drawing up a statement of financial position as at 6 March for Jerry and Company.

The statement of financial position as at 6 March, following the introduction of more funds, will be:

Jerry and Company
Statement of financial position as at 6 March

	£
ASSETS	
Cash at bank (13,000 + 4,000)	17,000
Motor van	5,000
Inventories	3,000
Total assets	25,000
EQUITY AND LIABILITIES	
Equity (6,000 + 4,000)	10,000
Liabilities − borrowing	12,000
Liabilities − trade payable	3,000
Total equity and liabilities	25,000

The introduction of more funds by the owner will result in an increase in the equity of £4,000 and an increase in the cash at bank by the same amount.

The example of Jerry and Company illustrates the point that the accounting equation (assets equals equity plus liabilities) will always hold true because it reflects the fact that, if a business wishes to acquire more assets, it must raise funds equal to the cost of those assets. The funds raised must be provided by the owners (equity), or by others (liabilities), or by a combination of the two. This means that the total cost of assets acquired should always equal the total equity plus liabilities.

It is worth pointing out that businesses do not normally draw up a statement of financial position after each day, as shown in the example. We have done this to illustrate the effect on the statement of financial position of each transaction. In practice, a statement of financial position for a business is usually prepared at the end of a defined reporting period. The period over which businesses measure their financial results is usually known as the **reporting period**, but it is sometimes called the 'accounting period' or 'financial period'.

Determining the length of the reporting period will involve weighing up the costs of producing the information against the perceived benefits of having that information for decision-making purposes. In practice, the reporting period will vary between businesses; it could be monthly, quarterly, half-yearly or annually. For external reporting purposes, an annual reporting period is the norm (although certain businesses, typically larger ones, report more frequently than this). For internal reporting purposes to managers, however, more frequent (perhaps monthly) financial statements may be prepared.

THE EFFECT OF TRADING TRANSACTIONS

In the example (Jerry and Company), we showed how various types of transactions affected the statement of financial position. However, one very important type of transaction – trading transactions – has yet to be considered. To show how this type of transaction affects the statement of financial position, let us return to Jerry and Company.

Example 2.2 (continued)

The statement of financial position that we drew up for Jerry and Company as at 6 March was as follows:

Jerry and Company
Statement of financial position as at 6 March

	£
ASSETS	
Cash at bank	17,000
Motor van	5,000
Inventories	3,000
Total assets	25,000
EQUITY AND LIABILITIES	
Equity	10,000
Liabilities – borrowing	12,000
Liabilities – trade payable	3,000
Total equity and liabilities	25,000

$\rightarrow$

On 7 March, the business managed to sell all of the inventories for £5,000 and received a bank transfer immediately from the customer for this amount. The statement of financial position on 7 March, after this transaction has taken place, will be:

Jerry and Company
Statement of financial position as at 7 March

	£
ASSETS	
Cash at bank (17,000 + 5,000)	22,000
Motor van	5,000
Inventories (3,000 − 3,000)	–
Total assets	27,000
EQUITY AND LIABILITIES	
Equity (10,000 + (5,000 − 3,000))	12,000
Liabilities – borrowing	12,000
Liabilities – trade payable	3,000
Total equity and liabilities	27,000

We can see that the inventories (£3,000) have now disappeared from the statement of financial position, but the cash at bank has increased by the selling price of the inventories (£5,000). The net effect has therefore been to increase assets by £2,000 (that is, £5,000 less £3,000). This increase represents the net increase in wealth (the profit) that has arisen from trading. Also note that the equity of the business has increased by £2,000, in line with the increase in assets. This increase in equity reflects the fact that wealth generated, as a result of trading or other operations, will be to the benefit of the owners and will increase their stake in the business.

Activity 2.6

What would have been the effect on the statement of financial position if the inventories had been sold on 7 March for £1,000 rather than £5,000?

The statement of financial position on 7 March would then have been:

Jerry and Company
Statement of financial position as at 7 March

	£
ASSETS	
Cash at bank (17,000 + 1,000)	18,000
Motor van	5,000
Inventories (3,000 − 3,000)	–
Total assets	23,000
EQUITY AND LIABILITIES	
Equity (10,000 + (1,000 − 3,000))	8,000
Liabilities – borrowing	12,000
Liabilities – trade payable	3,000
Total equity and liabilities	23,000

As we can see, the inventories (£3,000) will disappear from the statement of financial position but the cash at bank will rise by only £1,000. This will mean a net reduction in assets of £2,000. This reduction represents a loss arising from trading and will be reflected in a reduction in the equity of the owners.

What we have just seen means that the accounting equation can be extended as follows:

Assets (at the end of the period) = Equity (amount at the start of period)
+ Profit (or − Loss) for the period)
+ Liabilities (at the end of the period)

(This is assuming that the owner makes no injections or withdrawals of equity during the period.)

Any funds introduced or withdrawn by the owners also affect equity. If the owners withdrew £1,500 for their own use, the equity of the owners would be reduced by £1,500. If these drawings were in cash, the cash balance would decrease by £1,500 in the statement of financial position.

Like all items in the statement of financial position, the amount of equity is cumulative. This means that any profit not taken out as drawings by the owner(s) remains in the business. These retained (or 'ploughed-back') earnings have the effect of expanding the business.

CLASSIFYING ASSETS

On the statement of financial position, assets and claims are usually grouped into categories. This is designed to help users, as a haphazard listing of these items could be confusing. Assets may be categorised as being either current or non-current.

Current assets

Current assets are basically assets that are held for the short term. To be more precise, they are assets that meet any of the following conditions:

- they are held for sale or consumption during the business's normal operating cycle;
- they are expected to be sold within a year after the date of the relevant statement of financial position;
- they are held principally for trading;
- they are cash, or near cash such as easily marketable, short-term investments.

The operating cycle of a business, mentioned above, is the time between buying and/ or creating a product or service and receiving the cash on its sale. For most businesses, this will be less than a year. (It is worth mentioning that sales made by most businesses are made on credit. The customer pays at some point after the goods are received or the service is provided.)

The most common current assets are inventories, **trade receivables** (amounts owed by customers for goods or services supplied on credit) and cash. For businesses that sell goods, rather than render a service, the current assets of inventories, trade receivables and cash are interrelated. They circulate within a business as shown in Figure 2.3. We can see that cash can be used to buy inventories, which are then sold on credit. When the credit customers (trade receivables) pay, the business receives an injection of cash and so on.

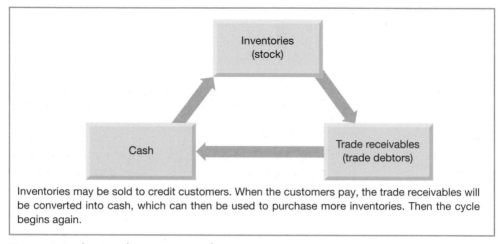

Inventories may be sold to credit customers. When the customers pay, the trade receivables will be converted into cash, which can then be used to purchase more inventories. Then the cycle begins again.

Figure 2.3 The circulating nature of current assets

For purely service businesses, the situation is similar, except that inventories are not involved.

Non-current assets

Non-current assets (also called *fixed assets*) are simply assets that do not meet the definition of current assets. They tend to be held for long-term operations. Non-current assets may be either tangible or intangible. Tangible non-current assets normally consist of **property, plant and equipment**. We shall refer to them in this way from now on. This is a rather broad term that includes items such as land and buildings, machinery, motor vehicles, and fixtures and fittings.

The distinction between those assets continuously circulating (current) and those used for long-term operations (non-current) may help when assessing the mix of assets held. Most businesses need a certain amount of both types of asset to operate effectively.

Activity 2.7

Can you think of two examples of assets that may be classified as non-current assets for an insurance business?

Examples of assets that may be defined as being non-current are:

- property;
- furniture;
- motor vehicles;
- computer equipment;
- computer software;
- reference books.

This is not an exhaustive list. You may have thought of others.

The way in which a particular asset is classified (that is, between current and non-current) may vary according to the nature of the business. This is because the *purpose* for which the asset is held may vary. For example, a motor vehicle manufacturer will normally hold inventories of the finished motor vehicles produced for resale; it would, therefore, classify them as part of the current assets. Meanwhile, a business that uses motor vehicles for delivering its goods to customers (that is, as part of its long-term operations) would classify them as non-current assets.

Activity 2.8

The assets of Kunalun and Co., a large advertising agency, are as follows:

- cash at bank;
- fixtures and fittings;
- office equipment;
- motor vehicles;
- property;
- computer equipment;
- work in progress (that is, partly completed work for clients).

Which of these do you think should be defined as non-current assets and which should be defined as current assets?

Your answer should be as follows:

Non-current assets	*Current assets*
Fixtures and fittings	Cash at bank
Office equipment	Work in progress
Motor vehicles	
Property	
Computer equipment	

CLASSIFYING CLAIMS

As we have already seen, claims are normally classified into equity (owner's claim) and liabilities (claims of outsiders). Liabilities are further classified as either current or non-current.

Current liabilities

Current liabilities are basically amounts due for settlement in the short term. To be more precise, they are liabilities that meet any of the following conditions:

- They are expected to be settled within the business's normal operating cycle.
- They are held principally for trading purposes.
- They are due to be settled within a year after the date of the relevant statement of financial position.
- There is no right to defer settlement beyond a year after the date of the relevant statement of financial position.

Non-current liabilities

Non-current liabilities represent amounts due that do not meet the definition of current liabilities and so represent longer-term liabilities.

Activity 2.9

Can you think of one example of a current liability and one of a non-current liability?

An example of a current liability would be amounts owing to suppliers for goods supplied on credit (trade payables) or a bank overdraft (a form of short-term bank borrowing that is repayable on demand). An example of a non-current liability would be long-term borrowings.

It is quite common for non-current liabilities to become current liabilities. For example, borrowings to be repaid 18 months after the date of a particular statement of financial position will normally appear as a non-current liability. Those same borrowings will, however, appear as a current liability in the statement of financial position as at the end of the following year, by which time they would be due for repayment after 6 months.

This classification of liabilities between current and non-current helps to highlight those financial obligations that must shortly be met. The amount of current liabilities can be compared with the amount of current assets (that is, the assets that are either cash or will turn into cash within the normal operating cycle). This should reveal whether a business can cover its maturing obligations.

The classification of liabilities between current and non-current also helps to highlight the proportion of total long-term finance that is raised through borrowings rather than equity. Where a business relies on long-term borrowings, rather than relying solely on funds provided by the owner(s), the financial risks increase. This is because borrowing normally brings a commitment to make periodic interest payments and capital repayments. The business may be forced to stop trading if this commitment cannot be fulfilled. Thus, when raising long-term finance, the right balance must be struck between long-term borrowings and owner's equity. We shall consider this issue in more detail in both Chapters 6 and 11.

STATEMENT LAYOUTS

Having looked at the classification of assets and liabilities, we shall now consider the layout of the statement of financial position. Although there is an almost infinite number of ways in which the same information on assets and claims could be presented, we shall consider two basic layouts. The first of these, which we shall refer to as the standard layout, follows the style that we adopted with Jerry and Company earlier (see pages 00 to 00). A more comprehensive example of this style is shown in Example 2.3.

Example 2.3

Brie Manufacturing
Statement of financial position as at 31 March 2016

	£000
ASSETS	
Non-current assets	
Property	45
Plant and equipment	30
Motor vans	19
	94
Current assets	
Inventories	23
Trade receivables	18
Cash at bank	12
	53
Total assets	147
EQUITY AND LIABILITIES	
Equity	60
Non-current liabilities	
Long-term borrowings	50
Current liabilities	
Trade payables	37
Total equity and liabilities	147

The non-current assets have a total of £94,000 which, together with the current assets total of £53,000, gives a total of £147,000 for assets. Similarly, the equity totals £60,000 which, together with the £50,000 for non-current liabilities and £37,000 for current liabilities, gives a total for equity and liabilities of £147,000.

Within each category of asset (non-current and current) shown in Example 2.3, the items are listed in reverse order of liquidity (nearness to cash). Thus, those assets furthest from cash come first and those assets closest to cash come last. In the case of non-current assets, property is listed first as this asset is usually the most difficult to turn into cash and motor vans are listed last as there is usually a ready market for them. In the case of current assets, we have already seen that inventories are converted to trade receivables and then trade receivables are converted to cash. As a result, under the heading of current assets, inventories are listed first, followed by trade receivables and finally cash itself. This ordering of assets will occur irrespective of the layout used.

Note that, in addition to a grand total for assets held, subtotals for non-current assets and current assets are shown. Subtotals are also used for non-current liabilities and current liabilities when more than one item appears within these categories.

A slight variation from the layout illustrated in Example 2.3 is as shown in Example 2.4.

Example 2.4

Brie Manufacturing
Statement of financial position as at 31 March 2016

	£000
ASSETS	
Non-current assets	
Property	45
Plant and equipment	30
Motor vans	19
	94
Current assets	
Inventories	23
Trade receivables	18
Cash at bank	12
	53
Total assets	147
LIABILITIES	
Non-current liabilities	
Long-term borrowings	(50)
Current liabilities	
Trade payables	(37)
Total liabilities	(87)
Net assets	60
EQUITY	60

We can see that the total liabilities are deducted from the total assets. This derives a figure for net assets – which is equal to equity. Using this format, the basic accounting equation is rearranged so that:

Assets − Liabilities = Equity

This rearranged equation highlights the fact that equity represents the residual interest of the owner(s) after deducting all liabilities of the business.

Figure 2.4 summarises the two types of layout discussed in this section.

The standard layout, which is very popular in practice, will be used throughout the book.

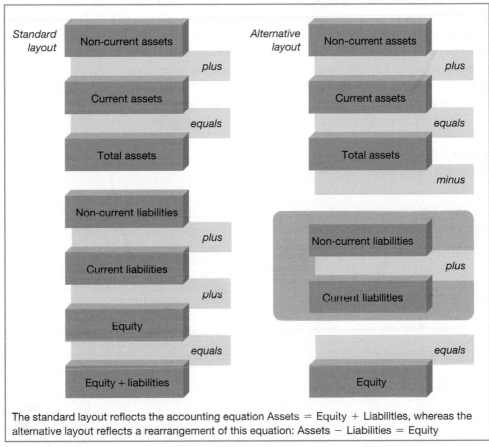

The standard layout reflects the accounting equation Assets = Equity + Liabilities, whereas the alternative layout reflects a rearrangement of this equation: Assets − Liabilities = Equity

Figure 2.4 Layouts for the statement of financial position

CAPTURING A MOMENT IN TIME

As we have already seen, the statement of financial position reflects the assets, equity and liabilities of a business at *a specified point in time.* It has been compared to a photograph. A photograph 'freezes' a particular moment in time and will represent the situation only at that moment. Hence, events may be quite different immediately before and immediately after the photograph was taken. When examining a statement of financial position, therefore, it is important to establish the date for which it has been drawn up. This information should be prominently displayed in the heading to the statement, as shown above in Example 2.4. The more recent the statement of financial position date, the better, when assessing current financial position.

A business will normally prepare a statement of financial position as at the close of business on the last day of its annual reporting period. In the UK, businesses are free to choose their reporting period and, once chosen, it will normally change only under exceptional circumstances. When making a decision on which year-end date to choose, commercial convenience can often be a deciding factor. For example, a business operating in the retail trade may choose to have a year-end date early in the calendar year (for example, 31 January) because trade tends to be slack during that period and more staff time is available to help with the tasks involved in the preparation of the annual financial statements (such as checking the amount of inventories held). Since trade is slack, it is also a time when the amount of inventories held by the retail business is likely to be unusually low as compared with other times of the year. Thus the statement of financial position, while portraying the actual inventories held, may not portray the typical inventories of the business.

Activity 2.10

In broad terms, when might the following types of business have a financial year-end:

1. A football club
2. A landscape gardening business
3. A tour operator?

1. A football club is likely to select a year-end that falls outside the football season. Tottenham Hotspur Football Club, for example, has a year-end of 30 June.
2. A landscape gardener will be busiest during the planting season. A year-end during the winter period is, therefore, likely to be most suitable.
3. A tour operator will be busiest during the summer and winter holiday seasons. Thus, a year-end that falls outside these seasons is likely to be most suitable. The tour operator Thomas Cook, for example, has a year-end of 30 September.

THE ROLE OF ACCOUNTING CONVENTIONS

Accounting has a number of conventions, or rules, that have evolved over time. They have evolved as attempts to deal with practical problems experienced by preparers and users of financial statements, rather than to reflect some theoretical ideal. In preparing the statements of financial position earlier, we have followed various **accounting conventions**, though they have not been explicitly mentioned. We shall now identify and discuss the major conventions that we have applied.

Business entity convention

For accounting purposes, the business and its owner(s) are treated as being quite separate and distinct. This is why owners are treated as being claimants against their own business in respect of their investment. The **business entity convention** must be distinguished from the legal position that may exist between businesses and their owners. For sole proprietorships and partnerships, the law does not make any distinction between the business and its owner(s). For limited companies, however, there is a clear legal distinction between the business and its owners. (As we shall see in Chapter 4, the limited company is regarded as having a separate legal existence.) For accounting purposes, these legal distinctions are irrelevant and the business entity convention applies to all businesses.

Historic cost convention

The **historic cost convention** holds that the value of assets shown on the statement of financial position should be based on their historic cost (that is, acquisition cost). The use of historic cost means that problems of measurement reliability are minimised as the amount paid for a particular asset is often a matter of demonstrable fact. Reliance on opinion is avoided, or at least reduced, which should enhance the credibility of the information in the eyes of users. A key problem, however, is that the information provided may not be relevant to user needs. Even quite early in the life of some assets, historic costs may become outdated compared with current market values. This may be misleading in assessing current financial position.

Many argue that recording assets at their current value would provide a more realistic view of financial position and would be relevant for a wide range of decisions. A system of measurement based on current value does, however, bring its own problems. The term 'current value' can be defined in different ways. It can be defined broadly as either the current replacement cost or the current realisable value (selling price) of an asset. These two types of valuation may result in quite different figures being produced to represent the current value of an item. Furthermore, the broad terms 'replacement cost' and 'realisable value' can be defined in different ways. We must therefore be clear about what kind of current value accounting we wish to use.

Activity 2.11 illustrates some of the problems associated with current value accounting.

Activity 2.11

Plumber and Company has a fleet of motor vans used for making deliveries to customers. The owners want to show these vans on the statement of financial position at their current values rather than at their historic cost. They would like to use either current replacement cost (based on how much would have to be paid to buy vans of a similar type and condition) or current realisable value (based on how much a motor van dealer would pay for the vans, if Plumber and Company sold them).

Why is the choice between the two current valuation methods important? Why would both current valuation methods present problems in establishing reliable values?

The choice between the two current valuation methods is important because the values derived under each method are likely to be quite different. Normally, replacement cost values for the motor vans will be higher than their current realisable values.

Establishing current values will usually rely on opinions, which may well vary from one dealer to another. Thus, instead of a single, unambiguous figure for, say, the current replacement cost for each van, a range of possible current replacement costs could be produced. The same problem will arise when trying to establish the current realisable value for each van.

We should bear in mind that the motor vans discussed in Activity 2.11 present less of a problem than many types of asset. There is a ready market for motor vans, which means that a value can be obtained by contacting a dealer. For a custom-built piece of equipment, however, identifying a replacement cost, or worse still a selling price, could be very difficult.

Where the current values of assets are based on the opinion of managers of the business, there is a greater risk that they will lack credibility. Some form of independent valuation, or verification, may therefore be required to reassure users.

Despite the problems associated with current values, they are increasingly used when reporting assets in the statement of financial position. This has led to a steady erosion in the importance of the historic cost convention. Thus, many businesses now prepare financial statements on a modified historic cost basis. We shall consider the valuation of assets in more detail a little later in the chapter.

Prudence convention

The **prudence convention** holds that caution should be exercised when making accounting judgements. The application of this convention normally involves recording all losses at once and in full; this refers to both actual losses and expected losses. Profits, meanwhile, are recognised only when they actually arise. Greater emphasis is therefore placed on expected losses than on expected profits. To illustrate the application of this convention, let us assume that certain inventories held by a business prove unpopular with customers and so a decision is made to sell them below their original cost. The prudence convention requires that the expected loss from future sales be recognised immediately rather than when the goods are eventually sold. Where, inventories can be sold above their original cost, however, profit will be recognised only at the time of sale.

The prudence convention evolved to counteract the excessive optimism of some managers and is designed to prevent an overstatement of financial position and performance. Applying this convention, however, requires judgement. This means that the way in which it is applied by preparers of financial statements may differ over time and between businesses. Where excessive prudence is applied, it will lead to an understatement of profits and financial position. This will mean a consistent bias in the reporting of both financial performance and position.

Activity 2.12

What might be the effect of applying excessive prudence on the quality of decisions made by the owners of a business who are considering selling their share of the business?

Being excessively prudent will tend to obscure the underlying financial reality and may lead to poor decisions being made. The owners may sell their stake in the business at a lower price than they would have received if a more balanced view of the financial health of the business had been presented.

In recent years, the prudence convention has weakened its grip on accounting and has become a less dominant force. The reason for this will be discussed later in the chapter. Nevertheless, it remains an important convention.

Going concern convention

The **going concern convention** holds that the financial statements should be prepared on the assumption that a business will continue operations for the foreseeable future, unless there is evidence to the contrary. In other words, it is assumed that there is no intention, or need, to sell off the non-current assets of the business.

Where a business is in financial difficulties, however, non-current assets may have to be sold to repay those with claims against the business. The realisable (sale) value of many non-current assets is often much lower than the values reported in the statement of financial position. In the event of a forced sale of assets, therefore, significant losses might arise. These losses must be anticipated and fully reported when a business's going concern status is called into question.

Dual aspect convention

The **dual aspect convention** asserts that each transaction has two aspects, both of which will affect the statement of financial position. This means that, for example, the purchase of a motor car for cash results in an increase in one asset (motor car) and a decrease in another (cash). The repayment of borrowings results in the decrease in a liability (borrowings) and the decrease in an asset (cash).

Activity 2.13

What are the two aspects of each of the following transactions?

1 Purchasing £1,000 of inventories on credit.
2 Owner withdrawing £2,000 in cash.
3 Paying a supplier for £1,000 of inventories bought on credit a few weeks earlier.

Your answer should be as follows:

1 Inventories increase by £1,000, trade payables increase by £1,000.
2 Equity reduces by £2,000, cash reduces by £2,000.
3 Trade payables reduce by £1,000, cash reduces by £1,000.

Recording the dual aspect of each transaction ensures that the statement of financial position will continue to balance.

Figure 2.5 summarises the main accounting conventions that exert an influence on the construction of the statement of financial position.

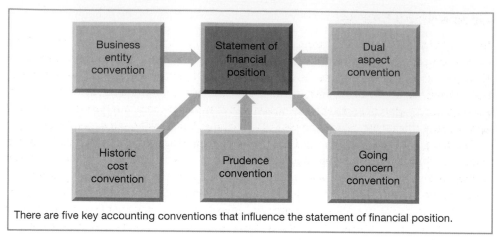

There are five key accounting conventions that influence the statement of financial position.

Figure 2.5 Accounting conventions influencing the statement of financial position

MONEY MEASUREMENT

We saw earlier that a resource will be regarded as an asset and included on the statement of financial position only if it can be measured in monetary terms, with a reasonable degree of reliability. Some resources of a business, however, do not meet this criterion and so are excluded from the statement of financial position. As a result, the scope of the statement of financial position is limited.

Activity 2.14

Can you think of resources of a business that cannot usually be measured reliably in monetary terms?

We thought of the following:

■ the quality of the human resources of the business;
■ the reputation of the business's products;
■ the beneficial location of the business;
■ the relationship the business enjoys with its customers.

You may have thought of others.

There have been occasional attempts to measure and report resources of a business that are normally excluded from the statement of financial position so as to provide a more complete picture of financial position. These attempts, however, usually fail the test of reliability. Unreliable measurements produce inconsistency in reporting and create doubts in the minds of users. The integrity and credibility of financial statements can, therefore, be undermined.

We shall now discuss some key resources of a business that normally defy reliable measurement.

Goodwill and brands

Some intangible non-current assets are similar to tangible non-current assets: they have a clear and separate identity and the cost of acquiring the asset can be reliably measured. Examples normally include patents, trademarks, copyrights and licenses. Other intangible non-current assets, however, are quite different. They lack a clear and separate identity and reflect a hotchpotch of attributes, which are part of the essence of the business. **Goodwill** and product brands are often examples of assets that lack a clear and separate identity.

The term 'goodwill' is often used to cover various attributes such as the quality of the products, the skill of employees and the relationship with customers. The term 'product brands' is also used to cover various attributes such as the brand image, the quality of the product, the trademark and so on. Where goodwill and product brands have been generated internally by the business, it is often difficult to determine their cost or to measure their current market value or even to be clear that they really exist. They are, therefore, excluded from the statement of financial position.

When such assets are acquired through an 'arm's-length transaction', however, the problems of uncertainty about their existence and measurement are resolved. (An arm's-length transaction is one that is undertaken between two unconnected parties.) If goodwill is acquired when taking over another business, or if a business acquires a particular product brand from another business, these items will have been separately identified and a price agreed for them. Under these circumstances, they can be regarded as assets (for accounting purposes) by the business that acquired them and included on the statement of financial position.

To agree a price for acquiring goodwill or product brands means that some form of valuation must take place and this raises the question as to how it is done. Usually, the valuation will be based on estimates of future earnings from holding the asset – a process that is fraught with difficulties. Nevertheless, a number of specialist businesses now exist that are prepared to take on this challenge. **Real World 2.1** shows how one specialist business ranked and valued the top ten brands in the world for 2015.

REAL WORLD 2.1

Brand leaders

Millward Brown Optimor, part of WPP plc, the marketing services group, produces an annual report that ranks and values the top world brands. For 2015, the top ten brands are as follows.

Ranking	Brand	Industry	Value ($m)
1	Apple	Technology	246,992
2	Google	Technology	173,652
3	Microsoft	Technology	115,500
4	IBM	Technology	93,987
5	Visa	Payments	91,962
6	AT&T	Telecom provider	89,492
7	Verizon	Telecom provider	86,009
8	Coca Cola	Soft drinks	83,841
9	McDonalds	Fast food	81,162
10	Marlboro	Tobacco	80,352

We can see that the valuations placed on the brands owned are quite staggering. We can also see how technology businesses dominate the rankings.

Source: BrandZ Top 100 Most Valuable Global Brands 2015, Millward Brown Optimor 2015, www. millwardbrown.com.

Human resources

Attempts have been made to place a monetary measurement on the human resources of a business, but without any real success. There are, however, certain limited circumstances in which human resources are measured and reported in the statement of financial position. Professional football clubs provide an example of where these circumstances normally arise. While football clubs cannot own players, they can own the rights to the players' services. Where these rights are acquired by compensating other clubs for releasing the players from their contracts, an arm's-length transaction arises and the amounts paid provide a reliable basis for measurement. This means that the rights to services can be regarded as an asset of the club for accounting purposes (assuming, of course, the player will bring benefits to the club).

Real World 2.2 describes how one leading club reports its investment in players on the statement of financial position.

REAL WORLD 2.2

Players on the pitch and on the statement of financial position

Tottenham Hotspur Football Club (Spurs) has acquired several key players as a result of paying transfer fees to other clubs. In common with most UK football clubs, Spurs reports the cost of acquiring the rights to the players' services on its statement of financial position. The club's statement as at 30 June 2014 shows the total cost of registering its squad of players at about £208 million. The club treats a proportion of each player's transfer fee as an expense each year. The exact proportion depends on the length of the particular player's contract.

The £208 million does not include 'home-grown' players such as Harry Kane and Andros Townsend, because Spurs did not pay a transfer fee for them and so no clear-cut value can be placed on their services. During the year to 30 June 2014, the club was active in the transfer market and spent around £110 million on acquiring new players, including Erik Lamela, Paulinho and Roberto Soldado. Some players also left the club during the year, including Gareth Bale, Tom Huddlestone, Clint Dempsey and Jermain Defoe.

The item of players' registrations is shown as an intangible asset in the statement of financial position as it is the rights to services, not the players, that are the assets. It is shown net of depreciation (or amortisation as it is usually termed for intangible non-current assets). The carrying amount at 30 June 2014 was £122 million and represented 28 per cent of Spurs' assets, as shown in the statement of financial position.

Source: Information taken from Tottenham Hotspur plc, Annual Report 2014 and Tottenham Hotspur Transfers, www.transferleague.com.

Monetary stability

When using money as the unit of measurement, we normally fail to recognise the fact that it will change in value over time. In the UK and throughout much of the world, however, inflation has been a persistent problem. This has meant that the value of money has declined in relation to other assets. In past years, high rates of inflation have resulted in statements of financial position, which were prepared on an historic cost basis, reflecting figures for assets that were much lower than if current values were employed. Rates of inflation have been relatively low in recent years and so the disparity between historic cost values and current values has been less pronounced. Nevertheless, it can still be significant. The problem of inflation has added fuel to the more general debate concerning how to measure asset values on the statement of financial position. It is to the issue of valuing assets that we now turn.

VALUING ASSETS

We saw earlier that, when preparing the statement of financial position, the historic cost convention is normally applied for the reporting of assets. This point requires further explanation as, in practice, things are a little more complex than this. Large businesses throughout much of the world adhere to asset valuation rules set out in International Financial Reporting Standards. We shall now consider the key valuation rules.

Non-current assets

Non-current assets have lives that are either *finite* or *indefinite*. Those with a finite life provide benefits to a business for a limited period of time, whereas those with an indefinite life provide benefits without a foreseeable time limit. This distinction between the two types of non-current assets applies to both tangible and intangible assets.

Initially non-current assets are recorded at their historic cost, which will include any amounts spent on getting them ready for use.

Non-current assets with finite lives

Benefits from assets with finite lives will be used up over time as a result of market changes, wear and tear and so on. The amount used up, which is referred to as *depreciation* (or *amortisation,* in the case of intangible non-current assets), must be measured for each reporting period for which the assets are held. Although we shall leave a detailed examination of depreciation until Chapter 3, we need to know that when an asset has been depreciated, this must be reflected in the statement of financial position.

The total depreciation that has accumulated over the period since the asset was acquired must be deducted from its cost. This net figure (that is, the cost of the asset less the total depreciation to date) is referred to as the *carrying amount.* It is sometimes also known as *net book value* or *written down value.* The procedure just described is not really a contravention of the historic cost convention. It is simply recognition of the fact that a proportion of the historic cost of the non-current asset has been consumed in the process of generating, or attempting to generate, benefits for the business.

Try to think of two non-current assets that have a finite life and which can be classified as:

1. tangible, and
2. intangible.

Tangible non-current assets with a finite life may include:

■ machinery and equipment;
■ motor vehicles; and
■ computers.

Inangible non-current assets with a finite life may include:

■ patents (many patents are granted for a period of 20 years);
■ leases taken out on assets (such as property); and
■ licences (such as a taxi licence).

Non-current assets with indefinite lives

Benefits from assets with indefinite lives may, or may not, be used up over time. Property, in the form of land, is usually an example of a tangible non-current asset with an indefinite life. Purchased goodwill could be an example of an intangible one, although this is not always the case. These assets are not subject to routine annual depreciation in each reporting period.

Fair values

Although initially historic cost is the standard or 'benchmark' treatment for recording non-current assets of all types (tangible and intangible, finite or indefinite lives), an alternative is allowed. Non-current assets may be recorded using **fair values** provided that these values can be measured reliably. The fair values, in this case, are the current market values (that is, the exchange values in an arm's-length transaction). The use of fair values, rather than cost figures, whether depreciated or not, can provide users with more up-to-date information, which may well be more relevant to their needs. It may also place the business in a better light, as assets such as property may have increased significantly in value over time. Increasing the statement of financial position value of an asset does not, of course, make that asset more valuable. Perceptions of the business may, however, be altered by such a move.

One consequence of upwardly revaluing non-current assets with finite lives is that the depreciation charge will be increased. This is because the depreciation charge is based on the new (increased) value of the asset.

Real World 2.3 shows the effect of the revaluation of non-current assets on the financial position of one large business.

Rising asset levels

During the year to 31 March 2010, Veolia Water UK plc, which owns Thames Water, changed its policy on the valuation of certain types of non-current assets. These assets included land and buildings, infrastructure assets and vehicles, plant and machinery. The business switched from the use of historic cost to the use of fair values and a revaluation exercise was carried out by independent qualified valuers.

The effect of this policy change was to report a revaluation gain of more than £436 million during the year. There was a 40 per cent increase in owners' (shareholders') equity, which was largely due to this gain.

Source: Information taken from Veolia Water UK plc, Annual Report 2009/10.

Activity 2.16

Refer to the statement of financial position of Brie Manufacturing shown earlier in Example 2.3 (page 47). What would be the effect on the statement of financial position of revaluing the property to a figure of £110,000?

The effect on the statement of financial position would be to increase the property to £110,000 and the gain on revaluation (that is, £110,000 − £45,000 = £65,000) would be added to equity, as it is the owner(s) who will have benefited from the gain. The revised statement of financial position would therefore be as follows:

Brie Manufacturing
Statement of financial position as at 31 March 2016

	£000
ASSETS	
Non-current assets (property, plant and equipment)	
Property	110
Plant and equipment	30
Motor vans	19
	159
Current assets	
Inventories	23
Trade receivables	18
Cash at bank	12
	53
Total assets	212
EQUITY AND LIABILITIES	
Equity (60 + 65)	125
Non-current liabilities	
Long-term borrowings	50
Current liabilities	
Trade payables	37
Total equity and liabilities	212

Once non-current assets are revalued, the frequency of revaluation becomes an important issue. Reporting assets on the statement of financial position at out-of-date revaluations is the worst of both worlds. It lacks the objectivity and verifiability of historic cost; it also lacks the realism of current values. Thus, where fair values are used, revaluations should be frequent enough to ensure that the carrying amount of the revalued asset does not differ materially from its true fair value at the statement of financial position date.

When an item of property, plant or equipment (a tangible asset) is revalued on the basis of fair values, all assets within that particular group must be revalued. It is not acceptable, therefore, to revalue some items of property but not others. Although this rule provides some degree of consistency within a particular group of assets, it does not prevent the statement of financial position from containing a mixture of valuations.

Intangible assets are not usually revalued to fair values. This is because revaluations can occur only where there is an active market, thereby permitting fair values to be properly determined. This kind of market rarely exists for intangible assets. There are, however, a few intangible assets, such as transferable taxi licences, fishing licences and production quotas, where an active market may exist.

Recent emphasis on the use of fair values in accounting has resulted in the prudence convention becoming less important. **Real World 2.4** is an extract from an article by John Kay which suggests why this change has taken place. The article, which is well worth reading in full, is highly critical of the change.

REAL WORLD 2.4

It's really not fair

Once upon a time, values were based on cost, unless assets were no longer worth their cost, in which case they had to be written down. A bird in the hand was worth more than any number in the bush: only when the bird emerged from the bush were you permitted to count it at all.

Like finance, however, accounting became cleverer, and worse. By the 1980s accounting had become the principal means by which UK graduates prepared for business. Many of these trainees found jobs in the finance sector; others took jobs in non-financial business — and, since they were smart, many rose to senior positions. Young accountants were smarter, greedier, less schooled in prudence and better schooled in economics. 'Fair value' increasingly replaced conservatism as a guiding principle. But this route to the 'true and fair view' – the traditional holy grail of the accountant – often led to an outcome that was just the opposite of fair.

 Source: Extract from Kay, J. (2015) 'Playing dice with your money', 4 September, Ft.com.
© The Financial Times Limited 2015. All Rights Reserved.

The impairment of non-current assets

All types of non-current asset are at risk of suffering a significant fall in value. This may be caused by changes in market conditions, technological obsolescence and so on. In some cases, this fall in value may lead to the carrying amount of the asset being higher than the amount that could be recovered from the asset through its continued use or through its sale. When this occurs, the asset value is said to be impaired and the general rule is to reduce the value on the statement of financial position to the recoverable amount. Unless this is done, the asset value will be overstated. The amount by which the asset value is reduced is known as an **impairment loss**. This type of impairment in value should not be confused with routine depreciation of assets with finite lives. Routine depreciation is concerned with the normal wear and tear of usage and/or the passage of time. An impairment loss is a reduction in the value of the asset through some fundamental change, sometimes a rapid one, in the commercial or technological environment.

Real World 2.5 provides an example of where one large mining business recently incurred large impairment losses on the value of its assets.

REAL WORLD 2.5

All going impaired shape

Anglo American is to slash billions of dollars from the value of a flagship iron ore asset, underscoring how the struggling group mistimed its entry into one of the most lucrative sectors of the global mining industry.

Anglo said on Thursday it expected to include the write downs on its Minas-Rio project in Brazil in next week's interim financial results, when the UK miner will also cut the value of coal assets in Australia. All told, Anglo is set to unveil between $3bn and $4bn of impairments at the results, with most attributed to Minas-Rio.

Miners are facing some of the toughest industry conditions for years, with slowing Chinese economic growth combining with ample supply of some commodities to drive down prices. Resources such as coal and iron ore were the main inputs for the Chinese steel plants that in turn powered the country's infrastructure-led growth.

That growth in demand turned iron ore into a vital source of profitability for the largest mining groups including Rio Tinto and BHP Billiton, as well as Anglo. However, iron ore prices have plummeted this year to their lowest levels since a spot market for the commodity developed — at under $50 a tonne, compared with a peak in 2011 of $190/t.

→

Anglo's impending impairment of Minas-Rio comes just months after a $3.5bn write down of its value. There was also a $4bn impairment in 2013. It means Anglo has written down most of the value it originally saw in the complex project, which cost the group more than $13bn in acquisition and construction costs.

Source: Wilson, J. (2015) 'Anglo American to write down value of mining assets by up to $4bn', FT.com, 16 July.
© The Financial Times Limited 2015. All Rights Reserved.

Intangible, non-current assets with indefinite lives should be tested for impairment on an annual basis. Other non-current assets, however, also must be tested where events suggest that impairment has taken place.

Activity 2.18

Why might it be a good idea to have impairment tests carried out by independent experts?

Impairment tests involve making judgements about the appropriate value to place on assets. Employing independent valuers to make these judgements will normally give users greater confidence in the information reported. There is always a risk that managers will manipulate impairment values to portray a picture that they would like users to see.

Where a non-current asset with a finite useful life has its value impaired, the future depreciation expense for that asset will be based on the new (lower) impaired value.

Inventories

It is not only non-current assets that run the risk of a significant fall in value. The **inventories** of a business could also suffer this fate as a result of changes in market taste, obsolescence, deterioration, damage and so on. Where a fall in value means that the amount likely to be recovered from the sale of the inventories will be lower than their cost, this loss must be reflected in the statement of financial position. Thus, if the net realisable value (that is, selling price less any selling costs) falls below the historic cost of inventories held, the former should be used as the basis of valuation. This reflects, once again, the influence of the prudence convention on the statement of financial position.

Real World 2.6 reveals how one well-known business wrote down some of its inventories.

Coming up Next

Next plc, the fashion and home furnishing retailer, saw some of its inventories fall in value during the year ended 24 January 2015. This led to a reported loss of £100.9 million, which represented the difference between their cost and net realisable value. (However, the operating profit for the year was £812.1 million overall.) To see this in context, the cost of inventories held at the 2014/15 year-end was £416.8 million and the cost of goods sold during the year £1,452.7 million. In the previous year, there was a reported loss of £80.7 million for the same reason. Inventories held at the end of 2013/2014 were £385.6 million and cost of goods sold during that year was £1,363.5 million.

The fashion business, particularly women's fashion, is very fast moving and so losses from holding such inventories are not altogether surprising.

Source: Information taken from Next plc, Annual Report and Accounts for the year ended 24 January 2015, pp. 82, 92.

MEETING USER NEEDS

The statement of financial position is the oldest of the three main financial statements and may help users in the following ways:

- *It provides insights about how the business is financed and how its funds are deployed.* The statement of financial position shows how much finance is contributed by the owners and how much is contributed by outside lenders. It also shows the different kinds of assets acquired and how much is invested in each kind.
- *It can provide a basis for assessing the value of the business.* Since the statement of financial position lists, and places a value on, the various assets and claims, it can provide a starting point for assessing the value of the business. We have seen earlier, however, that accounting rules may result in assets being shown at their historic cost and that the restrictive definition of assets may exclude certain business resources from the statement of financial position.
- *Relationships between assets and claims can be assessed.* It can be useful to look at relationships between various statement of financial position items, for example the relationship between how much wealth is tied up in current assets and how much is owed in the short term (current liabilities). From this relationship, we can see whether the business has sufficient short-term assets to cover its maturing obligations. We shall look at this and other relationships between statement of financial position items in some detail in Chapter 6.
- *Performance can be assessed.* The effectiveness of a business in generating wealth can usefully be assessed against the amount of investment that was involved. Thus, the relationship between profit earned during a period and the value of the net assets invested can be helpful to many users, particularly owners and managers. This and similar relationships will also be explored in detail in Chapter 6.

Once armed with the insights that a statement of financial position can provide, users are better placed to make investment and other decisions. **Real World 2.7** shows how a small business was able to obtain a loan because its bank was impressed by its strong statement of financial position.

REAL WORLD 2.7

A sound education

Sandeep Sud is a qualified solicitor who also runs a school uniform business based in Hounslow, in partnership with his parents. The business, which has four full-time employees, uses its statement of financial position to gauge how it is progressing. The statement has also been a key factor in securing a bank loan for the improvement and expansion of the business premises.

According to Sandeep:

Having a strong statement of financial position helped when it came to borrowing. When we first applied for a refurbishment loan we couldn't provide up-to-date accounts to the bank manager. This could have been a problem, but we quickly got our accounts in order and the loan was approved straight away. Because our statement of financial position was strong, the bank thought we were a good risk. Although we decided not to draw down on the loan – because we used cash flow instead – it did open our eyes to the importance of a strong statement of financial position.

Source: Adapted from: Balance sheets: the basics, www.businesslink.gov.uk, accessed 18 April 2016.

? SELF-ASSESSMENT QUESTION 2.1

The following information relates to Simonson Engineering as at 30 September 2016:

	£
Plant and equipment	25,000
Trade payables	18,000
Short-term borrowing	26,000
Inventories	45,000
Property	72,000
Long-term borrowing	51,000
Trade receivables	48,000
Equity at 1 October 2015	117,500
Cash in hand	1,500
Motor vehicles	15,000
Fixtures and fittings	9,000
Profit for the year to 30 September 2016	18,000
Drawings for the year to 30 September 2016	15,000

Required:
(a) Prepare a statement of financial position for the business as at 30 September 2016 using the standard layout illustrated in Example 2.3.
(b) Comment on the financial position of the business based on the statement prepared in (a).

(c) Show the effect on the statement of financial position shown in (a) above of a decision to revalue the property to £115,000 and to recognise that the net realisable value of inventories at the year end is £38,000.

The solution to this question can be found at the back of the book on page 523.

SUMMARY

The main points of this chapter may be summarised as follows.

The major financial statements

■ There are three major financial statements: the statement of cash flows, the income statement and the statement of financial position.

■ The statement of cash flows shows the cash movements over a particular period.

■ The income statement shows the wealth (profit) generated over a particular period.

■ The statement of financial position shows the accumulated wealth at a particular point in time.

The statement of financial position

■ This sets out the assets of the business, on the one hand, and the claims against those assets, on the other.

■ Assets are resources of the business that have certain characteristics, such as the ability to provide future economic benefits.

■ Claims are obligations on the part of the business to provide cash, or some other benefit, to outside parties.

■ Claims are of two types: equity and liabilities.

■ Equity represents the claim(s) of the owner(s) and liabilities represent the claims of others.

■ The statement of financial position reflects the accounting equation:

$$\text{Assets} = \text{Equity} + \text{Liabilities}$$

Classification of assets and liabilities

■ Assets are normally categorised as being current or non-current.

■ Current assets are cash or near cash or are held for sale or consumption in the normal course of business, or for trading, or for the short term.

■ Non-current assets are assets that are not current assets. They are normally held for the long-term operations of the business.

■ Liabilities are normally categorised as being current or non-current liabilities.

- Current liabilities represent amounts due in the normal course of the business's operating cycle, or are held for trading, or are to be settled within a year of, or cannot be deferred for at least a year after, the end of the reporting period.

- Non-current liabilities represent amounts due that are not current liabilities.

Statement of financial position layouts

- The standard layout begins with assets at the top of the statement of financial position and places equity and liabilities underneath.

- A variation of the standard layout also begins with the assets at the top of the statement of financial position, but then the non-current and current liabilities are deducted from the total assets figure to arrive at a net assets figure. Equity is placed underneath.

Accounting conventions

- Accounting conventions are the rules of accounting that have evolved to deal with practical problems experienced by those preparing financial statements.

- The main conventions relating to the statement of financial position include business entity, historic cost, prudence, going concern and dual aspect.

Money measurement

- Using money as the unit of measurement limits the scope of the statement of financial position.

- Certain resources such as goodwill, product brands and human resources are difficult to measure. An 'arm's-length transaction' is normally required before such assets can be reliably measured and reported on the statement of financial position.

- Money is not a stable unit of measurement – it changes in value over time.

Asset valuation

- The initial treatment is to show non-current assets at historic cost.

- Fair values may be used rather than historic cost, provided that they can be reliably obtained. This is rarely possible, however, for intangible non-current assets.

- Non-current assets with finite lives should be shown at cost (or fair value) less any accumulated depreciation (amortisation).

- Where the value of a non-current asset is impaired, it should be written down to its recoverable amount.

- Inventories are shown at the lower of cost or net realisable value.

The usefulness of the statement of financial position

■ It shows how finance has been raised and how it has been been deployed.

■ It provides a basis for valuing the business, though it can only be a starting point.

■ Relationships between various statement of financial position items can usefully be explored.

■ Relationships between wealth generated and wealth invested can be helpful indicators of business effectiveness.

KEY TERMS

For definitions of these terms, see Appendix A.

statement of cash flows p. 29
income statement p. 29
statement of financial
   position p. 29
final accounts p. 33
asset p. 34
claim p. 34
tangible asset p. 37
intangible asset p. 37
equity p. 37
liability p. 37
trade payable p. 39
reporting period p. 41
current asset p. 43
trade receivable p. 44

non-current (fixed) asset p. 44
property, plant and
   equipment p. 44
current liability p. 46
non-current liability p. 46
accounting convention p. 50
business entity convention p. 50
historic cost convention p. 51
prudence convention p. 52
going concern convention p. 53
dual aspect convention p. 53
goodwill p. 55
fair value p. 58
impairment loss p. 61
inventories p. 62

FURTHER READING

If you would like to explore the topics covered in this chapter in more depth, we recommend the following books:

Elliott, B. and Elliott, J. (2015), *Financial Accounting and Reporting,* 17th edn, Pearson, Chapters 17, 19 and 20.

International Accounting Standards Board, *A Guide through IFRS 2015* (Green Book), IAS 16 *Property, Plant and Equipment* and IAS 38 *Intangible Assets.*

KPMG, *Insights into IFRS,* 12th edn, Sweet and Maxwell, 2015/16, Sections 3.2, 3.3, 3.8 and 3.10 (a summarised version of this is available free at www.kpmg.com).

Melville, A. (2015) *International Financial Reporting: A Practical Guide,* 5th edn, Pearson, Chapters 5, 6, and 7.

REVIEW QUESTIONS

Solutions to these questions can be found at the back of the book on pages 000–000.

2.1 An accountant prepared a statement of financial position for a business. In this statement, the equity of the owner was shown next to the liabilities. This confused the owner, who argued: 'My equity is my major asset and so should be shown as an asset on the statement of financial position.' How would you explain this misunderstanding to the owner?

2.2 'The statement of financial position shows how much a business is worth.' Do you agree with this statement? Explain the reasons for your response.

2.3 What is meant by the accounting equation? How does the form of this equation differ between the two statement of financial position layouts mentioned in the chapter?

2.4 From time to time there have been attempts to place a value on the 'human assets' of a business in order to derive a figure that can be included on the statement of financial position. Do you think humans should be treated as assets? Would 'human assets' meet the conventional definition of an asset for inclusion on the statement of financial position?

EXERCISES

*Exercises 2.1 and 2.2 are basic level. Exercise 2.3 is intermediate level and Exercises 2.4 and 2.5 are advanced level. Those with **coloured numbers** have solutions at the back of the book, starting on page 550.*

2.1 On Thursday, the fourth day of his business venture, Paul, the street trader in wrapping paper (see earlier in the chapter, pages 29–37), bought more inventories for £53 cash. During the day he sold inventories that had cost £33 for a total of £47.

Required:
Draw up the three financial statements for Paul's business venture for Thursday.

2.2 While on holiday in Bridlington, Helen had her credit cards and purse stolen from the beach while she was swimming. She was left with only £40, which she had kept in her hotel room, but she had three days of her holiday remaining. She was determined to continue her holiday and decided to make some money to enable her to do so. She decided to sell orange juice to holidaymakers using the local beach. On the first day she bought 80 cartons of orange juice at £0.50 each for cash and sold 70 of these at £0.80 each. On the following day she bought 60 cartons at £0.50 each for cash and sold 65 at £0.80 each. On the third and final day she bought another 60 cartons at £0.50 each for cash. However, it rained and, as a result, business was poor. She managed to sell 20 at £0.80 each but sold off the rest of her inventories at £0.40 each.

Required:
Prepare an income statement and statement of cash flows for each day's trading and prepare a statement of financial position at the end of each day's trading.

2.3 On 1 March, Joe Conday started a new business. During March he carried out the following transactions:

1 March	Deposited £20,000 in a newly opened business bank account.
2 March	Bought fixtures and fittings for £6,000 cash and inventories £8,000 on credit.
3 March	Borrowed £5,000 from a relative and deposited it in the bank.
4 March	Bought a motor car for £7,000 cash and withdrew £200 in cash for his own use.
5 March	A further motor car costing £9,000 was bought. The motor car bought on 4 March was given in part exchange at a value of £6,500. The balance of purchase price for the new car was paid in cash.
6 March	Conday won £2,000 in a lottery and paid the amount into the business bank account. He also repaid £1,000 of the borrowings.

Required:
Draw up a statement of financial position for the business at the end of each day.

2.4 The following is a list of the assets and claims of Crafty Engineering as at 30 June last year:

	£000
Trade payables	86
Motor vehicles	38
Long-term borrowing from Industrial Finance Company	260
Equipment and tools	207
Short-term borrowings	116
Inventories	153
Property	320
Trade receivables	185

Required:
(a) Prepare the statement of financial position of the business as at 30 June last year from the above information using the standard layout. (*Hint:* There is a missing item that needs to be deduced and inserted.)
(b) Discuss the significant features revealed by this financial statement.

2.5 The statement of financial position of a business at the start of the week is as follows:

	£
ASSETS	
Property	145,000
Furniture and fittings	63,000
Inventories	28,000
Trade receivables	33,000
Total assets	269,000
EQUITY AND LIABILITIES	
Equity	203,000
Short-term borrowing (bank overdraft)	43,000
Trade payables	23,000
Total equity and liabilities	269,000

During the week the following transactions take place:
(a) Sold inventories for £11,000 cash; these inventories had cost £8,000.
(b) Sold inventories for £23,000 on credit; these inventories had cost £17,000.
(c) Received cash from trade receivables totalling £18,000.
(d) The owners of the business introduced £100,000 of their own money, which was placed in the business bank account.
(e) The owners brought a motor van, valued at £10,000, into the business.
(f) Bought inventories on credit for £14,000.
(g) Paid trade payables £13,000.

Required:
Show the statement of financial position after all of these transactions have been reflected.

Chapter 3

MEASURING AND REPORTING FINANCIAL PERFORMANCE

INTRODUCTION

In this chapter, we continue our examination of the major financial statements by looking at the income statement. This statement was briefly considered in Chapter 2, but we shall now look at it in some detail. We shall see how it is prepared and how it links with the statement of financial position. We shall also consider some of the key measurement problems to be faced when preparing the income statement.

Learning outcomes

When you have completed this chapter, you should be able to:

■ discuss the nature and purpose of the income statement;

■ prepare an income statement from relevant financial information and interpret the information that it contains;

■ discuss the main recognition and measurement issues that must be considered when preparing the income statement;

■ explain the main accounting conventions underpinning the income statement.

Businesses exist for the purpose of generating wealth, or profit. The income statement – or profit and loss account, as it is sometimes called – measures and reports how much **profit** a business has generated over a period. It is, therefore, an immensely important financial statement for many users.

To measure profit, the total revenue generated during a particular period must be identified. **Revenue** is simply a measure of the inflow of economic benefits arising from the ordinary operations of a business. These benefits will result in either an increase in assets (such as cash or amounts owed to the business by its customers) or a decrease in liabilities. Different forms of business enterprise will generate different forms of revenue. Some examples of the different forms that revenue can take are as follows:

- sales of goods (for example, by a manufacturer);
- fees for services (for example, of a solicitor);
- subscriptions (for example, of a club); and
- interest received (for example, on an investment fund).

Real World 3.1 shows the various forms of revenue generated by a leading football club.

REAL WORLD 3.1

Gunning for revenue

Arsenal Football Club generated total revenue of more than £344 million for the year ended 31 May 2015. Like other leading clubs, it relies on various forms of revenue to sustain its success. Figure 3.1 shows the contribution of each form of revenue for the year.

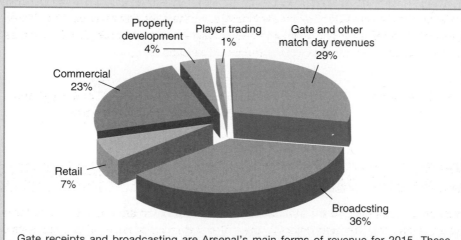

Gate receipts and broadcasting are Arsenal's main forms of revenue for 2015. These account for almost two thirds of the total revenue generated. Revenue from player trading was insignificant for the year.

Figure 3.1 Arsenal's revenue for the year ended 31 May 2015

Source: Based on information in Arsenal Holdings plc, Statement of Accounts and Annual Report 2014/15, p. 44.

The total expenses relating to each period must also be identified. **Expense** is really the opposite of revenue. It represents the outflow of economic benefits arising from the ordinary operations of a business. This loss of benefits will result in either a decrease in assets (such as cash) or an increase in liabilities (such as amounts owed to suppliers). Expenses are incurred in the process of generating revenue or, at least, in attempting to generate it. The nature of the business will again determine the type of expenses to be incurred. Examples of some of the more common types of expense are:

■ the cost of buying or making the goods that are sold during the period concerned – known as *cost of sales* or *cost of goods sold*;
■ salaries and wages;
■ rent;
■ motor vehicle running expenses.

Activity 3.1

Try to think of at least two other types of expense that a business may incur.

Other types of expense may include:

■ insurance;
■ printing and stationery;
■ heat and light;
■ telephone and postage.

You may have thought of others.

The income statement simply shows the total revenue generated during a particular period and deducts from this the total expenses incurred in generating that revenue. The difference between the total revenue and total expenses will represent either profit (if revenue exceeds expenses) or loss (if expenses exceed revenue). Therefore:

Profit (or loss) for the period = Total revenue for the period – Total expenses incurred in generating that revenue

DIFFERENT ROLES

The income statement and the statement of financial position are not substitutes for one another; rather, they perform different roles. The statement of financial position sets out the wealth held by the business at a single moment in time, whereas the income statement is concerned with the *flow* of wealth (profit) over a period of time. The two statements are, however, closely related.

The income statement links the statements of financial position at the beginning and the end of a **reporting period**. At the start of a new reporting period, the statement of financial position shows the opening wealth position of the business. At the end of the reporting period, an income statement is prepared to show the wealth generated for that period. A statement of financial position is then prepared to reveal the new wealth position at the end of the period. It will reflect changes in wealth that have occurred since the previous statement of financial position was drawn up.

We saw in Chapter 2 (pages 00 to 00) that the effect on the statement of financial position of making a profit (or loss) means that the accounting equation can be extended as follows:

Assets (at the end of the period) = **Equity (amount at the start of the period)**
+ Profit (or − Loss) (for the period)
+ Liabilities (at the end of the period)

(This is assuming that the owner makes no injections or withdrawals of equity during the period.)

Activity 3.2

Can you recall from Chapter 2 how a profit, or loss, for a period is shown in the statement of financial position?

It is shown as an adjustment to owners' equity. Profit is added and a loss is subtracted.

The equation above can be extended to:

Assets (at the end of the period) = **Equity (amount at the start of the period)**
+ (Sales revenue − Expenses) (for the period)
+ Liabilities (at the end of the period)

In theory, it is possible to calculate the profit (or loss) for the period by making all adjustments for revenue and expenses through the equity section of the statement of financial position. However, this would be rather cumbersome. A better solution is to have an 'appendix' to the equity section, in the form of an income statement. By deducting expenses from revenue for the period, the income statement derives the profit (or loss) by which the equity figure in the statement of financial position needs to be adjusted. This profit (or loss) figure represents the net effect of trading for the period. By providing this 'appendix', users are presented with a detailed and more informative view of performance.

INCOME STATEMENT LAYOUT

The layout of the income statement will vary according to the type of business to which it relates. To illustrate an income statement, let us consider the case of a retail business (that is, a business that buys goods in their completed state and resells them).

Example 3.1 sets out a typical layout for the income statement of a retail business.

Better-Price Stores
Income statement for the year ended 30 June 2016

	£
Sales revenue	232,000
Cost of sales	(154,000)
Gross profit	78,000
Salaries and wages	(24,500)
Rent	(14,200)
Heat and light	(7,500)
Telephone and postage	(1,200)
Insurance	(1,000)
Motor vehicle running expenses	(3,400)
Depreciation – fixtures and fittings	(1,000)
Depreciation – motor van	(600)
Operating profit	24,600
Interest received from investments	2,000
Interest on borrowings	(1,100)
Profit for the period	25,500

We saw in Chapter 2 that brackets are used to denote when an item is to be deducted in the financial statements. This convention is used by accountants in preference to + or − signs and will be used throughout the text.

We can see from the above statement that three measures of profit have been calculated. Let us now consider each of these in turn.

Gross profit

The first part of the income statement is concerned with calculating the **gross profit** for the period. Note that revenue, which arises from selling the goods, is the first item to appear. The cost of sales figure (also referred to as *cost of goods sold*) for the period is deducted from the revenue figure. This gives the gross profit, which represents the profit from buying and selling goods, without taking into account any other revenues or expenses associated with the business.

Operating profit

Operating expenses (overheads) incurred in running the business (salaries and wages, rent, stationery, insurance and so on) are deducted from the gross profit. The resulting figure is known as the **operating profit**. This represents the wealth generated during the period from the normal activities of the business. It does not take account of income from other activities. Better-Price Stores in Example 3.1 is a retailer, so interest received on some spare cash that the business has invested is not part of its operating profit. Costs of financing the business are also ignored in the calculation of the operating profit.

Profit for the period

Having established the operating profit, we add any non-operating income (such as rent receivable from letting property owned by the business) and deduct any non-operating expenses (such as interest payable on borrowings) to arrive at the **profit for the period** (or net profit). This final measure of wealth generated represents the amount attributable to the owner(s) and will be added to the equity figure in the statement of financial position. It is a residual: that is, the amount remaining after deducting all expenses incurred in generating the sales revenue and taking account of non-operating income and expenses.

Activity 3.3

Look back to Example 3.1 and assume that a trainee accountant prepared the income statement. Subsequent checking by the chief financial officer revealed the following errors:

1   Staff performance bonuses amounting to £12,500 had been charged to cost of sales.
2   The depreciation charge for fixtures and fittings should be £10,000 not £1,000.
3   Stationery costing £500 had been treated as interest on borrowings.

What will be the gross profit, operating profit and profit for the period after the above errors have been corrected?

Your answer should be as follows:

	Note	£
Corrected gross profit (78,000 + 12,500)	1	90,500
Corrected operating profit		
(24,600 − (10,000 − 1,000) − 500)	2	15,100
Corrected profit for the period		
(15,100 + 2,000 − (1,100 − 500))	3	16,500

Notes:

1   Staff bonuses should be treated as part of the salaries and wages of the business. This means that cost of sales will decrease by £12,500 and gross profit will increase by a corresponding amount. The corrected gross profit figure is, therefore, £90,500 (that is, £78,000 + £12,500). The operating profit and profit for the period, however, will not be affected by this correction. Although the salaries and wages operating expense will increase by £12,500, this is offset by a compensating increase in gross profit.

2   The increase in the depreciation charge from £1,000 to £10,000 will decrease operating profit by £9,000. Furthermore, by treating stationery correctly, operating expenses will

increase by £500, thereby decreasing operating profit by a corresponding amount. The corrected operating profit figure is, therefore, £15,100 (that is, £24,600 − £9,500).

3   The corrected profit for the period is calculated by taking the corrected operating profit £15,100, adding the interest received from investments £2,000, and then deducting the correct amount of interest on borrowing £600 (that is, £1,100 − £500) = £16,500.

FURTHER ISSUES

Having set out the main principles involved in preparing an income statement, we need to consider some further points.

Cost of sales

The **cost of sales** (or cost of goods sold) for a period can be identified in different ways. In some businesses, the cost of sales for each individual sale is identified at the time of the transaction. Each item of sales revenue is matched with the relevant cost of that sale. Many large retailers (for example, supermarkets) have point-of-sale (checkout) devices that not only record each sale but also simultaneously pick up the cost of the goods that are the subject of the particular sale. Businesses that sell a relatively small number of high-value items (for example, an engineering business that produces custom-made equipment) also tend to match sales revenue with the cost of the goods sold, at the time of sale. However, many businesses (for example, small retailers) may not find it practical to do this. Instead, they identify the cost of sales after the end of the reporting period.

To understand how this is done, we must remember that the cost of sales represents the cost of goods that were *sold* during the period rather than the cost of goods that were *bought* during the period. Part of the goods bought during the period may remain, as inventories, at the end of the period. These will normally be sold in the next period. To derive the cost of sales, we need to know the amount of opening and closing inventories for the period and the cost of goods bought during the period. Example 3.2 illustrates how the cost of sales is derived.

Example 3.2

Better-Price Stores, which we considered in Example 3.1 above, began the year with unsold inventories of £40,000 and during that year bought inventories at a cost of £189,000. At the end of the year, unsold inventories of £75,000 were still held by the business.

The opening inventories (at the beginning of the year) *plus* the goods bought during the year represent the total goods available for resale, as follows:

	£
Opening inventories	40,000
Purchases (goods bought)	189,000
Goods available for resale	229,000

The closing inventories represent that portion of the total goods available for resale that remains unsold at the end of the year. This means that the cost of goods actually sold during the year must be the total goods available for resale *less* the inventories remaining at the end of the year. That is:

	£
Goods available for resale	229,000
Closing inventories	(75,000)
Cost of sales (or cost of goods sold)	154,000

These calculations are sometimes shown on the face of the income statement as in Example 3.3.

Example 3.3

	£	£
Sales revenue		232,000
Cost of sales:		
Opening inventories	40,000	
Purchases (goods bought)	189,000	
Closing inventories	(75,000)	(154,000)
Gross profit		78,000

This is just an expanded version of the first section of the income statement for Better-Price Stores, as set out in Example 3.1. We have simply included the additional information concerning inventories balances and purchases for the year provided in Example 3.2.

Classifying expenses

The classification of expense items is often a matter of judgement. For example, the income statement set out in Example 3.1 could have included the insurance expense with the telephone and postage expense under a single heading – say, 'general expenses'. Such decisions are normally based on how useful a particular classification will be to users. This will usually mean that expense items of material size will be shown separately. For businesses that trade as limited companies, however, rules dictate the classification of expense items for external reporting purposes. These rules will be discussed in Chapter 4.

The following information relates to the activities of H&S Retailers for the year ended 30 April 2016:

	£
Motor vehicle running expenses	1,200
Closing inventories	3,000
Rent payable	5,000
Motor vans – cost less depreciation	6,300
Annual depreciation – motor vans	1,500
Heat and light	900
Telephone and postage	450
Sales revenue	97,400
Goods purchased	68,350
Insurance	750
Loan interest payable	620
Balance at bank	4,780
Salaries and wages	10,400
Opening inventories	4,000

Prepare an income statement for the year ended 30 April 2016. (*Hint*: Not all items listed should appear on the income statement.)

Your answer to this activity should be as follows:

H&S Retailers
Income statement for the year ended 30 April 2016

	£	£
Sales revenue		97,400
Cost of sales:		
Opening inventories	4,000	
Purchases	68,350	
Closing inventories	(3,000)	(69,350)
Gross profit		28,050
Salaries and wages		(10,400)
Rent payable		(5,000)
Heat and light		(900)
Telephone and postage		(450)
Insurance		(750)
Motor vehicle running expenses		(1,200)
Depreciation – motor vans		(1,500)
Operating profit		7,850
Loan interest		(620)
Profit for the period		7,230

Note that neither the motor vans nor the bank balance are included in this statement, because they are both assets and so neither revenues nor expenses.

Figure 3.2 summarises the layout of the income statement.

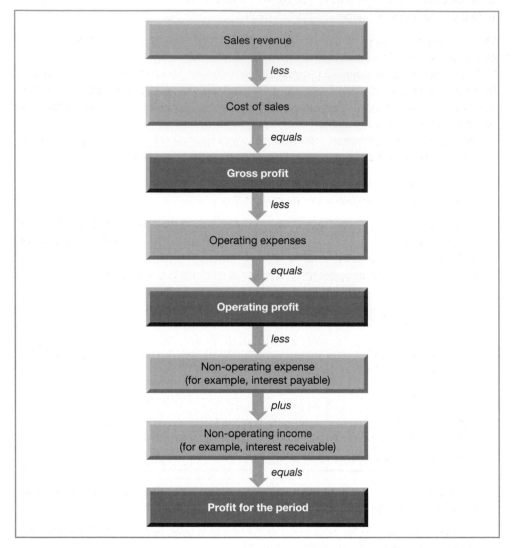

Figure 3.2 The layout of the income statement

RECOGNISING REVENUE

A key issue in the measurement of profit concerns the point at which revenue is recognised. Revenue arising from the sale of goods or provision of a service could be recognised at various points. Where, for example, a motor car dealer receives an order for a new car from one of its customers, the associated revenue could be recognised by the dealer:

- at the time that the order is placed by the customer;
- at the time that the car is collected by the customer; or
- at the time that the customer pays the dealer.

These three points could be quite far apart where, for example, the order relates to a specialist car that is sold to the customer on credit.

The point chosen can have a profound impact on total revenues and, in turn, the profit for the reporting period. If the sale transaction straddled the end of a reporting period, the point chosen for recognising revenue could determine whether it is included in an earlier reporting period or a later one.

There are two fundamental criteria for recognising revenue in the income statement. These are that an item of revenue should only be recognised where:

- it is probable that the economic benefits will be received, *and*
- the amount of revenue can be measured reliably.

There are, however, additional criteria that apply to certain categories of revenue. For example, when dealing with the sales of goods, two key criteria are that both ownership and control of the goods have been transferred to the buyer.

Activity 3.5 provides an opportunity to apply these criteria to a practical problem.

Activity 3.5

A manufacturing business sells goods on credit. Below are four points in the production/selling cycle at which revenue might be recognised:

1. when the goods are produced;
2. when an order is received from the customer;
3. when the goods are delivered to, and accepted by, the customer; and
4. when the cash is received from the customer.

At what point do you think the business should recognise revenue?

All of the criteria mentioned above will usually be fulfilled at point 3: when the goods are passed to, and accepted by, the customer. This is because:

- the selling price and the settlement terms will have been agreed and, therefore, the amount of revenue can be reliably measured;
- delivery and acceptance of the goods leads to ownership and control passing to the buyer; and
- transferring ownership gives the seller legally enforceable rights that makes it probable that the buyer will pay.

We can see that the effect of applying these criteria is that a sale on credit is usually recognised *before* the cash is received. This means that the total sales revenue shown in the income statement will, for most businesses (apart from retailers), include sales transactions for which the cash has yet to be received. The total sales revenue will often, therefore, be different from the total cash received from sales during the period. For cash sales (that is, sales where cash is paid at the same time as the goods are transferred), there will be no difference in timing between reporting sales revenue and cash received.

Long-term contracts

Some contracts for goods or services may take more than one reporting period to complete. If a business waits until the completion of a long-term contract before recognising revenue, a misleading impression may be given of performance over time.

Activity 3.6

Why might leaving revenue recognition until the contract is complete lead to a misleading impression?

It is because all the revenue would be shown in the final reporting period and none in the preceding reporting periods when work was also carried out.

It is possible, however, to recognise revenue *before* the contract is completed by identifying different stages of completion. A proportion of the total contract price, based on the work done, can then be treated as revenue of the reporting period during which each particular stage is completed. This approach can be used where contract revenue and costs, as well as the stages of completion, can be measured reliably.

Construction contracts often extend over a long period of time and so this staged approach to recognising revenues is often appropriate. Let us assume that a customer enters into a contract with a construction business to have a large factory built. It is estimated that the factory will take three years to complete. Building the factory can be broken down into the following stages of completion:

- Stage 1 – clearing and levelling the land and putting in the foundations.
- Stage 2 – building the walls.
- Stage 3 – putting on the roof.
- Stage 4 – putting in the windows and completing all the interior work.

It is expected that Stage 1 of the contract will be completed by the end of Year 1, Stages 2 and 3 will be completed by the end of Year 2 and Stage 4 by the end of Year 3.

Once a particular stage is completed, the agreed price for that stage can be recognised as revenue by the construction business. Thus, the revenue for completing Stage 1, along with any expenses incurred on that stage, will be incorporated in the income statement for Year 1 and so on. With such contracts, the customer will normally agree to an appropriate proportion of the total contract price being paid on completion of each stage.

Certain kinds of service may also take years to complete. One example is where a consultancy business installs a new computer system for a large organisation. If the outcome of the contract can be estimated reliably, a similar approach to that taken for construction contracts can be adopted. Thus, a proportion of the total contract price can be recognised as revenue as soon as a particular stage of completion has been reached.

Real World 3.2 sets out the revenue recognition criteria for one large construction business.

Continuous and non-continuous services

In some cases, a continuous service may be provided to customers. For example, a telecommunications business may provide open access to the internet for subscribers. Here, the benefits from providing the service are usually assumed to arise evenly over time and so revenue is recognised evenly over the subscription period.

Where it is not possible to break down a service into particular stages of completion, or to assume that benefits from providing the service accrue evenly over time, revenue is normally recognised after the service is completed. An example might be the work done by a solicitor on a house purchase for a client.

Real World 3.3 provides an example of how one major business recognises revenue for a period.

- Revenue from calls is recognised at the time the call is made over the group's network.
- Subscription fees, consisting primarily of monthly charges for access to broadband and other internet access or voice services, are recognised as revenue as the service is provided.
- Revenue from the interconnection of voice and data traffic between other telecommunications operators is recognised at the time of transit across the group's network.
- Revenue from the sale of equipment is recognised when all the significant risks and rewards of ownership are transferred to the buyer, which is normally the date the equipment is delivered and accepted by the customer.

Source: Information taken from BT Group plc, Annual Report 2014, p. 129.

Revenue for providing services is often recognised *before* the cash is received. There are occasions, however, when the business demands payment before providing the service.

Activity 3.7

Can you think of any examples where cash may be demanded in advance of a service being provided? (*Hint*: Try to think of services that you may use.)

Examples of cash being received in advance of the service being provided may include:

- rent received from letting premises;
- telephone line rental charges;
- TV licence (BBC) or subscription fees (for example, Sky);
- subscriptions received for the use of health clubs or golf clubs.

You may have thought of others.

RECOGNISING EXPENSES

Having considered the recognition of revenue, let us now turn to the recognition of expenses. The **matching convention** provides guidance on this. This convention states that expenses should be matched to the revenue that they helped to generate. In other words, the expenses associated with a particular item of revenue must be taken into account in the same reporting period as that in which the item of revenue is included. We saw how this convention is applied with Better-Price Stores' cost of sales expense in Example 3.2. The appropriate expense was just the cost of the inventories that were sold, not the cost of the inventories that were available for sale, during the period.

Applying this convention often means that an expense reported in the income statement for a period may not be the same as the cash paid for that item during the period. The expense reported might be either more or less than the cash paid during the period. Let us consider two examples that illustrate this point.

When the expense for the period is more than the cash paid during the period

Example 3.4

Domestic Ltd, a retailer, sells household electrical appliances. It pays its sales staff a commission of 2 per cent of sales revenue generated. Total sales revenue for last year amounted to £300,000. This means that the commission to be paid on sales for the year will be £6,000. However, by the end of the year, the amount of sales commission actually paid was only £5,000. If the business reported this amount, it would mean that the income statement would not reflect the full expense for the year. This would contravene the *matching convention* because not all of the expenses associated with the revenue of the year would have been matched with it in the income statement. This will be remedied as follows:

■ Sales commission expense in the income statement will include the amount paid plus the amount outstanding (that is, £6,000 = £5,000 + £1,000).

■ The amount outstanding (£1,000) represents an outstanding liability at the end of the year and will be included under the heading **accrued expenses**, or 'accruals', in the statement of financial position. As this item will have to be paid within 12 months of the year end, it will be treated as a current liability.

■ The cash will already have been reduced to reflect the commission paid (£5,000) during the period.

These points are illustrated in Figure 3.3.

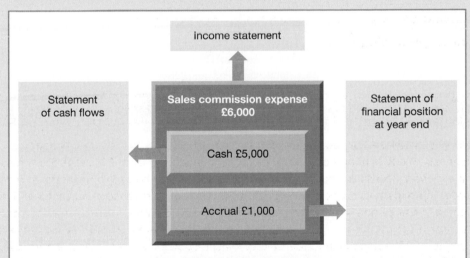

This illustrates the main points of Example 3.4. We can see that the sales commission expense of £6,000 (which appears in the income statement) is made up of a cash element of £5,000 and an accrued element of £1,000. The cash element appears in the statement of cash flows and the accrued element will appear as a year-end liability in the statement of financial position.

Figure 3.3 Accounting for sales commission

In principle, all expenses should be matched to the period in which the sales revenue to which they relate is reported. It is sometimes difficult, however, to match certain expenses to sales revenue in the same precise way that we have matched sales commission to sales revenue. For example, electricity charges incurred often cannot be linked directly to particular sales in this way. As a result, the electricity charges incurred by, say, a retailer would be matched to the *period* to which they relate. Example 3.5 illustrates this.

Example 3.5

Domestic Ltd has reached the end of its reporting period and has paid for electricity for only the first three quarters of the year (amounting to £1,900). This is simply because the electricity company has yet to produce bills for the quarter that ends on the same date as Domestic Ltd's year end. The amount of Domestic Ltd's bill for the last quarter of the year is £500. In this situation, the amount of the electricity expense outstanding is dealt with as follows:

■ Electricity expense in the income statement will include the amount paid, plus the amount of the bill for the last quarter of the year (that is, £1,900 + £500 = £2,400) in order to cover the whole year.
■ The amount of the outstanding bill (£500) represents a liability at the end of the year and will be included under the heading 'accruals' or 'accrued expenses' in the statement of financial position. This item would normally have to be paid within 12 months of the year end and will, therefore, be treated as a current liability.
■ The cash will already have been reduced to reflect the amount (£1,900) paid for electricity during the period.

This treatment will mean that the correct figure for the electricity expense for the year will be included in the income statement. It will also have the effect of showing that, at the end of the reporting period, Domestic Ltd owed the amount of the last quarter's electricity bill. Dealing with the outstanding amount in this way reflects the dual aspect of the item and will ensure that the accounting equation is maintained.

Domestic Ltd may wish to draw up its income statement before it is able to discover how much it owes for the last quarter's electricity. In this case it is quite normal to make an estimate of the amount of the bill and to use this amount as described above.

Activity 3.8

How will the eventual payment of the outstanding sales commission (Example 3.4) and the electricity bill for the last quarter (Example 3.5) be dealt with in the accounting records of Domestic Ltd?

When these amounts are eventually paid, they will be dealt with as follows:

■ reduce cash by the amounts paid;
■ reduce the amount of the accrued expense as shown on the statement of financial position by the same amounts.

Other expenses, apart from electricity charges, may also be matched to the period to which they relate.

Activity 3.9

Can you think of other expenses for a retailer that cannot be linked directly to sales revenue and for which matching will therefore be done on a time basis?

We thought of the following examples:

- rent payable;
- insurance;
- interest payable;
- licence fees payable.

This is not an exhaustive list. You may have thought of others.

When the amount paid during the period is more than the full expense for the period

It is not unusual for a business to be in a situation where it has paid more during the year than the full expense for that year. Example 3.6 illustrates how we deal with this.

Example 3.6

Images Ltd, an advertising agency, normally pays rent for its premises quarterly in advance (on 1 January, 1 April, 1 July and 1 October). On the last day of the last reporting period (31 December), it paid the next quarter's rent (£4,000) to the following 31 March, which was a day earlier than required. This would mean that a total of five quarters' rent was paid during the year. If Images Ltd reports all of the cash paid as an expense in the income statement, this would be more than the full expense for the year. This would contravene the matching convention because a higher figure than the expenses associated with the revenue of the year would appear in the income statement.

The problem is overcome by dealing with the rental payment as follows:

- Show the rent for four quarters as the appropriate expense in the income statement (that is, 4 × £4,000 = £16,000).
- The cash (that is, 5 × £4,000 = £20,000) would already have been paid during the year.
- Show the quarter's rent paid in advance (£4,000) as a prepaid expense under assets in the statement of financial position. (The rent paid in advance will appear as a current asset in the statement of financial position, under the heading **prepaid expenses** or 'prepayments'.)

→

In the next reporting period, this prepayment will cease to be an asset and will become an expense in the income statement of that period. This is because the rent prepaid relates to the next period during which it will be 'used up'.

These points are illustrated in Figure 3.4.

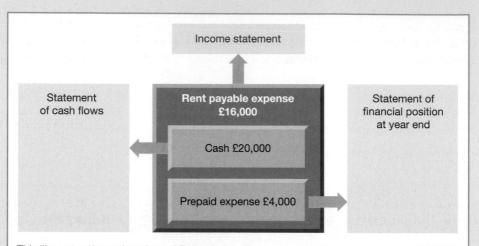

This illustrates the main points of Example 3.6. We can see that the rent expense of £16,000 (which appears in the income statement) is made up of four quarters' rent at £4,000 per quarter. This is the amount that relates to the period and is 'used up' during the period. The cash paid of £20,000 (which appears in the statement of cash flows) is made up of the cash paid during the period, which is five quarters at £4,000 per quarter. Finally, the prepayment of £4,000 (which appears on the statement of financial position) represents the payment made on 31 December and relates to the next reporting period.

Figure 3.4 Accounting for rent payable

In practice, the treatment of accruals and prepayments will be subject to the **materiality convention**. This convention states that, where the amounts involved are trivial, we should consider only what is expedient. This will usually mean treating an item as an expense in the period in which it is acquired, rather than strictly matching it to the revenue to which it relates. For example, a large business may find that, at the end of a reporting period, it holds £2 worth of unused stationery. The time and effort taken to record this as a prepayment would outweigh the negligible effect on the measurement of profit or financial position. As a result, it would be treated as an expense of the current period and ignored in the following period.

Profit, cash and accruals accounting

We have seen that, normally, for a particular reporting period, total revenue is not the same as total cash received and total expenses are not the same as total cash paid. As a result, the profit for the period (that is, total revenue minus total expenses) will not normally represent the net cash generated during that period. This reflects the difference between profit and liquidity. Profit is a measure of achievement, or productive effort, rather than a measure of cash generated. Although making a profit increases wealth, cash is only one possible form in which that wealth may be held.

These points are reflected in the **accruals convention**, which asserts that profit is the excess of revenue over expenses for a period, not the excess of cash receipts over cash payments. Leading on from this, the approach to accounting that is based on the accruals convention is frequently referred to as **accruals accounting**. The statement of financial position and the income statement are both prepared on the basis of accruals accounting.

Activity 3.10

What about the statement of cash flows? Is it prepared on an accruals accounting basis?

No. The statement of cash flows simply deals with cash receipts and payments.

DEPRECIATION

The expense of **depreciation**, which we have already come across, requires further examination. Most non-current assets do not have a perpetual existence, but have finite, or limited, lives. They are eventually 'used up' in the process of generating revenue for the business. This 'using up' may relate to physical deterioration (as with a motor vehicle). It may, however, be linked to obsolescence (as with some IT software that is no longer useful) or the mere passage of time (as with a purchased patent, which has a limited period of validity).

In essence, depreciation is an attempt to measure that portion of the cost (or fair value) of a non-current asset that has been depleted in generating the revenue recognised during a particular period. In the case of intangibles, we usually refer to the expense as **amortisation**, rather than depreciation. In the interests of brevity, we shall use the word depreciation for both tangibles and intangibles.

Calculating the depreciation expense

To calculate a depreciation expense for a period, four factors have to be considered:

- the cost (or fair value) of the asset;
- the useful life of the asset;
- the residual value of the asset; and
- the depreciation method.

The cost (or fair value) of the asset

The cost of an asset will include all costs incurred by the business to bring the asset to its required location and to make it ready for use. This means that, in addition to the cost of acquiring the asset, any delivery costs, installation costs (for example, setting up a new machine) and legal costs incurred in the transfer of legal title (for example, in purchasing a lease on property) will be included as part of the total cost of the asset. Similarly, any costs incurred in improving or altering an asset to make it suitable for use will also be included as part of the total cost.

Activity 3.11

Andrew Wu (Engineering) Ltd bought a new motor car for its marketing director. The invoice received from the motor car supplier showed the following:

	£
New BMW 325d	30,350
Delivery charge	180
Alloy wheels	660
Sun roof	400
Petrol	80
Number plates	130
Road fund licence	105
	31,905
Part exchange – Reliant Robin	(1,000)
Amount outstanding	30,905

What is the total cost of the new car to be treated as part of the business's property, plant and equipment?

The cost of the new car will be as follows:

	£
New BMW 325d	30,350
Delivery charge	180
Alloy wheels	660
Sun roof	400
Number plates	130
	31,720

This cost includes delivery charges, which are necessary to bring the asset into use, and it includes number plates, as they are a necessary and integral part of the asset. Improvements (alloy wheels and sun roof) are also regarded as part of the total cost of the motor car. The petrol and road fund licence, however, are costs of operating the asset. These amounts will, therefore, be treated as an expense in the period in which they were incurred (although part of the cost of the licence may be regarded as a prepaid expense in the period in which it was incurred).

The part-exchange figure shown is part payment of the total amount outstanding and so is not relevant to a consideration of the total cost.

The fair value of an asset was defined in Chapter 2 as the selling price that could be obtained in an orderly transaction under market conditions. As we saw, assets may be revalued to fair value only if this can be measured reliably. Where fair values have been applied, the depreciation expense should be based on those fair values, rather than on the historic costs.

The useful life of the asset

A non-current asset has both a *physical life* and an *economic life*. The physical life will be exhausted through the effects of wear and tear and/or the passage of time. The economic life is decided by the effects of technological progress, by changes in demand or changes in the way that the business operates. The benefits provided by the asset are eventually outweighed by the costs as it becomes unable to compete with newer assets, or becomes irrelevant to the needs of the business. The economic life of an asset may be much shorter than its physical life. For example, a computer may have a physical life of eight years and an economic life of three years.

The economic life determines the expected useful life of an asset for depreciation purposes. It is often difficult to estimate, however, as technological progress and shifts in consumer tastes can be swift and unpredictable.

Residual value (disposal value)

When a business disposes of a non-current asset that may still be of value to others, some payment may be received. This payment will represent the **residual value**, or *disposal value,* of the asset. To calculate the total amount to be depreciated, the residual value must be deducted from the cost (or fair value) of the asset. The likely amount to be received on disposal can, once again, be difficult to predict. The best guide is often past experience of similar assets sold.

Depreciation method

Once the amount to be depreciated (that is, the cost, or fair value, of the asset less any residual value) has been estimated, the business must select a method of allocating this depreciable amount between the reporting periods covering the asset's useful life. Although there are various ways in which this may be done, there are only two methods that are commonly used in practice.

The first of these is known as the **straight-line method**. This method simply allocates the amount to be depreciated evenly over the useful life of the asset. In other words, there is an equal depreciation expense for each year that the asset is held.

Example 3.7

To illustrate this method, consider the following information:

Cost of machine	£78,124
Estimated residual value at the end of its useful life	£2,000
Estimated useful life	4 years

→

To calculate the depreciation expense for each year, the total amount to be depreciated must be calculated. This will be the total cost less the estimated residual value: that is, £78,124 − £2,000 = £76,124. The annual depreciation expense can be derived by dividing the amount to be depreciated by the estimated useful life of the asset of four years. The calculation is therefore:

$$\frac{£76,124}{4} = £19,031$$

This means that the annual depreciation expense that appears in the income statement in relation to this asset will be £19,031 for each of the four years of the asset's life.

The amount of depreciation relating to the asset will be accumulated for as long as the asset continues to be owned by the business or until the accumulated depreciation amounts to the cost less residual value. This accumulated depreciation figure will increase each year as a result of the annual depreciation expense in the income statement. This accumulated amount will be deducted from the cost of the asset on the statement of financial position. At the end of the second year, for example, the accumulated depreciation will be £19,031 × 2 = £38,062. The asset details will appear on the statement of financial position as follows:

	£
Machine at cost	78,124
Accumulated depreciation	(38,062)
	40,062

As we saw in Chapter 2, this balance of £40,062 is referred to as the **carrying amount** (sometimes also known as the **written-down value** or **net book value**) of the asset. It represents that portion of the cost (or fair value) of the asset that has still to be treated as an expense (written off) in future years plus the residual value. This carrying-amount figure does not, except by coincidence, represent the current market value, which may be quite different. The only point at which the carrying amount is intended to represent the market value of the asset is at the time of its disposal. In Example 3.7, at the end of the four-year life of the machine, the carrying amount would be £2,000 – its estimated disposal value.

Activity 3.12

Can you figure out how the straight-line method derives its name?

It derives its name from the fact that the carrying amount of the asset at the end of each year, when plotted against time, will result in a straight line.

Figure 3.5 shows the carrying amount plotted over time using this method.

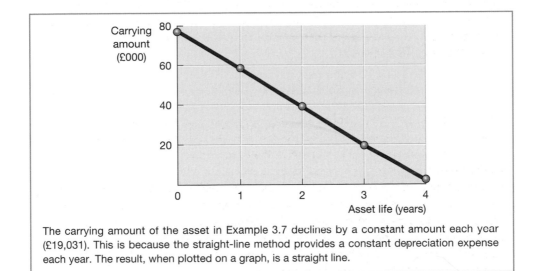

The carrying amount of the asset in Example 3.7 declines by a constant amount each year (£19,031). This is because the straight-line method provides a constant depreciation expense each year. The result, when plotted on a graph, is a straight line.

Figure 3.5 Graph of carrying amount against time using the straight-line method

The second approach to calculating the depreciation expense for a period is referred to as the **reducing-balance method**. This method applies a fixed percentage rate of depreciation to the carrying amount of the asset each year. The effect of this will be high annual depreciation expenses in the early years and lower expenses in the later years. To illustrate this method, let us take the same information that was used in Example 3.7. By using a fixed percentage of 60 per cent of the carrying amount to determine the annual depreciation expense, the effect will be to reduce the carrying amount to £2,000 after four years.

The calculations will be as follows:

	£
Cost of machine	78,124
Year 1 depreciation expense (60%* of cost)	(46,874)
Carrying amount	31,250
Year 2 depreciation expense (60% of carrying amount)	(18,750)
Carrying amount	12,500
Year 3 depreciation expense (60% of carrying amount)	(7,500)
Carrying amount	5,000
Year 4 depreciation expense (60% of carrying amount)	(3,000)
Residual value	2,000

*See the box on the following page for an explanation of how to derive the fixed percentage.

We can see that the pattern of depreciation is quite different between the two methods. If we plot the carrying amount of the asset, which has been derived using the reducing-balance method, against time, the result will be as shown in Figure 3.6.

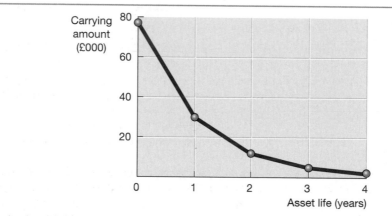

Under the reducing-balance method, the carrying amount of the asset in Example 3.7 falls by a larger amount in the earlier years than in the later years. This is because the depreciation expense is based on a fixed-rate percentage of the carrying amount.

Figure 3.6 Graph of carrying amount against time using the reducing-balance method

Your answer should be as follows:

Straight-line method

	(a) Profit before depreciation £	(b) Depreciation £	(a − b) Profit £
Year 1	40,000	19,031	20,969
Year 2	40,000	19,031	20,969
Year 3	40,000	19,031	20,969
Year 4	40,000	19,031	20,969

Reducing-balance method

	(a) Profit before depreciation £	(b) Depreciation £	(a − b) Profit/(loss) £
Year 1	40,000	46,874	(6,874)
Year 2	40,000	18,750	21,250
Year 3	40,000	7,500	32,500
Year 4	40,000	3,000	37,000

The straight-line method of depreciation results in the same profit figure for each year of the four-year period. This is because both the profit before depreciation and the depreciation expense are constant over the period. The reducing-balance method, however, results in very different profit figures for the four years, despite the fact that in this example the pre-depreciation profit is the same each year. In the first year a loss is reported and, thereafter, a rising profit.

Although the *pattern* of profit over the four-year period will be quite different, depending on the depreciation method used, the *total* profit for the period (£83,876) will remain the same. This is because both methods of depreciating will allocate the same amount of total depreciation (£76,124) over the four-year period. It is only the amount allocated *between* years that will differ.

In practice, the use of different depreciation methods may not have such a dramatic effect on profits as suggested in Activity 3.13. This is because businesses typically have more than one depreciating non-current asset. Where a business replaces some of its assets each year, the total depreciation expense calculated under the reducing-balance method will reflect a range of expenses (from high through to low), as assets will be at different points in their economic lives. This could mean that each year's total depreciation expense may not be significantly different from that which would have been derived under the straight-line method.

Selecting a depreciation method

The appropriate depreciation method to choose is the one that reflects the consumption of economic benefits provided by an asset. Where the economic benefits are consumed evenly over time (for example, with buildings), the straight-line method is usually appropriate. Where the economic benefits consumed decline over time (for example, with certain types of machinery that lose their efficiency), the reducing-balance method may be more appropriate. Where the pattern of economic benefits consumed is uncertain, the straight-line method is normally chosen.

There is an International Financial Reporting Standard (or International Accounting Standard) to deal with the depreciation of property, plant and equipment. As we shall see in Chapter 4, the purpose of accounting standards is to narrow areas of accounting difference and to try to ensure that information provided to users is transparent and comparable. The relevant standard endorses the view that the depreciation method chosen should reflect the pattern of consumption of economic benefits but does not specify particular methods to be used. It states that the useful life, depreciation method and residual values of non-current assets should be reviewed at least annually and adjustments made where appropriate. For intangible non-current assets with finite lives, there is a separate standard containing broadly similar rules.

Real World 3.4 sets out the depreciation policies of one large business.

REAL WORLD 3.4

Depreciating assets

Halfords Group plc is a major retailer of automotive and cycling products. It also operates a chain of auto repair centres. The business sells exclusive and own-branded products (such as C Boardman bikes) as well as third-party branded products.

The following describes how intangible non-current assets that have been acquired are amortised (depreciated) over time.

> Amortisation is recognised in profit or loss on a straight-line basis over the estimated useful lives of intangible assets, other than goodwill, from the date that they are available for use, since this most closely reflects the expected pattern of consumption of the future economic benefits embodied in the asset. The estimated useful lives for the current and comparative periods are as follows:

> ■ Brand names and trademarks 2 years, in respect of Autocentres, and 10 years in respect of C Boardman;
> ■ Customer relationships 5 to 15 years; and
> ■ Favourable leases over the term of the lease.

Halford's policy for depreciating property plant and equipment is described as follows.

> Depreciation of property, plant and equipment is provided to write off the cost, less residual value, on a straight-line basis over their useful economic lives as follows:

> ■ Leasehold premises with lease terms of 50 years or less are depreciated over the remaining period of the lease;
> ■ Leasehold improvements are depreciated over the period of the lease to a maximum of 25 years;

Halfords is typical of most UK businesses in that it uses the straight-line method. The reducing-balance method is much less popular.

The approach taken to calculating depreciation is summarised in Figure 3.7.

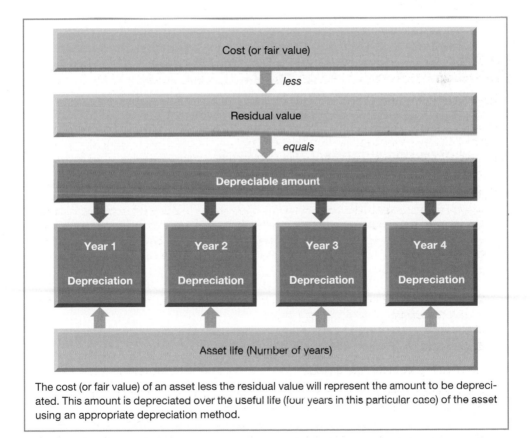

The cost (or fair value) of an asset less the residual value will represent the amount to be depreciated. This amount is depreciated over the useful life (four years in this particular case) of the asset using an appropriate depreciation method.

Figure 3.7 Calculating the annual depreciation expense

Impairment and depreciation

We saw in Chapter 2 that all non-current assets could be subjected to an impairment test. Where a non-current asset with a finite life has its carrying amount reduced as a result of an impairment test, depreciation expenses for future reporting periods should be based on the impaired value of that asset.

Depreciation and asset replacement

Some appear to believe that the purpose of depreciation is to provide the funds for the replacement of a non-current asset when it reaches the end of its useful life. However, this is not the case. It was mentioned earlier that depreciation represents an attempt to allocate the cost or fair value (less any residual value) of a non-current asset over its expected useful life. The depreciation expense for a particular reporting period is used in calculating profit for that period. If a depreciation charge is excluded from the income statement, we shall not have a fair measure of financial performance. Whether or not the business intends to replace the asset in the future is irrelevant.

Where an asset is to be replaced, the depreciation expense in the income statement will not ensure that liquid funds are set aside specifically for this purpose. Although the depreciation expense will reduce profit, and therefore reduce the amount that the owners may decide to withdraw, the amounts retained within the business as a result may be invested in ways that are unrelated to the replacement of the asset.

Depreciation and judgement

From our discussions about depreciation, it is clear that accounting is not as precise and objective as it is sometimes portrayed. There are areas where subjective judgement is required.

Activity 3.14

What judgements must be made to calculate a depreciation expense for a period?

You should have thought of the following:

- the expected residual or disposal value of the asset;
- the expected useful life of the asset;
- the choice of depreciation method.

Making different judgements on these matters would result in a different pattern of depreciation expenses over the life of the asset and, therefore, in a different pattern of reported profits. However, underestimations or overestimations that are made in relation to the above will be adjusted for in the final year of an asset's life. As a result, the total depreciation expense (and total profit) over the asset's life will not be affected by estimation errors.

Real World 3.5 describes the effect on annual performance of extending the useful life of a non-current asset held by a well-known business.

COSTING INVENTORIES

The cost of inventories is important in determining financial performance and position. The cost of inventories sold during a reporting period will affect the calculation of profit and the cost of inventories held at the end of the reporting period will affect the portrayal of assets held.

To calculate the cost of inventories, an assumption is made about the physical flow of inventories through the business. This assumption need not have anything to do with how inventories *actually* flow through the business; it is concerned only with providing useful measures of performance and position.

Three common assumptions used are:

- **first in, first out (FIFO)**, in which inventories are costed *as if* the earliest acquired inventories held are the first to be used;
- **last in, first out (LIFO)**, in which inventories are costed *as if* the latest acquired inventories held are the first to be used; and
- **weighted average cost (AVCO)**, in which inventories are costed *as if* inventories acquired lose their separate identity and go into a 'pool'. Any issues of inventories from this pool will reflect the weighted average cost of inventories held.

During a period of changing prices, the choice of assumption used in costing inventories can be important. Example 3.8 provides an illustration of how each assumption is applied and the effect of each on financial performance and position.

Example 3.8

A business commenced on 1 May to supply oil to factories. During the first month, the following transactions took place:

	Tonnes	Cost per tonne
May 2 Purchased	10,000	£10
May 10 Purchased	20,000	£13
May 18 Sold	9,000	

First in, first out (FIFO)

Using the first in, first out assumption, 9,000 tonnes of the 10,000 tonnes bought on 2 May are treated as if these are the ones to be sold. The remaining inventories bought on 2 May (1,000 tonnes) and the inventories bought on 10 May (20,000 tonnes) will become the closing inventories. Thus we have:

		£
Cost of sales	(9,000 @ £10 per tonne)	90,000
Closing inventories	(1,000 @ £10 per tonne)	10,000
	(20,000 @ £13 per tonne)	260,000
		270,000

Last in, first out (LIFO)

Using the last in, first out assumption, 9,000 tonnes of the inventories bought on 10 May will be treated as if these are the first to be sold. The earlier inventories bought on 2 May (10,000 tonnes) and the remainder of the inventories bought on 10 May (11,000 tonnes) will become the closing inventories. Thus we have:

		£
Cost of sales	(9,000 @ £13 per tonne)	117,000
Closing inventories	(11,000 @ £13 per tonne)	143,000
	(10,000 @ £10 per tonne)	100,000
		243,000

Figure 3.8 contrasts LIFO and FIFO.

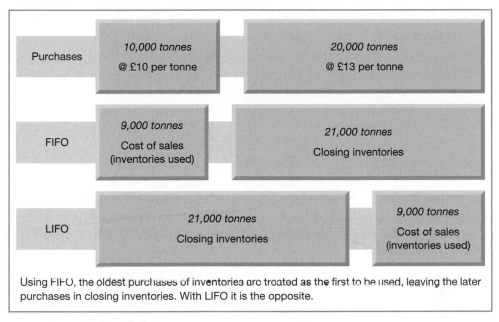

| Purchases | 10,000 tonnes @ £10 per tonne | 20,000 tonnes @ £13 per tonne |

Using FIFO, the oldest purchases of inventories are treated as the first to be used, leaving the later purchases in closing inventories. With LIFO it is the opposite.

Figure 3.8 FIFO and LIFO treatment of the inventories in Example 3.8

Weighted average cost (AVCO)

Under this assumption, newly acquired inventories are treated as if they lose their separate identity. A weighted average cost, based on the quantities of each batch purchased, is calculated. The weighted average cost is then used to derive both the cost of goods sold and the cost of remaining inventories held. This simply means that the cost of the inventories bought on 2 May and 10 May are added together and then divided by the total number of tonnes to obtain the weighted average cost per tonne. That is:

Average cost $=$ ((10,000 $\times$ £10) + (20,000 $\times$ £13))/(10,000 + 20,000) $=$ £12 per tonne

Both the cost of sales and the value of the closing inventories are then based on this average cost per tonne. Thus we have:

| Cost of sales | (9,000 @ £12 per tonne) | £108,000 |
| Closing inventories | (21,000 @ £12 per tonne) | £252,000 |

Suppose that the 9,000 tonnes of inventories in Example 3.8 were sold for £15 a tonne.

(a) Calculate the gross profit for the period under each of the three costing assumptions.
(b) What do you note about the different profit and closing inventories valuations when using each method, when prices are rising?

Your answer should be along the following lines:

(a) Gross profit calculation:

	FIFO £000	LIFO £000	AVCO £000
Sales revenue (9,000 @ £15)	135	135	135
Cost of sales	(90)	(117)	(108)
Gross profit	45	18	27
Closing inventories figure	270	243	252

(b) These figures show that FIFO will give the highest gross profit during a period of rising prices. This is because sales revenue is matched with the earlier (and cheaper) purchases. LIFO will give the lowest gross profit because sales revenue is matched against the more recent (and dearer) purchases. The AVCO assumption will normally give a figure that is between these two extremes.

The closing inventories figure in the statement of financial position will be highest with the FIFO assumption. This is because the cost of oil still held will be based on the more recent (and dearer) purchases. LIFO will give the lowest closing inventories figure, as the oil held will be based on the earlier (and cheaper) purchases. Once again, the AVCO assumption will normally give a figure that is between these two extremes. During a period of falling prices, the position of FIFO and LIFO is reversed.

The different costing assumptions have an effect on reported profit only from one reporting period to the next. The figure derived for closing inventories will be carried forward and matched with sales revenue in a later period. If the cheaper purchases of inventories are matched to sales revenue in the current period, it will mean that the dearer purchases will be matched to sales revenue in a later period. Over the life of the business, therefore, total profit will be the same either way.

Inventories – some further issues

We saw in Chapter 2 that the convention of prudence requires that inventories be valued at the lower of cost and net realisable value. (The net realisable value of inventories is the estimated selling price less any further costs needed to complete the goods and any costs involved in selling and distributing them.) In theory, this means that the valuation method applied to inventories could switch each year, depending on which of cost and net realisable value is the lower. In practice, however, the cost of the inventories held is usually below the current net realisable value – particularly during a period of rising prices. It is, therefore, the cost figure that will normally appear in the statement of financial position.

Activity 3.16

Can you think of any circumstances where the net realisable value will be lower than the cost of inventories held, even during a period of generally rising prices? Try to think of at least two.

The net realisable value may be lower where:

- goods have deteriorated or become obsolete;
- there has been a fall in the market price of the goods;
- the goods are being used as a 'loss leader', that is, they are deliberately going to be sold at a price lower than their cost;
- bad buying decisions have been made.

There is also an International Financial Reporting Standard that deals with inventories. It states that, when preparing financial statements for external reporting, the cost of inventories should normally be determined using either FIFO or AVCO; the LIFO assumption is not acceptable for external reporting. (There is no reason, however, that a business should not apply LIFO when preparing financial statements for use by its own managers.) The standard also requires the 'lower of cost and net realisable value' rule to be used and so endorses the application of the prudence convention.

Real World 3.6 sets out the inventories' costing methods used by some of the UK's leading businesses.

REAL WORLD 3.6

Counting the cost

Inventories costing methods used by some large UK businesses are as follows.

Name	Type of business	Costing method used
J Sainsbury plc	Supermarket	AVCO
Babcock International plc	Engineering support services	FIFO
Imperial Tobacco Group plc	Tobacco manufacturer	FIFO
WH Smith plc	Bookseller, stationer and travel	AVCO
Halfords Group plc	Automotive and leisure products	AVCO
Marks and Spencer plc	Food and clothing retailer	AVCO
Britvic plc	Soft drinks supplier	AVCO
AstraZeneca plc	Pharmaceuticals	FIFO or AVCO

Source: Annual reports of the relevant businesses for 2014 or 2015.

Note that AstraZeneca plc employs more than one inventories' costing method. This presumably means that the costing method will vary according to product type, location or some other key factor.

The table simply sets out a small, non-random sample of well-known businesses and so we cannot assess the relative popularity of the FIFO and LIFO methods in practice on the basis of this.

Costing inventories and depreciation provide two examples where the **consistency convention** should be applied. This convention holds that once a particular method of accounting is selected, it should be applied consistently over time. It would not be acceptable to switch from, say, FIFO to AVCO between periods (unless exceptional circumstances make it appropriate). The purpose of this convention is to help users make valid comparisons of performance and position from one period to the next.

Activity 3.17

Reporting inventories in the financial statements provides a further example of the need to apply subjective judgement. For the inventories of a retail business, what are the main judgements that are required?

The main judgements are:

- the choice of costing method (FIFO, LIFO, AVCO);
- deducing the net realisable value figure for inventories held.

Before leaving this topic, one final point should be made. Costing inventories using FIFO, LIFO and AVCO applies to items that are interchangeable. Where they are not, as would be the case with custom-made items, the specific cost of the individual items must be used.

TRADE RECEIVABLES PROBLEMS

We have seen that, when businesses sell goods or services on credit, revenue will usually be recognised before the customer pays the amounts owing. Recording the dual aspect of a credit sale will involve increasing sales revenue and increasing trade receivables by the amount of the revenue from the credit sale.

With this type of sale there is always the risk that the customer will not pay the amount due. Where it becomes reasonably certain that the customer will not pay, the amount owed is considered to be a **bad debt**, which must be taken into account when preparing the financial statements.

Activity 3.18

What would be the effect on the income statement, and on the statement of financial position, of not taking into account the fact that a debt is bad?

The effect would be to overstate the assets (trade receivables) on the statement of financial position and to overstate profit in the income statement, as the revenue that has been recognised will not result in any future benefit.

To provide a more realistic picture of financial performance and position, the bad debt must be 'written off'. This will involve reducing the trade receivables and increasing expenses (by creating an expense known as 'bad debts written off') by the amount of the bad debt. The matching convention requires that the bad debt is written off in the same period as the sale that gave rise to the debt is recognised.

Note that, when a debt is bad, the accounting response is not simply to cancel the original sale. If this were done, the income statement would not be so informative. Reporting the bad debts as an expense can be extremely useful in assessing management performance.

Activity 3.19

The treatment of bad debts represents a further example where judgement is needed to derive an appropriate expense figure. What will be the effect of different judgements concerning the appropriate amount of bad debts expense on the profit for a particular period and on the total profit reported over the life of the business?

The judgement concerning whether to write off a bad debt will affect the expenses for the period and, therefore, the reported profit. Over the life of the business, however, total reported profit would not be affected, as incorrect judgements made in one period will be adjusted for in a later period.

Suppose that a debt of £100 was written off in a period and that, in a later period, the amount owing was actually received. The increase in expenses of £100 in the period in which the bad debt was written off would be compensated for by an increase in revenue of £100 when the amount outstanding was finally received (bad debt recovered). If, however, the amount owing of £100 was never written off in the first place, the profit for the two periods would not be affected by the bad debt adjustment and would, therefore, be different – but the total profit for the two periods would be the same.

Real World 3.7 reveals average the level of bad debts among European businesses over time.

Bad debts getting worse

Figure 3.9 shows the average bad debt loss percentage for European businesses over an 11-year period.

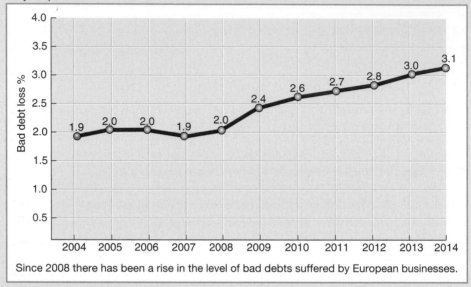

Since 2008 there has been a rise in the level of bad debts suffered by European businesses.

Figure 3.9 Average bad debt loss percentage for European businesses

The average bad debt loss percentages are based on a survey of more than 10,000 managers across 31 European countries. We can see that since 2008, there has been a rise in the level of bad debts incurred, presumably as a result of the difficult economic climate during this period.

According to Intrum Justitia, which produced the survey, the bad debt loss percentage of 3.1 per cent in 2014 translates into 360 billion euros of lost revenue.

Source: European Payment Index 2014, www.intrum.com.

USES AND USEFULNESS OF THE INCOME STATEMENT

The income statement may help in providing information on:

■ *How effective the business has been in generating wealth.* Since wealth generation is the primary reason for most businesses to exist, assessing how much wealth has been created is an important issue. The income statement reveals the profit for the period, or bottom line as it is sometimes called. This provides a measure of the wealth created for the owners. Gross profit and operating profit are also useful measures of wealth creation.

- *How profit was derived.* In addition to providing various measures of profit, the income statement provides other information needed for a proper understanding of business performance. It reveals the level of sales revenue and the nature and amount of expenses incurred, which can help in understanding how profit was derived. The analysis of financial performance will be considered in detail in Chapter 6.

? SELF-ASSESSMENT QUESTION 3.1

TT and Co. is a new business that started trading on 1 January 2015. The following is a summary of transactions that occurred during the first year of trading:

1 The owners introduced £50,000 of equity, which was paid into a bank account opened in the name of the business.
2 Premises were rented from 1 January 2015 at an annual rental of £20,000. During the year, rent of £25,000 was paid to the owner of the premises.
3 Rates (a tax on business premises) were paid during the year as follows:

For the period 1 January 2015 to 31 March 2015	£500
For the period 1 April 2015 to 31 March 2016	£1,200

4 A delivery van was bought on 1 January 2015 for £12,000. This is expected to be used in the business for four years and then to be sold for £2,000.
5 Wages totalling £33,500 were paid during the year. At the end of the year, the business owed £630 of wages for the last week of the year.
6 Electricity bills for the first three quarters of the year were paid totalling £1,650. After 31 December 2015, but before the financial statements had been finalised for the year, the bill for the last quarter arrived showing a charge of £620.
7 Inventories totalling £143,000 were bought on credit.
8 Inventories totalling £12,000 were bought for cash.
9 Sales revenue on credit totalled £152,000 (cost of sales £74,000).
10 Cash sales revenue totalled £35,000 (cost of sales £16,000).
11 Receipts from trade receivables totalled £132,000.
12 Payments of trade payables totalled £121,000.
13 Van running expenses paid totalled £9,400.

At the end of the year it was clear that a credit customer who owed £400 would not be able to pay any part of the debt. All of the other trade receivables were expected to be settled in full.

The business uses the straight-line method for depreciating non-current assets.

Required:
Prepare a statement of financial position as at 31 December 2015 and an income statement for the year to that date.

The solution to this question can be found at the back of the book on page 525.

SUMMARY

The main points of this chapter may be summarised as follows:

The income statement (profit and loss account)

- The income statement indicates how much profit (or loss) has been generated over a period and links the statements of financial position at the beginning and end of a reporting period.

- Profit (or loss) is the difference between total revenue and total expenses for a period.

- There are three main measures of profit:

  - *gross profit* – calculated by deducting the cost of sales from sales revenue;

  - *operating profit* – calculated by deducting overheads from gross profit;

  - *profit for the period* – calculated by adding non-operating income and deducting finance costs from operating profit.

Expenses and revenue

- Cost of sales may be identified by matching the cost of each sale to the particular sale or by adjusting the goods bought during a period by the opening and closing inventories.

- Classifying expenses is often a matter of judgement, although there are rules for businesses that trade as limited companies.

- Revenue is recognised when the amount of revenue can be measured reliably and it is probable that the economic benefits will be received.

- Where there is a sale of goods, there are additional criteria that ownership and control must pass to the buyer before revenue can be recognised.

- Revenue can be recognised before final completion of a contract provided that a particular stage of completion can be measured reliably.

- The matching convention states that expenses should be matched to the revenue that they help generate.

- A particular expense reported in the income statement may not be the same as the cash paid. This will result in accruals or prepayments appearing in the statement of financial position.

- The materiality convention states that where the amounts are immaterial, we should consider only what is expedient.

- The accruals convention states that profit = revenue − expenses (not cash receipts – cash payments).

Depreciation of non-current assets

- Depreciation requires a consideration of the cost (or fair value), useful life and residual value of an asset. It also requires a consideration of the method of depreciation.
- The straight-line method of depreciation allocates the amount to be depreciated evenly over the useful life of the asset.
- The reducing-balance method applies a fixed percentage rate of depreciation to the carrying amount of an asset each year.
- The depreciation method chosen should reflect the pattern of consumption of economic benefits of an asset.
- Depreciation allocates the cost (or fair value), less the residual value, of an asset over its useful life. It does not provide funds for replacement of the asset.

Costing inventories

- The way in which the cost of inventories is derived is important for the calculation of profit and the presentation of financial position.
- There are three major assumptions about the flow of inventories through a business:
  - *first in, first out* (FIFO) – the earliest inventories held are the first to be used;
  - *last in, first out* (LIFO) – the latest inventories are the first to be used;
  - *weighted average cost* (AVCO) – applies an average cost to all inventories used.
- When prices are rising, FIFO gives the lowest cost of sales figure and highest closing inventories figure and for LIFO it is the other way around. AVCO gives figures for cost of sales and closing inventories that lie between FIFO and LIFO.
- When prices are falling, the positions of FIFO and LIFO are reversed.
- Inventories are shown at the lower of cost and net realisable value.
- When a particular method of accounting, such as a depreciation method or inventories costing method, is selected, it should be applied consistently over time.

Bad debts

- Where it is reasonably certain that a credit customer will not pay, the debt is regarded as 'bad' and written off.

Uses of the income statement

- It provides measures of profit generated during a period.
- It provides information on how the profit was derived.

FURTHER READING

If you would like to explore the topics covered in this chapter in more depth, we recommend the following books:

Alexander, D. and Nobes, C. (2016) *Financial Accounting: An International Introduction,* 6th edn, Pearson, Chapters 2, 3, 9 and 10.

Elliott, B. and Elliott, J. (2015) *Financial Accounting and Reporting,* 17th edn, Pearson, Chapters 2, 8, 20 and 21.

International Accounting Standards Board, *A Guide through IFRS 2015* (Green Book), IAS 2 *Inventories* and IAS 18 *Revenue.*

KPMG, *Insights into IFRS,* 10th edn, Sweet and Maxwell, 2015/16, Sections 3.2, 3.3, 3.8, 3.10 and 4.2 (a summarised version of this is available free at www.kpmg.com).

? REVIEW QUESTIONS

Solutions to these questions can be found at the back of the book on pages 540.

3.1 'Although the income statement is a record of past achievement, the calculations required for certain expenses involve estimates of the future.' What does this statement mean? Can you think of examples where estimates of the future are used?

3.2 'Depreciation is a process of allocation and not valuation.' What do you think is meant by this statement?

3.3 What is the convention of consistency? Does this convention help users in making a more valid comparison between businesses?

3.4 'An asset is similar to an expense.' Do you agree? Explain your answer.

✳ EXERCISES

Exercise 3.1 is basic level. Exercises 3.2 and 3.3 are intermediate level and Exercises 3.4 to 3.5 are advanced level. Those with **coloured numbers** *have solutions at the back of the book, starting on page 552.*

3.1 You have heard the following statements made. Comment critically on them.

(a) 'Equity only increases or decreases as a result of the owners putting more cash into the business or taking some out.'
(b) 'An accrued expense is one that relates to next year.'
(c) 'Unless we depreciate this asset we shall be unable to provide for its replacement.'
(d) 'There is no point in depreciating the factory building. It is appreciating in value each year.'

3.2 Singh Enterprises, which started business on 1 January 2013, has a reporting period to 31 December and uses the straight-line method of depreciation. On 1 January 2013 the business bought a machine for £10,000. The machine had an expected useful life of four years and an estimated residual value of £2,000. On 1 January 2014 the business bought another machine for £15,000. This machine had an expected useful life of five years and an estimated residual value of £2,500. On 31 December 2015 the business sold the first machine bought for £3,000.

Required:
Show the relevant income statement extracts and statement of financial position extracts for the years 2013, 2014 and 2015.

3.3 Fill in the values (a) to (f) in the following table on the assumption that there were no opening balances involved.

	Relating to period		At end of period	
	Paid/received	Expense/revenue for period	Prepaid	Accruals/deferred revenues
	£	£	£	£
Rent payable	10,000	**(a)**	1,000	
Rates and insurance	5,000	**(b)**		1,000
General expenses	**(c)**	6,000	1,000	
Interest payable on borrowings	3,000	2,500	**(d)**	
Salaries	**(e)**	9,000		3,000
Rent receivable	**(f)**	1,500		1,500

3.4 The following is the statement of financial position of TT and Co. (see Self-assessment question 3.1 on page 107) at the end of its first year of trading:

Statement of financial position as at 31 December 2015

	£
ASSETS	
Non-current assets	
Property, plant and equipment	
Delivery van at cost	12,000
Depreciation	(2,500)
	9,500
Current assets	
Inventories	65,000
Trade receivables	19,600
Prepaid expenses*	5,300
Cash	750
	90,650
Total assets	100,150
EQUITY AND LIABILITIES	
Equity	
Original	50,000
Retained earnings	26,900
	76,900
Current liabilities	
Trade payables	22,000
Accrued expenses†	1,250
	23,250
Total equity and liabilities	100,150

* The prepaid expenses consisted of rates (£300) and rent (£5,000).
† The accrued expenses consisted of wages (£630) and electricity (£620).

During 2016, the following transactions took place:

1 The owners withdrew equity in the form of cash of £20,000.
2 Premises continued to be rented at an annual rental of £20,000. During the year, rent of £15,000 was paid to the owner of the premises.
3 Rates on the premises were paid during the year as follows: for the period 1 April 2016 to 31 March 2017, £1,300.
4 A second delivery van was bought on 1 January 2016 for £13,000. This is expected to be used in the business for four years and then to be sold for £3,000.
5 Wages totalling £36,700 were paid during the year. At the end of the year, the business owed £860 of wages for the last week of the year.
6 Electricity bills for the first three quarters of the year and £620 for the last quarter of the previous year were paid, totalling £1,820. After 31 December 2016, but before the

financial statements had been finalised for the year, the bill for the last quarter arrived showing a charge of £690.

7 Inventories totalling £67,000 were bought on credit.
8 Inventories totalling £8,000 were bought for cash.
9 Sales revenue on credit totalled £179,000 (cost £89,000).
10 Cash sales revenue totalled £54,000 (cost £25,000).
11 Receipts from trade receivables totalled £178,000.
12 Payments to trade payables totalled £71,000.
13 Van running expenses paid totalled £16,200.

The business uses the straight-line method for depreciating non-current assets.

Required:
Prepare a statement of financial position as at 31 December 2016 and an income statement for the year to that date.

3.5 The following is the statement of financial position of WW Associates as at 31 December 2014:

Statement of financial position as at 31 December 2014

	£
ASSETS	
Non-current assets	
Machinery	25,300
Current assets	
Inventories	12,200
Trade receivables	21,300
Prepaid expenses (rates)	400
Cash	8,300
	42,200
Total assets	67,500
EQUITY AND LIABILITIES	
Equity	
Original	25,000
Retained earnings	23,900
	48,900
Current liabilities	
Trade payables	16,900
Accrued expenses (wages)	1,700
	18,600
Total equity and liabilities	67,500

During 2015, the following transactions took place:

1 The owners withdrew equity in the form of cash of £23,000.
2 Premises were rented at an annual rental of £20,000. During the year, rent of £25,000 was paid to the owner of the premises.
3 Rates on the premises were paid during the year for the period 1 April 2015 to 31 March 2016 and amounted to £2,000.

4 Some machinery (a non-current asset), which was bought on 1 January 2014 for £13,000, has proved to be unsatisfactory. It was part-exchanged for some new machinery on 1 January 2015 and WW Associates paid a cash amount of £6,000. The new machinery would have cost £15,000 had the business bought it without the trade-in.

5 Wages totalling £23,800 were paid during the year. At the end of the year, the business owed £860 of wages.

6 Electricity bills for the four quarters of the year were paid, totalling £2,700.

7 Inventories totalling £143,000 were bought on credit.

8 Inventories totalling £12,000 were bought for cash.

9 Sales revenue on credit totalled £211,000 (cost £127,000).

10 Cash sales revenue totalled £42,000 (cost £25,000).

11 Receipts from trade receivables totalled £198,000.

12 Payments to trade payables totalled £156,000.

13 Van running expenses paid totalled £17,500.

The business uses the reducing-balance method of depreciation for non-current assets at the rate of 30 per cent each year.

Required:

Prepare an income statement for the year ended 31 December 2015 and a statement of financial position as at that date.

Chapter 4

ACCOUNTING FOR LIMITED COMPANIES

INTRODUCTION

Most businesses in the UK, from the very largest to some of the very smallest, operate in the form of limited companies. Around three and a half million limited companies exist, accounting for the majority of business activity and employment. The economic significance of this type of business is not confined to the UK; it can be seen in many of the world's developed countries.

In this chapter, we shall examine the main features of a limited company and how this form of business differs from sole proprietorship and partnership businesses. We consider the ways in which the owners provide finance, as well as the rules governing the way in which limited companies must account to their owners and to other interested parties. We shall also consider how the financial statements, which we discussed in the previous two chapters, are prepared for this type of business.

Learning outcomes

When you have completed this chapter, you should be able to:

■ discuss the nature and financing of a limited company;

■ describe the main features of the equity in a limited company and the restrictions placed on owners seeking to withdraw part of their equity;

■ discuss the framework of rules designed to safeguard the interests of shareholders;

■ explain how the income statement and statement of financial position of a limited company differ in detail from those of sole proprietorships and partnerships.

THE MAIN FEATURES OF LIMITED COMPANIES

Legal nature

Let us begin our examination of limited companies by discussing their legal nature. A **limited company** has been described as an artificial person that has been created by law. This means that a company has many of the rights and obligations that 'real' people have. It can, for example, enter into contracts in its own name. It can also sue other people (real or corporate) and it can be sued by them. This contrasts sharply with other types of businesses, such as sole proprietorships and partnerships (that is, unincorporated businesses), where it is the owner(s) rather than the business that must enter into contracts, sue and so on. This is because those businesses have no separate legal identity.

With the rare exceptions of those that are created by Act of Parliament or by Royal Charter, all UK companies are created (or *incorporated*) by registration. To create a company, the person or persons wishing to create it (usually known as *promoters*) fill in a few simple forms and pay a modest registration fee. After having ensured that the necessary formalities have been met, the Registrar of Companies, a UK government official, enters the name of the new company on the Registry of Companies. Thus, in the UK, companies can be formed very easily and cheaply (for about £100).

A limited company may be owned by just one person, but most have more than one owner and some have many owners. The owners are usually known as *members* or *shareholders.* The ownership of a company is normally divided into a number of **shares**, each of equal size. Each owner, or shareholder, owns one or more shares in the company. Large companies typically have a very large number of shareholders. For example, at 31 March 2015, BT Group plc, the international communications business, had almost 900,000 different shareholders and a total of 8,373 million shares in issue.

Since a limited company has its own legal identity, it is regarded as being quite separate from those that own and manage it. It is worth emphasising that this legal separateness of owners and the company has no connection with the business entity convention discussed in Chapter 2. This accounting convention applies equally well to all business types, including sole proprietorships and partnerships where there is certainly no legal distinction between the owner(s) and the business.

The legal separateness of the limited company and its shareholders leads to two important features of the limited company: perpetual life and limited liability. These are now explained.

Perpetual life

A company is normally granted a perpetual existence. This means that the life of a company is quite separate from the lives of those who own or manage it. It is not, therefore, affected by changes in ownership that arise when shares in the company are transferred between investors.

Assume that a company has a single owner (shareholder) who dies. What do you think will happen in these circumstances?

The company will still continue to exist. The shares of the deceased owner will simply pass to the beneficiary of his or her estate

Although a company may be granted a perpetual existence when it is first formed, it is possible for either the shareholders or the courts to bring this existence to an end. When this is done, the assets of the company are usually sold to generate cash to meet the outstanding liabilities. Any surplus arising after all liabilities have been met will then be used to pay the shareholders. Shareholders may agree to end the life of a company where it has achieved the purpose for which it was formed or where they feel that the company has no real future. (The London Organising Committee for the Olympic Games and Paralympic Games (LOCOG) Ltd, for example, was wound up in 2013 following successful completion of its task.) The courts may bring the life of a company to an end where creditors (those owed money by the company) have applied to the courts for this to be done because they have not been paid.

Where shareholders agree to end the life of a company, it is referred to as a 'voluntary liquidation'. **Real World 4.1** describes the demise of one company by this method.

REAL WORLD 4.1

Monotub Industries in a spin as founder gets Titan for £1

Monotub Industries, maker of the Titan washing machine, yesterday passed into corporate history with very little ceremony and with only a whimper of protest from minority shareholders.

At an extraordinary meeting held in a basement room of the group's West End headquarters, shareholders voted to put the company into voluntary liquidation and sell its assets and intellectual property to founder Martin Myerscough for £1. [The shares in the company were at one time worth 650p each.]

The only significant opposition came from Giuliano Gnagnatti who, along with other shareholders, has seen his investment shrink faster than a wool twin-set on a boil wash.

The not-so-proud owner of 100,000 Monotub shares, Mr Gnagnatti, the managing director of an online retailer, described the sale of Monotub as a 'free gift' to Mr Myerscough. This assessment was denied by Ian Green, the chairman of Monotub, who said the closest the beleaguered company had come to a sale was an offer for £60,000 that gave no guarantees against liabilities, which are thought to amount to £750,000.

The quiet passing of the washing machine, eventually dubbed the Titanic, was in strong contrast to its performance in many kitchens.

→

Originally touted as the 'great white goods hope' of the washing machine industry with its larger capacity and removable drum, the Titan ran into problems when it kept stopping during the spin cycle, causing it to emit a loud bang and leap into the air.

Summing up the demise of the Titan, Mr Green said: 'Clearly the machine had some revolutionary aspects, but you can't get away from the fact that the machine was faulty and should not have been launched with those defects.'

The usually-vocal Mr Myerscough, who has promised to pump £250,000 into the company and give Monotub shareholders £4 for every machine sold, refused to comment on his plans for the Titan or reveal who his backers were. But . . . he did say that he intended to 'take the Titan forward'.

 Source: Urquhart, Lisa (2003) 'Monotub Industries in a spin as founder gets Titan for £1', *Financial Times*, 23 January.
© The Financial Times Limited 2003. All Rights Reserved.

Limited liability

Since the company is a legal person in its own right, it must take responsibility for its own debts and losses. This means that, once the shareholders have paid what they have agreed to pay for the shares, their obligation to the company, and to the company's creditors, is satisfied. Thus shareholders can limit their losses to the amount that they have paid, or committed to pay, for their shares. This is of great practical importance to potential shareholders since they know that what they can lose, as part owners of the business, is limited.

Contrast this with the position of sole proprietors or partners. They cannot 'ring-fence' assets that they do not want to put into the business. If a sole proprietorship or partnership business finds itself in a position where liabilities exceed the business assets, the law gives unsatisfied creditors the right to demand payment out of what the sole proprietor or partner may have regarded as 'non-business' assets. Thus the sole proprietor or partner could lose everything – house, car, the lot. This is because the law sees Jill, the sole proprietor, as being the same as Jill the private individual.

Real World 4.2 gives an example of a well-known case where the shareholders of a particular company were able to avoid any liability to those that had lost money as a result of dealing with that company.

REAL WORLD 4.2

Carlton and Granada 1 – Nationwide Football League 0

Two television broadcasting companies, Carlton and Granada, each owned 50 per cent of a separate company, ITV Digital (formerly ON Digital). ITV Digital signed a contract to pay the Nationwide Football League (in effect the three divisions of English football below the Premiership) more than £89 million on both 1 August 2002 and 1 August 2003 for the rights to broadcast football matches over three seasons. ITV Digital was unable to sell enough subscriptions for the broadcasts and so collapsed because it was unable to meet its liabilities.

The Nationwide Football League tried to force Carlton and Granada (ITV Digital's only two shareholders) to meet ITV Digital's contractual obligations. It was unable to do so because the shareholders could not be held legally liable for the amounts owing.

Carlton and Granada subsequently merged into one business, but at the time of ITV Digital were two independent companies.

Activity 4.2

The fact that shareholders can limit their losses to that which they have paid, or have agreed to pay, for their shares, is of great practical importance to potential shareholders.

Can you think of any practical benefit to a private-sector economy, in general, of this ability of shareholders to limit losses?

Business is a risky venture – in some cases very risky. People will usually be happier to invest money when they know the limit of their liability. If investors are given limited liability, new businesses are more likely to be formed and existing ones are likely to find it easier to raise more finance. This is good for the private-sector economy and may ultimately lead to the generation of greater wealth for society as a whole.

Although **limited liability** benefits providers of equity finance (the shareholders), this may not be so for others with a stake in the business – as we saw in the case of the Nationwide Football League clubs in Real World 4.2. Limited liability allows shareholders to walk away from any unpaid debts of the company if the amount they agreed to pay is not enough to meet those debts. As a consequence, individuals, or businesses, may be wary of entering into a contract with a limited company. This can be a real problem for smaller, less established companies. Suppliers may insist on cash payment before delivery of goods or the rendering of a service. Alternatively, they may require a personal guarantee from a major shareholder that the debt will be paid before allowing trade credit. In the latter case, the supplier circumvents the company's limited liability status by demanding the personal liability of an individual. Larger, more established companies, on the other hand, find it easier to gain the confidence of suppliers.

Legal safeguards

Various safeguards exist to protect individuals and businesses contemplating dealing with a limited company. These include the requirement to indicate limited liability status in the name of the company. This should alert prospective suppliers and lenders to the potential risks involved.

A further safeguard is the restrictions placed on the ability of shareholders to withdraw their equity from the company.

Finally, limited companies are required to produce annual financial statements (income statements, statements of financial position and statements of cash flows) and make these publicly available. This means that anyone interested can gain an impression of the financial performance and position of the company. The form and content of the first two of these statements are considered in some detail later in the chapter. The statement of cash flows is considered in Chapter 5.

Public and private companies

When a company is registered with the Registrar of Companies, it must be registered either as a public or as a private company. The main practical difference between these is that a **public limited company** can offer its shares for sale to the general public, but a **private limited company** cannot. A public limited company must signal its status to all interested parties by having the words 'public limited company', or its abbreviation 'plc', in its name. For a private limited company, the word 'limited' or 'Ltd' must appear as part of its name.

Private limited companies tend to be smaller businesses where the ownership is divided among relatively few shareholders who are usually fairly close to one another – for example, family members. There are vastly more private limited companies than there are public ones. Of the nearly three and a half million UK limited companies in existence as at April 2015, fewer than 7,000 (representing just one in 500 of the total) were public limited companies.

Since public limited companies tend to be larger than private limited companies they are often economically more important. In some industry sectors, such as banking, insurance, oil refining and grocery retailing, they are completely dominant. Although there are some large private limited companies, many are little more than the vehicle through which one-person businesses operate.

Real World 4.3 shows the extent of the market dominance of public limited companies in one particular business sector.

REAL WORLD 4.3

A big slice of the market

The UK grocery sector is dominated by four large players: Tesco, Sainsbury, Morrisons and Asda. The first three are public limited companies and the fourth, Asda, is owned by a large US public company, Wal-Mart Inc. Figure 4.1 shows the share of the grocery market enjoyed by each during the 12-week period to 3 January 2016.

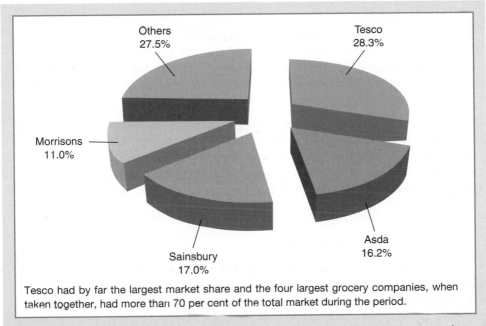

Tesco had by far the largest market share and the four largest grocery companies, when taken together, had more than 70 per cent of the total market during the period.

Figure 4.1 Market share of the UK's four largest grocery companies: 12 weeks to 3 January 2016

Source: Based on information in *Grocery market share for 12 weeks ending 3 January 2016*, Kantar World Panel, www.kantarworldpanel.com.

Taxation

A further consequence of the legal separation of the limited company from its owners is that companies must be accountable to the tax authorities for tax on their profits and gains. This leads to the reporting of tax in the financial statements of limited companies. The charge for tax is shown in the income statement. The tax charge for a particular year is based on that year's profit. For many companies, only 50 per cent of the tax liability is due for payment during the year concerned; the other 50 per cent will appear on the end-of-year statement of financial position as a current liability. This will be illustrated a little later in the chapter.

Companies are charged **corporation tax** on their profits and gains. It is levied on the company's taxable profit, which may differ from the profit shown on the income statement. This is because tax law does not follow normal accounting rules in every respect. Generally, however, taxable profit and accounting profit are pretty close to one another. The percentage rate of corporation tax tends to vary over time. For 2015/16, the corporation tax rate is 20 per cent.

The tax position of companies contrasts with that of sole proprietorships and partnerships, where tax is levied not on the business but on the owner(s). This means that tax will not be reported in the financial statements of unincorporated businesses as it is a matter between the owner(s) and the tax authorities.

THE ROLE OF THE STOCK EXCHANGE

The **London Stock Exchange** acts as both an important *primary* and *secondary* capital market for public companies. As a primary market, its function is to enable companies to raise new finance. As a secondary market, its function is to enable investors to sell their securities (including shares and loan notes) with ease. We have already seen that shares in a company may be transferred from one owner to another. The wish of some investors to sell their shares, coupled with the wish of others to buy those shares, has led to the creation of a formal market in which shares are bought and sold.

Only the shares of certain companies (*listed* companies) may be traded on the London Stock Exchange. As at March 2015, just over 900 UK companies were listed. This represents only about 1 in 3,900 of all UK companies (public and private) and roughly 1 in 7 public limited companies. However, many of these listed companies are massive. Nearly all of the UK businesses that are 'household names' (for example, Tesco, Next, BT, Vodafone, BP and so on) are listed companies.

Activity 4.4

If, as mentioned earlier, the change in ownership of shares does not directly affect a particular company, why do many public companies seek to have their shares traded in a recognised Stock Exchange?

Investors are generally reluctant to pledge their money unless they can see some way of turning their investment back into cash. The shares of a particular company may be valuable because it has bright prospects. Unless this value can be turned into cash, however, the benefit to investors is uncertain. After all, we cannot spend shares; we normally need cash. Thus, investors are more likely to buy new shares from a company where they can liquidate their investment (turn it into cash) as and when they wish. Stock Exchanges provide the means of liquidation and, by so doing, make it easier for a company to raise new share capital.

MANAGING A COMPANY

A limited company may have a legal personality, but it is not a human being capable of making decisions and plans about the business and exercising control over it. People must undertake these management tasks. The most senior level of management of a company is the board of directors.

The shareholders elect **directors** to manage the company on a day-to-day basis on their behalf. By law there must be at least one director for a private limited company and two for a public limited company. In a small company, the board may be the only level of management and consist of all of the shareholders. In larger companies, the board may consist of ten or so directors out of many thousands of shareholders. Indeed, directors are not even required to be shareholders, though they typically are. Below the board of directors of the typical large company could be several layers of management.

In recent years, the issue of **corporate governance** has generated much debate. The term is used to describe the ways in which companies are directed and controlled. The issue of corporate governance is important because, with larger companies, those who own the company (that is, the shareholders) are usually divorced from the day-to-day control of the business. The shareholders employ directors to manage the company for them. Given this position, it may seem reasonable to assume that the best interests of shareholders will guide the directors' decisions. In practice, however, this is not always the case. The directors may be more concerned with pursuing their own interests, such as increasing their pay and 'perks' (such as expensive motor cars, overseas visits and so on) and improving their job security and status. As a result, a conflict can occur between the interests of shareholders and the interests of directors.

Where directors pursue their own interests at the expense of the shareholders, there is clearly a problem for the shareholders. It may also be a problem, however, for society as a whole.

Activity 4.5

Can you think of a reason why directors pursuing their own interests may be a problem for society as a whole?

If shareholders feel that their funds are likely to be mismanaged, they will be reluctant to invest. This can have severe economic repercussions.

A shortage of funds will mean that companies can make fewer investments. It may also mean an increase in the costs of finance as businesses compete for what little funds are available. Thus, a lack of concern for shareholders can have a profound effect on the performance of individual companies and, with this, the health of the economy.

To avoid these problems, most competitive market economies have a framework of rules to help monitor and control the behaviour of directors. These rules are usually based around three guiding principles:

- *Disclosure.* This lies at the heart of good corporate governance. Adequate and timely disclosure can help shareholders to judge the performance of the directors. Where performance is considered unsatisfactory this will be reflected in the price of shares. Changes should then be made to ensure the directors regain the confidence of shareholders.
- *Accountability.* This involves setting out the duties of the directors and establishing an adequate monitoring process. In the UK, company law requires that the directors act in the best interests of the shareholders. This means, among other things, that they must not try to use their position and knowledge to make gains at the expense of the shareholders. The law also requires larger companies to have their annual financial statements independently audited. The purpose of an independent audit is to lend credibility to the financial statements prepared by the directors. We shall consider this point in more detail later in the chapter.

- *Fairness.* Directors should not be able to benefit from access to 'inside' information that is not available to shareholders. As a result, both the law and the Stock Exchange place restrictions on the ability of directors to buy and sell the shares of the company. This means, for example, that the directors cannot buy or sell shares immediately before the announcement of the annual profits or before the announcement of a significant event such as a planned merger.

These principles are set out in Figure 4.2.

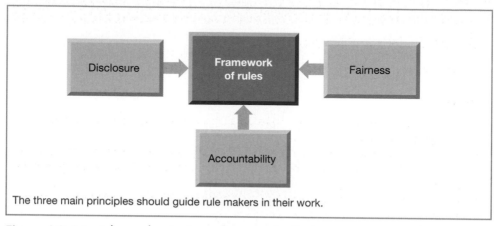

The three main principles should guide rule makers in their work.

Figure 4.2 Principles underpinning a framework of rules

Strengthening the framework of rules

The number of rules designed to safeguard shareholders has increased considerably over the years. This has been in response to weaknesses in corporate governance procedures, which have been exposed through well-publicised business failures and frauds, excessive pay increases to directors and evidence that some financial reports were being 'massaged' so as to mislead shareholders.

Many believe, however, that the shareholders must shoulder some of the blame for any weaknesses. Not all shareholders in large companies are private individuals owning just a few shares each. In fact, ownership, by market value, of the shares listed on the London Stock Exchange is dominated by investing institutions such as insurance businesses, banks and pension funds. These are often massive operations, owning large quantities of the shares of the companies in which they invest. These institutional investors employ specialist staff to manage their portfolios of shares in various companies. It has been argued that the large institutional shareholders, despite their size and relative expertise, have not been very active in corporate governance matters. As a result, there has been little monitoring of directors. However, things seem to be changing. There is increasing evidence that institutional investors are becoming more proactive in relation to the companies in which they hold shares.

THE UK CORPORATE GOVERNANCE CODE

In recent years there has been a real effort to address the problems of poor corporate governance. This has resulted in a code of best practice, known as the **UK Corporate Governance Code**. The UK Code sets out a number of principles underpinning its approach. **Real World 4.4** provides an outline of these.

REAL WORLD 4.4

The UK Corporate Governance Code

Key principles of the UK Code are as follows:

Leadership

- Every listed company should have a board of directors that is collectively responsible for its long-term success.
- There should be a clear division of responsibilities between the chairman, who leads the board, and the chief executive officer, who runs the company. No single person should have unbridled power.
- As part of their role as board members, non-executive directors should constructively challenge and help develop proposals on strategy.

Effectiveness

- There should be an appropriate balance of skills, experience, independence and knowledge to enable the board to carry out its duties effectively.
- Appointments to the board should be the subject of rigorous, formal and transparent procedures.
- All directors should allocate sufficient time to discharge their responsibilities.
- All board members should refresh their skills regularly and new board members should receive induction.
- The board should receive timely information that is of sufficient quality to enable it to carry out its duties.
- The board should undertake a formal and rigorous examination of its own performance each year, which will include its committees and individual directors.
- All directors should submit themselves for re-election at regular intervals, subject to satisfactory performance.

Accountability

- The board should present a fair, balanced and understandable assessment of the company's position and future prospects.
- The board should determine the nature and extent of the main risks to be taken in pursuit of the company's strategic objectives and should maintain sound risk management and internal control systems.

→

- The board should establish formal and transparent arrangements for corporate reporting, risk management and internal control and for maintaining an appropriate relationship with the company's auditors.

Remuneration

- Remuneration levels should be designed to promote the long-term success of the company. Performance-related elements should be transparent, stretching and rigorously applied.
- There should be formal and transparent procedures for developing policy on directors' remuneration. No director should determine his or her own level of remuneration.

Relations with shareholders

- The board as a whole has a responsibility for ensuring a satisfactory dialogue with shareholders.
- The board should use general meetings to communicate with investors and to encourage their participation.

Source: Adapted from the UK Corporate Governance Code, Financial Reporting Council, September 2014, pp. 5 and 6, www.frc.org.uk.

The Code has the backing of the London Stock Exchange. This means that companies listed on the London Stock Exchange are expected to comply with the requirements of the Code or must give their shareholders good reason why they do not. Failure to do one or other of these can lead to the company's shares being suspended from listing.

Activity 4.6

Why might this be an important sanction against a non-compliant company?

A major advantage of a Stock Exchange listing is that it enables investors to sell their shares whenever they wish. A company that is suspended from listing would find it hard and, therefore, expensive to raise funds from investors because there would be no ready market for the shares.

The Code has improved the quality of information available to shareholders. It has also imposed better checks on the powers of directors, and provided greater transparency in corporate affairs. However, rules can only be a partial answer. Many unacceptable business practices stem from a bad corporate culture. Only by changing this culture – that is, the shared values, beliefs and principles held within a business – can a positive change arise.

Rule makers must try to balance the need to protect shareholders against the need to foster the entrepreneurial spirit of directors, which could be stifled by excessive rules. Striking the right balance can be very difficult. Some argue that UK corporate governance has failed to do this and has become far too focused on rules and compliance.

Equity (the owners' claim)

The equity of a sole proprietorship is normally encompassed in one figure on the statement of financial position. In the case of companies, this is usually a little more complicated, although the same broad principles apply. With companies, equity is divided between shares (for example, the original investment), on the one hand, and **reserves** (that is, profits and gains), on the other. It is also possible that there will be more than one type of shares and of reserves. Thus, within the basic divisions of share capital and reserves, there might well be further subdivisions. This might seem quite complicated, but we shall shortly consider the reasons for these subdivisions and all should become clearer.

The basic division

When a company is first formed, those who take steps to form it (the promoters) will decide how much needs to be raised from potential shareholders to set the company up with the necessary assets to operate. Example 4.1 illustrates this.

Example 4.1

Some friends decide to form a company to operate an office cleaning business. They estimate that the company will need £50,000 to obtain the necessary assets. Between them, they raise the cash, which they use to buy shares in the company, on 31 March 2015, with a **nominal value** (or **par value**) of £1 each.

At this point the statement of financial position of the company would be:

Statement of financial position as at 31 March 2015

	£
Net assets (all in cash)	<u>50,000</u>
Equity	
Share capital	
50,000 shares of £1 each	<u>50,000</u>

The company now buys the necessary non-current assets (vacuum cleaners and so on) and inventories (cleaning materials) and starts to trade. During the first year, the company makes a profit of £10,000. This, by definition, means that the equity expands by £10,000. During the year, the shareholders (owners) make no drawings of their equity, so at the end of the year the summarised statement of financial position looks like this:

The profit is shown in a reserve, known as a **revenue reserve**, because it arises from generating revenue (making sales). Note that we do not simply merge the profit with the share capital: we must keep the two amounts separate (to satisfy company law). The reason for this is that there is a legal restriction on the maximum drawings of their equity (for example, as a **dividend**) that the shareholders can make. This is defined by the amount of revenue reserves and so it is helpful to show these separately. We shall look at why there is this restriction, and how it works, a little later in the chapter.

Share capital

Ordinary shares

Ordinary shares represent the basic units of ownership of a business. They are issued by all companies and are often referred to as *equities*. Ordinary shareholders are the primary risk takers as they share in the profits of the company only after other claims have been satisfied. There are no upper limits, however, on the amount by which they may benefit. The potential rewards available to ordinary shareholders reflect the risks that they are prepared to take. Since ordinary shareholders take most of the risks, power normally rests in their hands. Usually, only the ordinary shareholders are able to vote on issues that affect the company, such as the appointment of directors.

The nominal value of such shares is at the discretion of the people who start up the company. For example, if the initial share capital is to be £50,000, this could be two shares of £25,000 each, five million shares of one penny each or any other combination that gives a total of £50,000. All shares must have equal value.

be sold more easily to various investors. It would also be possible for the original shareholder to sell part of the shareholding and to retain a part.

In practice, £1 is the normal maximum nominal value for shares. Shares of 25 pence each and 50 pence each are probably the most common. BT's shares, which we mentioned earlier, have a nominal value of 5 pence each (although their market value at 7 November 2015 was £4.66 per share).

Preference shares

In addition to ordinary shares, some companies issue **preference shares**. These shares guarantee that *if a dividend is paid,* the preference shareholders will be entitled to the first part of it up to a maximum value. This maximum is normally defined as a fixed percentage of the nominal value of the preference shares. If, for example, a company issues one million preference shares of £1 each with a dividend rate of 6 per cent, this means that the preference shareholders are entitled to receive the first £60,000 (that is, 6 per cent of £1 million) of any dividend that is paid by the company for a particular year. The excess over £60,000 goes to the ordinary shareholders.

It is open to the company to issue other classes of shares – perhaps with some having unusual conditions – but in practice it is rare to find other than straightforward ordinary and preference shares. Even preference shares are not very common. While a company may have different classes of shares whose holders have different rights, within each class all shares must be treated equally. The rights of the various classes of shareholders, as well as other matters relating to a particular company, are contained in that company's set of rules, known as the *memorandum and articles of association.* A copy of these rules must be lodged with the Registrar of Companies, who makes it available for inspection by the general public.

Altering the nominal value of shares

As we have already seen, the promoters of a new company may make their own choice of the nominal (par) value of the shares. This value need not be permanent. At a later date the shareholders can decide to change it.

Suppose that a company has one million ordinary shares of £1 each and that shareholders decide to change the nominal value to £0.50 – in other words, to halve the value. To maintain the total nominal value of the share capital intact, the company would then issue each shareholder with twice as many shares as that previously held, each with half the original nominal value. Thus, each shareholder would retain a holding of the same total nominal value. This process is known, not surprisingly, as **splitting** the shares. The opposite, reducing the number of shares and increasing their nominal value per share to compensate, is known as **consolidating**. Since each shareholder would be left, after a split or consolidation, with exactly the same proportion of ownership of the company's assets as before, the process should have no effect on the total value of the shares held.

Both splitting and consolidating may be used to help make the shares more marketable. Splitting may help avoid share prices becoming too high and consolidating may help avoid share prices becoming too low. It seems that investors do not like either extreme. In addition, some Stock Exchanges do not permit shares to be traded at too low a price.

Reserves

The shareholders' equity consists of share capital and reserves. As mentioned earlier, reserves are profits and gains that a company has made and which still form part of the shareholders' equity. One reason that past profits and gains may no longer continue to be part of equity is that they have been paid out to shareholders (as dividends and so on). Another reason is that reserves will be reduced by the amount of any losses that the company might suffer. In the same way that profits increase equity, losses reduce it.

Activity 4.8

Are reserves amounts of cash? Can you think of a reason why this is an odd question?

To deal with the second point first, it is an odd question because reserves are a claim, or part of one, on the assets of the company, whereas cash is an asset. So reserves cannot be cash.

Reserves are classified as either revenue reserves or **capital reserves**. In Example 4.1 we came across a revenue reserve. We should recall that this reserve represents the company's retained trading profits as well as gains on the disposal of non-current assets. *Retained earnings,* as they are most often called, represent overwhelmingly the largest source of new finance for UK companies. Capital reserves arise for two main reasons:

- issuing shares at above their nominal value (for example, issuing £1 shares at £1.50);
- revaluing (upwards) non-current assets.

Where a company issues shares at above their nominal value, UK law requires that the excess of the issue price over the nominal value be shown separately.

Activity 4.9

Can you think why shares might be issued at above their nominal value? (*Hint*: This would not usually happen when a company is first formed and the initial shares are being issued.)

Once a company has traded and has been successful, the shares would normally be worth more than the nominal value at which they were issued. If additional shares are to be issued to new shareholders, unless they are issued at a value higher than the nominal value, the new shareholders will be gaining at the expense of the original ones.

Example 4.2 shows how this works.

Example 4.2

Based on future prospects, the net assets of a company are worth £1.5 million. There are currently 1 million ordinary shares in the company, each with a nominal value of £1. The company wishes to raise an additional £0.6 million of cash for expansion and has decided to raise it by issuing new shares. If the shares are issued for £1 each (that is 600,000 shares), the total number of shares will be:

$$1.0m + 0.6m = 1.6m$$

and their total value will be the value of the existing net assets plus the new injection of cash:

$$£1.5m + £0.6m = £2.1m$$

This means that the value of each share after the new issue will be:

$$£2.1m/1.6m = £1.3125$$

The current value of each share is:

$$£1.5m/1.0m = £1.50$$

so the original shareholders will lose:

$$£1.50 - £1.3125 = £0.1875 \text{ a share}$$

and the new shareholders will gain:

$$£1.3125 - £1.0 = £0.3125 \text{ a share}$$

The new shareholders will, no doubt, be delighted with this outcome; the original ones will not.

Things could be made fair between the two sets of shareholders described in Example 4.2 by issuing the new shares at £1.50 each. In this case, it would be necessary to issue 400,000 shares to raise the necessary £0.6 million. £1 a share of the £1.50 is the nominal value and will be included with share capital in the statement of financial position (£400,000 in total). The remaining £0.50 is a share premium, which will be shown as a capital reserve known as the **share premium account** (£200,000 in total).

It is not clear why UK company law insists on the distinction between nominal share values and the premium. In some other countries (for example, the United States) with similar laws governing the corporate sector, there is not this distinction. Instead, the total value at which shares are issued is shown as one comprehensive figure on the company's statement of financial position.

Real World 4.5 shows the equity structure of one very well-known business.

Bonus shares

It is always open to a company to take reserves of any kind (irrespective of whether they are capital or revenue) and turn them into share capital. This will involve transferring the desired amount from the reserve concerned to share capital and then distributing the appropriate number of new shares to the existing shareholders. New shares arising from such a conversion are known as **bonus shares**. Example 4.3 illustrates how bonus issues work.

Example 4.3

The summary statement of financial position of a company at a particular point in time is as follows:

Statement of financial position

	£
Net assets (various assets less liabilities)	128,000
Equity	
Share capital	
50,000 shares of £1 each	50,000
Reserves	78,000
Total equity	128,000

The directors decide that the company will issue existing shareholders with one new share for every share currently owned by each shareholder. The statement of financial position immediately following this will appear as follows:

Statement of financial position

	£
Net assets (various assets less liabilities)	128,000
Equity	
Share capital	
100,000 shares of £1 each (50,000 + 50,000)	100,000
Reserves (78,000 − 50,000)	28,000
Total equity	128,000

We can see that the reserves have decreased by £50,000 and share capital has increased by the same amount. Share certificates for the new 50,000 ordinary shares of £1 each, which have been created from reserves, will be issued to the existing shareholders to complete the transaction.

Activity 4.10

A shareholder of the company in Example 4.3 owned 100 shares before the bonus issue. How will things change for this shareholder as regards the number of shares owned and the value of the shareholding?

The answer should be that the number of shares would double, from 100 to 200. Now the shareholder owns one five-hundredth of the company (that is, 200/100,000). Before the bonus issue, the shareholder also owned one five-hundredth of the company (that is, 100/50,000). The company's assets and liabilities have not changed as a result of the bonus issue and so, logically, one five-hundredth of the value of the company should be identical to what it was before. Thus, each share is worth half as much as it used to be.

A bonus issue simply takes one part of the equity (a reserve) and puts it into another part (share capital). The transaction has no effect on the company's assets or liabilities, so there is no effect on shareholders' wealth.

Note that a bonus issue is not the same as a share split. A split does not affect the reserves.

Activity 4.11

Can you think why a company might want to make a bonus issue if it has no effect on shareholder wealth? Try to think of at least one reason.

We think that there are three possible reasons:

- *Share price.* To lower the value of each share without reducing the shareholders' collective or individual wealth. This has a similar effect to share splitting.
- *Shareholder confidence.* To provide the shareholders with a 'feel-good factor'. It is believed that shareholders like bonus issues because they seem to make them better off, although in practice they should not affect their wealth.
- *Lender confidence.* Where reserves arising from operating profits and/or realised gains on the sale of non-current assets (revenue reserves) are used to make the bonus issue, it has the effect of taking part of that portion of the shareholders' equity, that could be withdrawn by the shareholders, and locking it up. The amount transferred becomes part of the permanent equity base of the company. (We shall see a little later in this chapter that there are severe restrictions on the extent to which shareholders may make drawings from their equity.) An individual or business contemplating lending money to the company may insist that the extent, that shareholders can withdraw their funds is restricted as a condition of making the loan. This point will be explained shortly.

Real World 4.6 provides an example of a bonus share issue, where it seemed that the main motive was to make the share price more manageable. The 'feel-good' factor, however, also seems to be playing a part.

REAL WORLD 4.6

Is it really a bonus?

Medusa Mining is a gold producer that is listed on various international stock markets. In 2010, it announced a one-for-ten bonus issue of shares to all shareholders of the company.

In a statement, the company said it had achieved several significant milestones in the last calendar year and the bonus issue is in recognition of the invaluable support the company has received from its shareholders. The bonus issue was also designed to encourage greater liquidity in Medusa shares. Geoff Davis, managing director of Medusa, said: 'The board is extremely pleased to be in a position to reward shareholders as a result of the company having rapidly expanded its production over the last 12 months and having met all targets on time.'

Source: Adapted from 'Medusa Mining', www.proactiveinvestors.co.uk, 8 March 2010.

Share capital jargon

Before leaving our detailed discussion of share capital, it might be helpful to clarify some of the jargon relating to shares that is used in company financial statements.

Share capital that has been issued to shareholders is known as the **issued share capital** (or **allotted share capital**). Sometimes, but not very often, a company may not require shareholders to pay the whole amount that is due to be paid for the shares at the time of issue. This may happen where the company does not need the money all at once. Some money would normally be paid at the time of issue and the company would 'call' for further instalments until the shares were **fully paid shares**. That part of the total issue price that has been called is known as the **called-up share capital**. That part that has been called and paid is known as the **paid-up share capital**.

BORROWINGS

Most companies borrow money to supplement that raised from share issues and ploughed-back profits. Company borrowing is often on a long-term basis, perhaps on a ten-year contract. Lenders may be banks and other professional providers of loan finance, such as pension funds and insurance companies.

Usually, long-term loans are secured on assets of the company. This would give the lender the right, were the company to fail to make the contractual payments, to seize the assets concerned, sell them and use the cash to rectify this failure. A mortgage granted to a private individual buying a house or an apartment is a very common example of a secured loan.

Long-term financing of companies can be depicted as in Figure 4.3.

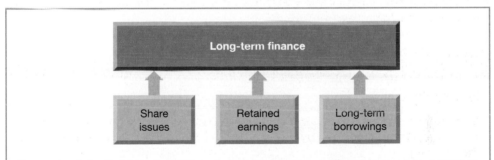

Companies derive their long-term finance from three sources: new share issues, retained earnings and long-term borrowings. For a typical company, the sum of the first two (jointly known as 'equity finance') exceeds the third. Retained earnings usually exceed either of the other two in terms of the amount of finance raised in most years.

Figure 4.3 Sources of long-term finance for a typical limited company

It is important to the prosperity and stability of a company that it strikes a suitable balance between finance provided by the shareholders (equity) and from borrowing. This topic will be explored in Chapters 6 and 11.

WITHDRAWING EQUITY

Companies, as we have seen, are legally obliged to distinguish, on the statement of financial position, between that part of the shareholders' equity that may be withdrawn and that part which may not. The withdrawable part consists of profits arising from trading and from the disposal of non-current assets. It is represented in the statement of financial position by *revenue reserves.* As already mentioned, withdrawals are usually made by shareholders through a dividend.

The non-withdrawable part consists of share capital plus profits arising from shareholders buying shares in the company and from upward revaluations of assets still held. It is represented in the statement of financial position by *share capital* and *capital reserves.* Figure 4.4 shows the important division between the part of the shareholders' equity that can be withdrawn and the part that cannot.

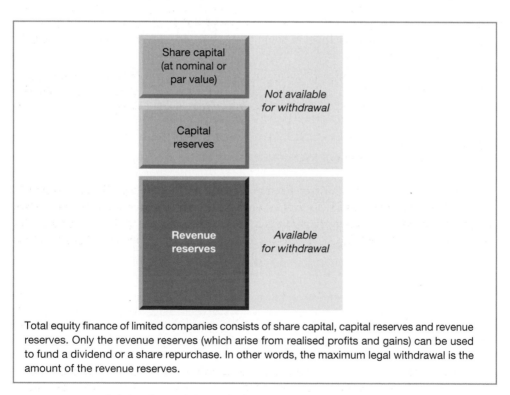

Total equity finance of limited companies consists of share capital, capital reserves and revenue reserves. Only the revenue reserves (which arise from realised profits and gains) can be used to fund a dividend or a share repurchase. In other words, the maximum legal withdrawal is the amount of the revenue reserves.

Figure 4.4 Availability for withdrawal of various parts of the shareholders' equity

Real World 4.7 describes how one company contravened the rules concerning the withdrawal of equity.

Ooops!

Betfair returned £80m to investors in violation of accounting rules, the gambling company has admitted. The embarrassing breach – which occurred in 2011, 2012 and 2013 before being noticed – consisted of Betfair paying out more in dividends and share buybacks than it was legally permitted to.

Betfair announced its first dividend as a public company in June 2011, partly to reassure investors who had seen the company's shares halve since its flotation six months earlier. It paid out £30m in relation to the 2011, 2012 and 2013 financial years, and also bought back £50m in shares. However, the payments did not comply with a rule change on how a company's realised profits and distributable reserves are defined.

Betfair said in its latest annual report that, 'as a result of certain changes to the technical guidance issued by the Institute of Chartered Accounts [sic] in England and Wales (the "ICAEW") in October 2010, the Company did not have sufficient distributable reserves to make those distributions and so they should not have been paid by the Company to its shareholders.'

Deed polls have now been used to ensure that investors do not have to repay the dividends, and the company's annual general meeting in September will be asked to approve the cancellation of ordinary shares affected by the buyback.

 Source: Extract from Mance, H. (2014) 'Betfair admits to £80m payouts mistake', ft.com, 3 August.
(c) The Financial Times Limited 2014. All Rights Reserved.

The law does not specify how large the non-withdrawable part of a particular company's shareholders' equity should be. However, when seeking to impress prospective lenders and credit suppliers, the larger this part, the better. Those considering doing business with the company must be able to see from the company's statement of financial position how large it is.

Why are limited companies required to distinguish different parts of their shareholders' equity, whereas sole proprietorship and partnership businesses are not?

The reason stems from the limited liability that company shareholders enjoy but which owners of unincorporated businesses do not. If a sole proprietor or partner withdraws equity, the position of the lenders and credit suppliers is not weakened since they can pursue their claims against the sole proprietor, or partner, as an individual. In the case of a limited company, however, claims cannot be pursued against individual shareholders. Thus, to protect the company's lenders and credit suppliers, the law insists the withdrawable and non-withdrawable elements of shareholder equity be separately disclosed.

Let us now look at an example that illustrates how this protection of creditors works.

Example 4.4

The summary statement of financial position of a company at a particular date is as follows:

Statement of financial position

	£
Total assets	43,000
Equity	
Share capital	
20,000 shares of £1 each	20,000
Reserves (revenue)	23,000
Total equity	43,000

A bank has been asked to make a £25,000 long-term loan to the company. If the loan were to be granted, the statement of financial position immediately following would appear as follows:

Statement of financial position (after the loan)

	£
Total assets (£43,000 + £25,000)	68,000
Equity	
Share capital	
20,000 shares of £1 each	20,000
Reserves (revenue)	23,000
	43,000
Non-current liability	
Borrowings – loan	25,000
Total equity and liabilities	68,000

As things stand, there are assets with a total carrying amount of £68,000 to meet the bank's claim of £25,000. It would be possible and perfectly legal, however, for the company to withdraw part of the shareholders' equity (through a dividend) equal to the total revenue reserves (£23,000). The statement of financial position would then appear as follows:

Statement of financial position

	£
Total assets (£68,000 − £23,000)	45,000
Equity	
Share capital	
20,000 shares of £1 each	20,000
Reserves (revenue) (£23,000 − £23,000)	-
	20,000
Non-current liabilities	
Borrowings – bank loan	25,000
Total equity and liabilities	45,000

This leaves the bank in a very much weaker position, in that there are now total assets with a carrying amount of £45,000 to meet a claim of £25,000. Note that the difference between the amount of the borrowings (bank loan) and the total assets equals the equity (share capital and reserves) total. Thus, the equity represents a margin of safety for lenders and suppliers. The larger the amount of the equity withdrawable by the shareholders, the smaller is the potential margin of safety for lenders and suppliers.

Activity 4.13

Can you recall the circumstances in which the non-withdrawable part of a company's equity could be reduced, without contravening the law? This was mentioned earlier in the chapter.

It can be reduced as a result of the company sustaining trading losses, or losses on disposal of non-current assets, which exceed the withdrawable amount of shareholders' equity.

THE MAIN FINANCIAL STATEMENTS

The financial statements of a limited company are, in essence, the same as those of a sole proprietor or partnership. There are, however, some differences of detail, which we shall now consider. Example 4.5 sets out the income statement and statement of financial position of a limited company.

Example 4.5

Da Silva plc
Income statement for the year ended 31 December 2015

	£m
Revenue	840
Cost of sales	(520)
Gross profit	320
Wages and salaries	(98)
Heat and light	(18)
Rent and rates	(24)
Motor vehicle expenses	(20)
Insurance	(4)
Printing and stationery	(12)
Depreciation	(45)
Audit fee	(4)
Operating profit	95
Interest payable	(10)
Profit before taxation	85
Taxation	(24)
Profit for the year	61

$\rightarrow$

Statement of financial position as at 31 December 2015

	£m
ASSETS	
Non-current assets	
Property, plant and equipment	203
Intangible assets	100
	303
Current assets	
Inventories	65
Trade receivables	112
Cash	36
	213
Total assets	516
EQUITY AND LIABILITIES	
Equity	
Ordinary shares of £0.50 each	200
Share premium account	30
Other reserves	50
Retained earnings	25
	305
Non-current liabilities	
Borrowings	100
Current liabilities	
Trade payables	99
Taxation	12
	111
Total equity and liabilities	516

Let us now go through these statements and pick out those aspects that are unique to limited companies.

The income statement

The main points for consideration in the income statement are as follows:

Profit

We can see that, following the calculation of operating profit, two further measures of profit are shown.

- The first of these is the **profit before taxation**. Interest charges are deducted from the operating profit to derive this figure. In the case of a sole proprietor or partnership business, the income statement would end here.
- The second measure of profit is the profit for the reporting period (usually a year). As the company is a separate legal entity, it is liable to pay tax (known as corporation tax) on the profits generated. This measure of profit represents the amount that is available for the shareholders.

Audit fee

Companies beyond a certain size are required to have their financial statements audited by an independent firm of accountants, for which a fee is charged. As mentioned earlier, the purpose of the audit is to lend credibility to the financial statements. Although it is also open to sole proprietorships and partnerships to have their financial statements audited, relatively few do so. Audit fee is, therefore, an expense that is most often seen in the income statement of a company.

Figure 4.5 shows an outline of the income statement for a limited company.

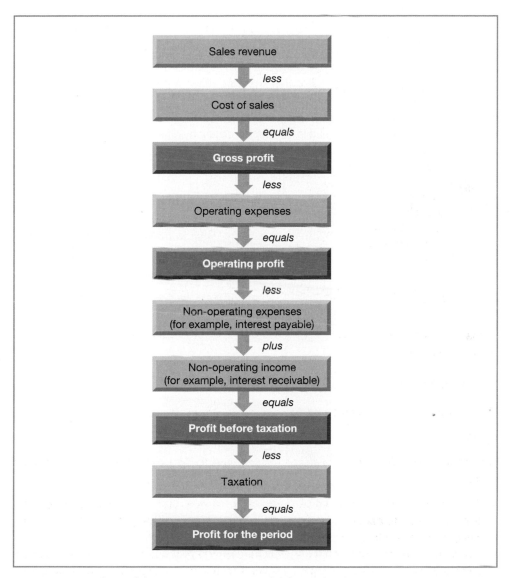

Figure 4.5 Outline of the income statement of a limited company

The statement of financial position

The main points for consideration in the statement of financial position are as follows:

Taxation

The amount that appears as part of the current liabilities represents 50 per cent of the tax on the profit for the year 2015. It is, therefore, 50 per cent (£12 million) of the charge that appears in the income statement (£24 million); the other 50 per cent (£12 million) will already have been paid. The unpaid 50 per cent will be paid shortly after the statement of financial position date. These payment dates are set down by law.

Other reserves

This will include any reserves that are not separately identified on the face of the statement of financial position. It may include a *general reserve,* which normally consists of trading profits that have been transferred to this separate reserve for reinvestment ('ploughing back') into the operations of the company. It is not at all necessary to set up a separate reserve for this purpose. The trading profits could remain unallocated and still swell the retained earnings of the company. It is not entirely clear why directors decide to make transfers to general reserves, since the profits concerned remain part of the revenue reserves, and as such they still remain available for dividend.

Activity 4.14

Can you think of a reason why the directors may wish to make a transfer to general reserves from retained earnings?

The most plausible explanation seems to be that directors feel that placing profits in a separate reserve indicates an intention to invest the funds, represented by the reserve, permanently in the company and, therefore, not to use them to pay a dividend or to fund a share repurchase.

The retained earnings appearing on the statement of financial position are, of course, also a reserve, but that fact is not indicated in its title.

DIVIDENDS

We have already seen that dividends represent drawings by the shareholders of the company. Dividends are paid out of the revenue reserves and should be deducted from these reserves (usually retained earnings) when preparing the statement of financial position. Shareholders are often paid an annual dividend, perhaps in two parts. An 'interim' dividend may be paid part way through the year and a 'final' dividend shortly after the year end.

Would you expect a company to pay all of its revenue reserves as a dividend?

It would be rare for a company to pay all of its revenue reserves as a dividend: the fact that it is legally possible does not necessarily make it a good idea. Most companies see ploughed-back profits as a major – usually *the* major – source of new finance.

Dividends declared by the directors during the year but still unpaid at the year end *may* appear as a liability in the statement of financial position. To be recognised as a liability, however, they must be properly authorised before the year-end date. This normally means that the shareholders must approve the dividend by that date, which is relatively rare in practice.

Large businesses tend to have a clear and consistent policy towards the payment of dividends. Any change in the policy provokes considerable interest and is usually interpreted by shareholders as a signal of the directors' views concerning the future. For example, an increase In dividends may be taken as a signal that future prospects are bright: a higher dividend providing tangible evidence of the directors' confidence.

Real World 4.8 provides an example of one business that increased its dividend after reporting good results.

REAL WORLD 4.8

Picking up a signal

WS Atkins, the UK engineering consultancy, on Thursday signalled confidence in its prospects by proposing to raise its dividend by 8.1 per cent.

Atkins, which counts the transformation of the London 2012 Olympic Park and redesign of Trafalgar Square among its high-profile projects, outlined a full-year payout to shareholders of 36.5p.

The dividend increase came as the 77-year-old company reported results that beat analysts' expectations. Pre-tax profit for the year to March 31 came to £106.7m, down 6.6 per cent compared to 2013–14, on flat revenue of £1.8bn. However, underlying pre-tax profit rose almost 14.6 per cent to £121.9m, surpassing analysts' expectations of £117.8m, following strong performances in Asia Pacific and the Middle East, where Atkins is building the Dubai metro.

Atkins said the overall outlook remained 'positive', despite challenging markets worldwide. It said it continued to see a 'good pipeline' of work across the nuclear and renewables sectors, offsetting markets hit by falling oil prices.

Source: Extracts from Powley, T. (2015) 'WS Atkins signals confidence by proposing 8.1% dividend rise', ft.com, 11 June.
© The Financial Times Limited 2015. All Rights Reserved.

ADDITIONAL FINANCIAL STATEMENTS

In the sections below, we turn our attention to two new financial statements that must be provided by those companies that are subject to International Financial Reporting Standards. We shall consider the nature and role of these standards a little later in the chapter.

Statement of comprehensive income

The **statement of comprehensive income** extends the conventional income statement to include certain other gains and losses that affect shareholders' equity. It may be presented either in the form of a single statement or as two separate statements, comprising an income statement (like the one shown in Example 4.5) and a statement of comprehensive income.

This new statement attempts to overcome the perceived weaknesses of the conventional income statement. In broad terms, the conventional income statement shows all *realised* gains and losses for the period. It also shows some unrealised losses. However, gains, and some losses, that remain *unrealised* (because the asset is still held) tend not to pass through the income statement, but will go, instead, directly to a reserve. We saw, in an earlier chapter, an example of such an unrealised gain.

Activity 4.16

Can you think of this example?

The example that we met earlier is where a business revalues its land and buildings. The gain arising is not shown in the conventional income statement, but is transferred to a revaluation reserve, which forms part of the equity. (See example in Activity 2.16 on page 00.) Land and buildings are not the only assets to which this rule relates, but revaluations of these types of asset are, in practice, the most common examples of unrealised gains.

An example of an unrealised gain, or loss, that has not been mentioned so far, arises from exchange differences when the results of foreign operations are translated into UK currency. Any gain, or loss, bypasses the income statement and is taken directly to a currency translation reserve.

A weakness of conventional accounting is that there is no robust principle that we can apply to determine precisely what should, and what should not, be included in the income statement. Thus, on the one hand, losses arising from the impairment of non-current assets normally appear in the income statement. On the other hand, losses arising from translating the carrying value of assets expressed in an overseas currency (because they are owned by an overseas branch) do not. In principle, there is no significant difference between the two types of loss, but the difference in treatment is ingrained in conventional accounting practice.

The statement of comprehensive income includes *all* gains and losses for a period and so will also take into account unrealised gains and any remaining unrealised losses. It extends the conventional income statement by including these items immediately beneath the measure of profit for the year. An illustration of this statement is shown in Example 4.6.

Example 4.6

Malik plc
Statement of comprehensive income for the year ended 31 July 2016

	£m
Revenue	97.2
Cost of sales	(59.1)
Gross profit	38.1
Distribution expenses	(13.0)
Administration expenses	(11.2)
Other expenses	(2.4)
Operating profit	11.5
Finance charges	(1.8)
Profit before tax	9.7
Tax	(2.4)
Profit for the year	7.3
Other comprehensive income	
Revaluation of property, plant and equipment	6.6
Foreign currency translation differences for foreign operations	4.0
Tax on other comprehensive income	(2.6)
Other comprehensive income for the year, net of tax	8.0
Total comprehensive income for the year	15.3

This example adopts a single-statement approach to presenting comprehensive income. The alternative two-statement approach simply divides the information shown into two separate parts. The income statement, which is the first statement, begins with the revenue and ends with the profit for the year. The statement of comprehensive income, which is the second statement, begins with the profit for the reporting period and ends with the total comprehensive income for the year.

Statement of changes in equity

The **statement of changes in equity** aims to help users to understand the changes in share capital and reserves that took place during the period. It reconciles the figures for these items at the beginning of the period with those at the end. This is achieved by showing the effect on the share capital and reserves of total comprehensive income as well as the effect of share issues and purchases during the period. The effect of dividends during the period may also be shown in this statement, although dividends can be shown in the notes instead.

To see how a statement of changes in equity may be prepared, let us consider Example 4.7.

Example 4.7

At 1 January 2015 Miro plc had the following equity:

Miro plc

	£m
Share capital (£1 ordinary shares)	100
Revaluation reserve	20
Translation reserve	40
Retained earnings	150
Total equity	**310**

During 2015, the company made a profit for the year from normal business operations of £42 million and reported an upward revaluation of property, plant and equipment of £120 million (net of any tax that would be payable were the unrealised gains to be realised). The company also reported a £10 million loss on exchange differences on translating the results of foreign operations. To strengthen its financial position, the company issued 50 million ordinary shares during the year at a premium of £0.40. Dividends for the year were £27 million.

This information for 2015 can be set out in a statement of changes in equity as follows:

Statement of changes in equity for the year ended 31 December 2015

	Share capital £m	Share premium £m	Revaluation reserve £m	Translation reserve £m	Retained earnings £m	Total £m
Balance as at 1 January 2015	100	–	20	40	150	310
Changes in equity for 2015						
Issue of ordinary shares (Note 1)	50	20	–	–	–	70
Dividends (Note 2)	–	–	–	–	(27)	(27)
Total comprehensive income for the year (Note 3)	–	–	120	(10)	42	152
Balance at 31 December 2015	150	20	140	30	165	505

Notes:

1 The premium on the share price is transferred to a specific reserve.

2 Dividends are shown in the statement of changes in equity. They are deducted from retained earnings. An alternative would be to show them as a note to the financial statements.

3 The effect of each component of comprehensive income on the various components of shareholders' equity must be separately disclosed. The revaluation gain and the loss on translating foreign operations are each allocated to a specific reserve. The profit for the year is added to retained earnings.

THE DIRECTORS' DUTY TO ACCOUNT

For companies of significant size, it is not practical for all shareholders to be involved in the management of the company. Instead, they appoint directors to act on their behalf. This separation of ownership from day-to-day control creates a need for directors to be accountable for their stewardship (management) of the company's assets. To fulfil this need, the directors must prepare financial statements that fairly represent the financial position and performance of the business. This involves selecting appropriate accounting policies, making reasonable accounting estimates and keeping to the relevant accounting rules when preparing the statements. To avoid misstatements in the financial statements, whether from fraud or error, appropriate internal control systems must also be maintained.

Each of the company's shareholders has the right to be sent a copy of the financial statements produced by the directors. A copy must also be sent to the Registrar of Companies, which is then made available for public inspection. A Stock Exchange listed company has the additional obligation to publish its financial statements on its website.

Activity 4.17

It can be argued that the publication of financial statements is vital to a well-functioning private sector. Why might this be the case? Try to think of at least one reason.

There are at least two reasons:

- Unless shareholders receive regular information about the performance and position of a business they will encounter problems in evaluating their investment. As a result, they would probably be reluctant to invest.
- Unless suppliers of labour, goods, services and loans receive information about the financial health of a business, they would probably be reluctant to engage in commercial relationships. The fact that a company has limited liability increases the risks involved in dealing with it.

THE NEED FOR ACCOUNTING RULES

The directors' duty to prepare and publish financial statements has led to the creation of a framework of rules concerning their form and content. Without rules, there is a much greater risk that unscrupulous directors will employ accounting policies and practices that portray an unrealistic view of financial health. There is also a much greater risk that the financial statements will not be comparable over time, or with those of other businesses. Accounting rules can narrow areas of differences and reduce the variety of accounting methods. This should help ensure that businesses treat similar transactions in a similar way.

Accounting rules should help to create greater confidence in the integrity of financial statements. This should make it easier to raise funds from investors and to build stronger relationships with customers and suppliers. We must be realistic, however, about what can be achieved through regulation. Problems of manipulation and of concealment can still occur even within a highly regulated environment. Nevertheless, the scale of these problems should be reduced where accounting rules are in place.

Problems of comparability between businesses can also still occur. Accounting is not a precise science. Even within a regulated environment, estimates and judgements must be made and these may vary according to who makes them. Furthermore, no two businesses are identical. Different accounting policies may therefore be applied to fit different circumstances.

SOURCES OF ACCOUNTING RULES

In recent years, there has been an increasing trend towards both the internationalisation of business and the integration of financial markets. This has given impetus to the international harmonisation of accounting rules. A common set of rules can help users when comparing the financial health of companies based in different countries. It can also relieve international companies of some of the burden of preparing financial statements. Different financial statements will no longer be needed to comply with the rules of the particular countries in which these companies operate.

The International Accounting Standards Board (IASB) is an independent body that is at the forefront of the move towards harmonisation. The Board, which is based in the UK, is dedicated to developing a single set of high-quality, globally-accepted, accounting rules. These aim to ensure transparent and comparable information in financial statements. The rules, which are known as **International Accounting Standards** (IASs) or **International Financial Reporting Standards** (IFRSs), deal with key issues such as:

- what information should be disclosed;
- how information should be presented;
- how assets should be valued; and
- how profit should be measured.

Activity 4.18

We have already come across some IASs and IFRSs in earlier chapters. Try to recall at least two topics where they were mentioned.

We came across financial reporting standards when considering:

- the valuation and impairment of assets (Chapter 2);
- depreciation and impairment of non-current assets (Chapter 3);
- the valuation of inventories (Chapter 3).

Over the years, the IASB has greatly extended its influence and authority. The point has now been reached where all major economies adopt IFRSs or have set time lines to adopt, or to converge with, IFRSs. Although, in the UK, the authority of the IASB extends only to listed companies, non-listed UK companies have the option to adopt IFRSs.

Company law also imposes rules on UK companies. These rules relate to corporate governance issues and go beyond anything required by IFRSs. There is, for example, a requirement to disclose details of directors' remuneration in the published financial statements. Furthermore, the Financial Conduct Authority (FCA), in its role as the UK (Stock Exchange) listing authority, imposes rules on Stock Exchange listed companies. These include the requirement to publish a condensed set of interim (half-year) financial statements in addition to the annual financial statements.

Figure 4.6 sets out the main sources of accounting rules for Stock Exchange listed companies discussed above.

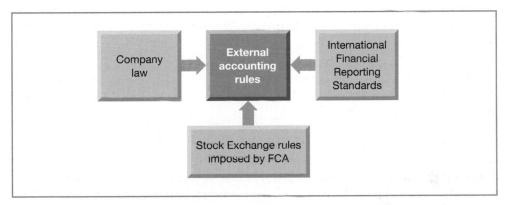

Figure 4.6 Sources of external accounting rules for a UK public limited company listed on the London Stock Exchange

THE AUDITORS' ROLE

Shareholders are required to elect a qualified and independent person or, more usually, a firm to act as **auditors**. The auditors' main duty is to report whether, in their opinion, the financial statements do what they are supposed to do, namely to show a true and fair view of the financial performance, position and cash flows of the company. To form an opinion, auditors must carefully scrutinise the financial statements and the underlying evidence upon which they are based. It will involve an examination of the accounting principles followed, the accounting estimates made and the robustness of the company's internal control systems. The auditors' opinion must accompany the financial statements sent to shareholders and to the Registrar of Companies.

The relationship between the shareholders, the directors and the auditors is illustrated in Figure 4.7. This shows that the shareholders elect the directors to act on their behalf, in the day-to-day running of the company. The directors are then required to 'account' to the shareholders on the performance, position and cash flows of the company, on an annual basis. The shareholders also elect the auditors, who then report back to the shareholders.

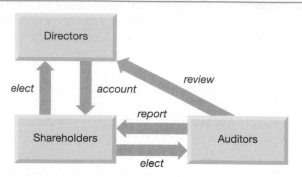

The directors are appointed by the shareholders to manage the company on the shareholders' behalf. The directors are required to report each year to the shareholders, principally by means of financial statements, on the company's performance, position and cash flows. To give greater confidence in the statements, the shareholders also appoint auditors to investigate the reports and to express an opinion on their reliability.

Figure 4.7 The relationship between the shareholders, the directors and the auditors

MANAGEMENT COMMENTARY

The organisational structures, operating systems and financing methods of businesses can be complex. Nevertheless, the financial statements must reflect these aspects if they are to faithfully portray financial position and performance. This can mean, however, that financial statements also become complex. To provide a clearer picture, a management commentary is often helpful. A narrative report can provide a review of the financial results as well as any further information needed to understand the financial health of the business.

Activity 4.19

What do you think are the main qualitative characteristics that information contained in a management commentary should possess? (*Hint*: Think back to Chapter 1.)

To be useful, the information should exhibit the characteristics for accounting information in general, which we identified in Chapter 1. Thus the information should be relevant and faithfully represented. It should also be comparable, verifiable, timely and understandable. The fact that we may be dealing with narrative information does not alter the need for these characteristics to be present.

In the UK, a management commentary has become part of the financial reporting landscape. In the sections below we consider two narrative reports, the directors' report and the strategic report, which both supplement and complement the main financial statements.

The directors' report

The directors are required to prepare a report to shareholders relating to each financial period. The content of the **directors' report** is prescribed by law and includes assorted topics such as current year's performance and position, future prospects of the business and social aspects. For companies of significant size, the report must cover, amongst other things, the following matters:

- the names of those who were directors during the reporting period;
- any recommended dividend;
- the involvement of employees in the affairs of the company;
- the employment and training of disabled persons;
- important events affecting the company since the year-end;
- likely future developments in the business; and
- research and development activities.

In addition to disclosing the information mentioned above, the directors' report must contain a declaration that the directors are not aware of any other information that the auditors might need in preparing their audit report. There must also be a declaration that the directors have taken steps to ensure that the auditors are aware of all relevant information. The auditors do not carry out an audit of the directors' report. However, they do check to see that the information in the report is consistent with that contained in the audited financial statements.

Strategic report

Until recently, an important element of the directors' report was the *business review*. This provided largely narrative information to help assess the performance and position of the business. To give greater prominence to this element, it has been separated out and is now contained within a **strategic report**. The overall aim of the report is to help shareholders understand how well the directors have performed in promoting the success of the company. Directors of all but the smallest companies are legally obliged to produce a balanced and comprehensive analysis of development and performance during the year, as well as the position of the company's business at the year-end. They must also describe the principal risks and uncertainties facing the company.

Strategic reports prepared by Stock Exchange listed companies must disclose more than those of other companies. **Figure 4.8** summarises their main features.

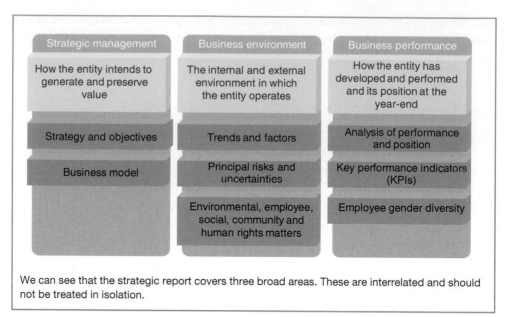

Strategic management	Business environment	Business performance
How the entity intends to generate and preserve value	The internal and external environment in which the entity operates	How the entity has developed and performed and its position at the year-end
Strategy and objectives	Trends and factors	Analysis of performance and position
Business model	Principal risks and uncertainties	Key performance indicators (KPIs)
	Environmental, employee, social, community and human rights matters	Employee gender diversity

We can see that the strategic report covers three broad areas. These are interrelated and should not be treated in isolation.

Figure 4.8 The strategic report

Source: *Guidance on the Strategic Report,* Financial Reporting Council, June 2014, p. 20.

Activity 4.20

Why do you think Stock Exchange listed companies are required to disclose more information about their business than other companies? Try to think of at least one reason.

Various arguments can be made in favour of greater accountability from listed companies. They include:

- Greater transparency concerning their operations should help investors make better decisions. Share prices may, therefore, be set in a more informed manner. This, in turn, should contribute towards the smooth functioning of capital markets.
- Listed companies tend to be larger, have more economic power and have more stakeholders than other companies. Their impact on the economy and society as a whole, therefore, tends to be greater. This, in turn, obliges them to account more fully for their actions and behaviour.

CREATIVE ACCOUNTING

Despite the proliferation of accounting rules and the independent checks that are imposed, concerns over the quality of published financial statements surface from time to time. There are occasions when directors apply particular accounting policies, or structure particular transactions, in such a way as to portray a picture of financial health that is in line with what they want users to see, rather than what is a true and fair view of financial position and performance. Misrepresenting the performance and position of a business in this way is referred to as **creative accounting** and it poses a major problem for accounting rule makers and for society generally.

Creative accounting methods

There are many ways in which unscrupulous directors can manipulate the financial statements. However, these methods usually involve adopting novel or unorthodox practices for reporting key elements of the financial statements such as revenue, expenses, assets and liabilities. They may also require the use of complicated or obscure transactions in an attempt to hide the underlying economic reality. The manipulation carried out may be designed either to bend the rules or to break them.

Many creative accounting methods are designed to overstate the revenue for a period. These methods often involve the early recognition of sales revenue or the reporting of sales transactions that have no real substance. **Real World 4.9** provides examples of both types of revenue manipulation that have been used in practice.

→

> *Hollow swaps:* Telecom businesses may agree to sell unused fibre optic capacity to each other – usually at the same price. Although this will not increase profits, it will increase revenues and give an impression that the business is growing.
>
> *Round tripping:* Energy businesses may agree to buy and sell energy between each other. Again this is normally for the same price and so no additional profits will be made. It will, however, boost revenues to give a false impression of business growth. This method is also known as 'in and out trading'.
>
> *Source*: Based on information in 'Dirty laundry: how companies fudge the numbers', *The Times, Business Section,* 22 September 2002.

Creative accounting and economic growth

Some years ago, there was a wave of creative accounting scandals, particularly in the United States but also in Europe. It seems, however, that this wave has now subsided. Action taken by different regulatory bodies has meant that company behaviour is now subject to stricter controls. Corporate governance procedures have been strengthened and tighter financial reporting rules have been imposed. Creative accounting is now a more risky and difficult process for those who attempt it. Nevertheless, it will never disappear completely and another wave of creative accounting scandals may occur in the future. The most recent wave coincided with a period of strong economic growth and, during good economic times, investors and auditors become less vigilant. The temptation to manipulate the figures, therefore, becomes greater. A weak corporate culture is needed, however, for such a temptation to become reality.

? SELF-ASSESSMENT QUESTION 4.1

This question requires you to correct some figures on a set of company financial statements. It should prove useful practice for the material that you covered in Chapters 2 and 3, as well as helping you to become more familiar with the financial statements of a company.

Presented below is a draft set of simplified financial statements for Pear Limited for the year ended 30 September 2016.

Income statement for the year ended 30 September 2016

	£000
Revenue	1,456
Cost of sales	(768)
Gross profit	688
Salaries	(220)
Depreciation	(249)
Other operating costs	(131)
Operating profit	88
Interest payable	(15)
Profit before taxation	73
Taxation at 30%	(22)
Profit for the year	51

Statement of financial position as at 30 September 2016

	£000
ASSETS	
Non-current assets	
Property, plant and equipment	
Cost	1,570
Depreciation	(690)
	880
Current assets	
Inventories	207
Trade receivables	182
Cash at bank	21
	410
Total assets	1,290
EQUITY AND LIABILITIES	
Equity	
Share capital	300
Share premium account	300
Retained earnings at beginning of year	104
Profit for year	51
	755
Non-current liabilities	
Borrowings (10% loan notes repayable 2019)	300
Current liabilities	
Trade payables	88
Other payables	20
Taxation	22
Borrowings (bank overdraft)	105
	235
Total equity and liabilities	1,290

The following information is available:

1 Depreciation has not been charged on office equipment with a carrying amount of £100,000. This class of assets is depreciated at 12 per cent a year using the reducing-balance method.

2 A new machine was purchased, on credit, for £30,000 and delivered on 29 September 2016 but has not been included in the financial statements. (Ignore depreciation.)

3 A sales invoice to the value of £18,000 for September 2016 has been omitted from the financial statements. (The cost of sales figure is stated correctly.)

4 A dividend of £25,000 had been approved by the shareholders before 30 September 2016, but was unpaid at that date. This is not reflected in the financial statements.

5 The interest payable on the loan notes for the second half-year was not paid until 1 October 2016 and has not been included in the financial statements.

6 Bad debts are to be written off representing 2 per cent of trade receivables outstanding at the year-end.

7 An invoice for electricity to the value of £2,000 for the quarter ended 30 September 2016 arrived on 4 October and has not been included in the financial statements.

8 The charge for taxation will have to be amended to take account of the above information. Make the simplifying assumption that tax is payable shortly after the end of the year, at the rate of 30 per cent of the profit before tax.

Required:

Prepare a revised set of financial statements for the year ended 30 September 2016 incorporating the additional information in 1 to 8 above. (Work to the nearest £1,000.)

The solution to this question can be found at the back of the book on page 526.

SUMMARY

The main points of this chapter may be summarised as follows:

Main features of a limited company

- It is an artificial person created by law.
- It has a separate life to its owners and is granted a perpetual existence.
- It must take responsibility for its own debts and losses but its owners are granted limited liability.
- To protect those dealing with it, limited liability is included in the name, restrictions are placed on the withdrawal of equity and annual financial statements are made publicly available.
- A public company can offer its shares for sale to the public; a private company cannot.
- The shares of public companies can be traded on the Stock Exchange.
- It is governed by a board of directors, which is elected by the shareholders.
- The UK Corporate Governance Code sets out how a Stock Exchange listed company should be directed and controlled.

Financing the limited company

- The share capital of a company can be of two main types: ordinary shares and preference shares.
- Holders of ordinary shares (equities) are the main risk takers and are given voting rights; they form the backbone of the company.
- Holders of preference shares are given a right to a fixed dividend before ordinary shareholders receive a dividend.
- Reserves are profits and gains made by the company and form part of the ordinary shareholders' equity.
- Borrowings provide another major source of finance.

Bonus share issues

■ Bonus shares are issued to existing shareholders when part of the reserves of the company is converted into share capital. No funds are raised.

■ The issue of bonus shares has no effect on shareholder wealth.

Reserves and the withdrawal of equity

■ Reserves are of two types: revenue reserves and capital reserves.

■ Revenue reserves arise from trading profits and from gains on the sale of non-current assets.

■ Capital reserves arise from the issue of shares above their nominal value or from the upward revaluation of non-current assets.

■ Revenue reserves can be withdrawn as dividends by the shareholders whereas capital reserves normally cannot.

Financial statements of limited companies

■ The financial statements of limited companies are based on the same principles as those of sole proprietorship and partnership businesses. However, there are differences in detail.

■ The income statement has two measures of profit displayed after the operating profit figure: *profit before taxation* and *profit for the period*.

■ The income statement also shows audit fees and tax on profits for the period.

■ Unpaid tax will normally appear in the statement of financial position as current liabilities.

■ The statement of comprehensive income extends the income statement to include all gains and losses, both realised and unrealised.

■ The statement of changes in equity reconciles the equity figures at the beginning and end of a reporting period.

Directors' duty

■ Separation of ownership from day-to-day control creates a need for directors to be accountable.

■ To fulfil this need, the directors have a duty to prepare and publish financial statements.

■ Shareholders have a right to receive a copy of the published financial statements.

The need for accounting rules

■ Rules are needed to avoid unacceptable accounting practices and to improve the comparability of financial statements.

■ Rules should give greater confidence in the integrity of financial statements.

→

Accounting rules

- The International Accounting Standards Board (IASB) has become an important source of rules.

- Company law and the London Stock Exchange are also sources of rules for UK companies.

Other statutory reports

- The auditors' report provides an opinion by independent auditors concerning whether the financial statements provide a true and fair view of the financial health of a business.

- The directors' report contains information of a financial and a non-financial nature, which goes beyond that contained in the financial statements.

- The strategic report provides largely narrative information to help assess the financial performance and position of the business.

- The directors' report and strategic report form part of a management commentary designed to both supplement and complement the main financial statements.

Creative accounting

- Despite the accounting rules in place there have been examples of creative accounting by directors.

- This involves using accounting practices to show what the directors would like users to see rather than what is a fair representation of reality.

KEY TERMS

For definitions of these terms, see Appendix A.

FURTHER READING

If you would like to explore the topics covered in this chapter in more depth, we recommend the following books:

Elliott, B. and Elliott, J. (2015) *Financial Accounting and Reporting,* 17th edn, Pearson, Chapters 3 and 12.

Financial Reporting Council, *The UK Corporate Governance Code*, FRC 2014, available free at www.frc.org.uk.

Melville, A. (2015) *International Financial Reporting,* 5th edn, Pearson, Chapters 1, 2 and 3.

Tricker, R. (2015) *Corporate Governance: Principles, Policies and Practices,* 3rd edn, OUP Chapters 4 and 7.

? REVIEW QUESTIONS

Solutions to these questions can be found at the back of the book on pages 540–541.

4.1 How does the liability of a limited company differ from the liability of a real person, in respect of amounts owed to others?

4.2 Some people are about to form a company, as a vehicle through which to run a new business. What factors should they bear in mind when deciding between forming a private limited company or a public limited company?

4.3 What is a reserve? Distinguish between a revenue reserve and a capital reserve.

4.4 Compare the main features of a preference share with those of:

   (a) an ordinary share; and
   (b) loan notes.

*Exercises 4.1 and 4.2 are basic level. Exercise 4.3 is intermediate level and Exercises 4.4 and 4.5 are advanced level. Those with **coloured numbers** have solutions at the back of the book, starting on page 555.*

4.1 Comment on the following quote:

> Limited companies can set a limit on the amount of debts that they will meet. They tend to have reserves of cash, as well as share capital and they can use these reserves to pay dividends to the shareholders. Some companies have preference as well as ordinary shares. The preference shares give a guaranteed dividend. The shares of some companies can be bought and sold on the Stock Exchange. Shareholders selling their shares provide a useful source of new finance to the company.

4.2 Briefly explain each of the following expressions that you have seen in the financial statements of a limited company:
(a) dividend;
(b) audit fee;
(c) share premium account.

4.3 The following information was extracted from the financial statements of I. Ching (Booksellers) plc for the year to 31 December 2015:

	£m
Finance charges	40
Cost of sales	460
Distribution expenses	110
Revenue	943
Administration expenses	212
Other expenses	25
Gain on revaluation of property, plant and equipment	20
Loss on foreign currency translations on foreign operations	15
Tax on profit for the year	24
Tax on other components of comprehensive income	1

Required:
Prepare a statement of comprehensive income for the year ended 31 December 2015.

4.4 Presented below is a draft set of financial statements for Chips Limited.

Chips Limited
Income statement for the year ended 30 June 2016

	£000
Revenue	1,850
Cost of sales	(1,040)
Gross profit	810
Depreciation	(220)
Other operating costs	(375)
Operating profit	215
Interest payable	(35)
Profit before taxation	180
Taxation	(60)
Profit for the year	120

Statement of financial position as at 30 June 2016

	Cost £000	Depreciation £000	£000
ASSETS			
Non-current assets			
Property, plant and equipment			
Buildings	800	(112)	688
Plant and equipment	650	(367)	283
Motor vehicles	102	(53)	49
	1,552	(532)	1,020
Current assets			
Inventories			950
Trade receivables			420
Cash at bank			16
			1,386
Total assets			2,406
EQUITY AND LIABILITIES			
Equity			
Ordinary shares of £1, fully paid			800
Reserves at beginning of the year			248
Profit for the year			120
			1,168
Non-current liabilities			
Borrowings (secured 10% loan notes)			700
Current liabilities			
Trade payables			361
Other payables			117
Taxation			60
			538
Total equity and liabilities			2,406

The following additional information is available:

1. Purchase invoices for goods received on 29 June 2016 amounting to £23,000 have not been included. This means that the cost of sales figure in the income statement has been understated.
2. A motor vehicle costing £8,000 with depreciation amounting to £5,000 was sold on 30 June 2016 for £2,000, paid by cheque. This transaction has not been included in the company's records.
3. No depreciation on motor vehicles has been charged. The annual rate is 20 per cent of cost at the year-end.
4. A sale on credit for £16,000 made on 1 July 2016 has been included in the financial statements in error. The cost of sales figure is correct in respect of this item.
5. A half-yearly payment of interest on the secured loan due on 30 June 2016 has not been paid.
6. The tax charge should be 30 per cent of the reported profit before taxation. Assume that it is payable, in full, shortly after the year-end.

Required:
Prepare a revised set of financial statements incorporating the additional information in 1 to 6 above. (Work to the nearest £1,000.)

4.5 Rose Limited operates a small chain of retail shops that sells high-quality teas and coffees. Approximately half of sales are on credit. Abbreviated and unaudited financial statements are as follows:

Rose Limited
Income statement for the year ended 31 March 2016

	£000
Revenue	12,080
Cost of sales	(6,282)
Gross profit	5,798
Labour costs	(2,658)
Depreciation	(625)
Other operating costs	(1,003)
Operating profit	1,512
Interest payable	(66)
Profit before taxation	1,446
Taxation	(434)
Profit for the year	1,012

Statement of financial position as at 31 March 2016

	£000
ASSETS	
Non-current assets	2,728
Current assets	
Inventories	1,583
Trade receivables	996
Cash	26
	2,605
Total assets	5,333
EQUITY AND LIABILITIES	
Equity	
Share capital (50p shares, fully paid)	750
Share premium	250
Retained earnings	1,468
	2,468
Non-current liabilities	
Borrowings – secured loan notes (2018)	300
Current liabilities	
Trade payables	1,118
Other payables	417
Tax	434
Borrowings – overdraft	596
	2,565
Total equity and liabilities	5,333

Since the unaudited financial statements for Rose Limited were prepared, the following information has become available:

1. An additional £74,000 of depreciation should have been charged on fixtures and fittings.
2. Invoices for credit sales on 31 March 2016 amounting to £34,000 have not been included; cost of sales is not affected.
3. Trade receivables totalling £21,000 are recognised as having gone bad, but they have not yet been written off.
4. Inventories which had been purchased for £2,000 have been damaged and are unsaleable. This is not reflected in the financial statements.
5. Fixtures and fittings to the value of £16,000 were delivered just before 31 March 2016, but these assets were not included in the financial statements and the purchase invoice had not been processed.
6. Wages for Saturday-only staff, amounting to £1,000, have not been paid for the final Saturday of the year. This is not reflected in the financial statements.
7. Tax is payable at 30 per cent of profit before taxation. Assume that it is payable shortly after the year-end.

Required:
Prepare revised financial statements for Rose Limited for the year ended 31 March 2016, incorporating the information in 1 to 7 above. (Work to the nearest £1,000.)

Chapter 5

MEASURING AND REPORTING CASH FLOWS

INTRODUCTION

This chapter is devoted to the first major financial statement identified in Chapter 2: the statement of cash flows. This statement reports the movements of cash during a period and the effect of these movements on the cash position of the business. It is an important financial statement because cash is vital to the survival of a business. Without cash, a business cannot operate.

In this chapter, we shall see how the statement of cash flows is prepared and how the information that it contains may be interpreted. We shall also see why the deficiencies of the income statement, in identifying and explaining cash flows, make a separate statement necessary.

The statement of cash flows is being considered after the chapters on limited companies because the format of the statement requires an understanding of this type of business. Most larger limited companies are required to provide a statement of cash flows for shareholders and other users as part of their annual financial reports.

Learning outcomes

When you have completed this chapter, you should be able to:

- discuss the crucial importance of cash to a business;
- explain the nature of the statement of cash flows and discuss how it can be helpful in identifying cash flow problems;
- prepare a statement of cash flows;
- interpret a statement of cash flows.

THE STATEMENT OF CASH FLOWS

The statement of cash flows is a fairly late addition to the annual published financial statements. At one time, companies were only required to publish an income statement and a statement of financial position. It seems the prevailing view was that all the financial information needed by users would be contained within these two statements. This view may have been based partly on the assumption that, if a business were profitable, it would also have plenty of cash. While in the long run this is likely to be true, it is not necessarily true in the short-to-medium term.

We saw in Chapter 3 that the income statement sets out the revenue and expenses, for the period, rather than the cash inflows and outflows. This means that the profit (or loss), which represents the difference between the revenue and expenses for the period, may have little or no relation to the cash generated for the period.

To illustrate this point, let us take the example of a business making a sale (generating revenue). This may well lead to an increase in wealth that will be reflected in the income statement. However, if the sale is made on credit, no cash changes hands – at least not at the time of the sale. Instead, the increase in wealth is reflected in another asset: an increase in trade receivables. Furthermore, if an item of inventories is the subject of the sale, wealth is lost to the business through the reduction in inventories. This means that an expense is incurred in making the sale, which will also be shown in the income statement. Once again, however, no cash changes hands at the time of sale. For such reasons, the profit and the cash generated during a period rarely go hand in hand.

Activity 5.1 helps to underline how particular transactions and events can affect profit and cash for a period differently.

Activity 5.1

The following is a list of business/accounting events. In each case, state the immediate effect (increase, decrease or none) on both profit and cash:

	Effect on profit	on cash
1 Repayment of borrowings	_____	_____
2 Making a profitable sale on credit	_____	_____
3 Buying a non-current asset on credit	_____	_____
4 Receiving cash from a credit customer (trade receivable)	_____	_____
5 Depreciating a non-current asset	_____	_____
6 Buying some inventories for cash	_____	_____
7 Making a share issue for cash	_____	_____

→

You should have come up with the following:

		Effect	
		on profit	on cash
1	Repayment of borrowings	none	decrease
2	Making a profitable sale on credit	increase	none
3	Buying a non-current asset on credit	none	none
4	Receiving cash from a credit customer (trade receivable)	none	increase
5	Depreciating a non-current asset	decrease	none
6	Buying some inventories for cash	none	decrease
7	Making a share issue for cash	none	increase

The reasons for these answers are as follows:

1 Repaying borrowings requires that cash be paid to the lender. This means that two figures in the statement of financial position will be affected, but none in the income statement.
2 Making a profitable sale on credit will increase the sales revenue and profit figures. No cash will change hands at this point, however.
3 Buying a non-current asset on credit affects neither the cash balance nor the profit figure.
4 Receiving cash from a credit customer increases the cash balance and reduces the credit customer's balance. Both of these figures are on the statement of financial position. The income statement is unaffected.
5 Depreciating a non-current asset means that an expense is recognised. This causes a decrease in profit. No cash is paid or received.
6 Buying some inventories for cash means that the value of the inventories will increase and the cash balance will decrease by a similar amount. Profit is not affected.
7 Making a share issue for cash increases the shareholders' equity and increases the cash balance. Profit is not affected.

From what we have seen so far, it is clear that the income statement is not the place to look if we are to gain insights about cash movements over time. We need a separate financial statement.

WHY IS CASH SO IMPORTANT?

It is worth asking why cash is so important. In one sense, it is just another asset that the business needs to enable it to function. Hence, it is no different from inventories or non-current assets.

The importance of cash lies in the fact that people will only normally accept cash in settlement of their claims. If a business wants to employ people, it must pay them in cash. If it wants to buy a new non-current asset, it must normally pay the seller in cash (perhaps after a short period of credit). When businesses fail, it is the lack of cash to pay amounts owed that really pushes them under. Cash generation is vital for businesses to survive and to be able to take advantage of commercial opportunities. These are the things that make cash the pre-eminent business asset. During an economic downturn, the ability to generate cash takes on even greater importance. Banks become more cautious in their lending and businesses with weak cash flows often find it difficult to obtain finance.

Real World 5.1 is taken from an article by Luke Johnson who is a 'serial entrepreneur'. Among other things, he was closely involved with taking Pizza Express from a business that owned just 12 restaurants to over 250 and, at the same time, increasing its share price from 40 pence to over £9. In the article he highlights the importance of cash flow in managing a business.

REAL WORLD 5.1

Cash flow is king

Wise entrepreneurs learn that profits are not necessarily cash. But many founders never understand this essential accounting truth. A cash flow projection is a much more important document than a profit and loss (income) statement. A lack of liquidity can kill you, whereas a company can make paper losses for years and still survive if it has sufficient cash. It is amazing how financial journalists, fund managers, analysts, bankers and company directors can still focus on the wrong numbers in the accounts – despite so many high-profile disasters over the years.

FT *Source*: Extract from Johnson, Luke (2013) 'The most dangerous unforced errors', ft.com, 9 July. © The Financial Times Limited 2013. All Rights Reserved.

Real World 5.2 is taken from a column written by John Timpson, which appeared in the *Daily Telegraph*. Timpson was the chief executive of the successful, high street shoe repairing and key cutting business that bears his name. In the column he highlights the importance of cash reporting in managing the business.

REAL WORLD 5.2

Cash is key

I look at our cash balance every day (not Saturdays and Sundays). It is the best way to test the financial temperature of our business. The trick is to compare with the same day last year, thus showing cash flow for the past 12 months.

It is not a perfect system (never forget that your finance department may secretly massage the cash by paying suppliers sooner or later than you anticipate) but a glance at the daily cash is more transparent than management accounts that are full of provisions and only appear once a month.

Finance and IT take a delight in producing a deluge of data. But being in possession of too many statistics is counterproductive. This daily cash report helps to clear the clutter created by computers – it's a simple report that helps you pose the right questions.

Why have things suddenly got worse? Are we in danger of breaking our bank borrowing limit? Why does the cash flow look so much better than in the management accounts? This cash report can also give you an early warning of changing financial circumstances.

It came to my rescue in 2004 when, through a major acquisition, the business doubled in size overnight and was going through a great deal of change. Our financial control suffered but I didn't realise how bad things were until I was waiting to board a plane to go on a Caribbean holiday. A quick look at my Blackberry (when my wife wasn't looking) showed an unexpected £500,000 deterioration in our overdraft. It wasn't a great start to the holiday and my wife was upset when I spent the first day on the telephone. However, we were able to tackle the problem six weeks before it would have been revealed in the management accounts.

Source: John Timpson (2010). The management column, *The Daily Telegraph Business*, 14 June.

THE MAIN FEATURES OF THE STATEMENT OF CASH FLOWS

The statement of cash flows summarises the inflows and outflows of cash (and cash equivalents) for a business over a period. To aid user understanding, these cash flows are divided into categories (for example, those relating to investments in non-current assets). Cash inflows and outflows falling within each category are added together to provide a total for that category. These totals are shown on the statement of cash flows and, when added together, reveal the net increase or decrease in cash (and cash equivalents) over the period.

When describing in detail how this statement is prepared and presented, we shall follow the requirements of International Accounting Standard (IAS) 7 *Statement of Cash Flows*.

A DEFINITION OF CASH AND CASH EQUIVALENTS

IAS 7 defines cash as notes and coins in hand and deposits in banks and similar institutions that are accessible to the business on demand. Cash equivalents are short-term, highly liquid investments that can be readily convertible to known amounts of cash. They are also subject to an insignificant risk of changes of value. Figure 5.1 sets out this definition of cash equivalents in the form of a decision chart.

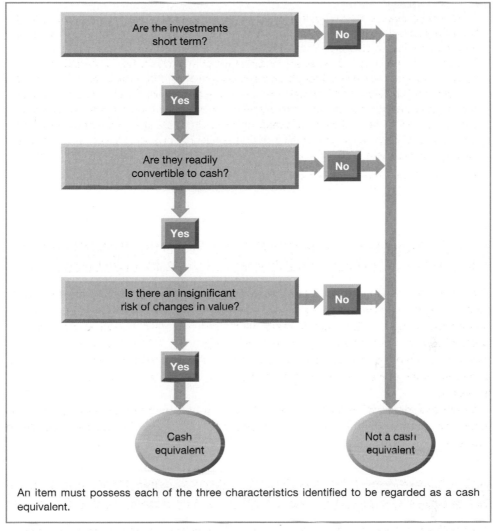

An item must possess each of the three characteristics identified to be regarded as a cash equivalent.

Figure 5.1 Decision chart for identifying cash equivalents

Activity 5.2 should clarify the types of items that fall within the definition of 'cash equivalents'.

At the end of its reporting period, Zeneb plc's statement of financial position included the following items:

1 A bank deposit account where one month's notice of withdrawal is required.
2 Ordinary shares in Jones plc (a Stock Exchange listed business).
3 A high-interest bank deposit account that requires six months' notice of withdrawal.
4 An overdraft on the business's bank current account.

Which (if any) of these four items would be included in the figure for cash and cash equivalents?

Your response should have been as follows:

1 A cash equivalent. It is readily withdrawable and there is no risk of a change of value.
2 Not a cash equivalent. It can be converted into cash because it is Stock Exchange listed. There is, however, a significant risk that the amount expected (hoped for!) when the shares are sold may not actually be forthcoming.
3 Not a cash equivalent because it is not readily convertible into liquid cash.
4 This is cash itself, albeit a negative amount of it. The only exception to this classification would be where the business is financed in the longer term by an overdraft, when it would be part of the financing of the business, rather than negative cash.

THE RELATIONSHIP BETWEEN THE MAIN FINANCIAL STATEMENTS

The statement of cash flows is, along with the income statement and the statement of financial position, a major financial statement. The relationship between the three statements is shown in Figure 5.2. The statement of financial position shows the various assets (including cash) and claims (including the shareholders' equity) of the business *at a particular point in time.* The statement of cash flows and the income statement explain the *changes over a period* to two of the items in the statement of financial position. The statement of cash flows explains the changes to cash. The income statement explains changes to equity, arising from trading operations.

THE LAYOUT OF THE STATEMENT OF CASH FLOWS

As mentioned earlier, the cash flows of a business are divided into categories. The various categories and the way in which they are presented in the statement of cash flows are shown in Figure 5.3.

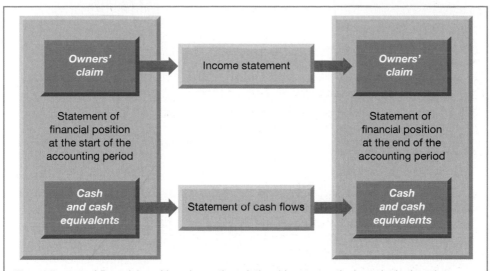

The statement of financial position shows the relationship, at a particular point in time, between the business's assets and claims. The income statement explains how, over a period between two statements of financial position, the equity figure in the first statement of financial position has altered as a result of trading operations. The statement of cash flows also looks at changes over the reporting period, but this statement explains the alteration in the cash (and cash equivalent) balances from the first to the second of the two consecutive statements of financial position.

Figure 5.2 The relationship between the statement of financial position, the income statement and the statement of cash flows

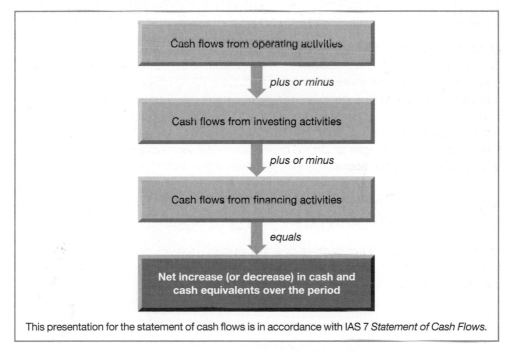

This presentation for the statement of cash flows is in accordance with IAS 7 *Statement of Cash Flows.*

Figure 5.3 Standard presentation for the statement of cash flows

Let us now consider each of the categories of cash flow that have been identified.

Cash flows from operating activities

These represent the cash inflows and outflows arising from normal day-to-day trading activities, after taking account of the tax paid and financing costs (equity and borrowings) relating to these activities. The cash inflows for the period are the amounts received from trade receivables (credit customers settling their accounts) and from cash sales for the period. The cash outflows for the period are the amounts paid for inventories, operating expenses (such as rent and wages), corporation tax, interest and dividends.

Note that it is the cash inflows and outflows during a period that appear in the statement of cash flows, not revenue and expenses for that period. Similarly, tax and dividends that appear in the statement of cash flows are those actually paid during the period. Many companies pay tax on their annual profits in four equal instalments. Two of these are paid during the year concerned and the other two are paid during the following year. Thus, by the end of each year, half of the tax will have been paid and the remaining half will still be outstanding, to be paid during the following year. This means that the tax payment during a year is normally equal to half of the previous year's tax charge and half of that of the current year.

Cash flows from investing activities

These include cash outflows to acquire non-current assets and cash inflows from their disposal. In addition to items such as property, plant and equipment, non-current assets might include financial investments made in loans or shares in another business.

These cash flows also include cash inflows *arising from* financial investments (loans and shares).

Activity 5.3

What might be included as cash inflows from financial investments?

This can include interest received from loans that have been made and dividends received from shares in other companies.

Under IAS 7, interest received and dividends received could be classified under 'Cash flows from operating activities'. This alternative treatment is available as these items appear in the calculation of profit. For the purpose of this chapter, however, we shall not use this alternative treatment.

Cash flows from financing activities

These represent cash inflows and outflows relating to the long-term financing of the business.

What might be included as cash inflows from financing activities?

These will include cash movements relating to the raising and redemption of long-term borrowings and to shares.

Under IAS 7, interest and dividend paid by the business could appear under this heading as outflows. This alternative to including them in 'Cash flows from operating activities' is available as they represent a cost of raising finance. For the purpose of this chapter, however, we shall not use this alternative treatment.

Whichever treatment for interest and dividends (both paid and received) is chosen, it should be applied consistently.

Net increase or decrease in cash and cash equivalents

The final total shown on the statement will be the net increase or decrease in cash and cash equivalents over the period. It will be deduced from the totals from each of the three categories mentioned above.

THE NORMAL DIRECTION OF CASH FLOWS

The effect on a business's cash and cash equivalents of activities relating to each category is shown in Figure 5.4. The arrows show the *normal* direction of cash flow for the typical, profitable, business in a typical reporting period.

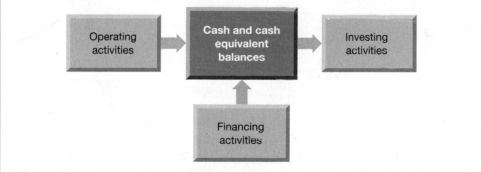

Various activities of the business each have their own effect on the total of the cash and cash equivalents, either positive (increasing the total) or negative (reducing it). The net increase or decrease in the cash and cash equivalents over a period will be the sum of these individual effects, taking account of the direction (cash in or cash out) of each activity.

Note that the direction of the arrow shows the normal direction of the cash flow in respect of each activity. In certain circumstances, each of these arrows could be reversed in direction.

Figure 5.4 Diagrammatical representation of the statement of cash flows

Normally, 'operating activities' provide positive cash flows and therefore increase the business's cash resources. For most UK businesses, cash generated from day-to-day trading, even after deducting tax, interest and dividends, is by far the most important source of new finance.

Activity 5.5

Last year's statement of cash flows for Angus plc showed a negative cash flow from operating activities. What could be the reason for this and should the business's management be alarmed by it? (*Hint*: We think that there are two broad possible reasons for a negative cash flow.)

The two reasons are:

1 The business is unprofitable. This leads to more cash being paid out to employees, to suppliers of goods and services, for interest and so on than is received from trade receivables. This should be of concern as a major expense for most businesses is depreciation. Since depreciation does not lead to a cash flow, it is not considered in 'net cash inflows from operating activities'. A negative operating cash flow might well indicate, therefore, a much larger trading loss – in other words, a significant loss of the business's wealth.

2 The business is expanding its activities (level of sales revenue). Although the business may be profitable, it may be spending more cash than is being generated from sales. Cash will be spent on acquiring more assets, non-current and current, to accommodate increased demand. For example, a business may need to have inventories in place before additional sales can be made. Similarly, staff will have to be employed and paid. Even when additional sales are made, they would normally be made on credit, with the cash inflow lagging behind the sales. This means that there would be no immediate cash benefit.

Expansion often causes cash flow strains for new businesses, which will be expanding inventories and other assets from zero. They would also need to employ and pay staff. To add to this problem, increased profitability may encourage a feeling of optimism, leading to a lack of attention being paid to the cash flows.

Investing activities typically cause net negative cash flows. This is because many non-current assets either wear out or become obsolete and need to be replaced. Businesses may also expand their asset base. Non-current assets may, of course, be sold, which would give rise to positive cash flows. In net terms, however, the cash flows are normally negative, with cash spent on new assets far outweighing that received from the sale of old ones.

Financing can go in either direction, depending on the financing strategy at the time. Since businesses seek to expand, there is a general tendency for this area to lead to cash coming into the business rather than leaving it.

Real World 5.3 shows the summarised statement of cash flows of Tesco plc, the UK-based supermarket company.

REAL WORLD 5.3

Cashing in

A summary of the statement of cash flows for the business for the year ended 28 February 2015 shows the cash flows of the business under each of the headings described above.

Summary group statement of cash flows
Year ended 28 February 2015

	£m
Cash generated from operations	1,467
Interest paid	(613)
Corporation tax paid	(370)
Net cash from operating activities	484
Net cash used in investing activities	(2015)
Net cash from financing activities	814
Net increase in cash and cash equivalents	(717)

Source: Adapted from: Tesco plc, Annual Report and Financial Statements 2015, www.tescoplc.com, p. 87.

As we shall see shortly, more detailed information under each of the main headings is provided in the statement of cash flows presented to shareholders and other users.

PREPARING THE STATEMENT OF CASH FLOWS

Deducing net cash flows from operating activities

As we have seen, the first category within the statement of cash flows is the 'cash flows from operating activities'. There are two approaches that can be taken to deriving this figure: the direct method and the indirect method.

The direct method

The **direct method** involves an analysis of the cash records of the business for the period, identifying all payments and receipts relating to operating activities. These are summarised to give the total figures for inclusion in the statement of cash flows. When a computer is used, this is a simple matter, though hardly any businesses adopt the direct method.

The indirect method

The **indirect method** is very much the more popular method. It relies on the fact that, sooner or later, sales revenue gives rise to cash inflows and expenses give rise to out-flows. This means that the figure for profit for the year will be linked to the net cash flows from operating activities. Since businesses have to produce an income statement, the information that it contains can be used as a starting point to deduce the cash flows from operating activities.

With credit sales, the cash receipt arises at some point after the sale is made. Thus, sales made towards the end of the current reporting period may result in the cash being received after the end of the period. The income statement for the current period will include all sales revenue generated during that period. Where cash relating to those sales is received after the end of the period, it will be included in the statement of cash flows for the following period. While profit for the period will not normally equal the net cash inflows from operating activities, there is a clear link between them. This means that we can deduce the cash inflows from sales if we have the relevant income statement and statements of financial position.

If we adjust the sales revenue figure by the increase or decrease in trade receivables over the period, we deduce the cash from sales for the period. Example 5.1 shows how this is done.

Example 5.1

The sales revenue figure for a business for the year was £34 million. The trade receivables totalled £4 million at the beginning of the year, but had increased to £5 million by the end of the year.

Basically, the trade receivables figure is dictated by sales revenue and cash receipts. It is increased when a sale is made and decreased when cash is received from a credit customer. If, over the year, the sales revenue and the cash receipts had been equal, the beginning-of-year and end-of-year trade receivables figures would have been equal. Since the trade receivables figure increased, it must mean that less cash was received than sales revenues were made. In fact, the cash receipts from sales must have been £33 million (that is, 34 − (5 − 4)).

Put slightly differently, we can say that as a result of sales, assets of £34 million flowed into the business. If £1 million of this went to increasing the asset of trade receivables, this leaves only £33 million that went to increase cash.

The same general point is true in respect of nearly all of the other items that are taken into account in deducing the operating profit figure. The main exception is depreciation.

The depreciation expense for a reporting period is not necessarily associated with any movement in cash during that same period.

All of this means that we can take the *profit before taxation* (that is, the profit after interest but before taxation) for the year, add back the depreciation and interest expense charged in arriving at that profit, and adjust this total by movements in inventories, trade (and other) receivables and payables. If we then go on to deduct payments made during the reporting period for taxation, interest on borrowings and dividends, we have the net cash from operating activities.

Example 5.2

The relevant information from the financial statements of Dido plc for last year is as follows:

	£m
Profit before taxation (after interest)	122
Depreciation charged in arriving at profit before taxation	34
Interest expense	6
At the beginning of the year:	
Inventories	15
Trade receivables	24
Trade payables	18
At the end of the year:	
Inventories	17
Trade receivables	21
Trade payables	19

The following further information is available about payments during last year:

	£m
Taxation paid	32
Interest paid	5
Dividends paid	9

The cash flow from operating activities is derived as follows:

	£m
Profit before taxation (after interest)	122
Depreciation	34
Interest expense	6
Increase in inventories (17 − 15)	(2)
Decrease in trade receivables (21 − 24)	3
Increase in trade payables (19 − 18)	1
Cash generated from operations	164
Interest paid	(5)
Taxation paid	(32)
Dividends paid	(9)
Net cash from operating activities	110

As we can see, the net increase in **working capital*** (that is, current assets less current liabilities) as a result of trading was £162 million (that is, 122 + 34 + 6). Of this, £2 million went into increased inventories. More cash was received from trade receivables than sales revenue was made. Similarly, less cash was paid to trade payables than purchases of goods and services on credit. Both of these had a favourable effect on cash. Over the year, therefore, cash increased by £164 million. When account was taken of the payments for interest, tax and dividends, the net cash from operating activities was £118 million (inflow).

Note that we needed to adjust the profit before taxation (after interest) by the depreciation and interest expenses to derive the profit before depreciation, interest and taxation.

* Working capital is a term widely used in accounting and finance, not just in the context of the statement of cash flows. We shall encounter it several times in later chapters.

Activity 5.7

In deriving the cash generated from operations, we add the depreciation expense for the period to the profit before taxation. Does this mean that depreciation is a source of cash?

No. Depreciation is a not source of cash. The periodic depreciation expense is irrelevant to cash flow. Since the profit before taxation is derived *after* deducting the depreciation expense for the period, we need to eliminate the impact of depreciation by adding it back to the profit figure. This will give us the profit before tax *and before* depreciation, which is what we need.

We should be clear why we add back an amount for interest at the start of the derivation of cash flow from operating activities only to deduct an amount for interest further down. The reason is that the first is the *interest expense* for the reporting period, whereas the second is the amount of *cash paid out for interest* during that period. These may well be different amounts, as was the case in Example 5.2.

The indirect method of deducing the net cash flow from operating activities is summarised in Figure 5.5.

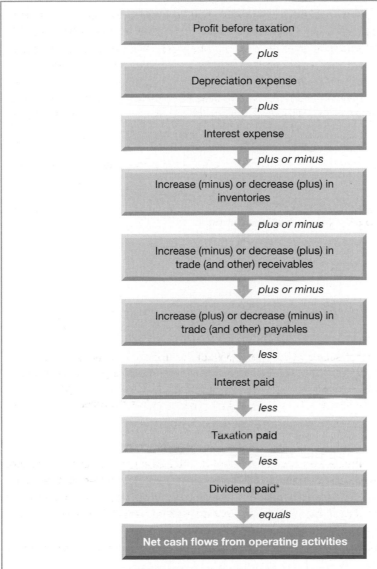

Determining the net cash from operating activities firstly involves adding back the depreciation and the interest expense to the profit before taxation. Next, adjustment is made for increases or decreases in inventories, receivables and payables. Lastly, cash paid for interest, taxation and dividends is deducted.

* Note that dividends could alternatively be included under the heading 'Cash flows from financing activities'.

Figure 5.5 The indirect method of deducing the net cash flows from operating activities

The relevant information from the financial statements of Pluto plc for last year is as follows:

	£m
Profit before taxation (after interest)	165
Depreciation charged in arriving at operating profit	41
Interest expense	21
At the beginning of the year:	
Inventories	22
Trade receivables	18
Trade payables	15
At the end of the year:	
Inventories	23
Trade receivables	21
Trade payables	17

The following further information is available about payments during last year:

	£m
Taxation paid	49
Interest paid	25
Dividends paid	28

What figure should appear in the statement of cash flows for 'Cash flows from operating activities'?

Net cash inflows from operating activities:

	£m
Profit before taxation (after interest)	165
Depreciation	41
Interest expense	21
Increase in inventories (23 − 22)	(1)
Increase in trade receivables (21 − 18)	(3)
Increase in trade payables (17 − 15)	2
Cash generated from operations	225
Interest paid	(25)
Taxation paid	(49)
Dividends paid	(28)
Net cash from operating activities	123

Real World 5.4 explains how one well-known business uses operating cash flow as a performance target.

Turning energy into cash

BP plc, the energy business, frames one of its key financial performance targets in terms of operating cash flows (that is, net cash flows after operating activity). Its performance over the five years ending 31 December 2014 is set out in Figure 5.6.

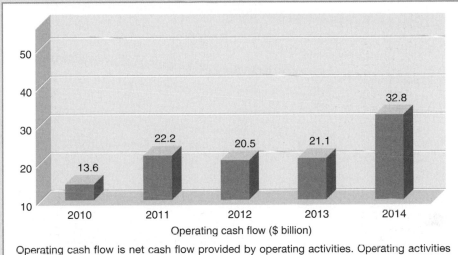

Operating cash flow is net cash flow provided by operating activities. Operating activities are the principal revenue-generating activities of the group and other activities that are not investing or financing activities.

Figure 5.6 BP plc operating cash flows 2010–2014

The 2014 performance was much better than in previous years. It was, however, in line with planned performance for that year.

Source: Information taken from BP plc, Annual Report 2014, www.bp.com, p.18.

Deducing the other areas of the statement of cash flows

Determining the investing and financing activities of a business is much easier than determining 'cash flows from operating activities'. It largely involves a comparison of the opening and closing statements of financial position to detect movements in non-current assets, non-current liabilities and equity over the period. We show how this is done in Example 5.3, which prepares a complete statement of cash flows.

Example 5.3

Torbryan plc's income statement for the year ended 31 December 2015 and the statements of financial position as at 31 December 2014 and 2015 are as follows:

Income statement for the year ended 31 December 2015

	£m
Revenue	576
Cost of sales	(307)
Gross profit	269
Distribution expenses	(65)
Administrative expenses	(26)
	178
Other operating income	21
Operating profit	199
Interest receivable	17
Interest payable	(23)
Profit before taxation	193
Taxation	(46)
Profit for the year	147

Statements of financial position as at 31 December 2014 and 2015

	2014 £m	2015 £m
ASSETS		
Non-current assets		
Property, plant and equipment		
Land and buildings	241	241
Plant and machinery	309	325
	550	566
Current assets		
Inventories	44	41
Trade receivables	121	139
	165	180
Total assets	715	746
EQUITY AND LIABILITIES		
Equity		
Called-up ordinary share capital	150	200
Share premium account	–	40
Retained earnings	26	123
	176	363
Non-current liabilities		
Borrowings – loan notes	400	250
Current liabilities		
Borrowings (all bank overdraft)	68	56
Trade payables	55	54
Taxation	16	23
	139	133
Total equity and liabilities	715	746

During 2015, the business spent £95 million on additional plant and machinery. There were no other non-current-asset acquisitions or disposals. A dividend of £50 million was paid on ordinary shares during the year. The interest receivable revenue and the interest payable expense for the year were each equal to the cash inflow and outflow respectively. £150 million of loan notes were redeemed at their nominal (par) value.

The statement of cash flows would be:

Torbryan plc
Statement of cash flows for the year ended 31 December 2015

	£m
Cash flows from operating activities	
Profit before taxation (after interest) (see Note 1 below)	193
Adjustments for:	
Depreciation (Note 2)	79
Interest receivable (Note 3)	(17)
Interest payable (Note 4)	23
Increase in trade receivables (139 − 121)	(18)
Decrease in trade payables (55 − 54)	(1)
Decrease in inventories (44 − 41)	3
Cash generated from operations	262
Interest paid	(23)
Taxation paid (Note 5)	(39)
Dividend paid	(50)
Net cash from operating activities	150
Cash flows from investing activities	
Payments to acquire tangible non-current assets	(95)
Interest received (Note 3)	17
Net cash used in investing activities	(78)
Cash flows from financing activities	
Repayments of loan notes	(150)
Issue of ordinary shares (Note 6)	90
Net cash used in financing activities	(60)
Net increase in cash and cash equivalents	12
Cash and cash equivalents at 1 January 2015 (Note 7)	(68)
Cash and cash equivalents at 31 December 2015	(56)

To see how this relates to the cash of the business at the beginning and end of the year it can be useful to provide a reconciliation as follows:

Analysis of cash and cash equivalents during the year ended 31 December 2015

	£m
Overdraft balance at 1 January 2015	(68)
Net cash inflow	12
Overdraft balance at 31 December 2015	(56)

Notes:

1 This is simply taken from the income statement for the year.
2 Since there were no disposals, the depreciation charges must be the difference between the start and end of the year's plant and machinery (non-current assets) values, adjusted by the cost of any additions.

	£m
Carrying amount at 1 January 2015	309
Additions	95
	404
Depreciation (balancing figure)	(79)
Carrying amount at 31 December 2015	325

3 Interest receivable must be deducted to work towards what the profit would have been before it was added in the income statement, because it is not part of operations but of investing activities. The cash inflow from this source appears under the 'Cash flows from investing activities' heading.
4 The interest payable expense must be taken out, by adding it back to the profit figure. We subsequently deduct the cash paid for interest payable during the year. In this case the two figures are identical.
5 Taxation is paid by many companies 50 per cent during their reporting year and 50 per cent in the following year. As a result, the 2015 payment would have been half the tax on the 2014 profit (that is, the figure that would have appeared in the current liabilities at the end of 2014), plus half of the 2015 taxation charge (that is, $16 + (^1/_2 \times 46) = 39$). Probably the easiest way to deduce the amount paid during the year to 31 December 2015 is by following this approach:

	£m
Taxation owed at start of the year (from the statement of financial position as at 31 December 2014)	16
Taxation charge for the year (from the income statement)	46
	62
Taxation owed at the end of the year (from the statement of financial position as at 31 December 2015)	(23)
Taxation paid during the year	39

This follows the logic that if we start with what the business owed at the beginning of the year, add what was owed as a result of the current year's taxation charge and then deduct what was owed at the end, the resulting figure must be what was paid during the year.

6 The share issue raised £90 million, of which £50 million went into the share capital total on the statement of financial position and £40 million into share premium.
7 There were no 'cash equivalents', just cash (though negative).

WHAT DOES THE STATEMENT OF CASH FLOWS TELL US?

The statement of cash flows tells us how the business has generated cash during the period and where that cash has gone. This is potentially very useful information. Tracking the sources and uses of cash over several years could show financing trends that a reader of the statements could use to help to make judgements about the likely future behaviour of the business.

Looking specifically at the statement of cash flows for Torbryan plc, in Example 5.3, we can see the following:

- Net cash flow from operations seems strong, much larger than the profit for the year, after taking account of the dividend paid. This might be expected as depreciation is deducted in arriving at profit. Working capital has absorbed some cash, which may indicate an expansion of activity (sales revenue) over the year. As we have only one year's income statement, however, we cannot tell whether this has occurred.
- There were net outflows of cash for investing activities, but this would not be unusual. Many types of non-current assets have limited lives and need to be replaced. Expenditure during the year was not out of line with the depreciation expense for the year, which is to be expected for a business with a regular replacement programme for its non-current assets.
- There was a major outflow of cash to redeem borrowings, which was partly offset by the proceeds of a share issue. This may well represent a change of financing strategy.

Activity 5.9

Why might this be the case? What has been the impact of these changes on the long-term financing of the business?

The financing changes, together with the retained earnings for the year, have led to a significant shift in the equity/borrowings balance.

Real World 5.5 identifies the important changes in the cash flows of Ryanair plc during the year ended 31 March 2015.

REAL WORLD 5.5

Flying high

Ryanair's summarised cash flow statement for the year ended 31 March 2015

	€m
Net cash provided by operating activities	1,689.4
Net cash from (used in) investing activities	(2,888.2)
Net cash from (used in) financing activities	653.3
Net decrease in cash and cash equivalents	(545.5)

We can see that there was a net decrease in cash and cash equivalents of €545.5 million during the year. Cash and cash equivalents decreased from €1,730.1 million at 31 March 2014 to €1,184.6 million at 31 March 2015. Both, however, are very large balances and represent 20 per cent and 10 per cent respectively of total assets held.

The net cash inflow from operating activities during the year to 31 March 2015 was €1,689.4 million. This was significantly higher than the previous year of €1,044.6 million. The increase was largely due to an increase in profit after tax of €343.9 million and an increase in accrued expenses of €364.4 million. The latter amount is mostly made up of increases in amounts received in advance for flight bookings and increases in payables.

The net cash outflow from investing activities during the year totalled €2,888.2 million. This included an outflow of €788.5 million for the purchase of property, plant and equipment (mostly new aircraft). The major outflow, however, was €2,106.3 million for financial investments with a maturity of more than three months.

The net cash inflow from financing activities was €653.3 million. During the year there were issues of unsecured bonds totalling €1,690.9 million. This large inflow was partly offset, however, by a large dividend of €520.3 million, repayments of long-term borrowings of €419.7 million and shares repurchases of €112.0 million.

Source: Information taken from Ryanair plc, Annual Report 2015, pp. 161, 108 and 109.

? SELF-ASSESSMENT QUESTION 5.1

Touchstone plc's income statements for the years ended 31 December 2014 and 2015 and statements of financial position as at 31 December 2014 and 2015 are as follows:

Income statements for the years ended 2014 and 2015

	2014	2015
	£m	£m
Revenue	173	207
Cost of sales	(96)	(101)
Gross profit	77	106
Distribution expenses	(18)	(20)
Administrative expenses	(24)	(26)
Other operating income	3	4
Operating profit	38	64
Interest payable	(2)	(4)
Profit before taxation	36	60
Taxation	(8)	(16)
Profit for the year	28	44

Statements of financial position as at 31 December 2014 and 2015

	2014 £m	2015 £m
ASSETS		
Non-current assets		
Property, plant and equipment		
Land and buildings	94	110
Plant and machinery	53	62
	147	172
Current assets		
Inventories	25	24
Treasury bills (short-term investments)	–	15
Trade receivables	16	26
Cash at bank and in hand	4	4
	45	69
Total assets	192	241
EQUITY AND LIABILITIES		
Equity		
Called-up ordinary share capital	100	100
Retained earnings	30	56
	130	156
Non-current liabilities		
Borrowings – loan notes (10%)	20	40
Current liabilities		
Trade payables	38	37
Taxation	4	8
	42	45
Total equity and liabilities	192	241

Notes:

1 Included in 'cost of sales', 'distribution expenses' and 'administrative expenses', depreciation was as follows:

	2014 £m	2015 £m
Land and buildings	5	6
Plant and machinery	6	10

2 There were no non-current-asset disposals in either year.
3 The interest payable expense equalled the cash payment made during each of the years.
4 The business paid dividends on ordinary shares of £14 million during 2014 and £18 million during 2015.
5 The Treasury bills represent a short-term investment of funds that will be used shortly in operations. There is insignificant risk that this investment will lose value.

Required:
Prepare a statement of cash flows for the business for 2015.

The solution to this question can be found at the back of the book on page 527.

SUMMARY

The main points of this chapter may be summarised as follows:

The need for a statement of cash flows

- Cash is important because no business can operate without it.
- The statement of cash flows is designed to reveal movements in cash over a period.
- Cash movements cannot be readily detected from the income statement, which focuses on revenue and expenses rather than on cash inflows and outflows.
- Profit (or loss) and cash generated for the period are rarely equal.
- The statement of cash flows is a major financial statement, along with the income statement and the statement of financial position.

Preparing the statement of cash flows

- The statement of cash flows has three major categories of cash flows: cash flows from operating activities, cash flows from investing activities and cash flows from financing activities.
- The total of the cash movements under these three categories will provide the net increase or decrease in cash and cash equivalents for the period.
- A reconciliation can be undertaken to check that the opening balance of cash and cash equivalents plus the net increase (or decrease) for the period equals the closing balance.
- 'Cash and cash equivalents' include certain short-term investments and, perhaps, bank overdrafts.

Calculating the cash generated from operations

- The net cash flows from operating activities can be derived by either the direct method or the indirect method.
- The direct method is based on an analysis of the cash records for the period, whereas the indirect method uses information contained within the income statement and statements of financial position.
- The indirect method takes the profit before taxation for the period, adds back any depreciation and interest payable charge (and/or deducts any interest receivable), deducts the actual interest paid during the period (and/or adds the actual interest received) and then adjusts for changes in inventories, receivables and payables during the period.

Interpreting the statement of cash flows

- The statement of cash flows shows the main sources and uses of cash.
- Tracking the cash movements over several periods may reveal financing and investing patterns and may help predict future management action.

FURTHER READING

If you would like to explore the topics covered in this chapter in more depth, we recommend the following books:

Alexander, D. and Nobes, C. (2016) *Financial Accounting: An International Introduction,* 6th edn, Pearson, Chapter 13.

Elliott, B. and Elliott, J. (2015) *Financial Accounting and Reporting,* 17th edn, Pearson, Chapter 5.

International Accounting Standards Board, *A guide through IFRS 2015* (Green Book), IAS 7 *Statement of Cash Flows.*

KPMG, *Insights* into IFRS, 11th edn, Sweet and Maxwell, 2014/15, Section 2.3 (a summary of this book is available free at www.kpmg.com).

 REVIEW QUESTIONS

Solutions to these questions can be found at the back of the book on pages 541–542.

5.1 The typical business outside the service sector has about 50 per cent more of its resources tied up in inventories than in cash, yet there is no call for a 'statement of inventories flows' to be prepared. Why is cash regarded as more important than inventories?

5.2 What is the difference between the direct and indirect methods of deducing cash generated from operations?

5.3 Taking each of the categories of the statement of cash flows in turn, in which direction would you normally expect the cash flow to be? Explain your answer.

(a) Cash flows from operating activities.
(b) Cash flows from investing activities.
(c) Cash flows from financing activities.

5.4 What causes the profit for the reporting period not to equal the net cash inflow?

Exercises 5.1 and 5.2 are basic level. Exercise 5.3 is intermediate level and Exercises 5.4 and 5.5 are advanced level. Those with coloured numbers have solutions at the back of the book, starting on page 556.

5.1 How will each of the following events ultimately affect the amount of cash?

(a) an increase in the level of inventories;

(b) a rights issue of ordinary shares;

(c) a bonus issue of ordinary shares;

(d) writing off part of the value of some inventories;

(e) the disposal of a large number of the business's shares by a major shareholder;

(f) depreciating a non-current asset.

5.2 The following information has been taken from the financial statements of Juno plc for last year and the year before last:

	Year before last £m	Last year £m
Operating profit	156	187
Depreciation charged in arriving at operating profit	47	55
Inventories held at end of year	27	31
Trade receivables at end of year	24	23
Trade payables at end of year	15	17

Required:

What is the figure for cash generated from the operations for Juno plc for last year?

5.3 Torrent plc's income statement for the year ended 31 December 2015 and the statements of financial position as at 31 December 2014 and 2015 are as follows:

Income statement for the year ended 31 December 2015

	£m
Revenue	623
Cost of sales	(353)
Gross profit	270
Distribution expenses	(71)
Administrative expenses	(30)
Rental income	27
Operating profit	196
Interest payable	(26)
Profit before taxation	170
Taxation	(36)
Profit for the year	134

Statements of financial position as at 31 December 2014 and 2015

	2014 £m	2015 £m
ASSETS		
Non-current assets		
Property, plant and equipment		
Land and buildings	310	310
Plant and machinery	325	314
	635	624
Current assets		
Inventories	41	35
Trade receivables	139	145
	180	180
Total assets	815	804
EQUITY AND LIABILITIES		
Equity		
Called-up ordinary share capital	200	300
Share premium account	40	–
Revaluation reserve	69	9
Retained earnings	123	197
	432	506
Non-current liabilities		
Borrowings – loan notes	250	150
Current liabilities		
Borrowings (all bank overdraft)	56	89
Trade payables	54	41
Taxation	23	18
	133	148
Total equity and liabilities	815	804

During 2015, the business spent £67 million on additional plant and machinery. There were no other non-current asset acquisitions or disposals.

There was no share issue for cash during the year. The interest payable expense was equal in amount to the cash outflow. A dividend of £60 million was paid.

Required:

Prepare the statement of cash flows for Torrent plc for the year ended 31 December 2015.

5.4 Chen plc's income statements for the years ended 31 December 2014 and 2015 and the statements of financial position as at 31 December 2014 and 2015 are as follows:

Income statements for the years ended 31 December 2014 and 2015

	2014 £m	2015 £m
Revenue	207	153
Cost of sales	(101)	(76)
Gross profit	106	77
Distribution expenses	(22)	(20)
Administrative expenses	(20)	(28)
Operating profit	64	29
Interest payable	(4)	(4)
Profit before taxation	60	25
Taxation	(16)	(6)
Profit for the year	44	19

Statements of financial position as at 31 December 2014 and 2015

	2014 £m	2015 £m
ASSETS		
Non-current assets		
Property, plant and equipment		
Land and buildings	110	130
Plant and machinery	62	56
	172	186
Current assets		
Inventories	24	25
Trade receivables	26	25
Cash at bank and in hand	19	–
	69	50
Total assets	241	236
EQUITY AND LIABILITIES		
Equity		
Called-up ordinary share capital	100	100
Retained earnings	56	57
	156	157
Non-current liabilities		
Borrowings – loan notes (10%)	40	40
Current liabilities		
Borrowings (all bank overdraft)	–	2
Trade payables	37	34
Taxation	8	3
	45	39
Total equity and liabilities	241	236

Included in 'cost of sales', 'distribution expenses' and 'administrative expenses', depreciation was as follows:

	2014 £m	2015 £m
Land and buildings	6	10
Plant and machinery	10	12

There were no non-current asset disposals in either year. The amount of cash paid for interest equalled the expense in each year. Dividends were paid totalling £18 million in each year.

Required:
Prepare a statement of cash flows for the business for 2015.

5.5 The following financial statements for Blackstone plc are a slightly simplified set of published accounts. Blackstone plc is an engineering business that developed a new range of products in 2013. These products now account for 60 per cent of its sales revenue.

Income statement for the years ended 31 March

	Notes	2015 £m	2016 £m
Revenue		7,003	11,205
Cost of sales		(3,748)	(5,809)
Gross profit		3,255	5,396
Operating expenses		(2,205)	(3,087)
Operating profit		1,050	2,309
Interest payable	1	(216)	(456)
Profit before taxation		834	1,853
Taxation		(210)	(390)
Profit for the year		624	1,463

Statements of financial position as at 31 March

	Notes	2015 £m	2016 £m
ASSETS			
Non-current assets			
Property, plant and equipment	2	4,300	7,535
Intangible assets	3	–	700
		4,300	8,235
Current assets			
Inventories		1,209	2,410
Trade receivables		641	1,173
Cash at bank		123	–
		1,973	3,583
Total assets		6,273	11,818

	2015 £m	2016 £m
EQUITY AND LIABILITIES		
Equity		
Share capital	1,800	1,800
Share premium	600	600
Capital reserves	352	352
Retained earnings	685	1,748
	3,437	4,500
Non-current liabilities		
Borrowings – bank loan (repayable 2018)	1,800	3,800
Current liabilities		
Trade payables	931	1,507
Taxation	105	195
Borrowings (all bank overdraft)	–	1,816
	1,036	3,518
Total equity and liabilities	6,273	11,818

Notes:

1 The expense and the cash outflow for interest payable are equal for each year.

2 The movements in property, plant and equipment during the year are:

	Land and buildings £m	Plant and machinery £m	Fixtures and fittings £m	Total £m
Cost				
At 1 April 2015	4,500	3,850	2,120	10,470
Additions	–	2,970	1,608	4,578
Disposals	–	(365)	(216)	(581)
At 31 March 2016	4,500	6,455	3,512	14,467
Depreciation				
At 1 April 2015	1,275	3,080	1,815	6,170
Charge for year	225	745	281	1,251
Disposals	–	(305)	(184)	(489)
At 31 March 2016	1,500	3,520	1,912	6,932
Carrying amount				
At 31 March 2016	3,000	2,935	1,600	7,535

3 Intangible assets represent the amounts paid for the goodwill of another engineering business acquired during the year.

4 Proceeds from the sale of non-current assets in the year ended 31 March 2016 amounted to £54 million.

5 Dividends were paid on ordinary shares of £300 million in 2015 and £400 million in 2016.

Required:

Prepare a statement of cash flows for Blackstone plc for the year ended 31 March 2016. (*Hint:* A loss (deficit) on disposal of non-current assets is simply an additional amount of depreciation and should be dealt with as such in preparing the statement of cash flows.)

Chapter 6

ANALYSING AND INTERPRETING FINANCIAL STATEMENTS

INTRODUCTION

In this chapter, we consider the analysis and interpretation of the financial statements discussed in Chapters 2 and 3. We shall see how the use of financial (or accounting) ratios can help to assess the financial performance and position of a business. We shall also take a look at the problems encountered when applying financial ratios.

Financial ratios can be used to examine various aspects of financial health and are widely used by external users, such as shareholders and lenders, and by managers. They can be very helpful to managers in a wide variety of decision areas, such as profit planning, working capital management, financial structure.

Learning outcomes

When you have completed this chapter, you should be able to:

■ identify the major categories of ratios that can be used for analysing financial statements;

■ calculate key ratios for assessing the financial performance and position of a business;

■ explain the significance of the ratios calculated;

■ discuss the limitations of ratios as a tool of financial analysis.

FINANCIAL RATIOS

Financial ratios provide a quick and relatively simple means of assessing the financial health of a business. A ratio simply relates one figure appearing in the financial statements to another figure appearing there (for example, operating profit in relation to sales revenue) or, perhaps, to some resource of the business (for example, operating profit per employee).

Ratios can be very helpful when comparing the financial health of different businesses. Differences may exist between businesses in the scale of operations. As a result, a direct comparison of, say, the operating profit generated by each business may be misleading. By expressing operating profit in relation to some other measure (for example, capital employed), the problem of scale is eliminated. This means that a business with an operating profit of £10,000 and capital employed of £100,000 can be compared with a much larger business with an operating profit of £80,000 and capital employed of £1,000,000 by the use of a simple ratio. The operating profit to capital employed ratio for the smaller business is 10 per cent (that is, (10,000/100,000) × 100%) and the same ratio for the larger business is 8 per cent (that is, (80,000/1,000,000) × 100%). These ratios can be directly compared, whereas a comparison of the absolute operating profit figures might be much less meaningful. The need to eliminate differences in scale through the use of ratios can also apply when comparing the performance of the same business from one time period to another.

By calculating a small number of ratios it is often possible to build up a revealing picture of the position and performance of a business. It is not surprising, therefore, that ratios are widely used by those who have an interest in businesses and business performance. Ratios are not difficult to calculate but they can be difficult to interpret.

Ratios help us to identify which questions to ask, rather than provide the answers. They help to highlight the financial strengths and weaknesses of a business, but cannot explain why those strengths or weaknesses exist or why certain changes have occurred. They provide a starting point for further analysis. Only a detailed investigation will reveal the underlying reasons.

Ratios can be expressed in various forms, for example as a percentage or as a proportion. The way that a particular ratio is presented will depend on the needs of those who will use the information. Although it is possible to calculate a large number of ratios, only a few, based on key relationships, tend to be helpful to a particular user. Many of the ratios that could be calculated from the financial statements (for example, rent payable in relation to current assets) may not be considered because there is not usually any clear or meaningful relationship between the two items.

There is no generally accepted list of ratios that can be applied to the financial statements, nor is there a standard method of calculating many ratios. Variations in both the choice of ratios and their calculation will be found in practice. It is important, therefore, to be consistent in the way in which ratios are calculated for comparison purposes. The ratios that we shall discuss are very popular – presumably because they are seen as useful for decision-making purposes.

FINANCIAL RATIO CLASSIFICATIONS

Ratios can be grouped into categories, with each category relating to a particular aspect of financial performance or position. The following broad categories provide a useful basis for explaining the nature of the financial ratios to be dealt with. There are five of them:

- *Profitability.* Businesses generally exist with the primary purpose of creating wealth for their owners. Profitability ratios provide some indication of the degree of success in achieving this purpose. They normally express the profit made in relation to other key figures in the financial statements or to some business resource.
- *Efficiency.* Ratios may be used to measure the efficiency with which particular resources, such as inventories or employees, have been used within the business. These ratios are also referred to as *activity* ratios.
- *Liquidity.* It is vital to the survival of a business that there are sufficient liquid resources available to meet maturing obligations (that is, amounts owing that must be paid in the near future). Liquidity ratios examine the relationship between liquid resources and amounts due for payment in the near future.
- *Financial gearing.* This is the relationship between the contribution to financing a business made by the owners and the contribution made by others, in the form of loans. This relationship is important because the level of gearing has an important effect on the level of risk associated with a business. Gearing ratios help to reveal the extent to which loan finance is utilised and the consequent effect on the level of risk borne by a business.
- *Investment.* Certain ratios are concerned with assessing the returns and performance of shares in a particular business from the perspective of shareholders who are not involved with the management of the business.

These five key aspects of financial health that ratios seek to examine are summarised in Figure 6.1.

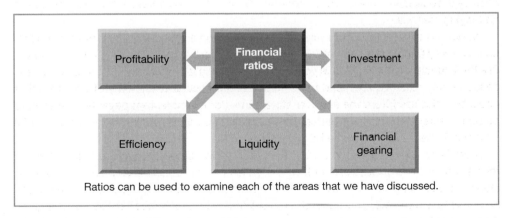

Ratios can be used to examine each of the areas that we have discussed.

Figure 6.1 The key aspects of financial health

The analyst must be clear *who* the target users are and *why* they need the information. Different users of financial information are likely to have different information needs. This will, in turn, determine the ratios that they find useful. Shareholders, for example, are likely to be interested in their returns in relation to the level of risk associated with their investment. Profitability, investment and gearing ratios should, therefore, be of particular interest. Long-term lenders are likely to be concerned with the long-term viability of the business and, to assess this, profitability and gearing ratios should be of interest. Short-term lenders, such as suppliers of goods and services on credit, are likely to be interested in the ability of the business to repay the amounts owing in the short term.

Activity 6.1

Which one of the above category of ratios should be of most value for short-term lenders?

Liquidity ratios, which focus on the ability to meet maturing obligations, are likely to be of most value.

THE NEED FOR COMPARISON

Merely calculating a ratio will not tell us very much about the position or performance of a business. If, for example, a ratio revealed that a retail business was generating £100 in sales revenue per square metre of floor space, it would not be possible to deduce from this information alone whether this particular level of performance was good, bad or indifferent. It is only when we compare this ratio with some 'benchmark' that the information can be interpreted and evaluated.

Activity 6.2

Can you think of any bases that could be used to compare a ratio that you have calculated from the financial statements of your business for a particular period? (*Hint*: There are three main possibilities.)

You may have thought of the following bases:

- past periods for the same business;
- similar businesses for the same or past periods; and/or
- planned performance for the business.

We shall now take a closer look at these three in turn.

Past periods

By comparing the ratio that we have calculated with the same ratio, but for a previous period, it is possible to detect whether there has been an improvement or deterioration in performance. Indeed, it is often useful to track particular ratios over time (say, five or ten years) to see whether it is possible to detect trends. The comparison of ratios from different periods brings certain problems, however. In particular, there is always the possibility that trading conditions were quite different in the periods being compared. There is the further problem that, when comparing the performance of a single business over time, operating inefficiencies may not be clearly exposed. For example, the fact that sales revenue per employee has risen by 10 per cent over the previous period may at first sight appear to be satisfactory. This may not be the case, however, if similar businesses have shown an improvement of 50 per cent for the same period or had much better sales revenue per employee ratios to start with. Finally, there is the problem that inflation may have distorted the figures on which the ratios are based. Inflation can lead to an overstatement of profit and an understatement of asset values, as will be discussed later in the chapter.

Similar businesses

In a competitive environment, a business must consider its performance in relation to that of other businesses operating in the same industry. Survival may depend on its ability to achieve comparable levels of performance. A useful basis for comparing a particular ratio, therefore, is the ratio achieved by similar businesses during the same period. This basis is not, however, without its problems. Competitors may have different year-ends and so trading conditions may not be identical. They may also have different accounting policies, which can have a significant effect on reported profits and asset values (for example, different methods of calculating depreciation or valuing inventories). Finally, it may be difficult to obtain the financial statements of competitor businesses. Sole proprietorships and partnerships, for example, are not obliged to make their financial statements available to the public. In the case of limited companies, there is a legal obligation to do so. However, a diversified business may not provide a breakdown of activities that is sufficiently detailed to enable comparisons with other businesses.

Planned performance

Ratios may be compared with targets that management developed before the start of the period under review. The comparison of actual performance with planned performance can be a useful way of assessing the level of achievement attained. Indeed, planned performance often provides the most valuable benchmark against which managers may assess their own business. However, planned performance must be based on realistic assumptions if it is to be worthwhile for comparison purposes.

Planned, or target, ratios may be prepared for each aspect of the business's activities. When developing these ratios, account will normally be taken of past performance and the performance of other businesses. This does not mean, however, that the business should seek to achieve either of these levels of performance. Neither of them may provide an appropriate target.

We should bear in mind that those outside the business do not normally have access to the business's plans. For such people, past performance and the performances of other, similar, businesses may provide the only practical benchmarks.

CALCULATING THE RATIOS

Probably the best way to explain financial ratios is through an example. Example 6.1 provides a set of financial statements from which we can calculate important ratios.

Example 6.1

The following financial statements relate to Alexis plc, which operates a wholesale carpet business:

Statements of financial position (balance sheets) as at 31 March

	2015 £m	2016 £m
ASSETS		
Non-current assets		
Property, plant and equipment (at cost less depreciation)		
Land and buildings	381	427
Fixtures and fittings	129	160
	510	587
Current assets		
Inventories	300	406
Trade receivables	240	273
Cash at bank	4	–
	544	679
Total assets	1,054	1,266
EQUITY AND LIABILITIES		
Equity		
£0.50 ordinary shares (Note 1)	300	300
Retained earnings	263	234
	563	534
Non-current liabilities		
Borrowings – 9% loan notes (secured)	200	300
Current liabilities		
Trade payables	261	354
Taxation	30	2
Short-term borrowings (all bank overdraft)	–	76
	291	432
Total equity and liabilities	1,054	1,266

Income statements for the year ended 31 March

	2015 £m	2016 £m
Revenue (Note 2)	2,240	2,681
Cost of sales (Note 3)	(1,745)	(2,272)
Gross profit	495	409
Operating expenses	(252)	(362)
Operating profit	243	47
Interest payable	(18)	(32)
Profit before taxation	225	15
Taxation	(60)	(4)
Profit for the year	165	11

Notes:

1 The market value of the shares of the business at the end of the reporting period was £2.50 for 2015 and £1.50 for 2016.
2 All sales and purchases are made on credit.
3 The cost of sales figure can be analysed as follows:

	2015 £m	2016 £m
Opening inventories	241	300
Purchases (Note 2)	1,804	2,378
	2,045	2,678
Closing inventories	(300)	(406)
Cost of sales	1,745	2,272

4 At 1 April 2014, the trade receivables stood at £223 million and the trade payables at £183 million.
5 A dividend of £40 million had been paid to the shareholders in respect of each of the years.
6 The business employed 13,995 staff at 31 March 2015 and 18,623 at 31 March 2016.
7 The business expanded its capacity during 2016 by setting up a new warehouse and distribution centre.
8 At 1 April 2014, the total of equity stood at £438 million and the total of equity and non-current liabilities stood at £638 million.

A BRIEF OVERVIEW

Before we start our detailed examination of the ratios for Alexis plc (in Example 6.1), it is helpful to take a quick look at what information is obvious from the financial statements. This will usually pick up some issues that ratios may not be able to identify. It may also highlight some points that could help us in our interpretation of the ratios. Starting at the top of the statement of financial position, the following points can be noted:

- *Expansion of non-current assets.* These have increased by about 15 per cent (from £510 million to £587 million). Note 7 mentions a new warehouse and distribution centre, which may account for much of the additional investment in non-current assets. We are not told when this new facility was established, but it is quite possible that it was well into the year. This could mean that not much benefit was reflected in terms of additional sales revenue or cost saving during 2016. Sales revenue, in fact, expanded by about 20 per cent (from £2,240 million to £2,681 million) – greater than the expansion in non-current assets.
- *Major expansion in the elements of working capital.* Inventories increased by about 35 per cent, trade receivables by about 14 per cent and trade payables by about 36 per cent between 2015 and 2016. These are major increases, particularly in inventories and payables (which are linked because the inventories are all bought on credit – see Note 2).
- *Reduction in the cash balance.* The cash balance fell from £4 million (in funds) to a £76 million overdraft, between 2015 and 2016. The bank may be putting the business under pressure to reverse this, which could create difficulties.
- *Apparent debt capacity.* Comparing the non-current assets with the long-term borrowings implies that the business may well be able to offer security on further borrowing. This is because potential lenders usually look at the value of assets that can be offered as security when assessing loan requests. Lenders seem particularly attracted to land and buildings as security. For example, at 31 March 2016, non-current assets had a carrying amount (the value at which they appeared in the statement of financial position) of £587 million, but long-term borrowing was only £300 million (though there was also an overdraft of £76 million). Carrying amounts are not normally, of course, market values. On the other hand, land and buildings tend to have a market value higher than their value as shown on the statement of financial position due to a general tendency to inflation in property values.
- *Lower operating profit.* Though sales revenue expanded by 20 per cent between 2015 and 2016, both cost of sales and operating expenses rose by a greater percentage, leaving both gross profit and, particularly, operating profit massively reduced. The level of staffing, which increased by about 33 per cent (from 13,995 to 18,623 employees – see Note 6), may have greatly affected the operating expenses. (Without knowing when the additional employees were recruited during 2016, we cannot be sure of the effect on operating expenses.) Increasing staffing by 33 per cent must put an enormous strain on management, at least in the short term. It is not surprising, therefore, that 2016 was not successful for the business – not, at least, in profit terms.

Having had a quick look at what is fairly obvious, without calculating any financial ratios, we shall now go on to calculate and interpret those relating to profitability, efficiency, liquidity, gearing and investment.

PROFITABILITY

The following ratios may be used to evaluate the profitability of the business:

- return on ordinary shareholders' funds;
- return on capital employed;
- operating profit margin; and
- gross profit margin.

We shall now look at each of these in turn.

Return on ordinary shareholders' funds (ROSF)

The **return on ordinary shareholders' funds ratio** compares the amount of profit for the period available to owners, with their average investment in the business during that same period. The ratio (which is normally expressed in percentage terms) is as follows:

$$\text{ROSF} = \frac{\text{Profit for the year (less any preference dividend)}}{\text{Ordinary share capital} + \text{Reserves}} \times 100$$

The profit for the year (less any preference dividend) is used in calculating the ratio, because this figure represents the amount of profit that is attributable to the owners.

In the case of Alexis plc, the ratio for the year ended 31 March 2015 is:

$$\text{ROSF} = \frac{165}{(438 + 563)/2} \times 100 - 33.0\%$$

Note that, when calculating the ROSF, the average of the figures for ordinary shareholders' funds as at the beginning and at the end of the year has been used. This is because an average figure is normally more representative. The amount of shareholders' funds was not constant throughout the year, yet we want to compare it with the profit earned during the whole period. We know, from Note 8, that the amount of shareholders' funds at 1 April 2014 was £438 million. By a year later, however, it had risen to £563 million, according to the statement of financial position as at 31 March 2015.

The easiest approach to calculating the average amount of shareholders' funds is to take a simple average based on the opening and closing figures for the year. This is often the only information available, as is the case for us with Alexis plc. Averaging is normally appropriate for all ratios that combine a figure for a period (such as profit for the year) with one taken at a point in time (such as shareholders' funds).

Where not even the beginning-of-year figure is available, it will be necessary to rely on just the year-end figure. This is not ideal but, when this approach is consistently applied, it can still produce useful ratios.

Calculate the ROSF for Alexis plc for the year to 31 March 2016.

The ratio for 2016 is:

$$ROSF = \frac{11}{(563 + 534)/2} \times 100 = 2.0\%$$

Broadly, businesses seek to generate as high a value as possible for this ratio. This is provided that it is not achieved at the expense of jeopardising future returns by, for example, taking on more risky activities. In view of this, the 2016 ratio is very poor by any standards; a bank deposit account will normally yield a better return. We need to find out why things went so badly wrong in 2016. As we look at other ratios, we should find some clues.

Return on capital employed (ROCE)

The **return on capital employed ratio** is a fundamental measure of business performance. This ratio expresses the relationship between the operating profit generated during a period and the average long-term capital invested in the business.

The ratio is expressed in percentage terms and is as follows:

$$\textbf{ROCE} = \frac{\textbf{Operating profit}}{\textbf{Share capital} + \textbf{Reserves} + \textbf{Non-current liabilities}} \times \textbf{100}$$

Note, in this case, that the profit figure used is the operating profit (that is, the profit *before* interest and taxation), because the ratio attempts to measure the returns to all suppliers of long-term finance before any deductions for interest payable on borrowings, or payments of dividends to shareholders, are made.

For the year ended 31 March 2015, the ratio for Alexis plc is:

$$ROCE = \frac{243}{(638 + 763)/2} \times 100 = 34.7\%$$

(The capital employed figure, which is the total equity plus non-current liabilities, at 1 April 2014 is given in Note 8.)

ROCE is considered by many to be a primary measure of profitability. It compares inputs (capital invested) with outputs (operating profit) so as to reveal the effectiveness with which funds have been deployed. Once again, an average figure for capital employed should be used where the information is available.

Calculate the ROCE for Alexis plc for the year to 31 March 2016.

The ratio for 2016 is:

$$\text{ROCE} = \frac{47}{(763 + 834)/2} \times 100 = 5.9\%$$

This ratio tells much the same story as ROSF; namely a poor performance, with the return on the assets being less than the rate that the business pays for most of its borrowed funds (that is, 9 per cent for the loan notes).

Real World 6.1 shows how financial ratios are used by businesses as a basis for setting profitability targets.

REAL WORLD 6.1

Targeting profitability

The ROCE ratio is widely used by businesses when establishing targets for profitability. These targets are sometimes made public and here are some examples:

- Barratt Developments plc, the builder, has a target return on capital employed of at least 25 per cent for 2017.
- FirstGroup plc, the passenger transport business, has a medium-term target ROCE of 10 to 12 per cent.
- Rexam plc, the beverage can maker, has a target ROCE of 15 per cent.
- Anglo American plc, the mining business, has a target ROCE of 16 per cent for 2016.
- Smurfitt Kappa Group plc, the packaging manufacturer, has a target ROCE of 15 per cent.
- Severfield plc, the structural steel specialist whose major works include the Shard in London, has a target ROCE of more than 10 per cent over the economic cycle.

Sources: Information taken from 'Key performance indicators', www.barrattdevelopments.co.uk, accessed 12 November 2015; FirstGroup plc, 'Preliminary results for the year ended 31 March 2014' 21 May 2014, www.firstgroupplc.com; 'Rexam warns on currency volatility', ft.com, 20 February 2014; 'Miners: If you're in a hole', ft.com, 6 January 2014; Smurfit Kappa Group plc, Q3 2015 Results, 4 November 2015 www.midlandpaper.com; and Severfield plc, 'Full year results 2015', 17 June 2015, p.11, www.severfield.com.

Real World 6.2 provides some indication of the levels of ROCE achieved by UK businesses.

Achieving profitability

ROCE ratios for UK manufacturing and service companies for each of the seven years ending in 2014 are shown in Figure 6.2.

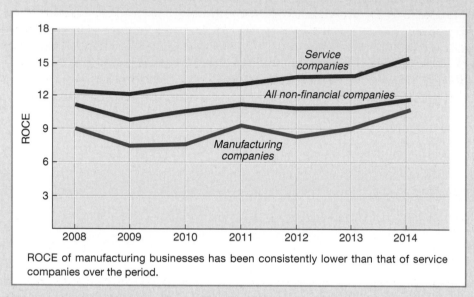

ROCE of manufacturing businesses has been consistently lower than that of service companies over the period.

Figure 6.2 The ROCE of UK companies

According to the Office of National Statistics, the difference in ROCE between the two sectors is accounted for by the higher capital intensity of manufacturing.

Source: Figure compiled from information taken from Office of National Statistics, 'Profitability of UK companies Q1 2015', www.statistics.gov.uk, 8 July 2015.

Operating profit margin

The **operating profit margin ratio** relates the operating profit for the period to the sales revenue. The ratio is expressed as follows:

$$\text{Operating profit margin} = \frac{\text{operating profit}}{\text{sales revenue}} \times 100$$

Operating profit (that is, profit before interest and taxation) is used in this ratio as it represents the profit from trading operations before interest payable is taken into account. It is normally the most appropriate measure of operational performance, when making comparisons. This is because differences arising from the way in which the business is financed will not influence the measure.

For the year ended 31 March 2015, the ratio for Alexis plc is:

$$\text{Operating profit margin} = \frac{243}{2,240} \times 100 = 10.8\%$$

This ratio compares one output of the business (operating profit) with another output (sales revenue). It can vary considerably between types of business. Supermarkets, for example, tend to operate on low prices and, therefore, low operating profit margins. This is done in an attempt to stimulate sales and thereby increase the total amount of operating profit generated. Jewellers, on the other hand, tend to have high operating profit margins but have much lower levels of sales volume. Factors such as the degree of competition, the type of customer, the economic climate and industry characteristics (such as the level of risk) will influence the operating profit margin of a business. This point is picked up again later in the chapter.

Activity 6.5

Calculate the operating profit margin for Alexis plc for the year to 31 March 2016.

The ratio for 2016 is:

$$\text{Operating profit margin} = \frac{47}{2,081} \times 100 = 1.8\%$$

Once again, a very weak performance compared with that of 2015. In 2015, for every £1 of sales revenue an average of 10.8p (that is, 10.8 per cent) was left as operating profit, after paying the cost of the carpets sold and other expenses of operating the business. By 2016, however, this had fallen to only 1.8p for every £1. The reason for the poor ROSF and ROCE ratios appears to have been partially, if not wholly, due to a high level of other expenses relative to sales revenue. The next ratio should provide us with a clue as to how the sharp decline in this ratio occurred.

Real World 6.3 sets out the target operating profit margins for some well-known car manufacturers.

REAL WORLD 6.3

Profit driven

- BMW has a target operating profit margin of between 8 and 10 per cent.
- Volvo has a target operating profit margin of 8 per cent by 2020.
- Nissan has a target operating profit margin of between 8 and 10 per cent by 2017.
- Audi has a target operating profit margin of 8–10 per cent.
- Mercedes has a medium-term target profit margin of 10 per cent.
- Renault has set a target operating profit margin of 5 per cent for 2017.

- Ford has a long-term target of achieving an operating profit margin target of between 8 and 9 per cent. It also aims to achieve an 8 per cent margin by 2020.

We can see that, with the exception of Renault, target operating profit margins fall within the 8 to 10 per cent range. The dates by which these targets are to be achieved, however, vary.

Sources: Information taken from 'BMW targets continuing success in 2015', Corporate News BMW Group, www.bmwgroup.com, 18 March 2015; 'Volvo pins hopes on its, "all-in" car', ft.com, 17 August 2014; 'Nissan to focus on boosting profit margin over market share', 12 May 2014, Reuters, www.reuters.com; 'Audi's race to catch up with BMW hurts profit margin', 4 May 2015, www.reuters.com; 'These three scenarios could significantly impact Daimler's valuation', Forbes Investing, www.forbes.com 15 April 2015; 'European recovery lifts Renault profit despite weaker pricing', 30 July 2015, Reuters, www.cnbc.com; and 'Ford's 2020 vision: improved operating margin more geographic profitability, strong sales growth', 29 September 2014, mediaford.com.

Gross profit margin

The **gross profit margin ratio** relates the gross profit of the business to the sales revenue generated for the same period. Gross profit represents the difference between sales revenue and the cost of sales. The ratio is therefore a measure of profitability in buying (or producing) and selling goods or services before any other expenses are taken into account. As cost of sales represents a major expense for many businesses, a change in this ratio can have a significant effect on the 'bottom line' (that is, the profit for the year). The gross profit margin ratio is calculated as follows:

$$\text{Gross profit margin} = \frac{\text{Gross profit}}{\text{Sales revenue}} \times 100$$

For the year ended 31 March 2015, the ratio for Alexis plc is:

$$\text{Gross profit margin} = \frac{495}{2{,}240} \times 100 = 22.1\%$$

Activity 6.6

Calculate the gross profit margin for Alexis plc for the year to 31 March 2016.

The ratio for 2016 is:

$$\text{Gross profit margin} = \frac{409}{2{,}681} \times 100 = 15.3\%$$

The decline in this ratio means that gross profit was lower *relative* to sales revenue in 2016 than it had been in 2015. Bearing in mind that:

Gross profit = Sales revenue − Cost of sales (or cost of goods sold)

This means that cost of sales was higher *relative* to sales revenue in 2016 than in 2015. This could mean that sales prices were lower and/or that the purchase price of carpets had increased. It is possible that both sales prices and purchase prices had reduced, but the former at a greater rate than the latter. Similarly they may both have increased, but with sales prices having increased at a lesser rate than purchase prices.

Clearly, part of the decline in the operating profit margin ratio is linked to the dramatic decline in the gross profit margin ratio. Whereas, after paying for the carpets sold, for each £1 of sales revenue, 22.1p was left to cover other operating expenses in 2015, this was only 15.3p in 2016.

The profitability ratios for the business over the two years can be set out as follows:

	2015	2016
	%	%
ROSF	33.0	2.0
ROCE	34.7	5.9
Operating profit margin	10.8	1.8
Gross profit margin	22.1	15.3

Activity 6.7

What do you deduce from a comparison of the declines in the operating profit and gross profit margin ratios?

We can see that the difference in the operating profit margin was 9 per cent (that is, 10.8 per cent to 1.8 per cent), whereas that of the gross profit margin was only 6.8 per cent (that is, from 22.1 per cent to 15.3 per cent). This can only mean that operating expenses were greater, compared with sales revenue in 2016, than they had been in 2015. The decline in both ROSF and ROCE was caused partly, therefore, by the business incurring higher inventories' purchasing costs relative to sales revenue and partly through higher operating expenses compared with sales revenue. We need to compare each of these ratios with their planned levels, however, before we can usefully assess the business's success.

An investigation is needed to discover what caused the increases in both cost of sales and operating expenses, relative to sales revenue, from 2015 to 2016. This will involve checking on what has happened with sales and inventories prices over the two years. Similarly, it will involve looking at each of the individual areas that make up operating expenses to discover which ones were responsible for the increase, relative to sales revenue. Here, further ratios, for example, staff expenses (wages and salaries) to sales revenue, could be calculated in an attempt to isolate the cause of the change from 2015 to 2016. As mentioned earlier, the increase in staffing may well account for most of the increase in operating expenses.

Real World 6.4 discusses how some operating expenses can be controlled by unusual means.

EFFICIENCY

Efficiency ratios are used to try to assess how successfully the various resources of the business are managed. The following ratios consider some of the more important aspects of resource management:

- average inventories' turnover period;
- average settlement period for trade receivables;
- average settlement period for trade payables;
- sales revenue to capital employed; and
- sales revenue per employee.

We shall now look at each of these in turn.

Average inventories' turnover period

Inventories often represent a significant investment for a business. For some types of business (for example, manufacturers and certain retailers), inventories may account for a substantial proportion of the total assets held (see Real World 12.1 on page 000). The **average inventories' turnover period ratio** measures the average period for which inventories are being held. The ratio is calculated as follows:

$$\text{Average inventories turnover period} = \frac{\text{Average inventories held}}{\text{Cost of sales}} \times 365$$

The average inventories for the period can be calculated as a simple average of the opening and closing inventories levels for the year. In the case of a highly seasonal business, however, where inventories levels vary considerably over the year, a monthly average would be more appropriate. Such information may not, however, be available. This point about monthly averaging is equally relevant to any asset or claim that tends to vary over the reporting period, including trade receivables and trade payables.

In the case of Alexis plc, the inventories' turnover period for the year ended 31 March 2015 is:

$$\text{Average inventories turnover period} = \frac{(241 + 300)/2}{1,745} \times 365 = 56.6 \text{ days}$$

(The opening inventories figure was taken from Note 3 to the financial statements.)

This means that, on average, the inventories held are being 'turned over' every 56.6 days. So, a carpet bought by the business on a particular day would, on average, have been sold about eight weeks later. A business will normally prefer a short inventories' turnover period to a long one, because holding inventories has costs, for example the opportunity cost of the funds tied up. When judging the amount of inventories to carry, the business must consider such things as the likely demand for them, the possibility of supply shortages, the likelihood of price rises, the amount of storage space available and their perishability or susceptibility to obsolescence.

This ratio is sometimes expressed in terms of weeks or months rather than days: multiplying by 52 or 12, rather than 365, will achieve this.

Activity 6.8

Calculate the average inventories turnover period for Alexis plc for the year ended 31 March 2016.

The ratio for 2016 is:

$$\text{Average inventories turnover period} = \frac{(300 + 406)/2}{2,272} \times 365 = 56.7 \text{ days}$$

The inventories turnover period is virtually the same in both years.

Average settlement period for trade receivables

Selling on credit is the norm for most businesses, except for retailers. Trade receivables are a necessary evil. A business will naturally be concerned with the amount of funds tied up in trade receivables and try to keep this to a minimum. The speed of payment can have a significant effect on the business's cash flow. The **average settlement period for trade receivables ratio** calculates how long, on average, credit customers take to pay the amounts that they owe to the business. The ratio is as follows:

$$\frac{\text{Average settlement period}}{\text{for trade receivables}} = \frac{\text{Average trade receivables}}{\text{Credit sales revenue}} \times 365$$

A business will normally prefer a shorter average settlement period to a longer one as, once again, funds are being tied up that may be used for more profitable purposes. Although this ratio can be useful, it is important to remember that it produces an *average* figure for the number of days for which debts are outstanding. This average may be badly distorted by, for example, a few large customers who are very slow or very fast payers.

Since all sales made by Alexis plc are on credit, the average settlement period for trade receivables for the year ended 31 March 2015 is:

$$\text{Average settlement period for trade receivables} = \frac{(223 + 240)/2}{2{,}240} \times 365 = 37.7 \text{ days}$$

(The opening trade receivables figure was taken from Note 4 to the financial statements.)

Activity 6.9

Calculate the average settlement period for Alexis plc's trade receivables for the year ended 31 March 2016.

The ratio for 2016 is:

$$\text{Average settlement period for trade receivables} = \frac{(240 + 273)/2}{2{,}681} \times 365 = 34.9 \text{ days}$$

On the face of it, this reduction in the settlement period is welcome. It means that less cash was tied up in trade receivables for each £1 of sales revenue in 2016 than in 2015. Only if the reduction were achieved at the expense of customer goodwill or through high out-of-pocket cost might its desirability be questioned. For example, the reduction may have been due to chasing customers too vigorously or giving large discounts to customers for prompt payment.

Average settlement period for trade payables

The **average settlement period for trade payables ratio** measures how long, on average, the business takes to pay those who have supplied goods and services to it on credit. The ratio is calculated as follows:

$$\text{Average settlement period for trade payables} = \frac{\text{Average trade payables}}{\text{Credit purchases}} \times 365$$

This ratio provides an average figure, which, like the average settlement period for trade receivables ratio, can be distorted by the payment period for one or two large suppliers.

As trade payables provide a free source of finance for the business, it is perhaps not surprising that some businesses attempt to increase their average settlement period for trade payables. Such a policy can be taken too far, however, and can result in a loss of goodwill of suppliers.

For the year ended 31 March 2015, Alexis plc's average settlement period for trade payables is:

$$\text{Average settlement period for trade payables} = \frac{(183 + 261)/2}{1{,}804} \times 365 = 44.9 \text{ days}$$

(The opening trade payables figure was taken from Note 4 to the financial statements and the purchases figure from Note 3.)

Activity 6.10

Calculate the average settlement period for trade payables for Alexis plc for the year ended 31 March 2016.

The ratio for 2016 is:

$$\text{Average settlement period for trade payables} = \frac{(261 + 354)/2}{2{,}378} \times 365 = 47.2 \text{ days}$$

There was an increase, between 2015 and 2016, in the average length of time that elapsed between buying goods and services and paying for them. On the face of it, this is beneficial because the business is using free finance provided by suppliers. This may not be so, however, where it results in a loss of supplier goodwill and Alexis plc suffers adverse consequences.

Small businesses often suffer acute cash flow problems because large business customers refuse to pay within a reasonable period. This has led the UK government to introduce a Prompt Payment Code to help small businesses. Large businesses do not have to sign up to this Code, which sets standards for payment practices, but they are actively encouraged to do so. To date, however, the Code has achieved only limited success. **Real World 6.5** describes the nature of the problems still facing small businesses and recent attempts to strengthen the Code in order to improve matters.

REAL WORLD 6.5

Feeling the squeeze

The UK government's measures to improve late payments to suppliers have had some impact, but the burden on small businesses of chasing those payments remains severe, according to new figures. The total owed in late payments to UK companies of all sizes has fallen from an estimated £45bn to £31bn since this time last year, according to Bacs, the direct debit company. However, four-fifths of those are having to wait one month or longer beyond the agreed terms before receiving payment.

$\rightarrow$

For smaller businesses – employing fewer than 250 people – late payments totalled £26.8bn, down from £32.4bn this time last year. But these companies were spending nearly £11bn a year – an average of £11,500 each – in their attempts to recover overdue payments, up from £8.2bn in July 2014.

In his March budget, the Chancellor of the Exchequer promised to extend the voluntary Prompt Payment Code, which seeks to encourage large businesses to set out clearly defined payment terms and to which more than 1,700 companies have signed up. Meanwhile, the EU late payment directive stipulates that public authorities and private companies must pay their suppliers within 30 and 60 days respectively, or explain why.

The Chancellor's move came after companies such as Heinz and 2 Sisters Food Group, the UK's biggest Christmas pudding maker, were exposed for extending payment terms and imposing punitive terms on suppliers. The government claimed victory in March in its drive to name and shame big businesses that failed to commit to fair treatment of suppliers after Diageo, the world's biggest drinks company, backed down on a plan to lengthen payment terms.

While SMEs can charge penalties and interest for late payment, they fear losing business from big customers in retaliation.

In February, the government announced plans to make 30-day payment terms the standard in the UK, with 60 days the new maximum limit, as part of a crackdown on late payment of bills.

FT *Source:* Gordon S. (2015), 'UK small businesses spend £11bn chasing payments', ft.com, 16 July. © The Financial Times Limited 2015. All Rights Reserved.

Sales revenue to capital employed

The **sales revenue to capital employed ratio** (or net asset turnover ratio) examines how effectively the assets of the business are being used to generate sales revenue. It is calculated as follows:

$$\text{Sales revenue to capital employed ratio} = \frac{\text{Sales revenue}}{\text{Share capital} + \text{Reserves} + \text{Non-current liabilities}}$$

Generally speaking, a higher sales revenue to capital employed ratio is preferred to a lower one. A higher ratio will normally suggest that assets are being used more productively in the generation of revenue. However, a very high ratio may suggest that the business is **overtrading** on its assets. In other words, it has insufficient assets to sustain the level of sales revenue achieved.

When comparing the sales revenue to capital employed ratio for different businesses, factors such as the age and condition of assets held, the valuation bases for assets and whether assets are leased or owned outright can complicate interpretation.

A variation of this formula is to use the total assets less current liabilities (which is equivalent to long-term capital employed) in the denominator (lower part of the fraction). The same result is obtained.

For the year ended 31 March 2015, this ratio for Alexis plc is:

$$\text{Sales revenue to capital employed} = \frac{2,240}{(638 + 763)/2} = 3.20 \text{ times}$$

Calculate the sales revenue to capital employed ratio for Alexis plc for the year ended 31 March 2016.

The ratio for 2016 is:

$$\text{Sales revenue to capital employed} = \frac{2,681}{(763 + 834)/2} = 3.36 \text{ times}$$

This seems to be an improvement, since, in 2016, more sales revenue was being generated for each £1 of capital employed (£3.36) than was the case in 2015 (£3.20). Provided that overtrading is not an issue, and that the additional sales are generating an acceptable profit, this is to be welcomed.

Sales revenue per employee

The **sales revenue per employee ratio** relates sales revenue generated during a reporting period to a particular business resource – labour. It provides a measure of the productivity of the workforce. The ratio is:

$$\textbf{Sales revenue per employee} = \frac{\textbf{Sales revenue}}{\textbf{Number of employees}}$$

Generally, businesses would prefer a high value for this ratio, implying that they are deploying their staff efficiently.

For the year ended 31 March 2015, the ratio for Alexis plc is:

$$\text{Sales revenue per employee} = \frac{£2,240m}{13,995} = £160,057$$

Activity 6.12

Calculate the sales revenue per employee for Alexis plc for the year ended 31 March 2016.

The ratio for 2016 is:

$$\text{Sales revenue per employee} = \frac{£2,681m}{18,623} = £143,962$$

This represents a fairly significant decline, which merits further investigation. As already mentioned, the number of employees increased quite notably (by about 33 per cent) during 2016. We need to know why this had not generated additional sales revenue sufficient to maintain the ratio at its 2015 level. It may be because the extra employees were not appointed until late in the year ended 31 March 2016.

The efficiency, or activity, ratios may be summarised as follows:

	2015	2016
Average inventories turnover period	56.6 days	56.7 days
Average settlement period for trade receivables	37.7 days	34.9 days
Average settlement period for trade payables	44.9 days	47.2 days
Sales revenue to capital employed (net asset turnover)	3.20 times	3.36 times
Sales revenue per employee	£160,057	£143,962

Activity 6.13

What do you deduce from a comparison of the efficiency ratios over the two years?

Maintaining the inventories turnover period at the 2015 level may be reasonable, though to assess whether this is a satisfactory period we need to know the planned inventories turnover period. The inventories turnover period for other businesses operating in carpet retailing, particularly those regarded as the market leaders, may have been helpful in formulating the plans. On the face of things, a shorter trade receivables settlement period and a longer trade payables settlement period are both desirable. These may, however, have been achieved at the cost of a loss of the goodwill of customers and suppliers, respectively.

The increased sales revenue to capital employed ratio seems beneficial, provided the business can manage this increase. The decline in the sales revenue per employee ratio is undesirable but is probably related to the dramatic increase in the number of employees. As with the inventories turnover period, these other ratios need to be compared with planned, or target, ratios.

RELATIONSHIP BETWEEN PROFITABILITY AND EFFICIENCY

In our earlier discussions concerning profitability ratios, we saw that return on capital employed (ROCE) is regarded as a key ratio by many businesses. The ratio is:

$$\text{ROCE} = \frac{\text{Operating profit}}{\text{Long-term capital employed}} \times 100$$

where long-term capital comprises share capital plus reserves plus long-term borrowings. This ratio can be broken down into two elements, as shown in Figure 6.3. The first ratio is the operating profit margin ratio and the second is the sales revenue to capital employed (net asset turnover) ratio, both of which we discussed earlier.

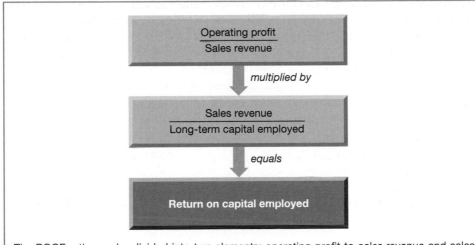

The ROCE ratio can be divided into two elements: operating profit to sales revenue and sales revenue to capital employed. By analysing ROCE in this way, we can see the influence of both profitability and efficiency on this important ratio.

Figure 6.3 The main elements of the ROCE ratio

By breaking down the ROCE ratio in this manner, we highlight the fact that the overall return on funds employed within the business will be determined both by the profitability of sales and by efficiency in the use of capital.

Example 6.2

Consider the following information, for last year, concerning two different businesses operating in the same industry:

	Antler plc £m	Baker plc £m
Operating profit	20	15
Average long-term capital employed	100	75
Sales revenue	200	300

The ROCE for each business is identical (20 per cent). However, the manner in which that return was achieved by each business is quite different. In the case of Antler plc, the operating profit margin is 10 per cent and the sales revenue to capital employed ratio is 2 times (so, ROCE = 10% × 2 = 20%). In the case of Baker plc, the operating profit margin is 5 per cent and the sales revenue to capital employed ratio is 4 times (and so, ROCE = 5% × 4 = 20%).

Example 6.2 demonstrates that a relatively high sales revenue to capital employed ratio can compensate for a relatively low operating profit margin. Similarly, a relatively low sales revenue to capital employed ratio can be overcome by a relatively high operating profit margin. In many areas of retail and distribution (for example, supermarkets and delivery services), operating profit margins are quite low, but the ROCE can be high, provided that assets are used productively (that is, low margin, high sales revenue to capital employed).

Show how the ROCE ratio for Alexis plc can be analysed into the two elements for each of the years 2015 and 2016. What conclusions can you draw from your figures?

	ROCE	=	Operating profit margin	×	Sales revenue to capital employed
2015	34.7%		10.8%		3.20
2016	5.9%		1.8%		3.36

As we can see, the relationship between the three ratios holds for Alexis plc for both years. The small apparent differences arise because the three ratios are stated here only to one or two decimal places.

In 2016, the business was more effective at generating sales revenue (sales revenue to capital employed ratio increased). However, it fell well below the level needed to compensate for the sharp decline in the profitability of sales (operating profit margin). As a result, the 2016 ROCE was well below the 2015 value.

LIQUIDITY

Liquidity ratios are concerned with the ability of the business to meet its short-term financial obligations. The following ratios are widely used:

- current ratio; and
- acid test ratio.

These ratios will now be considered.

Current ratio

The **current ratio** compares the 'liquid' assets (that is, cash and those assets held that will soon be turned into cash) of the business with the current liabilities. The ratio is calculated as follows:

$$\text{Current ratio} = \frac{\text{Current assets}}{\text{Current liabilities}}$$

It seems to be believed by some that there is an 'ideal' current ratio (usually 2 times or 2:1) for all businesses. However, this is not the case. Different types of business require different current ratios. A manufacturing business, for example, will normally have a relatively high current ratio because it will hold inventories of finished goods, raw materials and work-in-progress. It will also sell goods on credit, thereby giving rise to trade receivables. A supermarket chain, on the other hand, will have a relatively low ratio, as it will hold only fast-moving inventories of finished goods and its sales will be for cash rather than on credit.

The higher the current ratio, the more liquid the business is considered to be. As liquidity is vital to the survival of a business, a higher current ratio might be thought to be preferable to a lower one. If a business has a very high ratio, however, it may be that excessive funds are tied up in cash or other liquid assets and are not, therefore, being used as productively as they might otherwise be.

For the year ended 31 March 2015, the ratio for Alexis plc is:

$$\text{Current ratio} = \frac{544}{291} = 1.9 \text{ times (or 1.9:1)}$$

Activity 6.15

Calculate the current ratio for Alexis plc as at 31 March 2016.

The ratio for 2016 is:

$$\text{Current ratio} = \frac{679}{432} = 1.6 \text{ times (or 1.6:1)}$$

Although this is a decline from 2015 to 2016, it may not be a matter for concern. The next ratio may provide a clue as to whether there seems to be a problem.

Acid test ratio

The **acid test ratio** is very similar to the current ratio, but it represents a more stringent test of liquidity. For many businesses, inventories cannot be converted into cash quickly. (Note that, in the case of Alexis plc, the inventories turnover period was about 57 days in both years (see page 211).) As a result, it is usually better to exclude this particular asset from this measure of liquidity.

The acid test ratio is calculated as follows:

$$\text{Acid test ratio} = \frac{\textbf{Current assets (excluding inventories)}}{\textbf{Current liabilities}}$$

For the year ended 31 March 2015, the ratio for Alexis plc is:

$$\text{Acid test ratio} = \frac{544 - 300}{291} = 0.8 \text{ times (or 0.8:1)}$$

We can see that the 'liquid' current assets do not quite cover the current liabilities, so the business may be experiencing some liquidity problems.

The minimum level for this ratio is often stated as 1.0 times (or 1:1; that is, current assets (excluding inventories) equal current liabilities). However, for many highly successful businesses, it is not unusual for the acid test ratio to be below 1.0 without causing liquidity problems.

Activity 6.16

Calculate the acid test ratio for Alexis plc as at 31 March 2016.

The ratio for 2016 is:

$$\text{Acid test ratio} = \frac{679 - 406}{432} = 0.6 \text{ times}$$

The 2016 ratio is significantly below that for 2015. The 2016 level may well be a cause for concern. The rapid decline in this ratio should lead to steps being taken, at least, to investigate the reason for this and, perhaps, to stop it falling further.

The liquidity ratios for the two-year period may be summarised as follows:

	2015	2016
Current ratio	1.9	1.6
Acid test ratio	0.8	0.6

Activity 6.17

What do you deduce from these liquidity ratios?

There has clearly been a decline in liquidity from 2015 to 2016. This is indicated by both ratios. The decline in the acid test ratio is particularly worrying as it suggests that the business may struggle to meet its short-term obligations. The apparent liquidity problem may, however, be planned, short term and linked to the increase in non-current assets and the number of employees. When the benefits of the expansion come on stream, liquidity may improve. On the other hand, short-term lenders and suppliers may become anxious by the decline in liquidity. This could lead them to press for payment, which is likely to cause further problems.

FINANCIAL GEARING

Financial gearing occurs when a business is financed, at least in part, by borrowing rather than by owners' equity. The extent to which a business is geared (that is, financed from borrowing) is an important factor in assessing risk. Borrowing involves taking on a commitment to pay interest charges and to make capital repayments. Where the borrowing is heavy, this can be a significant financial burden; it can increase the risk of the business becoming insolvent. Nevertheless, most businesses are geared to some extent. (Costain Group plc, the builders and construction business, is a rare example of a UK business with little or no borrowings.)

Given the risks involved, we may wonder why a business would want to take on gearing. One reason is that the owners have insufficient funds, so the only way to finance the business adequately is to borrow. Another reason is that gearing can be used to increase the returns to owners. This is possible provided the returns generated from borrowed funds exceed the cost of paying interest. Example 6.3 illustrates this point.

Example 6.3

The long-term capital structures of two new businesses, Lee Ltd and Nova Ltd, are as follows:

	Lee Ltd £	Nova Ltd £
£1 ordinary shares	100,000	200,000
10% loan notes	200,000	100,000
	300,000	300,000

In their first year of operations, they each make an operating profit (that is, profit before interest and taxation) of £50,000. The tax rate is 20 per cent of the profit before taxation (but after interest).

Lee Ltd would probably be considered relatively highly geared, as it has a high proportion of borrowed funds in its long-term capital structure. Nova Ltd is much lower geared. The profit available to the shareholders of each business in the first year of operations will be:

	Lee Ltd £	Nova Ltd £
Operating profit	50,000	50,000
Interest payable	(20,000)	(10,000)
Profit before taxation	30,000	40,000
Taxation (20%)	(6,000)	(8,000)
Profit for the year (available to ordinary shareholders)	24,000	32,000

The return on ordinary shareholders' funds (ROSF) for each business will be:

Lee Ltd
$$\frac{24,000}{100,000} \times 100 = 24\%$$

Nova Ltd
$$\frac{32,000}{200,000} \times 100 = 16\%$$

We can see that Lee Ltd, the more highly geared business, has generated a better ROSF than Nova Ltd. This is despite the fact that the ROCE (return on capital employed) is identical for both businesses (that is, (£50,000/£300,000) × 100 = 16.7%).

→

Note that at the £50,000 level of operating profit, the shareholders of both businesses have generated higher returns as a result of gearing. If both businesses were totally financed by equity, the profit for the year (that is, after taxation) would be £40,000 (that is, £50,000 less 20 per cent taxation), giving an ROSF of 13.3 per cent (that is, £40,000/£300,000).

An effect of gearing is that returns to shareholders become more sensitive to changes in operating profits. For a highly geared business, a change in operating profits will lead to a proportionately greater change in the ROSF ratio.

Activity 6.18

Assume that the operating profit £70,000 rather than £50,000. What would be the effect of this on ROSF?

The revised profit available to the shareholders of each business in the first year of operations will be:

	Lee Ltd	Nova Ltd
	£	£
Operating profit	70,000	70,000
Interest payable	(20,000)	(10,000)
Profit before taxation	50,000	60,000
Taxation (20%)	(10,000)	(12,000)
Profit for the year (available to ordinary shareholders)	40,000	48,000

The ROSF for each business will now be:

$$\text{Lee Ltd} \quad \frac{40,000}{100,000} \times 100 = 40\% \qquad \text{Nova Ltd} \quad \frac{48,000}{200,000} \times 100 = 24\%$$

We can see that for Lee Ltd, the higher-geared business, the returns to shareholders have increased by two thirds (from 24 per cent to 40 per cent), whereas for the lower-geared business, Nova Ltd, the benefits of gearing are less pronounced, increasing by only half (from 16 per cent to 24 per cent). The effect of gearing can, of course, work in both directions. So, for a highly geared business, a small decline in operating profit will bring about a much greater decline in the returns to shareholders.

The reason that gearing seems to be beneficial to shareholders is that interest rates for borrowings are low by comparison with the returns that the typical business can earn. On top of this, interest expenses are tax deductible, in the way shown in Example 6.3 and Activity 6.17. This makes the effective cost of borrowing quite cheap. It is debatable, however, whether low interest rates really are beneficial to shareholders. Since borrowing increases the risk to shareholders, there is a hidden cost involved. Many argue that this cost is precisely compensated by the higher returns, giving no net benefit to shareholders. In other words, the apparent benefits of higher returns from gearing are illusory. What are not illusory, however, are the benefits to shareholders from the tax deductibility of interest payments.

Activity 6.19

If shareholders gain from the tax-deductibility of interest on borrowings, who loses?

The losers are the tax authority (ultimately the government) and, therefore, other taxpayers.

The effect of gearing is like that of two intermeshing cogwheels of unequal size (see Figure 6.4). The movement in the larger cog (operating profit) causes a more than proportionate movement in the smaller cog (returns to ordinary shareholders).

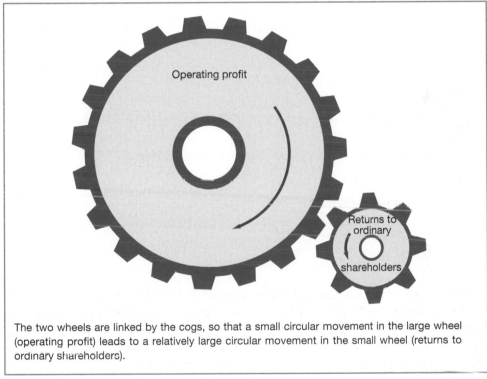

Operating profit

Returns to ordinary shareholders

The two wheels are linked by the cogs, so that a small circular movement in the large wheel (operating profit) leads to a relatively large circular movement in the small wheel (returns to ordinary shareholders).

Figure 6.4 The effect of financial gearing

Two ratios are widely used to assess gearing:

■ gearing ratio;
■ interest cover ratio.

Gearing ratio

The **gearing ratio** measures the contribution of long-term lenders to the long-term capital structure of a business:

$$\text{Gearing ratio} = \frac{\text{Long-term (non-current) liabilities}}{\text{Share capital} + \text{Reserves} + \text{Long-term (non-current) liabilities}} \times 100$$

For the year ended 31 March 2015, the ratio for Alexis plc is:

$$\text{Gearing ratio} = \frac{200}{(563 + 200)} \times 100 = 26.2\%$$

This is a level of gearing that would not normally be considered to be very high.

Activity 6.20

Calculate the gearing ratio of Alexis plc as at 31 March 2016.

The ratio for 2016 is:

$$\text{Gearing ratio} = \frac{300}{(534 + 300)} \times 100 = 36.0\%$$

This is a substantial increase in the level of gearing over the year.

Interest cover ratio

The **interest cover ratio** measures the amount of operating profit available to cover interest payable. The ratio may be calculated as follows:

$$\text{Interest cover ratio} = \frac{\text{Operating profit}}{\text{Interest payable}}$$

For the year ended 31 March 2015, the ratio for Alexis plc is:

$$\text{Interest cover ratio} = \frac{243}{18} = 13.5 \text{ times}$$

This ratio shows that the level of operating profit is considerably higher than the level of interest payable. This means that a large fall in operating profit could occur before operating profit levels failed to cover interest payable. The lower the level of operating profit coverage, the greater the risk to lenders that interest payments will not be met. There will also be a greater risk to the shareholders that the lenders will take action against the business to recover the interest due.

Calculate the interest cover ratio of Alexis plc for the year ended 31 March 2016.

The ratio for 2016 is:

$$\text{Interest cover ratio} = \frac{47}{32} = 1.5 \text{ times}$$

Alexis plc's gearing ratios are:

	2015	2016
Gearing ratio	26.2%	36.0%
Interest cover ratio	13.5 times	1.5 times

What do you deduce from a comparison of Alexis plc's gearing ratios over the two years?

The gearing ratio has changed significantly. This is mainly due to the substantial increase in the contribution of long-term lenders to financing the business. The gearing ratio at 31 March 2016 would not be considered very high for a business that is trading successfully. It is the low profitability that is the problem. The interest cover ratio has fallen dramatically from 13.5 times in 2015 to 1.5 times in 2016. This was partly caused by the increase in borrowings in 2016, but mainly caused by the dramatic fall in profitability in that year. The situation in 2016 looks hazardous. Only a small decline in future operating profits would result in them being unable to cover interest payments.

Without knowledge of the planned ratios, it is not possible to reach a valid conclusion on Alexis plc's gearing.

INVESTMENT RATIOS

There are several ratios available that are designed to help shareholders assess the returns on their investment. The following are widely used:

- dividend payout ratio;
- dividend yield ratio;
- earnings per share; and
- price/earnings ratio.

Dividend payout ratio

The **dividend payout ratio** measures the proportion of earnings that is paid out to shareholders in the form of dividends. The ratio is calculated as follows:

$$\text{Dividend payout ratio} = \frac{\textbf{Dividends announced for the year}}{\textbf{Earnings for the year available for dividends}} \times 100$$

In the case of ordinary shares, the earnings available for dividend will normally be the profit for the year (that is, the profit after taxation) less any preference dividends relating to the year. This ratio is normally expressed as a percentage.

For the year ended 31 March 2015, the ratio for Alexis plc is:

$$\text{Dividend payout ratio} = \frac{40}{165} \times 100 = 24.2\%$$

Activity 6.23

Calculate the dividend payout ratio of Alexis plc for the year ended 31 March 2016.

The ratio for 2016 is:

$$\text{Dividend payout ratio} = \frac{40}{11} \times 100 = 363.6\%$$

This would normally be considered to be a very alarming increase in the ratio over the two years. Paying a dividend of £40 million in 2016 would probably be widely regarded as very imprudent.

The information provided by this ratio is often expressed slightly differently as the **dividend cover ratio**. Here the calculation is:

$$\text{Dividend cover ratio} = \frac{\textbf{Earnings for the year available for dividend}}{\textbf{Dividend announced for the year}}$$

For 2015, the ratio for Alexis plc would be 165/40 = 4.1 times. That is to say, the earnings available for dividend cover the actual dividend paid by just over four times. For 2016, the ratio is 11/40 = 0.3 times.

Dividend yield ratio

The **dividend yield ratio** relates the cash return from a share to its current market value. This can help investors to assess the cash return on their investment in the business. The ratio, expressed as a percentage, is:

$$\text{Dividend yield} = \frac{\textbf{Dividend per share}}{\textbf{Market value per share}} \times 100$$

For the year ended 31 March 2015, the dividend yield for Alexis plc is:

$$\text{Dividend yield} = \frac{0.067^*}{2.50} \times 100 = 2.7\%$$

The shares' market value is given in Note 1 to Example 6.1 (page 200).

* Dividend proposed/number of shares = 40/(300 × 2) = £0.067 dividend per share (the 300 is multiplied by 2 because they are £0.50 shares).

Earnings per share

The **earnings per share (EPS)** ratio relates the earnings generated by the business, and available to shareholders, during a period, to the number of shares in issue. For equity (ordinary) shareholders, the amount available will be represented by the profit for the year (profit after taxation) less any preference dividend, where applicable. The ratio for equity shareholders is calculated as follows:

$$\text{Earnings per share} = \frac{\text{Earnings available to ordinary shareholders}}{\text{Number of ordinary shares in issue}}$$

For the year ended 31 March 2015, the earnings per share for Alexis plc, is:

$$\text{EPS} = \frac{£165m}{600m} = 27.5p$$

Many investment analysts regard the EPS ratio as a fundamental measure of share performance. The trend in earnings per share over time is used to help assess the investment potential of a business's shares. Although it is possible to make total profit increase through ordinary shareholders investing more in the business, by the business issuing more shares for cash, this will not necessarily lead to an increase in the profitability *per share*.

Real World 6.6 points out the danger of placing too much emphasis on this ratio. The equity fund manager, Terry Smith, argues that, had more attention been paid to ROCE rather than EPS, investors would have spotted that all was not well with Tesco plc, the supermarket giant. He also takes to task, Warren Buffett, the legendary investor, for ignoring his own advice and investing heavily in the business.

A trolley load of problems

In his 1979 letter to shareholders, Mr Buffett stated: 'The primary test of managerial economic performance is the achievement of a high earnings rate on equity capital employed (without undue gearing, accounting gimmickry, etc) and not the achievement of consistent gains in earnings per share.'

This makes it all the more surprising to me that both Mr Buffett and the many acolytes who have seemingly followed him to the gates of hell in Tesco, ignored this chart:

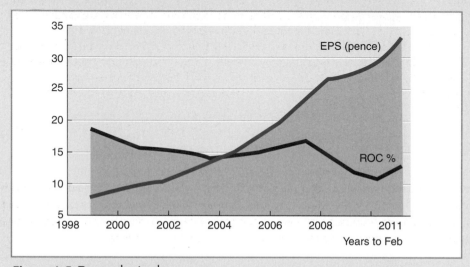

Figure 6.5 Tesco: the Leahy years

This is not the first such chart that I have come across in which a company reports steadily rising earnings per share (EPS), on which most analysts and 'investors' focus. For them, the rise in EPS seems to have a mesmeric effect like Kaa the snake in *The Jungle Book*. But they ignore the point that more capital is being employed to generate those earnings at ever lower returns. Add in the fact that Tesco has changed its definition of return on capital employed (ROCE) eight times during those years, and there's more than enough material to send investors running for cover – even those who have less aversion than I do to retailers.

Yet much of the commentary about what has gone wrong at Tesco focuses on Philip Clarke, who took over as chief executive from Sir Terry Leahy in 2011, as if everything was going swimmingly until then. Looking at the ROCE line in the chart it is clear that this was not the case.

Moreover, one thing to bear in mind is that if Tesco's ROCE during the Leahy years fell from a very good 19 per cent to a less than adequate 10 per cent, this is an average of returns on capital employed, which includes both capital invested years ago and more recent commitments. To drag the average ROCE down so dramatically it is likely that returns on new investments in those years were not just inadequate, but in some cases negative – as the ill-starred US expansion proved to be.

Even if return on capital employed does not have the same importance for you as it does for me, or Mr Buffett (at least in 1979), consider this: in 14 of the past 18 years (taking us back to 1997 when Sir Terry became chief executive) Tesco's free cash flow less its dividend (with free cash defined as operating cash flow less gross capital expenditure) was a negative number. In plain English, Tesco was not generating enough cash both to invest and to pay its dividend. In half of those 14 years, the proceeds of fixed asset disposals took the numbers back into the black, but that is not exactly a sustainable source of financing.

So guess what they did instead? Yes, they borrowed it. Tesco's gross debt, which was £894 million when Sir Terry took over, peaked at nearly £15.9 billion in 2009. The company spent much of its free cash on fixed-asset investment and raised debt to help pay the dividend. This is neither healthy nor sustainable, as investors in Tesco have now come to realise.

The concept that this might not be sustainable hardly requires much thought. Neither does charting the ROCE versus the growth in EPS. Yet it is evident that many investors, including it seems Mr Buffett (who has been trimming his Tesco stake in recent years) either didn't do this or ignored the results if they did. It makes me wonder what else they are ignoring.

Source: Extract from Smith, T (2014) 'How investors ignored the warning signs at Tesco', ft.com, 5 September.

It is not usually very helpful to compare the EPS of one business with that of another. Differences in financing arrangements (for example, in the nominal value of shares issued) can render any such comparison meaningless. However, it can be very useful to monitor the changes that occur in this ratio for a particular business over time.

Activity 6.25

Calculate the earnings per share of Alexis plc for the year ended 31 March 2016.

The ratio for 2016 is:

$$\text{EPS} = \frac{£11m}{600m} = 1.8p$$

Price/earnings (P/E) ratio

The **price/earnings ratio** relates the market value of a share to the earnings per share. This ratio can be calculated as follows:

$$\text{P/E ratio} = \frac{\text{Market value per share}}{\text{Earnings per share}}$$

For the year ended 31 March 2015, the ratio for Alexis plc is:

$$\text{P/E ratio} = \frac{£2.50}{27.5p^*} = 9.1 \text{ times}$$

* The EPS figure (27.5p) was calculated on page 000.

This ratio indicates that the market value of the share is 9.1 times higher than its current level of earnings. It is a measure of market confidence in the future of a business. The higher the P/E ratio, the greater the confidence in the future earning power of the business and, consequently, the more investors are prepared to pay in relation to that current earning power.

Activity 6.26

Calculate the P/E ratio of Alexis plc as at 31 March 2016.

The ratio for 2016 is:

$$\text{P/E ratio} = \frac{£1.50}{1.8p} = 83.3 \text{ times}$$

As P/E ratios provide a useful guide to market confidence about the future, they can be helpful when comparing different businesses. However, differences in accounting policies between businesses can lead to different profit and earnings per share figures. This can distort comparisons.

The investment ratios for Alexis plc over the two-year period are as follows:

	2015	2016
Dividend payout ratio	24.2%	363.6%
Dividend yield ratio	2.7%	4.5%
Earnings per share	27.5p	1.8p
P/E ratio	9.1 times	83.3 times

Activity 6.27

What do you deduce from the investment ratios set out above? Can you offer an explanation why the share price has not fallen as much as it might have done, bearing in mind the much poorer trading performance in 2016?

Although the EPS has fallen dramatically, and the dividend payment for 2016 seems very imprudent, the share price has held up reasonably well (fallen from £2.50 to £1.50). Moreover, the dividend yield and P/E ratios have improved in 2016. This is an anomaly of these two ratios, which stems from using a forward-looking value (the share price) in conjunction with historic data (dividends and earnings). Share prices are based on investors' assessments of the business's future. It seems that the 'market' was less happy with Alexis plc at the end of 2016 than at the end of 2015. This is evidenced by the fact that the share price had fallen by £1 a share. The decline in share price, however, was less dramatic than the decline in profit for the year. This suggests that investors believe the business will perform better in the future. Perhaps they are confident that the large increase in assets and employee numbers occurring in 2016 will yield benefits in the future; benefits that the business was not able to generate in 2016.

Real World 6.7 provides information about the share performance of a selection of large, well-known UK businesses. This type of information is provided on a daily basis by several newspapers, notably the *Financial Times.*

REAL WORLD 6.7

Market statistics for some well-known businesses

The following data was extracted from the *Financial Times* of 11 February 2016, relating to the previous day's trading of the shares of some well-known businesses on the London Stock Exchange:

Share	Price	Chng	52 Week		Yld	P/E	Volume
			High	Low			000s
Marks and Spencer	413.00	+1.80	600.00	403.60	4.36	15.82	7168.70
Royal Mail	422.10	−0.30	532.50	414.90	4.98	14.68	2918.0
National Express	286.00	+3.10	334.70	257.60	3.60	17.72	377.9
Tesco	181.30	+7.50	252.52	137.00	0.64	−2.61	48711.3
Coca Cola	1305	+28.00	1638	1075	3.88	20.73	517.5
National Grid	941.80	−1.90	992.50	806.40	4.55	16.41	10329.9

The column headings are as follows:

Price	Mid-market price in pence (that is, the price midway between buying and selling price) of the shares at the end of trading on 10 February 2016
Chng	Gain or loss in the mid-market price during 10 February 2016
High/Low	Highest and lowest prices reached by the share during the 52 weeks ended on 10 February 2016
Yld	Dividend yield, based on the most recent year's dividend and the current share price
P/E	Price/earnings ratio, based on the most recent year's (after-tax) profit for the year and the current share price
Volume	The number of shares (in thousands) that were bought/sold on 10 February 2016

So, for example for Marks and Spencer plc, the retail business:

- the shares had a mid-market price of 413.00p each at the close of Stock Exchange trading on 10 February 2016;
- the shares had increased in price by 1.80p during trading on 10 February 2016;
- the shares had highest and lowest prices during the previous 52 weeks of 600.00p and 403.60p, respectively;
- the shares had a dividend yield, based on the 10 February 2016 price (and the dividend for the most recent year) of 4.36 per cent;
- the shares had a P/E ratio, based on the 10 February 2016 price (and the after-taxation earnings per share for the most recent year), of 15.82;
- during trading on 10 February 2016, 7,168,700 of the business's shares had changed hands between buyers and sellers.

Source: Based on data from *Financial Times*, 11 February 2016, p 26.

Real World 6.8 shows how investment ratios can vary between different industry sectors.

REAL WORLD 6.8

Yielding dividends

Investment ratios can vary significantly between businesses and between industries. To give some indication of the range of variations that occur, the average dividend yield ratios and average P/E ratios for listed businesses in 12 different industries are shown in Figures 6.6 and 6.7, respectively.

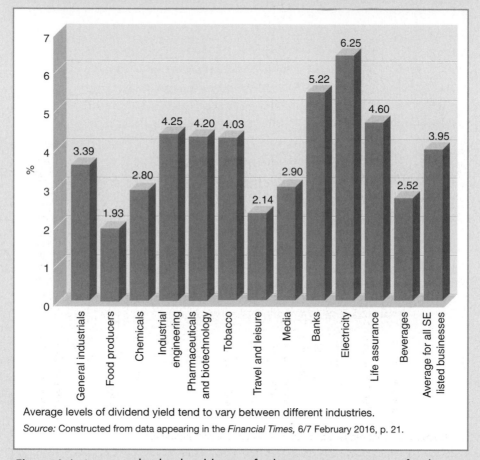

Average levels of dividend yield tend to vary between different industries.

Source: Constructed from data appearing in the *Financial Times*, 6/7 February 2016, p. 21.

Figure 6.6 Average dividend yield ratios for businesses in a range of industries

These dividend yield ratios are calculated from the current market value of the shares and the most recent year's dividend paid.

Some industries tend to pay out lower dividends than others, leading to lower dividend yield ratios. The average for all Stock Exchange listed businesses was 3.95 per cent (as is shown in Figure 6.6), but there is a wide variation with Food Producers at 1.93 per cent and Electricity at 6.25 per cent.

Some types of businesses tend to invest heavily in developing new products, hence their tendency to pay low dividends compared with their share prices. Some of the inter-industry differences in the dividend yield ratio can be explained by the nature of the calculation of the ratio. The prices of shares at any given moment are based on expectations of their economic futures; dividends are actual past events. A business that had a good trading year recently may have paid a dividend that, in the light of investors' assessment of the business's economic future, may be high (a high dividend yield).

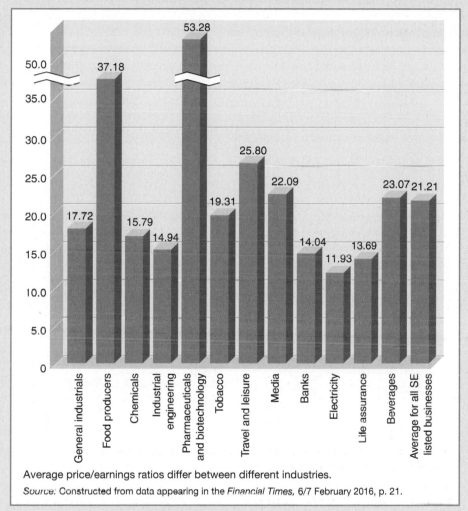

Average price/earnings ratios differ between different industries.

Source: Constructed from data appearing in the *Financial Times*, 6/7 February 2016, p. 21.

Figure 6.7 Average price/earnings ratios for businesses in a range of industries

These P/E ratios are calculated from the current market value of the shares and the most recent year's earnings per share (EPS).

Businesses that have a high share price relative to their recent historic earnings have high P/E ratios. This may be because their future is regarded as economically bright, which may be the result of investing heavily in the future at the expense of recent profits (earnings). On the other hand, high P/Es also arise where businesses have recent low earnings, but

→

investors believe that their future is brighter. The average P/E for all Stock Exchange listed businesses was 21.21 times, but Electricity was as low as 11.93 times and Pharmaceuticals and Biotechnology as high as 53.28 times.

TREND ANALYSIS

It is often helpful to see whether ratios are indicating trends. Key ratios can be plotted on a graph to provide a simple visual display of changes occurring over time. The trends occurring within a business may, for example, be plotted against trends for rival businesses or for the industry as a whole for comparison purposes. An example of trend analysis is shown in **Real World 6.9**.

REAL WORLD 6.9

Trend setting

In Figure 6.8, the current ratio of three of the UK's leading supermarkets is plotted over time. We can see that the current ratios of the three businesses have tended to move closer. Tesco plc was lower than that of its main rivals, until 2005, when it overtook Morrison and 2009, when it overtook Sainsbury. Since then Tesco's current ratio has decreased and is now, once again, lower than Sainsbury's. The current ratio of Sainsbury shows a fairly consistent downward path until 2009 after which it begins to fluctuate. Morrison has tended to maintain the lowest current ratio over time. With well-managed businesses like these, it is highly likely that any changes are the result of deliberate policy.

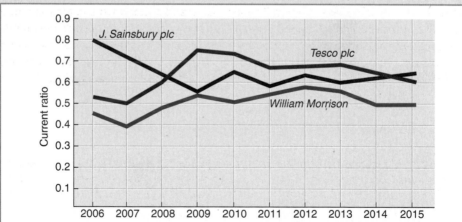

The current ratio for three leading UK supermarket businesses is plotted for the financial years ended during 2006–2015. This enables comparison to be made regarding the ratio, both for each of the three businesses over time and between the businesses.

Source: Ratios calculated from information in the annual reports of the three businesses for each of the years 2005 to 2015.

Figure 6.8 Graph plotting current ratio against time

USING RATIOS TO PREDICT FINANCIAL FAILURE

Financial ratios, based on current or past performance, are often used to help predict the future. Normally, both the choice of ratios and the interpretation of results are dependent on the judgement and opinion of the analyst. In recent years, however, attempts have been made to develop a more rigorous and systematic approach to the use of ratios for prediction purposes. In particular, researchers have shown an interest in the ability of ratios to predict the financial failure of a business.

By financial failure, we mean a business either being forced out of business or being severely adversely affected by its inability to meet its financial obligations. It is often referred to as 'going bust' or 'going bankrupt'. This is, of course, a likely area of concern for all those connected with the business.

LIMITATIONS OF RATIO ANALYSIS

Although ratios offer a quick and useful method of analysing the position and performance of a business, they are not without their problems and limitations. We shall now review some of their shortcomings.

Quality of financial statements

It must always be remembered that ratios are based on financial statements. The results of ratio analysis are, therefore, dependent on the quality of these underlying statements. Ratios will inherit the limitations of the financial statements on which they are based. In Chapter 2 we saw that one important limitation of financial statements is their failure to include all resources controlled by the business. Internally-generated goodwill and brands, for example, are excluded from the statement of financial position because they fail to meet the strict definition of an asset. This means that, even though these resources may be of considerable value, key ratios such as ROSF, ROCE and the gearing ratio will fail to acknowledge their presence.

Activity 6.28

Assume that a business has internally generated goodwill that had been created in earlier years. If this resource were introduced as a non-current asset with an indefinite life in the current statement of financial position, what would be the effect on ROSF, ROCE and the gearing ratio?

The effect of introducing internally-generated goodwill will be similar to that of an asset revaluation, which we considered in Chapter 2. Total assets will increase and equity will also increase. An increase in equity will increase the denominator (lower part of the fraction) for all three ratios. This will, in turn, lead to lower ratios than would be the case if the goodwill were not introduced.

There is also the problem of deliberate attempts to make the financial statements misleading. We discussed this problem of 'creative accounting' in Chapter 4.

Inflation

A persistent, though recently less severe, problem, in most countries is that the financial results of businesses can be distorted as a result of inflation. One effect of inflation is that the reported value of assets held for any length of time may bear little relation to current values. Generally speaking, the reported value of assets will be understated relative to current prices during a period of inflation. This occurs because they are usually reported at their original cost (less any amounts written off for depreciation). This means that comparisons, either between businesses or between periods, will be hindered. A difference in, say, ROCE may simply be owing to the fact that assets shown in one of the statements of financial position being compared were acquired more recently.

Another effect of inflation is to distort the measurement of profit. In the calculation of profit, sales revenue is often matched with costs incurred at an earlier time. This is because there is often a time lag between acquiring a particular resource and using it to help generate sales revenue. For example, inventories may well be acquired several months before they are sold. During a period of inflation, this will mean that the expense does not reflect prices that are current at the time of the sale. The cost of sales figure is usually based on the historic cost of the inventories concerned. As a result, expenses will be understated in the income statement and this, in turn, means that profit will be overstated. One effect of this will be to distort the profitability ratios discussed earlier.

The restricted view given by ratios

It is important not to rely exclusively on ratios, thereby losing sight of information contained in the underlying financial statements. As we saw earlier in this chapter, some items reported in these statements can be vital in assessing position and performance. For example, the total sales revenue, capital employed and profit figures may be useful in assessing changes in absolute size that occur over time, or in assessing differences in scale between businesses. Ratios do not provide such information. When comparing one figure with another, ratios measure *relative* performance and position and, therefore, provide only part of the picture. When comparing two businesses, therefore, it will often be useful to assess the absolute size of profits, as well as the relative profitability of each business. For example, Business A may generate £1 million operating profit and have a ROCE of 15 per cent and Business B may generate £100,000 operating profit and have a ROCE of 20 per cent. Although Business B has a higher level of *profitability,* as measured by ROCE, it generates lower total operating profits and that fact should not be overlooked.

The basis for comparison

We saw earlier that if ratios are to be useful they require a basis for comparison. Moreover, it is important that we compare like with like. Where the comparison is with another business, there can be difficulties. No two businesses are identical: the greater the differences between the businesses being compared, the greater are the limitations of ratio analysis. Furthermore, any differences in accounting policies, financing methods (gearing levels) and financial year-ends will add to the problems of making comparisons between businesses.

Statement of financial position ratios

Because the statement of financial position is only a 'snapshot' of the business at a particular moment in time, any ratios based on statement of financial position figures, such as the liquidity ratios, may not be representative of the financial position of the business for the year as a whole. It is common, for example, for a seasonal business to have a financial year-end that coincides with a low point in business activity. Inventories and trade receivables may therefore be low at the year-end. As a result, the liquidity ratios may also be low. A more representative picture of liquidity can only really be gained by taking additional measurements at other points in the year.

Real World 6.10 points out another way in which ratios are limited.

REAL WORLD 6.10

Remember, it's people that really count . . .

Lord Weinstock (1924–2002) was an influential industrialist whose management style and philosophy helped to shape management practice in many UK businesses. During his long and successful reign at GEC plc, a major engineering business, Lord Weinstock relied heavily on financial ratios to assess performance and to exercise control. In particular, he relied on ratios relating to sales revenue, expenses, trade receivables, profit margins and inventories turnover. However, he was keenly aware of the limitations of ratios and recognised that, ultimately, people produce profits.

In a memo written to GEC managers he pointed out that ratios are an aid to good management rather than a substitute for it. He wrote:

> The operating ratios are of great value as measures of efficiency but they are only the measures and not efficiency itself. Statistics will not design a product better, make it for a lower cost or increase sales. If ill-used, they may so guide action as to diminish resources for the sake of apparent but false signs of improvement.
>
> Management remains a matter of judgement, of knowledge of products and processes and of understanding and skill in dealing with people. The ratios will indicate how well all these things are being done and will show comparison with how they are done elsewhere. But they will tell us nothing about how to do them. That is what you are meant to do.

Source: Extract from *Arnold Weinstock and the Making of GEC*, Stephen Aris (Aurum Press, 1998), published in the *Sunday Times*, 22 February 1998, p. 3.

Both Ali plc and Bhaskar plc operate wholesale electrical stores throughout the UK. The financial statements of each business for the year ended 31 December last year are as follows:

Statements of financial position as at 31 December last year

	Ali plc £m	Bhaskar plc £m
ASSETS		
Non-current assets		
Property, plant and equipment (cost less depreciation)		
Land and buildings	360.0	510.0
Fixtures and fittings	87.0	91.2
	447.0	601.2
Current assets		
Inventories	592.0	403.0
Trade receivables	176.4	321.9
Cash at bank	84.6	91.6
	853.0	816.5
Total assets	1,300.0	1,417.7
EQUITY AND LIABILITIES		
Equity		
£1 ordinary shares	320.0	250.0
Retained earnings	367.6	624.6
	687.6	874.6
Non-current liabilities		
Borrowings – Loan notes	190.0	250.0
Current liabilities		
Trade payables	406.4	275.7
Taxation	16.0	17.4
	422.4	293.1
Total equity and liabilities	1,300.0	1,417.7

Income statements for the year ended 31 December last year

	Ali plc £m	Bhaskar plc £m
Revenue	1,478.1	1,790.4
Cost of sales	(1,018.3)	(1,214.9)
Gross profit	459.8	575.5
Operating expenses	(308.5)	(408.6)
Operating profit	151.3	166.9
Interest payable	(19.4)	(27.5)
Profit before taxation	131.9	139.4
Taxation	(32.0)	(34.8)
Profit for the year	99.9	104.6

All purchases and sales were on credit. The market values of a share in Ali plc and Bhaskar plc at the end of the year were £6.50 and £8.20, respectively.

Required:

For each business, calculate two ratios that are concerned with each of the following aspects:

- profitability;
- efficiency;
- liquidity;
- gearing;
- investment (ten ratios in total).

What can you conclude from the ratios that you have calculated?

The solution to this question can be found at the back of the book on page 528.

SUMMARY

The main points of this chapter may be summarised as follows:

Ratio analysis

- Compares two related figures, usually both from the same set of financial statements.
- Is an aid to understanding what the financial statements really mean.
- Is an inexact science so results must be interpreted cautiously.
- Usually requires the business's performance for past periods, the performance of similar businesses and/or planned performance as benchmark ratios.
- Can often benefit from a brief overview of the financial statements to provide insights that may not be revealed by ratios and/or may help in the interpretation of them.

Profitability ratios

- Are concerned with assessing the effectiveness of the business in generating profit.
- Most commonly found in practice are the return on ordinary shareholders' funds (ROSF), return on capital employed (ROCE), operating profit margin and gross profit margin.

Efficiency ratios

- Are concerned with assessing the efficiency of using assets/resources.
- Most commonly found in practice are the average inventories turnover period, average settlement period for trade receivables, average settlement period for trade payables, sales revenue to capital employed and sales revenue per employee.

Liquidity ratios

- Are concerned with assessing the ability to meet short-term obligations.
- Most commonly found in practice are the current ratio and the acid test ratio.

Gearing ratios

- Are concerned with assessing the relationship between equity and debt financing.
- Most commonly found in practice are the gearing ratio and interest cover ratio.

Investment ratios

- Are concerned with assessing returns to shareholders.
- Most commonly found in practice are the dividend payout ratio, the dividend yield ratio, earnings per share (EPS) and the price/earnings ratio.

Uses of ratios

- Individual ratios can be tracked to detect trends, for example by plotting them on a graph.
- Ratios can be used to detect signs of overtrading.
- Ratios can be used to predict financial failure.

Limitations of ratio analysis

- Ratios are only as reliable as the financial statements from which they derive.
- Inflation can distort the information.
- Ratios give a restricted view.
- It can be difficult to find a suitable benchmark (for example, another business) to compare with.
- Some ratios could mislead due to the 'snapshot' nature of the statement of financial position.

KEY TERMS

For definitions of these terms, see Appendix A.

FURTHER READING

If you would like to explore the topics covered in this chapter in more depth, try the following books:

Cope, A., Robinson, T., Henry, E., Pirie, W. and Broihahn, M. (2015) *International Financial Statement Analysis,* 3rd edn, CFA Institute, Chapter 7.

Elliott, B. and Elliott, J. (2015) *Financial Accounting and Reporting,* 17th edn, Pearson, Chapters 28 and 29.

Schoenebeck, K. and Holtzman, M. (2012) *Interpreting and Analyzing Financial Statements,* 6th edn, Prentice Hall, Chapters 2 to 5.

Subramanyam, K. and Wild, J. (2015) *Financial Statement Analysis,* 11th edn, McGraw-Hill Higher Education, Chapters 6 and 8.

? REVIEW QUESTIONS

Solutions to these questions can be found at the back of the book on page 541.

6.1 Some businesses operate on a low operating profit margin (for example, a supermarket chain). Does this mean that the return on capital employed from the business will also be low?

6.2 What potential problems arise particularly for the external analyst from the use of statement of financial position figures in the calculation of financial ratios?

6.3 Two businesses operate in the same industry. One has an inventories turnover period that is longer than the industry average. The other has an inventories turnover period that is shorter than the industry average. Give three possible explanations for each business's inventories turnover period ratio.

6.4 In the chapter it was mentioned that ratios help to eliminate some of the problems of comparing businesses of different sizes. Does this mean that size is irrelevant when interpreting and analysing the position and performance of different businesses?

EXERCISES

Exercises 6.1 and 6.2 are basic level. Exercise 6.3 is intermediate level and Exercises 6.4 and 6.5 are advanced level. Those with **coloured numbers** have solutions at the back of the book, starting on page 559.

6.1 Set out below are ratios relating to three different businesses. Each business operates within a different industrial sector.

Ratio	A plc	B plc	C plc
Operating profit margin	3.6%	9.7%	6.8%
Sales to capital employed	2.4 times	3.1 times	1.7 times
Average inventories turnover period	18 days	–*	44 days
Average settlement period for trade receivables	2 days	12 days	26 days
Current ratio	0.8 times	0.6 times	1.5 times

*There is no average inventories ratio calculated for B Ltd because it holds no inventories.

Required:

State, with reasons, which one of the three businesses is:
(a) A holiday tour operator
(b) A supermarket chain
(c) A food manufacturer.

6.2 Amsterdam Ltd and Berlin Ltd are both wholesalers serving broadly the same market, but they seem to take a different approach to it according to the following information:

Ratio	Amsterdam Ltd	Berlin Ltd
Return on capital employed (ROCE)	20%	17%
Return on ordinary shareholders' funds (ROSF)	30%	18%
Average settlement period for trade receivables	63 days	21 days
Average settlement period for trade payables	50 days	45 days
Gross profit margin	40%	15%
Operating profit margin	10%	10%
Average inventories turnover period	52 days	25 days

Required:
Describe what this information indicates about the differences in approach between the two businesses. If one of them prides itself on customer service and one of them on competitive prices, which do you think is which and why?

6.3 The directors of Helena Beauty Products Ltd have been presented with the following abridged financial statements:

Helena Beauty Products Ltd
Income statement for the year ended 31 December

	Year before last £000	Year before last £000	Last year £000	Last year £000
Sales revenue		3,600		3,840
Cost of sales				
Opening inventories	320		400	
Purchases	2,240		2,350	
	2,560		2,750	
Closing inventories	(4 00)	(2,160)	(500)	(2,250)
Gross profit		1,440		1,590
Expenses		(1,360)		(1,500)
Operating profit		80		90
Corporation tax		(15)		(20)
Profit before taxation		65		70
Interest payable		–		–
Profit for the year		65		70

Statement of financial position as at 31 December

	Year before last £000	Last year £000
ASSETS		
Non-current assets		
Property, plant and equipment	1,900	1,860
Current assets		
Inventories	400	500
Trade receivables	750	960
Cash at bank	8	4
	1,158	1,464
Total assets	3,058	3,324
EQUITY AND LIABILITIES		
Equity		
£1 ordinary shares	1,650	1,700
Share premium account	-	116
Retained earnings	1,018	1,058
	2,668	2,874
Current liabilities	390	450
Total equity and liabilities	3,058	3,324

Required:

Using six ratios, comment on the profitability (three ratios) and efficiency (three ratios) of the business.

6.4 Threads Limited manufactures nuts and bolts, which are sold to industrial users. The abbreviated financial statements for each of the last two years are as follows:

Income statements for the year ended 31 December

	Year before last £000	Last year £000
Revenue	1,180	1,200
Cost of sales	(680)	(750)
Gross profit	500	450
Operating expenses	(200)	(208)
Depreciation	(66)	(75)
Operating profit	234	167
Interest	(–)	(8)
Profit before taxation	234	159
Taxation	(80)	(48)
Profit for the year	154	111

Statements of financial position as at 31 December

	Year before last £000	Last year £000
ASSETS		
Non-current assets		
Property, plant and equipment	702	687
Current assets		
Inventories	148	236
Trade receivables	102	156
Cash	3	4
	253	396
Total assets	955	1,083
EQUITY AND LIABILITIES		
Equity		
Ordinary share capital (£1 shares, fully paid)	500	500
Retained earnings	256	295
	756	795
Non-current liabilities		
Borrowings – Bank loan	–	50
Current liabilities		
Trade payables	60	76
Other payables and accruals	18	16
Taxation	40	24
Short-term borrowings (all bank overdraft)	81	122
	199	238
Total equity and liabilities	955	1,083

Dividends were paid on ordinary shares of £70,000 and £72,000 in respect of the year before last and last year, respectively.

Required:

(a) Calculate the following financial ratios for *both* years (using year-end figures for statement of financial position items):

- return on capital employed
- operating profit margin
- gross profit margin
- current ratio
- acid test ratio
- settlement period for trade receivables
- settlement period for trade payables
- inventories turnover period.

(b) Comment on the performance of Threads Limited from the viewpoint of a business considering supplying a substantial amount of goods to Threads Limited on usual trade credit terms.

6.5 The financial statements for Harridges plc are given below for the two years ended 31 December for each of the last two years. Harridges plc operates a large chain of retail stores.

Harridges plc
Income statement for the years ended 31 December

	Year before last	Last year
	£m	£m
Sales revenue	2,600	3,500
Cost of sales	(1,560)	(2,350)
Gross profit	1,040	1,150
Wages and salaries	(320)	(350)
Overheads	(260)	(200)
Depreciation	(150)	(250)
Operating profit	310	350
Interest payable	(50)	(50)
Profit before taxation	260	300
Taxation	(105)	(125)
Profit for the year	155	175

Statement of financial position as at 31 December

	Year before last £m	Last year £m
ASSETS		
Non-current assets		
Property, plant and equipment	1,265	1,525
Current assets		
Inventories	250	400
Trade receivables	105	145
Cash at bank	380	115
	735	660
Total assets	2,000	2,185
EQUITY AND LIABILITIES		
Equity		
Share capital: £1 shares fully paid	490	490
Share premium	260	260
Retained earnings	350	450
	1,100	1,200
Non-current liabilities		
Borrowings – 10% loan notes	500	500
Current liabilities		
Trade payables	300	375
Other payables	100	110
	400	485
Total equity and liabilities	2,000	2,185

Dividends were paid on ordinary shares of £65 million and £75 million in respect of the year before last and last year, respectively.

Required:
(a) Choose and calculate eight ratios that would be helpful in assessing the performance of Harridges plc. Use end-of-year values and calculate ratios for both years.
(b) Using the ratios calculated in (a) and any others you consider helpful, comment on the business's performance from the viewpoint of a prospective purchaser of a majority of shares.

PART TWO

MANAGEMENT ACCOUNTING

Chapter 7

THE RELEVANCE AND BEHAVIOUR OF COSTS

INTRODUCTION

In this chapter, we shall consider the relevance of costs when making management decisions. Not all costs (and revenues) that appear to be linked to a business decision may actually be relevant to it. It is important to distinguish between costs (and revenues) that are relevant and those that are not. Failure to do this can lead to poor decisions being made.

We shall also consider the behaviour of cost in the face of changes in activity. Broadly, cost can be analysed between an element that is fixed in relation to the volume of activity and an element that varies according to the volume of activity. We shall see how knowledge of the way in which costs behave can be used to make short-term decisions and to assess risk.

The principles outlined here will provide the basis for much of the rest of the book.

Learning outcomes

When you have completed this chapter, you should be able to:

- define and distinguish between relevant costs, outlay costs and opportunity costs;

- distinguish between fixed cost and variable cost and use this distinction to explain the relationship between cost, volume and profit;

- deduce the break-even point for some activity and discuss its usefulness;

- demonstrate the way in which marginal analysis can be used when making short-term decisions.

WHAT IS MEANT BY 'COST'?

Cost represents the amount sacrificed to achieve a particular business objective. Measuring cost may seem, at first sight, to be a straightforward process: it is simply the amount paid for the item of goods being supplied or the service being provided. When measuring cost *for decision-making purposes,* however, things are not quite that simple. The following activity illustrates why this is the case.

Activity 7.1

You own a motor car, for which you paid a purchase price of £5,000 – much below the list price – at a recent car auction. You have just been offered £6,000 for this car.

What is the cost to you of keeping the car for your own use? *Note:* Ignore running costs and so on; just consider the 'capital' cost of the car.

By retaining the car, you are forgoing a cash receipt of £6,000. Thus, the real sacrifice, or cost, incurred by keeping the car for your own use is £6,000.

Any decision that is made with respect to the car's future should logically take account of this figure. This cost is known as the 'opportunity cost' since it is the value of the opportunity forgone in order to pursue the other course of action. (In this case, the other course of action is to retain the car.)

We can see that the cost of retaining the car is not the same as the purchase price. In one sense, of course, the cost of the car in Activity 7.1 is £5,000 because that is how much was paid for it. However, this cost, which for obvious reasons is known as the **historic cost**, is only of academic interest. It cannot logically ever be used to make a decision on the car's future.

If we disagree with this point, we should ask ourselves how we should assess an offer of £5,500, from another person, for the car. The answer is that we should compare the offer price of £5,500 with the **opportunity cost** of £6,000. This amount represents the value of being deprived of the next best opportunity by pursuing a particular course of action. By making this comparison, we should reject the offer as it is less than the £6,000 opportunity cost. In these circumstances, it would not be logical to accept the offer of £5,500 on the basis that it was more than the £5,000 that we originally paid. (The only other figure that should concern us is the value to us, in terms of pleasure, usefulness and so on, of retaining the car. If we valued this more highly than the £6,000 opportunity cost, we should reject both offers.)

We may still feel, however, that the £5,000 is relevant here because it will help us in assessing the profitability of the decision. If we sold the car, we should make a profit of either £500 (£5,500 − £5,000) or £1,000 (£6,000 − £5,000) depending on which offer we accept. Since we should aim to make the higher profit, the right decision is to sell the car for £6,000. However, we do not need to know the historic cost of the car to make the right decision. What decision should we make if the car cost us £4,000 to buy? Clearly we should still sell the car for £6,000 rather than for £5,500 as the important comparison is between the offer price and the opportunity cost.

Activity 7.2

Assume that the car cost £10,000. Would this alter the relevance of the historic cost?

Even in this case, the historic cost would still be irrelevant. Had we just bought a car for £10,000 and found that shortly after it is only worth £6,000, we may well be fuming with rage at our mistake, but this does not make the £10,000 relevant to the present decision.

Whatever the historic cost of the car, we should reach the same conclusion. The only relevant factors, in a decision on whether to sell the car or to keep it, are the £6,000 opportunity cost and the value of the benefits of keeping it. Thus, the historic cost can never be a **relevant cost** regarding a future decision.

To say that historic cost is an **irrelevant cost** is not to say that *the effects of having incurred that cost* are always irrelevant. The fact that we own the car, and are thus in a position to exercise choice as to how to use it, is not irrelevant. It is absolutely relevant.

Opportunity costs are rarely taken into account in financial accounting, as they do not involve any out-of-pocket expenditure. They are normally only calculated where they are relevant to a particular management decision. Historic costs, on the other hand, do involve out-of-pocket expenditure and are recorded. They are used in preparing the annual financial statements, such as the statement of financial position and the income statement. This is logical, however, since these statements are intended to be accounts of what has actually happened and are drawn up after the event.

RELEVANT COSTS: OPPORTUNITY AND OUTLAY COSTS

We have just seen that, when we are making decisions concerning the future, **past costs** (that is, historic costs) are irrelevant. It is future opportunity costs and future **outlay costs** (future amounts spent to achieve an objective) that are of concern. In more formal terms, we can say that, to be relevant to a particular decision, a cost must satisfy all three of the following criteria:

1 *It must relate to the objectives of the business.* Businesses exist primarily to increase their owners' (shareholders) wealth. Thus, to be relevant to a particular decision, a cost must relate to this wealth objective.
2 *It must be a future cost.* Past costs cannot be relevant to decisions being made about the future.
3 *It must vary with the decision.* Only costs (and revenues) that differ between outcomes are relevant.

To illustrate the final criterion, let us take the example of a road haulage business that has decided to buy an additional lorry and the final decision lies between two different models. The load capacity, fuel costs and maintenance costs are different for each lorry.

These potential revenues and costs are all relevant items. The lorry will require a driver, who will need to be employed, but a suitably qualified driver could drive either lorry for the same wage. Thus the cost of employing the driver will be irrelevant to the decision as to which lorry to buy. This is despite the fact that this cost is a future one.

Activity 7.3

Assume that the decision did not concern a choice between two models of lorry but rather whether to operate an additional lorry or not. Would this make a difference to the view taken concerning the cost of employing a driver?

In this case, the cost of employing the additional driver would be relevant. It would now be a cost that would vary with the decision made.

Figure 7.1 shows a decision flow diagram for deciding which costs are relevant.

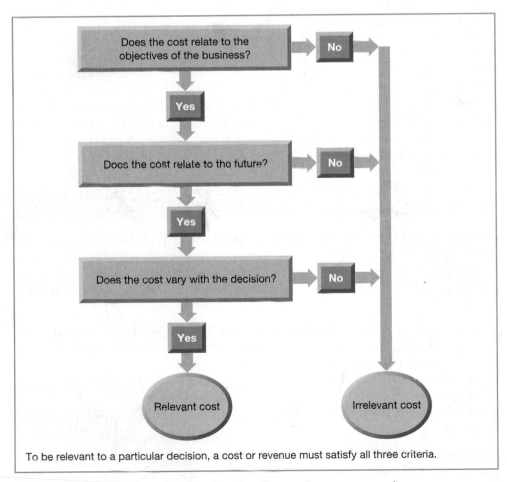

To be relevant to a particular decision, a cost or revenue must satisfy all three criteria.

Figure 7.1 Decision flow diagram for identifying relevant costs and revenues

A garage business has an old car that it bought several months ago. The car needs a replacement engine before it can be driven. It is possible to buy a reconditioned engine for £300. This would take seven hours to fit by a mechanic who is paid £15 an hour. At present the garage is short of work but the owners are reluctant to lay off any mechanics or even to cut down their basic working week. This is because skilled labour is difficult to find and an upturn in repair work is expected soon.

The garage paid £3,000 to buy the car. Without the engine it could be sold for an estimated £3,500. What is the minimum price at which the garage should sell the car with a reconditioned engine fitted?

The minimum price is the amount required to cover the relevant costs of the job. At this price, the business will make neither a profit nor a loss. Any price that is lower than this amount will mean that the wealth of the business is reduced. Thus, the minimum price is:

	£
Opportunity cost of the car	3,500
Cost of the reconditioned engine	300
Total	3,800

Note that in Activity 7.4, the original cost of the car is irrelevant for the reasons already discussed. It is the opportunity cost of the car that concerns us. The cost of the new engine is relevant because, if the work is done, the garage will have to pay £300 for the engine, but will pay nothing if the job is not done. The £300 is an example of a future outlay cost.

Labour cost is irrelevant because the same cost will be incurred whether the mechanic undertakes the engine-replacement work or not. This is because the mechanic is being paid to do nothing if this job is not undertaken; thus the additional labour cost arising from this job is zero.

It should be emphasised that the garage will not seek to sell the car with its reconditioned engine for £3,800. It will try to charge as much as possible for it. However, any price above £3,800 will make the garage better off financially than if the engine replacement had not been undertaken.

Assume exactly the same circumstances as in Activity 7.4, except that the garage is busy at the moment. If a mechanic undertakes the engine-replacement job, it will mean that other work the mechanic could have done during the seven hours, and which could have been charged to a customer, will not be undertaken. The garage's labour charge is £60 an hour, although the mechanic is only paid £15 an hour.

What is the minimum price at which the garage should sell the car, with a reconditioned engine fitted, under these altered circumstances?

The minimum price is:

	£
Opportunity cost of the car	3,500
Cost of the reconditioned engine	300
Labour cost (7 × £60)	420
Total	4,220

In Activity 7.5, we can see that the opportunity cost of the car and the cost of the engine are the same as they were in Activity 7.4, but a charge for labour has been added to obtain the minimum price. There, the relevant labour cost is that which the garage will have to sacrifice in making the time available to undertake the engine-replacement job. While the mechanic is working on this job, the garage is losing the opportunity to do work for which a customer would pay £420. Note that the £15 an hour mechanic's wage is still not relevant. The mechanic will be paid £15 an hour irrespective of whether it is the engine-replacement work or some other job that is undertaken.

Real World 7.1 is based on a *Financial Times* article that discusses the financial benefit of having a university education. When assessing this benefit, opportunity costs must be taken into account.

REAL WORLD 7.1

Gaining by degrees

There is a considerable amount of conjecture and anxiety as to whether a university education represents good value for money. With tuition fees in the US having more than tripled, when adjusted for inflation, since the 1970s, potential students and their parents are questioning the value of a degree. With tuition fees going in the same direction in the UK and in many other countries, this is now a key issue for very many people worldwide.

According to a research study carried out by two US statisticians, things are not necessarily as gloomy as they look. The study concluded that the inflation-adjusted value of a university education has remained close to its all-time high, despite soaring tuition fees and the downturn in employment prospects following the economic recession that started in 2008. The study showed that a university degree is worth a net $300,000. This is calculated as the additional lifetime earning power of graduates over their non-graduate counterparts, less fees and other costs, including the opportunity cost of earning little or nothing during their student days, compared with their non-student equivalents.

As the FT article says:

> While the political controversy focuses on tuition fees, by far the largest component of the cost of higher education is the opportunity cost of being out of the labour force for four years, and that has actually shrunk in real terms because of the decline in the earnings power of those without a degree.

FT *Source*: Based on Foley, S. (2014), 'Is a university degree a good investment?', ft.com, 7 September.

COST BEHAVIOUR

Costs incurred by a business may be classified in various ways and one useful way is according to how they behave in relation to changes in the volume of activity. Costs may be classified according to whether they:

- remain constant (fixed) when changes occur to the volume of activity; or
- vary according to the volume of activity.

These are known as **fixed costs** and **variable costs** respectively. Thus, in the case of a restaurant, part of the manager's salary would normally be a fixed cost of a particular meal while the cost of the unprepared food would be a variable cost.

As we shall see, knowing how much of each type of cost is associated with a particular activity can be of great value to the decision maker.

FIXED COST

The way in which a fixed cost behaves can be shown by preparing a graph that plots the fixed cost of a business against the level of activity, as in Figure 7.2. The distance 0F represents the amount of fixed cost, and this stays the same irrespective of the volume of activity.

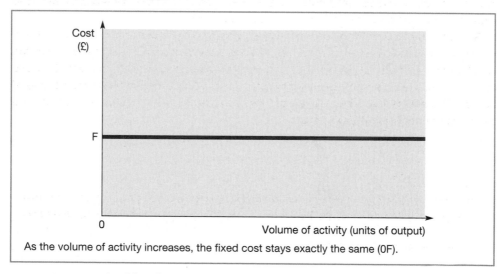

As the volume of activity increases, the fixed cost stays exactly the same (0F).

Figure 7.2 Graph of fixed cost against the volume of activity

Activity 7.6

Can you give some examples of items of cost that are likely to be fixed for a hairdressing business?

We came up with the following:

- rent;
- insurance;
- cleaning cost;
- employee salaries.

These items of cost are likely to be the same irrespective of the number of customers having their hair cut or styled.

Employee salaries (or wages) are sometimes assumed to be a variable cost. In practice, however, they tend to be fixed. Employees are not normally paid according to the volume of output and it is unusual to dismiss them when there is a temporary downturn in activity. Where there is, or at least appears to be, a permanent downturn, redundancies may be made with fixed-cost savings. This, however, is true of all types of fixed cost. For example, management may decide to close some branches to make rental cost savings.

Whether labour cost is fixed or variable depends on the particular terms of employment. There are circumstances in which the labour cost is variable (that is, where employees are paid according to how much output they produce), but this is unusual.

It is important to be clear that 'fixed', in this context, means only that the cost is unaffected by changes in the volume of activity. Fixed cost is likely to be affected by inflation. If rent (a typical fixed cost) goes up because of inflation, a fixed cost will have increased, but not because of a change in the volume of activity.

Similarly, the level of fixed cost does not stay the same, irrespective of the time period involved. Fixed cost elements are almost always *time based:* that is, they vary with the length of time concerned. The rental charge for two months is normally twice that for one month. Thus, fixed cost normally varies with time, but (of course) not with the volume of output. This means that when we talk of fixed cost being, say, £1,000, we must add the period concerned, say, £1,000 a month.

Activity 7.7

Does fixed cost stay the same irrespective of the volume of output, even where there is a massive rise in that volume? Think in terms of the rent cost for the hairdressing business.

No. The fixed cost is likely to increase.

In fact, the rent is only fixed over a particular range (known as the 'relevant' range). If the number of people wanting to have their hair cut by the business increased, and the business wished to meet this increased demand, it would eventually have to expand its physical size. This might be achieved by opening an additional branch, or perhaps by moving the existing business to larger accommodation nearby. It may be possible to cope with relatively minor increases in activity by using existing space more efficiently, or by having longer opening hours. If activity continued to expand, however, increased rent charges would seem inevitable.

In practice, the situation described in Activity 7.7 would look something like Figure 7.3.

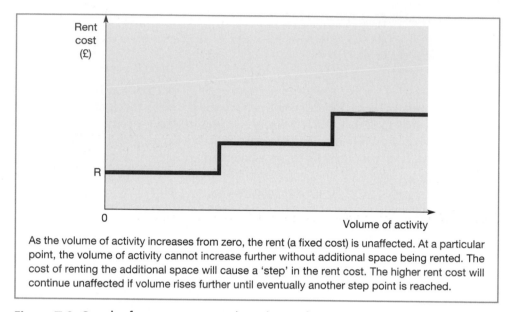

As the volume of activity increases from zero, the rent (a fixed cost) is unaffected. At a particular point, the volume of activity cannot increase further without additional space being rented. The cost of renting the additional space will cause a 'step' in the rent cost. The higher rent cost will continue unaffected if volume rises further until eventually another step point is reached.

Figure 7.3 Graph of rent cost against the volume of activity

At lower volumes of activity, the rent cost shown in Figure 7.3 would be 0R. As the volume of activity expands, the accommodation becomes inadequate and further expansion requires an increase in the size of the accommodation and, therefore, its cost. This higher level of accommodation provision will enable further expansion to take place. Eventually, additional cost will need to be incurred if further expansion is to occur. Elements of fixed cost that behave in this way are often referred to as **stepped fixed costs**.

VARIABLE COST

We saw earlier that variable cost varies with the volume of activity. In a manufacturing business, for example, this would include the cost of raw materials used.

Variable cost can be represented graphically as in Figure 7.4. At zero volume of activity, the variable cost is zero. It then increases in a straight line as activity increases.

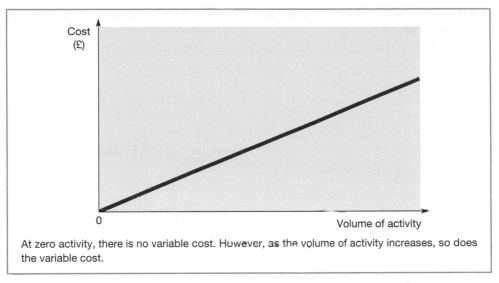

At zero activity, there is no variable cost. However, as the volume of activity increases, so does the variable cost.

Figure 7.4 Graph of variable cost against the volume of activity

As with many types of business activity, the variable cost incurred by hairdressers tends to be low in comparison with the fixed cost: that is, fixed cost tends to make up the bulk of total cost.

The straight line for variable cost, in Figure 7.4, implies that this type of cost will be the same per unit of activity, irrespective of the volume of activity. We shall consider the practicality of this assumption a little later in this chapter.

SEMI-FIXED (SEMI-VARIABLE) COST

In some cases, a particular cost has an element of both fixed and variable cost. These can be described as **semi-fixed (semi-variable) costs**. An example might be the electricity cost for the hairdressing business. Some of this will be for heating and lighting, and this part is probably fixed, at least until the volume of activity expands to a point where longer opening hours or larger accommodation is necessary. The other part of the cost will vary with the volume of activity. Here we are talking about such things as power for hairdryers.

Analysing semi-fixed (semi-variable) costs into the fixed and variable elements is a relatively easy matter in practice.

FINDING THE BREAK-EVEN POINT

Armed with knowledge of how much each element of cost represents for a particular product or service, it is possible to make predictions regarding total and per-unit cost at various projected levels of output. This information can be very useful to decision makers. Much of the rest of this chapter will be devoted to seeing how it can be useful, starting with **break-even analysis**.

If, for a particular product or service, we know the fixed cost for a period and the variable cost per unit, we can produce a graph like the one shown in Figure 7.5. This graph shows the total cost over the possible range of volume of activity.

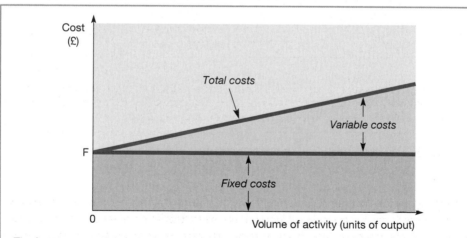

The bottom part of the graph represents the fixed cost element. To this is added the wedge-shaped top portion, which represents the variable cost. The two parts together represent total cost. At zero activity, the variable cost is zero, so total cost equals fixed cost. As activity increases, so does total cost, but only because variable cost increases. We are assuming that there are no steps in the fixed cost.

Figure 7.5 Graph of total cost against the volume of activity

The bottom part of Figure 7.5 shows the fixed cost area. Added to this is the variable cost, the wedge-shaped portion at the top of the graph. The uppermost line represents the total cost over a range of volume of activity. For any particular volume, the total cost can be measured by the vertical distance between the graph's horizontal axis and the relevant point on the uppermost line.

Logically, the total cost at zero activity is the amount of the fixed cost. This is because, even where there is nothing happening, the business will still be paying rent, salaries and so on, at least in the short term. On the other hand, no variable cost will be incurred. As the volume of activity increases from zero, the fixed cost is augmented by the relevant variable cost to give the total cost.

If we take this total cost graph in Figure 7.5, and superimpose on it a line representing total revenue over the range of volume of activity, we obtain the **break-even chart**. This is shown in Figure 7.6.

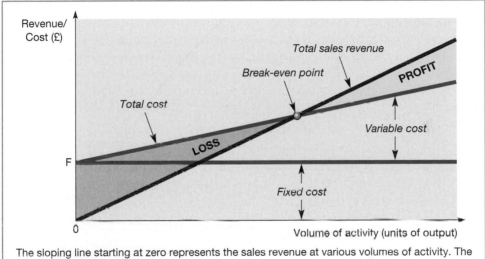

The sloping line starting at zero represents the sales revenue at various volumes of activity. The point at which this finally catches up with the sloping total cost line, which starts at F, is the break-even point (BEP). Below this point a loss is made, above it a profit.

Figure 7.6 Break-even chart

Note in Figure 7.6 that, at zero volume of activity (zero sales), there is zero sales revenue. The profit (loss), which is the difference between total sales revenue and total cost, for a particular volume of activity, is the vertical distance between the total sales revenue line and the total cost line at that volume of activity. Where there is no vertical distance between these two lines (total sales revenue equals total cost) the volume of activity is at **break-even point (BEP)**. At this point there is neither profit nor loss; that is, the activity *breaks even*. Where the volume of activity is below BEP, a loss will be incurred because total cost exceeds total sales revenue. Where the business operates at a volume of activity above BEP, there will be a profit because total sales revenue will exceed total cost. The further the volume of activity is below BEP, the higher the loss: the further above BEP it is, the higher the profit.

Deducing BEPs graphically is a laborious business. Since, however, the relationships in the graph are all linear (that is, the lines are all straight), it is easy to calculate the BEP.

We know that at BEP (but not at any other volume of activity):

Total sales revenue = Total cost

(At all other volumes of activity except the BEP, either total sales revenue will exceed total cost or the other way round. Only at BEP are they equal.) The above formula can be expanded so that:

Total sales revenue = Fixed cost + Variable cost

If we call the number of units of output at BEP *b,* then

$$b \times \text{Sales revenue per unit} = \text{Fixed cost} + (b \times \text{Variable cost per unit})$$

so:

$$(b \times \text{Sales revenue per unit}) - (b \times \text{Variable cost per unit}) = \text{Fixed cost}$$

and:

$$b \times (\text{Sales revenue per unit} - \text{Variable cost per unit}) = \text{Fixed cost}$$

giving:

$$b = \frac{\text{Fixed cost}}{\text{Sales revenue per unit} - \text{Variable cost per unit}}$$

If we look back at the break-even chart in Figure 7.6, this formula seems logical. The total cost line starts off at point F, higher than the starting point for the total sales revenue line (zero) by amount F (the amount of the fixed cost). Because the sales revenue per unit is greater than the variable cost per unit, the sales revenue line will gradually catch up with the total cost line. The rate at which it will catch up is dependent on the relative steepness of the two lines. Bearing in mind that the slopes of the two lines are the variable cost per unit and the selling price per unit, the above equation for calculating *b* looks perfectly logical.

Though the BEP can be calculated quickly and simply without resorting to graphs, this does not mean that the break-even chart is without value. The chart clearly shows the relationship between cost, volume and profit over a range of activity and in a form that can easily be understood by non-financial managers. The break-even chart can therefore be a useful device for explaining this relationship.

Example 7.1

Cottage Industries Ltd makes baskets. The fixed cost of operating the workshop for a month totals £500. Each basket requires materials that cost £2 and takes one hour to make. The business pays the basket makers £10 an hour. The basket makers are all on contracts such that if they do not work for any reason, they are not paid. The baskets are sold to a wholesaler for £14 each.

What is the BEP for basket making for the business?

Solution

The BEP (in number of baskets) is:

$$\text{BEP} = \frac{\text{Fixed cost}}{(\text{Sales revenue per unit} - \text{Variable cost per unit})}$$

$$= \frac{£500}{£14 - (£2 + £10)}$$

$$= 250 \text{ baskets per month}$$

Note that the BEP must be expressed with respect to a period of time.

Real World 7.2 shows information on the BEPs of two well-known businesses.

REAL WORLD 7.2

BE at Ryanair (and BA)

Commercial airlines seem to pay a lot of attention to their BEPs and their 'load factors', that is, their actual level of activity. A load factor of 88 per cent means that, on average, the planes were flying with 88 per cent of the seats occupied by a paying customer. A BEP of 72 per cent means that the flight would break even with only 72 per cent occupancy.

Figure 7.7 shows the BEPs and load factors for Ryanair, the 'no frills' carrier, for recent years.

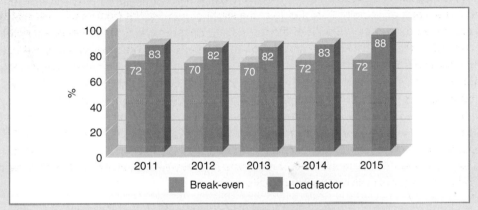

Figure 7.7 Break-even points and load factors at Ryanair

We can see that Ryanair made operating profits, in each of the five years considered. This is because the airline's load factor was consistently greater than its BEP. Over recent years, Ryanair's BEPs and load factors have been remarkably consistent. In 2015, however, while the BEP stayed in line with recent previous years, the load factor was significantly higher.

Unlike Ryanair, most airlines do not publish their break-even points. British Airways plc (BA) used to do so. In the most recent year that BA disclosed, its BEP (2008) it was 64 per cent, with a load factor of 71 per cent. Those figures were quite typical of BA's results during the years immediately preceding 2008.

Ryanair's 2015 surge in profit has been linked to its more customer-friendly approach. This prompted Michael O'Leary, the business's chief executive, to say: If I'd only known that being nice to customers was going to be so good for my business I would have done it years ago.

Sources: Based on information contained in the Ryanair Holdings plc, Annual Report 2015; British Airways plc, Annual Report 2008; and Bloomberg Business (2015), www.bloomberg.com, 26 May.

Activity 7.9

In Real World 7.2, we saw that Ryanair's break-even point varied from one year to the next. Why wasn't it exactly the same each year?

The break-even point depends on three broad factors. These are: sales revenue, variable cost and fixed cost. Each if these can vary quite significantly from one year to another.

In the case of Ryanair, sales revenue could be greatly affected by the level of disposable income among the travelling public and/or by levels of competition from other airlines. Costs can vary from one year to another, particularly the cost of aviation fuel. [Interestingly, Ryanair's average fuel cost was €2.45 per gallon in 2014, but only €1.76 per gallon in 2011.]

Activity 7.10

Can you think of reasons why the managers of a business might find it useful to know the BEP of some activity that they are planning to undertake?

By knowing the BEP, it is possible to compare the expected, or planned, volume of activity with the BEP and so make a judgement about risk. If the volume of activity is expected to be only just above the break-even point, this may suggest that it is a risky venture. Only a small fall from the expected volume of activity could lead to a loss.

Activity 7.11

Cottage Industries Ltd (see Example 7.1) expects to sell 500 baskets a month. The business has the opportunity to rent a basket-making machine. Doing so would increase the total fixed cost of operating the workshop for a month to £3,000. Using the machine would reduce the labour time to half an hour per basket. The basket makers would still be paid £10 an hour.

(a) How much profit would the business make each month from selling baskets:
 - without the machine; and
 - with the machine?
(b) What is the BEP if the machine is rented?
(c) What do you notice about the figures that you calculate?

(a) Estimated monthly profit from basket making:

	Without the machine		With the machine	
	£	£	£	£
Sales revenue (500 × £14)		7,000		7,000
Materials (500 × £2)	(1,000)		(1,000)	
Labour (500 × 1 × £10)	(5,000)			
(500 × ½ × £10)			(2,500)	
Fixed cost	(500)		(3,000)	
		(6,500)		(6,500)
Profit		500		500

(b) The BEP (in number of baskets) with the machine:

$$\text{BEP} = \frac{\text{Fixed cost}}{(\text{Sales revenue per unit} - \text{Variable cost per unit})}$$

$$= \frac{£3,000}{£14 - (£2 + £5)}$$

$$= 429 \text{ baskets a month}$$

The BEP without the machine is 250 baskets per month (see Example 7.1).

(c) There seems to be nothing to choose between the two manufacturing strategies regarding profit, at the expected sales volume. There is, however, a distinct difference between the two strategies regarding the BEP. Without the machine, the actual volume of sales could fall by a half of that which is expected (from 500 to 250) before the business would fail to make a profit. With the machine, however, just a 14 per cent fall (from 500 to 429) would be enough to cause the business to fail to make a profit. On the other hand, for each additional basket sold above the estimated 500, an additional profit of only £2 (that is, £14 − (£2 + £10)) would be made without the machine, whereas £7 (that is, £14 − (£2 + £5)) would be made with the machine. (Note that knowledge of the BEP and the planned volume of activity gives some basis for assessing the riskiness of the activity.)

Real World 7.3 discusses the effect of reduced selling prices and high extraction costs of oil.

Not oiling the wheels

The reduction in oil prices during 2014 and 2015 is a serious problem for many of the world's oil producers. Figure 7.8 shows the current price of crude oil, in September 2015, compared with the price at which various oil producers would break even, given their production costs.

At the September 2015 crude oil market price, only onshore Middle East oil is profitable. This is a cause of great concern for businesses producing crude oil elsewhere in the world. A large proportion of oil producers' costs tend to be fixed. Many of the North American shale oil 'frackers' are new businesses established when the oil price was very much higher.

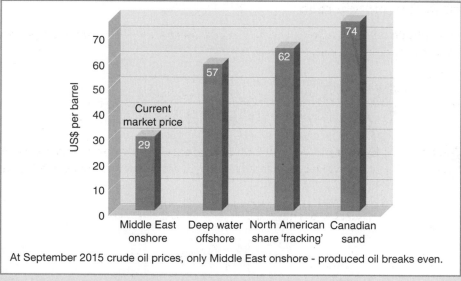

At September 2015 crude oil prices, only Middle East onshore - produced oil breaks even.

Figure 7.8 Break-even prices of crude oil production

Source: Information taken from Crooks, E. (2015), 'Takeover activity in the oil industry shows signs of revival', ft.com, 23 June.

We shall take a closer look at the relationship between fixed cost, variable cost and profit together with any advice that we might give the management of Cottage Industries Ltd after we have briefly considered the notion of contribution.

CONTRIBUTION

The bottom part of the break-even formula (sales revenue per unit less variable cost per unit) is known as the **contribution per unit**. Thus, for the basket-making activity, without the machine the contribution per unit is £2 and with the machine it is £7. This can be quite a useful figure to know in a decision-making context. It is called 'contribution' because it contributes to meeting the fixed cost and, if there is any excess, it then contributes to profit.

We shall see, a little later in this chapter, how knowing the amount of the contribution generated by a particular activity can be valuable when making short-term decisions, as well as being useful in the BEP calculation.

Contribution margin ratio

The **contribution margin ratio** is the contribution from an activity expressed as a percentage of the sales revenue, thus:

$$\text{Contribution margin ratio} = \frac{\text{Contribution}}{\text{Sales revenue}} \times 100\%$$

Contribution and sales revenue can both be expressed in per-unit or total terms. For Cottage Industries Ltd (Example 7.1 and Activity 7.11), the contribution margin ratios are:

$$\text{Without the machine:} \frac{14 - 12}{14} \times 100\% = 14\%$$

$$\text{With the machine:} \frac{14 - 7}{14} \times 100\% = 50\%$$

The ratio reveals the extent to which sales revenue is eaten away by variable cost.

MARGIN OF SAFETY

The **margin of safety** is the extent to which the planned volume of output or sales lies above the BEP. To illustrate how the margin of safety is calculated, we can use the information in Activity 7.11 relating to each option.

	Without the machine (number of baskets)	With the machine (number of baskets)
(a) Expected volume of sales	500	500
(b) BEP	250	429
Margin of safety (the difference between (a) and (b))	250	71
Expressed as a percentage of expected volume of sales	50%	14%

The margin of safety can be used as a partial measure of risk.

Activity 7.12

What advice would you give Cottage Industries Ltd about renting the machine, on the basis of the values for margin of safety?

It is a matter of personal judgement, which in turn is related to individual attitudes to risk, as to which strategy to adopt. Most people, however, would prefer the strategy of not renting the machine, since the margin of safety between the expected volume of activity and the BEP is much greater. Thus, for the same level of return, the risk will be lower without renting the machine.

The relative margins of safety are directly linked to the relationship between the selling price per basket, the variable cost per basket and the fixed cost per month. Without the machine the contribution (selling price less variable cost) per basket is £2; with the machine it is £7. On the other hand, without the machine the fixed cost is £500 a month; with the machine it is £3,000. This means that, with the machine, the contributions have more fixed cost to 'overcome' before the activity becomes profitable. However, the rate at which the contributions can overcome fixed cost is higher with the machine, because variable cost is lower. Thus, one additional, or one less, basket sold has a greater impact on profit than it does if the machine is not rented. The contrast between the two scenarios is shown graphically in Figures 7.9(a) and 7.9(b).

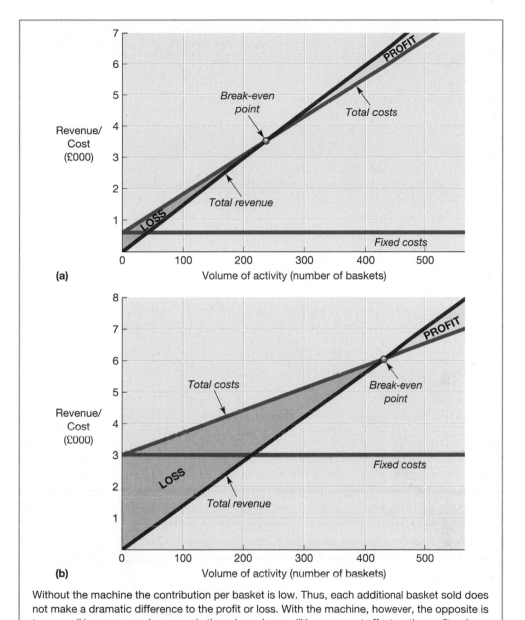

(a)

(b)

Without the machine the contribution per basket is low. Thus, each additional basket sold does not make a dramatic difference to the profit or loss. With the machine, however, the opposite is true; small increases or decreases in the sales volume will have a great effect on the profit or loss.

Figure 7.9 Break-even charts for Cottage Industries Ltd's basket-making activities (a) without the machine and (b) with the machine

If we look back to Real World 7.2 (page 000) we can see that Ryanair typically had a much larger margin of safety than BA.

Real World 7.4 goes into more detail on Ryanair's margin of safety and operating profit, over recent years.

Ryanair's margin of safety

As we saw in Real World 7.2, commercial airlines pay a lot of attention to BEPs. They are also interested in their margin of safety (the difference between load factor and BEP).

Figure 7.10 shows Ryanair's margin of safety and its operating profit over a five-year period. In each of these years, the load factors were comfortably greater than the BEP. This led to strong operating profits.

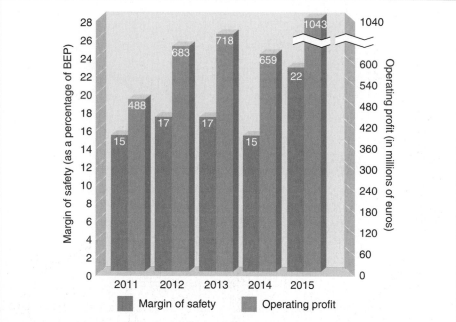

The margin of safety is expressed as the difference between the load factor and the BEP (for each year), expressed as a percentage of the BEP. Generally, the higher the margin of safety, the higher the operating profit.

Figure 7.10 Ryanair's margin of safety

Source: Derived from information contained in Ryanair Holdings plc, Annual Report 2015.

OPERATING GEARING

The relationship between contribution and fixed cost is known as **operating gearing** (or operational gearing). An activity with a relatively high fixed cost compared with its total variable cost, at its normal level of activity, is said to have high operating gearing. Thus, Cottage Industries Ltd has higher operating gearing using the machine than it has if not using it. Renting the machine increases the level of operating gearing quite dramatically because it causes an increase in fixed cost. At the same time, however, it leads to a reduction in variable cost per basket.

Operating gearing and its effect on profit

The reason why the word 'gearing' is used in this context is that, as with intermeshing gear wheels of different circumferences, a movement in one of the factors (volume of output) causes a more-than-proportionate movement in the other (profit) as illustrated by Figure 7.11.

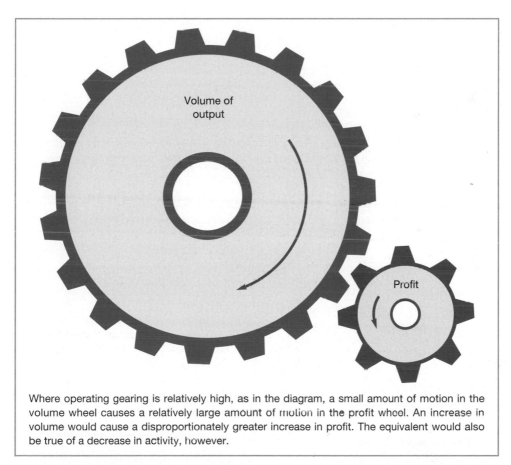

Where operating gearing is relatively high, as in the diagram, a small amount of motion in the volume wheel causes a relatively large amount of motion in the profit wheel. An increase in volume would cause a disproportionately greater increase in profit. The equivalent would also be true of a decrease in activity, however.

Figure 7.11 The effect of operating gearing

Increasing the level of operating gearing makes profit more sensitive to changes in the volume of activity. We can demonstrate operating gearing with Cottage Industries Ltd's basket-making activities as follows:

	Without the machine			With the machine		
Volume (number of baskets)	500	1,000	1,500	500	1,000	1,500
	£	£	£	£	£	£
Contributions*	1,000	2,000	3,000	3,500	7,000	10,500
Fixed cost	(500)	(500)	(500)	(3,000)	(3,000)	(3,000)
Profit	500	1,500	2,500	500	4,000	7,500

* £2 per basket without the machine and £7 per basket with it.

Note that, without the machine (low operating gearing), a doubling of the output from 500 to 1,000 units brings a trebling of the profit. With the machine (high operating gearing), a doubling of output from 500 units causes profit to rise by eight times. At the same time, reductions in the volume of output tend to have a more damaging effect on profit where the operating gearing is higher.

Activity 7.13

What types of business activity are likely to have high operating gearing? (*Hint*: Cottage Industries Ltd might give you some idea.)

Activities that are capital intensive tend to have high operating gearing. This is because renting or owning capital equipment gives rise to additional fixed cost, but it can also give rise to lower variable cost.

Real World 7.5 shows how a very well-known business has benefited from high operating gearing.

REAL WORLD 7.5

Making more dough

Greggs plc, the high street bakery retailer, reported an increase in sales revenue of 5.5 per cent for its reporting period ended 3 January 2015. This led to a 49 per cent increase in its operating profit. The business ascribed this to a lower-than-expected increase in its costs and to the effect of operating gearing.

Greggs, like most retailers, has a high proportion of its costs that are fixed, such as premises occupancy costs, salaries and wages, plant depreciation, motor vehicle running costs and training.

Source: Information from Greggs plc, Preliminary results statement for the 53 weeks ended 3 January 2015, 4 March 2015.

FAILING TO BREAK EVEN

Where a business fails to reach its BEP, steps must be taken to remedy the problem: there must be an increase in sales revenue or a reduction in cost, or both. **Real World 7.6** discusses how the ill-fated Malaysian Airlines, which has failed to reach its BEP since 2010, aims to be profitable by 2018.

REAL WORLD 7.6

Taking off

Malaysian Airways, which has been unprofitable since 2010, suffered two air disasters during 2014 that had a serious adverse effect on the business's profitability.

The business appointed a new chief executive officer (CEO), Christopher Mueller, with the aim of getting it profitable again. To achieve this, the new CEO is planning to:

- reduce the workforce from 20,000 employees to 14,000;
- reduce the number of flights and the size of the fleet;
- focus on domestic and regional routes;
- stop some long-haul, loss-making routes, for example, its only US route from Kuala Lumpur to Los Angeles;
- renegotiate some key contracts, including some of those with airports.

These are drastic steps. However, the new CEO believes they are necessary to achieve break even and to save the business.

Source: Information taken from McGee, P. and Parker, A. (2015) 'Disaster-plagued Malaysian Airways seeks break even by 2018', ft.com, 1 June.

WEAKNESSES OF BREAK-EVEN ANALYSIS

Although break-even analysis can provide useful insights concerning the relationship between cost, volume and profit, it does have its weaknesses. There are three general problems:

1. *Non-linear relationships.* Break-even analysis assumes that total variable cost and total revenue lines are perfectly straight when plotted against volume of output. In real life, this is unlikely to be the case. We shall look at the reason for this in Activity 7.14. Non-linearity is probably not a major problem, since, as we have just seen:
   - break-even analysis is normally conducted in advance of the activity actually taking place. Predicting future cost, revenue and so on, however, can be extremely difficult. Thus, what are probably minor variations from strict linearity, are unlikely to be significant when compared with other forecasting errors; and

- most businesses operate within a narrow range of volume of activity; over short ranges, curved lines tend to be relatively straight;

2. *Stepped fixed cost.* Most types of fixed cost are not fixed over the whole range of activity. They tend to be 'stepped' in the way depicted in Figure 7.3. This means that, in practice, great care must be taken in making assumptions about fixed cost. The problem is heightened because many activities will involve various types of fixed cost (for example rent, supervisory salaries, administration cost), all of which are likely to have steps at different points.

3. *Multi-product businesses.* Most businesses provide more than one product (or service). This can be a problem for break-even analysis since additional sales of one product may affect sales of another of the business's products. There is also the problem of identifying the fixed cost associated with a particular product. Fixed cost may relate to more than one product – for example, work on two products may be carried out in the same rented accommodation. There are ways of dividing the fixed cost between products, but these tend to be arbitrary, which undermines the value of the break-even analysis.

Activity 7.14

We have just seen that, in practice, relationships between costs, revenues and volumes of activity are not necessarily straight-line ones.
Can you think of at least two reasons, with examples, why this may be the case?

We thought of the following:

- *Economies of scale with labour.* A business may operate more economically at a higher volume of activity. For example, employees may be able to increase productivity by specialising in particular tasks.
- *Economies of scale with buying goods or services.* A business may find it cheaper to buy in goods and services where it is buying in bulk as discounts are often given.
- *Diseconomies of scale.* This may mean that the per-unit cost of output is higher at higher levels of activity. For example, it may be necessary to pay higher rates of pay to recruit the additional employees needed, or to pay overtime rates, at higher volumes of activity.
- *Lower sales prices at high levels of activity.* Some consumers may only be prepared to buy the particular product or service at a lower price. Thus, it may not be possible to achieve high levels of sales activity without lowering the selling price.

You may have thought of others.

Despite some practical problems, break-even analysis seems to be widely used. The media frequently refer to the BEP for businesses and activities. There is seemingly constant discussion, for example, about Eurotunnel's BEP and whether it will ever be reached. Similarly, the number of people regularly needed to pay to watch a football team so that the club breaks even is often mentioned.

This latter point is illustrated in **Real World 7.7,** which is taken from an article discussing how Plymouth Argyle FC, the English Football League 2 club, is managing to break even on the basis of its average attendance for home games.

REAL WORLD 7.7

Enough Pilgrims

The Plymouth Argyle owner, James Brent, said that the attendance at home matches, which averages about 7,300, is around the figure that enables the club to break even. He went on to say that he is comfortable with the situation.

Source: Information taken from Errington, C. (2015), 'James Brent: Plymouth Argyle can be competitive in League 1', *Western Morning News*, 10 March.

Real World 7.8 is an extract from the annual report of JD Sports Fashion plc, which owns the outdoor clothing outlets Blacks and Millets. It describes how these outlets struggled towards break even during 2014.

REAL WORLD 7.8

Still not in the black

Our pre-existing Blacks and Millets Outdoor fascias have had a mixed year. We started the year with an excess of heavy winter jackets and a lack of Spring / Summer product, particularly in camping and Peter Storm own brand. We had to trade our way out of this position with the significant (profit) margin sacrifice required to clear the Winter and earlier season stocks (inventories) leading to a poor first half trading result. However, the second half of the year, which we acknowledge is traditionally the stronger part of the year, has been much more promising and, ultimately, a breakeven position was achieved in this six month period compared to a loss of £4.9 million in the same period of the previous year.

Source: JD Sports Fashion plc, Annual Report and Accounts 2014, p. 25.

Real World 7.9 provides evidence concerning the extent to which managers use break-even analysis.

REAL WORLD 7.9

Break-even analysis in practice

A survey of management accounting practice in the United States was conducted in 2003. Nearly 2,000 businesses replied to the survey. These tended to be larger businesses, of which about 40 per cent were manufacturers and about 16 per cent financial services; the remainder were across a range of other industries.

The survey revealed that 62 per cent use break-even analysis extensively, with a further 22 per cent considering using the technique in the future.

Though the survey relates to the US and was undertaken several years ago, in the absence of more recent UK evidence, it provides some indication of what is likely also to be current practice in the UK and elsewhere in the developed world.

Source: Information from the '2003 Survey of Management Accounting' by Ernst and Young, 2003.

USING CONTRIBUTION TO MAKE DECISIONS: MARGINAL ANALYSIS

We saw at the start of this chapter that, when deciding between two or more possible courses of action, *only costs that vary with the decision should be included in the analysis.* This principle can be applied to the consideration of fixed cost.

For many decisions that involve:

- relatively small variations from existing practice, and/or
- relatively limited periods of time,

fixed cost is not relevant. This element of cost will be the same irrespective of the decision made. This is because the fixed cost element cannot, or will not, be altered in the short term.

Activity 7.15

Ali plc owns a workshop from which it provides a PC repair and maintenance service. There has recently been a downturn in demand for the service. It would be possible for Ali plc to carry on the business from smaller, cheaper accommodation.

Can you think of any reasons why the business might not immediately move to smaller, cheaper accommodation?

We thought of broadly three reasons:

1. It is not usually possible to find a buyer for the existing accommodation at very short notice and it may be difficult to find an available alternative quickly.
2. It may be difficult to move accommodation quickly where there is, say, delicate equipment to be moved.
3. Management may feel that the downturn might not be permanent, and so would be reluctant to take such a dramatic step and deny itself the opportunity to benefit from a possible revival of trade.

You may have thought of others.

We shall now consider some types of decisions where fixed cost can be regarded as irrelevant. In making these decisions, we should have as our key strategic objective the enhancement of owners' (shareholders') wealth. Since these decisions are short term in nature, wealth will normally be increased by generating as much net cash inflow as possible.

In **marginal analysis** only costs and revenues that vary with the decision are considered. This usually means that fixed cost can be ignored. This is because marginal analysis is usually applied to minor alterations in the level of activity. It tends to be true, therefore, that the variable cost per unit will be equal to the **marginal cost**, which is the additional cost of producing one more unit of output. While marginal cost normally equals variable cost, there may be times when producing one more unit will involve a step in the fixed cost. If this occurs, the marginal cost is not just the variable cost; it will include the increment, or step, in the fixed cost as well.

Marginal analysis may be used in four key areas of decision making:

- pricing/assessing opportunities to enter contracts;
- determining the most efficient use of scarce resources;
- make-or-buy decisions; and
- closing or continuation decisions.

Let us consider each of these areas in turn.

Pricing/assessing opportunities to enter contracts

To understand how marginal analysis may be used in assessing an opportunity, consider the following activity.

Activity 7.16

Cottage Industries Ltd (see Example 7.1, page 000) has spare capacity in that its basket makers have some spare time. An overseas retail chain has offered the business an order for 300 baskets at a price of £13 each.

Without considering any wider issues, should the business accept the order? (Assume that the business does not rent the machine.)

Since the fixed cost will be incurred in any case, it is not relevant to this decision. All we need to do is to see whether the price offered will yield a contribution. If it will, the business will be better off by accepting the contract than by refusing it.

	£
Additional revenue per unit	13
Additional cost per unit	(12)
Additional contribution per unit	1

For 300 units, the additional contribution will be £300 (that is, 300 × £1). Since no fixed cost increase is involved, irrespective of what else is happening to the business, it will be £300 better off by taking this contract than by refusing it.

As ever with decision making, there are other factors that are either difficult or impossible to quantify. These should be taken into account before reaching a final decision. In the case of Cottage Industries Ltd's decision concerning the overseas customer, these could include the following:

- The possibility that spare capacity will have been 'sold off' cheaply when there might be another potential customer who will offer a higher price. There is the danger that, by the time the higher-priced offer is made, the capacity will be fully committed. It is a matter of commercial judgement as to how likely this will be.

- Selling the same product, but at different prices to different customers, could lead to a loss of customer goodwill. The fact that a different price will be set for customers in different countries (that is, in different markets) may be sufficient to avoid this potential problem.
- If the business is going to suffer continually from being unable to sell its full production potential at the 'usual' price, it might be better, in the long run, to reduce capacity and make fixed cost savings. Using the spare capacity to produce marginal benefits may result in the business failing to address this issue.
- On a more positive note, the business may see this as a way of breaking into the overseas market. This is something that might be impossible to achieve if the business charges its usual price.

The most efficient use of scarce resources

In many cases, the output of a business is determined by customer demand for the particular goods or services. In some cases, however, output will be restricted by the capacity of the business to supply as much of the product as the customers demand. Limited capacity to supply might stem from a shortage of any factor of production – labour, raw materials, space, machine capacity and so on. Such scarce factors are often known as *key* or *limiting* factors.

Where capacity to supply acts as a brake on output, management must decide on how best to deploy the scarce resource. That is, it must decide which products, from the range available, should be provided and how many of each should be provided. Marginal analysis can be useful to management in such circumstances. The guiding principle is that the most profitable combination of products will occur where the *contribution per unit of the scarce factor* is maximised. Example 7.2 illustrates this point.

Example 7.2

A business provides three different services, the details of which are as follows:

	Service (code name)		
	AX107	AX109	AX220
	£	£	£
Selling price per unit	50	40	65
Variable cost per unit	(25)	(20)	(35)
Contribution per unit	25	20	30
Labour time per unit	5 hours	3 hours	6 hours

Within reason, the market will take as many units of each service as can be provided, but the ability to provide the service is limited by the availability of labour, all of which needs to be skilled. Fixed cost is not affected by the choice of service provided because all three services use the same facilities.

The most profitable service is AX109 because it generates a contribution of £6.67 (£20/3) an hour. The other two generate only £5.00 each an hour (£25/5 and £30/6). So, to maximise profit, priority should be given to the production that maximises the contribution per unit of limiting factor.

Our first reaction might be that the business should provide only service AX220, as this is the one that yields the highest contribution per unit sold. If so, we would have been making the mistake of thinking that it is the ability to sell that is the limiting factor. If the above analysis is not convincing, we can take a random number of available labour hours and ask ourselves what is the maximum contribution (and, therefore, profit) that could be made by providing each service exclusively. Bear in mind that there is no shortage of anything else, including market demand, just a shortage of labour.

Activity 7.17

A business makes three different products, the details of which are as follows:

	Product (code name)		
	B14	B17	B22
Selling price per unit (£)	25	20	23
Variable cost per unit (£)	10	8	12
Weekly demand (units)	25	20	30
Machine time per unit (hours)	4	3	4

Fixed cost is not affected by the choice of product because all three products use the same machine. Machine time is limited to 148 hours a week.
Which combination of products should be manufactured if the business is to produce the highest profit?

	Product (code name)		
	B14	B17	B22
Selling price per unit (£)	25	20	23
Variable cost per unit (£)	(10)	(8)	(12)
Contribution per unit (£)	15	12	11
Machine time per unit (hours)	4	3	4
Contribution per machine hour (£)	3.75	4.00	2.75
Order of priority	2nd	1st	3rd

Therefore produce:

20 units of product B17 using	60 hours
22 units of product B14 using	88 hours
	148 hours

This leaves unsatisfied the market demand for a further 3 units of product B14 and 30 units of product B22.

What practical steps could be taken that might lead to a higher level of contribution for the business in Activity 7.17?

The possibilities for improving matters that occurred to us are as follows:

- Consider obtaining additional machine time. This could mean obtaining a new machine, subcontracting the machining to another business or, perhaps, squeezing a few more hours a week out of the business's own machine. Perhaps a combination of two or more of these is a possibility.
- Redesign the products in a way that requires less time per unit on the machine.
- Increase the price per unit of the three products. This might well have the effect of dampening demand, but the existing demand cannot be met at present. It may, therefore, be more profitable, in the long run, to make a greater contribution on each unit sold than to take one of the other courses of action to overcome the problem.

Going back to Activity 7.17, what is the maximum price that the business concerned would logically be prepared to pay to have the remaining B14s machined by a subcontractor, assuming that no fixed or variable cost would be saved as a result of not doing the machining itself?

Would there be a different maximum if we were considering the B22s?

If the remaining three B14s were subcontracted at no cost, the business would be able to earn a contribution of £15 a unit, which it would not otherwise be able to gain. Therefore, any price up to £15 a unit would be worth paying to a subcontractor to undertake the machining. Naturally, the business would prefer to pay as little as possible, but anything up to £15 would still make it worthwhile subcontracting the machining.

This would not be true of the B22s because they have a different contribution per unit; £11 would be the relevant figure in their case.

Make-or-buy decisions

Businesses are frequently confronted by the need to decide whether to produce the product or service that they sell themselves, or to buy it in from some other business. Thus, a producer of electrical appliances might decide to subcontract the manufacture of one of its products to another business, perhaps because there is a shortage of production capacity in the producer's own factory. Alternatively, the producer may believe it to be cheaper to subcontract than to make the appliance itself. Obtaining services or products from a subcontractor is often called **outsourcing**.

In many cases, whether to outsource or not is a longer-term, strategic decision. In that case, it needs to be assessed as such. In the present context, we are considering more tactical make-or-buy decisions that can be taken quickly for the short term.

Activity 7.20

Shah Ltd needs a component for one of its products. It can subcontract production of the component to another business that will provide the components for £20 each. Shah Ltd can produce the components internally for a total variable cost of £15 per component. Shah Ltd has spare capacity.

Should the component be subcontracted or produced internally?

The answer is that Shah Ltd should produce the component internally, since the variable cost of subcontracting is greater by £5 (that is, £20 − £15) than the variable cost of internal manufacture.

Activity 7.21

Now assume that Shah Ltd (Activity 7.20) has no spare capacity, so it can only produce the component internally by reducing its output of another of its products. While it is making each component, it will lose contributions of £12 from the other product.

Should the component be subcontracted or produced internally?

The answer is to subcontract. In this case, both the variable cost of production and the opportunity cost of lost contributions must be taken into account.

Thus, the relevant cost of internal production of each component is:

	£
Variable cost of production of the component	15
Opportunity cost of lost production of the other product	12
	27

This is obviously more costly than the £20 per component that will have to be paid to the subcontractor.

Activity 7.22

What factors, other than the immediately financially quantifiable, would you consider when making a make-or-buy decision?

We feel that there are two major factors:

1 *General problems of subcontracting.* These include
   (a) loss of control of quality;
   (b) potential unreliability of supply.
2 *Expertise and specialisation.* Businesses should normally focus on their core competences.

Picking up the second point in Activity 7.22, it is possible for most businesses, with sufficient determination, to do virtually everything in-house. This may, however, require a level of skill and facilities that most businesses neither have nor feel inclined to acquire. For example, though it is true that most businesses could generate their own electricity, their managements tend to take the view that this is better done by a specialist generator business. Specialists can often do things more cheaply, with less risk of things going wrong.

Closing or continuation decisions

It is quite common for businesses to produce separate financial statements for each department or section, to try to assess their relative performance. Example 7.3 considers how marginal analysis can help decide how to respond where it is found that a particular department underperforms.

Example 7.3

Goodsports Ltd is a retail shop that operates through three departments, all in the same accommodation. The three departments occupy roughly equal-sized areas of the accommodation. The projected trading results for next year are:

	Total £000	Sports equipment £000	Sports clothes £000	General clothes £000
Sales revenue	534	254	183	97
Cost	(482)	(213)	(163)	(106)
Profit/(loss)	52	41	20	(9)

It would appear that if the general clothes department were to close, the business would be more profitable, by £9,000 a year.

When the cost is analysed between that part that is variable and that part that is fixed, however, the contribution of each department can be deduced and the following results obtained:

	Total £000	Sports equipment £000	Sports clothes £000	General clothes £000
Sales revenue	534	254	183	97
Variable cost	(344)	(167)	(117)	(60)
Contribution	190	87	66	37
Fixed cost (rent and so on)	(138)	(46)	(46)	(46)
Profit/(loss)	52	41	20	(9)

Now it is obvious that closing the general clothes department, without any other developments, would make the business worse off by £37,000 (the department's contribution). The department should not be closed, because it makes a positive contribution. The fixed cost would continue whether the department was closed or not. As can be seen from the above analysis, distinguishing between variable and fixed cost, and deducing the contribution, can make the picture a great deal clearer.

In considering Goodsports Ltd (in Example 7.3), we saw that the general clothes department should not be closed 'without any other developments'.

What 'other developments' could affect this decision, making continuation either more attractive or less attractive?

The things that we could think of are as follows:

- Expansion of the other departments or replacing the general clothes department with a completely new activity. This would make sense only if the space currently occupied by the general clothes department could generate contributions totalling at least £37,000 a year.
- Subletting the space occupied by the general clothes department. Once again, this would need to generate a net rent greater than £37,000 a year to make it more financially beneficial than keeping the department open.
- Keeping the department open, even if it generated no contribution whatsoever (assuming that there is no other use for the space), may still be beneficial. If customers are attracted into the shop because it has general clothing, they may then buy something from one of the other departments. In the same way, the activity of a sub-tenant might attract customers into the shop. (On the other hand, it might drive them away!)

Figure 7.12 summarises the four key decision-making areas where marginal analysis tends to be used.

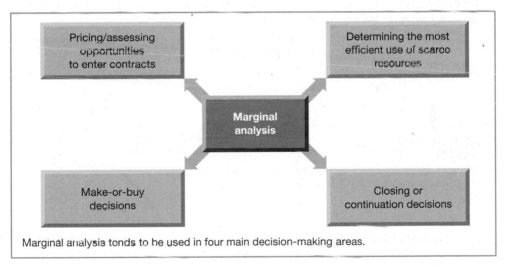

Marginal analysis tends to be used in four main decision-making areas.

Figure 7.12 The four key areas of decision making using marginal analysis

Khan Ltd can render three different types of service (Alpha, Beta and Gamma) using the same staff. Various estimates for next year have been made as follows:

	Service		
	Alpha	Beta	Gamma
Selling price (£/unit)	30	39	20
Variable material cost (£/unit)	15	18	10
Other variable costs (£/unit)	6	10	5
Share of fixed cost (£/unit)	8	12	4
Staff time required (hours)	2	3	1

Fixed cost for next year is expected to total £40,000.

Required:

(a) If the business were to render only service Alpha next year, how many units of the service would it need to provide in order to break even? (Assume for this part of the question that there is no effective limit to market size and staffing level.)

(b) If the business has limited staff hours available next year, in which order of preference would the three services come?

(c) The maximum market for next year for the three services is as follows:

Alpha	3,000 units
Beta	2,000 units
Gamma	5,000 units

Khan Ltd has a maximum of 10,000 staff hours available next year.

What quantities of each service should the business provide next year and how much profit would this be expected to yield?

The solution to this question can be found at the back of the book on page 529.

SUMMARY

The main points in this chapter may be summarised as follows:

> *Cost = amount of resources, usually measured in monetary terms, sacrificed to achieve a particular objective*

Relevant and irrelevant costs

- Relevant costs must:

  - relate to the objective being pursued by the business;

  - be future costs;

  - differ from one possible decision outcome to the next.

- Relevant costs therefore include:
  - future opportunity costs;
  - differential future outlay costs.
- Irrelevant costs therefore include:
  - all past (or sunk) costs;
  - all committed costs;
  - non-differential future outlay costs.

Cost behaviour

- Fixed cost is independent of the level of activity (for example, rent).
- Variable cost varies with the level of activity (for example, raw materials).
- Semi-fixed (semi-variable) cost is a mixture of fixed and variable costs (for example, electricity).

Break-even analysis

- The break-even point (BEP) is the level of activity (in units of output or sales revenue) at which total cost (fixed + variable) = total sales revenue.
- Calculation of BEP is as follows:

$$\text{BEP (in units of output)} = \frac{\text{Fixed cost for the period}}{\text{Contribution per unit}}$$

- Knowledge of the BEP for a particular activity can be used to help assess risk.
- Contribution per unit = sales revenue per unit less variable cost per unit.
- Contribution margin ratio = contribution/sales revenue ($\times$ 100%).
- Margin of safety = excess of planned volume (or sales revenue) of activity over volume (or sales revenue) at BEP.
- Operating gearing is the extent to which the total cost of some activity is fixed rather than variable.

Weaknesses of BE analysis

- There are non-linear relationships between costs, revenues and volume.
- There may be stepped fixed costs. Most fixed costs are not fixed over all volumes of activity.
- Multi-product businesses have problems in allocating fixed costs to particular activities.

> **Marginal analysis (ignores fixed costs where these are not affected by the decision)**
>
> - Assessing contracts – we consider only the effect on contributions.
> - Using scarce resources – the limiting factor is most effectively used by maximising its contribution per unit.
> - Make-or-buy decisions – we take the action that leads to the highest total contributions.
> - Closing/continuing an activity – should be assessed by net effect on total contributions.

KEY TERMS

For definitions of these terms, see Appendix A.

cost p. 249	**break-even analysis** p. 258
historic cost p. 249	**break-even chart** p. 259
opportunity cost p. 249	**break-even point (BEP)** p. 259
relevant cost p. 250	**contribution per unit** p. 265
irrelevant cost p. 250	**contribution margin ratio** p. 265
past cost p. 250	**margin of safety** p. 265
outlay cost p. 250	**operating gearing** p. 269
fixed cost p. 254	**marginal analysis** p. 274
variable cost p. 254	**marginal cost** p. 274
stepped fixed cost p. 256	**outsourcing** p. 278
semi-fixed (semi-variable) cost p. 258	

FURTHER READING

If you would like to explore the topics covered in this chapter in more depth, we recommend the following books:

Bhimani A., Horngren, C., Datar, S. and Rajan, M. (2015), *Management and Cost Accounting,* 6th edn, Pearson, Chapters 8 and 10.

Drury, C. (2015), *Management and Cost Accounting,* 9th edn, Cengage Learning EMEA, Chapters 8 and 9.

Hilton, R. and Platt, D. (2014), *Managerial Accounting,* Global edn, McGraw-Hill Higher Education, Chapters 6 and 7.

McWatters, C. and Zimmerman, J. (2016), *Management Accounting in a Dynamic Environment,* Routledge, Chapters 2 and 3.

Solutions to these questions can be found at the back of the book on pages 543–544.

7.1 Define the terms *fixed cost* and *variable cost.* Explain how an understanding of the distinction between fixed cost and variable cost can be useful to managers.

7.2 What is meant by the BEP for an activity? How is the BEP calculated? Why is it useful to know the BEP?

7.3 When we say that some business activity has *high operating gearing,* what do we mean? What are the implications for the business of high operating gearing?

7.4 If there is a scarce resource that is restricting sales, how will the business maximise its profit? Explain the logic of the approach that you have identified for maximising profit.

? EXERCISES

*Exercise 7.1 is basic level. Exercises 7.2 and 7.3 are intermediate level and Exercises 7.4 and 7.5 are advanced level. Those with **coloured numbers** have solutions at the back of the book, starting on page 561.*

7.1 Lombard Ltd has been offered a contract for which there is available production capacity. The contract is for 20,000 identical items, manufactured by an intricate assembly operation, to be produced and delivered in the next few months at a price of £80 each. The specification for one item is as follows:

Assembly labour	4 hours
Component X	4 units
Component Y	3 units

There would also be the need to hire equipment, for the duration of the contract, at an outlay cost of £200,000.

The assembly is a highly skilled operation and the workforce is currently underutilised. It is the business's policy to retain this workforce on full pay in anticipation of high demand next year, for a new product currently being developed. There is sufficient available skilled labour to undertake the contract now under consideration. Skilled workers are paid £15 an hour.

Component X is used in a number of other sub-assemblies produced by the business. It is readily available. 50,000 units of Component X are currently held in inventories. Component Y was a special purchase in anticipation of an order that did not in the end materialise. It is, therefore, surplus to requirements and the 100,000 units that are currently held may have to be sold at a loss. An estimate of various values for Components X and Y provided by the materials planning department is as follows:

	Component	
	X	Y
	£/unit	£/unit
Historic cost	4	10
Replacement cost	5	11
Net realisable value	3	8

It is estimated that any additional relevant costs associated with the contract (beyond the above) will amount to £8 an item.

Required:
Analyse the information and advise Lombard Ltd on the desirability of the contract.

7.2 The management of a business is concerned about its inability to obtain enough fully trained labour to enable it to meet its present budget projection.

	Service			
	Alpha	Beta	Gamma	Total
	£000	£000	£000	£000
Variable costs				
Materials	6	4	5	15
Labour	9	6	12	27
Expenses	3	2	2	7
Allocated fixed costs	6	15	12	33
Total cost	24	27	31	82
Profit	15	2	2	19
Sales revenue	39	29	33	101

The amount of labour likely to be available amounts to £20,000. All of the variable labour is paid at the same hourly rate. You have been asked to prepare a statement of plans, ensuring that at least 50 per cent of the budgeted sales revenues are achieved for each service and the balance of labour is used to produce the greatest profit.

Required:
(a) Prepare the statement, with explanations, showing the greatest profit available from the limited amount of skilled labour available, within the constraint stated. (*Hint:* Remember that all labour is paid at the same rate.)
(b) What steps could the business take in an attempt to improve profitability, in the light of the labour shortage?

7.3 A hotel group prepares financial statements on a quarterly basis. The senior management is reviewing the performance of one hotel and making plans for next year.

The managers have in front of them the results for this year (based on some actual results and some forecasts to the end of this year):

Quarter	Sales revenue	Profit/(loss)
	£000	£000
1	400	(280)
2	1,200	360
3	1,600	680
4	800	40
Total	4,000	800

The total estimated number of guests (guest nights) for this year is 50,000, with each guest night being charged at the same rate. The results follow a regular pattern; there are no unexpected cost fluctuations beyond the seasonal trading pattern shown above.

For next year, management anticipates an increase in unit variable cost of 10 per cent and a profit target for the hotel of £1 million. These will be incorporated into its plans.

Required:
(a) Calculate the total variable and total fixed cost of the hotel for this year. Show the provisional annual results for this year in total, showing variable and fixed cost separately. Show also the revenue and cost per guest.
(b) (i) If there is no increase in guests for next year, what will be the required revenue rate per hotel guest to meet the profit target?
(ii) If the required revenue rate per guest is not raised above this year's level, how many guests will be required to meet the profit target?
(c) Outline and briefly discuss the assumptions that are made in typical profit-volume or break-even analysis and assess whether they limit its usefulness.

7.4 A business makes three products, A, B and C. All three products require the use of two types of machine: cutting machines and assembling machines. Estimates for next year include the following:

	Product		
	A	B	C
Selling price (£ per unit)	25	30	18
Sales demand (units)	2,500	3,400	5,100
Material cost (£ per unit)	12	13	10
Variable production cost (£ per unit)	7	4	3
Time required per unit on cutting machines (hours)	1.0	1.0	0.5
Time required per unit on assembling machines (hours)	0.5	1.0	0.5

Fixed cost for next year is expected to total £42,000.

The business has cutting machine capacity of 5,000 hours a year and assembling machine capacity of 8,000 hours a year.

Required:

(a) State, with supporting workings, which products in which quantities the business should plan to make next year on the basis of the above information. (*Hint:* First determine which machines will be a limiting factor (scarce resource).)

(b) State the maximum price per product that it would be worth the business paying to a subcontractor to carry out that part of the work that could not be done internally.

7.5 Darmor Ltd has three products, which require the same production facilities. Information about the production cost for one unit of its products is as follows:

	Product		
	X	Y	Z
	£	£	£
Labour: Skilled	6	9	3
Unskilled	2	4	10
Materials	12	25	14
Other variable costs	3	7	7
Fixed cost	5	10	10

All labour and materials are variable costs. Skilled labour is paid £12 an hour and unskilled labour is paid £8 an hour. All references to labour cost above are based on basic rates of pay. Skilled labour is scarce, which means that the business could sell more than the maximum that it is able to make of any of the three products.

Product X is sold in a regulated market and the regulators have set a price of £30 per unit for it.

Required:

(a) State, with supporting workings, the price that must be charged for Products Y and Z, such that the business would find it equally profitable to make and sell any of the three products.

(b) State, with supporting workings, the maximum rate of overtime premium that the business would logically be prepared to pay its skilled workers to work beyond the basic time.

Chapter 8

FULL COSTING

INTRODUCTION

Full (absorption) costing takes into account of all of the cost of producing a particular product or service. In this chapter, we shall see how this approach is used to deduce the cost of some activity, such as making a unit of product (for example, a tin of baked beans), providing a unit of service (for example, a car repair) or creating a facility (for example, building a high speed rail link from London to Birmingham).

We shall first look at how the traditional, but still widely used, approach to full (or absorption) costing is carried out and consider its usefulness for management purposes. We shall then go on to consider activity-based costing. This is a more recently developed approach that offers an alternative to the traditional one.

Learning outcomes

When you have completed this chapter, you should be able to:

■ deduce the full (absorption) cost of a cost unit in a single-product and a multi-product environment, using the traditional approach;

■ discuss the problems of deducing full (absorption) cost in practice;

■ discuss the usefulness of full (absorption) cost information to managers;

■ explain the role and nature of activity-based costing.

WHAT IS FULL COSTING?

Full cost is the total amount of resources, usually measured in monetary terms, sacrificed to achieve a given objective. It takes account of all resources sacrificed to achieve that objective. Thus, if the objective were to supply a customer with a product or service, the cost of all aspects of making the product or rendering the service would be included as part of the full cost. To derive the full cost figure, we must accumulate the elements of cost incurred and then assign them to the particular product or service.

The logic of **full costing** is that the entire cost of running a facility, such as an office or factory, is part of the cost of the output that it helps to generate. Take, for example, the cost of renting an office incurred by an architect. Although this will not alter if the architect undertakes one more assignment, there would be nowhere to work unless the office was available. Thus, rent of the office must be taken into account when assessing the full cost of each assignment undertaken by the architect. A **cost unit** is one unit of whatever is having its cost determined. This is usually one unit of output of a particular product or service.

WHY DO MANAGERS WANT TO KNOW THE FULL COST?

We saw in Chapter 1 that the only point in providing management accounting information is to improve the quality of management decisions. There are four main areas where information relating to the full cost of the business's products or services may prove useful. These are:

- *Pricing and output decisions.* Having full cost information can help managers make decisions on the price to charge customers for the business's products or services. Full cost information, along with relevant information concerning prices, can also be used to determine the number of units of products or services to be produced.
- *Exercising control.* Determining the full cost of a product or service is often a useful starting point for exercising cost control. Where the reported full cost figure is considered too high, for example, individual elements of full cost may then be examined to see whether there are opportunities for reduction. This may lead to re-engineering the production process, finding new sources of supply and so on. Also, budgets and plans are often expressed in full cost terms. Budgets are typically used to help managers exercise control by comparing planned (budgeted) performance, with actual performance.
- *Assessing relative efficiency.* Full cost information can help managers compare the cost of carrying out an activity in a particular way, or particular place, with its cost if carried out in a different way, or place. A car manufacturer, for example, may wish to compare the cost of building a particular model of car in one manufacturing plant, rather than in another. This could help in determining where to locate future production.
- *Assessing performance.* Profit is an important measure of business performance. To measure the profit arising from providing a particular product or service, the sales revenue that it generates should be compared with the costs consumed in generating that revenue. This can help in assessing past decisions. It can also help in guiding future decisions, such as continuing with, or abandoning, the particular product or service.

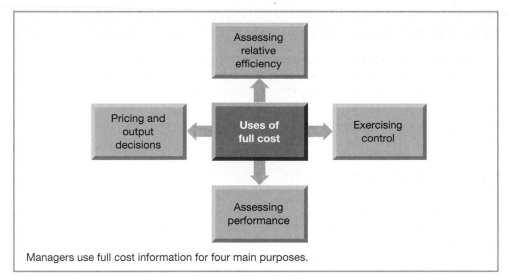

Managers use full cost information for four main purposes.

Figure 8.1 Uses of full cost by managers

Now let us consider **Real World 8.1.**

When considering the information in Real World 8.1, an important question that arises is 'what does the full cost of a particular medical procedure include?' Does it simply include the cost of the salaries earned by doctors and nurses during the time spent with the patient or does it also include the cost of other items? If the cost of other items is included, how is it determined? Would it include, for example, a charge for:

- the artificial knee and drugs provided for the patient;
- equipment used in the operating theatre;
- administrative and support staff within the hospital;
- heating and lighting;
- maintaining the hospital buildings; and
- laundry and cleaning?

If the cost of such items is included, how can an appropriate charge for the procedure be determined? If, on the other hand, the costs are not included, is the figure of £5,148 potentially misleading? Addressing questions such as these is the focus of this chapter.

In the sections that follow, we shall firstly see how full costing is applied to a single product business and then look at a multi-product one.

SINGLE-PRODUCT BUSINESSES

The simplest case for which to deduce the full cost per unit is where the business has only one product or service, that is, each unit of output is identical. Here it is simply a question of adding up all of the elements of cost of production incurred in a particular period (materials, labour, rent, fuel, power and so on) and dividing this total by the total number of units of output for that period.

Activity 8.1

Fruitjuice Ltd has just one product, a sparkling orange drink that is marketed as 'Orange Fizz'. During last month the business produced 7,300 litres of the drink. The cost incurred was made up as follows:

	£
Ingredients (oranges and so on)	390
Fuel	85
Rent of accommodation	350
Depreciation of equipment	75
Labour	880

What is the full cost per litre of producing 'Orange Fizz'?

This figure is found simply by adding together all of the elements of cost incurred and then dividing by the number of litres produced:

$$£(390 + 85 + 350 + 75 + 880)/7,300 = £0.24 \text{ per litre}$$

In practice, there can be problems in deciding exactly how much cost was incurred. In the case of Fruitjuice Ltd, for example, how is the cost of depreciation deduced? It is certainly an estimate and so its reliability is open to question. The cost of raw materials may also be a problem. Should we use the 'relevant' cost of the raw materials (in this case, almost certainly the replacement cost) or the actual price paid for it (historic cost)? If the cost per litre is to be used for some decision-making purpose (which it should be), the replacement cost is probably more logical. In practice, however, it seems that historic cost is more often used to deduce full cost. It is not clear why this should be the case.

There can also be problems in deciding precisely how many units of output were produced. If making Orange Fizz is not a very fast process, some of the drink will probably be in the process of being made at any given moment. This, in turn, means that some of the cost incurred last month was for some Orange Fizz that was work in progress at the end of the month, so is not included in last month's output quantity of 7,300 litres. Similarly, part of the 7,300 litres might well have been started and incurred cost in the previous month, yet all of those litres were included in the 7,300 litres that we used in our calculation of the cost per litre. Work in progress is not a serious problem, but some adjustment for the value of opening and closing work in progress for the particular period needs to be made if reliable full cost information is to be obtained.

This approach to full costing, which can be taken where all of the output consists of identical, or nearly identical, items (of goods or services), is usually referred to as **process costing**.

Activity 8.2

Can you think of at least two types of industry where process costing may apply?

Suitable industries are likely to include:

- paint manufacturing;
- chemical processing;
- oil extraction;
- plastic manufacturing;
- paper manufacturing;
- brick manufacturing;
- beverages;
- semiconductor chips.

You may have thought of others.

MULTI-PRODUCT BUSINESSES

Many businesses provide products or services that are distinct rather than identical. In this situation, the process costing approach that we used with litres of 'Orange Fizz' (in Activity 8.1) would be inappropriate. While it may be appropriate to assign an average cost to each *identical* unit of output, it is not appropriate where the units of output are quite different. It would be illogical, for example, to assign the same cost to each car repair carried out by a garage, irrespective of the complexity and size of the repair.

Where a business offers distinct products or services, a **job costing** approach is normally used. This involves accumulating costs for each individual unit of output to determine its full cost. To understand how this can be done, we first need to understand the difference between direct and indirect cost.

Direct and indirect cost

To provide full cost information, the various elements of cost must be accumulated and then assigned to particular cost units on some reasonable basis. Where cost units are not identical, the starting point is to separate cost into two categories: direct cost and indirect cost.

- **Direct cost**. This is a cost that can be identified with specific cost units. That is to say, the cost can be traced to a particular cost unit and can be measured reliably. The main examples of a direct cost are direct materials and direct labour. Thus, in determining the cost of a car repair by a garage, both the cost of spare parts used in the repair and the cost of the mechanic's time would be part of the direct cost of that repair. Collecting elements of direct cost is a simple matter of having a cost-recording system that is capable of capturing the cost of direct materials used on each job and the cost, based on the hours worked and the rate of pay, of direct workers.
- **Indirect cost** (or **overheads**). This is all other elements of cost, that is, those items that cannot be identified with each particular cost unit (job). Thus, the amount paid to rent the garage would be an indirect cost of a particular car repair.

We shall use the terms 'indirect cost' and 'overheads' interchangeably for the remainder of this book. Indirect cost is also sometimes known as **common cost** because it is common to all of the output of the production unit (for example, factory or department) for the period.

Real World 8.2 gives some indication of the relative importance of direct and indirect costs in practice.

REAL WORLD 8.2

Counting the cost

A survey of 176 UK businesses operating in various industries, all with annual sales of more than £50 million, was conducted by Al-Omiri and Drury. They discovered that the full cost of the businesses' output on average is split between direct and indirect costs as shown in Figure 8.2.

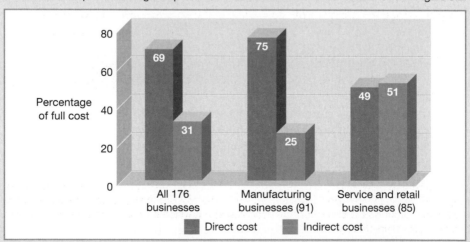

Figure 8.2 Percentage of full cost contributed by direct and indirect cost

For the manufacturers, the 75 per cent direct cost was, on average, made up as follows:

	Per cent
Direct materials	52
Direct labour	14
Other direct costs	9

Source: Al-Omiri, M. and Drury, C. (2007) 'A survey of factors influencing the choice of product costing systems in UK organisations', *Management Accounting Research,* December, pp. 399–424.

Activity 8.3

A garage owner wishes to know the direct cost of each job (car repair) that is carried out. How could the direct cost (labour and materials) information concerning a particular job be collected?

Usually, direct workers are required to record how long was spent on each job. Thus, the mechanic doing the job would record the length of time worked on the car. The stores staff would normally be required to keep a record of the cost of parts and materials used on each job.

A 'job sheet' will normally be prepared – usually on the computer – for each individual job. The quality of the information generated relies on staff faithfully recording all elements of direct labour and materials applied to the job.

Job costing

To deduce the full cost of a particular cost unit, we first identify the direct cost of the cost unit, which, from the definition of direct cost, is fairly straightforward. We then seek to 'charge' each cost unit with an 'appropriate' share of indirect cost (overheads). Put another way, cost units will absorb overheads. This leads to full costing also being called **absorption costing**. The absorption process is shown graphically in Figure 8.3.

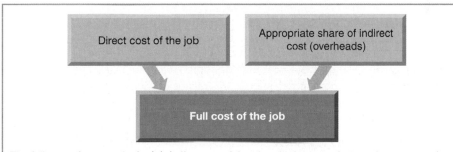

The full cost of any particular job is the sum of those cost elements that can be measured specifically in respect of the job (direct cost) and a share of the cost of creating the environment in which production (of an object or service) can take place, but which do not relate specifically to any particular job (indirect cost).

Figure 8.3 The relationship between direct cost and indirect cost

Sparky Ltd employs a number of electricians. The business undertakes a range of work for its customers, from replacing fuses to installing complete wiring systems in new houses.

In respect of a particular job done by Sparky Ltd, into which category (direct or indirect) would each of the following cost elements fall?

- the wages of the electrician who did the job;
- depreciation of the tools used by the electrician;
- the cost of cable and other materials used on the job;
- rent of the building where Sparky Ltd stores its inventories of cable and other materials.

The electrician's wages earned while working on the particular job and the cost of the materials used on the job are included in direct cost. This is because it is possible to measure how much time was spent on the particular job (and therefore its direct labour cost) and the amount of materials used (and therefore the direct material cost) in the job.

The others are included in the general cost of running the business and, as such, must form part of the indirect cost of doing the job. They cannot be directly measured in respect of the particular job, however.

It is important to note that whether a cost is direct or indirect depends on the item being costed – the cost objective. To refer to indirect cost without identifying the cost objective is potentially misleading.

Into which category, direct or indirect, would each of the elements of cost listed in Activity 8.4 fall, if we were seeking to find the cost of operating the entire business of Sparky Ltd for a month?

The answer is that all of them will form part of the direct cost, since they can all be related to, and measured in respect of, running the business for a month.

Broader-reaching cost objectives, such as operating Sparky Ltd for a month, tend to include a higher proportion of direct cost than do more limited ones, such as a particular job done by Sparky Ltd. As we shall see shortly, this makes costing broader cost objectives more straightforward than costing narrower ones. This is because direct cost is normally easier to deal with than indirect cost.

Full (absorption) costing and the behaviour of cost

We saw in Chapter 7 that the full **cost** of doing something (or total cost, as it is usually known in the context of marginal analysis) can be analysed between its fixed and the variable elements. This is illustrated in Figure 8.4.

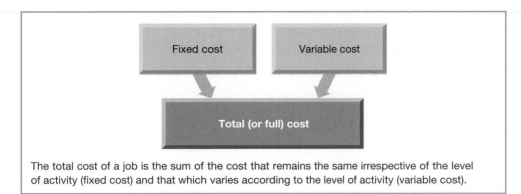

The total cost of a job is the sum of the cost that remains the same irrespective of the level of activity (fixed cost) and that which varies according to the level of activity (variable cost).

Figure 8.4 The relationship between fixed cost, variable cost and total cost

The apparent similarity of what is shown in Figure 8.4 to that shown in Figure 8.3 may create the impression that variable cost and direct cost are the same, and that fixed cost and indirect cost (overheads) are the same. This, however, is not the case.

Fixed cost and variable cost are defined in terms of how costs behave in the face of changes in the volume of activity. Direct cost and indirect cost, on the other hand, are defined in terms of the extent to which they can be identified with, and measured in respect of, particular cost units (jobs). These two sets of notions are entirely different. While a fixed cost can often be an indirect cost and a variable cost can often be a direct cost, this is far from being a hard and fast rule. Take, for example, most manufactured products. They are likely to have indirect cost, such as power for machinery, which is variable, and direct cost, such as labour, which is fixed. Thus, identifying a cost as being either indirect or direct tells us nothing about whether it is fixed or variable.

The relationship between the reaction of cost to volume changes, on the one hand, and how cost elements must be gathered to deduce the full cost for a particular job, on the other, is shown in Figure 8.5.

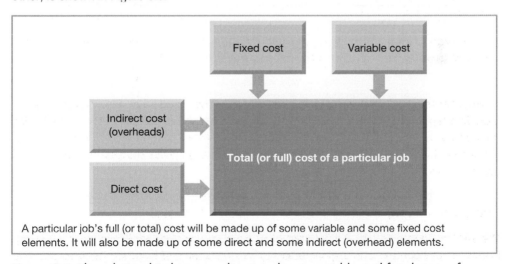

A particular job's full (or total) cost will be made up of some variable and some fixed cost elements. It will also be made up of some direct and some indirect (overhead) elements.

Figure 8.5 The relationship between direct, indirect, variable and fixed costs of a particular job

Total cost is the sum of direct and indirect costs. It is also the sum of fixed and variable costs. These two facts are not connected.

The problem of indirect cost

It is worth emphasising that the distinction between direct and indirect cost is only important in a job-costing environment, that is, where units of output differ. This distinction was of no consequence when costing a litre of 'Orange Fizz' drink (Activity 8.1) as all of the cost was shared equally between the individual litres of 'Orange Fizz'. Where units of output are not identical, however, this cannot be done if we wish to achieve a useful measure of the full cost of a particular job.

While indirect cost must form part of the full cost of each cost unit, it cannot, by definition, be identified directly with particular cost units. This raises a major practical issue: how can indirect cost be assigned to individual cost units?

OVERHEADS AS SERVICE RENDERERS

Indirect cost (overheads) can be viewed as rendering a service to cost units. Take, for example, a legal case undertaken by a firm of solicitors for a particular client. This case can be regarded as receiving a service from the office in which the work is done. It seems reasonable, therefore, to charge each case (cost unit) with a share of the cost of running the office (rent, lighting, heating, cleaning, building maintenance and so on). It also seems reasonable for this charge to be related to the amount of service received by each particular case from the office.

The next step is the difficult one. How might the cost of running the office, which is a cost incurred for all the work undertaken by the firm, be divided between individual legal cases that differ in size and complexity?

The easiest way would be to share this overhead cost equally between each case handled by the firm within the period. This method, however, has little to commend it.

Activity 8.6

Can you think why sharing overheads equally has little to commend it?

It is because it is highly unlikely that each case will have received identical service from the office.

Where they have not received identical service, we must identify something, which is both observable and measurable, about the various individual cases that allows us to distinguish between them. In practice, time spent working on each individual case by direct labour tends to be used. It must be stressed, however, that this is not the 'correct' way and it is certainly not the only way.

Job costing: a worked example

To see how job costing works, let us consider Example 8.1.

Example 8.1

Johnson Ltd, a business that provides a personal computer maintenance and repair service, has overheads of £10,000 each month. Each month 1,000 direct labour hours are worked and charged to cost units (jobs carried out by the business). A particular PC repair undertaken by the business used direct materials costing £15. Direct labour worked on the repair was 3 hours and the wage rate is £16 an hour. Johnson Ltd charges overheads to jobs on a direct labour hour basis. What is the full (absorption) cost of the repair?

Solution

First, let us establish the **overhead absorption (recovery) rate**, that is, the rate at which individual repairs will be charged with overheads. This is £10 (that is, £10,000/1,000) per direct labour hour.

Thus, the full cost of the repair is:

	£
Direct materials	15
Direct labour (3 × £16)	48
	63
Overheads (3 × £10)	30
Full cost of the job	93

Note, in Example 8.1, that the number of labour hours (3 hours) appears twice in deducing the full cost: once to deduce the direct labour cost and a second time to deduce the overheads to be charged to the repair. These are really two separate issues, though they are both based on the same number of labour hours.

Note also that, if all the jobs undertaken during the month are assigned overheads in a similar manner, all £10,000 of overheads will be charged between the various jobs. Jobs that involve a lot of direct labour will be assigned a large share of overheads. Similarly, jobs that involve little direct labour will be assigned a small share of overheads.

Activity 8.7

Can you think of reasons why direct labour hours tend to be regarded as the most appropriate basis for sharing overheads between cost units?

The reasons that occurred to us are as follows:

- Large jobs should logically attract large amounts of overheads because they are likely to have been rendered more 'service' by the overheads than small ones. The length of time that they are worked on by direct labour may be seen as a rough way of measuring relative size, though other means of doing this may be found – for example, relative physical size, where the cost unit is a physical object, like a manufactured product.

■ Most overheads are related to time. Rent, heating, lighting, non-current asset depreciation, supervisors' and managers' salaries, which are all typical overheads, are all more or less time-based. That is to say that the overheads for one week tend to be about half of those for a similar two-week period. Thus, a basis of allotting overheads to jobs that takes account of the length of time that the units of output benefited from the 'service' rendered by the overheads seems logical.

■ Direct labour hours are capable of being measured for each job. They will normally be measured to deduce the direct labour element of cost in any case. Thus, a direct labour hour basis of dealing with overheads is practical to apply in the real world.

It cannot be emphasised enough that there is no 'correct' way to allot overheads to jobs. Overheads cannot, by definition, automatically be identified with individual jobs. If, nevertheless, we wish to take account of the fact that overheads are part of the full cost of all jobs, we must find some way of allotting a share of the total overheads to each job. In practice, the direct labour hour method seems to be the most popular way of doing so. Real World 8.4, which we consider later in the chapter, provides some evidence of this.

Now let us consider **Real World 8.3,** which gives an example of one well-known organisation that does not use direct labour hours to cost its output.

REAL WORLD 8.3

Recovering costs

As we saw in Real World 8.1, the UK National Health Service (NHS) seeks to ascertain the cost of various medical and surgical procedures that it undertakes for its patients. In determining the costs of a procedure that requires time in hospital as an 'in patient', the NHS identifies the full cost of the particular procedure (for example, a knee replacement operation). To this it adds a share of the hospital overheads to cover the cost of the patient's stay in hospital. The proportion of total ward overheads absorbed by an individual patient is arrived at by dividing the overhead total figure by the number of 'bed days' throughout the hospital for the period in order to establish a 'bed-day rate'. A bed day is one patient spending one day occupying a bed in the hospital. Thus the full cost of a particular patient's treatment is the cost of the procedure plus the cost of the appropriate number of bed days.

Note that the NHS does not use the direct labour hour basis of absorption. The bed-day rate is, however, an alternative, logical, time-based approach.

Source: NHS England (2014), *NHS Better care, better value indicators,* 15 May, http://www.productivity.nhs.uk.

Activity 8.8

Marine Suppliers Ltd undertakes a range of work, including making sails for small sailing boats on a made-to-measure basis.

The business expects the following to arise during the next month:

Direct labour cost	£60,000
Direct labour time	6,000 hours
Indirect labour cost	£9,000
Depreciation of machinery	£3,000
Rent	£5,000
Heating, lighting and power	£2,000
Machine time	2,000 hours
Indirect materials	£500
Other miscellaneous indirect production cost elements (overheads)	£200
Direct materials cost	£3,000

The business has received an enquiry about a sail. It is estimated that the particular sail will take 12 direct labour hours to make and will require 20 square metres of sailcloth, which costs £2 per square metre.

The business normally uses a direct labour hour basis of charging indirect cost (overheads) to individual jobs.

What is the full (absorption) cost of making the sail?

The direct cost of making the sail can be identified as follows:

	£
Direct materials (20 × £2)	40.00
Direct labour (12 × (£60,000/6,000))	120.00
	160.00

To deduce the indirect cost (overhead) element that must be added to derive the full cost of the sail, we first need to total these cost elements as follows:

	£
Indirect labour	9,000
Depreciation	3,000
Rent	5,000
Heating, lighting and power	2,000
Indirect materials	500
Other miscellaneous indirect production cost (overhead) elements	200
Total indirect cost (overheads)	19,700

Since the business uses a direct labour hour basis of charging indirect cost to jobs, we need to deduce the indirect cost (or overhead) recovery rate per direct labour hour. This is simply:

$$£19,700/6,000 = £3.28 \text{ per direct labour hour}$$

Thus, the full cost of the sail is expected to be:

	£
Direct materials (20 × £2)	40.00
Direct labour (12 × (£60,000/6,000))	120.00
Indirect cost (12 × £3.28)	39.36
Full cost	199.36

Figure 8.6 shows the process for applying indirect (overhead) and direct costs to the sail that was the subject of Activity 8.8.

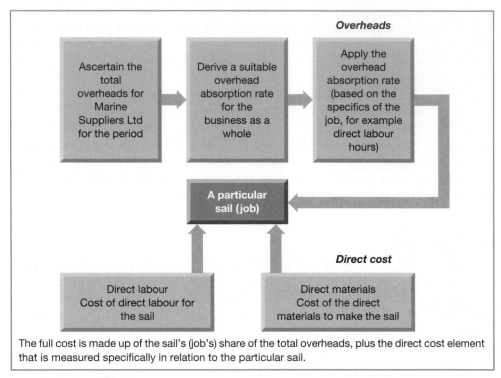

Overheads

| Ascertain the total overheads for Marine Suppliers Ltd for the period | Derive a suitable overhead absorption rate for the business as a whole | Apply the overhead absorption rate (based on the specifics of the job, for example direct labour hours) |

A particular sail (job)

Direct cost

| Direct labour Cost of direct labour for the sail | Direct materials Cost of the direct materials to make the sail |

The full cost is made up of the sail's (job's) share of the total overheads, plus the direct cost element that is measured specifically in relation to the particular sail.

Figure 8.6 How the full cost is derived for the sail by Marine Suppliers Ltd in Activity 8.8

Activity 8.9

Suppose that Marine Suppliers Ltd (see Activity 8.8) used a machine hour basis of charging overheads to jobs. What would be the cost of the particular job if it was expected to take 5 machine hours (as well as 12 direct labour hours)?

The total overheads of the business will of course be the same irrespective of the method of charging them to jobs. Thus, the overhead recovery rate, on a machine hour basis, will be:

£19,700/2,000 = £9.85 per machine hour

The full cost of the sail is, therefore, expected to be:

	£
Direct materials (20 × £2)	40.00
Direct labour (12 × (£60,000/6,000))	120.00
Indirect cost (5 × £9.85)	49.25
Full cost	209.25

Selecting a basis for charging overheads

We saw earlier that there is no single correct way of charging overheads. The final choice is a matter of judgement. It is reasonable to suggest, however, that the nature of the overheads should influence how overheads are charged to jobs. Where production is capital intensive and overheads are primarily machine based (such as depreciation, machine maintenance, power and so on), machine hours might be favoured. Otherwise direct labour hours might be preferred.

It would be irrational to choose one of these methods in preference to the other simply because it apportions either a higher or a lower amount of overheads to a particular job. The total overheads will be the same irrespective of how they are apportioned between individual jobs and so a method that gives a higher share of overheads to some jobs must give a lower share to the other jobs. There is one cake of fixed size: if one person receives a relatively large slice, others must on average receive relatively small slices. To illustrate further this issue of apportioning overheads, consider Example 8.2.

Example 8.2

A business, that provides a service, expects to incur overheads totalling £20,000 next month. The total direct labour time worked is expected to be 1,600 hours and machines are expected to operate for a total of 1,000 hours.

During the next month, the business expects to do just two large jobs. Information concerning each job is as follows:

	Job 1	Job 2
Direct labour hours	800	800
Machine hours	700	300

How much of the total overheads will be charged to each job if overheads are to be charged on:

(a) a direct labour hour basis; and
(b) a machine hour basis?

What do you notice about the two sets of figures that you calculate?

Solution

(a) Direct labour hour basis

Overhead recovery rate = £20,000/1,600 = £12.50 per direct labour hour.

Job 1	£12.50 × 800 = £10,000
Job 2	£12.50 × 800 = £10,000

(b) Machine hour basis

Overhead recovery rate = £20,000/1,000 = £20.00 per machine hour.

Job 1	£20.00 × 700 = £14,000
Job 2	£20.00 × 300 = £6,000

$\rightarrow$

It is clear from these calculations that the total overheads charged to jobs is the same (that is, £20,000), whichever method is used. Whereas the machine hour basis gives Job 1 a higher share of these overheads than the direct labour hour method, the opposite is true for Job 2.

It is not feasible to charge overheads using one method for one job and using the other method for the other job. This would mean either total overheads would not be fully charged to the jobs, or the jobs would be overcharged with overheads. If, for example, the direct labour hour method was used for Job 1 (£10,000) and the machine hour basis was used for Job 2 (£6,000), only £16,000 of a total £20,000 of overheads would be charged to jobs. As a result, the objective of full (absorption) costing, which is to charge *all* overhead costs to jobs carried out during the period, would not be achieved. Furthermore, if selling prices are based on full cost, there is a risk that this particular business would not charge high enough prices to cover all of its costs.

Figure 8.7 shows the effect of the two different methods of charging overheads to Jobs 1 and 2.

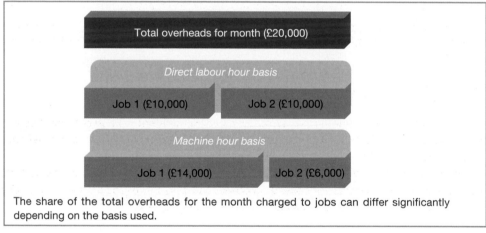

The share of the total overheads for the month charged to jobs can differ significantly depending on the basis used.

Figure 8.7 The effect of different bases of charging overheads to jobs in Example 8.2

Activity 8.10

The point has just been made that it would normally be irrational to prefer one basis of charging overheads to jobs simply because it apportions either a higher or a lower amount of overheads to a particular job. This is because the total overheads are the same irrespective of the method of charging the total to individual jobs. Can you think of any circumstances where it may not be so irrational?

This might occur where a customer has agreed to pay a price for a particular job based on full cost plus an agreed fixed percentage for profit. Here it would be beneficial to the producer for the total cost of the job to be as high as possible.

The circumstances outlined in the answer to Activity 8.10 would be relatively unusual, but sometimes public sector organisations, particularly central and local government departments, have been known to enter into such **cost-plus pricing** contracts. They are, however, now pretty rare as they are so open to abuse. Normally, contract prices are agreed in advance, typically in conjunction with competitive tendering.

Real World 8.4 provides some insight into the basis of overhead recovery in practice.

REAL WORLD 8.4

Overhead recovery rates in practice

A survey of 129 UK manufacturing businesses showed that the direct labour hour basis (or a close approximation to it) of charging indirect cost (overheads) to cost units was overwhelmingly the most popular. It was used by 72 per cent of the respondents to the survey.

Fifteen per cent of respondents used a 'production-time based overhead rate'. This is presumably something like a machine-hour rate.

Though this survey applied only to manufacturing businesses, in the absence of other information it provides some impression of what happens in practice.

Source: Based on information taken from, Brierley, J., Cowton, C. and Drury, C. (2007) Product costing practices in different manufacturing industries: A British survey, *International Journal of Management*, December pp. 667–675.

Segmenting the overheads

We have just seen that charging the same overheads to different jobs on different bases is not feasible. It is perfectly feasible, however, to charge one segment of the total overheads on one basis and another segment on another basis.

Segmenting the overheads in this way is quite common. A business may be divided into separate areas (cost centres) for costing purposes, charging overheads differently from one area to the next, according to the nature of the work done in each.

Activity 8.11

Taking the same business as in Example 8.2 (page 000), on closer analysis we find that of the overheads totalling £20,000 next month, £8,000 relate to machines (depreciation, maintenance, rent of the space occupied by the machines and so on) and the remaining £12,000 to more general overheads. The other information about the business is exactly as it was before.

How much of the total overheads will be charged to each job if the machine-related overheads are to be charged on a machine hour basis and the remaining overheads are charged on a direct labour hour basis?

Direct labour hour basis

> Overhead recovery rate = £12,000/1,600 = £7.50 per direct labour hour

Machine hour basis

> Overhead recovery rate = £8,000/1,000 = £8.00 per machine hour

Overheads charged to jobs

	Job 1 £	Job 2 £
Direct labour hour basis:		
£7.50 × 800	6,000	
£7.50 × 800		6,000
Machine hour basis:		
£8.00 × 700	5,600	
£8.00 × 300		2,400
Total	11,600	8,400

We can see from this that all the overheads of £20,000 have been charged.

Dealing with overheads on a cost centre basis

In practice, all but the smallest businesses tend to be divided into departments with each department dealing with a separate activity. The reasons for departmentalising the business include the following:

- *Size and complexity.* Many businesses are too large and complex to be managed as a single unit. It is usually more practical to operate each business as a series of relatively independent units with each one having its own manager.
- *Expertise.* Each department normally has its own area of specialism and is managed by a specialist.
- *Accountability.* Each department can have its own accounting records that enable its performance to be assessed. This can lead to greater management control and motivation among the staff.

As is shown in Real World 8.5, which we shall consider shortly, in practice most businesses charge overheads to cost units on a department-by-department basis. They do this because they expect that it will give rise to a more useful way of charging overheads. It is probably only in a minority of cases that it leads to any great improvement in the usefulness of the resulting full cost figures. Although it may not be of enormous benefit, applying overheads on a departmental basis is probably not an expensive exercise. Since cost elements are collected department by department for other purposes (particularly control), to apply overheads on a department-by-department basis is a relatively simple matter.

We shall now take a look at how the departmental approach to deriving full cost works, in a service industry context, through Example 8.3.

Example 8.3

Autosparkle Ltd offers a motor vehicle paint-respray service. The jobs that it undertakes range from painting a small part of a saloon car, usually following a minor accident, to a complete respray of a double-decker bus.

Each job starts life in the Preparation Department, where it is prepared for the Paintshop. Here, the job is worked on by direct workers, in most cases taking some direct materials from the stores with which to treat the old paintwork and, generally, to render the vehicle ready for respraying. Thus the job will be charged with direct materials, direct labour and with a share of the Preparation Department's overheads. The job then passes into the Paintshop Department, already valued at the cost that it picked up in the Preparation Department.

In the Paintshop, the staff draw direct materials (mainly paint) from the stores and direct workers spend time respraying the job, using sophisticated spraying apparatus as well as working by hand. So, in the Paintshop, the job is charged with direct materials, direct labour and a share of that department's overheads. The job now passes into the Finishing Department, valued at the cost of the materials, labour and overheads that it accumulated in the first two departments.

In the Finishing Department, jobs are cleaned and polished ready to go back to the customers. Further direct labour and, in some cases, materials are added. All jobs also pick up a share of that department's overheads. The job, now complete, passes back to the customer.

Figure 8.8 shows graphically how this works for a particular job.

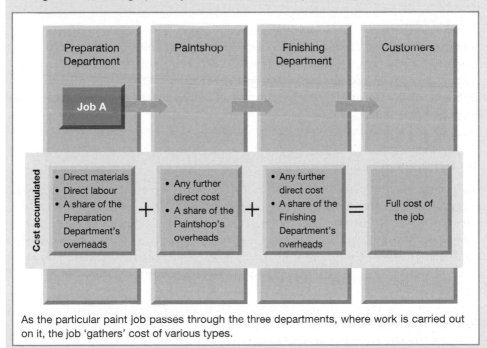

As the particular paint job passes through the three departments, where work is carried out on it, the job 'gathers' cost of various types.

Figure 8.8 A cost unit (Job A) passing through Autosparkle Ltd's process

→

The approach to charging overheads to jobs (for example, direct labour hours) might be the same for all three departments, or it might be different from one department to another. It is possible that cost elements relating to the spraying apparatus dominate the Paintshop overhead cost, so the Paintshop's overheads might well be charged to jobs on a machine hour basis. The other two departments are probably labour intensive, so that direct labour hours may be seen as being appropriate there.

The passage of a job through the departments, picking up cost as it goes, can be compared to a snowball being rolled across snow: as it rolls, it picks up more and more snow.

Where cost determination is dealt with departmentally, each department is known as a **cost centre**. This can be defined as a particular physical area or some activity or function for which the cost is separately identified. Charging direct cost to jobs, in a departmental system, is exactly the same as where the whole business is one single cost centre. It is simply a matter of keeping a record of:

- the number of hours of direct labour worked on the particular job and the grade of labour, where there are different grades with different rates of pay;
- the cost of the direct materials taken from stores and applied to the job; and
- any other direct cost elements, for example some subcontracted work, associated with the job.

This record keeping will normally be done cost centre by cost centre.

It is obviously necessary to break down the production overheads of the entire business on a cost centre basis. This means that the total overheads of the business must be divided between the cost centres, such that the sum of the overheads of all of the cost centres equals the overheads for the entire business. By charging all of their overheads to jobs, the cost centres will, between them, charge all of the overheads of the business to jobs. **Real World 8.5** provides an indication of the number of different cost centres that businesses tend to use in practice.

REAL WORLD 8.5

Cost centres in practice

It is usual for businesses to have several cost centres. A survey of 186 larger UK businesses involved in various activities by Drury and Tayles showed the following:

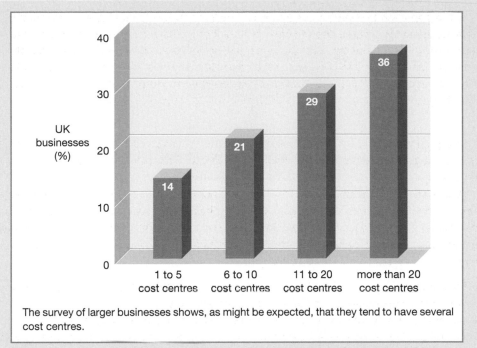

The survey of larger businesses shows, as might be expected, that they tend to have several cost centres.

Figure 8.9 Analysis of the number of cost centres within a business

We can see that 86 per cent of businesses surveyed had six or more cost centres and that 36 per cent of businesses had more than 20 cost centres. Although not shown on the diagram, 3 per cent of businesses surveyed had a single cost centre (that is, there was a business-wide or overall overhead rate used). Clearly, businesses that deal with overheads on a business-wide basis are relatively rare.

Source: Based on information taken from Drury, C. and Tayles, M. 'Profitability analysis in UK organisations', (2006), *British Accounting Review*, December, pp. 405–425.

Batch costing

Many types of goods and some services are produced in a batch of identical, or nearly identical, units of output. Each batch produced, however, is distinctly different from other batches. A theatre, for example, may put on a production whose nature and cost is very different from that of other productions. On the other hand, ignoring differences in the desirability of the various types of seating, all of the individual units of output (tickets to see the production) are identical.

In these circumstances, the cost per ticket is calculated using **batch costing** and involves:

- using a job costing approach (taking account of direct and indirect costs and so on) to find the cost of mounting the production; and then
- dividing the cost of mounting the production by the expected number of tickets to be sold to find the cost per ticket.

Figure 8.10 shows the process for deriving the cost of one cost unit (product) in a batch.

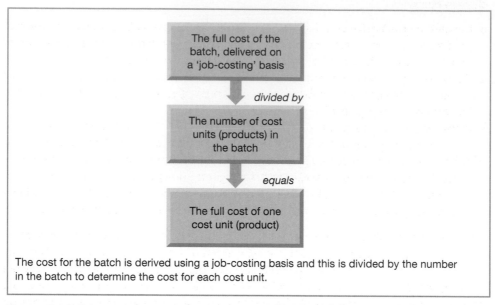

The full cost of the batch, delivered on a 'job-costing' basis

divided by

The number of cost units (products) in the batch

equals

The full cost of one cost unit (product)

The cost for the batch is derived using a job-costing basis and this is divided by the number in the batch to determine the cost for each cost unit.

Figure 8.10 Deriving the cost of one cost unit where production is in batches

Batch costing is used in a variety of industries, including clothing manufacturing, engineering component manufacturing, tyre manufacturing, bakery goods and footwear manufacturing.

The forward-looking nature of full (absorption) costing

Although deducing full cost can be done after the work has been completed, it is frequently predicted in advance. This is often because an idea of the full cost is needed as a basis for setting a selling price. Predictions, however, rarely turn out to be 100 per cent accurate. Where actual outcomes differ from predicted outcomes an over-recovery or under-recovery of overheads will normally occur.

ACTIVITY-BASED COSTING

We have seen that the traditional approach to job/batch costing involves identifying that part of the cost that can be measured in respect of a particular job/batch (direct cost). Other cost elements (overheads) are thrown into a pool of cost. These are then charged to individual jobs/batches according to some formula, such as the number of direct labour hours worked.

Costing and pricing: the traditional way

The traditional, and still widely used, approach to job costing and product pricing developed when the notion of trying to determine the cost of industrial production first emerged. This was around the time of the UK Industrial Revolution when industry displayed the following characteristics:

- *Direct-labour-intensive and direct-labour-paced production.* Labour was at the heart of production. To the extent that machinery was used, it tended to support the efforts of direct labour and the speed of production was dictated by direct labour.
- *A low level of indirect cost relative to direct cost.* Little was spent on power, personnel services, machinery (leading to low depreciation charges) and other areas typical of the indirect cost (overheads) of modern businesses.
- *A relatively uncompetitive market.* Transport difficulties, limited industrial production worldwide and a lack of knowledge by customers of competitors' prices meant that businesses could prosper without being too scientific in their approach to deriving full costs. Typically they could simply add a margin for profit to arrive at the selling price (cost-plus pricing). In addition, customers would have tended to accept those products that the supplier had to offer, rather than demanding precisely what they wanted.

Since overheads at that time represented a pretty small element of total cost, it was acceptable and practical to deal with them in a fairly arbitrary manner. Not too much effort was devoted to trying to control overheads because the potential rewards of better control were relatively small, certainly when compared with the benefits from firmer control of direct labour and material costs. It was also reasonable to charge overheads to individual jobs on a direct labour hour basis. Most of the overheads were incurred in support of direct labour: providing direct workers with a place to work, heating and lighting the workplace, employing people to supervise the direct workers and so on. Direct workers, perhaps aided by machinery, carried out all production.

At that time, service industries were a relatively unimportant part of the economy and would have largely consisted of self-employed individuals. These individuals would probably have been uninterested in trying to do more than work out a rough hourly/daily rate for their time and to try to base prices on this.

Costing and pricing: the new environment

In recent years, the world of industrial production has fundamentally changed. Most of it is now characterised by the following:

- *Capital-intensive and machine-paced production.* Machines are at the heart of much production, including both the manufacture of goods and the rendering of services. Most labour supports the efforts of machines, for example, technically maintaining them. Also, machines often dictate the pace of production. According to evidence provided in Real World 8.2 (page 000), direct labour accounts on average for just 14 per cent of manufacturers' total cost.
- *A high level of indirect cost relative to direct costs.* Modern businesses tend to have very high depreciation, servicing and power costs. There are also high costs of personnel and staff welfare, which were scarcely envisaged in the early days of industrial production. At the same time, there are very low (sometimes no) direct labour costs. Although direct material cost often remains an important element of total cost, more efficient production and quality control methods lead to less waste and, therefore, to a lower total material

cost, again tending to make indirect cost (overheads) more dominant. We saw in Real World 8.2, overheads account for 25 per cent of manufacturers' total cost and 51 per cent of service sector total cost.

■ *A highly competitive international market.* Production, much of it highly sophisticated, is carried out worldwide. Transport, including fast airfreight, is easy and relatively cheap. Fax, telephone and, particularly, the Internet ensure that potential customers can quickly and cheaply find the prices of a range of suppliers. Markets now tend to be highly price competitive. Customers increasingly demand products custom made to their own requirements. This means that businesses need to know their product costs with a greater degree of accuracy than historically has been the case. Businesses also need to take a considered and informed approach to pricing their output.

In the UK, as in many developed countries, service industries now dominate the economy, employing the great majority of the workforce and producing most of the value of productive output. Though there are still many self-employed individuals supplying services (for example, plumbers), many service providers are vast businesses.

Activity 8.12

Can you think of two types of service provider that are vast businesses?

Examples include:

■ banks
■ insurance businesses
■ cinema operators
■ supermarkets
■ restaurant chains

You may have thought of others.

For many of these larger service providers, the activities very closely resemble modern manufacturing activity. They too are characterised by high capital intensity, overheads dominating direct costs and a competitive international market.

In the past, the traditional approach to determining product costs has worked reasonably well, mainly because overhead recovery rates (that is, rates at which overheads are absorbed by jobs) were typically of a much lower value for each direct labour hour than the rate paid to direct workers as wages or salaries. It is now, however, becoming increasingly common for overhead recovery rates to be between five and ten times the hourly rate of pay, because overheads are now much more significant. When production is dominated by direct labour paid, say, £8 an hour, it might be reasonable to have an overhead recovery rate of, say, £1 an hour. When, however, direct labour plays a relatively small part in production, to have an overhead recovery rate of, say, £50 for each direct labour hour is likely to lead to very arbitrary product costing. Even a small change in the amount of direct labour worked on a job could massively affect the total cost deduced. This is not because the direct worker is very highly paid, but because of the effect of the direct labour hours on the overhead cost loading. A further problem is that overheads are still typically charged on a direct labour hour basis even though the overheads may not be closely related to direct labour.

Real World 8.6 provides a rather disturbing view of costing and cost control in large banks.

REAL WORLD 8.6

Bank accounts

In a study of the cost structures of 52 international banks, the German consultancy firm, Droege, found that indirect cost (overheads) could represent as much as 85 per cent of total cost. However, whilst direct costs were generally under tight management control, overheads were not. The overheads, which include such items as IT development, risk control, auditing, marketing and public relations, were often not allocated between operating divisions or were allocated in a rather arbitrary manner.

Source: Based on information in Skorecki, A. (2004) 'Banks have not tackled indirect costs', ft.com, 7 January.

Taking a closer look

The changes in the competitive environment discussed above have led to much closer attention being paid to the issue of overheads. There has been increasing recognition of the fact that overheads do not just happen; something must be causing them. To illustrate this point, let us consider Example 8.4.

Example 8.4

Modern Producers Ltd has a storage area that is set aside for its inventories of finished goods. The cost of running the stores includes a share of the factory rent and other establishment costs, such as heating and lighting. It also includes the salaries of staff employed to look after the inventories and the cost of financing the inventories held in the stores.

The business has just two product lines: A and B. Product A tends to be made in small batches and low levels of finished inventories are held. The business prides itself on its ability to supply Product B, in relatively large quantities, instantly. As a consequence, most of the space in the finished goods store is filled with finished Product Bs, ready to be despatched immediately an order is received.

Traditionally, the whole cost of operating the stores would have been treated as a part of general overheads and included in the total of overheads charged to jobs, probably on a direct labour hour basis. This means that, when assessing the cost of Products A and B, the cost of operating the stores has fallen on them according to the number of direct labour hours worked on manufacturing each one; a factor that has nothing to do with storage. In fact, most of the stores' cost should be charged to Product B, since this product causes (and benefits from) the stores' cost much more than Product A.

→

> Failure to account more precisely for the cost of running the stores is masking the fact that Product B is not as profitable as it seems to be. It may even be leading to losses as a result of the relatively high stores-operating cost that it causes. However, much of this cost is charged to Product A, without regard to the fact that Product A causes little of it.

ABC contrasted with the traditional approach

Activity-based costing (ABC) aims to overcome the kind of problem just illustrated in Example 8.4. There is a basic philosophical difference between the traditional and the ABC approaches. The traditional approach views overheads as *rendering a service to cost units,* the cost of which must be charged to those units. (Products A and B are the cost units in Example 8.4.) ABC, on the other hand, views overheads as being *caused by* activities, like operating a store to house the cost units. Since it is the cost units that cause these activities, it is, therefore, the cost units that must be charged with the costs that they cause. The more cost that they cause, the more of the overheads they are charged with.

With the traditional approach, overheads are apportioned to product cost centres. For each product cost centre an overhead recovery rate would be derived, typically overheads per direct labour hour. Overheads would then be applied to units of output according to how many direct labour hours were worked on them.

With ABC, the overheads are analysed into cost pools, with one cost pool for each cost-driving activity. The overheads are then charged to units of output, through activity cost driver rates. These rates are an attempt to represent the extent to which each particular cost unit is assessed as having caused the particular part of the overheads.

Cost pools are much the same as cost centres, except that each cost pool is linked to a particular *activity* (operating the stores in Example 8.4), rather than being more general, as is the case with cost centres in traditional job (or product) costing.

Directly linking the cost of all support activities (that is, activities that cause overheads) to particular products or services, potentially provides a more realistic, and more finely measured, account of the overhead cost element for a particular product or service. For a manufacturing business, these support activities may include materials ordering, materials handling, storage, inspection and so on. The cost of the support activities makes up the total overheads cost.

To implement a system of ABC, managers must begin by carefully examining the business's operations. They will need to identify:

- each of the various support activities involved in the process of making products or providing services;
- the costs to be attributed to each support activity; and
- the factors that cause a change in the costs of each support activity, that is the **cost drivers**.

Identifying the cost drivers is a vital element of a successful ABC system. They have a cause-and-effect relationship with activity costs and so are used as a basis for attaching activity costs to a particular product or service. This point is now discussed further.

Attributing overheads

Once the various support activities, their costs and the factors that drive these costs have been identified, ABC requires:

1. An overhead **cost pool** to be established for each activity. Thus, Modern Producers Ltd, the business in Example 8.4, will create a cost pool for operating the finished goods store. There will be just one cost pool for each separate cost driver.
2. The total cost associated with each support activity to be allocated to the relevant cost pool.
3. The total cost in each pool to then be charged to output (Products A and B, in the case of Example 8.4) using the relevant cost driver.

Step 3 (above) involves dividing the amount in each cost pool by the estimated total usage of the cost driver to derive a cost per unit of the cost driver. This unit cost figure is then multiplied by the number of units of the cost driver used by a particular product, or service, to determine the amount of overhead cost to be attached to it (or absorbed by it).

Example 8.5 should make this last step clear.

Example 8.5

The management accountant at Modern Producers Ltd (see Example 8.4) has estimated that the cost of running the finished goods stores for next year will be £90,000. This will be the amount allocated to the 'finished goods stores cost pool'.

It is estimated that each Product A will spend an average of one week in the stores before being sold. With Product B, the equivalent period is four weeks. Both products are of roughly similar size and have very similar storage needs. It is felt, therefore, that the period spent in the stores ('product weeks') is the cost driver.

Next year, 50,000 Product As and 25,000 Product Bs are expected to pass through the stores. The estimated total usage of the cost driver will be the total number of 'product weeks' that the products will be in store. For next year, this will be:

Product	A	50,000 × 1 week	=	50,000
Product	B	25,000 × 4 weeks	=	100,000
				150,000

The cost per unit of cost driver is the total cost of the stores divided by the number of 'product weeks', as calculated above. This is:

$$£90,000/150,000 = £0.60$$

To determine the cost to be attached to a particular unit of product, the figure of £0.60 must be multiplied by the number of 'product weeks' that a product stays in the finished goods store. Thus, each unit of Product A will be charged with £0.60 (that is, £0.60 × 1) and each Product B with £2.40 (that is, £0.60 × 4).

The traditional and ABC approaches are illustrated in Figure 8.11.

Traditional approach

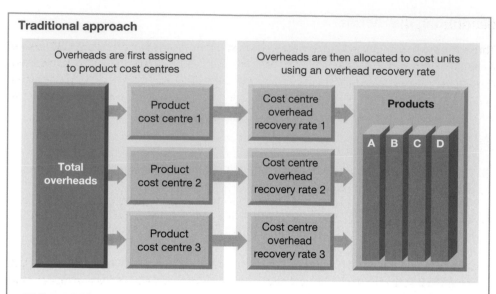

ABC approach

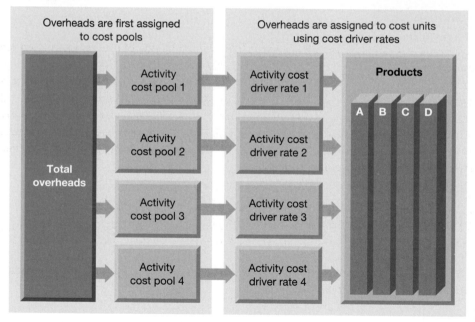

With the traditional approach, overheads are first assigned to product cost centres and then absorbed by cost units based on an overhead recovery rate (using direct labour hours worked on the cost units or some other approach) for each cost centre. With activity-based costing, overheads are assigned to cost pools and then cost units are charged with these elements to the extent that they drive the costs in the various pools.

Source: Adapted from *Activity Based Costing: A Review with Case Studies*, J. Innes and F. Mitchell, CIMA Publishing, 1990.

Figure 8.11 Traditional versus activity-based costing

Benefits of ABC

Through the direct tracing of overheads to products in the way described, ABC seeks to establish a more accurate cost for each unit of product or service. This should help managers in assessing product profitability. It should also help them in making decisions concerning pricing and the appropriate product mix. Further benefits may also flow from adopting an ABC approach.

Can you think of any further benefits that an ABC approach to costing may provide?

By identifying the various support activities' costs and analysing what causes them to change (what drives them), managers should gain a better understanding of the business. This, in turn, should help them in controlling overheads and improving efficiency.

Identifying support activities and their cost drivers should also help managers in forward planning. They may, for example, be in a better position to assess the likely effect of new products and processes on activities and costs.

ABC and service industries

Much of our discussion of ABC has concentrated on the manufacturing industry, perhaps because early users of ABC were manufacturing businesses. In fact, ABC is probably even more relevant to service industries because, in the absence of a direct material element, a service business's total cost is likely to be largely made up of overheads. Real World 8.2 (page 000) shows that, for the businesses included in that survey, overheads represent 51 per cent of total cost for service providers, but only 25 per cent for manufacturers. There is certainly evidence that ABC has been adopted more readily by businesses that sell services rather than products, as we shall see later.

What is the difference in the way in which direct costs are accounted for when using ABC, relative to their treatment taking a traditional approach to full costing?

The answer is no difference at all. ABC is concerned only with the way in which overheads are charged to jobs to derive the full cost.

Criticisms of ABC

Critics of ABC argue that analysing overheads in order to identify cost drivers can be time-consuming and costly. The costs of setting up the ABC system, as well as costs of running and updating it, must be incurred. These costs can be very high, particularly where the business's operations are complex and involve a large number of activities and cost drivers. Furthermore, where the products produced are quite similar, the finer measurements provided by ABC may not lead to strikingly different outcomes than under the traditional approach. Supporters of ABC may argue, however, that identifying the activities that cause the costs may still be well worth doing. As mentioned earlier, knowing what drives the costs may make cost control more effective.

ABC is also criticised for the same reason that full costing is generally criticised, which is that it does not provide relevant information for decision making. We shall address this point very shortly

Real World 8.7 shows how ABC came to be used at the Royal Mail.

REAL WORLD 8.7

Delivering ABC

Early in the 2000s, the previously publicly-owned Royal Mail adopted ABC and used it to find the cost of making postal deliveries. Royal Mail identified 340 activities that gave rise to costs, created a cost pool and identified a cost driver for each of these.

Royal Mail plc continues to use an ABC approach to deriving its costs. The volume of mail is obviously a major driver of costs.

Source: Information from Royal Mail Group Ltd (2015), Regulatory Financial Statements 2014/15 (July).

Real World 8.8 provides some indication of the extent to which ABC is used in practice.

REAL WORLD 8.8

ABC in practice

A survey of 176 UK businesses operating in various industries, all with an annual sales revenue of more than £50 million, was conducted by Al-Omiri and Drury. This indicated that 29 per cent of larger UK businesses use ABC.

The adoption of ABC in the UK varies widely between industries, as is shown in Figure 8.12.

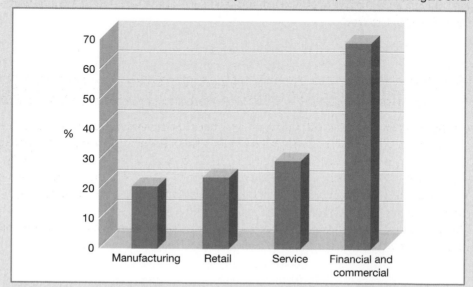

Figure 8.12 ABC in practice

Al-Omiri and Drury took their analysis a step further by looking at the factors that tend to characterise businesses that adopt ABC. They found that businesses that used ABC tended to be:

- large;
- sophisticated, in terms of using advanced management accounting techniques generally;
- in an intensely competitive market for their products;
- operating in a service industry, particularly in the financial services.

[It is interesting that Royal Mail (see Real World 8.7) closely fits this description.]

A more recent UK survey undertaken by the Chartered Institute of Management Accountants (CIMA) emphatically supported the finding that larger businesses tend to use ABC more than smaller ones. It showed that only 22 per cent of businesses with fewer than 50 employees use ABC, whereas 46 per cent of businesses with more than 10,000 employees use the technique.

A still more recent survey of the practices of 11 small and medium-sized UK businesses found that none of them assigned overheads to their output, using neither the traditional approach nor ABC.

All of these findings are broadly in line with other recent research evidence involving businesses from around the world.

Sources: Al-Omiri, M. and Drury, C. (2007), 'A survey of factors influencing the choice of product costing systems in UK organisations', *Management Accounting Research*, December, pp. 399–424; CIMA (2009) 'Management accounting tools for today and tomorrow', p. 12; and Lucas, M., Prowle, M. and Lowth, G. (2013), 'Management accounting practices of UK small-medium-sized enterprises', CIMA, p. 7.

The CIMA survey referred to in Real World 8.8 was conducted in July 2009. Broadly the survey asked management accountants in a wide range of business types and sizes to indicate the extent to which their business used a range of management accounting techniques. 439 management accountants completed the survey. We shall be making reference to this survey on a number of occasions throughout the book. When we do, we shall refer to it as the 'CIMA survey'.

USING FULL (ABSORPTION) COST INFORMATION

Both the traditional and the ABC methods have been criticised because, in practice, they tend to use past (historic) costs. It can be argued that past costs are irrelevant, irrespective of the purpose for which the information is to be used. This is basically because it is not possible to make decisions about the past, only about the future. Advocates of full costing methods would argue, however, that they provide a useful guide to long-run average cost.

Despite the criticisms made of full costing methods, the CIMA study suggests that their use is widespread, as is indicated in **Real World 8.9**.

The use of full cost information

The businesses surveyed by CIMA derived full cost information to the following extent (see Figure 8.13):

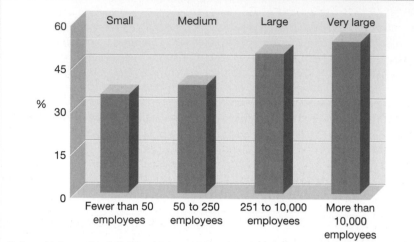

Full cost information is fairly widely used and the size of the business seems to be a factor. It is used by about 45 per cent of all of the businesses surveyed.

The Lucas, Prowle and Lowth survey mentioned in Real World 8.8 found that none of the 11 businesses surveyed derives full cost information.

Figure 8.13 The use of full cost information

Source: Figure adapted from CIMA (2009) 'Management accounting tools for today and tomorrow', p. 12.

An International Accounting Standard (IAS 2 *Inventories*) requires that all inventories, including work in progress, be valued at full cost in the published financial statements. This fact demands the use of full costing. As a result, businesses that have work in progress and/ or inventories of finished goods at the end of their financial periods apply full costing for profit measurement purposes. (This will include the many service providers that tend to have work in progress.) This requirement alone may explain the widespread use of full costing.

Psilis Ltd makes a product in two qualities, called 'Basic' and 'Super'. The business is able to sell these products at a price that gives a standard profit mark-up of 25 per cent of full cost. Full cost is derived using a traditional batch costing approach.

Management is concerned by the lack of profit.

To derive the full cost for each product, overheads are absorbed on the basis of direct labour hours. The costs are as follows:

	Basic £	Super £
Direct labour (all £10 an hour)	40	60
Direct material	15	20

The total annual overheads are £1,000,000.

Based on experience over recent years, in the forthcoming year the business expects to make and sell 40,000 Basics and 10,000 Supers.

Recently, the business's management accountant has undertaken an exercise to try to identify activities and cost drivers in an attempt to be able to deal with the overheads on a more precise basis than had been possible before. This exercise has revealed the following analysis of the annual overheads:

Activity (and cost driver)	Cost	Annual number of activities		
	£000	Total	Basic	Super
Number of machine set-ups	280	100	20	80
Number of quality-control inspections	220	2,000	500	1,500
Number of sales orders processed	240	5,000	1,500	3,500
General production (machine hours)	260	500,000	350,000	150,000
Total	1,000			

The management accountant explained the analysis of the £1,000,000 overheads as follows:

- The two products are made in relatively small batches, so that the amount of the finished product held in inventories is negligible. The Supers are made in particularly small batches because the market demand for this product is relatively low. Each time a new batch is produced, the machines have to be reset by skilled staff. Resetting for Basic production occurs about 20 times a year and for Supers about 80 times: about 100 times in total. The cost of employing the machine-setting staff is about £280,000 a year. It is clear that the more set-ups that occur, the higher the total set-up costs; in other words, the number of set-ups is the factor that drives set-up costs.
- All production has to be inspected for quality and this costs about £220,000 a year. The higher specifications of the Supers mean that there is more chance that there will be quality problems. Thus the Supers are inspected in total 1,500 times annually, whereas the Basics only need about 500 inspections. The number of inspections is the factor that drives these costs.

- Sales order processing (dealing with customers' orders, from receiving the original order to dispatching the products) costs about £240,000 a year. Despite the larger amount of Basic production, there are only 1,500 sales orders each year because the Basics are sold to wholesalers in relatively large-sized orders. The Supers are sold mainly direct to the public by mail order, usually in very small-sized orders. It is believed that the number of orders drives the costs of processing orders.

Required:
(a) Deduce the full cost of each of the two products on the basis used at present and, from these, deduce the current selling price.
(b) Deduce the full cost of each product on an ABC basis, taking account of the management accountant's recent investigations.
(c) What conclusions do you draw? What advice would you offer the management of the business?

The solution to this question can be found at the back of the book on pages 530–531.

SUMMARY

The main points in this chapter may be summarised as follows:
Full (absorption) cost = the amount of resources sacrificed to achieve a particular objective.

Uses of full (absorption) cost information

- Pricing and output decisions
- Exercising control
- Assessing relative efficiency
- Profit measurement

Single-product businesses

- Where all the units of output are identical, the full cost can be calculated as follows:

$$\text{Cost per unit} = \frac{\text{Total cost of output}}{\text{Number of units produced}}$$

Multi-product businesses – job costing

- Where units of output are not identical, it is necessary to divide the cost into two categories: direct cost and indirect cost (overheads).
- Direct cost = cost that can be identified with specific cost units (for example, labour of a garage mechanic, in relation to a particular job).
- Indirect cost (overheads) = cost that cannot be directly measured in respect of a particular job (for example, the rent of a garage).

- Full (absorption) cost = direct cost + indirect cost.
- Direct/indirect is not linked to variable/fixed.
- Indirect cost is difficult to relate to individual cost units – arbitrary bases are used and there is no single correct method.
- Traditionally, indirect cost is seen as the cost of providing a 'service' to cost units.
- Direct labour hour basis of applying indirect cost to cost units is the most popular in practice.

Dealing with indirect cost on a cost centre (departmental) basis

- Indirect cost (overheads) can be segmented – usually on a cost centre basis – and each product cost centre has its own overhead recovery rate.
- Cost centres are areas, activities or functions for which cost is separately determined.

Batch costing

- A variation of job costing where each job consists of a number of identical (or near identical) cost units:

$$\text{Cost per unit} = \frac{\text{Cost of the batch (direct + indirect)}}{\text{Number of units in the batch}}$$

Activity-based costing

- Activity-based costing is an approach to dealing with overheads (in full costing) that treats all costs as being caused or 'driven' by activities.
- Advocates argue that it is more relevant to the modern commercial environment than is the traditional approach.
- Identification of the cost drivers can lead to more relevant indirect cost treatment in full costing.
- Identification of the cost drivers can also lead to better control of overheads.
- Critics argue that ABC is time-consuming and expensive to apply – not justified by the possible improvement in the quality of information.
- Full cost information is seen by some as not very useful because it can be backward looking: it includes information irrelevant to decision making, but excludes some relevant information.

FURTHER READING

If you would like to explore the topics covered in this chapter in more depth, we recommend the following books:

Atrill, P. and McLaney, E. (2015) *Management Accounting for Decision Makers,* 9th edn, Pearson, Chapters 4 and 5.

Bhimani A., Horngren, C., Datar, S. and Rajan, M. (2015) *Management and Cost Accounting,* 6th edn, Pearson, Chapters 3, 4 and 5.

Drury, C. (2015) *Management and Cost Accounting,* 9th edn, Cengage Learning EMEA, Chapters 3, 5 and 11.

Hilton, R. and Platt, D. (2014) *Managerial Accounting,* Global edn, McGraw-Hill Higher Education, Chapters 3, 4 and 5.

? REVIEW QUESTIONS

Solutions to these questions can be found at the back of the book on pages 544–545.

8.1 What problem does the existence of work in progress cause in process costing?

8.2 What is the point of distinguishing direct cost from indirect cost? Why is this not necessary in process costing environments?

8.3 Are direct cost and variable cost the same thing? Explain your answer.

8.4 How does activity-based costing (ABC) differ from the traditional approach? What is the underlying difference in the philosophy of each of them?

Exercises 8.1 and 8.2 are basic level. Exercise 8.3 is intermediate level and Exercises 8.4 and 8.5 are advanced level. Those with **coloured numbers** have solutions at the back of the book, starting on page 563.

8.1 Distinguish between

- job costing;
- process costing; and
- batch costing.

Fully explain each approach.

8.2 Pieman Products Ltd makes road trailers to the precise specifications of individual customers.

The following are predicted to occur during the forthcoming year, which is about to start:

Direct materials cost	£50,000
Direct labour cost	£160,000
Direct labour time	16,000 hours
Indirect labour cost	£25,000
Depreciation of machine	£8,000
Rent	£10,000
Heating, lighting and power	£5,000
Indirect materials	£2,000
Other indirect cost (overhead) elements	£1,000
Machine time	3,000 hours

All direct labour is paid at the same hourly rate.

A customer has asked the business to build a set of trailers for transporting racing motorcycles to race meetings. It is estimated that this will require materials and components that will cost £1,150. It will take 250 direct labour hours to do the job, of which 50 will involve the use of machinery.

Required:
Deduce a logical cost for the job and explain the basis of dealing with overheads that you propose.

8.3 Athena Ltd is an engineering business doing work for its customers to their particular requirements and specifications. It determines the full cost of each job taking a 'job costing' approach, accounting for overheads on a cost centre (departmental) basis. It bases its prices to customers on this full cost figure. The business has two departments (both of which are cost centres): a Machining Department, where each job starts, and a Fitting Department, which completes all of the jobs. Machining Department overheads are charged to jobs on a machine hour basis and those of the Fitting Department on a direct labour hour basis. The budgeted information for next year is as follows:

Heating and lighting	£25,000	(allocated equally between the two departments)
Machine power	£10,000	(all allocated to the Machining Department)
Direct labour	£200,000	(£150,000 allocated to the Fitting Department and £50,000 to the Machining Department. All direct workers are paid £10 an hour)
Indirect labour	£50,000	(apportioned to the departments in proportion to the direct labour cost)
Direct materials	£120,000	(all applied to jobs in the Machining Department)
Depreciation	£30,000	(all relates to the Machining Department)
Machine time	20,000 hours	(all worked in the Machining Department)

Required:

(a) Prepare a statement showing the budgeted overheads for next year, analysed between the two cost centres. This should be in the form of three columns: one for the total figure for each type of overhead and one column each for the two cost centres, where each type of overhead is analysed between the two cost centres. Each column should also show the total of overheads for the year.

(b) Derive the appropriate rate for charging the overheads of each cost centre to jobs (that is, a separate rate for each cost centre).

(c) Athena Ltd has been asked by a customer to specify the price that it will charge for a particular job that will be undertaken early next year, if the job goes ahead. The job is expected to use direct materials costing Athena Ltd £1,200, to need 50 hours of machining time, 10 hours of Machine Department direct labour and 20 hours of Fitting Department direct labour. Athena Ltd charges a profit loading of 20% to the full cost of jobs to determine the selling price.

Show workings to derive the proposed selling price for this job.

8.4 Moleskin Ltd manufactures a range of products used in the building industry. Manufacturing is undertaken using one of two processes: the Alpha Process and the Omega process. All of the products are manufactured in batches. The current pricing policy has been to absorb all overheads using direct labour hours to obtain total cost. Price is then calculated as total cost plus a 35 per cent mark-up.

A recent detailed analysis has examined overhead cost; the results are:

Analysis of overhead costs

	Cost per month £	Monthly volume
Alpha Process cost	96,000	480 hours
Omega Process cost	44,800	1,280 hours
Set-up cost	42,900	260 set-ups
Handling charges	45,600	380 movements
Other overheads	50,700	(see below)
	280,000	

There are 4,000 direct labour hours available each month.

Two of Moleskin's products are a joist (JT101) and a girder (GR27). JT101s are produced by the Alpha Process in a simple operation. GR27s are manufactured by the Omega Process, a more complex operation with more production stages. Both products are sold by the metre.

Details for the two products are:

	JT101	GR27
Monthly volume	1,000 metres	500 metres
Batch size	1,000 metres	50 metres
Processing time per batch		
– Alpha	100 hours	–
– Omega	–	25 hours
Set-ups per batch	1	2
Handling charges per batch	1 movement	5 movements
Materials per metre	£16	£15
Direct labour per metre	1/2 hour	1/2 hour

Direct labour is paid £16 per hour.

Required:

(a) Calculate the price per metre for both JT101s and GR27s detailed above, using traditional absorption costing based on direct labour hours.
(b) Calculate the price per metre for both JT101s and GR27s using activity-based costing. Assume that 'Other overheads' are allocated using direct labour hours.
(c) Outline the points that you would raise with the management of Moleskin in the light of your answers to (a) and (b).
(d) Outline the practical problems that may be encountered in implementing activity-based techniques and comment on how they may be overcome.

8.5 A business manufactures refrigerators for domestic use. There are three models: Lo, Mid and Hi. The models, their quality and their price are aimed at different markets.

Product costs are computed using a blanket (business-wide) overhead-rate. Products absorb overheads on a labour hour basis. Prices, as a general rule, are set based on cost plus 20 per cent. The following information is provided:

	Lo	Mid	Hi
Material cost (£/unit)	25	62.5	105
Direct labour hours (per unit)	1/2	1	1
Budget production/sales (units)	20,000	1,000	10,000

The budgeted overheads for the business, for the year, amount to £4,410,000. Direct labour is costed at £8 an hour.

The business is currently facing increasing competition, especially from imported goods. As a result, the selling price of Lo has been reduced to a level that produces a very low profit margin. To address this problem, an activity-based costing approach has been suggested. The overheads have been analysed and it has been found that these are grouped around main business activities of machining (£2,780,000), logistics (£590,000) and establishment costs (£1,040,000). It is maintained that these costs could be allocated based respectively on cost drivers of machine hours, material orders and space, to reflect the use of resources in each of these areas. After analysis, the following proportionate statistics are available related to the total volume of products:

	Lo	Mid	Hi
	%	%	%
Machine hours	40	15	45
Material orders	47	6	47
Space	42	18	40

Required:
(a) Calculate for each product the full cost and selling price determined by:
   (i) The original (traditional) costing method.
   (ii) The activity-based costing method.
(b) What are the implications of the two systems of costing in the situation given?
(c) What business/strategic options exist for the business in the light of the new information?

Chapter 9

BUDGETING

INTRODUCTION

In its 2015 annual report, BSkyB Group plc, the satellite television broadcaster, stated:

> There is a comprehensive budgeting and forecasting process, and the annual budget, which is regularly reviewed and updated, is approved by the board [of directors]. Performance is monitored against budget through weekly and monthly reporting cycles.

As we shall see, the practice at BSkyB is typical of many businesses.

What is a budget? What is it for? How is it prepared? Who prepares it? How is it used? Why does the board regard it as important enough to spend time on? How and why is performance monitored? Who does the monitoring? We shall be looking at the answers to each of these questions in the course of this chapter.

We shall see that budgets set out short-term plans to help managers run the business. They provide the means to assess whether actual performance was as planned and, if not, the reasons for this. Budgets do not exist in a vacuum; they are an integral part of a planning framework adopted by well-run businesses. To understand fully the nature of budgets we must, therefore, understand the planning framework within which they are set.

The chapter begins with a discussion of the budgeting framework and then goes on to consider detailed aspects of the budgeting process. It ends with considering the use of budgets in monitoring performance and exercising control.

Learning outcomes

When you have completed this chapter, you should be able to:

■ define a budget and show how budgets, strategic objectives and strategic plans are related;

■ explain the budgeting process and the interlinking of the various budgets within the business;

■ indicate the uses of budgeting and construct various budgets, including the cash budget, from relevant data;

■ show how the budget can be used to exercise control over the business.

HOW BUDGETS LINK WITH STRATEGIC PLANS AND OBJECTIVES

It is vital that businesses develop plans for the future. Whatever a business is trying to achieve, it is unlikely to happen unless its managers are clear what the future direction of the business is going to be. The development of plans Involves five key steps:

1 *Establish mission and objectives* The ultimate purpose of the business is usually set out in a **mission statement**. This is a broad statement of intent, which attempts to capture the essence of the business. The strategic objectives state how the mission of the business can be achieved and will usually include quantifiable goals.

2 *Undertake a position analysis* This involves an assessment of where the business is currently placed in relation to where it wants to be, as set out in its mission and strategic objectives.

3 *Identify and assess the strategic options* The business must explore the various ways in which it might move from where it is now (identified in Step 2) to where it wants to be (identified in Step 1).

4. *Select strategic options and formulate plans* This involves selecting what seems to be the best of the courses of action or strategies (identified in Step 3) and formulating a long-term strategic plan. This strategic plan is then normally broken down into a series of short-term plans, one for each element of the business. These plans are the budgets. Thus, a **budget** is a business plan for the short term – typically one year – and is expressed mainly in financial terms. Its role is to convert the strategic plans into actionable blueprints for the immediate future. Budgets will define precise targets concerning such things as:
   - cash receipts and payments;
   - sales volumes and revenues, broken down into amounts and prices for each of the products or services provided by the business;
   - detailed inventories requirements;
   - detailed labour requirements; and
   - specific production requirements.

5. *Perform, review and control* Here the business pursues the budgets derived in step 4. By comparing the actual outcome with the budgets, managers can see if things are going according to plan. Action would be taken to exercise control where actual performance appears not to be matching the budgets.

From the above description of the planning process, we can see that the relationship between the mission, strategic objectives, strategic plans and budgets can be summarised as follows:

- the mission sets the overall direction and, once set, is likely to last for quite a long time – perhaps throughout the life of the business;
- the strategic objectives, which are also long term, will set out how the mission can be achieved;
- the strategic plans identify how each objective will be pursued; and
- the budgets set out, in detail, the short-term plans and targets necessary to fulfil the strategic objectives.

An analogy might be found in terms of a student enrolling on a course of study. The student's mission might be to have a happy and fulfilling life. A key strategic objective flowing from this mission might be to embark on a career that will be rewarding in various ways. The particular study course might have been identified as the most effective way to work towards this objective. Successfully completing the course would then be the strategic plan. In working towards this strategic plan, passing a particular stage of the course might be identified as the target for the forthcoming year. This short-term target is analogous to the budget. Having achieved the 'budget' for the first year, the student's budget for the second year becomes passing the second stage and so on.

Figure 9.1 shows the planning and control process in diagrammatic form.

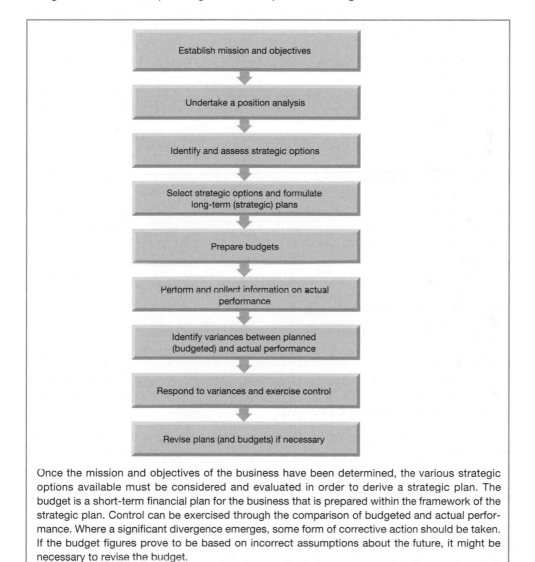

Establish mission and objectives

Undertake a position analysis

Identify and assess strategic options

Select strategic options and formulate long-term (strategic) plans

Prepare budgets

Perform and collect information on actual performance

Identify variances between planned (budgeted) and actual performance

Respond to variances and exercise control

Revise plans (and budgets) if necessary

Once the mission and objectives of the business have been determined, the various strategic options available must be considered and evaluated in order to derive a strategic plan. The budget is a short-term financial plan for the business that is prepared within the framework of the strategic plan. Control can be exercised through the comparison of budgeted and actual performance. Where a significant divergence emerges, some form of corrective action should be taken. If the budget figures prove to be based on incorrect assumptions about the future, it might be necessary to revise the budget.

Figure 9.1 The planning and control process

Do you think that planning (including budgeting) within a business should be the responsibility of managers or accountants?

It should be the responsibility of managers. Although accountants play a role in the planning process, by supplying relevant information to managers and by contributing to decision making as part of the management team, they should not dominate the process.

Despite the fact that managers should be responsible for planning, in practice accountants often seem to dominate the process. Managers are failing in their responsibilities if they allow this to happen. Accountants should not have an excessive influence in the budgeting process, despite their skills at handling financial information.

TIME HORIZON OF PLANS AND BUDGETS

Setting strategic plans is a major exercise normally performed every five years or so, and budgets are usually set for the forthcoming year. These planning horizons, however, may vary according to the needs of the particular business. Businesses involved in certain industries – say, information technology – may find that a strategic planning horizon of five years is too long since new developments can, and do, occur virtually overnight. Two or three years may be more appropriate. Similarly, a budget need not be set for one year, although this is a widely used time horizon.

One business that keeps its strategic planning under frequent review is Greene King plc, the brewery, pub and hotel business. **Real World 9.1,** which is an extract from the annual report for the business, explains how strategic planning is a regular annual event.

REAL WORLD 9.1

Strategic planning at the pub

According to its annual report, Greene King has the following approach to strategic planning:

There is a two-day meeting for the board in February each year focusing on strategy, with the business unit managing directors and heads of the main functional areas, namely commercial, HR (Human Resources) and property, attending for part thereof. The strategy sessions include an in-depth review of relevant economic factors, management's projections for the medium term and provide the board with an opportunity to agree the strategic plans across all areas for the short and medium term. Following approval of the company's strategy, budgets are prepared for the next financial year to be approved by the board in April. The board also has a programme to review each business unit and main functional area in detail on a regular basis, with particular focus on the achievement of strategic objectives. The relevant managing director or functional head attends such meetings to present and answer questions.

Source: Greene King plc, Annual Report 2015, p. 40.

Can you think of any reason why most businesses prepare detailed budgets for the forthcoming year, rather than for a shorter or longer period?

This is probably because a year represents a long enough time for the budget preparation exercise to be worthwhile, yet short enough into the future for detailed plans to be capable of being made. The process of formulating budgets can be a time-consuming exercise, but there are economies of scale – for example, preparing the budget for the next year would not normally take twice as much time and effort as preparing the budget for the next six months.

An annual budget sets targets for the forthcoming year for all aspects of the business. It is usually broken down into monthly budgets, which define monthly targets. Indeed, in many instances, the annual budget will be built up from monthly figures. Thus, the sales staff may be required to set sales targets for each month of the budget period. These targets may vary from month to month, perhaps due to variations in seasonal demand.

HOW BUDGETS HELP MANAGERS

Budgets are generally regarded as having five areas of usefulness. These are:

1 *Budgets tend to promote forward thinking and the possible identification of short-term problems.* Focusing on the future may well enable managers to spot potential problems and to do so at an early enough stage for steps to be taken to avoid or otherwise deal with each problem. For example, the budgeting process may bring to light a potential shortage of production capacity. Identifying such a problem, at a very early stage, gives managers time for calm and rational consideration of the best way of overcoming it. The best solution to the potential problem may only be feasible if action can be taken well in advance.
2 *Budgets can be used to help co-ordination between the various sections of the business.* It is crucially important that the activities of the various departments and sections of the business are linked so that the activities of one are complementary to those of another. The activities of the purchasing/procurement department of a manufacturing business, for example, should dovetail with the raw materials needs of the production departments. If they do not, production could run out of raw materials, leading to expensive production stoppages. Possibly, just as undesirable, excessive amounts of raw materials could be bought, leading to large and unnecessary inventories holding costs. We shall see how this co-ordination tends to work in practice later in this chapter.
3 *Budgets can motivate managers to better performance.* Having a stated task can motivate managers and staff in their performance. Simply telling managers to do their best is not very motivating, but to define a required level of achievement is more likely to be so. Managers will be better motivated by being able to relate their particular role to the business's overall objectives. Since budgets are directly derived from strategic objectives, budgeting makes this possible. It is clearly not possible to allow managers to operate in an unconstrained environment. Having to operate in a way that matches the goals of the business is a price of working in an effective business.

4 *Budgets can provide a basis for a system of control.* **Control** can be defined as compelling events to conform to plan. This definition is valid in any context. For example, when we talk about controlling a car, we mean making the car do what we plan that it should do. If managers wish to control and monitor their own performance, and that of more junior staff, they need some yardstick against which to measure and assess performance. Current performance could possibly be compared with past performance or perhaps with what happens in another business. However, planned performance is usually the most logical yardstick. If there is information available concerning the actual performance for a period, and this can be compared with the planned performance (the budget), then a basis for control will have been established. Since it is possible to state *actual* outcomes in the same terms as the budget, making comparison between actual and planned outcomes is a relatively simple matter. Where actual outcomes are at variance with budgets, this variance will be highlighted. Managers can then take steps to get the business back on track towards the achievement of the budgets.

Comparing the budget with actual outcomes also enables the use of **management by exception**, an approach where senior managers can spend most of their time dealing with those staff or activities that have failed to achieve the budget (the exceptions). Thus, senior managers do not have to spend too much time on those that are performing well. It also allows managers to exercise self-control. By knowing what is expected of them and what they have actually achieved, they can assess how well they are performing and take steps to correct matters where they are failing to achieve.

5 *Budgets can provide a system of authorisation for managers to spend up to a particular limit.* Some activities (for example, staff development and research and development) are allocated a fixed amount of funds at the discretion of senior management. This provides the authority to spend.

Figure 9.2 shows the benefits of budgets in diagrammatic form.

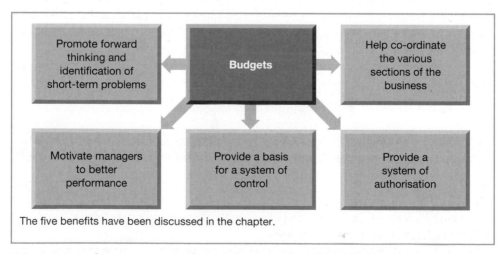

Figure 9.2 Budgets are seen as having five main benefits to the business

The following two activities pick up issues that relate to some of the uses of budgets.

The third point on the list of the uses of budgets (motivation) implies that managers are set stated tasks. Do you think there is a danger that requiring managers to work towards such predetermined targets will stifle their skill, flair and enthusiasm?

If the budgets are set in such a way as to offer challenging yet achievable targets, the manager is still required to show skill, flair and enthusiasm. There is the danger, however, that if targets are badly set (either unreasonably demanding or too easy to achieve), they could be demotivating and have a stifling effect.

The fourth point on the list of the uses of budgets (control) implies that current management performance is compared with some yardstick. What is wrong with comparing actual performance with past performance, or the performance of others, in an effort to exercise control?

What happened in the past, or is happening elsewhere, does not necessarily represent a sensible target for this year in this business. Considering what happened last year, and in other businesses (as with benchmarking), may help in the formulation of plans, but past events and the performance of others should not automatically be seen as the target.

The five identified uses of budgets can conflict with one another on occasion. Using the budget as a motivational device provides an example of this. Some businesses set the budget targets at a more difficult level than the managers are expected to achieve in an attempt to motivate managers to strive to reach their targets. For control purposes, however, the budget becomes less meaningful as a benchmark against which to compare actual performance. Incidentally, there is good reason to doubt the effectiveness of setting excessive targets as a motivational device, as we shall see later in the chapter.

Conflict between the different uses will mean that managers must decide which particular uses for budgets should be given priority. Managers must be prepared, if necessary, to trade off the benefits resulting from one particular use for the benefits of another.

BUDGETS AND FORECASTS

We have seen that a budget is a business plan for the short term, which is mainly expressed in financial terms. Note particularly that a budget is a *plan,* not a forecast. To talk of a plan suggests an intention or determination to achieve the targets; **forecasts** tend to be predictions of the future state of the environment.

Clearly, forecasts are very helpful to the planner/budget setter. If, for example, a reliable forecaster has predicted the number of new cars to be purchased in the UK during next year, it will be valuable for a manager in a car manufacturing business to take account of this information when setting next year's sales budgets. However, a forecast and a budget are distinctly different.

LIMITING FACTORS

Some aspect of the business will, inevitably, stop it achieving its objectives to the maximum extent. This is often a limited ability of the business to sell its products. Sometimes, however, it is some production shortage (such as labour, materials or plant) that is the **limiting factor**. Production shortages can often be overcome by an increase in funds – for example, more plant can be bought or leased. This is not always a practical solution, however, because no amount of money will buy certain labour skills or increase the world supply of some raw material. As a last resort, it might be necessary to revise the sales budget to a lower level to match the production limitation.

While easing an initial limiting factor may be possible, another limiting factor will replace it, though at a higher level of output. In the end, the business will hit a ceiling; some limiting factors will prove impossible to ease.

Activity 9.5

Can you think of any ways in which a short-term shortage of production facilities of a manufacturer might be overcome?

We thought of the following:

- Higher production in previous months and increasing inventories ('stockpiling') to meet periods of higher demand.
- Increasing production capacity, perhaps by working overtime and/or acquiring (buying or leasing) additional plant.
- Subcontracting some production.
- Encouraging potential customers to change the timing of their purchases by offering discounts or other special terms during the months that have been identified as quiet.

You might well have thought of other approaches.

The limiting factor should try to be identified at the outset. All managers can then be informed and can take it into account when preparing their budgets.

HOW BUDGETS LINK TO ONE ANOTHER

Larger businesses will prepare more than one budget for a particular period. Each budget prepared will relate to a specific aspect of the business. The ideal situation is probably that there should be a separate operating budget for each person who is in a managerial position, no matter how junior. The contents of all of the individual operating budgets will be summarised in **master budgets** consisting of a budgeted income statement and statement of financial position (balance sheet). The cash budget is, however, considered by some to be a third master budget.

Figure 9.3 illustrates the interrelationship and interlinking of individual operating budgets, in this particular case using a manufacturing business as an example.

The sales budget is usually the first one to be prepared (at the left of Figure 9.3), as the level of sales often determines the overall level of activity for the forthcoming period. This is because it is the most common limiting factor. The finished inventories requirement tends to be set by the level of sales, though it would also be dictated by the policy of the business on the level of the finished products inventories. The requirement for finished inventories will define the required production levels, which will, in turn, dictate the requirements of the individual production departments or sections. The demands of manufacturing, in conjunction with the business's policy on how long it holds raw materials before they enter production, define the raw materials inventories budget.

The purchases budget will be dictated by the materials inventories budget, which will, in conjunction with the policy of the business on taking credit from suppliers, dictate the trade payables budget. One of the determinants of the cash budget will be the trade payables budget; another will be the trade receivables budget, which itself derives, through the business's policy on credit periods granted to credit customers, from the sales budget. Cash will also be affected by overheads and direct labour costs (themselves linked to production) and by capital expenditure – that is, investment in non-current assets such as property, plant and equipment.

Cash will also be affected by new finance and redemption of existing sources. (This is not shown in Figure 9.3 because the diagram focuses only on budgets concerned with operational matters.) The factors that affect policies on matters such as inventories holding

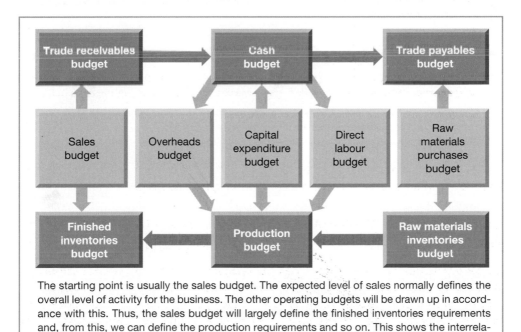

The starting point is usually the sales budget. The expected level of sales normally defines the overall level of activity for the business. The other operating budgets will be drawn up in accordance with this. Thus, the sales budget will largely define the finished inventories requirements and, from this, we can define the production requirements and so on. This shows the interrelationship of operating budgets for a manufacturing business.

Figure 9.3 The interrelationship of operating budgets

and trade receivables collection and trade payables payment periods will be discussed in some detail in Chapter 12.

The way in which budgets link to one another results in the co-ordination that was mentioned earlier as one of the main uses of budgets to managers.

A manufacturing business has been used as the example in Figure 9.3 simply because it has all of the types of operating budgets found in practice. Service businesses, however, have similar types of budgets, with the exception perhaps of inventories budgets.

There will be the horizontal relationships between budgets, which we have just looked at, but there will usually be vertical ones as well. Breaking down the sales budget into a number of subsidiary budgets, perhaps one for each regional sales manager, is a common approach. The overall sales budget will be a summary of the subsidiary ones. The same may be true of virtually all of the other budgets, most particularly the production budget.

Figure 9.4 shows the vertical relationship of the sales budgets for a business. The business has four geographical sales regions, each one the responsibility of a separate manager. Each regional manager is responsible to the overall sales manager of the business. The overall sales budget will be the sum of the budgets for the four sales regions and will be the responsibility of, say, the marketing director.

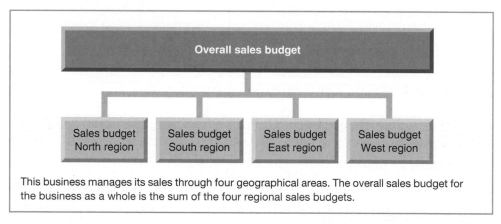

This business manages its sales through four geographical areas. The overall sales budget for the business as a whole is the sum of the four regional sales budgets.

Figure 9.4 The vertical relationship between a business's sales budgets

Although sales are often managed on a geographical basis, they may be managed on some other basis. For example, a business that sells a range of products may employ a specialist manager for each type of product. Thus, an insurance business may have separate sales managers, and so separate sales budgets, for life insurance, household insurance, motor insurance and so on. Large businesses may even have separate product-type managers for each geographical region. Each of these managers would have a separate budget, which would combine to form the overall sales budget for the business as a whole.

All of the operating budgets that we have just reviewed must mesh with the master budgets, that is, the budgeted income statement and statement of financial position.

USING BUDGETS IN PRACTICE

This section provides a flavour of how budgets are used, the extent to which they are used and their level of accuracy.

Real World 9.2 shows how Rolls-Royce Holdings plc, the UK engine manufacturer, undertakes its budgeting process.

REAL WORLD 9.2

Budgeting at Rolls-Royce

According to its annual report Rolls-Royce has:

- a comprehensive planning and financial reporting procedure including annual budgets and periodic strategic plans, both of which are reviewed and approved by the board;
- ongoing monitoring by both the board and senior management of performance against budgets, through the periodic reporting of detailed management accounts and key performance indicators;

Source: Rolls-Royce Holdings plc, Annual Report 2014, p. 62.

There is quite a lot of survey evidence that shows the extent to which budgeting is used by businesses in practice. **Real World 9.3** reviews some of this evidence, which shows that most businesses, certainly larger ones, prepare and use budgets.

REAL WORLD 9.3

Budgeting in practice

A survey of 41 UK manufacturing businesses found that 40 of the 41 prepared budgets.

Source: Dugdale, D., Jones, C. and Green, S. (2006), 'Contemporary management accounting practices in UK manufacturing', CIMA Publication, Elsevier.

Another survey of UK businesses, but this time businesses involved in the food and drink sector, found that virtually all of them used budgets.

Source: Abdel-Kader, M. and Luther, R. (2004) 'An empirical investigation of the evolution of management accounting practices', Working paper No. 04/06, University of Essex, October.

A survey of the opinions of senior finance staff at 340 businesses of various sizes and operating in a wide range of industries in North America revealed that 97 per cent of those businesses had a formal budgeting process.

Source: BPM Forum (2008), 'Perfect how you project'.

On the other hand, a survey of seven small and four medium-sized UK businesses found that not all of the small ones had a formal-budgeting process, though all of the medium-sized ones did.

Source: Lucas, M., Prowle, P. and Lowth, G. (2013), 'Management accounting practices of UK small and medium-sized enterprises', CIMA, July, p. 6.

Though these surveys relate to UK and North American businesses, they provide some idea of what is also likely to be practice elsewhere in the developed world.

Real World 9.4 gives some insight regarding the accuracy of budgets.

REAL WORLD 9.4

Budget accuracy

The survey of senior finance staff of North American businesses, mentioned in Real World 9.3 above, asked them to compare the actual revenues with the budgeted revenues for 2007. Figure 9.5 shows the results:

We can see that only 66 per cent of revenue budgets were accurate within 10 per cent. The survey also revealed (but not shown in Figure 9.5) that budgets for expenses were generally more accurate, with 74 per cent being accurate within 10 per cent.

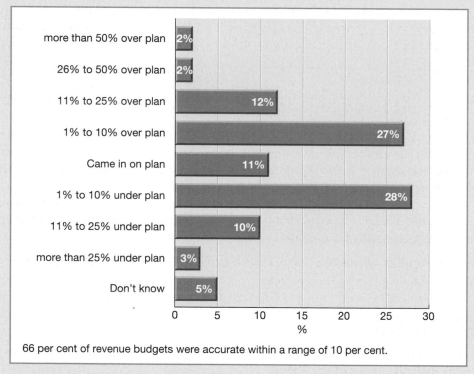

66 per cent of revenue budgets were accurate within a range of 10 per cent.

Figure 9.5 The accuracy of revenue budgets

Source: Information from BPM Forum (2008), 'Perfect how you project'.

PREPARING BUDGETS

We shall now look in some detail at how the various budgets used by the typical business are prepared, starting with the cash budget and then looking at others.

The cash budget

It is helpful for us to start with the cash budget for the following reasons:

- It is a key budget (some people see it as a 'master budget' along with the budgeted income statement and budgeted statement of financial position); most economic aspects of a business are reflected in cash sooner or later. This means that, for a typical business, the cash budget reflects the whole business more comprehensively than any other single budget.
- A very small, unsophisticated business (for example, a corner shop) may feel that full-scale budgeting is not appropriate to its needs, but almost certainly it should prepare a cash budget as a minimum.

Since budgets are documents that are to be used only internally by a business, their layout is a matter of management choice and will vary from one business to the next. However, as managers, irrespective of the business, are likely to be using budgets for similar purposes, some consistency of approach tends to be found. In most businesses, the cash budget will probably possess the following features:

1 The budget period would be broken down into sub-periods, typically months.
2 The budget would be in columnar form, with one column for each month.
3 Receipts of cash would be identified under various headings and a total for each month's receipts shown.
4 Payments of cash would be identified under various headings and a total for each month's payments shown.
5 The surplus of total cash receipts over payments, or of payments over receipts, for each month would be identified.
6 The running end-of-month cash balance would be identified. This would be achieved by taking the balance at the end of the previous month and adjusting it for the surplus (or deficit) of receipts over payments for the current month.

Typically, all of the pieces of information in points 3 to 6 in this list would be useful to management for one reason or another.

Probably the best way to deal with this topic is through an example.

Example 9.1

Vierra Popova Ltd is a wholesale business. The budgeted income statements for each of the next six months are as follows:

	Jan £000	Feb £000	Mar £000	Apr £000	May £000	June £000
Sales revenue	52	55	55	60	55	53
Cost of goods sold	(30)	(31)	(31)	(35)	(31)	(32)
Salaries and wages	(10)	(10)	(10)	(10)	(10)	(10)
Electricity	(5)	(5)	(4)	(3)	(3)	(3)
Depreciation	(3)	(3)	(3)	(3)	(3)	(3)
Other overheads	(2)	(2)	(2)	(2)	(2)	(2)
Total expenses	(50)	(51)	(50)	(53)	(49)	(50)
Profit for the month	2	4	5	7	6	3

$\rightarrow$

The business allows all of its customers one month's credit (this means, for example, that cash from January sales will be received in February). Sales revenue during December totalled £60,000.

The business plans to maintain inventories at their existing level until some time in March, when they are to be reduced by £5,000. Inventories will remain at this lower level indefinitely. Inventories purchases are made on one month's credit. December purchases totalled £30,000. Salaries, wages and 'other overheads' are paid in the month concerned. Electricity is paid quarterly in arrears in March and June. The business plans to buy and pay for a new delivery van in March. This will cost a total of £15,000, but an existing van will be traded in for £4,000 as part of the deal.

The business expects to have £12,000 in cash at the beginning of January.

The cash budget for the six months ending in June will look as follows:

	Jan £000	Feb £000	Mar £000	Apr £000	May £000	June £000
Receipts						
Trade receivables (Note 1)	60	52	55	55	60	55
Payments						
Trade payables (Note 2)	(30)	(30)	(31)	(26)	(35)	(31)
Salaries and wages	(10)	(10)	(10)	(10)	(10)	(10)
Electricity			(14)			(9)
Other overheads	(2)	(2)	(2)	(2)	(2)	(2)
Van purchase	–	–	(11)	–	–	–
Total payments	(42)	(42)	(68)	(38)	(47)	(52)
Cash surplus for the month	18	10	(13)	17	13	3
Opening balance (Note 3)	12	30	40	27	44	57
Closing balance	30	40	27	44	57	60

Notes:

1 The cash receipts from credit customers (trade receivables) lag a month behind sales because customers are given a month in which to pay for their purchases. So, December sales will be paid for in January and so on.

2 In most months, the purchases of inventories will equal the cost of goods sold. This is because the business maintains a constant level of inventories. For inventories to remain constant at the end of each month, the business must replace exactly the amount that has been used. During March, however, the business plans to reduce its inventories by £5,000. This means that inventories purchases will be lower than inventories usage in that month. The payments for inventories purchases lag a month behind purchases because the business expects to be allowed a month to pay for what it buys.

3 Each month's cash balance is the previous end-of-month figure plus the cash surplus (or minus the cash deficit) for the current month. The balance at the start of January is £12,000 according to the information provided earlier.

4 Depreciation does not give rise to a cash payment. In the context of profit measurement (in the income statement), depreciation is a very important aspect. Here, however, we are interested only in cash.

Looking at the cash budget of Vierra Popova Ltd (Example 9.1), what conclusions do you draw and what possible course of action do you recommend regarding the cash balance over the period concerned?

Given the size of the business, there is a fairly large cash balance that seems to be increasing. Management might consider:

- putting some of the cash into an income-yielding deposit;
- increasing the investment in non-current (fixed) assets;
- paying a dividend to the owners; and/or
- repaying borrowings.

Vierra Popova Ltd (Example 9.1) now wishes to prepare its cash budget for the second six months of the year. The budgeted income statements for each month of the second half of the year are as follows:

	July £000	Aug £000	Sept £000	Oct £000	Nov £000	Dec £000
Sales revenue	57	59	62	57	53	51
Cost of goods sold	(32)	(33)	(35)	(32)	(30)	(29)
Salaries and wages	(10)	(10)	(10)	(10)	(10)	(10)
Electricity	(3)	(3)	(4)	(5)	(6)	(6)
Depreciation	(3)	(3)	(3)	(3)	(3)	(3)
Other overheads	(2)	(2)	(2)	(2)	(2)	(2)
Total expenses	(50)	(51)	(54)	(52)	(51)	(50)
Profit for the month	7	8	8	5	2	1

The business will continue to allow all of its customers one month's credit.

It plans to increase inventories from the 30 June level by £1,000 each month until, and including, September. During the following three months, inventories levels will be decreased by £1,000 each month.

Inventories purchases, which had been made on one month's credit until the June payment, will, starting with the purchases made in June, be made on two months' credit.

Salaries, wages and 'other overheads' will continue to be paid in the month concerned. Electricity is paid quarterly in arrears in September and December.

At the end of December, the business intends to pay off part of some borrowings. This payment is to be such that it will leave the business with a cash balance of £5,000 with which to start next year.

Prepare the cash budget for the six months ending in December. (Remember that any information you need that relates to the first six months of the year, including the cash balance that is expected to be brought forward on 1 July, is given in Example 9.1.)

→

The cash budget for the six months ended 31 December is:

	July £000	Aug £000	Sept £000	Oct £000	Nov £000	Dec £000
Receipts						
Trade receivables	53	57	59	62	57	53
Payments						
Trade payables (Note 1)	–	(32)	(33)	(34)	(36)	(31)
Salaries and wages	(10)	(10)	(10)	(10)	(10)	(10)
Electricity	–	–	(10)	–	–	(17)
Other overheads	(2)	(2)	(2)	(2)	(2)	(2)
Borrowings repayment (Note 2)	–	–	–	–	–	(131)
Total payments	(12)	(44)	(55)	(46)	(48)	(191)
Cash surplus for the month	41	13	4	16	9	(138)
Opening balance	60	101	114	118	134	143
Closing balance	101	114	118	134	143	5

Notes:

1 There will be no payment to suppliers (trade payables) in July because the June purchases will be made on two months' credit and will therefore be paid in August. The July purchases, which will equal the July cost of sales figure plus the increase in inventories made in July, will be paid for in September and so on.

2 The borrowings repayment is simply the amount that will cause the balance at 31 December to be £5,000.

Preparing other budgets

Although each one will have its own particular features, other budgets will tend to follow the same sort of pattern as the cash budget, that is, they will show inflows and outflows during each month and the opening and closing balances in each month.

Example 9.2

To illustrate some of the other budgets, we shall continue to use the example of Vierra Popova Ltd that we considered in Example 9.1. To the information given there, we need to add the fact that the inventories balance at 1 January was £30,000.

Trade receivables budget
This would normally show the planned amount owed to the business by credit customers at the beginning and at the end of each month, the planned total credit sales revenue for each month and the planned total cash receipts from credit customers (trade receivables). The layout would be something like this:

	Jan £000	Feb £000	Mar £000	Apr £000	May £000	June £000
Opening balance	60	52	55	55	60	55
Sales revenue	52	55	55	60	55	53
Cash receipts	(60)	(52)	(55)	(55)	(60)	(55)
Closing balance	52	55	55	60	55	53

The opening and closing balances represent the amount that the business plans to be owed (in total) by credit customers (trade receivables) at the beginning and end of each month, respectively.

Trade payables budget

Typically this shows the planned amount owed to suppliers by the business at the beginning and at the end of each month, the planned credit purchases for each month and the planned total cash payments to trade payables. The layout would be something like this:

	Jan £000	Feb £000	Mar £000	Apr £000	May £000	June £000
Opening balance	30	30	31	26	35	31
Purchases	30	31	26	35	31	32
Cash payment	(30)	(30)	(31)	(26)	(35)	(31)
Closing balance	30	31	26	35	31	32

The opening and closing balances represent the amount planned to be owed (in total) by the business to suppliers (trade payables), at the beginning and end of each month respectively.

Inventories budget

This would normally show the planned amount of inventories to be held by the business at the beginning and at the end of each month, the planned total inventories purchases for each month and the planned total monthly inventories usage. The layout would be something like this:

	Jan £000	Feb £000	Mar £000	Apr £000	May £000	June £000
Opening balance	30	30	30	25	25	25
Purchases	30	31	26	35	31	32
Inventories used	(30)	(31)	(31)	(35)	(31)	(32)
Closing balance	30	30	25	25	25	25

The opening and closing balances represent the amount of inventories, at cost, planned to be held by the business at the beginning and end of each month respectively.

A *raw materials inventories budget,* for a manufacturing business, would follow a similar pattern to the (finished) inventories budget in Example 9.2, with the 'inventories usage' being the cost of the inventories put into production. A *finished inventories budget* for a manufacturer would also be similar to the above, except that 'inventories manufactured' would replace 'purchases'. A manufacturing business would normally prepare both a raw materials inventories budget and a finished inventories budget. Each of these would typically be based on the full cost of the inventories (that is, including overheads). There is no reason why the inventories should not be valued on the basis of either variable cost or direct costs, should managers feel that this would provide more useful information.

The inventories budget will normally be expressed in financial terms, but may also be expressed in physical terms (for example, kg or metres) for individual inventories items.

Note how the trade receivables, trade payables and inventories budgets in Example 9.2 link to one another, and to the cash budget, for the same business in Example 9.1. Note particularly that:

- the purchases figures in the trade payables budget and in the inventories budget are identical;
- the cash payments figures in the trade payables budget and in the cash budget are identical; and
- the cash receipts figures in the trade receivables budget and in the cash budget are identical.

Other values would link different budgets in a similar way. For example, the row of sales revenue figures in the trade receivables budget would be identical to the sales revenue figures that will be found in the sales budget. This is how the linking (co-ordination), which was discussed earlier in this chapter, is achieved.

Activity 9.8

Have a go at preparing the trade receivables budget for Vierra Popova Ltd for the six months from July to December (see Activity 9.7 and Example 9.2).

The trade receivables budget for the six months ended 31 December is:

	July £000	Aug £000	Sept £000	Oct £000	Nov £000	Dec £000
Opening balance (Note 1)	53	57	59	62	57	53
Sales revenue (Note 2)	57	59	62	57	53	51
Cash receipts (Note 3)	(53)	(57)	(59)	(62)	(57)	(53)
Closing balance (Note 4)	57	59	62	57	53	51

Notes:

1. The opening trade receivables figure is the previous month's sales revenue figure (sales are on one month's credit).
2. The sales revenue is the current month's figure.
3. The cash received each month is equal to the previous month's sales revenue figure.
4. The closing balance is equal to the current month's sales revenue figure.

Note that if we knew any three of the four figures each month, we could deduce the fourth.

This budget could be set out in any manner that would have given the sort of information that management would require in respect of planned levels of trade receivables and associated transactions.

Activity 9.9

Have a go at preparing the trade payables budget for Vierra Popova Ltd for the six months from July to December (see Activity 9.7 and Exercise 9.2). (*Hint*: Remember that the trade payables payment period alters from the June purchases onwards.)

The trade payables budget for the six months ended 31 December is:

	July £000	Aug £000	Sept £000	Oct £000	Nov £000	Dec £000
Opening balance	32	65	67	70	67	60
Purchases	33	34	36	31	29	28
Cash payments	–	(32)	(33)	(34)	(36)	(31)
Closing balance	65	67	70	67	60	57

This, again, could be set out in any manner that would have given the sort of information that management would require in respect of planned levels of trade payables and associated transactions.

NON-FINANCIAL MEASURES IN BUDGETING

The efficiency of internal operations and customer satisfaction levels have become of critical importance to businesses striving to survive in an increasingly competitive environment. Non-financial performance indicators have an important role to play in assessing performance in these key areas. Such indicators might include customer/supplier delivery times, machine set-up times, product defect levels and customer satisfaction levels.

There is no reason why budgeting needs be confined to financial targets and measures. Non-financial measures can also be used as the basis for targets and these can be brought into the budgeting process and reported alongside the financial targets for the business.

BUDGETING FOR CONTROL

We have seen that budgets provide a useful basis for exercising control over a business as they provide a yardstick against which performance can usefully be assessed. Unless we measure actual performance in the same terms as those in which the budget is stated, however, valid comparison will not be possible.

Exercising control involves finding out where and why things did not go according to plan and then seeking ways to put them right for the future. One reason why things may not have gone according to plan is that the budget targets were unachievable.

In this case, it may be necessary to revise the budgets for future periods so that targets become achievable.

This last point should not be taken to mean that budget targets can simply be ignored if the going gets tough; rather that they should be adaptable. Unrealistic budgets cannot form a basis for exercising control and little can be gained by sticking with them. Budgets may become unrealistic for a variety of reasons, including unexpected changes in the commercial environment (for example, an unexpected collapse in demand for services of the type that the business provides).

Real World 9.5 discusses how one budget, which was revised in the light of cost overruns, was still too ambitious.

REAL WORLD 9.5

Digging itself out of a hole

DiamondCorp plc owns, and is now developing, the Lace diamond mine in South Africa. An update on progress by the business revealed that the tunnelling budget had been revised. Nevertheless, tunnelling costs were exceeding the revised budget. The company stated:

> Tunnel development costs to date are averaging Rand 39,135/metre against a revised budget of Rand 37,000/metre. The over spend continues to be the result of increased operating costs on the company's underground mining fleet. However, cost saving initiatives, including the introduction of chains to the tyres of the underground loaders and computerisation of maintenance scheduling, are starting to show a positive impact which should be reflected in improvements in the cost per metre rate going forward. The overall mine development expenditure is within budget.

Source: DiamondCorp plc (2014), Lace Diamond Mine Project Update, 30 October, http://www.londonstockexchange.com/exchange/news/market-news/market-newsdetail/DCP/12133439.html.

We saw earlier that budgets enable a management-by-exception environment to be created where senior management can focus on areas where things are not going according to plan (the exceptions – it is to be hoped). To create this environment, a comparison of the budget and the actual results must be undertaken to see whether any variances between the two exist. We are now going to discuss the way in which this is usually done.

MEASURING VARIANCES FROM BUDGET

We saw in Chapter 1 that the key financial objective of a business is to increase the wealth of its owners (shareholders). Since profit is the net increase in wealth from business operations, the most important budget target to meet is the profit target. We shall therefore take this as our starting point when comparing the budget with the actual results. Example 9.3 shows the budgeted and actual income statement for Baxter Ltd for the month of May.

Example 9.3

The following are the budgeted and actual income statements for Baxter Ltd, a manufacturing business, for the month of May:

	Budget	Actual
Output (production and sales)	1,000 units	900 units
	£	£
Sales revenue	100,000	92,000
Direct materials	(40,000) (40,000 metres)	(36,900) (37,000 metres)
Direct labour	(20,000) (2,500 hours)	(17,500) (2,150 hours)
Fixed overheads	(20,000)	(20,700)
Operating profit	20,000	16,900

From these figures it is clear that the budgeted profit was not achieved. As far as May is concerned, this is a matter of history. However, the business (or at least one aspect of it) is out of control. Senior management must discover where things went wrong during May and try to ensure that these mistakes are not repeated in later months. It is not enough to know that things went wrong overall. We need to know where and why. The approach taken is to compare the budgeted and actual figures for the various items (sales revenue, raw materials and so on) in the above statement.

Can you see any problems in comparing the various items (sales, direct materials and so on) for the budget and the actual performance of Baxter Ltd in order to draw conclusions as to which aspects were out of control?

The problem is that the actual level of output was not as budgeted.

Baxter Ltd's actual level of output for May was 10 per cent less than budget. This means that we cannot, for example, say that there was a labour cost saving of £2,500 (that is, £20,000 − £17,500) and conclude that all is well in that area.

Flexing the budget

One practical way to overcome our difficulty is to 'flex' the budget to what it would have been had the planned level of output been 900 units rather than 1,000 units. **Flexing the budget** simply means revising it, assuming a different volume of output.

To exercise control, the budget is usually flexed to reflect the volume that actually occurred, where this is higher or lower than that originally planned. This means that we need to know which revenues and costs are fixed and which ones are variable, relative to the volume of output. Once we know this, flexing is a simple operation. We shall assume that sales revenue, material cost and labour cost vary strictly with volume. Fixed overheads, by definition, will not. Whether, in real life, labour cost does vary with the volume of output is not so certain, but it will serve well enough as an assumption for our purposes. Where labour costs are actually fixed, we simply take this into account in the flexing process.

On the basis of our assumptions regarding the behaviour of revenues and costs, the flexed budget would be as follows:

	Flexed budget
Output (production and sales)	900 units
	£
Sales revenue	90,000
Direct materials	(36,000) (36,000 metres)
Direct labour	(18,000) (2,250 hours)
Fixed overheads	(20,000)
Operating profit	16,000

This is simply the original budget, with the sales revenue, raw materials and labour cost figures scaled down by 10 per cent (the same factor as the actual output fell short of the budgeted one).

Putting the original budget, the flexed budget and the actual for May together, we obtain the following:

	Original budget	Flexed budget	Actual
Output (production and sales)	1,000 units	900 units	900 units
	£	£	£
Sales revenue	100,000	90,000	92,000
Direct materials	(40,000)	(36,000) (36,000m)	(36,900) (37,000m)
Direct labour	(20,000)	(18,000) (2,250 hr)	(17,500) (2,150 hr)
Fixed overheads	(20,000)	(20,000)	(20,700)
Operating profit	20,000	16,000	16,900

Flexible budgets enable us to make a more valid comparison between the budget (using the flexed figures) and the actual results. Key differences, or variances, between budgeted and actual results for each aspect of the business's activities can then be calculated.

It may seem as if we are saying that it does not matter if there are volume shortfalls because we just revise the budget and carry on as if all is well. However, this is not the case, because losing sales normally means losing profit. The first point that we must pick up therefore is the loss of profit arising from the loss of sales of 100 units.

Activity 9.11

What will be the loss of profit arising from the sales volume shortfall, assuming that everything except sales volume was as planned?

The answer is simply the difference between the original budget and the flexed budget profit figures. The only difference between these two profit figures is the volume of sales; everything else was the same. (That is to say that the flexing was carried out assuming that the per-unit sales revenue, material cost and labour cost were all as originally budgeted.) This means that the figure for the loss of profit due to the volume shortfall, taken alone, is £4,000 (that is, £20,000 − £16,000).

This difference between the two budgeted profit figures is known as a **variance** (the sales volume variance, in this case). A variance is simply the difference between the actual results and the original budget, relating to a particular factor (sales volume, in the case of Activity 9.11).

Where a variance has the effect of making the actual profit lower than the budgeted profit, it is known as an **adverse variance**. The variance arising from the sales volume shortfall is, therefore, an adverse variance. Where a variance has the opposite effect, it is known as a **favourable variance**. We can say, therefore, that a variance is the effect of that factor (taken alone) on the budgeted profit. When looking at some particular aspect, such as sales volume, we assume that all other factors went according to plan.

Variances explain the difference between what profit was planned (budgeted profit) and what profit was achieved (actual profit). If, therefore, we take the budgeted profit and adjust it for the totals for both favourable and unfavourable variances, we should arrive at the actual profit. This is shown in Figure 9.6.

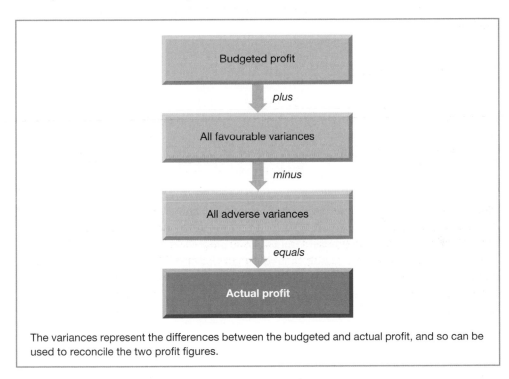

The variances represent the differences between the budgeted and actual profit, and so can be used to reconcile the two profit figures.

Figure 9.6 Relationship between the budgeted and actual profit

For the month of May, we have already identified one of the reasons that the budgeted profit of £20,000 was not achieved and that the actual profit was only £16,900. This was the £4,000 loss of profit (adverse variance) that arose from the sales volume shortfall. Now that the budget is flexed, and the variance arising from the sales volume difference has been stripped out, we can compare like with like and reach further conclusions about May's trading.

The fact that the sales revenue, materials and labour figures differ between the flexed budget and the actual results (see page 000) suggests that the adverse sales volume variance was not the only problem area. To identify the value of the differences that arose from these other three areas (sales revenue, materials and labour), we need to compare the flexed budget and actual values for each of them.

Activity 9.12

Compare the sales revenue, raw materials and labour values between the flexed budget and the actual results and reconcile the original budget and the actual profit for Baxter Ltd. Remember that the sales volume variance is also part of the difference.

This is calculated as follows:

	£
Budgeted profit	20,000
Favourable variances	
Sales price (92,000 − 90,000)	2,000
Direct labour (18,000 − 17,500)	500
Total favourable variances	2,500
Adverse variances	
Sales volume (as above)	(4,000)
Direct materials (36,000 − 36,900)	(900)
Fixed overheads (20,000 − 20,700)	(700)
Total adverse variances	(5,600)
Actual profit	16,900

The variance between flexed budget sales revenue and actual sales revenue (£2,000) can only arise from higher prices being charged than were envisaged in the original budget. This is because any variance arising from volume difference has already been isolated in the flexing process. Less was spent on labour than was allowed for a volume of 900 units. More was spent on materials than should have been for an output of 900 units. There was also an overspend on fixed overheads.

Activity 9.13

If you were the chief executive of Baxter Ltd, what attitude would you take to the overall variance between the budgeted profit and the actual one?

How would you react to the five individual variances that are the outcome of the analysis shown in the solution to Activity 9.12?

You would probably be concerned about how large the variances are and their direction (favourable or adverse). In particular you may have thought of the following:

- The overall adverse profit variance is £3,100 (that is £20,000 − £16,900). This represents 15.5 per cent of the budgeted profit (that is (£3,100/£20,000) × 100%) and you (as chief executive) would pretty certainly see it as significant and worrying.

- The £4,000 adverse sales volume variance represents 20 per cent of budgeted profit and it too would be a major cause of concern.
- The £2,000 favourable sales price variance represents 10 per cent of budgeted profit. Since this is favourable it might be seen as a cause for celebration rather than concern. On the other hand, it means that Baxter's output was, on average, sold at prices 2 per cent above the planned price. This could have been the cause of the worrying adverse sales volume variance. Baxter may have sold fewer units because it charged higher prices.
- The £900 adverse direct materials variance represents 4.5 per cent of budgeted profit. It would be unrealistic to expect the actuals to hit the precise budget figure each month. The question is whether 4.5 per cent for this variance represents a significant amount and a cause for concern.
- The £500 favourable direct labour variance represents 2.5 per cent of budgeted profit. Since this is favourable and relatively small it may be seen as not being a major cause for concern.
- The £700 fixed overhead adverse variance represents 3.5 per cent of budgeted profit. The chief executive may be concerned about this.

The chief executive will now need to ask some questions as to why things went so badly wrong in several areas and what can be done to improve things for the future.

The variance between the actual and flexed figures that has been calculated for both materials and labour overheads can be broken down further.

The total direct materials variance (£900) can be analysed to see the extent to which it is caused by a difference (between budget and actual):

- in the amount of raw material used; and/or
- in the prices at which the materials were bought.

A similar analysis can be carried out for the total direct labour variance (£500). These further analyses may provide much more helpful information than the broad variances for each of these two areas. Overhead variances can also be broken down further. These further analyses are beyond the scope of this book. If you would like to pursue this topic, the further reading at the end of the chapter provides some appropriate references.

Real World 9.6 shows how two UK-based businesses, Associated British Foods Group plc, the food processor, and Tate and Lyle plc, the sugar refiner, use **variance analysis** to exercise control over their operations. Many businesses explain in their annual reports how they operate systems of budgetary control.

REAL WORLD 9.6

Variance analysis in practice

Food for thought

In its 2015 annual report, Associated British Foods Group plc state:

> All businesses prepare annual operating plans and budgets which are updated regularly. Performance against budget is monitored at operational level and centrally, with variances being reported promptly.

Refined controls

Tate and Lyle plc makes it clear that it too uses budgets and variance analysis to help keep control over its activities. The 2015 annual report states that there is:

A comprehensive planning and budgeting system for all items of expenditure with an annual budget approved by the Board. Performance is reported monthly against budget and prior year results; significant variances are investigated.

The board of directors of neither of these businesses will seek explanations of variances arising at each branch/department, but they will be looking at figures for the businesses as a whole or the results for major divisions of them.

Equally certainly, branch/department managers will receive a monthly (or perhaps more frequent) report of variances arising within their area of responsibility alone.

Sources: Associated British Foods Group plc, Annual report 2015, p.67; and Tate and Lyle plc, Annual Report 2015, p. 51.

Real World 9.7 gives some indication of the importance of flexible budgeting in practice.

REAL WORLD 9.7

Being flexible about budgeting

A study of the UK food and drink industry by Abdel-Kader and Luther provides some insight as to the importance attached by management accountants to flexible budgeting. The study asked those in charge of the management accounting function to rate the importance of flexible budgeting by selecting one of three possible categories: 'not important', 'moderately important' or 'important'. Figure 9.7 sets out the results, from the sample of 117 respondents.

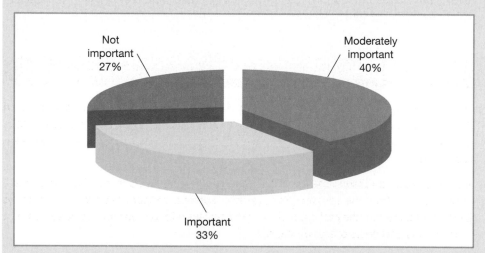

Figure 9.7 Degree of importance attached to flexible budgeting

Respondents were also asked to state the frequency with which flexible budgeting was used within the business, using a five-point scale ranging from 1 (never) through to 5 (very often). Figure 9.8 sets out the results.

We can see that although flexible budgeting is regarded as important by a significant proportion of management accountants and is being used in practice, not all businesses use it.

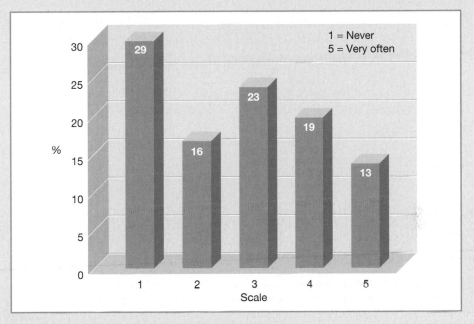

Figure 9.8 Frequency of use of flexible budgets

Source: Based on information in Abdel-Kader, M. and Luther, R. (2006), 'Management accounting practices in the food and drinks industry', CIMA Research.

MAKING BUDGETARY CONTROL EFFECTIVE

It should be clear from what we have seen of **budgetary control** that a system, or a set of routines, must be put in place to enable the potential benefits to be gained. Most businesses that operate successful budgetary control systems tend to share some common features. These include the following:

■ *A serious attitude taken to the system.* This approach should apply to all levels of management, right from the very top. For example, senior managers need to make clear to junior managers that they take notice of the monthly variance reports and base some of their actions and decisions upon them.

- *Clear demarcation between areas of managerial responsibility.* It needs to be clear which manager is responsible for each business area, so that accountability can more easily be ascribed for any area that seems to be going out of control.
- *Budget targets that are challenging yet achievable.* Setting unachievable targets is likely to have a demotivating effect. There may be a case for getting managers to participate in establishing their own targets to help create a sense of 'ownership'. This, in turn, can increase the managers' commitment and motivation.
- *Established data collection, analysis and reporting routines.* These should take the actual results and the budget figures, and calculate and report the variances. This should be part of the business's regular accounting information system, so that the required reports are automatically produced each month.
- *Reports aimed at individual managers, rather than general-purpose documents.* This avoids managers having to wade through a large report to find the small part that is relevant to them.
- *Fairly short reporting periods.* These would typically be one month long, so that things cannot go too far wrong before they are picked up.
- *Timely variance reports.* Reports should be produced and made available to managers shortly after the end of the relevant reporting period. If it is not until the end of June that a manager is informed that the performance in May was below the budgeted level, it is quite likely that the performance for June will be below target as well. Reports on the performance in May ideally need to emerge in early June.
- *Action being taken to get operations back under control if they are shown to be out of control.* The report will not change things by itself. Managers need to take action to try to ensure that the reporting of significant adverse variances leads to action to put things right for the future.

BEHAVIOURAL ISSUES

Budgets are prepared with the objective of affecting the attitudes and behaviour of managers. We saw earlier that budgets are intended to motivate managers, and research evidence generally shows that budgets can be effective in achieving this. More specifically, the research shows that:

- the existence of budgets generally tends to improve performance;
- demanding, yet achievable, budget targets tend to motivate better than less demanding targets – it seems that setting the most demanding targets that will be accepted by managers is a very effective way to motivate them;
- unrealistically demanding targets tend to have an adverse effect on managers' performance; and
- the participation of managers in setting their targets tends to improve motivation and performance. This is probably because those managers feel a sense of commitment to the targets and a moral obligation to achieve them.

These points suggest that care must be taken in the extent to which managers have unfettered choice of their own targets.

Activity 9.14

Can you think of any arguments against allowing managers to have too much influence over setting their own targets?

It may lead to slack (that is, easily achievable targets) being introduced. This may mean that the potential of the business will not be fully achieved. On the other hand, in an effort to impress, a manager may select a target that is not really achievable.

THE USE OF VARIANCE ANALYSIS

Variance analysis is a very popular management accounting technique. **Real World 9.8** provides some evidence of this.

REAL WORLD 9.8

Using variance analysis

The CIMA survey examined the extent to which the use of variance analysis varies with business size. Figure 9.9 shows the results.

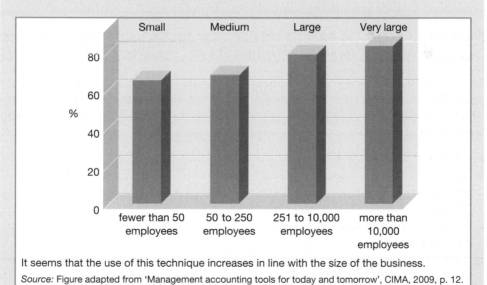

It seems that the use of this technique increases in line with the size of the business.

Source: Figure adapted from 'Management accounting tools for today and tomorrow', CIMA, 2009, p. 12.

Figure 9.9 Variance analysis and business size

→

The survey also indicated that variance analysis was the most widely used of a variety of management accounting tools examined (which included the techniques covered in previous chapters). Overall, more than 70 per cent of respondents used this technique.

The CIMA survey indicated that there is a tendency for smaller businesses to be less likely to use variance analysis. This was emphasised by the survey of seven small and four medium-sized UK businesses that we met earlier in the chapter, which found that none of these eleven businesses used variance analysis.

Sources: Al-Omiri, M. and Drury, C. (2007), 'A survey of factors influencing the choice of product costing systems in UK organisations', *Management Accounting Research,* December, pp. 399–424; and Lucas, M., Prowle, P. and Lowth, G. (2013), 'Management accounting practices of UK small and medium-sized enterprises', CIMA, July, p. 7.

Self-assessment question 9.1 should pull together what we have just seen about preparing budgets.

? SELF-ASSESSMENT QUESTION 9.1

Antonio Ltd has planned production and sales for the next nine months as follows:

	Production units	Sales units
May	350	350
June	400	400
July	500	400
August	600	500
September	600	600
October	700	650
November	750	700
December	750	800
January	750	750

During the period, the business plans to advertise so as to generate these increases in sales. Payments for advertising of £1,000 and £1,500 will be made in July and October respectively.

The selling price per unit will be £20 throughout the period. Forty per cent of sales are normally made on two months' credit. The other 60 per cent are settled within the month of the sale.

Raw materials will be held for one month before they are taken into production. Purchases of raw materials will be on one month's credit (buy one month, pay the next). The cost of raw materials is £8 per unit of production.

The direct labour cost will be £6 per unit of production. This is a variable cost. It will be paid in the month concerned.

Various fixed production overheads, which during the period to 30 June had run at £1,800 a month, are expected to rise to £2,000 each month from 1 July to 31 October. These are expected to rise again from 1 November to £2,400 a month and to remain at that level for the foreseeable future. These overheads include a steady £400 each month for depreciation.

Overheads are planned to be paid 80 per cent in the month of production and 20 per cent in the following month.

To help to meet the planned increased production, a new item of plant will be bought and delivered in August. The cost of this item is £6,600; the contract with the supplier will specify that this will be paid in three equal amounts in September, October and November.

The business plans to hold raw materials inventories of 500 units on 1 July. The balance at the bank on the same day is planned to be £7,500.

Required:

(a) Draw up the following for the six months ending 31 December:

(i) A raw materials inventories budget, showing both physical quantities and financial values.

(ii) A trade payables budget.

(iii) A cash budget.

(iv) A budgeted income statement for the month of May.

(b) The cash budget reveals a potential cash deficiency during October and November. Can you suggest any ways in which a modification of plans could overcome this problem?

(c) Calculate the actual profit for May and reconcile it with the budgeted profit for the month calculated in (a) (iv), above. The reconciliation should include the following variances:

- sales volume
- sales price
- direct materials
- direct labour
- fixed overheads.

The following information is relevant:

During May, 360 units were sold for a total of £7,400. The raw material cost was £2,810. The labour cost was £2,250. The fixed production overheads cost was £1,830.

The solution to this question can be found at the back of the book on p. 531.

SUMMARY

The main points of this chapter may be summarised as follows:

Budgets

- A budget is a short-term business plan, mainly expressed in financial terms.
- Budgets are the short-term means of working towards the business's mission and objectives.
- They are usually prepared for a one-year period with sub-periods of a month.
- There is usually a separate budget for each key area.

- The budgets for each area are summarised in master budgets (budgeted income statement and statement of financial position).
- Budgets are plans rather than forecasts.

Uses of budgets

- Promote forward thinking.
- Help co-ordinate the various aspects of the business.
- Motivate performance.
- Provide the basis of a system of control.
- Provide a system of authorisation.

Preparing budgets

- There is no standard style – practicality and usefulness are the key issues.
- They are usually prepared in columnar form, with a column for each month (or similarly short period).
- Each budget must link (co-ordinate) with others.
- The starting point for preparing budgets is to identify the limiting factor. This will determine the overall level of activity.
- Non-financial measures (such as units of output) can be used when budgeting.

Controlling through budgets

- Control is achieved through a comparison of budget performance and actual performance.
- To exercise control, budgets can be flexed to match actual volume of output.
- A variance is an increase (favourable) or decrease (adverse) in profit, relative to the budgeted profit, as a result of some aspect of the business's activities when taken alone.
- Budgeted profit plus all favourable variances less all adverse variances equals actual profit.

Effective budgetary control

- Good budgetary control requires establishing systems and routines to ensure such things as a clear distinction between individual managers' areas of responsibility; prompt, frequent and relevant variance reporting; and senior management commitment.
- Behavioural aspects of control relating to management style, participation in budget-setting and the failure to meet budget targets should be taken into account by senior managers.

FURTHER READING

If you would like to explore the topics covered in this chapter in more depth, we recommend the following books:

Atrill, P. and McLaney, E. (2015) *Management Accounting for Decision Makers,* 8th edn, Pearson, Chapters 6 and 7.

Bhimani A., Horngren, C., Datar, S. and Rajan, M. (2015) *Management and Cost Accounting* 6th edn, Pearson, Chapters 14, 15 and 16.

Drury, C. (2015) *Management and Cost Accounting,* 9th edn, Cengage Learning EMEA, Chapter 15.

Hilton, R. and Platt, D. (2014) *Managerial Accounting,* Global edn, McGraw-Hill Higher Education, Chapters 9, 10 and 11.

? REVIEW QUESTIONS

Solutions to these questions can be found at the back of the book, on pages. 545–546.

9.1 Define a budget. How is a budget different from a forecast?

9.2 What were the five uses of budgets that were identified in the chapter?

9.3 What is meant by a *variance*? What is the point in analysing variances?

9.4 What is the point in flexing the budget in the context of variance analysis? Does flexing imply that differences between budget and actual in the volume of output are ignored in variance analysis?

*Exercise 9.1 is basic level. Exercises 9.2 and 9.3 are intermediate level and Exercises 9.4 and 9.5 are advanced level. Those with **coloured numbers** have solutions at the back of the book, starting on page 566.*

9.1 You have overheard the following statements:

(a) 'A budget is a forecast of what is expected to happen in a business during the next year.'

(b) 'Monthly budgets must be prepared with a column for each month so that you can see the whole year at a glance, month by month.'

(c) 'Budgets are OK but they stifle all initiative. No manager worth employing would work for a business that seeks to control through budgets.'

(d) 'Any sensible person would start with the sales budget and build up the other budgets from there.'

Required:
Critically discuss these statements, explaining any technical terms.

9.2 A nursing home, which is linked to a large hospital, has been examining its budgetary control procedures, with particular reference to overhead costs.

The level of activity in the facility is measured by the number of patients treated in the budget period. For the current year, the budget stands at 6,000 patients and this is expected to be met.

For months 1 to 6 of this year (assume 12 months of equal length), 2,700 patients were treated. The actual variable overhead costs incurred during this six-month period are as follows:

Expense	£
Staffing	59,400
Power	27,000
Supplies	54,000
Other	8,100
Total	148,500

The hospital accountant believes that the variable overhead costs will be incurred at the same rate during months 7 to 12 of the year.

Fixed overheads are budgeted for the whole year as follows:

Expense	£
Supervision	120,000
Depreciation/financing	187,200
Other	64,800
Total	372,000

Required:
(a) Present an overheads budget for months 7 to 12 of the year. You should show each expense, but should not separate individual months. What is the total overheads cost for each patient that would be incorporated into any statistics?
(b) The home actually treated 3,800 patients during months 7 to 12, the actual variable overheads were £203,300 and the fixed overheads were £190,000. In summary form, examine how well the home exercised control over its overheads.
(c) Interpret your analysis and point out any limitations or assumptions.

9.3 Linpet Ltd is to be incorporated on 1 June. The opening statement of financial position (balance sheet) of the business will then be as follows:

Assets	£
Cash at bank	60,000
Share capital	
£1 ordinary shares	60,000

During June, the business intends to make payments of £40,000 for a leasehold property, £10,000 for equipment and £6,000 for a motor vehicle. The business will also purchase initial trading inventories costing £22,000 on credit.
 The business has produced the following estimates:

1 Sales revenue for June will be £8,000 and will increase at the rate of £3,000 a month until September. In October, sales revenue will rise to £22,000 and in subsequent months will be maintained at this figure.
2 The gross profit percentage on goods sold will be 25 per cent.
3 There is a risk that supplies of trading inventories will be interrupted towards the end of the accounting year. The business, therefore, intends to build up its initial level of inventories (£22,000) by purchasing £1,000 of inventories each month in addition to the monthly purchases necessary to satisfy monthly sales requirements. All purchases of inventories (including the initial inventories) will be on one month's credit.
4 Sales revenue will be divided equally between cash and credit sales. Credit customers are expected to pay two months after the sale is agreed.
5 Wages and salaries will be £900 a month. Other overheads will be £500 a month for the first four months and £650 thereafter. Both types of expense will be payable when incurred.
6 80 per cent of sales revenue will be generated by salespeople who will receive 5 per cent commission on sales revenue. The commission is payable one month after the sale is agreed.
7 The business intends to purchase further equipment in November for £7,000 cash.
8 Depreciation will be provided at the rate of 5 per cent a year on property and 20 per cent a year on equipment. (Depreciation has not been included in the overheads mentioned in 5 above.)

Required:
(a) State why a cash budget is required for a business.
(b) Prepare a cash budget for Linpet Ltd for the six-month period to 30 November.

9.4 Newtake Records Ltd owns a small chain of shops selling DVDs and CDs. At the beginning of June the business had an overdraft of £35,000 and the bank had asked for this to be eliminated by the end of November. As a result, the directors have recently decided to review their plans for the next six months.

The following plans were prepared for the business some months earlier:

	May £000	June £000	July £000	Aug £000	Sept £000	Oct £000	Nov £000
Sales revenue	180	230	320	250	140	120	110
Purchases	135	180	142	94	75	66	57
Administration expenses	52	55	56	53	48	46	45
Selling expenses	22	24	28	26	21	19	18
Taxation payment	–	–	–	22	–	–	–
Finance payments	5	5	5	5	5	5	5
Shop refurbishment	–	–	14	18	6	–	–

Notes:
1 The inventories level at 1 June was £112,000. The business believes it is preferable to maintain a minimum inventories level of £40,000 over the period to 30 November.
2 Suppliers allow one month's credit.
3 The gross profit margin is 40 per cent.
4 All sales proceeds are received in the month of sale. However, 50 per cent of customers pay with a credit card. The charge made by the credit card business to Newtake Records Ltd is 3 per cent of the sales revenue value. These charges are in addition to the selling expenses identified above. The credit card business pays Newtake Records Ltd in the month of sale.
5 The business has a bank loan, which it is paying off in monthly instalments of £5,000. The interest element represents 20 per cent of each instalment.
6 Administration expenses are paid when incurred. This item includes a charge of £15,000 each month in respect of depreciation.
7 Selling expenses are payable in the following month.

Required (working to the nearest £1,000):
(a) Prepare an inventories budget for the six months to 30 November also based on the table of plans above.
(b) Prepare a cash budget for the six months ending 30 November which shows the cash balance at the end of each month also based on the plans set out in the table above.
(c) Prepare a budgeted income statement for the whole of the six-month period ending 30 November. (A monthly breakdown of profit is *not* required.)
(d) What problems is Newtake Records Ltd likely to face in the next six months? Can you suggest how the business might deal with these problems?

9.5 Daniel Chu Ltd, a new business, will start production on 1 April, but sales will not start until 1 May. Planned sales for the next nine months are as follows:

	Sales units
May	500
June	600
July	700
August	800
September	900
October	900
November	900
December	800
January	700

The selling price of a unit will be a consistent £100 and all sales will be made on one month's credit. It is planned that sufficient finished goods inventories for each month's sales should be available at the end of the previous month.

Raw materials purchases will be such that there will be sufficient raw materials inventories available at the end of each month precisely to meet the following month's planned production. This planned policy will operate from the end of April. Purchases of raw materials will be on one month's credit. The cost of raw material is £40 a unit of finished product.

The direct labour cost, which is variable with the level of production, is planned to be £20 a unit of finished production. Production overheads are planned to be £20,000 each month, including £3,000 for depreciation. Non-production overheads are planned to be £11,000 a month, of which £1,000 will be depreciation.

Various non-current (fixed) assets costing £250,000 will be bought and paid for during April.

Except where specified, assume that all payments take place in the same month as the cost is incurred.

The business will raise £300,000 in cash from a share issue in April.

Required:
Draw up the following for the six months ending 30 September:

(a) A finished inventories budget, showing just physical quantities.
(b) A raw materials inventories budget showing both physical quantities and financial values.
(c) A trade payables budget.
(d) A trade receivables budget.
(e) A cash budget.

PART THREE
FINANCE

Chapter 10

MAKING CAPITAL INVESTMENT DECISIONS

INTRODUCTION

The chapter is the first of three dealing with the area generally known as *finance* or *financial management*.

In this chapter, we shall look at how businesses should assess proposed investments in new plant, machinery, buildings and other long-term assets. This is a very important area; expensive and far-reaching consequences can flow from bad investment decisions. We shall also consider some of the practical aspects to be taken into account when evaluating investment proposals.

Learning Outcomes

When you have completed this chapter, you should be able to:

- Explain the nature and importance of investment decision making.
- Identify and evaluate the four main investment appraisal methods found in practice.
- Use each of the four methods to reach a decision on a particular investment opportunity.
- Discuss the attributes of each of the four methods.

THE NATURE OF INVESTMENT DECISIONS

The essential feature of investment decisions is *time.* Investment involves making an outlay of something of economic value, usually cash, at one point in time, which is expected to yield economic benefits to the investor at some other point in time. Usually, the outlay precedes the benefits. Furthermore, the outlay is typically a single large amount while the benefits arrive as a series of smaller amounts over a fairly protracted period.

Investment decisions tend to be of profound importance to the business because:

- *Large amounts of resources are often involved.* Many investments made by businesses involve laying out a significant proportion of their total resources (see Real World 10.2). If mistakes are made with the decision, the effects on the businesses could be significant, if not catastrophic.
- *It is often difficult and/or expensive to bail out of an investment once it has been undertaken.* Investments made by a business are often specific to its needs. A hotel business, for example, may invest in a new, custom-designed hotel complex. If the business found, after having made the investment, that room occupancy rates were too low, the only course of action might be to sell the complex. The specialist nature of the complex may, however, lead to it having a rather limited resale value. This could mean that the amount recouped from the investment is much less than it had originally cost.

Real World 10.1 gives an illustration of a major investment by a well-known business operating in the UK.

REAL WORLD 10.1

Launching an investment

Brittany Ferries, the cross-Channel ferry operator, has ordered an additional ferry. The ferry is costing the business £225 million and will be used on the Portsmouth to Santander route from 2017. Although Brittany Ferries is a substantial business, this level of outlay is significant. Clearly, the business believes that acquiring the new ferry will be worthwhile, but how would it have reached this conclusion?

Presumably, the anticipated future benefits from carrying passengers and freight, as well as the costs of operating the ferry, will have been major inputs to the decision.

Source: www.brittany-ferries.co.uk.

The issues raised by Brittany Ferries' investment will be the main subject of this chapter.

Real World 10.2 indicates the level of annual net investment for a number of randomly selected, well-known UK businesses. We can see that the scale of investment varies from one business to another. (It also tends to vary from one year to another for a particular business.) In nearly all of these businesses the scale of investment was significant, despite the fact that many businesses were cutting back on investment during the economic recession.

REAL WORLD 10.2

The scale of investment by UK businesses

	Expenditure on additional non-current assets as a percentage of:	
	Annual sales revenue	End-of-year non-current assets
British Sky Broadcasting plc (television)	74	69
J D Wetherspoon (pub operator)	11	14
Marks and Spencer plc (stores)	6	10
Ryanair Holdings plc (airline)	19	12
Severn Trent Water plc (water and sewerage)	23	6
Vodafone plc (telecommunications)	24	10
Wm Morrison Supermarkets plc (supermarkets)	3	7

Note that the very large figure for investment outlay at BSkyB was linked to the business's major acquisions of Sky Deutschland and Sky Italia. Of course, expenditure to take over another business is making an investment and is much the same, in principle, as making an investment in individual items of property, plant and equipment and other assets.

Source: Annual reports of the businesses concerned for the financial year ending in 2015.

Real World 10.2 considers only expenditure on non-current assets, but this type of investment often requires a significant outlay on current assets to support it (additional inventories, for example). This suggests that the real scale of investment is even greater than indicated above.

Activity 10.1

When managers are making decisions involving capital investments, what should the decision seek to achieve?

Investment decisions must be consistent with the objectives of the particular organisation. For a private-sector business, maximising the wealth of the owners (shareholders) is normally assumed to be the key financial objective.

INVESTMENT APPRAISAL METHODS

Given the importance of investment decisions, it is essential that proper screening of investment proposals takes place. An important part of this screening process is to ensure that appropriate methods of evaluation are used.

Research shows that there are basically four methods used by businesses to appraise investment opportunities. They are:

- accounting rate of return (ARR);
- payback period (PP);
- net present value (NPV); and
- internal rate of return (IRR).

It is possible to find businesses that use variants of these four methods. It is also possible to find businesses, particularly smaller ones, that do not use any formal appraisal method but rely instead on the 'gut feeling' of their managers. Most businesses, however, seem to use one (or more) of these four methods.

We shall evaluate each of the appraisal methods, but will see that only one of them (NPV) offers a wholly logical approach. The other three are flawed to a greater or lesser extent. Nevertheless, all four methods are fairly widely used by managers, as we shall see later in the chapter.

To help in examining each of the methods, it might be useful to see how each of them would cope with a particular investment opportunity. Let us consider the following example.

Example 10.1

Billingsgate Battery Company has carried out some research that shows there to be a market for a standard service that it has recently developed.

Provision of the service would require investment in a machine that would cost £100,000, payable immediately. Sales of the service would take place throughout the next five years. At the end of that time, it is estimated that the machine could be sold for £20,000.

Inflows and outflows from sales of the service would be expected to be:

Time		£000
Immediately	Cost of machine	(100)
1 year's time	Operating profit before depreciation	20
2 years' time	Operating profit before depreciation	40
3 years' time	Operating profit before depreciation	60
4 years' time	Operating profit before depreciation	60
5 years' time	Operating profit before depreciation	20
5 years' time	Disposal proceeds from the machine	20

Note that, broadly speaking, the operating profit before deducting depreciation (that is, before non-cash items) equals the net amount of cash flowing into the business. Broadly, apart from depreciation, all of this business's expenses cause cash to flow out of the business. Sales revenues tend to lead to cash flowing in. Expenses tend to lead to it flowing out. For the time being, we shall assume that working capital – which is made up of inventories, trade receivables and trade payables – remains constant. This means that operating profit before depreciation will tend to equal the net cash inflow.

→

To simplify matters, we shall assume that the cash from sales and for the expenses of providing the service are received and paid, respectively, at the end of each year. This is clearly unlikely to be true in real life. Money will have to be paid to employees (for salaries and wages) on a weekly or a monthly basis. Customers will pay within a month or two of buying the service. On the other hand, making the assumption probably does not lead to a serious distortion. It is a simplifying assumption, that is often made in real life, and it will make things more straightforward for us now. We should be clear, however, that there is nothing about any of the four methods that *demands* that this assumption is made.

Having set up the example, let us now go on to consider how each of the appraisal methods works.

ACCOUNTING RATE OF RETURN (ARR)

The first of the four methods that we shall consider is the **accounting rate of return (ARR)**. This method takes the average accounting operating profit that the investment will generate and expresses it as a percentage of the average investment made over the life of the project. In other words:

$$\textbf{ARR} = \frac{\textbf{Average annual operating profit}}{\textbf{Average investment to earn that profit}} \times \textbf{100\%}$$

We can see from the equation that, to calculate the ARR, we need to deduce two pieces of information about the particular project:

- the annual average operating profit; and
- the average investment.

In our example, the average annual operating profit *before depreciation* over the five years is £40,000 (that is, £000(20 + 40 + 60 + 60 + 20)/5). Assuming 'straight-line' depreciation (that is, equal annual amounts), the annual depreciation charge will be £16,000 (that is, £(100,000 − 20,000)/5). Therefore, the average annual operating profit *after depreciation* is £24,000 (that is, £40,000 − £16,000).

The average investment over the five years can be calculated as follows:

$$\text{Average investment} = \frac{\text{Cost of machine} + \text{Disposal value*}}{2}$$

$$= \frac{\pounds100,000 + \pounds20,000}{2}$$

$$= \pounds60,000$$

* *Note*: To find the average investment we are simply adding the value of the amount invested at the beginning and end of the investment period together and dividing by two.

The ARR of the investment, therefore, is:

$$ARR = \frac{£24,000}{£60,000} \times 100\% = 40\%$$

The following decision rules apply when using ARR:

- For any project to be acceptable, it must achieve a target ARR as a minimum.
- Where there are competing projects that all seem capable of exceeding this minimum rate (that is, where the business must choose between more than one project), the one with the higher (or highest) ARR should be selected.

To decide whether the 40 per cent return is acceptable, we need to compare this percentage return with the minimum rate required by the business.

Chaotic Industries is considering an investment in a fleet of ten delivery vans to take its products to customers. The vans will cost £15,000 each to buy, payable immediately. The annual running costs are expected to total £50,000 for each van (including the driver's salary). The vans are expected to operate successfully for six years, at the end of which period they will all have to be sold, with disposal proceeds expected to be about £3,000 a van. At present, the business outsources transport, for all of its deliveries, to a commercial carrier. It is expected that this carrier will charge a total of £530,000 each year for the next six years to undertake the deliveries.

What is the ARR of buying the vans? (Note that cost savings are as relevant a benefit from an investment as are net cash inflows.)

The vans will save the business £30,000 a year (that is, £530,000 − (£50,000 × 10)), before depreciation, in total. Therefore, the inflows and outflows will be:

Time		£000
Immediately	Cost of vans (10 × £15,000)	(150)
1 year's time	Saving before depreciation	30
2 years' time	Saving before depreciation	30
3 years' time	Saving before depreciation	30
4 years' time	Saving before depreciation	30
5 years' time	Saving before depreciation	30
6 years' time	Saving before depreciation	30
6 years' time	Disposal proceeds from the vans (10 × £3,000)	30

The total annual depreciation expense (assuming a straight-line method) will be £20,000 (that is, (£150,000 − £30,000)/6). Therefore, the average annual saving, *after depreciation*, is £10,000 (that is, £30,000 − £20,000).

The average investment will be

$$\text{Average investment} = \frac{£150,000 + £30,000}{2}$$

$$= £90,000$$

and the ARR of the investment is

$$\text{ARR} = \frac{£10,000}{£90,000} \times 100\%$$

$$= 11.1\%$$

ARR and ROCE

In essence, ARR and the return on capital employed (ROCE) ratio take the same approach to measuring business performance. Both relate operating profit to the cost of assets used to generate that profit. ROCE , however, typically assesses the performance of the entire business *after* it has performed, while ARR assesses the potential performance of a particular investment *before* it has performed.

We saw that investments are required to achieve a minimum target ARR. Given the link between ARR and ROCE, this target could be based on overall rates of returns previously achieved – as measured by ROCE. It could also be based on the industry-average ROCE.

The link between ARR and ROCE strengthens the case for adopting ARR as the appropriate method of investment appraisal. ROCE is a widely-used measure of profitability and some businesses express their financial objective in terms of a target ROCE. It may seem sensible, therefore, to use a method of investment appraisal that is consistent with this overall measure of business performance. A secondary point in favour of ARR is that it provides a result expressed percentage terms, which many managers seem to prefer.

Problems with ARR

Activity 10.3

ARR suffers from a major defect as a means of assessing investment opportunities. Can you reason out what this is? Consider the three competing projects whose profits are shown below. All three involve investment in a machine that is expected to have no residual value at the end of the five years. Note that all of the projects have the same total operating profits after depreciation over the five years.

Time		Project A £000	Project B £000	Project C £000
Immediately	Cost of machine	(160)	(160)	(160)
1 year's time	Operating profit after depreciation	20	10	160
2 years' time	Operating profit after depreciation	40	10	10
3 years' time	Operating profit after depreciation	60	10	10
4 years' time	Operating profit after depreciation	60	10	10
5 years' time	Operating profit after depreciation	20	160	10

In this example, each project has the same total operating profit over the five years (£200,000) and the same average investment of £80,000 (that is, £160,000/2). This means that each project will give rise to the same ARR of 50 per cent (that is, £40,000/£80,000).

ARR, therefore, fails to distinguish between them even though they are not of equal merit. This is because ARR ignores the time factor and, therefore, the cost of financing the project.

To maximise the wealth of the owners, a manager faced with a choice between the three projects set out in Activity 10.3 should select Project C. This is because most of the benefits arise within 12 months of making the initial investment. Project A would rank second and Project B would come a poor third. Any appraisal technique that is not capable of distinguishing between these three situations is seriously flawed. We shall look at why timing is so important later in the chapter.

There are further problems associated with the ARR method, which we shall now discuss.

Use of average investment

Using the average investment in calculating ARR can lead to daft results. Example 10.2 illustrates the kind of problem that can arise.

Example 10.2

George put forward an investment proposal to his boss. The business uses ARR to assess investment proposals using a minimum 'hurdle' rate of 27 per cent. Details of the proposal were:

Cost of equipment	£200,000
Estimated residual value of equipment	£40,000
Average annual operating profit before depreciation	£48,000
Estimated life of project	10 years
Annual straight-line depreciation charge	£16,000 (that is, (£200,000 − £40,000)/10)

The ARR of the project will be:

$$ARR = \frac{48,000 - 16,000}{(200,000 + 40,000)/2} \times 100\% = 26.7\%$$

The boss rejected George's proposal because it failed to achieve an ARR of at least 27 per cent. Although George was disappointed, he realised that there was still hope. In fact, all that the business had to do was to give away the piece of equipment at the end of its useful life rather than sell it. The residual value of the equipment then became zero and the annual depreciation charge became ([£200,000 − £0]/10) = £20,000 a year. The revised ARR calculation was then:

$$ARR = \frac{48,000 - 20,000}{(200,000 + 0)/2} \times 100\% = 28\%$$

Use of accounting profit

We have seen that ARR is based on accounting profit. When measuring performance over the whole life of a project, however, it is cash flows rather than accounting profits that are important. Cash is the ultimate measure of the economic wealth generated by an investment. It is cash that is used to acquire resources and for distribution to owners. As a result, cash provides the appropriate measure when considering performance over the life of a project. Accounting profit is more appropriate for reporting achievement on a periodic basis. It is a useful measure of productive effort for a relatively short period, such as a year or half year.

Target ARR

We saw earlier a target ARR against which to assess investment opportunities must be chosen. This cannot be objectively determined and so will depend on the judgement of managers. The target ARR may, therefore, vary over time and may vary between businesses.

Competing investments

The ARR method can create problems when considering competing investments of different size. Consider Activity 10.4.

Activity 10.4

Sinclair Wholesalers plc is currently considering opening a new sales outlet in Coventry. Two possible sites have been identified for the new outlet. Site A has an area of 30,000 square metres. It will require an average investment of £6 million and will produce an average operating profit of £600,000 a year. Site B has an area of 20,000 square metres. It will require an average investment of £4 million and will produce an average operating profit of £500,000 a year.

What is the ARR of each investment opportunity? Which site would you select and why?

The ARR of Site A is £600,000/£6m = 10 per cent. The ARR of Site B is £500,000/£4m = 12.5 per cent. Site B, therefore has the higher ARR. In terms of the absolute operating profit generated, however, Site A is the more attractive. If the ultimate objective is to increase the wealth of the shareholders of Sinclair Wholesalers plc, it would be better to choose Site A even though the percentage return is lower. It is the absolute size of the return rather than the relative (percentage) size that is important. This is a general problem of using comparative measures, such as percentages, when the objective is measured in absolute terms, such as an amount of money.

Real World 10.3 illustrates how using percentage measures can lead to confusion.

REAL WORLD 10.3

Increasing road capacity by sleight of hand

During the 1970s, the Mexican government wanted to increase the capacity of a major four-lane road. It came up with the idea of repainting the lane markings so that there were six narrower lanes occupying the same space as four wider ones had previously done. This increased the capacity of the road by 50 per cent (that is, $^2/_4 \times 100$). A tragic outcome of the narrower lanes was an increase in deaths from road accidents. A year later the Mexican government had the six narrower lanes changed back to the original four wider ones. This reduced the capacity of the road by 33 per cent (that is, $^2/_6 \times 100$). The Mexican government reported that, overall, it had increased the capacity of the road by 17 per cent (that is, 50% − 33%), despite the fact that its real capacity was identical to that which it had been originally. The confusion arose because each of the two percentages (50 per cent and 33 per cent) is based on different bases (four and six).

Source: Gigerenzer, G. (2002) *Reckoning with Risk: learning to live with uncertainty*, Penguin.

PAYBACK PERIOD (PP)

Another approach to appraising possible investments is the **payback period (PP)**. This is the time taken for an initial investment to be repaid out of the net cash inflows from a project. As the PP method takes time into account and it deals with cash, rather than accounting profit, it appears, at first glance, to overcome two key weaknesses of the ARR method.

Let us consider PP in the context of the Billingsgate Battery example. We should recall that the project's cash flows are:

Time		£000
Immediately	Cost of machine	(100)
1 year's time	Operating profit before depreciation	20
2 years' time	Operating profit before depreciation	40
3 years' time	Operating profit before depreciation	60
4 years' time	Operating profit before depreciation	60
5 years' time	Operating profit before depreciation	20
5 years' time	Disposal proceeds	20

Note that all of these figures are amounts of cash to be paid or received (we saw earlier that operating profit before depreciation is a rough measure of the cash flows from the project).

The payback period can be derived by calculating the cumulative cash flows as follows:

Time		Net cash flows £000	Cumulative cash flows £000	
Immediately	Cost of machine	(100)	(100)	
1 year's time	Operating profit before depreciation	20	(80)	(−100 + 20)
2 years' time	Operating profit before depreciation	40	(40)	(−80 + 40)
3 years' time	Operating profit before depreciation	60	20	(−40 + 60)
4 years' time	Operating profit before depreciation	60	80	(20 + 60)
5 years' time	Operating profit before depreciation	20	100	(80 + 20)
5 years' time	Disposal proceeds	20	120	(100 + 20)

We can see that the cumulative cash flows become positive at the end of the third year. If we assume that the cash flows arise evenly over the year, the precise payback period would be:

$$2 \text{ years} + (^{40}/_{60}) \text{ years} = 2^2/_3 \text{ years}$$

where 40 represents the cash flow still required at the beginning of the third year to repay the initial outlay and 60 is the projected cash flow during the third year.

The following decision rules apply when using PP:

- For a project to be acceptable it should have a payback period no longer than a maximum payback period set by the business.
- If there were two (or more) competing projects whose payback periods were all shorter than the maximum payback period requirement, the project with the shorter (or shortest) payback period should be selected.

If, for example, Billingsgate Battery had a maximum acceptable payback period of four years, the project would be undertaken. A project with a payback period of longer than four years would not be acceptable.

Activity 10.5

What is the payback period of the Chaotic Industries project from Activity 10.2?

The inflows and outflows are expected to be:

Time		Net cash flows £000	Cumulative net cash flows £000	
Immediately	Cost of vans	(150)	(150)	
1 year's time	Saving before depreciation	30	(120)	(−150 + 30)
2 years' time	Saving before depreciation	30	(90)	(−120 + 30)
3 years' time	Saving before depreciation	30	(60)	(−90 + 30)
4 years' time	Saving before depreciation	30	(30)	(−60 + 30)
5 years' time	Saving before depreciation	30	0	(−30 + 30)
6 years' time	Saving before depreciation	30	30	(0 + 30)
6 years' time	Disposal proceeds from the vans	30	60	(30 + 30)

The payback period here is five years; that is, it is not until the end of the fifth year that the vans will pay for themselves out of the savings that they are expected to generate.

The logic of using PP is that projects that can recoup their cost quickly are economically more attractive than those with longer payback periods. In other words, it emphasises liquidity.

The PP method has certain advantages. It is quick and easy to calculate. Also, it can easily be understood by managers. PP is an improvement on ARR in respect of timing and of the use cash flows (rather than accounting flows). It is not, however, a complete answer to the problem.

Problems with PP

The cumulative cash flows of each project in Activity 10.6 are set out in Figure 10.1.

Activity 10.6

In what respect is PP not a complete answer as a means of assessing investment opportunities? Consider the cash flows arising from three competing projects:

Time		Project 1 £000	Project 2 £000	Project 3 £000
Immediately	Cost of machine	(200)	(200)	(200)
1 year's time	Operating profit before depreciation	70	20	70
2 years' time	Operating profit before depreciation	00	20	100
3 years' time	Operating profit before depreciation	70	160	30
4 years' time	Operating profit before depreciation	80	30	200
5 years' time	Operating profit before depreciation	50	20	440
5 years' time	Disposal proceeds	40	10	20

(*Hint*: Again, the defect is not concerned with the ability of the manager to forecast future events. This is a problem, but it is a problem whatever approach we take.)

The PP for each project is three years and so the PP method would regard the projects as being equally acceptable. It cannot distinguish between those projects that pay back a significant amount early within the three-year payback period and those that do not.

In addition, this method ignores cash flows after the payback period. Managers concerned with increasing owners' wealth would greatly prefer Project 3 because the cash inflows are received earlier. In fact, most of the initial cost of making the investment has been repaid by the end of the second year. Furthermore, the cash inflows are very much greater in total.

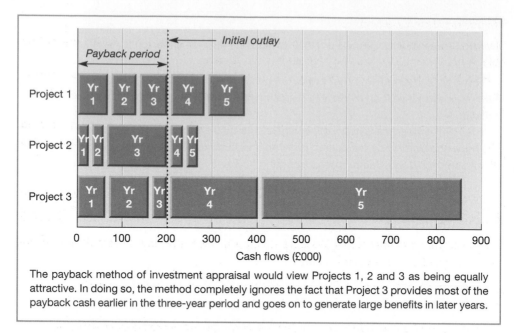

The payback method of investment appraisal would view Projects 1, 2 and 3 as being equally attractive. In doing so, the method completely ignores the fact that Project 3 provides most of the payback cash earlier in the three-year period and goes on to generate large benefits in later years.

Figure 10.1 The cumulative cash flows of each project in Activity 10.6

Some additional points concerning the PP method are considered below.

Relevant information

We saw earlier that the PP method is simply concerned with how quickly the initial investment can be recouped. Cash flows arising beyond the payback period are ignored. While this neatly avoids the practical problems of forecasting cash flows over a long period, it means that not all relevant information may be taken into account.

Risk

By favouring projects with a short payback period, the PP method appears to provide a means of dealing with the problem of risk. This is, however, a fairly crude approach to assessing risk. It looks only at the risk that the project will end earlier than expected. This is only one of many risk areas. What, for example, about the risk that the demand for the product may be less than expected? There are more systematic approaches to dealing with risk that can be used.

Wealth maximisation

Although the PP method takes some note of the timing of project costs and benefits, it is not concerned with maximising the wealth of the business owners. Instead, it favours projects that pay for themselves quickly.

Target payback period

Managers must decide what maximum payback period is acceptable. As this cannot be objectively determined, it is really a matter of judgement.

Real World 10.4 explains that Next plc, the well-known fashion and household retailer, uses the payback period approach to assessing the opening of new stores. It also seems to use ARR.

According to its 2015 annual report, Next plc, the well-known fashion and household retailer, uses the payback period approach to assessing the opening of new stores. It also seems to use ARR.

NET PRESENT VALUE (NPV)

From what we have seen so far, it seems that to make sensible investment decisions, we need a method of appraisal that both:

- considers *all* of the costs and benefits of each investment opportunity; and
- makes a logical allowance for the *timing* of those costs and benefits.

The **net present value (NPV)** method of Investment appraisal provides us with this.

Consider the Billingsgate Battery example's cash flows, which we should recall are:

Time		£000
Immediately	Cost of machine	(100)
1 year's time	Operating profit before depreciation	20
2 years' time	Operating profit before depreciation	40
3 years' time	Operating profit before depreciation	60
4 years' time	Operating profit before depreciation	60
5 years' time	Operating profit before depreciation	20
5 years' time	Disposal proceeds	20

Given a financial objective of maximising owners' wealth, it would be easy to assess this investment if all cash inflows and outflows were to occur immediately. It would then simply be a matter of adding up the cash inflows (total £220,000) and comparing them with the cash outflows (£100,000). This would lead us to conclude that the project should go ahead because the owners would be better off by £120,000. Of course, it is not as easy as this because time is involved. The cash outflow will occur immediately, whereas the cash inflows will arise at different times in the future.

Why does time matter?

Time is an important issue because people do not normally see an amount paid out now as equivalent in value to the same amount being received in a year's time. Thus, if we were offered £100 in one year's time in exchange for paying out £100 now, we would not be interested, unless we wished to do someone a favour.

Activity 10.7

Why would you see £100 to be received in a year's time as not equal in value to £100 to be paid immediately?

The reason is that, if the investor had the £100 now, it could be invested so that it would generate income during that year.

Income lost

The income that is foregone represents an *opportunity cost*. As we saw in Chapter 7, an opportunity cost occurs where one course of action deprives us of the opportunity to derive some benefit from an alternative action.

An investment must exceed the opportunity cost of the funds invested if it is to be worthwhile. If Billingsgate Battery Company sees investing money elsewhere as the alternative to investment in the machine, the return from investing in the machine must be better than that from the alternative investment. If this is not the case, there is no economic reason to buy the machine.

All investments expose their investors to **risk**. Hence buying a machine, on the strength of estimates made before its purchase, exposes a business to risk. Things may not turn out as expected. We saw in Chapter 1 that people normally expect greater returns in exchange for taking on greater risk. Examples of this in real life are not difficult to find. One such example is that banks tend to charge higher rates of interest to borrowers whom the bank perceives as more risky. Those offering good security for a loan and in receipt of a regular income tend to be charged lower rates of interest.

Going back to Billingsgate Battery Company's investment opportunity, it is not enough to say that we should buy the machine providing the expected returns are higher than those from an alternative investment. The logical equivalent of investing in the machine would be an investment that is of similar risk. Determining the riskiness of a particular project and, therefore, how large the **risk premium** should be, is a difficult task, however.

What will logical investors do?

To summarise, logical investors seeking to increase their wealth will only invest when they believe they will be adequately compensated for the loss of income that the alternative investment will generate. This normally involves checking to see whether the proposed investment will yield a return greater than the basic rate of interest (which will normally include an allowance for inflation) plus an appropriate risk premium.

Dealing with the time value of money

Let us now return to the Billingsgate Battery Company example. We should recall that the cash flows expected from this investment are:

Time		£000
Immediately	Cost of machine	(100)
1 year's time	Operating profit before depreciation	20
2 years' time	Operating profit before depreciation	40
3 years' time	Operating profit before depreciation	60
4 years' time	Operating profit before depreciation	60
5 years' time	Operating profit before depreciation	20
5 years' time	Disposal proceeds	20

We have already seen that it is not enough simply to compare the basic cash inflows and outflows for the investment. Each of these cash flows must be expressed in similar terms, so that a direct comparison can be made between the sum of the inflows over time and the immediate £100,000 investment. Fortunately, we can do this.

To explain how it is done, let us assume that, instead of making this investment, the business could make an alternative investment with similar risk and obtain a return of 20 per cent a year.

Activity 10.8

We know that Billingsgate Battery Company could alternatively invest its money at a rate of 20 per cent a year. How much do you judge the present (immediate) value of the expected first year receipt of £20,000 to be? In other words, if instead of having to wait a year for the £20,000, and being deprived of the opportunity to invest it at 20 per cent, you could have some money now, what sum to be received now would you regard as exactly equivalent to getting £20,000 but having to wait a year for it?

We should obviously be happy to accept a lower amount if we could get it immediately than if we had to wait a year. This is because we could invest it at 20 per cent (in the alternative project). Logically, we should be prepared to accept the amount that, with a year's income, will grow to £20,000. If we call this amount PV (for present value) we can say:

$$PV + (PV \times 20\%) = £20,000$$

that is, the amount plus income from investing the amount for the year equals the £20,000. If we rearrange this equation we find:

$$PV \times (1 + 0.2) = £20,000$$

(Note that 0.2 is the same as 20 per cent, but expressed as a decimal.) Further rearranging gives:

$$PV = £20,000/(1 + 0.2) = £16,667$$

Therefore, logical investors who have the opportunity to invest at 20 per cent a year would not mind whether they have £16,667 now or £20,000 in a year's time. In this sense, we can say that, given a 20 per cent alternative investment opportunity, the present value of £20,000 to be received in one year's time is £16,667.

If we derive the present value (PV) of each of the cash flows associated with Billingsgate's machine investment, we could easily make the direct comparison between the cost of making the investment (£100,000) and the various benefits that will derive from it during years 1 to 5.

Using the same logic as was used to derive the PV of a cash flow expected after one year, it can be shown that the PV of a particular cash flow is:

PV of the cash flow of year n = actual cash flow of year n divided by $(1 + r)^n$

where n is the year of the cash flow (that is, how many years into the future) and r is the opportunity financing cost expressed as a decimal (instead of as a percentage).

We have already seen how this works for the £20,000 inflow for year 1 for the Billingsgate project. For year 2 the calculation would be:

$$\text{PV of year 2 cash flow (that is, £40,000)} = £40,000/(1 + 0.2)^2 = £40,000/(1.2)^2$$

$$= £40,000/1.44 = £27,778$$

This means that the present value of the £40,000 to be received in two years' time is £27,778.

Activity 10.9

See if you can show that an investor would find £27,778, receivable now, as equally acceptable to receiving £40,000 in two years' time, assuming that there is a 20 per cent investment opportunity.

The reasoning goes like this:

	£
Amount available for immediate investment	27,778
Income for year 1 (20% × 27,778)	5,556
	33,334
Income for year 2 (20% × 33,334)	6,667
	40,001

(The extra £1 is only a rounding error.)

This is to say that since the investor can turn £27,778 into £40,000 in two years, these amounts are equivalent. We can say that £27,778 is the present value of £40,000 receivable after two years (given a 20 per cent cost of finance).

The act of reducing the value of a cash flow, to take account of the period between the present time and the time that the cash flow is expected, is known as **discounting**. Discounting, in effect charges the project with the cost of financing it. Ignoring this financing cost would be to overlook a significant cost of undertaking the project.

Calculating the net present value

Now let us calculate the present values of all of the cash flows associated with the Billingsgate machine project and, from them, the *net present value (NPV)* of the project as a whole. The relevant cash flows and calculations are:

Time	Cash flow £000	Calculation of PV	PV £000
Immediately (time 0)	(100)	$(100)/(1 + 0.2)^0$	(100.00)
1 year's time	20	$20/(1 + 0.2)^1$	16.67
2 years' time	40	$40/(1 + 0.2)^2$	27.78
3 years' time	60	$60/(1 + 0.2)^3$	34.72
4 years' time	60	$60/(1 + 0.2)^4$	28.94
5 years' time	20	$20/(1 + 0.2)^5$	8.04
5 years' time	20	$20/(1 + 0.2)^5$	8.04
Net present value (NPV)			24.19

Note that $(1 + 0.2)^0 = 1$.

Once again, we must decide whether the machine project is acceptable to the business. To help us, the following decision rules for NPV should be applied:

- If the NPV is positive the project should be accepted; if it is negative the project should be rejected.
- If there are two (or more) competing projects that have positive NPVs, the project with the higher (or highest) NPV should be selected.

In this case, the NPV is positive, so we should accept the project and buy the machine. The reasoning behind this decision rule is quite straightforward. Investing in the machine will make the business, and its owners, £24,190 better off than they would be by taking up the next best available opportunity. The total benefits from investing in this machine are worth a total of £124,190 today. Since the business can 'buy' these benefits for just £100,000 today, the investment should be made. If, however, the present value of the benefits were below £100,000, it would be less than the cost of 'buying' those benefits and the opportunity should, therefore, be rejected.

Activity 10.10

What is the *maximum* the Billingsgate Battery Company would be prepared to pay for the machine, given the potential benefits of owning it?

The business would logically be prepared to pay up to £124,190 since the wealth of the owners of the business would be increased up to this price – although the business would prefer to pay as little as possible.

Using present value tables

To deduce each PV in the Billingsgate Battery Company project, we took the relevant cash flow and multiplied it by $1/(1 + r)^n$. There is a slightly different way to do this. Tables exist that show values of this **discount factor** for a range of values of r and n. Such a table appears in at the end of this book, in Appendix E on page 000. Take a look at it.

Look at the column for 20 per cent and the row for one year. We find that the factor is 0.833. This means that the PV of a cash flow of £1 receivable in one year is £0.833. So the present value of a cash flow of £20,000 receivable in one year's time is £16,660 (that is, 0.833 × £20,000). This is the same result, ignoring rounding errors, as we found earlier by using the equation.

Activity 10.11

What is the NPV of the Chaotic Industries project from Activity 10.2, assuming a 15 per cent opportunity cost of finance (discount rate)? (Use the present value table in Appendix E, page 000)

Remember that the inflows and outflows are expected to be:

Time		£000
Immediately	Cost of vans	(150)
1 year's time	Saving before depreciation	30
2 years' time	Saving before depreciation	30
3 years' time	Saving before depreciation	30
4 years' time	Saving before depreciation	30
5 years' time	Saving before depreciation	30
6 years' time	Saving before depreciation	30
6 years' time	Disposal proceeds from the vans	30

The calculation of the NPV of the project is as follows:

Time	Cash flows	Discount factor (15%)	Present value
	£000		£000
Immediately	(150)	1.000	(150.00)
1 year's time	30	0.870	26.10
2 years' time	30	0.756	22.68
3 years' time	30	0.658	19.74
4 years' time	30	0.572	17.16
5 years' time	30	0.497	14.91
6 years' time	30	0.432	12.96
6 years' time	30	0.432	12.96
		NPV	(23.49)

Activity 10.12

How would you interpret this result?

The fact that the project has a negative NPV means that the present values of the benefits from the investment are worth less than they cost. Any cost up to £126,510 (the present value of the benefits) would be worth paying, but not £150,000.

The present value table in Appendix E shows how the value of £1 diminishes as its receipt goes further into the future. Assuming an opportunity cost of finance of 20 per cent a year, £1 to be received immediately, obviously, has a present value of £1. However, as the time before it is to be received increases, the present value diminishes significantly, as is shown in Figure 10.2.

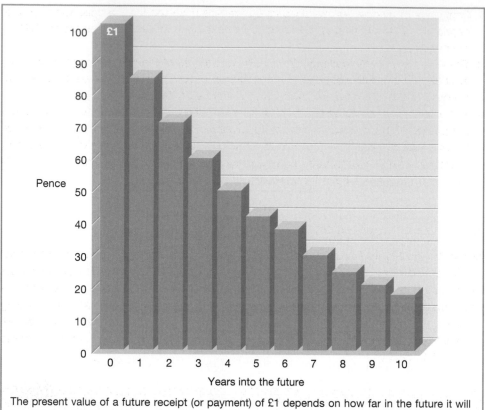

The present value of a future receipt (or payment) of £1 depends on how far in the future it will occur. Those that occur in the near future will have a larger present value than those occurring at a more distant point in time.

Figure 10.2 Present value of £1 receivable at various times in the future, assuming an annual financing cost of 20 per cent

The discount rate and the cost of capital

We have seen that the appropriate discount rate to use in NPV assessments is the opportunity cost of finance. This is, in effect, the cost to the business of the finance needed to fund the investment. It will normally be the cost of a mixture of funds (shareholders' funds and borrowings) employed by the business and is often referred to as the **cost of capital**. We shall refer to it as cost of capital from now on.

WHY NPV IS BETTER

From what we have seen, NPV offers a better approach to appraising investment opportunities than either ARR or PP. This is because it fully takes account of each of the following:

■ *The timing of the cash flows.* By discounting the various cash flows associated with each project according to when they are expected to arise, NPV takes account of the time value of money. As the discounting process incorporates the opportunity cost of capital, the net benefit *after* financing costs have been met is identified (as the NPV of the project).

■ *The whole of the relevant cash flows.* NPV includes *all* of the relevant cash flows. They are treated differently according to their date of occurrence, but they are all taken into account. In this way, they can all have an influence on the decision.

■ *The objectives of the business.* NPV is the only method of appraisal in which the output of the analysis has a direct bearing on the wealth of the owners of the business. Positive NPVs enhance wealth; negative ones reduce it. Since we assume that private sector businesses seek to increase owners' wealth, NPV is superior to the other two methods (ARR and PP) that we have discussed so far.

NPV's wider application

NPV is the most logical approach to making business decisions about investments in productive assets. It also provides the basis for valuing any economic asset, that is, any asset capable of yielding financial benefits. This definition will include such things as equity shares and loans. In fact, when we talk of *economic value,* we mean the value derived by adding together the discounted (present) values of all future cash flows from the asset concerned.

Real World 10.5 describes a mining project where the NPV has been used to assess its financial viability.

REAL WORLD 10.5

Fully charged

The El Sauz/Fleur mining project in northern Mexico is being undertaken to produce lithium carbonate. This is an important industrial chemical that is used, amongst other things, for the production of battery cathodes. The project is 30 per cent owned by Rare Earth Minerals plc and 70 per cent owned by Bacanora Minerals Ltd. On 10 February 2015 it was announced that the net present value (NPV) of the mining project, at an 8 per cent discount rate, is estimated to be $US2,023 million. The NPV calculation assumes an output of 75,600 tonnes of battery grade lithium carbonate over a 20 year open pit life. It also assumes an average lithium carbonate price of $US6,500/tonne for the life of the mine.

Source: Based on information in www.rareearthmineralsplc.com, 10 February 2015.

INTERNAL RATE OF RETURN (IRR)

This is the last of the four major methods of investment appraisal found in practice. It is closely related to the NPV method in that both involve discounting future cash flows. The **internal rate of return (IRR)** of an investment is the discount rate that, when applied to its future cash flows, will produce an NPV of precisely zero. In essence, it represents the yield from an investment opportunity.

We should recall that, when we discounted the cash flows of the Billingsgate Battery Company machine project at 20 per cent, we found that the NPV was a positive figure of £24,190 (see page 000). What does the NPV of the machine project tell us about the rate of return that the investment will yield for the business (that is, the project's IRR)?

As the NPV is positive when discounting at 20 per cent, it implies that the rate of return that the project generates is more than 20 per cent. The fact that the NPV is a pretty large figure implies that the actual rate of return is quite a lot above 20 per cent. The higher the discount rate, the lower will be the NPV: this is because a higher discount rate gives a lower discounted figure.

IRR cannot usually be calculated directly. Iteration (trial and error) is the approach normally adopted. Although doing this manually is fairly laborious, computer spreadsheet packages can do this with ease.

Despite it being labourious, we shall now go on and derive the IRR for the Billingsgate project manually, to show how it works.

Let us try a higher rate, say 30 per cent and see what happens.

Time	Cash flow £000	Discount factor 30%	PV £000
Immediately (time 0)	(100)	1.000	(100.00)
1 year's time	20	0.769	15.38
2 years' time	40	0.592	23.68
3 years' time	60	0.455	27.30
4 years' time	60	0.350	21.00
5 years' time	20	0.269	5.38
5 years' time	20	0.269	5.38
		NPV	(1.88)

By increasing the discount rate from 20 per cent to 30 per cent, we have reduced the NPV from £24,190 (positive) to £1,880 (negative). Since the IRR is the discount rate that will give us an NPV of exactly zero, we can conclude that the IRR of Billingsgate Battery Company's machine project is very slightly below 30 per cent. Further trials could lead us to the exact rate, but there is probably not much point, given the likely inaccuracy of the cash flow estimates. For most practical purposes, it is good enough to say that the IRR is about 30 per cent.

The relationship between the NPV and the IRR is shown graphically in Figure 10.3 using the information relating to the Billingsgate Battery Company.

In Figure 10.3, if the discount rate is equal to zero, the NPV will be the sum of the net cash flows. In other words, no account is taken of the time value of money. However, as the discount rate increases there is a corresponding decrease in the NPV of the project. When the NPV line crosses the horizontal axis there will be a zero NPV. That point represents the IRR.

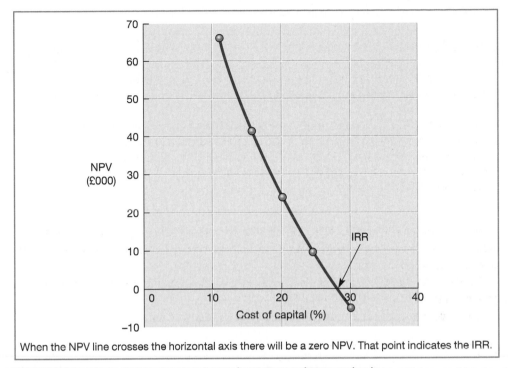

When the NPV line crosses the horizontal axis there will be a zero NPV. That point indicates the IRR.

Figure 10.3 The relationship between the NPV and IRR methods

Activity 10.14

What is the internal rate of return of the Chaotic Industries project from Activity 10.2?

(Hint: Remember that you already know the NPV of this project at 15 per cent (from Activity 10.11).)

Since we know that, at a 15 per cent discount rate, the NPV is a relatively large negative figure, our next trial should use a lower discount rate, say 10 per cent:

Time	Cash flows £000	Discount factor (10% – from the table)	Present value £000
Immediately	(150)	1.000	(150.00)
1 year's time	30	0.909	27.27
2 years' time	30	0.826	24.78
3 years' time	30	0.751	22.53
4 years' time	30	0.683	20.49
5 years' time	30	0.621	18.63
6 years' time	30	0.564	16.92
6 years' time	30	0.564	16.92
		NPV	(2.46)

This figure is close to zero NPV. However, the NPV is still negative and so the precise IRR will be a little below 10 per cent.

We could undertake further trials to derive the precise IRR. If, however, we have to do this manually, further trials can be time consuming.

We can get an acceptable approximation to the answer fairly quickly by first calculating the change in NPV arising from a 1 per cent change in the discount rate. This can be done by taking the difference between the two trials (that is, 15 per cent and 10 per cent) that have already been carried out (in Activities 10.12 and 10.15):

Trial	Discount factor %	Net present value £000
1	15	(23.49)
2	10	(2.46)
Difference	5	21.03

The change in NPV for every 1 per cent change in the discount rate will be:

$$(21.03/5) = 4.21$$

The amount by which the IRR would need to fall below the 10% discount rate in order to achieve a zero NPV would therefore be:

$$(2.46/4.21) \times 1\% = 0.58\%$$

The IRR is therefore:

$$(10.00 - 0.58) = 9.42\%$$

To say that the IRR is about 9 or 10 per cent, however, is near enough for most purposes.

Note that this approach to obtaining a more accurate figure for IRR assumes a straight-line relationship between the discount rate and NPV. We can see from Figure 10.3 that this assumption is not strictly correct. Over a relatively short range, however, this simplification is not usually a problem and so we can still arrive at a reasonable approximation using the approach that we took.

In practice, most businesses would use a computer spreadsheet, which will derive a project's IRR very quickly. It is not usually necessary, therefore, to use a series of trial discount rates manually or to make the approximation just described.

The following decision rules are applied when using IRR:

- For any project to be acceptable, it must meet a minimum IRR requirement. This is often referred to as the *hurdle rate* and, logically, this should be the opportunity cost of capital.
- Where there are competing projects, the one with the higher (or highest) IRR should be selected.

Real World 10.6 illustrates how IRR is used to assess the economic effectiveness of environmental initiatives.

REAL WORLD 10.6

IRR from reducing carbon footprint

Companies like to highlight their commitment to the environment and the communities in which they operate, but it is all too easy for them to forget such commitment under the pressure of cutting costs and keeping shareholders happy. It is a pressure they should resist. As Thomas Cook discovered last month, prioritising short-term profits over a broader responsibility to society can cause damage to a brand, which may dent those profits in the long run. It is unlikely to be the last time a company's actions end up causing damage to its reputation. From food contamination to banking scandals, headlines frequently offer evidence that business is not always very responsible.

However, there are also signs that many in the corporate sector are committed to minimising their environmental impact and to ensuring the benefits of their activities extend to the broader community. Celebrating these efforts, the Responsible Business Awards recognise companies for everything from supporting an ageing workforce at home to contributing to emergency relief operations overseas.

Run by Business in the Community (BITC), the UK charity that promotes corporate responsibility, the awards judge companies on how well they are integrating responsible practices into their businesses in areas that include the environment, education, enterprise, unemployment and workplace diversity. As the finalists demonstrate, companies increasingly regard such investment less in terms of charitable use of spare cash and more as an integral part of their business, enhancing their long-term financial success.

Looking at environmental initiatives, the business benefits can be relatively easy to calculate. Cutting carbon emissions reduces expenditure on energy, while generating less waste saves money. Companies participating in Carbon Action, part of the CDP investor engagement initiative (formerly the Carbon Disclosure Project) found that carbon reduction and energy-efficiency investments could generate an average internal rate of return of 33 per cent, delivering a payback in just three years.

Source: Extracts from: Murray, S. (2015), 'It pays for companies to be part of the scenery', ft.com, 2 June.
© The Financial Times Limited 2015. All Rights Reserved.

Real World 10.7 gives some examples of IRRs sought in practice.

REAL WORLD 10.7

Rates of return

IRRs for investment projects can vary considerably. Here are a few examples of the expected or target returns from investment projects of large businesses.

- GlaxoSmithKline plc, the leading pharmaceuticals business, is aiming to increase its annual IRR from investments in new products to 14 per cent.
- Next plc, the fashion retailer, requires an annual IRR of 15 per cent when appraising new stores.

- Carillion plc, a facilities management and construction business, seeks a 15 per cent IRR on new public–private partnership projects.
- Rentokil Initial plc, the business services provider, has an after-tax required IRR of 15 per cent for any takeover targets that it may be considering in pest control in emerging markets.
- Marks and Spencer plc, the stores chain, has targeted a 'hurdle' internal rate of return of 12 to 15 per cent on a new investment programme.

These values seem surprisingly high. A study of returns made by all of the businesses listed on the London Stock Exchange between 1900 and 2014 showed an average annual return of 5.3 per cent. This figure is the *real* return (that is, ignoring inflation). It would probably be fair to add a percentage (say, 1 or 2 per cent) to cover inflation to compare it with the targets for the businesses listed above. Also, the targets for five of the businesses are probably pre-tax (the businesses do not specify, except Rentokil Initial). In that case it is probably reasonable to add about a quarter to the average Stock Exchange returns. This would give us around 9 per cent per year. It appears that the targets for the five businesses, listed above, are rather ambitious. This may be more understandable in the case of Rentokil Initial, given that the rate is for takeover targets, which they may regard as being particularly risky. For the other businesses, they are targeting an IRR well above what businesses have actually achieved over the past century.

Sources: Information taken from GlaxoSmithKline plc, Annual Report 2014. p. 27; Next plc, Annual Report 2015, p. 6; Carillion plc, Annual Report 2014, p. 26; Rentokil Initial plc, Annual Report 2014, p. 10; Press release on 2012 annual results, Marks and Spencer plc, 22 May 2012; and Dimson, E., Marsh, P. and Staunton, M. (2015) *Credit Suisse Global Investments Returns Yearbook*, p. 57.

Problems with IRR

IRR has certain key attributes in common with NPV. All cash flows are taken into account and their timing is logically handled. The main problem of IRR, however, is that it does not directly address the question of wealth generation. It can, therefore, lead to the wrong decision being made. This is because the IRR approach will always rank a project with, for example, an IRR of 25 per cent above that of a project with an IRR of 20 per cent. Although accepting the project with the higher percentage return will often generate more wealth, this may not always be the case. This is because IRR completely ignores the *scale of investment*.

With a 15 per cent cost of capital, £15 million invested at 20 per cent for one year will make us wealthier by £0.75 million (that is, $15 \times (20 - 15)\% = 0.75$). With the same cost of capital, £5 million invested at 25 per cent for one year will make us only £0.5 million (that is, $5 \times (25 - 15)\% = 0.50$). IRR does not recognise this.

Competing projects do not usually show such large differences in scale and so IRR and NPV normally give the same signal. However, as NPV will always give the correct signal, it is difficult to see why any other method should be used.

Activity 10.15

Which other investment appraisal method ignores the scale of investment?

We saw earlier that the ARR method suffers from this problem.

That ARR and IRR both suffer from the same problem is not coincidence. Their problem stems from the fact that they are both relative rates of return. Given the wealth-generating objective of most businesses, absolute returns, measured in monetary terms, are much more relevant than relative returns measured as percentages.

A further problem with the IRR method is that it has difficulty handling projects with unconventional cash flows. In the examples studied so far, each project has a negative cash flow arising at the start of its life and then positive cash flows thereafter. In practice, however, a project may have both positive and negative cash flows at future points in its life. This pattern of cash flows can result in more than one IRR, or even no IRR at all. Although this problem is also quite rare, it is never a problem for NPV.

SOME PRACTICAL POINTS

When undertaking an investment appraisal, there are several practical points to bear in mind:

- *Past costs.* As with all decisions, we should take account only of relevant costs in our analysis. Only costs that vary with the decision should be considered, as we discussed at length in Chapter 7. This means that, all past and common future costs should be ignored as they cannot vary with the decision. Opportunity costs should, of course, be taken into account.
- *Taxation.* Owners will be interested in the after tax returns generated from the business. As a result, taxation will usually be an important consideration when making an investment decision. The profits from the project will be taxed, the capital investment may attract tax relief and so on. Tax is levied on these at significant rates. This means that, in real life, unless tax is formally taken into account, the wrong decision could easily be made. The timing of the tax outflow should also be taken into account when preparing the cash flows for the project.
- *Cash flows not profit flows.* We have seen that for the NPV, IRR and PP methods, it is cash flows rather than profit flows that are relevant to the assessment of investment projects. In an investment appraisal requiring the application of any of these methods, details of the profits for the investment period may be given. These need to be adjusted in order to derive the cash flows. We should remember that the operating profit *before* non-cash items (such as depreciation) is an approximation to the cash flows for the period. We should, therefore, work back to this figure.

  When the data are expressed in profit rather than cash flow terms, an adjustment in respect of working capital may also be necessary. Some adjustment should be made to take account of changes in working capital. For example, launching a new product may give rise to an increase in the net investment made in trade receivables and inventories less trade payables. This working capital investment would normally require an immediate outlay of cash. This outlay for additional working capital should be shown in the NPV calculations as an initial cash outflow. However, at the end of the life of the project, the additional working capital will be released. This divestment results in an effective inflow of cash at the end of the project. It should also be taken into account at the point at which it is received.

- *Year-end assumption.* In the examples and activities considered so far, we have assumed that cash flows arise at the end of the relevant year. This simplifying assumption is used to make the calculations easier. As we saw earlier, this assumption is clearly unrealistic, as money will have to be paid to employees on a weekly or monthly basis, credit customers will pay within a month or two of buying the product or service and so on. It is probably not a serious distortion, however. We should be clear that there is nothing about any of the four appraisal methods that demands that this assumption be made. It is perfectly possible to deal more precisely with the timing of the cash flows.
- *Interest payments.* When using discounted cash flow techniques (NPV and IRR), interest payments should not be taken into account in deriving cash flows for the period. Discounting already takes account of the costs of financing. To include interest charges in deriving cash flows for the period would therefore be double counting.
- *Other factors.* Investment decision making must not be viewed as simply a mechanical exercise. The results derived from a particular investment appraisal method will be only one input to the decision-making process. There may be broader issues connected to the decision that have to be taken into account but which may be difficult or impossible to quantify.

The reliability of the forecasts and the validity of the assumptions used in the evaluation will also have a bearing on the final decision.

Activity 10.16

The directors of Manuff (Steel) Ltd are considering closing one of the business's factories. There has been a reduction in the demand for the products made at the factory in recent years. The directors are not optimistic about the long-term prospects for these products. The factory is situated in an area where unemployment is high.

The factory is leased with four years of the lease remaining. The directors are uncertain whether the factory should be closed immediately or at the end of the period of the lease. Another business has offered to sublease the premises from Manuff (Steel) Ltd at a rental of £40,000 a year for the remainder of the lease period.

The machinery and equipment at the factory cost £1,500,000. The value at which they appear in the statement of financial position is £400,000. In the event of immediate closure, the machinery and equipment could be sold for £220,000. The working capital at the factory is £420,000. It could be liquidated for that amount immediately, if required. Alternatively, the working capital can be liquidated in full at the end of the lease period. Immediate closure would result in redundancy payments to employees of £180,000.

If the factory continues in operation until the end of the lease period, the following operating profits (losses) are expected:

	Year 1	Year 2	Year 3	Year 4
	£000	£000	£000	£000
Operating profit (loss)	160	(40)	30	20

These figures are derived after deducting a charge of £90,000 a year for depreciation of machinery and equipment. The residual value of the machinery and equipment at the end of the lease period is estimated at £40,000.

Redundancy payments are expected to be £150,000 at the end of the lease period if the factory continues in operation. The business has an annual cost of capital of 12 per cent. Ignore taxation.

Required:

(a) Determine the relevant cash flows arising from a decision to continue operations until the end of the lease period rather than to close immediately.
(b) Calculate the net present value of continuing operations until the end of the lease period, rather than closing immediately.
(c) What other factors might the directors take into account before making a final decision on the timing of the factory closure?
(d) State, with reasons, whether or not the business should continue to operate the factory until the end of the lease period.

Your answer should be:

(a) Relevant cash flows

			Years		
	0	1	2	3	4
	£000	£000	£000	£000	£000
Operating cash flows (Note 1)		250	50	120	110
Sale of machinery (Note 2)	(220)				40
Redundancy costs (Note 3)	180				(150)
Sublease rentals (Note 4)		(40)	(40)	(40)	(40)
Working capital invested (Note 5)	(420)				420
	(460)	210	10	80	380

Notes:

1 Each year's operating cash flows are calculated by adding back the depreciation charge for the year to the operating profit for the year. In the case of the operating loss, the depreciation charge is deducted.
2 In the event of closure, machinery could be sold immediately. As a result, an opportunity cost of £220,000 is incurred if operations continue.
3 By continuing operations, there will be a saving in immediate redundancy costs of £180,000. However, redundancy costs of £150,000 will be paid in four years' time.
4 By continuing operations, the opportunity to sublease the factory will be foregone.
5 Immediate closure would mean that working capital could be liquidated. By continuing operations this opportunity is foregone. However, working capital can be liquidated in four years' time.

(b)

	Years				
	0	1	2	3	4
Discount rate 12 per cent	1.000	0.893	0.797	0.712	0.636
Present value	(460)	187.5	8.0	57.0	241.7
Net present value	<u>34.2</u>				

(c) Other factors that may influence the decision include:

■ *The overall strategy of the business.* The business may need to set the decision within a broader context. It may be necessary to manufacture the products at the factory because they are an integral part of the business's product range. The business may wish to avoid redundancies in an area of high unemployment for as long as possible.

■ *Flexibility.* A decision to close the factory is probably irreversible. If the factory continues, however, there may be a chance that the prospects for the factory will brighten in the future.

■ *Creditworthiness of sub-lessee.* The business should investigate the creditworthiness of the sub-lessee. Failure to receive the expected sublease payments would make the closure option far less attractive.

■ *Accuracy of forecasts.* The forecasts made by the business should be examined carefully. Inaccuracies in the forecasts or any underlying assumptions may change the expected outcomes.

(d) The NPV of the decision to continue operations rather than close immediately is positive. Hence, shareholders would be better off if the directors took this course of action. The factory should therefore continue in operation rather than close down. This decision is likely to be welcomed by employees and would allow the business to maintain its flexibility.

The main methods of investment appraisal are summarised in Figure 10.4.

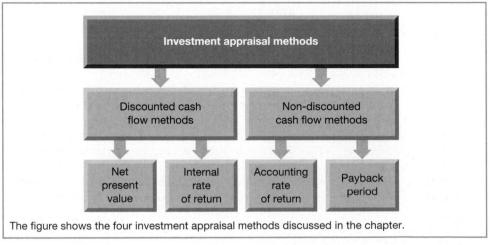

The figure shows the four investment appraisal methods discussed in the chapter.

Figure 10.4 The main investment appraisal methods

INVESTMENT APPRAISAL IN PRACTICE

Many surveys have been conducted in the UK, and elsewhere in the world, into the methods of investment appraisal used by businesses. They have shown the following features:

- Businesses tend to use more than one method to assess each investment decision.
- The discounting methods (NPV and IRR) have become increasingly popular over time. NPV and IRR are now the most popular of the four methods.
- PP continues to be popular and, to a lesser extent, so does ARR. This is despite the theoretical shortcomings of both methods.
- Larger businesses tend to rely more heavily on discounting methods than smaller businesses.

A survey of large businesses in five leading industrialised countries, including the UK, also shows considerable support for the NPV and IRR methods. There is less support for the payback method but it still seems to be fairly widely used. **Real World 10.8** sets out some key findings.

REAL WORLD 10.8

A multinational survey of business practice

A survey of investment and financing practices in five different countries was carried out by Cohen and Yagil. This survey, based on a sample of the largest 300 businesses in each country, revealed the following concerning the popularity of three of the investment appraisal methods discussed in this chapter.

Frequency of the use of investment appraisal techniques

	USA	UK	Germany	Canada	Japan	Average
IRR	4.00	4.16	4.08	4.15	3.29	3.93
NPV	3.88	4.00	3.50	4.09	3.57	3.80
PP	3.46	3.89	3.33	3.57	3.52	3.55

Response scale: 1 = never, 5 = always.

Key findings of the survey include the following:

- IRR is more popular than NPV in all countries, except Japan. The difference between the two methods, however, is not statistically significant.
- Managers of UK businesses use investment appraisal techniques the most, while managers of Japanese businesses use them the least. This may be related to business traditions within each country.
- There is a positive relationship between business size and the popularity of the IRR and NPV methods. This may be related to the greater experience and understanding of financial theory of managers of larger businesses. A more recent survey (by Lucas, Prowle and Lowth) of some much smaller UK businesses indicated that none of them carried out any investment appraisal. This adds emphasis to the size/sophistication relationship in this context.

Sources: Cohen, G. and Yagil, J. (2007) 'A multinational survey of corporate financial policies', Working Paper, Haifa University; and Lucas, M., Prowle, M. and Lowth, G. (2013) 'Management accounting practices of UK small-medium-sized enterprises', *CIMA*, July.

Earlier in the chapter, we discussed the limitations of the PP method. Can you suggest reasons that might explain why it is still a reasonably popular method of investment appraisal among managers?

There seem to be several possible reasons:

- PP is easy to understand and use.
- It can avoid the problems of forecasting far into the future.
- It gives emphasis to the early cash flows when there is greater certainty concerning the accuracy of their predicted value.
- It emphasises the importance of liquidity. Where a business has liquidity problems, a short payback period for a project is likely to appear attractive.

The popularity of PP may suggest a lack of sophistication by managers, concerning investment appraisal. This criticism is most often made against managers of smaller businesses. This point is borne out by both of the surveys discussed in Real World 10.8 which found that smaller businesses are much less likely to use discounted cash flow methods (NPV and IRR) than larger ones. Other surveys have tended to reach a similar conclusion.

IRR may be popular because it expresses outcomes in percentage terms rather than in absolute terms. This form of expression seems to be preferred by managers, despite the problems of percentage measures discussed earlier. This may be because managers are used to using percentage figures as targets (for example, return on capital employed).

Real World 10.9 shows extracts from the 2014 annual report of a well-known business, Rolls-Royce plc, the builder of engines for aircraft and other purposes.

REAL WORLD 10.9

The use of NPV at Rolls-Royce

In its 2014 annual report and accounts, Rolls-Royce plc stated that:

> The Group subjects all major investments and capital expenditure to a rigorous examination of risks and future cash flows to ensure that they create shareholder value. All major investments require Board approval.
>
> The Group has a portfolio of projects at different stages of their life cycles. Discounted cash flow analysis of the remaining life of projects is performed on a regular basis.

Source: Rolls-Royce Holdings plc, Annual Report 2014, p. 160.

Rolls-Royce indicates that it uses NPV (the report refers to creating shareholder value and to discounted cash flow, which strongly imply NPV). It is interesting to note that Rolls-Royce not only assesses new projects but also reassesses existing ones. This must be a sensible commercial approach. Businesses should not continue with existing projects unless those projects have a positive NPV based on future cash flows. Just because a project seemed to have a positive NPV before it started does not mean that this will persist, in the light of changing circumstances. Activity 10.16 (page 000) considered a decision to close down a project.

INVESTMENT APPRAISAL AND STRATEGIC PLANNING

So far, we have tended to view investment opportunities as unconnected, independent, projects. In practice, however, successful businesses are those that set out a clear strategic framework for the selection of investment projects. Unless this framework is in place, it may be difficult to identify those projects that are likely to generate a positive NPV. The best investment projects are usually those that match the business's internal strengths (for example, skills, experience, access to finance) with the opportunities available. In areas where this match does not exist, other businesses, for which the match does exist, are likely to have a distinct competitive advantage. This means that they will be able to provide the product or service at a better price and/or quality.

Real World 10.10 shows how Irish-based building materials business, CRH plc, made an investment that fitted its strategic objectives.

REAL WORLD 10.10

Windows are a good fit

CRH plc, the Irish building materials business, bought the California-based glazing business C R Laurence Co Inc for $1.3 billion in August 2015.

CRH will become the world's third largest building materials group, partly as a result of this and other acquisitions. The business already has a major presence in the US and Canada, which is why CRH's management described C R Laurence as an 'exceptional strategic fit' for it. This means that CRH believes that the acquisition represented a good deal. That may not be true, however, for another purchaser, paying the same price, for whom there was not that degree of strategic fit.

Source: Information taken from Grant, J. (2015), 'CRH adds CR Laurence to acquisitions tally for $1.3bn', ft.com, 27 August.

Beacon Chemicals plc is considering buying some equipment to produce a chemical named X14. The new equipment's capital cost is estimated at £100 million. If its purchase is approved now, the equipment can be bought and production can commence by the end of this year. £50 million has already been spent on research and development work. Estimates of revenues and costs arising from the operation of the new equipment are:

	Year 1	Year 2	Year 3	Year 4	Year 5
Sales price (£/litre)	100	120	120	100	80
Sales volume (million litres)	0.8	1.0	1.2	1.0	0.8
Variable cost (£/litre)	50	50	40	30	40
Fixed cost (£m)	30	30	30	30	30

If the equipment is bought, sales of some existing products will be lost resulting in a loss of contribution of £15 million a year, over the life of the equipment.

The accountant has informed you that the fixed cost includes depreciation of £20 million a year on the new equipment. It also includes an allocation of £10 million for fixed overheads. A separate study has indicated that if the new equipment were bought, additional overheads, excluding depreciation, arising from producing the chemical would be £8 million a year. Production would require additional working capital of £30 million.

For the purposes of your initial calculations ignore taxation.

Required:

(a) Deduce the relevant annual cash flows associated with buying the equipment.
(b) Deduce the payback period.
(c) Calculate the net present value using a discount rate of 8 per cent.

(*Hint:* You should deal with the investment in working capital by treating it as a cash outflow at the start of the project and an inflow at the end.)

The solution to this question can be found at the back of the book on page 533.

SUMMARY

The main points of this chapter may be summarised as follows:

Accounting rate of return (ARR)

ARR is the average accounting profit from the project expressed as a percentage of the average investment.

■ Decision rule – projects with an ARR above a defined minimum are acceptable; the greater the ARR, the more attractive the project becomes.

- Conclusion on ARR:
  - does not relate directly to shareholders' wealth – can lead to illogical conclusions;
  - takes almost no account of the timing of cash flows;
  - ignores some relevant information and may take account of some irrelevant;
  - relatively simple to use;
  - much inferior to NPV.

Payback period (PP)

PP is the length of time that it takes for the cash outflow for the initial investment to be repaid out of resulting cash inflows.

- Decision rule – projects with a PP up to a defined maximum period are acceptable; the shorter the PP, the more attractive the project.
- Conclusion on PP:
  - does not relate to shareholders' wealth;
  - ignores inflows after the payback date;
  - takes little account of the timing of cash flows;
  - ignores much relevant information;
  - does not always provide clear signals and can be impractical to use;
  - much inferior to NPV, but it is easy to understand and can offer a liquidity insight.

Net present value (NPV)

NPV is the sum of the discounted values of the net cash flows from the investment.

- Money has a time value.
- Decision rule – all positive NPV investments enhance shareholders' wealth; the greater the NPV, the greater the enhancement and the greater the attractiveness of the project.
- PV of a cash flow = cash flow $\times$ $1/(1 + r)^n$, assuming a constant discount rate.
- Discounting brings cash flows at different points in time to a common valuation basis (their present value), which enables them to be directly compared.
- Conclusion on NPV:
  - relates directly to shareholders' wealth objective;
  - takes account of the timing of cash flows;
  - takes all relevant information into account;
  - provides clear signals and is practical to use.

Internal rate of return (IRR)

IRR is the discount rate that, when applied to the cash flows of a project, causes it to have a zero NPV.

- Represents the average percentage return on the investment, taking account of the fact that cash may be flowing in and out of the project at various points in its life.
- Decision rule – projects that have an IRR greater than the cost of capital are acceptable; the greater the IRR, the more attractive the project.
- Cannot normally be calculated directly; a trial and error approach is usually necessary.
- Conclusion on IRR:
  - does not relate directly to shareholders' wealth. Usually gives the same signals as NPV but can mislead where there are competing projects of different size;
  - takes account of the timing of cash flows;
  - takes all relevant information into account;
  - problems of multiple IRRs when there are unconventional cash flows;
  - inferior to NPV.

Use of appraisal methods in practice

- All four methods identified are widely used.
- The discounting methods (NPV and IRR) show a steady increase in usage over time.
- Many businesses use more than one method.
- Larger businesses seem to be more sophisticated in their choice and use of appraisal methods than smaller ones.

Investment appraisal and strategic planning

- It is important that businesses invest in a strategic way so as to play to their strengths.

KEY TERMS

For definitions of these terms, see Appendix A.

FURTHER READING

If you would like to explore the topics covered in this chapter in more depth, we recommend the following books:

Arnold, G. (2012) *Corporate Financial Management*, 5th edn, Pearson, Chapters 2, 3 and 4.

Drury, C. (2015) *Management and Cost Accounting*, 9th edn, Cengage Learning, Chapters 13 and 14.

McLaney, E. (2014) *Business Finance: Theory and practice*, 10th edn, Pearson, 2014, Chapters 4, 5 and 6.

Pike, R., Neale, B. and Linsley, P. (2015), *Corporate Finance and Investment*, 8th edn, Pearson, Chapters 3 to 6.

 REVIEW QUESTIONS

Solutions to these questions can be found at the back of the book on pages 546–547.

10.1 Why is the net present value method of investment appraisal considered to be theoretically superior to other methods that are found in practice?

10.2 The payback period method has been criticised for not taking the time value of money into account. Could this limitation be overcome? If so, would this method then be preferable to the NPV method?

10.3 Research indicates that the IRR method is extremely popular even though it has shortcomings when compared to the NPV method. Why might managers prefer to use IRR rather than NPV when carrying out discounted cash flow evaluations?

10.4 Why are cash flows rather than profit flows used in the IRR, NPV and PP methods of investment appraisal?

EXERCISES

*Exercise 10.1 is basic level. Exercises 10.2 and 10.3 are intermediate level and Exercises 10.4 and 10.5 are advanced level. Those with **coloured numbers** have solutions at the back of the book starting on page 569.*

10.1 The directors of Mylo Ltd are currently considering two mutually exclusive investment projects. Both projects are concerned with the purchase of new plant. The following data are available for each project:

	Project 1 £000	Project 2 £000
Cost (immediate outlay)	100	60
Expected annual operating profit (loss):		
Year 1	29	18
2	(1)	(2)
3	2	4
Estimated residual value of the plant after 3 years	7	6

The business has an estimated cost of capital of 10 per cent. It uses the straight-line method of depreciation for all non-current (fixed) assets when calculating operating profit. Neither project would increase the working capital of the business. The business has sufficient funds to meet all investment expenditure requirements.

Required:

(a) Calculate for each project:
  (i)   the net present value;
  (ii) the approximate internal rate of return;
  (iii) The payback period.

(b) State, with reasons, which, if any, of the two investment projects the directors of Mylo Ltd should accept.

10.2   Newton Electronics Ltd has incurred expenditure of £5 million over the past three years researching and developing a miniature hearing aid. The hearing aid is now fully developed. The directors are considering which of three mutually exclusive options should be taken to exploit the potential of the new product. The options are:

1   The business could manufacture the hearing aid itself. This would be a new departure, since the business has so far concentrated on research and development projects. However, the business has manufacturing space available that it currently rents to another business for £100,000 a year. This space will not continue to be leased if the decision is not to manufacture. The business would have to purchase plant and equipment costing £9 million and invest £3 million in working capital immediately for production to begin.

A market research report, for which the business paid £50,000, indicates that the new product has an expected life of five years. Sales of the product during this period are predicted as:

	Predicted sales for the year ended 30 November				
	Year 1	Year 2	Year 3	Year 4	Year 5
Number of units (000s)	800	1,400	1,800	1,200	500

The selling price per unit will be £30 in the first year but will fall to £22 in the following three years. In the final year of the product's life, the selling price will fall to £20. Variable production costs are predicted to be £14 a unit. Fixed production costs (including depreciation) will be £2.4 million a year. Marketing costs will be £2 million a year.

The business intends to depreciate the plant and equipment using the straight-line method and based on an estimated residual value at the end of the five years of £1 million. The business has a cost of capital of 10 per cent a year.

2   Newton Electronics Ltd could agree to another business manufacturing and marketing the product under licence. A multinational business, Faraday Electricals plc, has offered to undertake the manufacture and marketing of the product. In return it will make a royalty payment to Newton Electronics Ltd of £5 per unit. It has been estimated that the annual number of sales of the hearing aid will be 10 per cent higher if the multinational business, rather than if Newton Electronics Ltd, manufactures and markets the product.

3   Newton Electronics Ltd could sell the patent rights to Faraday Electricals plc for £24 million, payable in two equal instalments. The first instalment would be payable immediately and the second at the end of two years. This option would give Faraday Electricals the exclusive right to manufacture and market the new product.
Ignore taxation.

Required:
(a) Calculate the net present value (as at the beginning of Year 1) of each of the options available to Newton Electronics Ltd.
(b) Identify and discuss any other factors that Newton Electronics Ltd should consider before arriving at a decision.
(c) State, with reasons, what you consider to be the most suitable option.

10.3   Chesterfield Wanderers is a professional football club that has enjoyed considerable success in recent years. As a result, the club has accumulated £10 million to spend on its further development. The board of directors is currently considering two mutually exclusive options for spending the funds available.

The first option is to acquire another player. The team manager has expressed a keen interest in acquiring Basil ('Bazza') Ramsey, a central defender, who currently plays for a rival club. The rival club has agreed to release the player immediately for £10 million if required. A decision to acquire 'Bazza' Ramsey would mean that the existing central defender, Vinnie Smith, could be sold to another club. Chesterfield Wanderers has recently received an offer of £2.2 million for this player. This offer is still open but will only be accepted if 'Bazza' Ramsey joins Chesterfield Wanderers. If this does not happen, Vinnie Smith will be expected to stay on with the club until the end of his playing career in five years' time. During this period, Vinnie will receive an annual salary of £400,000 and a loyalty bonus of £200,000 at the end of his five-year period with the club.

Assuming 'Bazza' Ramsey is acquired, the team manager estimates that gate receipts will increase by £2.5 million in the first year and £1.3 million in each of the four following years. There will also be an increase in advertising and sponsorship revenues of £1.2 million for each of the next five years if the player is acquired. At the end of five years, the player can be sold to a club in a lower division and Chesterfield Wanderers will expect to receive £1 million as a transfer fee. 'Bazza' will receive an annual salary of £800,000 during his period at the club and a loyalty bonus of £400,000 after five years.

The second option is for the club to improve its ground facilities. The west stand could be extended and executive boxes could be built for businesses wishing to offer corporate hospitality to clients. These improvements would also cost £10 million and would take one year to complete. During this period, the west stand would be closed, resulting in a reduction of gate receipts of £1.8 million. However, gate receipts for each of the following four years would be £4.4 million higher than current receipts. In five years' time, the club has plans to sell the existing grounds and to move to a new stadium nearby. Improving the ground facilities is not expected to affect the ground's value when it comes to be sold. Payment for the improvements will be made when the work has been completed at the end of the first year.

Whichever option is chosen, the board of directors has decided to take on additional ground staff. The additional wages bill is expected to be £350,000 a year over the next five years.

The club has a cost of capital of 10 per cent. Ignore taxation.

Required:

(a) Calculate the incremental cash flows arising from each of the options available to the club, and calculate the net present value of each of the options.

(b) On the basis of the calculations made in (a) above, which of the two options would you choose and why?

(c) Discuss the validity of using the net present value method in making investment decisions for a professional football club.

10.4 C. George (Controls) Ltd manufactures a thermostat that can be used in a range of kitchen appliances. The manufacturing process is, at present, semi-automated. The equipment used cost £540,000 and has a carrying amount (as shown on the statement of financial position) of £300,000. Demand for the product has been fairly stable at 50,000 units a year in recent years.

The following data, based on the current level of output, have been prepared in respect of the product:

	Per unit	
	£	£
Selling price		12.40
Labour	(3.30)	
Materials	(3.65)	
Overheads: Variable	(1.58)	
Fixed	(1.60)	
		(10.13)
Operating profit		2.27

Although the existing equipment is expected to last for a further four years before it is sold for an estimated £40,000, the business has recently been considering purchasing new equipment that would completely automate much of the production process. The new equipment would cost £670,000 and would have an expected life of four years, at the end of which it would be sold for an estimated £70,000. If the new equipment is purchased, the old equipment could be sold for £150,000 immediately.

The assistant to the business's accountant has prepared a report to help assess the viability of the proposed change, which includes the following data:

	Per unit	
	£	£
Selling price		12.40
Labour	(1.20)	
Materials	(3.20)	
Overheads: Variable	(1.40)	
Fixed	(3.30)	
		(9.10)
Operating profit		3.30

Depreciation charges will increase by £85,000 a year as a result of purchasing the new machinery; however, other fixed costs are not expected to change.

In the report the assistant wrote:

> The figures shown above that relate to the proposed change are based on the current level of output and take account of a depreciation charge of £150,000 a year in respect of the new equipment. The effect of purchasing the new equipment will be to increase the operating profit to sales revenue ratio from 18.3 per cent to 26.6 per cent. In addition, the purchase of the new equipment will enable us to reduce our inventories level immediately by £130,000.
>
> In view of these facts, I recommend purchase of the new equipment.

The business has a cost of capital of 12 per cent. Ignore taxation.

Required:

(a) Prepare a statement of the incremental cash flows arising from the purchase of the new equipment.

(b) Calculate the net present value of the proposed purchase of new equipment.

(c) State, with reasons, whether the business should purchase the new equipment.

(d) Explain why cash flow, rather than profit, projections are used to assess the viability of proposed capital expenditure projects.

10.5 The accountant of your business has recently been taken ill through overwork. In his absence, his assistant has prepared some calculations of the profitability of a project, which are to be discussed soon at the board meeting of your business. His workings, which are set out below, include some errors of principle. You can assume that there are no arithmetical errors.

Year	0	1	2	3	4	5
	£000	£000	£000	£000	£000	£000
Sales revenue		450	470	470	470	470
Less costs						
Materials		126	132	132	132	132
Labour		90	94	94	94	94
Overheads		45	47	47	47	47
Depreciation		120	120	120	120	120
Working capital	180					
Interest on working capital		27	27	27	27	27
Write-off of development costs	–	30	30	30	–	–
Total costs	180	438	450	450	420	420
Operating profit/(loss)	(180)	12	20	20	50	50

$$\frac{\text{Total profit (loss)}}{\text{Cost of equipment}} = \frac{(£28,000)}{£600,000} = \text{Return on investment (4.7\%)}$$

You ascertain the following additional information:

1 The cost of equipment includes £100,000, being the carrying value of an old machine. If it were not used for this project it would be scrapped with a zero net realisable value. New equipment costing £500,000 will be purchased on 31 December Year 0. You should assume that all other cash flows occur at the end of the year to which they relate.
2 The development costs of £90,000 have already been spent.
3 Overheads have been costed at 50 per cent of direct labour, which is the business's normal practice. An independent assessment has suggested that incremental overheads are likely to amount to £30,000 a year.
4 The business's cost of capital is 12 per cent.

Ignore taxation in your answer.

Required:
(a) Prepare a corrected statement of the incremental cash flows arising from the project. Where you have altered the assistant's figures you should attach a brief note explaining your alterations.
(b) Calculate:
(i)   the project's payback period;
(ii) The project's net present value as at 31 December Year 0.
(c) Write a memo to the board advising on the acceptance or rejection of the project.

Chapter 11

FINANCING A BUSINESS

INTRODUCTION

In this chapter, we shall examine various aspects of financing a business. We begin by considering the main sources of finance available. Some of these sources have already been touched upon when we discussed the financing of limited companies in Chapter 4. We shall now look at these in more detail as well as discussing other sources of finance not yet mentioned. The factors to be taken into account when choosing an appropriate source of finance are also considered.

Following our consideration of the main sources of finance, we shall examine how long-term finance may be raised. We shall take a look at various aspects of the capital markets, including the ways in which share capital may be issued, the role of the Stock Exchange and the financing of smaller businesses.

Learning outcomes

When you have completed this chapter, you should be able to:

■ identify the main sources of finance available to a business and explain the advantages and disadvantages of each;

■ outline the ways in which share capital may be issued;

■ explain the role and nature of the Stock Exchange;

■ discuss the ways in which smaller businesses may raise finance.

THE MAIN OBJECTIVE OF FINANCING POLICY

Managers should aim to raise finance in such a way that the wealth of the business and its owners is maximised. To do this, they should select sources of finance that combine cost and risk such that the overall cost of capital is minimised. The value of a business can be viewed as the sum of the discounted future cash flows that it generates, where the discount rate is the business's overall cost of capital. By minimising the cost of capital, the discount rate is minimised, which means, in turn, that the value of the business will be maximised.

SOURCES OF FINANCE

When considering the various sources of finance available to a business, it is useful to distinguish between *internal* and *external* sources of finance. By internal sources we mean sources that do not require the agreement of anyone beyond the directors of the business. Thus, retained earnings are considered an internal source because directors have the power to retain earnings without the explicit agreement of the shareholders, whose earnings they are. Finance from an issue of new shares, on the other hand, is an external source because it requires the agreement of potential investors.

Within each of the two categories just described, we can further distinguish between *long-term* and *short-term* sources of finance. There is no agreed definition concerning each of these terms but, for the purpose of this chapter, long-term sources are defined as those that provide finance for at least one year. Short-term sources are therefore defined as those that provide finance for up to one year. As we shall see, sources that are regarded as short-term when first used often end up being used by the business for quite long periods.

We begin the chapter by considering the various sources of internal finance available. We then go on to consider the various sources of external finance. This is probably the appropriate order since businesses tend to look first to internal sources before going outside for new funds.

INTERNAL SOURCES OF FINANCE

Internal sources of finance usually have the advantage of flexibility. They may also be obtained quickly; particularly sources from working capital. The main internal sources of funds are summarised in Figure 11.1 and are described below.

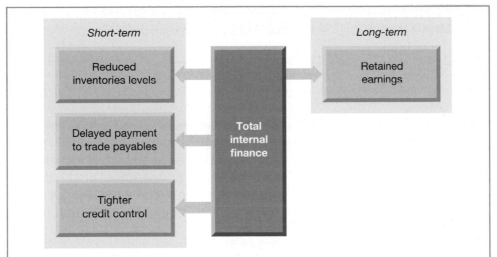

The major internal source of long-term finance is the earnings that are retained rather than distributed to shareholders. The major internal sources of short-term finance involve reducing the level of trade receivables and inventories and increasing the level of trade payables.

Figure 11.1 Major internal sources of finance

INTERNAL SOURCES OF LONG-TERM FINANCE

Retained earnings

Earnings retained within the business, rather than distributed to shareholders in the form of dividends, represent much the most important source of new finance for UK businesses in terms of amounts raised.

Activity 11.1

Are retained earnings a free source of finance for the business? Explain.

No. This is because they have an opportunity cost to shareholders. If shareholders receive a dividend, they can use the cash to make other income-yielding investments. If the business retains the cash, shareholders are deprived of this potential income.

In view of the opportunity cost involved, shareholders will expect a rate of return from retained earnings that is equivalent to what they would receive had the funds been invested in another opportunity with the same level of risk.

Although the reinvestment of earnings incurs a cost to the business, it may be better to raise finance from equity (ordinary share) investors in this way rather than by an issue of shares. No issue costs are incurred and the amount raised is certain, once the earnings have been generated. Where new shares are issued, issue costs may be substantial and the success of the issue may be uncertain, as we shall see later in this chapter. In addition, any new shares issued to outside investors will result in a dilution of control for existing shareholders.

Retaining earnings may be an easier option than asking investors to subscribe to a new share issue. These earnings are already held by the business and so there is no delay in receiving the funds. Moreover, there is often less scrutiny when earnings are retained for reinvestment purposes compared to when new shares are issued. Investors tend to examine closely the reasons for any new share issue. A problem with the use of earnings as a source of finance, however, is that their timing and future level cannot always be reliably determined.

It would be wrong to gain the impression that businesses either retain their entire earnings or pay them all out as dividends. Larger businesses, for example, tend to pay dividends but normally pay out no more than 50 per cent of their earnings.

Not all businesses pay dividends every year, even when they have been profitable. One such business is Asos plc (the online fashion retailer). It has never paid a dividend, because it has needed the funds to expand. **Real World 11.1,** an extract from its 2015 annual report, explains the situation.

INTERNAL SOURCES OF SHORT-TERM FINANCE

The major internal forms of short-term finance are:

- tighter credit control;
- reducing inventories levels; and
- delaying payments to trade payables (suppliers).

These are shown in Figure 11.1.

We saw in Chapter 5, in the context of statements of cash flows, that increases and decreases in these working capital items will have a direct and rapid effect on cash. Having funds tied up in trade receivables and inventories and failing to take advantage of free credit from suppliers creates a financing opportunity cost.

Activity 11.2

Why does it create an opportunity cost? Explain.

It is because those funds could be used for profit-generating activities or for returning funds to shareholders or lenders.

Tighter credit control

By exerting tighter control over amounts owed by credit customers, a business may be able to reduce the funds tied up. It is important, however, to weigh the benefits of tighter credit control against the likely costs in the form of lost customer goodwill and lost sales.

To remain competitive, a business must take account of the needs of its customers and the credit policies adopted by rival businesses.

Reducing inventories levels

This internal source of funds may prove attractive to a business. It must ensure, however, that there are sufficient inventories available to meet likely future production and sales demand. Failure to do this can result in costly dislocation of production, lost customer goodwill and/or lost sales revenue.

The nature and condition of the inventories held will determine whether this form of finance is available. A business may hold excessive inventories as a result of poor buying decisions. This may mean that a large part of inventories held is slow moving or obsolete and cannot be easily liquidated.

Delaying payment to trade payables

By providing a period of credit, suppliers are in effect offering their customers interest-free loans. If the business delays payment, the period of the 'loan' is extended and funds are retained within the business. This can be highly beneficial for a business, although it is not always the case. If a business fails to pay within the agreed credit period, there may be significant costs. For example, buying on credit may become difficult once it has a reputation as a slow payer.

Activity 11.3 concerns the cash flow benefit of more efficient management of the working capital elements.

Activity 11.3

Trader Ltd is a wholesaler of imported washing machines. The business is partly funded by a bank overdraft and the bank is putting pressure on Trader Ltd to reduce this as soon as possible.

Sales revenue is £14.6 million a year and is all on credit. Purchases and cost of sales are roughly equal at £7.3 million a year. Current investments in the relevant working capital elements are:

	£m
Inventories	1.5
Trade receivablevs	3.8
Trade payables	0.7

Trader Ltd's accountant believes that much of the overdraft could be eliminated through better control of working capital. As a result, she has investigated and benchmarked several successful businesses that are similar to Trader Ltd and found the following averages:

	Days
Average inventories turnover period	22
Average settlement period for trade receivables	57
Average settlement period for trade payables	55

How much cash could Trader Ltd generate if it were able to bring its ratios into line with those of similar businesses?

The cash that could be generated is as follows:

	£m	£m
Inventories		
Current level	1.5	
Target level: $^{22}/_{365} \times 7.3 =$	0.4	1.1
Trade receivables		
Current level	3.8	
Target level: $^{57}/_{365} \times 14.6 =$	2.3	1.5
Trade payables		
Current level	0.7	
Target level: $^{55}/_{365} \times 7.3 =$	1.1	0.4
Total		3.0

Some further points

The so-called short-term sources just described are short-term to the extent that they can be reversed at short notice. For example, a reduction in the level of trade receivables can be reversed within a couple of weeks. Typically, however, once a business has established a reduced receivables settlement period, a reduced inventories holding period and/or an expanded payables settlement period, it will tend to maintain these new levels.

In Chapter 12, we shall see how these three elements of working capital may be managed. We shall also see that, for many businesses, the funds invested in working capital items are vast and, in many cases, needlessly so. There is often considerable scope for generating funds through more efficient management of working capital.

EXTERNAL SOURCES OF FINANCE

The main external sources of long-term and short-term finance are summarised in Figure 11.2.

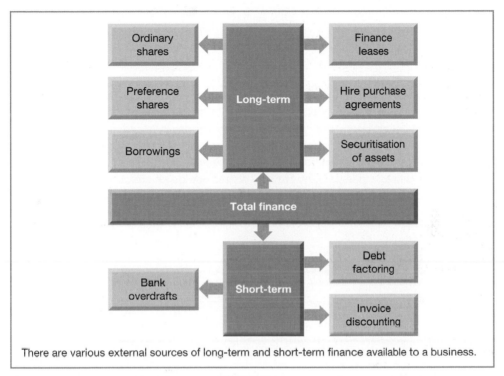

There are various external sources of long-term and short-term finance available to a business.

Figure 11.2 Major external sources of finance

EXTERNAL SOURCES OF LONG-TERM FINANCE

The major external sources of long-term finance are:

■ ordinary shares;
■ preference shares;
■ borrowing;
■ finance leases (including sale-and-leaseback arrangements);
■ hire-purchase agreements; and
■ securitisation of assets.

We shall now look at each of these sources in turn.

Ordinary shares

Ordinary (equity) shares represent the risk capital of a business and form the backbone of a business's financial structure. There is no fixed rate of dividend. Furthermore, ordinary shareholders will only receive a dividend if profits available for distribution still remain after other investors (preference shareholders and lenders) have received their dividend or interest payments. If the business is wound up, the ordinary shareholders will receive only proceeds from asset disposals after lenders and creditors, and in some cases preference shareholders, have received their entitlements. Because of the high risks associated with this form of investment, ordinary shareholders normally expect a relatively high rate of return.

Although ordinary shareholders' potential losses are limited to the amount that they have invested or agreed to invest, the potential returns from their investment are unlimited. After preference shareholders and lenders have received their returns, all remaining profits accrue to the ordinary shareholders. Thus, while their 'downside' risk is limited, their 'upside' potential is not. Ordinary shareholders control the business through their voting rights, which give them the power to elect the directors and to remove them from office.

From the business's perspective, ordinary shares can be an effective form of financing compared to borrowing. It is possible to avoid paying a dividend, whereas it is not usually possible to avoid interest payments.

Activity 11.4

From the business's point of view, ordinary shares represent a less risky form of financing than borrowing. Why is this?

It is because the obligation to make interest payments and capital repayments could put the business in financial jeopardy. There is no such risk with ordinary shares.

Preference shares

Preference shares offer investors a lower level of risk than ordinary shares. Provided there are sufficient profits available, preference shares will normally receive a fixed rate of dividend each year and will also receive the first slice of any dividend paid. If the business is wound up, preference shareholders may be given priority over the claims of ordinary shareholders. (The business's own documents of incorporation will state the precise rights of preference shareholders in this respect.)

Preference shareholders are not usually given voting rights, although these may be granted where the preference dividend is in arrears. Both preference shares and ordinary shares are, in effect, redeemable. The business is allowed to buy back the shares from shareholders at any time.

Preference shares are no longer an important source of new finance. A major reason for this is that dividends are not allowable against taxable profits, whereas loan interest is an allowable expense. From the business's point of view, preference shares and loans are quite similar, so their different tax treatment is an important issue. Furthermore, in recent years, interest rates on borrowing have been at historically low levels.

Borrowings

Most businesses rely on borrowings as well as share capital to finance operations. Lenders enter into a contract with the business in which the rate of interest, dates of interest payments, capital repayments and security for the loan are clearly stated. If a business is successful, lenders will not benefit beyond the fact that their claim will become more secure. If, on the other hand, the business experiences financial difficulties, there is a risk that the agreed interest payments and capital repayments will not be made. To protect themselves against this risk, lenders often seek some form of **security** from the business. This may take the form of assets pledged either by a **fixed charge** on particular assets held by the business, or by a **floating charge**, which 'hovers' over the whole of the business's assets. A floating charge will only fix on particular assets in the event that the business defaults on its obligations.

Activity 11.5

What do you think is the advantage for the business of having a floating charge rather than a fixed charge on its assets?

A floating charge on assets will allow the managers of the business greater flexibility in their day-to-day operations than a fixed charge. Individual assets can be sold without reference to the lenders.

Not all assets are acceptable to lenders as security. To be acceptable, they must normally be non-perishable, easy to sell and of high and stable value. (Property normally meets these criteria and so is often favoured by lenders.) In the event of default, lenders have the right to seize the assets pledged and to sell them. Any surplus from the sale, after lenders have been paid, will be passed to the business. In some cases, security offered may take the form of a personal guarantee by the owners of the business or, perhaps, by some third party. This most often occurs with small businesses.

Lenders may seek further protection through the use of **loan covenants**. These are obligations, or restrictions, on the business that form part of the loan contract. Covenants may impose:

- the right of lenders to receive regular financial reports concerning the business;
- an obligation to insure the assets being offered as security;
- a restriction on the right to make further borrowings (for example, issue further loan notes) without prior permission of the existing lenders;
- a restriction on the right to sell certain assets held;
- a restriction on dividend payments and/or payments made to directors; and
- minimum levels of liquidity and/or maximum levels of financial gearing.

Any breach of these covenants can have serious consequences. Lenders may demand immediate repayment of the loan in the event of a material breach.

Real World 11.2 describes how one well-known retailer, HMV, struggled to generate profits, which, in turn, led to the risk that it would breach its loan covenants.

REAL WORLD 11.2

HMV faces extinction

The CD and DVD chain said it was facing a 'probable covenant breach at the end of January 2013', and blamed poor sales in the run-up to the crucial Christmas trading period. Trevor Moore, chief executive, said: 'In light of current trading performance, and market conditions, it is probable that the banking covenants will not be complied with at that time.' 'HMV has had a difficult first half,' he added, but said that the retailer was in 'constructive discussions with the group's banks, including keeping them fully informed in relation to current trading'.

Mr Moore, who recently took over at HMV, insisted that HMV had a future, and he planned to outline his strategic blueprint for the group in due course. The latest set-backs come despite HMV moving more into entertainment and selling assets in an effort to turn round its fortunes. 'I don't think we have tried everything,' he said. 'If I thought we had tried everything I would not have joined.'

HMV has become a high-profile victim of the move away from high street entertainment sales, as consumers increasingly download music and internet competition reduces its market share.

In fact, HMV weighed down by its debts, went into administration on 13 January 2013. However, HMV's high street presence has not totally disappeared. In April 2013, Hilco, a business that specialises in resurrecting collapsed businesses, bought the HMV business from the liquidator. Since then HMV has gone from strength to strength. By 2015 it had overtaken Amazon to become the UK's leading seller of physical music (CDs and vinyl).

 Sources: Extracts from Wembridge, M. and Felsted, A. (2012), 'HMV plunges 40% on covenant warning', ft.com, 13 December; information contained in both Felstead, A. and Sakoui, A. (2013) 'Hilco strikes deal to rescue HMV', ft.com, 5 April and Masters, B. (2015) 'HMV proves that down does not mean out, ft.com, 16 January.
© The Financial Times Limited 2012. All Rights Reserved. Pearson Education Ltd. is responsible for providing this adaptation of the original article.

Loan covenants and the availability of security can lower the risk for lenders and can make the difference between a successful and an unsuccessful loan issue. They can also lower the cost of borrowing as the rate of return will depend on the perceived level of risk to which lenders are exposed.

From an investor's perspective, the risk/return characteristics of loan, preference share and ordinary share finance are shown graphically in Figure 11.3.

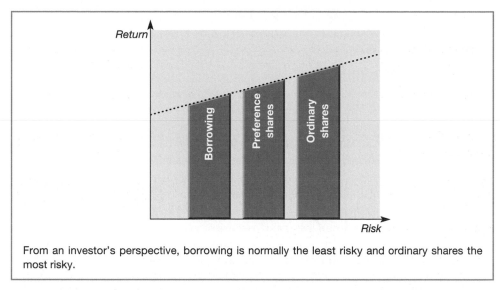

From an investor's perspective, borrowing is normally the least risky and ordinary shares the most risky.

Figure 11.3 The risk/return characteristics of sources of long-term finance

Activity 11.7

Now consider these three forms of finance from the viewpoint of a business. Will a business rank them, according to risk, in the same order?

For a business, the level of risk associated with each form of finance is in reverse order. Borrowing is the most risky because it exposes shareholders to the legally enforceable obligation to make regular interest payments and, usually, repayment of the amount borrowed.

FORMS OF BORROWING

Borrowing may take various forms and among the most important are:

- term loans;
- loan notes (or loan stock);
- Eurobonds;
- convertible loan notes; and
- mortgages.

Term loans

A **term loan** is a type of loan offered by banks and other financial institutions that can be tailored to the needs of the client business. The amount of the loan, time period, repayment terms and interest rate are all open to negotiation and agreement – which can be very useful. Where, for example, the whole amount borrowed is not required immediately, a business may agree with the lender that sums are drawn only when required. This means that interest will be paid only on amounts actually drawn and there is no need to pay interest on amounts borrowed that are not yet needed. Term loans tend to be cheap to set up (from the borrower's perspective) and can be quite flexible as to conditions. For these reasons, they tend to be popular in practice.

Loan notes (or loan stock)

Many businesses borrow in such a way that various investors are able to lend part of the amount required by the borrower. This is particularly the case with the larger, Stock Exchange listed, companies and involves them making an issue of **loan notes** (or **loan stock**). Although such an issue may be large in total, it can be taken up in small slices by individual investors, both private individuals and investing institutions such as pension funds and insurance businesses. In some cases, these slices of loans can be bought and sold through the Stock Exchange. This means that investors do not have to wait the full term of their loan to obtain repayment, but can sell their slice of it to another would-be lender at intermediate points in the term of the loan. This flexibility can make loan notes an attractive investment to certain investors. Loan notes are sometimes known as *debentures*.

Loan notes may be redeemable or irredeemable. Where loan notes are traded on the Stock Exchange, their listed value will fluctuate according to the fortunes of the business, movements in interest rates and so on.

Loan notes are usually referred to as **bonds** in the USA and, increasingly so, in the UK.

Real World 11.3 is extracts from an article which describes how, in 2015, Manchester United redeemed its relatively high interest, secured bonds. It financed this through an issue of lower interest bearing bonds. This resulted in a substantial net saving in annual interest payments. The article concluded by making the point that the estimated £10 million annual interest cost saving would pay Wayne Rooney's salary for a few months.

REAL WORLD 11.3

Manchester United win

Football can be a brutal business. Top assets are prone to lose form, get hurt or break contracts. A club can miss out on huge prizes by the thickness of a goalpost, or a hashed clearance from defence.

And yet lenders seem very keen to back the beautiful game. Last week Manchester United told holders of its senior secured bonds–paying interest of 8.375 per cent a year–that it wanted to buy them all back by the end of this month, two years ahead of schedule. To raise the cash to redeem the $269 million outstanding, it will issue $425 million in 12-year notes paying just 3.79 per cent.

At the same time, the club said it would replace a two year old bank loan with one about a quarter smaller ($225 million), while cutting the interest-rate range and extending the term six years to 2025. In exchange, the bank gets another covenant–a promise that earnings before interest, tax, depreciation and amortisation will not drop below £65 million a year. The closest United came to that in recent years was £91 million in 2012, so it is hardly an imposition.

Activity 11.8

Would you expect the market price of ordinary shares or of loan notes to be the more volatile? Why?

Price movements will normally be much less volatile for loan notes than for ordinary shares. The price of loan notes and ordinary shares will reflect the expected future returns from each. Interest from loan notes is fixed by contract over time. Returns from ordinary shares, on the other hand, are very much less certain.

Activity 11.9

Would you expect the returns on loan notes to be higher or lower than those of ordinary shares?

Loan note holders will expect to receive a lower level of return than ordinary shareholders. This is because of the lower level of risk associated with this form of investment (loan interest is fixed by contract and security will often be available).

Some of the features of financing by loan notes, particularly the possibility that the loan notes may be traded on the Stock Exchange, can lead to confusing loan notes with shares. We should be clear that shares and loan notes are not the same thing. It is the shareholders who own the company and, therefore, who share in its losses and profits. Holders of loan notes lend money to the company under a legally binding contract that normally specifies the rate of interest, the interest payment dates and the date of repayment of the loan itself.

Eurobonds

Eurobonds are unsecured loan notes denominated in a currency other than the home currency of the business that issued them. They are issued by listed businesses (and other large organisations) in various countries, and the finance is raised on an international basis. They are often denominated in US dollars, but many are issued in other major currencies. They are bearer bonds (that is, the owner of the bond is not registered and the holder of the bond certificate is regarded as the owner) and interest is normally paid, without deduction of tax, on an annual basis.

Eurobonds are part of an international capital market that is not restricted by regulations imposed by authorities in particular countries. This partly explains why the cost of servicing eurobonds is usually lower than the cost of similar domestic bonds. Numerous banks and other financial institutions throughout the world have created a market for the purchase and sale of eurobonds. These bonds are made available to financial institutions, which may retain them as an investment or sell them to clients.

The extent of borrowing, by UK businesses, in currencies other than sterling has expanded greatly in recent years. Businesses are often attracted to eurobonds because of the size of the international capital market. Access to a wider pool of potential investors can increase the chances of a successful issue.

Convertible loan notes

Convertible loan notes (or convertible bonds) give investors the right to convert loan notes into ordinary shares at a specified price and at a given future date (or range of dates). The share price specified, which is known as the *exercise price,* will normally be higher than the market price of the ordinary shares at the time of the loan notes issue. The investor remains a lender to the business and will receive interest on the amount of the loan notes, until such time as the conversion takes place. If and when conversion takes place, in effect, the investor swaps the loan notes for a particular number of shares. There is no obligation to convert to ordinary shares. This will be done only if the market price of the shares at the conversion date exceeds the agreed conversion price.

An investor may find this form of investment a useful 'hedge' against risk (that is, it can reduce the level of risk). This may be particularly useful when investment in a new business is being considered. Initially, the investment will be in the form of loan notes, and regular interest payments will be received. If the business is successful, the investor can then convert the investment into ordinary shares.

A business may also find this form of financing useful. If the business is successful, the loan notes become self-liquidating (that is, no cash outlay is required to redeem them) as investors will exercise their option to convert. It may also be possible to offer a lower rate of interest on the loan notes because of the expected future benefits arising from conversion. There will be, however, some dilution of control and, possibly, a dilution of earnings for existing shareholders if holders of convertible loan notes exercise their option to convert. (Dilution of earnings available to shareholders will not automatically occur as a result of the conversion of borrowings to share capital. There will be a saving in interest charges that will have, at least a partially, offsetting effect.)

Real World 11.4 outlines a recent convertible loan note (bond) issue. It was fairly unusual in that no interest was payable during the life of the bond. Investors, therefore, relied on the hope that the business's share price would rise sufficiently during the conversion period.

REAL WORLD 11.4

The name's Bond, convertible bond

Oh, James. Bonds of two kinds have produced good things for Sony. Mr Bond's latest outing in Skyfall, on course to be the most lucrative film in the spy franchise, will be a nice earner for Sony Pictures. And its parent's latest convertible bond, issued this week, netted the company ¥150 billion, or $1.8 billion. But while Skyfall's Japanese premiere in Tokyo next week will produce some good publicity, the financial kind of bond is sending very negative signals.

While 007 has never needed to do bond maths, Sony's shareholders do not get that luxury. Its zero-coupon convertible bonds were its first such debt in almost a decade. The bonds can be converted to shares at ¥957, a 10 per cent premium to Wednesday's close, any time in the next five years from mid-December. Sony shares, however, fell almost 9 per cent on Thursday to ¥793 in by far the heaviest day of trading the company has seen. But the fall should have been half as bad again, taking the shares to ¥753 all else being equal, if it were to have fully reflected expectations that the bonds would be converted. The result instead suggests that investors are not very sure that Sony can even lift its shares to a point where it makes more sense to take a punt on future profitability than to hold an IOU that does not even offer interest.

Sony's troubles are well known, as are those of Sharp and Panasonic, its rivals. Its finances are at least on a somewhat sounder footing, thanks to its film, music, gaming and financial services units. But all the efforts of Mr Bond or even Sony's new film signing, the boy band, One Direction, will not convince investors a corner has been turned until its electronics business produces its equivalent of a Skyfall-sized hit – a best-selling phone or tablet. Until then, Mr Bond will continue to make miraculous recoveries from disaster-laden scenarios but Sony's shares are unlikely to follow suit.

FT *Source*: Lex column (2012) 'Sony – group bonding', ft.com, 15 November.
© The Financial Times Limited 2012. All Rights Reserved.

Convertibles are an example of a **financial derivative**. This is any form of financial instrument, based on equity or loans, which can be used by investors to increase their returns or reduce risk.

Mortgages

A **mortgage** is a form of loan that is secured on an **asset**, typically land and property. Financial institutions such as banks, insurance businesses and pension funds are often prepared to lend to businesses on this basis. The mortgage may be over a long period (20 years or more).

Interest rates

Interest rates may be either floating or fixed. A **floating interest rate** means that the rate of return will rise and fall with market rates of interest. Interest rates may be either floating or fixed. A floating interest rate means that the rate of return will rise and fall with market rates of interest. (However, a condition of a floating rate loan can be that there would be a maximum and/or a minimum rate of interest payable.) The market value of floating loan notes is likely to remain fairly stable over time.

The converse will normally be true for loans with a **fixed interest rate**. Interest payments will remain unchanged with rises and falls in market rates of interest. This means that the value of the loan notes will fall when interest rates rise, and will rise when interest rates fall.

Activity 11.10

Why does the value of fixed-interest loan notes rise and fall with rises and falls in interest rates?

This is because investors will be prepared to pay less for loan notes that pay a rate of interest below the market rate of interest and will be prepared to pay more for loan notes that pay a rate of interest above the market rate of interest.

Movements in interest rates can be a significant issue for businesses that have high levels of borrowing. A business with a floating rate of interest may find that rate rises will place real strains on cash flows and profitability. Conversely, a business that has a fixed rate of interest will find that, when rates are falling, it will not enjoy the benefits of lower interest charges.

Finance leases

When a business needs a particular asset, such as a piece of equipment, instead of buying it direct from a supplier, the business either:

- arranges for a bank (or other financial institution) to buy it and then lease it to the business; or
- leases it from the supplier (perhaps the manufacturer of the asset), instead of buying it in the normal way.

The party (financial institution or supplier) that owns the asset, and then leases it to the business, is known as a 'lessor'. The business that leases the asset from the bank and then uses it is known as the 'lessee'.

A **finance lease**, as such an arrangement is known, is in essence a form of lending. This is because, had the business borrowed the funds and then used them to buy the asset itself, the effect would be much the same. The business would have use of the asset, but would also have a financial obligation to the lender – just as with a leasing arrangement.

With finance leasing, legal ownership of the asset remains with the lessor. However, the lease agreement transfers to the lessee virtually all the rewards and risks associated with the item being leased. The finance lease agreement will cover a substantial part of the life of the leased item and, often, cannot be cancelled. **Real World 11.5** gives an example of the use of finance leasing by a large international business.

REAL WORLD 11.5

Leased assets take off

Many airline businesses use finance leasing as a means of acquiring new aeroplanes. This includes International Airlines Group (IAG), the business that owns British Airways, Iberia and Aer Lingus. At 31 December 2014, the carrying amount of AIG's fleet of planes was made up of roughly 54 per cent leased and 46 per cent owned outright.

Source: Based on information in International Airlines Group, Annual Report 2014, p. 120.

A finance lease can be contrasted with an **operating lease**, where the rewards and risks of ownership stay with the owner and where the lease is short-term. An example of an operating lease is where a builder hires some earth-moving equipment for a week to carry out a particular job.

Over the years, some important benefits associated with finance leasing have disappeared. Changes in the tax laws mean that it is no longer quite such a tax-efficient form of financing, and changes in accounting disclosure requirements make it no longer possible to conceal this form of 'borrowing' from investors. Nevertheless, the popularity of finance leases has continued. Other reasons must, therefore, exist for businesses to adopt this form of financing. These reasons are said to include the following:

■ *Ease of borrowing.* Leasing may be obtained more easily than other forms of long-term finance. Lenders normally require some form of security and a profitable track record before making advances to a business. However, a lessor may be prepared to lease assets to a new business without a track record and to use the leased assets as security for the amounts owing.

■ *Cost.* Leasing agreements may be offered at reasonable cost. As the asset leased is used as security, standard lease arrangements can be applied and detailed credit checking of lessees may be unnecessary. This can reduce administration costs for the lessor and thereby help in providing competitive lease rentals.

■ *Flexibility.* Leasing can help provide flexibility where there are rapid changes in technology. If an option to cancel can be incorporated into the lease, the business may be able to exercise this option and invest in new technology as it becomes available. This will help the business to avoid the risk of obsolescence. Avoiding this risk will come at a cost to the lessee, however, because the risk is passed to the lessor, who will expect this increased risk to be rewarded.

■ *Cash flows.* Leasing, rather than buying an asset outright, means that large cash outflows can be avoided. The leasing option allows cash outflows to be smoothed out over the asset's life. In some cases, it is possible to arrange for low lease payments to be made in the early years of the asset's life, when cash inflows may be low, and for these to increase over time as the asset generates higher cash flows.

These benefits are summarised in diagrammatic form in Figure 11.4.

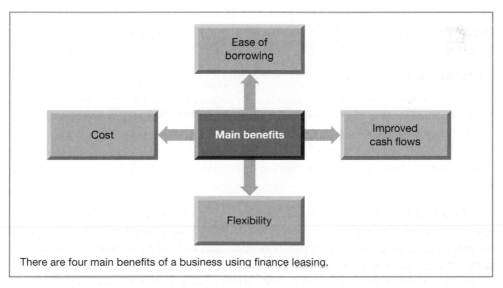

There are four main benefits of a business using finance leasing.

Figure 11.4 Benefits of finance leasing

Sale-and-leaseback arrangements

A **sale-and-leaseback** arrangement involves a business raising finance by selling an asset to a financial institution. The sale is accompanied by an agreement to lease the asset back to the business to allow it to continue to use the asset. The lease rental payment is a business expense that is allowable against profits for taxation purposes.

There are usually rental reviews at regular intervals throughout the period of the lease, and the amounts payable in future years may be difficult to predict. At the end of the lease agreement, the business must either try to renew the lease or find an alternative asset. Although the sale of the asset will result in an immediate injection of cash for the business, it will lose benefits from any future capital appreciation on the asset. Where a capital gain arises on the sale of the asset to the financial institution, a liability for taxation may also arise.

Activity 11.11

Can you think which type of asset is often subject to a sale-and-leaseback arrangement?

Property (real estate) is often the asset that is subject to such an arrangement.

Many of the well-known UK high street retailers (for example, Boots, Debenhams, Marks and Spencer, Tesco and Sainsbury) have sold off their store sites under sale-and-leaseback arrangements.

Sale-and-leaseback agreements can be used to help a business focus on its core areas of competence. In recent years, many hotel businesses have entered into sale-and-leaseback arrangements to enable them to become hotel operators rather than a combination of hotel operators and owners.

Real World 11.6 explains how a leading European mobile phone operator raised funds through the sale-and-leaseback of some of its mobile masts.

REAL WORLD 11.6

The future of sale-and-leaseback is Orange

Orange has opened discussions with infrastructure groups about a sale of its mobile masts in Spain as it looks to cut costs in European markets. The French telecoms group could sell about 9,400 towers, or 53 per cent of its Spanish network, according to Expansion, the Spanish newspaper that first reported the sale.

Such deals are typically structured as a sale and leaseback arrangement where Orange would become a tenant that uses the masts. Telecoms groups in markets in the US and Africa have been active in selling their mast network, although the trend is not as prevalent in Europe.

Orange has spoken to tower operators to gauge interest in the sale, although no firm decision has been taken to sell the infrastructure. A decision will depend on the level of interest, according to a person familiar with the situation.

The value of tower deals can be difficult to estimate, although in a comparable deal in 2013 Albertis acquired 4,227 mobile telephone towers for €385 million from Telefonica and Yoigo in Spain. Orange declined to comment.

FT *Source*: Extract from Thomas, D. (2014) 'Orange looks to offload Spanish mobile masts to cut costs', ft.com, 14 August.
© The Financial Times Limited 2014. All Rights Reserved.

Hire purchase

Hire purchase is a form of credit used to acquire an asset. Under the terms of a hire-purchase (HP) agreement a customer pays for the asset by instalments over an agreed period. Normally, the customer will pay an initial deposit (down payment) and then make instalment payments at regular intervals, perhaps monthly, until the balance outstanding has been paid. The customer will usually take possession of the asset after payment of the initial deposit, although legal ownership of the asset will not be transferred until the final instalment has been paid. HP agreements will often involve three parties.

- the supplier;
- the customer; and
- a financial institution.

Although the supplier will deliver the asset to the customer, the financial institution will buy the asset from the supplier and then enter into an HP agreement with the customer. This intermediary role played by the financial institution enables the supplier to receive immediate payment for the asset but allows the customer a period of extended credit.

Figure 11.5 sets out the main steps in the hire purchase process.

Activity 11.12

In what way is an HP agreement:

(a) similar to,
(b) different from,

a finance lease?

HP agreements are similar to finance leases in so far as they allow a customer to obtain immediate possession of the asset without paying its full cost. HP agreements differ from finance leases because, under the terms of an HP agreement, the customer will eventually become the legal owner of the asset, whereas under the terms of a finance lease, ownership will stay with the lessor.

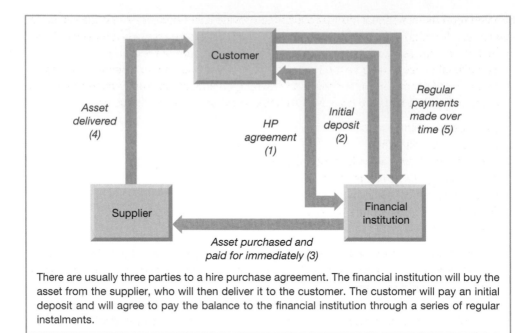

There are usually three parties to a hire purchase agreement. The financial institution will buy the asset from the supplier, who will then deliver it to the customer. The customer will pay an initial deposit and will agree to pay the balance to the financial institution through a series of regular instalments.

Figure 11.5 The hire purchase process

HP agreements are, perhaps, most commonly associated with private consumers acquiring large household items or cars. It is also, however, a significant form of financing for businesses. **Real World 11.7** shows the extent to which one large UK business depends on hire purchase to finance its main assets.

REAL WORLD 11.7

Getting there by instalments

Stagecoach Group plc, the transport business, reported in its 2015 annual report, passenger service vehicles with a carrying amount of £776.6 million, of which £90.5 million related to assets purchased under HP agreements. This amounts to around 12 per cent of the total.

Source: Information taken from Stagecoach Group plc, Annual Report 2015, p. 81.

Securitisation

Securitisation involves bundling together illiquid financial or physical assets of the same type so as to provide financial backing for an issue of bonds. 'Illiquid' in this sense means not readily able to be sold. This financing method was notably used by US banks, which bundled together residential mortgage loans to provide asset backing for bonds issued to investors. (Mortgage loans held by a bank are financial assets that provide future cash flows in the form of interest receivable and repayment of the amount of the loan.)

Securitisation has spread beyond the banking industry and has now become an important source of finance for businesses in a wide range of industries. Future cash flows from a variety of illiquid assets are now used as backing for bond issues, including:

- credit card receipts;
- water industry charges;
- rental income from university accommodation;
- ticket sales for football matches;
- royalties from music copyright;
- consumer instalment contracts; and
- beer sales to pub tenants.

The effect of securitisation is to capitalise future cash flows arising from illiquid assets. This capitalised amount is sold to investors, through the financial markets, to raise finance for the business holding these assets.

Securitisation may also be used to help manage risk. Where, for example, a bank has lent a lot of funds to a particular industry, its industry exposure can be reduced by bundling together some of the outstanding loan contracts and making a securitisation issue. This means that those who invested in the securitised bonds will bear the risk relating to the loan contracts concerned and not the bank.

The main elements of the securitisation process are set out in Figure 11.6.

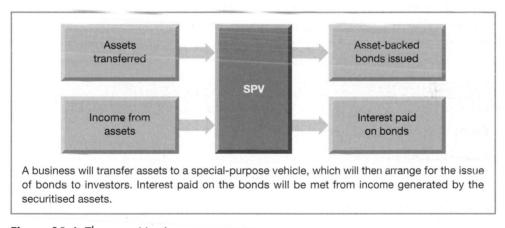

A business will transfer assets to a special-purpose vehicle, which will then arrange for the issue of bonds to investors. Interest paid on the bonds will be met from income generated by the securitised assets.

Figure 11.6 The securitisation process

Securitisation and the financial crisis

Securitising mortgage loan repayments became popular among US mortgage lenders during the early years of the 2000s. Where this approach was adopted, the monthly repayments due to be made by the relevant mortgage borrowers were 'securitised' and sold to many of the major banks, particularly in the USA. Unfortunately, many of the mortgage loans were made to people on low incomes who were not good credit risks (sub-prime loans). When the borrowers started to default on their obligations, it became clear that the securities, now owned by the banks, were worth much less than the banks had paid the mortgage lenders for them. This led to the so-called 'sub-prime' crisis that triggered the worldwide economic problems that emerged during 2008. There is, however, no inherent reason for securitisation to be the cause of such a problem and it is unfortunate that the practice is linked with the sub-prime crisis. It can be a perfectly legitimate and practical way for a business to raise finance.

EXTERNAL SOURCES OF SHORT-TERM FINANCE

Short-term, in this context, is usually taken to mean up to one year. The major external sources of short-term finance (as were shown in Figure 11.2) are:

- bank overdrafts;
- debt factoring; and
- invoice discounting.

We shall now discuss each of these.

Bank overdrafts

A **bank overdraft** enables a business to maintain a negative balance on its bank account. It represents a very flexible form of borrowing as the size of an overdraft can (subject to bank approval) be increased or decreased more or less instantaneously. It is relatively inexpensive to arrange and interest rates are often very competitive, though often higher than those for a term loan. As with all loans, the rate of interest charged will vary according to how creditworthy the customer is perceived to be by the bank. An overdraft is fairly easy to arrange – sometimes it can be agreed by a telephone call to the bank. In view of these advantages, it is not surprising that an overdraft is an extremely popular form of short-term finance.

Banks prefer to grant overdrafts that are self-liquidating, that is, the funds are used in such a way as to extinguish the overdraft balance by generating cash inflows. The banks may want to examine the business's cash budget to see when the overdraft should be repaid and how much finance is required. They may also require some form of security on amounts advanced.

One potential drawback with this form of finance is that it is repayable on demand. This may pose problems for a business that is illiquid. **Real World 11.8** describes how one small business found itself in severe difficulties following the withdrawal of overdraft facilities by its bank, the Royal Bank of Scotland (RBS).

Backs to the wall

Clive May believes that the closure of the bricklaying business he founded with his brother Nick 17 years ago is only a matter of time after he says RBS withdrew their overdraft and pulled a £70,000 loan facility. 'The vultures are circling,' Mr May says. 'As a direct result of the bank's actions we are going to have to go into liquidation to stave off a threat from HMRC regarding VAT. We've asked for a time to pay arrangement but to no avail.'

The situation is a reversal of fortune for the company, based in Mold, Flintshire, which three years ago had a £220,000 overdraft and sales of £2.6 million. After withdrawing its overdraft facility, RBS offered a loan under the wrapper of the enterprise finance guarantee scheme, which means the government would back the debt. But instead of providing capital for the business, Mr May says the money was used to pay off its overdraft balance, leaving him in need of extra cash to service his order book. 'Once drawn down they said unless you secure your assets, the facility will be pulled, which is what they did,' Mr May explains. 'Their actions have destroyed this company.'

Mr May has tried to avoid collapse by taking an invoice discounting facility with Bibby Financial Services, but the charges involved have eaten up nearly 50 per cent of the money offered by this facility. If the company could secure finance at a reasonable rate there would be no reason for it to be in dire straits, Mr May claims, adding that he has £750,000 in secured orders for a number of building projects. 'There is a good possibility that we will now have to close with the 30 lads who work for us thrown on the scrap heap just before Christmas,' Mr May says. 'This isn't right.'

RBS did not immediately respond to a request for comment.

 Source: Moules, J. (2013) 'RBS has driven us to wall, says bricks business', ft.com, 25 November. © The Financial Times Limited 2013. All Rights Reserved.

Despite the problems suffered by the May brothers' business, many businesses operate for many years using an overdraft, simply because the bank remains confident of their ability to repay and the arrangement suits the business. Thus, bank overdrafts, though in theory regarded as short-term, can, in practice, often become a source of long-term finance.

Debt factoring and invoice discounting

Debt factoring and **invoice discounting** are quite similar services offered by financial institutions, many of which are subsidiaries of commercial banks.

Debt factoring involves outsourcing the business's trade receivables management to a specialist subcontractor. In addition to operating normal credit control procedures, a factor may offer to undertake credit investigations and advise on the creditworthiness of customers. It may also offer protection for approved credit sales. The factor is usually prepared to make an advance to the business of up to around 80 per cent of approved trade receivables. This advance is usually paid immediately after the goods have been supplied to the customer.

The balance of the debt, less any deductions for fees and interest, will be paid after an agreed period or when the debt is collected. The charge made for the factoring service is based on total sales revenue and is often around 2 or 3 per cent of sales revenue. Any advances made to the business by the factor will attract a rate of interest similar to the rate charged on bank overdrafts.

Many businesses find a factoring arrangement very convenient. It can result in savings in credit management and create more certainty with the cash flows. It can also release the time of key personnel for more profitable activities. This may be extremely important for smaller businesses that rely on the talent and skills of a few key individuals. However, there is a possibility that a factoring arrangement will be seen as an indication that the business is experiencing financial difficulties. This may have an adverse effect on the confidence of customers, suppliers and staff. For this reason, some businesses try to conceal the factoring arrangement by collecting debts on behalf of the factor. When considering a factoring agreement, the costs and likely benefits arising must be identified and carefully weighed.

Figure 11.7 shows the debt factoring process diagrammatically.

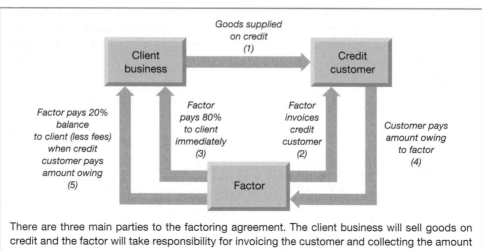

There are three main parties to the factoring agreement. The client business will sell goods on credit and the factor will take responsibility for invoicing the customer and collecting the amount owing. The factor will then pay the client business the invoice amount, less fees and interest, in two stages. The first stage typically represents 80 per cent of the invoice value and will be paid immediately after the goods have been delivered to the customer. The second stage will represent the balance outstanding and will usually be paid when the customer has paid the factor the amount owing.

Figure 11.7 The debt-factoring process

With invoice discounting, the institution provides a loan based on a proportion of the face value of a business's credit sales outstanding. The amount advanced is usually 75 to 80 per cent of the value of the approved sales invoices outstanding. The business must agree to repay the advance within a relatively short period – perhaps 60 or 90 days. Responsibility for collecting the trade receivables outstanding remains with the business and repayment of the advance is not dependent on the trade receivables being collected. The service charge for invoice discounting is only about 0.2 to 0.3 per cent of sales revenue; much lower that debt factoring, but for a much less comprehensive service.

Invoice discounting is a much more important source of funds to businesses than is factoring. Both factoring and invoice discounting are forms of **asset-based finance** as the trade receivables are, in effect, used as security for the cash advances received by the business.

LONG-TERM VERSUS SHORT-TERM BORROWING

Where it is clear that some form of borrowing is required to finance the business, a decision must be made as to whether long-term or short-term borrowing is more appropriate. There are many factors to be taken into account, which include the following:

- *Matching.* The business may attempt to match the type of borrowing with the nature of the assets held. Thus, long-term borrowing may be used to finance assets that form part of the permanent operating base of the business. These normally include non-current assets and a certain level of current assets. This leaves assets held for a short period, such as current assets used to meet seasonal increases in demand, to be financed by short-term borrowing, which tends to be more flexible in that funds can be raised and repaid at short notice. Figure 11.8 shows this funding division graphically.

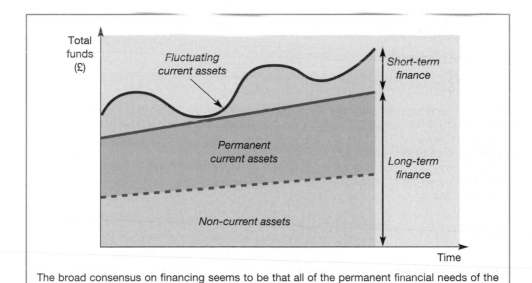

The broad consensus on financing seems to be that all of the permanent financial needs of the business should come from long-term sources. Only that part of current assets that fluctuates in the short term, probably on a seasonal basis, should be financed from short-term sources.

Figure 11.8 Short-term and long-term financing requirements

A business may wish to match the period of borrowing exactly with the asset life. This may not be possible, however, because of the difficulty of predicting the life of many assets.

- *Flexibility.* Short-term borrowing may be used as a means of postponing a commitment to long-term borrowing. Short-term borrowing does not usually incur a financial penalty for early repayment, whereas this may arise if long-term borrowing is repaid early.
- *Refunding risk.* Short-term borrowing has to be renewed more frequently than long-term borrowing. This may create problems for the business if it is in financial difficulties or if there is a shortage of funds available for borrowing.
- *Interest rates.* Interest payable on long-term borrowing is often higher than for short-term borrowing, as lenders require a higher return where their funds are locked up for a long period. This fact may make short-term borrowing a more attractive source of finance for a business. However, there may be other costs associated with borrowing (arrangement fees, for example) to be taken into account. The more frequently borrowings are renewed, the higher these costs will be.

Activity 11.13

Some businesses may take up a less cautious financing position than that shown in Figure 11.8 and others may take up a more cautious one. How would the diagram differ under each of these options?

A less cautious position would mean relying on short-term finance to help fund part of the permanent capital base. A more cautious position would mean relying on long-term finance to help finance the fluctuating assets of the business.

GEARING AND THE FINANCING DECISION

In Chapter 6 we saw that financial gearing (also known as 'leverage') occurs when a business is financed, in part, by contributions from borrowing. We also saw that the level of gearing associated with a business is often an important factor in assessing the risk and returns to ordinary shareholders. In Example 11.1, we consider the implications of making a choice between different levels of financial gearing.

Example 11.1

Blue plc is a newly formed business. Although there is some uncertainty as to the exact amount, operating profit of £40 million a year seems most likely. The business will have long-term finance totalling £300 million, but it has yet to be decided whether to raise:

- all £300 million from £1 ordinary shares (the 'all-equity option'); or
- £150 million from £1 ordinary shares and £150 million from the issue of secured loan notes paying interest at 10 per cent a year (the 'geared option').

The rate of corporation tax is 20 per cent.

It is useful to look at the outcomes, under each financing option, for the shareholders for a range of possible operating profits.

All-equity option

	£m	£m	£m	£m	£m
Operating profit	20.00	30.00	40.00	50.00	60.00
Interest	–	–	–	–	–
Profit before taxation	20.00	30.00	40.00	50.00	60.00
Taxation (20%)	(4.00)	(6.00)	(8.00)	(10.00)	(12.00)
Profit for the year	16.00	24.00	32.00	40.00	48.00
Earnings per share	£0.053	£0.080	£0.107	£0.133	£0.160

Geared option

	£m	£m	£m	£m	£m
Operating profit	20.00	30.00	40.00	50.00	60.00
Interest	(15.00)	(15.00)	(15.00)	(15.00)	(15.00)
Profit before taxation	5.00	15.00	25.00	35.00	45.00
Taxation (20%)	(1.00)	(3.00)	(5.00)	(7.00)	(9.00)
Profit for the year	4.00	12.00	20.00	28.00	36.00
Earnings per share	£0.027	£0.080	£0.133	£0.187	£0.240

Activity 11.14

What do you notice about the earnings per share (EPS) values for each of the two financing options, in the light of different possible operating profits?

The obvious point is that, with the geared option, the EPS values are more sensitive to changes in the level of operating profit. An increase in £10 million from the most likely operating profit of £40 million will increase EPS with the geared option by 41 per cent (from £0.133 to £0.187). With the all-equity option, the increase is only 24 per cent (from £0.107 to £0.133).

Activity 11.15

Given that a £40 million operating profit is the most likely, what advice would you give the shareholders as to the better financing option?

The geared option will give the shareholders £0.026 more EPS and so appears to be more attractive. If the operating profit proves to be greater than £40 million, shareholders would be still better off than under the all-equity option. If, however, the operating profit falls below £40 million, the reduction in EPS would be much more dramatic under the geared option.

Note in Example 11.1 that, with an operating profit of £30 million, the EPS figures are the same irrespective of the financing option chosen (£0.080). This is because the rate of return (operating profit/long-term investment) is 10 per cent. This is the same as the interest rate for the loan notes. Where a business is able to generate a rate of return greater than the interest rate on the borrowings, the effect of gearing is to increase EPS. Where the opposite is the case, the effect of gearing is to decrease EPS.

Activity 11.16

In Chapter 7, we came across *operating gearing*. Is this the same thing as *financial gearing*?

No. Operating gearing is the relationship between fixed and variable costs in the total cost of some activity. Financial gearing is the relationship between the amount of equity and the amount of fixed return finance in the long-term funding of a business.

Activity 11.17

If a business's main activity has high operating gearing, would we expect it also to have high financial gearing?

A business with high operating gearing will find that its operating profit is particularly sensitive to changes in the level of sales revenue. A business with high financial gearing will find that its profit after interest is particularly sensitive to changes in the level of operating profit. Thus, returns to shareholders in a business that has both high operating gearing and high financial gearing will be highly sensitive to changes in the level of sales revenue. To avoid this degree of sensitivity, a business whose activities have high operating gearing will not usually have high financial gearing.

RAISING LONG-TERM FINANCE

We shall now consider ways in which long-term finance may be raised by a business. We begin by looking at various forms of share issue and then go on to examine the role of capital markets.

Share issues

A business may issue shares in a number of ways. These may involve direct appeals to investors or the use of financial intermediaries. The most common methods of share issues are set out in Figure 11.9.

We shall now discuss each of these methods in turn.

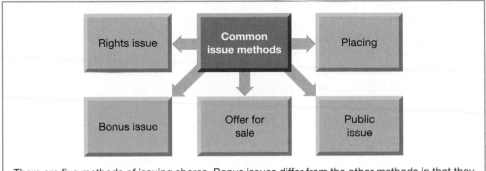

There are five methods of issuing shares. Bonus issues differ from the other methods in that they do not lead to an injection of cash for the business.

Figure 11.9 Common methods of share issue

Rights issues

A **rights issue** can be made by established businesses that seek to raise additional funds by issuing new shares to their existing shareholders. Company law gives existing shareholders the first right of refusal to buy any new shares issued by a company. Hence, new shares should be offered to shareholders in proportion to their existing holding. Only where the existing shareholders agree to waive their right can the shares be offered to other investors.

Rights issues are a fairly common form of share issue. During 2014, they accounted for approximately 22 per cent of all finance raised from share issues by businesses already listed on the London Stock Exchange (see Reference 1 at the end of the chapter). The business (in effect, the existing shareholders) would typically prefer that existing shareholders buy the shares through a rights issue, irrespective of the legal position. This is for two reasons:

- Ownership (and, therefore, control) of the business remains in the same hands; there is no 'dilution' of control.
- Issue costs (advertising, complying with various company law requirements) tend to be lower where new shares are offered to existing shareholders. It is estimated that the average cost of a rights issue is between 2 and 3 per cent of the funds raised. A lot of the cost is fixed and so this percentage will be higher for smaller rights issues and lower for larger rights issues (see Reference 2 at the end of the chapter). This compares with up to 4 per cent for an issue to the public (see Reference 3 at the end of the chapter).

To encourage existing shareholders to take up their 'rights' to buy new shares, they are offered at a price below the current market price of existing shares. Rights shares are typically offered at between 30 and 40 per cent below the current market price (see Reference 4 at the end of the chapter).

In Chapter 4 (Example 4.2, p. 000), the point was made that issuing new shares at below their current value is to the benefit of new shareholders and to the detriment of existing ones. In view of this, does it matter that rights issues are always made below the current value of the shares?

The answer is that it does not matter *in these particular circumstances,* because the existing shareholders and the new shareholders are exactly the same people. Moreover, the shareholders will hold the new shares in the same proportion as they currently hold the existing shares. Thus, shareholders will gain on the new shares exactly as much as they lose on the existing ones: in the end, no one is better or worse off as a result of the rights issue being made at a discount.

Shareholders do not have to buy the rights shares. They can sell their entitlement to these shares to another investor. They can even choose to take up part of their rights entitlement (by buying some of the new shares) and to sell the remaining part.

Calculating the value of the rights offer received by shareholders is quite straightforward, as shown in Example 11.2.

Example 11.2

Shaw Holdings plc has 20 million ordinary shares of 50p in issue. These shares are currently valued on the Stock Exchange at £1.60 per share. The directors have decided to make a one-for-four issue (that is, one new share for every four shares already held) at £1.30 per share.

The first step in the valuation process is to calculate the price of a share following the rights issue. This is known as the *ex-rights price,* and is simply a weighted average of the price of shares before the rights issue and the price of the rights issue shares. In this example, we have a one-for-four rights issue. The theoretical ex-rights price is therefore calculated as follows:

	£
Price of four shares before the rights issue (4 × £1.60)	6.40
Price of taking up one rights share	1.30
	7.70

$$\text{Theoretical ex-rights price} = \frac{£7.70}{5} \qquad = £1.54$$

As the price of each share, in theory, should be £1.54 following the rights issue, and the price of a rights share is £1.30, the value of the rights offer will be the difference between the two:

$$£1.54 - £1.30 = £0.24 \text{ per share}$$

Market forces will usually ensure that the actual and theoretical price of rights shares will be fairly close.

An investor with 2,000 shares in Shaw Holdings plc (see Example 11.2) has contacted you for investment advice. She is undecided whether to take up the rights issue, sell the rights or allow the rights offer to lapse.

Calculate the effect on the net wealth of the investor of each of the options being considered.

Before the rights issue the position of the investor was:

	£
Value of shares (2,000 × £1.60)	3,200

If she takes up the rights issue, she will be in the following position:

	£
Value of holding after rights issue ((2,000 + 500) × £1.54)	3,850
Cost of buying the rights shares (500 × £1.30)	(650)
	3,200

If the investor sells the rights, she will be in the following position:

	£
Value of holding after rights issue (2,000 × £1.54)	3,080
Sale of rights (500 × £0.24)	120
	3,200

If the investor lets the rights offer lapse, she will be in the following position:

	£
Value of holding after rights issue (2,000 × £1.54)	3,080

As we can see, the first two options should leave her in the same position concerning net wealth as before the rights issue. Before the rights issue she had 2,000 shares worth £1.60 each, or £3,200 in total. However, she will be worse off if she allows the rights offer to lapse than under the other two options.

In practice, businesses usually sell the rights on behalf of those shareholders who allow them to lapse. It will then pass on the proceeds to ensure that they are not disadvantaged by the issue.

When considering a rights issue, the directors must first consider the amount of funds needing to be raised. This will depend on the future plans and needs of the business. The directors must then decide on the issue price of the rights shares. Normally, this decision is not critical. In Example 11.2, the business made a one-for-four issue with the price of the rights shares set at £1.30. However, it could have raised the same amount by making a one-for-two issue with the rights price at £0.65, a one-for-one issue with the price at £0.325, and so on. The issue price that is finally decided upon will not affect the value of the underlying assets of the business or the proportion of the underlying assets and earnings to which each shareholder is entitled. The directors must try to ensure that the issue price is not above the current market price of the shares, however, or the issue will be unsuccessful.

Offers for sale and public issues

When a business wishes to sell new shares to the general investing public, it may make an **offer for sale** or a **public issue**. In the case of the former, the shares are sold to an *issuing house* (in effect, a wholesaler of new shares), which then sells them on to potential investors. With the latter, the shares are sold by the business making the share issue direct to potential investors. The advantage of an offer for sale, from the business's viewpoint, is that the sale proceeds of the shares are certain.

In practical terms, the net effect on the business is much the same whether there is an offer for sale or a public issue. As we have seen, the costs of a public issue can be pretty large. Some share issues by Stock Exchange listed businesses arise from the initial listing of the business, often known as an *initial public offering (IPO)*. Other share issues are undertaken by businesses that are already listed and are seeking additional finance from investors; these are usually known as a *seasoned equity offering (SEO)*. IPOs tend to be more widely used than SEOs.

Private placings

A **private placing** does not involve an invitation to the public to subscribe for shares. Instead the shares are 'placed' with selected investors, such as large financial institutions. This can be a quick and relatively cheap way of raising funds, because savings can be made in advertising and legal costs. However, it can result in the ownership of the business being concentrated in a few hands.

Real World 11.9 describes how a placing was used by a well known toy manufacturer to finance more efficient inventories management.

REAL WORLD 11.9

Placed on the right track

During 2015, Hornby plc, which owns the model railway, Scalextric, Airfix and Corgi car brands, made a share placing that raised £15 million. Hornby used the funds raised to establish a new warehouse in Canterbury, with a new inventories control, sales and distribution system.

Hornby used to manufacture its products at a factory in Margate, but moved production to China in the 1990s.

Source: Information taken from Murray Brown, J. (2015) 'Hornby signals third profit warning in three years', ft.com, 10 November.

Placings are used by both newly listed and more seasoned listed businesses. Unlisted businesses may also make this form of issue. During 2014, 95 per cent of the total finance raised from shares issued by companies that were newly listed on the London Stock Exchange came from placings.

Placings are also fairly popular for seasoned offerings (as with the case of Hornby in Real World 11.9). Well over 50 per cent of finance raised by seasoned businesses was through placings. These were much higher percentages than in the recent past (see Reference 1 at the end of the chapter). Placings have comfortably overtaken rights issues in their popularity for seasoned businesses making share issues.

Bonus issues

We should recall from Chapter 4 that a bonus issue is not a means of raising finance. It is simply converting one part of the equity (reserves) into another (ordinary shares). No cash changes hands and there is no direct benefit to either the business or shareholders.

THE ROLE OF THE STOCK EXCHANGE

We have considered the various forms of long-term capital that are available to a business. In this section we shall consider the role that the **Stock Exchange** plays in providing finance for businesses. The Stock Exchange acts as both an important *primary* and *secondary* capital market for businesses. As a primary market, its function is to enable businesses to raise new finance. As a secondary market, its function is to enable investors to sell their securities (including shares and loan notes) with ease. Thus, it provides a 'second-hand' market where shares and loan notes already in issue may be bought and sold.

In order to issue shares or loan notes through the Stock Exchange, or for existing shares and loan notes to be bought and sold through it, a business must become 'listed'. To obtain a listing, a business must meet fairly stringent requirements concerning size, profit history, information disclosure, and so on.

Advantages of a listing

The secondary market role of the Stock Exchange means that shares and other financial claims are easily transferable. Nevertheless, the Stock Exchange is not the only means of transferring shares in a listed business. Existing shareholders could sell their shares directly to other investors. Using the facility offered by the Stock Exchange, however, is usually the most convenient way of buying or selling shares.

The Stock Exchange can be a useful vehicle for a successful entrepreneur wishing to realise the value of the business that has been built up. By successfully floating (listing) the shares on the Stock Exchange, and thereby making the shares available to the public, the entrepreneur can realise the value of the shares held. The 'paper' value of some, or all, of the shares can be turned into cash.

The Stock Exchange is often cited as an example of an **efficient capital market**. This is a market where share prices at all times rationally reflect all available, relevant information.

It implies that any new information coming to light which bears on a particular business and its share price will be taken into account quickly and accurately, in terms of size and direction of share price movement. As a result, the price quoted for a share, at any time, will tend to be the best estimate of its true worth.

Activity 11.20

What benefits might a listed business gain from having its shares efficiently priced?

If shares can easily be sold for prices that tend to reflect their true worth, investors will have more confidence to invest. The business may benefit from this greater investor confidence by finding it easier to raise long-term finance and by obtaining this finance at a lower cost, as investors will view their investment as being less risky.

Disadvantages of a listing

A Stock Exchange listing can have certain disadvantages for a business. These include:

■ Strict rules are imposed on listed businesses, including requirements for levels of financial disclosure additional to those already imposed by International Financial Reporting Standards (for example, the listing rules require that half-yearly financial reports are published).

■ Financial analysts, financial journalists and others tend to monitor closely the activities of listed businesses, particularly larger ones. Such scrutiny may not be welcome, especially if the business is dealing with sensitive issues or is experiencing operational problems.

■ There may be pressure to perform well over the short term. This pressure may detract from undertaking projects that will yield benefits only in the longer term. If the market becomes disenchanted with the business, and the price of its shares falls, this may make it vulnerable to a takeover bid from another business.

■ The costs of obtaining and retaining a listing are huge, which can be a real deterrent for some businesses. To make an initial public offering, a business will rely on the help of various specialists such as lawyers, accountants and bankers. As we have seen, this represents a significant cost to the business.

Although there are over 900 UK businesses listed on the London Stock Exchange, in terms of equity market value, the market is dominated by just a few large ones, as is shown in **Real World 11.10.**

REAL WORLD 11.10

Listing to one side

At 31 January 2016, there were 918 businesses that had a London Stock Exchange Main Market listing. Just 149 of these (16 per cent) accounted for 86 per cent of their total equity market value.

Source: London Stock Exchange (2016), Market Statistics, Table 8 (January).

Real World 11.11 provides an analysis of the ownership of shares in UK listed businesses at the end of 2014.

REAL WORLD 11.11

Ownership of UK listed shares

At the end of 2014, the proportion of shares of UK listed businesses held by various investors was as shown in Figure 11.10.

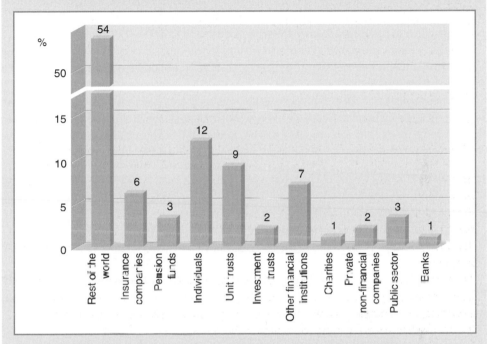

Figure 11.10 Beneficial ownership of UK shares at 31 October 2014

A striking feature of the ownership of UK shares is the extent of overseas ownership. At the end of 2014, this accounted for 54 per cent of the total; in 1963, it was 7 per cent and in 1998, still only 31 per cent. This overseas investors ownership of shares in UK businesses is broadly mirrored by the extent to which UK investors own shares of businesses based elsewhere in the world. It reflects the high level of the globalisation of business.

Another striking feature is the extent to which large financial institutions now dominate the ownership of UK listed shares. In 1963, 58 per cent of those UK shares owned by UK investors were owned by individuals. At the end of 2014, it was only 25 per cent though it had been even lower in recent years.

Information on the types of overseas investors that own UK shares is not available, but it seems reasonable to speculate that the make-up is broadly similar to that of UK investors. This is to say that individuals probably make up a relatively small part of the total and professionally managed funds make up the bulk of it.

Source: Office for National Statistics (2015) Ownership of quoted shares for UK domiciled companies 2014, 2 September. Adapted from data from the office for National Statistics licensed under the open Government License v. 3.0.

Going private

Such are the disadvantages of a stock market listing that many businesses have 'de-listed'. This has obviously denied them the advantages of a listing, but it has avoided the disadvantages.

THE ALTERNATIVE INVESTMENT MARKET

The **Alternative Investment Market (AIM)** was established by the London Stock Exchange to meet the needs of smaller, young and growing businesses. It serves a similar function to the main Stock Exchange in so far that it helps businesses to raise new finance and allows their securities to be traded. It is cheaper for a business to enter AIM than the main Stock Exchange: obtaining an AIM listing and raising funds costs the typical business about £500,000. Furthermore, the listing requirements of AIM are less stringent than those of a full Stock Exchange listing.

Businesses listed on AIM, though generally smaller than those listed on the main market, tend to be large by the standards of the typical small business. Their market values often fall within the range £1 million to £250 million. Some AIM listed businesses, however, have market values greater than £1,000 million, as shown by **Real World 11.12.**

REAL WORLD 11.12

Take AIM

At 31 October 2015, there were 1,056 businesses that had shares that were listed on AIM. Their distribution according to market value is shown in Figure 11.11.

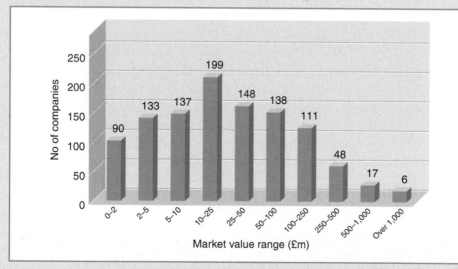

Figure 11.11 Distribution of AIM listed companies by equity market value

The figure shows that few AIM listed businesses (fewer than one in three) have a market capitalisation greater than £50 million. The most popular range is £10 million to £25 million.

Source: London Stock Exchange (2015) Main Market Factsheet (November).

As AIM listed businesses are generally smaller and younger than those on the main Stock Exchange, they tend to be higher-risk investments. Nevertheless, many investors are attracted to this market.

AIM listed companies include Majestic Wine plc, the wine retailer, Asos plc, the online fashion retailer, and Hornby plc, the model railway business that we discussed in Real World 11.9.

PROVIDING LONG-TERM FINANCE FOR THE SMALL BUSINESS

Although the Stock Exchange and AIM provide an important source of long-term finance for larger businesses, they are not really suitable for smaller businesses. In practice, the costs of obtaining and retaining a listing are high, even with AIM. Thus, small businesses must look elsewhere for help in raising long-term finance.

The original owners of smaller businesses provide the vast majority of equity finance. Finance raised from outsiders is normally through loans from banks and credit card businesses (by making business purchases with a credit card). Loans from family and friends also play a part along with leasing and HP finance. **Real World 11.13** shows the main sources of finance for small businesses in the UK.

REAL WORLD 11.13

Small business funding

Bank finance, such as overdrafts and loans, is the main source of external finance for small businesses, as the pie chart in Figure 11.12 shows.

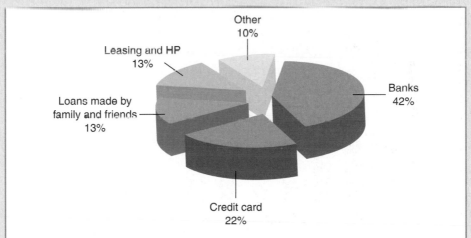

The chart shows the sources of finance other than that provided as equity capital by the owners of the businesses. Borrowing from banks and others provides the overwhelming proportion of this finance. Equity capital provided by venture capitalists, business angels and the like makes up only 1 per cent of the total (included in 'Other').

Source: British Business Bank (2015) 'Small business finance markets 2014'.

Figure 11.12 External financing of small businesses (2012 to 2014)

Where equity finance is provided by 'outside' investors, it will normally be by venture capitalists and business angels.

Venture capital and business angels

Venture capital is long-term capital provided to small and medium-sized businesses that wish to grow but do not have ready access to stock markets. Businesses of interest to the venture capitalist often have higher levels of risk than would normally be acceptable to traditional providers of finance, such as the major clearing banks. The attraction for the venture capitalist of investing in higher-risk businesses is the prospect of higher returns.

The venture capitalist will often make a substantial investment in the business (usually more than £100,000), and this will often take the form of ordinary shares. To monitor the sum invested, the venture capitalist will usually require a representative on the board of directors as a condition of the investment. The venture capitalist may not be looking for a very quick return, and may well be prepared to invest in a business for five years or more. The return may take the form of a capital gain on the realisation of the investment (typically selling the shares).

Business angels are often wealthy individuals who have been successful in business. They are usually willing to invest, through a shareholding, between £10,000 and £750,000 in a start-up business or in a business that is wishing to expand. They normally have a minority stake in the business and, although they do not usually become involved in its day-to-day management, they tend to take an interest, more generally, in the way that the business is managed.

Business angels fill an important gap in the market as the size and nature of investments they find appealing are often not so appealing to venture capitalists. The panellists on the BBC TV programme *Dragons' Den* are business angels.

Although venture capital and business angel finance may be vital to some small businesses, their overall significance as a form of business finance is small.

Government assistance

One of the most effective ways in which the UK government assists small businesses is through the Enterprise Finance Guarantee (EFG) Scheme (formerly the Small Firms Loan Guarantee Scheme). This aims to help small businesses that have viable business plans but lack the security to enable them to borrow. The scheme, which is available for businesses with annual sales revenue of up to £41 million, guarantees:

- 75 per cent of the amount borrowed, for which the borrower pays a premium of 2 per cent on the outstanding borrowing; and
- loans ranging from £1,000 to £1.2 million for a maximum period of ten years.

More recently, in 2013, the UK government set up the British Business Bank (BBB). Its aim is to support economic growth by bringing together public and private funds so as to create a more effective and efficient finance market for small and medium-sized businesses.

As well as taking new initiatives, the Bank has taken over existing commitments of the UK government in the area of financing smaller businesses. The finance can be either in the form of loans or equity finance of the venture capital/business angel type.

In November 2014, the UK government increased its commitment to both EFG and BBB by pledging additional public finance to each of them. EFG is now managed by BBB.

In addition to other forms of financial assistance, such as government grants and tax incentives for investors to buy shares in small businesses, the government also helps by providing information concerning sources of finance available.

Footnote on finance for small businesses

Raising finance has traditionally been seen as a particular area of concern for smaller businesses. Survey evidence of the views of smaller business owners, however, suggests that this is not a particular problem. They expressed the view that it rated only in seventh place in their list of 'obstacles to business success', with only 5 per cent of those surveyed seeing it as a main obstacle. Raising finance was well behind 'the economy', 'competition', 'taxation' and 'red tape' as obstacles to business success (see Reference 5 at the end of the chapter).

ISLAMIC FINANCE

The increasing economic importance of those who follow the Islamic faith has led to greater attention being paid to their needs concerning the financing of businesses. Many of these individuals are citizens of Islamic states, but many others are nationals of the USA and Western European countries, particularly the UK and France.

A key feature of Islamic finance is the belief, based on the teachings of the Islamic holy book (the Quran), that charging pure interest is wrong. This stems from the notion that it is immoral to gain income (in the form of interest) merely because money has been lent. Sharia law, which guides Islamic practice, is not against free enterprise capitalism; it is the lack of risk taking that is the problem. Sharia is, however, also hostile to pure speculation. It is probably fair to say that Sharia looks favourably on profits earned through hard work and enterprise, but shuns gains from pure financing and speculation.

We can see that normal interest-bearing loans to businesses, such as term loans and loan notes, are contrary to Sharia law. All investors, not just equity investors, are required to bear part of the risk associated with operating the business. In recent years, special types of bonds have emerged to meet this requirement. This has enabled Tesco plc, the supermarket business, to make an issue of Sharia-compliant bonds in Malaysia.

Sharia law also forbids investing in businesses that contravene Islamic principles, such as those that produce alcoholic drinks, pornography and tobacco. This is not, however, different in essence from ethical investing practiced by many non-Islamic investors, for example the Church of England.

Helsim Ltd is a wholesaler and distributor of electrical components. The most recent draft financial statements of the business included the following:

Income statement for the year

	£m	£m
Sales revenue		14.2
Opening inventories	3.2	
Purchases	8.4	
	11.6	
Closing inventories	(3.8)	(7.8)
Gross profit		6.4
Administration expenses		(3.0)
Distribution expenses		(2.1)
Operating profit		1.3
Finance costs		(0.8)
Profit before taxation		0.5
Tax		(0.2)
Profit for the period		0.3

Statement of financial position as at the end of the year

	£m
ASSETS	
Non-current assets	
Property, plant and equipment	
Land and buildings	3.8
Equipment	0.9
Motor vehicles	0.5
	5.2
Current assets	
Inventories	3.8
Trade receivables	3.6
Cash at bank	0.1
	7.5
Total assets	12.7
EQUITY AND LIABILITIES	
Equity	
Share capital	2.0
Retained earnings	1.8
	3.8
Non-current liabilities	
Loan notes (secured on property)	3.5
Current liabilities	
Trade payables	1.8
Short-term borrowings	3.6
	5.4
Total equity and liabilities	12.7

Notes:
1 Land and buildings are shown at their current market value. Equipment and motor vehicles are shown at cost less accumulated depreciation.
2 No dividends have been paid to ordinary shareholders for the past three years.

In recent months, trade payables have been pressing for payment. The managing director has therefore decided to reduce the level of trade payables to an average of 40 days outstanding. To achieve this, he has decided to approach the bank with a view to increasing the overdraft (the short-term borrowings comprise only a bank overdraft). The business is currently paying 10 per cent a year interest on the overdraft.

Required:
(a) Comment on the liquidity position of the business.
(b) Calculate the amount of finance required to reduce trade payables, from the level shown on the statement of financial position, to an average of 40 days outstanding.
(c) State, with reasons, how you consider the bank would react to the proposal to grant an additional overdraft facility.
(d) Identify four sources of finance (internal or external, but excluding a bank overdraft) that may be suitable to finance the reduction in trade payables, and state, with reasons, which of these you consider the most appropriate.

The solution to this question can be found at the back of the book on p. 534.

SUMMARY

The main points in this chapter may be summarised as follows:

Sources of finance

- Long-term finance is for at least one year whereas short-term finance is for a shorter period.
- External sources of finance require the agreement of outside parties, whereas internal sources do not.
- The higher the risk associated with a source of finance, the higher the expected return from investors.

Internal sources of finance

- Retained earnings are by far the most important source of new long-term finance (internal or external) for UK businesses.
- Retained earnings are not a free source of finance, as investors will require returns similar to those from ordinary shares.
- Internal sources of short-term finance include tighter control of trade receivables, reducing inventories levels and delaying payments to trade payables.

→

External sources of finance

■ External sources of long-term finance include ordinary shares, preference shares, borrowings, leases, hire purchase agreements and securitisation.

■ From an investor's perspective, ordinary shares are normally the most risky form of investment and provide the highest expected returns to investors. Borrowings (loans) are normally the least risky and provide the lowest expected returns to investors.

■ Loans are relatively low-risk because lenders usually have security for their loan. Loan covenants can further protect lenders.

■ Types of loans include term loans, convertible loan notes, mortgages, eurobonds and deep discount bonds.

■ Convertible loan notes offer the right of conversion to ordinary shares at a specified date and a specified price.

■ Interest rates may be floating or fixed.

■ A finance lease is really a form of lending that gives the lessee the use of an asset over most of its useful life in return for regular payments.

■ A sale-and-leaseback arrangement involves the sale of an asset to a financial institution accompanied by an agreement to lease the asset back to the business.

■ Hire purchase is a form of credit to acquire an asset. Under the terms of a hire purchase agreement, a customer pays for an asset by instalments over an agreed period.

■ Securitisation involves bundling together similar, illiquid assets to provide backing for the issue of bonds.

■ External sources of short-term finance include bank overdrafts, debt factoring and invoice discounting.

■ Bank overdrafts are flexible and cheap but are repayable on demand.

■ Debt factoring and invoice discounting use trade receivables as a basis for borrowing, with the latter more popular because of cost and flexibility.

■ When choosing between long-term and short-term borrowing, important factors include matching the type of borrowing to the type of assets, flexibility, refunding risk and interest rates.

Financial gearing

■ Most businesses have some fixed return element in their long-term financial structures.

■ Financial gearing increases the risk to shareholders.

■ Gearing is beneficial to shareholders because interest payments to lenders are tax-deductible.

Share issues

- Share issues that involve the payment of cash by investors can take the form of a rights issue, public issue, offer for sale or a private placing.

- A rights issue is made to existing shareholders. This is a fairly popular approach to issuing shares. The law requires that shares that are to be issued for cash must first be offered to existing shareholders. Rights issue costs are relatively low.

- A public issue involves a direct issue to the public and an offer for sale involves an indirect issue to the public.

- A private placing is an issue of shares to selected investors. This has become a popular approach to issuing shares, both with businesses new to the market and for seasoned offerings.

- A bonus issue of shares does not involve the receipt of cash in exchange for the shares issued.

The Stock Exchange

- The Stock Exchange is an important primary and secondary market in capital for large businesses. However, obtaining a Stock Exchange listing can have certain drawbacks for a business.

- The Stock Exchange is broadly seen as an *efficient capital market*. This means that new information that becomes publicly available is quickly and accurately reflected in share prices. This helps share prices to reflect the best estimate of their 'true' value.

The Alternative Investment Market (AIM)

- AIM is an important primary and secondary market managed by the London Stock Exchange for smaller, growing businesses. It tends to be a cheaper way for a business to become listed.

Small businesses

- Apart from funds invested by the owners, loans (particularly bank overdrafts and term loans) make up the overwhelming majority of small business financing.

- Venture capital and funds provided by business angels can provide long-term capital for small or medium-sized businesses not listed on the Stock Exchange.

- The government assists small businesses through guaranteeing loans and by providing grants and tax incentives.

- The British Business Bank has been set up, by the government, to support small businesses in their quest for funding by bringing together public and private funds.

→

Islamic finance

■ The teachings of the Islamic faith are opposed to investors receiving pure interest on amounts that are lent to businesses and where risk is not shared; they are also opposed to investors making purely speculative gains.

■ Special types of investment vehicles have been devised to try to ensure that returns to all investors are compliant with Sharia law.

KEY TERMS

For definitions of these terms, see Appendix A.

security p. 419
fixed charge p. 419
floating charge p. 419
loan covenant p. 419
term loan p. 421
loan note p. 422
loan stock p. 422
bond p. 422
Eurobond p. 423
convertible loan note p. 424
financial derivative p. 425
mortgage p. **425**
floating interest rate p. 425
fixed interest rate p. 425
finance lease p. 426
operating lease p. 426
sale and leaseback p. 428

hire purchase p. 429
securitisation p. 430
bank overdraft p. 432
debt factoring p. 433
invoice discounting p. 433
asset-based finance p. 435
rights issue p. 439
offer for sale p. 442
public issue p. 442
private placing p. 442
Stock Exchange p. 443
efficient capital market p. 443
Alternative Investment Market (AIM) p. 446
venture capital p. 448
business angel p. 448

REFERENCES

1 London Stock Exchange, Main Market Factsheet, November 2014, Table 3, page 5.
2 Association of British Insurers (2013) Encouraging equity investment, page 36.
3 Association of British Insurers (2013) Encouraging equity investment, page 24.
4 Association of British Insurers (2013) Encouraging equity investment, page 32.
5 Department of Business, Innovation and Skills (2015) Small business survey 2014, BIS research paper 214, page 7.

FURTHER READING

If you would like to explore the topics discussed in this chapter in more depth, we recommend the following:

Arnold, G. (2012) *Corporate Financial Management,* 5th edn, Pearson, Chapters 11 and 12.

Brealey, R. and Myers, S. (2013) *Principles of Corporate Finance, Global edition,* 11th edn, McGraw-Hill Education, Chapters 13 to 19 and 23 to 25.

Hillier, D., Clacher I., Ross, S., Westerfield, R. and Jordan, B. (2014) *Fundamentals of Corporate Finance,* 2nd European edn, McGraw-Hill Education, Chapters 14 to 16.

McLaney, E. (2014) *Business Finance: Theory and Practice* , 10th edn, Financial Times Prentice Hall, Chapters 8, 9, 11 and 12.

Pike, R., Neale, B. and Linsley, P. (2015) *Corporate Finance and Investment*, 7th edn, Pearson, Chapters 15 and 16.

❓ REVIEW QUESTIONS

Solutions to these questions can be found at the back of the book on pages 547–548.

11.1 What are the potential disadvantages of raising finance through a sale-and-leaseback arrangement?

11.2 Why might a business that has a Stock Exchange listing revert to being unlisted?

11.3 Distinguish between an offer for sale and a public issue of shares.

11.4 Distinguish between invoice discounting and factoring.

✳ EXERCISES

*Exercises 11.1 and 11.2 are basic level. Exercise 11.3 is intermediate level and Exercises 11.4 to 11.5 are advanced level. Those with **coloured numbers** have solutions at the back of the book starting on page 572.*

11.1 Provide reasons why a business may decide to:
  (a) lease rather than buy an asset which is to be held for long-term use;
  (b) use retained earnings to finance growth rather than issue new shares;
  (c) repay long-term borrowings earlier than the specified repayment date.

11.2 H. Brown (Portsmouth) Ltd produces a range of central heating systems for sale to builders' merchants. As a result of increasing demand for the business's products, the directors have decided to expand production. The cost of acquiring new plant and machinery and the increase in working capital requirements are planned to be financed by a mixture of long-term and short-term borrowing.

Required:

(a) Discuss the major factors that should be taken into account when deciding on the appropriate mix of long-term and short-term borrowing necessary to finance the expansion programme.

(b) Discuss the major factors that a lender should take into account when deciding whether to grant a long-term loan to the business.

(c) Identify three conditions that might be included in a long-term loan agreement.

11.3 Devonian plc has the following equity as at 30 November Year 4:

	£m
Ordinary shares 25p fully paid	50.0
General reserve	22.5
Retained earnings	25.5
	98.0

In the year to 30 November Year 4, the operating profit (profit before interest and taxation) was £40 million and it is expected that this will increase by 25 per cent during the forthcoming year. The business is listed on the London Stock Exchange and the share price as at 30 November Year 4 was £2.10.

The business wishes to raise £72 million in order to re-equip one of its factories and is considering two possible financing options. The first option is to make a 1-for-5 rights issue at a discount price of £1.80 per share. The second option is to borrow long-term at an interest rate of 10 per cent a year. If the first option is taken, it is expected that the price/earnings (P/E) ratio will remain the same for the forthcoming year. If the second option is taken, it is estimated that the P/E ratio will fall by 10 per cent of its Year 4 value by the end of the forthcoming year.

Assume a tax rate of 30 per cent.

Required:

(a) Assuming a rights issue of shares is made, calculate:
    (i) the theoretical ex-rights price of an ordinary share in Devonian plc; and
    (ii) the value of the rights for each original ordinary share.

(b) Calculate the price of an ordinary share in Devonian plc in one year's time assuming:
    (i) a rights issue is made; and
    (ii) the required funds are borrowed.
    Comment on your findings.

(c) Explain why rights issues are usually made at a discount.

(d) From the business's viewpoint, how critical is the pricing of a rights issue likely to be?

11.4 Russell Ltd installs and services heating and ventilation systems for commercial premises. The business's most recent statement of financial position and income statement are as follows:

Statement of financial position

	£000
ASSETS	
Non-current assets	
Property, plant and equipment	741.8
Current assets	
Inventories at cost	293.2
Trade receivables	510.3
	803.5
Total assets	1,545.3
EQUITY AND LIABILITIES	
Equity	
£1 ordinary shares	400.0
General reserve	50.2
Retained earnings	382.2
	832.4
Non-current liabilities	
Borrowings – 12% loan notes (repayable in 5 years' time)	250.0
Current liabilities	
Trade payables	199.7
Taxation	128.0
Borrowings – bank overdraft	135.2
	462.9
Total equity and liabilities	1,545.3

Income statement for the year

	£000
Sales revenue	5,207.8
Operating profit	542.0
Interest payable	(30.0)
Profit before taxation	512.0
Taxation (25%)	(128.0)
Profit for the year	384.0

Note:

Dividend paid during the year	153.6

The business wishes to invest in more machinery and equipment to enable it to cope with an upsurge in demand for its services. An additional operating profit of £120,000 a year is expected if an investment of £600,000 is made in plant and machinery.

The directors are considering an offer from venture capitalists to finance the expansion programme. The finance will be made available immediately through either:

- an issue of £1 ordinary shares at a premium on nominal value of £3 a share; or
- an issue of £600,000 10 per cent loan notes at nominal value.

The directors wish to maintain the same dividend payout ratio in future years as in past years whichever method of finance is chosen.

Required:

(a) For each of the financing schemes:
   (i)   prepare a projected income statement for next year;
   (ii) calculate the projected earnings per share for next year;
   (iii) calculate the projected level of gearing as at the end of next year.
(b) Briefly assess both of the financing schemes under consideration from the viewpoint of the existing shareholders.

11.5 Gainsborough Fashions Ltd operates a chain of fashion shops. In recent months the business has been under pressure from its suppliers to reduce the average credit period taken from three months to one month. As a result, the directors have approached the bank to ask for an increase in the existing overdraft for one year to be able to comply with the suppliers' demands. The most recent financial statements of the business are as follows:

Statement of financial position as at 31 May

	£m
ASSETS	
Non-current assets	
Property, plant and equipment	74
Current assets	
Inventories at cost	198
Trade receivables	3
	201
Total assets	275
EQUITY AND LIABILITIES	
Equity	
£1 ordinary shares	20
General reserve	4
Retained earnings	17
	41
Non-current liabilities	
Borrowings – loan notes repayable in just over one year's time	40
Current liabilities	
Trade payables	162
Accrued expenses	10
Borrowings – bank overdraft	17
Taxation	5
	194
Total equity and liabilities	275

Abbreviated income statement for the year ended 31 May

	£m
Sales revenue	740
Operating profit	38
Interest charges	(5)
Profit before taxation	33
Taxation	(10)
Profit for the year	23

A dividend of £23 million was paid for the year.

Notes:

1 The loan notes are secured by personal guarantees from the directors.

2 The current overdraft bears an interest rate of 12 per cent a year.

Required:

(a) Identify and discuss the major factors that a bank would take into account before deciding whether to grant an increase in the overdraft of a business.

(b) State whether, in your opinion, the bank should grant the required increase in the overdraft for Gainsborough Fashions Ltd. You should provide reasoned arguments and supporting calculations where necessary.

Chapter 12

MANAGING WORKING CAPITAL

INTRODUCTION

This chapter considers the factors to be taken into account when managing the working capital of a business. Each element of working capital will be identified and the major issues surrounding them will be discussed. Working capital represents a significant investment for many businesses and so its proper management and control can be vital. We saw in Chapter 10 that an investment in working capital is typically an important aspect of many new investment proposals.

Learning outcomes

When you have completed this chapter, you should be able to:

- identify the main elements of working capital;

- discuss the purpose of working capital and the nature of the working capital cycle;

- explain the importance of establishing policies for the control of working capital;

- explain the factors that have to be taken into account when managing each element of working capital.

WHAT IS WORKING CAPITAL?

Working capital is usually defined as current assets less current liabilities. The major elements of current assets are:

- inventories;
- trade receivables; and
- cash (in hand and at bank).

The major elements of current liabilities are:

- trade payables; and
- bank overdrafts.

The size and composition of working capital can vary between industries. For some types of business, the investment in working capital can be substantial. A manufacturing business, for example, will often be heavily invested in raw material, work in progress and finished goods. It will also normally sell its goods on credit, giving rise to trade receivables. A retailer, on the other hand, holds only one form of inventories (finished goods) and will normally sell its goods for cash rather than on credit. Many service businesses hold no inventories. Few, if any, businesses operate without a cash balance. In some cases, however, it is a negative one (a bank overdraft). Most businesses buy goods and/or services on credit, giving rise to trade payables.

The amount and composition of working capital can also vary between businesses of similar size within the same industry. This may reflect different approaches towards the management of working capital and its individual elements, which, in turn, is often linked to different attitudes towards risk.

Working capital represents a net investment in short-term assets. These assets are continually flowing into and out of the business and are essential for day-to-day operations. The various elements of working capital are interrelated and can be seen as part of a short-term cycle. For a manufacturing business, the working capital cycle can be depicted as shown in Figure 12.1.

For a retailer, the situation would be as in Figure 12.1 except that there will be only inventories of finished goods. There will be no work in progress or raw materials. For a purely service business, the working capital cycle would also be similar to that depicted in Figure 12.1 except that there would be no inventories of finished goods or raw materials. There may well be work in progress, however, since many forms of service take time to complete. A case handled by a firm of solicitors, for example, may take several months. During this period, costs will build up before the client is billed for them.

Managing working capital

The management of working capital is an essential part of the business's short-term planning and control process. Management must decide how much of each element should be held. As we shall see later, there are costs associated with holding either too much or too little of each element. In order to manage working capital effectively, management must be aware of these costs, which include opportunity costs. Potential benefits must then be weighed against likely costs in an attempt to achieve the optimum level of each working capital element.

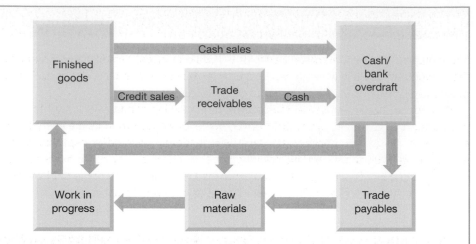

Cash is used to pay trade payables for raw materials, or raw materials are bought for immediate cash settlement. Cash is also spent on labour and other items that turn raw materials into work in progress and, finally, into finished goods. The finished goods are sold to customers either for cash or on credit. In the case of credit customers, there will be a delay before the cash is received from the sales. Receipt of cash completes the cycle.

Figure 12.1 The working capital cycle

The working capital needs of a business may vary over time as a result of changes in the business environment. These changes should be constantly monitored to ensure that the business retains an appropriate level of investment in working capital.

Activity 12.1

What kinds of changes in the business environment might lead to altering the level of investment in working capital? Try to identify at least two changes that could affect the working capital needs of a business.

These may include the following:

- changes in interest rates;
- changes in market demand for the business's output;
- changes in the seasons; and
- changes in the state of the economy.

You may have thought of others.

Changes arising within the business could also alter working capital needs. These internal changes might include using different production methods (resulting, perhaps, in a need to hold a lower level of inventories) and changes in the level of risk that managers are prepared to take.

THE SCALE OF WORKING CAPITAL

It is tempting to think that, compared with the scale of investment in non-current assets, the amounts invested in working capital are trivial. However, this is not the case. For many businesses, the scale of investment in working capital is vast.

Real World 12.1 gives some impression of the working capital investment for five UK businesses that are either very well known by name, or whose products are everyday commodities for most of us. These businesses were randomly selected, except that each one is high profile and from a different industry. For each business, the major items appearing on the statement of financial position are expressed as a percentage of the total investment by the providers of long-term finance (equity and non-current liabilities).

REAL WORLD 12.1

A summary of the statements of financial position of five UK businesses

Business:	Next plc	Ryanair Holdings plc	Babcock Int Group plc	Tesco plc	Severn Trent plc
Statement of financial position date:	24.1.15	31.3.15	31.3.15	28.2.15	31.3.15
Non-current assets	40	73	105	132	103
Current assets					
Inventories	30	–	4	12	–
Trade and other receivables	60	1	17	9	7
Other current assets	6	10	1	17	2
Cash and near cash	20	54	3	11	3
	116	65	25	49	12
Total assets	164	138	130	181	115
Equity and non-current liabilities	100	100	100	100	100
Current liabilities					
Trade and other payables	46	24	27	41	7
Other short-term liabilities	10	9	1	32	1
Overdrafts and short-term borrowings	8	5	2	8	7
	64	38	30	81	15
Total equity and non-current liabilities	164	138	130	181	115

→

The non-current assets, current assets and current liabilities are expressed as a percentage of the total long-term investment (equity plus non-current liabilities) of the business concerned. Next plc is a major retail and home shopping business. Ryanair Holdings plc is a leading airline. Babcock International Group plc is a large engineering and support business. Tesco plc is one of the UK's leading supermarkets. Severn Trent plc is an important supplier of water, sewerage services and waste management, mainly in the UK.

Source: Table constructed from information appearing in the financial statements for the year ended during 2015 for each of the five businesses concerned.

Real World 12.1 reveals quite striking differences in the make-up of the statement of financial position from one business to the next. Take, for example, the current assets and current liabilities. Although the totals for current assets are pretty large when compared with the total long-term investment, these percentages vary considerably between businesses. When looking at the mix of current assets, we can see that only Next, Babcock and Tesco, which produce and/or sell goods, hold significant amounts of inventories. The other two businesses are service providers and so inventories are not a significant item. We can also see that very few of the sales of Tesco, Ryanair and Severn Trent are on credit, as they have relatively little invested in trade receivables.

Note that Tesco's trade payables are much higher than its trade receivables. They are also very high compared to its inventories. Since trade payables represent amounts due to suppliers of inventories, it means that Tesco receives the cash from a typical trolley load of groceries well in advance of paying for them. The relatively large 'Other current assets' and 'Other short-term liabilities' for Tesco arises from advances to and deposits from customers, respectively, that arise from the business's involvement in banking.

In the sections that follow, we consider each element of working capital separately and how they might be properly managed. Before doing so, however, it is worth looking at **Real World 12.2,** which suggests that there is scope for improving working capital management among European businesses.

REAL WORLD 12.2

Working capital not working hard enough

According to a survey of 1,000 of Europe's largest businesses (excluding financial and auto manufacturing businesses), working capital is not as well managed as it could be. The survey, conducted in 2014 by Ernst and Young, suggests that larger European businesses had, in total, between €275 billion and €475 billion tied up in working capital that could be released through better management of inventories, trade receivables and trade payables. The potential for savings represents between 12 per cent and 21 per cent of the total working capital invested and between 3 per cent and 6 per cent of total sales. The lower figure of each range is calculated by comparing the results for each business with the results for the average for the industry, and the higher figure is calculated comparing the results for each business with the upper quartile (that is the best performing 25 per cent of businesses) of the industry within which that business operates.

The report suggests that the higher figure for each range probably represents an ambitious target for savings as there are wide variations in payment terms, customer types, discount practices and so on across Europe.

The average investment (in days) for each of the five years to 2014, by the largest 1,000 European businesses, for each of the main elements of working capital is set out in Figure 12.2. As the figure shows, the average performance, in terms of working capital management, has not altered very much over the four years. Within each average, however, some businesses have improved and some have deteriorated.

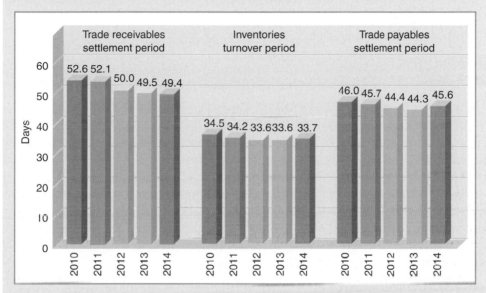

Figure 12.2 Average investment (in days) for the main working capital elements

The survey results suggest that working capital is rather better managed in the USA than it is in Europe.

Source: Compiled from information in Ernst and Young (2015) *All Tied Up: Working Capital Management Report 2015*, www.ey.com.

Real World 12.2 focuses on the working capital problems of large businesses. For smaller businesses, however, these problems may be even more acute.

Activity 12.2

Why might smaller businesses carry more excess working capital than larger ones? Try to think of at least one reason.

Two possible reasons are:

1 Smaller businesses tend to be less well managed than larger ones. They often lack the resources to employ people with the same level of expertise as those employed by larger businesses.

2 Economies of scale may be a factor. For example, a business with twice the sales revenue of a competitor business would not normally need twice the level of inventories.

You may have thought of other reasons.

MANAGING INVENTORIES

A business may hold inventories for various reasons, the most common of which is to meet the immediate day-to-day requirements of customers and production. However, a business may hold more than needed for this purpose where there is a risk that future supplies may be interrupted or scarce. Similarly, if there is a risk that the cost of inventories will increase in the future, a business may buy in larger quantities.

For some businesses, inventories can represent a substantial proportion of total assets held. For example, a car dealership that rents its premises may have nearly all of its assets in the form of inventories. Manufacturers also tend to invest heavily in inventories, as they must hold three different types: raw materials, work in progress and finished goods. Each type represents a particular stage in the production cycle.

For businesses with seasonal demand, the level of inventories held may vary substantially over the year. One such example might be greetings card manufacturers. For those businesses with fairly stable demand, the level of inventories held may vary little throughout the year.

Businesses that hold inventories simply to meet the day-to-day requirements of their customers, and for production, will normally seek to minimise the amount of inventories held. This is because there are significant costs associated with holding inventories. These costs include:

- storage and handling costs;
- the cost of financing the inventories;
- the cost of pilferage and obsolescence; and
- the cost of opportunities forgone in tying up funds in this form of asset.

To gain some impression of the cost involved in holding inventories, **Real World 12.3** estimates the *financing* cost of inventories for five large businesses.

Inventories financing cost

The financing cost of inventories for each of five large businesses, based on their respective opportunity costs of capital, is calculated below.

Business	Type of operations	Cost of capital (a) %	Average inventories held* (b) £m	Financing cost of holding inventories (a) × (b) £m	Operating profit £m	Financing cost as a % of operating profit/(loss) %
Associated British Foods plc	Food producer	12.2**	1,729	210	947	22.2
Babcock International Group plc	Engineering and business support	9.1**	131	11.9	352.3	3.4
Go-ahead Group plc	Transport operator	8.8	16.8	1.5	96.8	1.5
Kingfisher plc	DIY retailer	8.7	2,037	177	652	27.1
J Sainsbury plc	Supermarket	9.0	1,001	90	81	111.1

* Based on opening and closing inventories for the relevant financial period.
** Based on mid-point of range quoted.

We can see that for three of the five businesses, inventories financing costs are significant in relation to their operating profits. The nature of their businesses requires Associated British Foods, Kingfisher and Sainsbury to invest heavily in inventories. J Sainsbury, however, is likely to turn over its inventories more quickly than the other three. (Note that the information in the table for Sainsbury is untypical of that business because it suffered a particularly difficult year of trading for its reporting period ended during 2015.) For Go-ahead, inventories financing costs are not significant. This is because it is a service provider with a much lower investment in inventories.

These figures do not take account of other costs of inventories' holding mentioned earlier, such as the cost of providing secure storage. As these other costs may easily outweigh the costs of finance, the total cost of maintaining inventories may be very high in relation to operating profits.

The five businesses were not selected because they have particularly high inventories' costs but simply because they are among the relatively few that publish their costs of capital.

Source: Annual reports of the businesses for the years ended during 2014 or 2015.

Given that the potentially high cost of holding inventories, it may be tempting to think that a business should seek to hold few or no inventories. There are, however, costs that may arise when the level of inventories is too low.

To help manage inventories, a number of procedures and techniques may be employed. We shall now consider the more important of these.

Budgeting future demand

Preparing appropriate budgets is one of the best ways to ensure that inventories will be available to meet future production and sales requirements. These budgets should deal with each product that the business makes and/or sells. It is important that they are realistic, as they will determine future ordering and production levels. The budgets may be derived in various ways. They may be developed using statistical techniques, such as time series analysis, or may be based on the judgement of the sales and marketing staff.

Financial ratios

One of the ratios that we met in Chapter 6 can be used to help monitor inventories levels: the **average inventories' turnover period ratio**. This ratio is calculated as follows:

$$\text{Average inventories turnover period} = \frac{\text{Average inventories held}}{\text{Cost of sales}} \times 365$$

The ratio provides a picture of the average period for which inventories are held. This can be useful as a basis for comparison. The average inventories turnover period can be calculated for individual product lines as well as for inventories as a whole.

Recording and reordering systems

A sound system of recording inventories movements is a key element in managing inventories. There should be proper procedures for recording inventories purchases and usages. Periodic checks should be made to ensure that the amount of physical inventories held corresponds with what is indicated by the inventories' records.

Clear procedures for the reordering of inventories should also be in place. Authorisation for both the purchase and the issue of inventories should be confined to a few nominated members of staff. This should avoid problems of duplication and lack of coordination. To determine the point at which inventories should be reordered, information will be required concerning the **lead time** (that is, the time between the placing of an order and the receipt of the goods) and the likely level of demand.

Activity 12.4

An electrical wholesaler sells a particular type of light switch. The annual demand for the light switch is 10,400 units and the lead time for orders is four weeks. Demand for the light switch is steady throughout the year. At what level of inventories of the light switch should the business reorder, assuming that it is confident of the information given above?

The average weekly demand for the switch is 10,400/52 = 200 units. During the time between ordering new switches and receiving them, the quantity sold will be 4 × 200 units = 800 units. So the business should reorder no later than when the level held reaches 800 units. This should avoid running out of this inventories item.

For most businesses, there will be some uncertainty surrounding the level of demand, pattern of demand and lead time. To avoid the risk of running out of inventories, a buffer, or safety, inventories level may be maintained. The amount of buffer inventories is a matter of judgement. In forming this judgement, the following should be taken into account:

- the degree of uncertainty concerning demand factors and the lead time;
- the likely costs of running out of the item concerned; and
- the cost of holding the buffer inventories.

The effect of holding a buffer will be to raise the inventories level at which an order for new inventories is placed (the reorder point).

Activity 12.5

Assume the same facts as in Activity 12.4. However, we are also told that the business maintains buffer inventories of 300 units. At what level should the business reorder?

Reorder point = expected level of demand during the lead time *plus* the level of buffer inventories
= 800 + 300 units
= 1,100 units

Carrying buffer inventories will increase the cost of holding inventories. This must, however, be weighed against the cost of running out of inventories, in terms of lost sales, production problems and so on.

Hora plc holds inventories of a particular type of motor car tyre, which is ordered in batches of 1,200 units. The supply lead times and usage rates for the tyres are:

	Maximum	Most likely	Minimum
Supply lead times	25 days	15 days	8 days
Daily usage	30 units	20 units	12 units

The business wishes to avoid completely the risk of running out of inventories.

At what minimum level of inventories should Hora place a new order, such that it can guarantee not to run out?

What is the size of the buffer inventories based on the most likely lead times and usages?

If Hora were to place an order based on the maximum lead time and usage, but only the minimum lead time and usage were actually to occur, what would be the level of inventories immediately following the delivery of the new inventories? What does this inventories figure represent?

To be certain of avoiding running out of inventories, the business must assume a reorder point based on the maximum usage and lead time. This is a reorder point of 750 units (that is, 30 × 25).

The most likely usage during the lead time will only be 300 units (that is, 20 × 15). Thus, the buffer inventories based on most likely usage and lead time is 450 units (that is, 750 − 300).

The level of inventories when a new order of 1,200 units is received, immediately following the minimum supply lead time and minimum daily usage during the lead time, is 1,854 units (that is, 1,200 + 750 − (8 × 12)). This represents the maximum inventories holding for the business.

Levels of control

Deciding on the appropriate level of inventories' control to adopt requires a careful weighing of costs and benefits. This may lead to the implementation of different levels of control according to the nature of the inventories held. The **ABC system of inventories control** is based on the idea of selective levels of control.

A particular business, for example, may find it possible to divide its inventories into three broad categories: A, B and C. Each category will be based on the value of inventories held, as illustrated in Example 12.1.

Categorising inventories, in the way illustrated in Example 12.1, helps to direct management effort to the most important areas. It also helps to ensure that the costs of controlling inventories are proportionate to their value.

Example 12.1

Alascan Products plc makes door handles and door fittings. It makes them in brass, in steel and in plastic. The business finds that brass fittings account for 10 per cent of the physical volume of the finished inventories that it holds, but these represent 65 per cent of the total value. These are treated as Category A inventories. There are sophisticated recording procedures, tight control is exerted over inventories movements and there is a high level of security where the brass inventories are stored. This is economically viable because these inventories represent a relatively small proportion of the total volume.

The business finds that steel fittings account for 30 per cent of the total volume of finished inventories and represent 25 per cent of the total value. These are treated as Category B inventories, with a lower level of recording and management control being applied.

The remaining 60 per cent of the volume of inventories is plastic fittings, which represent the least valuable items, that account for only 10 per cent of the total value of finished inventories held. These are treated as Category C inventories, so the level of recording and management control would be lower still. Applying to these inventories the level of control that is applied to Category A or even Category B inventories would be uneconomic.

Figure 12.3 provides a graphical depiction of the ABC approach to inventories control.

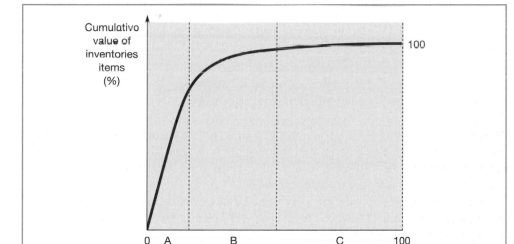

Category A contains inventories that, though relatively few in quantity, account for a large proportion of the total value. Category B inventories consists of those items that are less valuable, but more numerous. Category C comprises those inventories items that are very numerous, but relatively low in value. Different inventories' control rules would be applied to each category. For example, only Category A inventories would attract the more expensive and sophisticated controls.

Figure 12.3 ABC method of analysing and controlling inventories

Inventories' management models

Economic order quantity

Decision models may be used to help manage inventories. The **economic order quantity (EOQ)** model is concerned with determining the quantity of a particular inventories item that should be ordered each time. In its simplest form, the EOQ model assumes that demand is constant. This implies that inventories will be depleted evenly over time to be replenished just at the point that they run out. These assumptions would lead to a 'saw-tooth' pattern to represent inventories' movements, as shown in Figure 12.4.

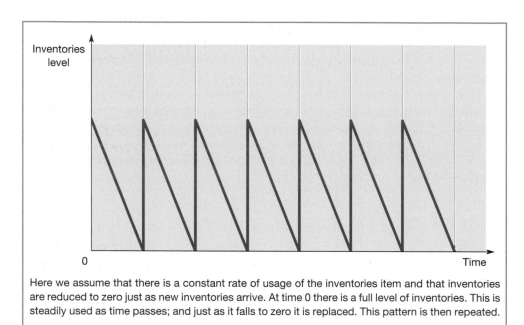

Here we assume that there is a constant rate of usage of the inventories item and that inventories are reduced to zero just as new inventories arrive. At time 0 there is a full level of inventories. This is steadily used as time passes; and just as it falls to zero it is replaced. This pattern is then repeated.

Figure 12.4 Patterns of inventories movements over time

The EOQ model recognises that the key costs associated with inventories' management are the cost of holding the inventories and the cost of ordering them. The cost of holding inventories can be substantial. Management may, therefore, try to minimise the average amount of inventories held and, with it, the holding cost. It will, however, increase the number of orders placed during the period and so ordering costs will rise. The EOQ model seeks to calculate the optimum size of a purchase order that will balance both of these cost elements.

Figure 12.5 shows how, as the level of inventories and the size of inventories orders increase, the annual costs of placing orders will decrease because fewer orders will be placed. However, the cost of holding inventories will increase, as there will be higher average inventories levels. The total costs curve, which is based on the sum of holding costs and ordering costs, will fall until the point E, which represents the minimum total cost. Thereafter, total costs begin to rise. The EOQ model seeks to identify point E, at which total costs are minimised. This will represent half of the optimum amount that should be ordered

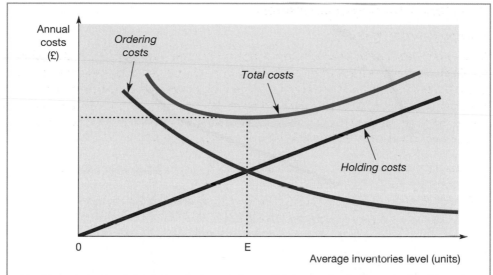

Small inventories' levels imply frequent reordering and high annual ordering costs. Small inventories levels also imply relatively low inventories holding costs. High inventories levels imply exactly the opposite. There is, in theory, an optimum order size that will lead to the sum of ordering and holding costs (total costs) being at a minimum.

Figure 12.5 Inventories holding and order costs

on each occasion. Assuming, as we are doing, that inventories are used evenly over time and that they fall to zero before being replaced, the average inventories level equals half of the order size.

The EOQ model, which can be used to derive the most economic order quantity, is:

$$EOQ = \sqrt{\frac{2DC}{H}}$$

where:

D = the annual demand for the inventories item (expressed in units of the inventories item);

C = the cost of placing an order;

H = the cost of holding one unit of the inventories item for one year.

Activity 12.7

HLA Ltd sells 2,000 bags of cement each year. It has been estimated that the cost of holding one bag of cement for a year is £4. The cost of placing an order for new inventories is estimated at £250.

Calculate the EOQ for bags of cement.

→

Your answer to this activity should be as follows:

$$EOQ = \sqrt{\frac{2 \times 2{,}000 \times 250}{4}} = 500 \text{ bags}$$

This will mean that the business will have to order bags of cement four times each year (that is 2,000/500) in batches of 500 bags so that sales demand can be met.

Note that the cost of inventories, which is the price paid to the supplier, does not directly affect the EOQ model. The model is concerned only with the administrative costs of placing and handling each order and the costs of holding the inventories. However, more expensive inventories items tend to have greater holding costs. This may be because an ABC system of inventories control is in place or because they tie up more finance than less expensive inventories, or both. The cost of inventories may, therefore, have an indirect influence on the economic order size that is calculated.

The basic EOQ model has a number of limiting assumptions. In particular, it assumes that:

- demand for an inventories item can be predicted with accuracy;
- demand is constant over the period and does not fluctuate through seasonality or for other reasons;
- no 'buffer' inventories are required; and
- there are no discounts for bulk purchasing.

The model can, however, be modified to overcome each of these limiting assumptions. Many businesses use this model (or a development of it) to help in the management of inventories.

Activity 12.8

Petrov plc sells 10,000 tonnes of sand each year and demand is constant over time. The purchase cost of each tonne is £15 and the cost of placing and handling an order is estimated to be £32. The cost of holding one tonne of sand for one year is estimated to be £4. The business uses the EOQ model to determine the appropriate order quantity and holds no buffer inventories.

Calculate the total annual cost of trading in this product.

The total annual cost will be made up of three elements:

- the cost of purchases;
- the cost of ordering; and
- the cost of holding this item in inventories.

The annual cost of purchases is 10,000 × £15 = £150,000.

The annual cost of ordering is calculated as follows:

The EOQ is:

$$EOQ = \sqrt{\frac{2 \times 10,000 \times 32}{4}} = 400 \text{ tonnes}$$

This will mean that 10,000/400 = 25 orders will be placed each year. The annual cost of ordering is therefore 25 × £32 = £800.

The annual cost of holding inventories is calculated as follows:

The average quantity of inventories held will be half the optimum order size, as mentioned earlier. That is, 400/2 = 200 tonnes.

The annual holding cost is therefore 200 × £4 = £800.

The total annual cost of trading in this product is therefore:£150,000 + £800 + £800 = £151,600*

* Note that the annual ordering cost and annual holding cost are the same. This is no coincidence. If we look back at Figure 12.5 we can see that the economic order quantity represents the point at which total costs are minimised. At this point, annual order costs and annual holding costs are equal.

Just-in-time inventories management

In recent years, many businesses have tried to eliminate the need to hold inventories by adopting **just-in-time (JIT) inventories management**. This approach was originally used in the US defence industry during the Second World War, but was first used on a wide scale by Japanese manufacturing businesses. The essence of JIT is, as the name suggests, to have supplies delivered to the business just in time for them to be used in the production process or in a sale. The effect of adopting this approach can be that the inventories holding cost shifts from the business itself to the suppliers. A failure by a particular supplier to deliver on time, however, could cause enormous problems and costs to the business. Thus JIT may save cost, but it tends to increase risk.

For JIT to be successful, there needs to be a close relationship between a business and its suppliers. It is important that a business informs suppliers of its inventories' requirements in advance so that suppliers can schedule their own production to that of the business. Suppliers must then deliver materials of the right quality at the agreed times. Any delivery failures could lead to a dislocation of production and could be very costly. Successful JIT tends to require that suppliers are geographically near to the business.

Superlec plc makes electrical appliances. One of its major component suppliers is Technicalities Ltd. The two businesses have recently established a comprehensive JIT relationship.

Would you expect that the *total* inventories held between the two businesses to:

■ increase,
■ reduce, or
■ stay the same

as a result of the change of relationship?

The close working relationship required by JIT requires should lead to a reduction in the total amount of inventories between the two businesses. Knowing Superlec's inventories, requirements should help Technicalities to schedule its own production and inventories to those requirements.

Adopting JIT may well require re-engineering a business's production process. To ensure that orders are quickly fulfilled, factory production must be flexible and responsive. This may require changes to both the production layout and to working practices. Production flows may have to be redesigned and employees may have to be given greater responsibility and allow them to deal with unanticipated problems and encourage greater commitment. Information systems must also be installed that facilitate an uninterrupted production flow.

Although a business that applies JIT will not have to hold inventories, there may be other costs associated with this approach. For example, the close relationship necessary between the business and its suppliers may prevent the business from taking advantage of cheaper sources of supply that become available. Furthermore, suppliers may need to hold inventories for the customer and so may try to recoup this additional cost through increased prices. As we saw in Activity 12.9, however, the close relationship between customer and supplier should enable the supplier to predict its customers' inventories needs. This means that suppliers can tailor their own production to that of the customer.

JIT is widely viewed as more than simply an inventories control system. The philosophy underpinning this approach is that of *total quality management.* This is concerned with eliminating waste and striving for excellence. There is an expectation that suppliers will always deliver inventories on time and that there will be no defects in the items supplied. There is also an expectation that, for manufacturers, the production process will operate at maximum efficiency. This means that there will be no production breakdowns and the queuing and storage times of products manufactured will be eliminated, as only time spent directly on processing the products is seen as adding value. While these expectations may be impossible to achieve, they can help to create a culture that is dedicated to the pursuit of excellence and quality.

Real World 12.4 shows how a very well-known business operating in the UK uses JIT to advantage.

JIT at Nissan

Nissan Motors UK limited, the UK manufacturing arm of the world famous Japanese car business, has a plant in Sunderland in the north east of England. Here it operates a fairly well-developed JIT system. For example, Calsonic Kansei supplies car exhausts from a factory close to the Nissan plant. It makes deliveries to Nissan once every 30 minutes on average, so as to arrive exactly as they are needed in production. This is fairly typical of all of the 200 suppliers of components and materials to the Nissan plant.

The business used to have a comprehensive JIT system. More recently, however, Nissan has drawn back from its total adherence to JIT. By using only local suppliers it had cut itself off from the opportunity to exploit low-cost suppliers, particularly those located in China. A change in policy has led the business to hold buffer inventories for certain items to guard against disruption of supply arising from sourcing parts from the Far East.

Sources: Information taken from Tighe, C. (2006), 'Nissan reviews just-in-time parts policy', *Financial Times,* 23 October; and Ludwig, C. (2014) Local logistics and engineering partnership at Nissan Europe', *Automotive Logistics,* 5 February.

MANAGING TRADE RECEIVABLES

Selling goods or services on credit will result in costs being incurred by a business. These costs include the costs of credit administration, of bad debts and of opportunities forgone to use the funds for other purposes. However, these costs must be weighed against the benefits of increased sales revenue resulting from the opportunity for customers to delay payment.

Selling on credit is the norm outside the retail industry. When a business offers to sell its goods or services on credit, it must have clear policies concerning:

- which customers should receive credit;
- how much credit should be offered;
- what length of credit it is prepared to offer;
- whether discounts will be offered for prompt payment;
- what collection policies should be adopted; and
- how the risk of non-payment can be reduced.

In this section, we shall consider each of these issues.

Which customers should receive credit and how much should they be offered?

A business offering credit runs the risk of not receiving payment for goods or services supplied. Care must, therefore be taken over the type of customer to whom credit facilities are offered and how much credit is allowed. When considering a proposal from a customer for the supply of goods or services on credit, a business should take a number of factors into account. The following **five Cs of credit** provide a useful checklist.

- *Capital.* The customer must appear to be financially sound before any credit is extended. Where the customer is a business, its financial statements should be examined. Particular regard should be given to the customer's likely future profitability and liquidity. In addition, any major financial commitments (such as outstanding borrowings, capital expenditure commitments and contracts with suppliers) should be taken into account.
- *Capacity.* The customer must appear to have the capacity to pay for the goods acquired on credit. The payment record of the customer to date should be examined to provide important clues. To help further assess capacity, the type of business and the amount of credit required in relation to the customer's total financial resources should be taken into account.
- *Collateral.* On occasions, it may be necessary to ask for some kind of security for goods supplied on credit. When this occurs, the business must be convinced that the customer is able to offer a satisfactory form of security.
- *Conditions.* The state of the industry in which the customer operates, as well as the general economic conditions of the particular region or country, should be considered. The sensitivity of the customer's business to changes in economic conditions can also have an important influence on the ability of the customer to pay on time.
- *Character.* It is important to make some assessment of the customer's character. The willingness to pay will depend on the honesty and integrity of the individual with whom the business is dealing. Where the customer is a business, this will mean assessing the characters of its senior managers as well as their reputation within the industry. The selling business must feel confident that the customer will make every effort to pay any amounts owing.

To help assess the above factors, various sources of information are available. They include:

- *Trade references.* Some businesses ask potential customers to provide references from other suppliers that have extended credit to them. This can be extremely useful where the references provided are truly representative of the opinions of all the customer's suppliers. There is a danger that a potential customer will be selective when giving details of other suppliers, in an attempt to create a more favourable impression than is deserved.
- *Bank references.* It is possible to ask the potential customer for a bank reference. Although banks are usually prepared to supply references, their contents are not always very informative. The bank will usually charge a fee for providing a reference.
- *Published financial statements.* A limited company is obliged by law to file a copy of its annual financial statements with the Registrar of Companies. These are available for public inspection and can provide a useful insight to performance and financial position. Many companies also publish their annual financial statements on their websites or on computer-based information systems.
- *The customer.* Interviews with the directors of the customer business and visits to its premises may be carried out to gain an impression of the way that the customer conducts its business. Where a significant amount of credit is required, the business may ask

the customer for access to internal budgets and other unpublished financial information to help assess the level of risk involved.

- *Credit agencies.* Specialist agencies exist to provide information that can be used to assess the creditworthiness of a potential customer. The information that a credit agency supplies may be gleaned from various sources, including the financial statements of the customer and news items relating to the customer from both published and unpublished sources. The credit agencies may also provide a credit rating for the business. Agencies will charge a fee for their services.
- *Register of County Court Judgments.* Any money judgments given against the business or an individual in a county court will be maintained on the register for six years. This register is available for inspection by any member of the public for a small fee.
- *Other suppliers.* Similar businesses will often be prepared to exchange information concerning slow payers or defaulting customers through an industry credit circle. This can be a reliable and relatively cheap way of obtaining information.

Activity 12.10

It was mentioned above that, although banks are usually prepared to supply references, their contents are not always very informative. Why might this be the case?

If a bank customer is in financial difficulties, the bank may be unwilling to add to its problems by supplying a poor reference. It is worth remembering that the bank's loyalty is likely to be with its customer rather than the enquirer.

Once a customer is considered creditworthy, credit limits for the customer should be established. When doing so, the business must take account of its own financial resources and risk appetite. Unfortunately, there are no theories or models to guide a business when deciding on the appropriate credit limit to adopt; it is really a matter of judgement. Some businesses adopt simple 'rule of thumb' methods based on the amount of sales made to the customer (say, twice the monthly sales figure for the customer) or the maximum the business is prepared to be owed (say, a maximum of 20 per cent of its working capital) by all of its customers.

Length of credit period

A business must determine what credit terms it is prepared to offer its customers. The length of credit offered to customers can vary significantly between businesses. It may be influenced by such factors as:

- the typical credit terms operating within the industry;
- the degree of competition within the industry;
- the bargaining power of particular customers;
- the risk of non-payment;
- the capacity of the business to offer credit; and
- the marketing strategy of the business.

A word of explanation may be helpful with this last point. If, for example, a business wishes to increase its market share, it may decide to be more generous in its credit policy in an attempt to stimulate sales. Potential customers may be attracted by the offer of a longer credit period. However, any such change in policy must take account of the likely costs and benefits arising.

To illustrate this point, consider Example 12.2.

Example 12.2

Torrance Ltd produces a new type of golf putter. The business sells the putter to wholesalers and retailers and has an annual sales revenue of £600,000. The following data relate to each putter produced:

	£
Selling price	40
Variable cost	(20)
Fixed cost apportionment	(6)
Profit	14

The business's cost of capital is estimated at 10 per cent a year.

Torrance Ltd wishes to expand the sales volume of the new putter. It believes that offering a longer credit period can achieve this. The business's average trade receivables settlement period is currently 30 days. It is considering three options in an attempt to increase sales revenue. These are as follows:

	Option		
	1	2	3
Increase in average settlement period (days)	10	20	30
Increase in sales revenue (£)	30,000	45,000	50,000

To help the business to decide on the best option, the benefits of the various options should be weighed against their respective costs. Benefits will be represented by the increase in profit from the sale of additional putters. From the information supplied we can see that the contribution to profit (that is, selling price (£40) less variable costs (£20)) is £20 a putter. This represents 50 per cent of the selling price. So, whatever increase occurs in sales revenue, the additional contribution to profit will be half of that figure. The fixed cost can be ignored in our calculations, as it will remain the same whichever option is chosen.

The increase in contribution under each option will therefore be:

	Option		
	1	2	3
50% of the increase in sales revenue (£)	15,000	22,500	25,000

The increase in trade receivables under each option will be as follows:

	Option		
	1	*2*	*3*
	£	£	£
Projected level of trade receivables:			
40 × £630,000/365 (Note 1)	69,041		
50 × £645,000/365		88,356	
60 × £650,000/365			106,849
Current level of trade receivables:			
30 × £600,000/365	(49,315)	(49,315)	(49,315)
Increase in trade receivables	19,726	39,041	57,534

The increase in receivables that results from each option will mean an additional finance cost to the business.

The net increase in the business's profit arising from the projected change is:

	Option		
	1	*2*	*3*
	£	£	£
Increase in contribution (see above)	15,000	22,500	25,000
Increase in finance cost (Note 2)	(1,973)	(3,904)	(5,753)
Net increase in profits	13,027	18,596	19,247

The calculations show that Option 3 will be the most profitable one.

Notes:
1 If the annual sales revenue totals £630,000 and 40 days' credit is allowed (both of which will apply under Option 1), the average amount that will be owed to the business by its customers, at any point during the year, will be the daily sales revenue (that is, £630,000/365) multiplied by the number of days that the customers take to pay (that is 40). Exactly the same logic applies to Options 2 and 3 and to the current level of trade receivables.
2 The increase in the finance cost for Option 1 will be the increase in trade receivables (£19,726) × 10 per cent. The equivalent figures for the other options are derived in a similar way.

Example 12.2 illustrates the broad approach that a business should take when assessing changes in credit terms. However, by extending the length of credit, other costs may be incurred. These may include bad debts and additional collections costs, which should also be taken into account in the calculations.

Cash discounts

To encourage prompt payment from its credit customers, a business may offer a **cash discount** (or discount for prompt payment). The size of any discount will be an important influence on whether a customer decides to pay promptly.

From the business's viewpoint, the cost of offering discounts must be weighed against the likely benefits in the form of a reduction both in the cost of financing trade receivables and in the amount of bad debts. Example 12.3 shows how this may be done.

Example 12.3

Williams Wholesalers Ltd currently asks its credit customers to pay by the end of the month after the month of delivery. In practice, customers take rather longer to pay; on average 70 days. Sales revenue amounts to £4 million a year and bad debts to £20,000 a year.

It is planned to offer customers a cash discount of 2 per cent for payment within 30 days. Williams estimates that 50 per cent of customers will accept this facility but that the remaining customers, who tend to be slow payers, will not pay until 80 days after the sale. At present the business has an overdraft facility at an interest rate of 13 per cent a year. If the plan goes ahead, bad debts will be reduced to £10,000 a year and there will be savings in credit administration expenses of £6,000 a year.

Should the new credit terms be offered to customers?

Solution

The first step is to determine the reduction in trade receivables arising from the new policy.

		£	£
Existing level of trade receivables	(£4m × 70/365)		767,123
New level of trade receivables:	£2m × 80/365	438,356	
	£2m × 30/365	164,384	(602,740)
Reduction in trade receivables			164,383

The costs and benefits of offering the discount can be set out as follows:

	£	£
Cost and benefits of policy		
Cost of discount (£2m × 2%)		40,000
Less		
Interest saved on the reduction in trade receivables		
(£164,383[*] × 13%)	21,370	
Administration cost saving	6,000	
Cost of bad debts saved (20,000 − 10,000)	10,000	(37,370)
Net cost of policy		2,630

These calculations show that the business will be worse off by offering the new credit terms.

[*] It could be argued that the interest should be based on the amount expected to be received; that is the value of the trade receivables *after* taking account of the discount. However, basing it on the expected receipt figure would not, in this case, alter the conclusion that the business should not offer the new credit terms.

In practice, there is always the danger that a customer may be slow to pay and yet may still take the discount offered. Where the customer is important to the business, it may be difficult to insist on full payment. How might a business overcome this problem?

Instead of allowing customers to deduct a discount, customers who pay promptly can be rewarded separately, say on a three-monthly basis. The reward could be a cash payment to the customer or, perhaps, a credit note. The value of the reward would be equal to the cash discounts earned by each customer during the three months.

Debt factoring and invoice discounting

Trade receivables can, in effect, be turned into cash by either factoring them or having sales invoices discounted. Both are forms of asset-based finance, which involves a financial institution providing a business with an advance up to 80 per cent or more of the value of the trade receivables outstanding. These methods, which seem to be fairly popular approaches to managing receivables, were discussed in Chapter 11.

Credit insurance

It is often possible for a supplier to insure its entire trade receivables, individual customer accounts or the outstanding balance relating to a particular transaction.

Collection policies

A business offering credit must ensure that receivables are collected as quickly as possible so that non-payment risk is minimised and operating cash flows are maximised. Various steps can be taken to achieve this, including the following:

Develop customer relationships

For major customers it is often useful to cultivate a relationship with the key staff responsible for paying sales invoices. By so doing, the chances of prompt payment may be increased. For less important customers, the business should at least identify the key members of staff responsible for paying invoices, who can be contacted in the event of a payment problem.

Publicise credit terms

The credit terms of the business should be made clear in all relevant correspondence, such as order acknowledgements, invoices and statements. In early negotiations with the prospective customer, credit terms should be openly discussed and an agreement reached.

Issue invoices promptly

An efficient collection policy requires an efficient accounting system. Invoices (bills) must be sent out promptly to customers, as must monthly statements. Reminders must also be despatched promptly to customers who are late in paying. If a customer fails to respond to a reminder, the accounting system should alert managers so that a stop can be placed on further deliveries.

Monitor outstanding receivables

Management can monitor the effectiveness of collection policies in a number of ways. One method is to calculate the **average settlement period for trade receivables ratio**. This ratio, is calculated as follows:

$$\textbf{Average settlement period for trade receivables} = \frac{\textbf{Average trade receivables}}{\textbf{Credit sales}} \times \textbf{365}$$

Although this ratio can be useful, it is important to remember that it produces an *average* figure for the number of days for which debts are outstanding. This average may be badly distorted by a few large customers who are very slow, or very fast, payers.

Produce an ageing schedule of trade receivables

A more detailed and informative approach to monitoring receivables may be to produce an **ageing schedule of trade receivables**. Receivables are divided into categories according to the length of time they have been outstanding. An ageing schedule can be produced, on a regular basis, to help managers see the pattern of outstanding receivables. An example of an ageing schedule is set out in Example 12.4.

Example 12.4

Ageing schedule of trade receivables at 31 December

Customer	*Days outstanding*				*Total*
	1 to 30 days	*31 to 60 days*	*61 to 90 days*	*More than 90 days*	
	£	£	£	£	£
A Ltd	12,000	13,000	14,000	18,000	57,000
B Ltd	20,000	10,000	–	–	30,000
C Ltd	–	24,000	–	–	24,000
Total	32,000	47,000	14,000	18,000	111,000

This shows a business's trade receivables figure at 31 December, which totals £111,000. Each customer's balance is analysed according to how long the amount has been outstanding. (This business has just three credit customers.) To help focus management attention, accounts may be listed in order of size, with the largest debts first.

We can see from the schedule,for example, that A Ltd still has £14,000 outstanding for between 61 and 90 days (that is, arising from sales during October) and £18,000 outstanding for more than 90 days (that is, arising from sales during September or even before). This information can be very useful for credit control purposes.

Many accounting software packages now include this ageing schedule as one of the routine reports available to managers. Such packages often have the facility to put customers 'on hold' when they reach their credit limits. Putting a customer on hold means that no further credit sales will be made to that customer until amounts owing from past sales have been settled.

Many businesses use ageing summaries to assess the effectiveness of their receivables collection processes. Increasingly some of these businesses show the end-of-reporting period summary in their annual report.

Identify the pattern of receipts

A slightly different approach to exercising control over receivables is to identify the pattern of receipts from credit sales on a monthly basis. This involves monitoring the percentage of credit sales that are paid in the month of sale and the percentage that is paid in subsequent months. To do this, credit sales for each month must be examined separately. Example 12.5 illustrates this.

Example 12.5

A business made credit sales of £250,000 in June. It received 30 per cent of that amount during June, 40 per cent during July, 20 per cent during August and 10 per cent during September. The pattern of credit sales receipts and amounts owing is:

Pattern of credit sales receipts

	Receipts from June credit sales	Amounts received	Amount outstanding from June sales at month end	Amount outstanding
	£	%	£	%
June	75,000	30	175,000	70
July	100,000	40	75,000	30
August	50,000	20	25,000	10
September	25,000	10	0	0

This information can be used as a basis for control. Budgets may be established for the pattern of cash received from credit sales. The actual pattern can then be compared with the budget pattern of receipts to see whether there is any significant deviation (see Figure 12.6). Where this is the case, managers should consider corrective action.

Answer queries quickly

It is important for relevant staff to deal with customer queries on goods and services supplied quickly and efficiently. Payment is unlikely to be made by customers until their queries have been dealt with.

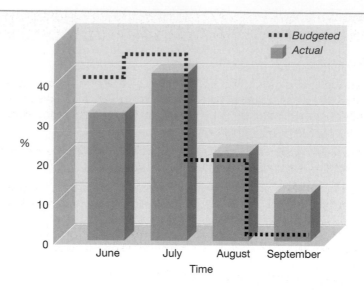

It can be seen that 30 per cent of the sales income for June is received in that month; the remainder is received in the following three months. The expected (budgeted) pattern of cash receipts for June sales, which has been assumed, is also depicted. By comparing the actual and expected pattern of receipts, it is possible to see whether credit sales are being properly controlled and to decide whether corrective action is required.

Figure 12.6 Comparison of actual and expected (budgeted) receipts over time for Example 12.5

Deal with slow payers

A business making significant sales on credit will, almost inevitably, be faced with customers who do not pay. When this occurs, there should be established procedures for dealing with the problem. There should be a timetable for sending out reminders and for adding customers to a 'stop list' for future supplies. The timetable may also specify the point at which the unpaid amount is passed to a collection agency for recovery. These agencies often work on a 'no collection – no fee' basis. Charges for their services vary but can be up to 15 per cent of the amounts collected.

Legal action may also be considered against delinquent credit customers. The cost of such action, however, must be weighed against likely returns. There is little point, for example, in incurring large legal expenses to try to recoup amounts owing if there is evidence that the customer has no money. Where possible, an estimate of the cost of bad debts should be taken into account when setting prices for products or services.

As a footnote to our consideration of managing receivables, **Real World 12.5** outlines some of the excuses that long-suffering credit managers must listen to when chasing payment for outstanding debts.

It's in the post

The Atradius Group provides trade credit insurance and trade receivables collections services worldwide. It has a presence in 40 countries. Its products and services aim to reduce its customers' exposure to buyers who cannot pay for the products and services customers purchase. In a press release Atradius stated:

> Although it happens rarely, some debtors (credit customers) still manage to surprise even us. These excuses have actually been used by credit customers:
>
> - It's not a valid debt as my vindictive ex-wife ran off with the company credit card.
> - I just got back from my luxury holiday, it cost more than I thought so I no longer have the funds to pay.
> - I wanted to pay but all the invoices were in my briefcase, which was stolen on the street.
> - My wife has been kidnapped and I need the money to get her back.

Source: www.atradius.us/news/press-releases, 13 August 2008.

MANAGING CASH

Why hold cash?

Most businesses hold a certain amount of cash. There are broadly three reasons why they do so.

Can you think what these reasons may be?

The three reasons are:

1. *To meet day-to-day commitments.* A business needs a certain amount of cash to pay for wages, overhead expenses, goods purchased and so on, when they fall due. Cash has been described as the lifeblood of a business. Unless it circulates through the business and is available to meet maturing obligations, the survival of the business will be put at risk. Simply being profitable is not enough to ensure survival.
2. *For precautionary purposes.* If future cash flows are uncertain, it would be prudent to hold a balance of cash. For example, a major customer that owes a large sum to the business may be in financial difficulties. This could lead to an expected large receipt not arriving. By holding cash, the business could still retain its capacity to meet its obligations. Similarly, if there is some uncertainty concerning future outlays, a cash balance will be needed.
3. *To exploit opportunities.* A business may decide to hold cash to put itself in a position to exploit profitable opportunities as and when they arise. For example, it may enable the acquisition of a competitor business that suddenly becomes available at an attractive price.

How much cash should be held?

The amount of cash held tends to vary considerably between businesses. The decision as to how much cash a business should hold is a difficult one. Various factors can influence the final decision.

Try to think of four possible factors that might influence the amount of cash that a particular business holds.

You may have thought of the following:

- *The nature of the business.* Some businesses, such as utilities (for example, water, electricity and gas suppliers), have cash flows that are both predictable and reasonably certain. This will enable them to hold lower cash balances. For some businesses, cash balances may vary greatly according to the time of year. A seasonal business may accumulate cash during the high season to enable it to meet commitments during the low season.
- *The opportunity cost of holding cash.* Where there are profitable opportunities in which to invest, either within or outside the business, it may not be economically prudent to hold a large cash balance.
- *The level of inflation.* Holding cash during a period of rising prices will lead to a loss of purchasing power. The higher the level of inflation, the greater will be this loss.
- *The availability of near-liquid assets.* If a business has marketable securities or inventories that may easily be liquidated, a high cash balance may not be necessary.
- *The availability of borrowing.* If a business can borrow easily (and quickly) – for example, through a bank overdraft – there may be less need to hold cash.
- *The cost of borrowing.* When interest rates are high, the option of borrowing becomes less attractive.
- *Economic conditions.* When the economy is in recession, businesses may prefer to hold cash so that they can be well placed to invest when the economy improves. In addition, during a recession, businesses may experience difficulties in collecting trade receivables. They may, therefore, prefer to hold higher cash balances than usual in order to meet commitments.
- *Relationships with suppliers.* Too little cash may hinder the ability of the business to pay suppliers promptly. This can lead to a loss of goodwill. It may also lead to discounts being forgone.

Cash budgets and managing cash

To manage cash effectively, it is useful for a business to prepare a cash budget. This is a very important tool for both planning and control purposes. Cash budgets were considered in Chapter 9 and so we shall not consider them again in detail. However, it is worth repeating that these statements enable managers to see how planned events are expected to affect the cash balance. The cash budget will identify periods when cash surpluses and cash deficits are expected.

When a cash surplus is expected to arise, managers must decide on the best use of the surplus funds. When a cash deficit is expected, managers must make adequate provision by borrowing, liquidating assets or rescheduling cash payments or receipts to deal with this. Cash budgets can help to control the cash held. Actual cash flows can be compared with the planned cash flows for the period. If there is a significant divergence between the planned cash flows and the actual cash flows, explanations must be sought and corrective action taken where necessary.

To refresh your memory on cash budgets it would probably be worth looking back at Chapter 9, pages 340–344.

Operating cash cycle

When managing cash, it is important to be aware of the **operating cash cycle (OCC)** of the business. For a business that purchases goods on credit for subsequent resale on credit, such as a wholesaler, it represents the period between the outlay of cash for the purchase of inventories and the ultimate receipt of cash from their sale. The OCC for this type of business is as shown in Figure 12.7.

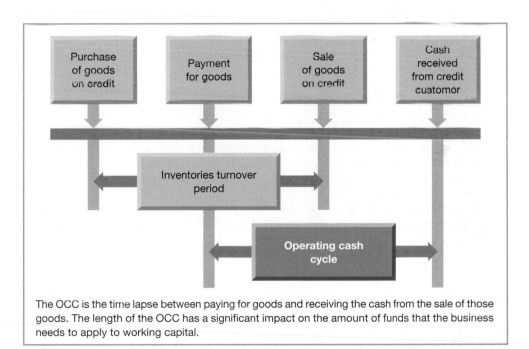

The OCC is the time lapse between paying for goods and receiving the cash from the sale of those goods. The length of the OCC has a significant impact on the amount of funds that the business needs to apply to working capital.

Figure 12.7 The operating cash cycle

Figure 12.7 shows that payment for inventories acquired on credit occurs some time after those inventories have been purchased. Therefore, no immediate cash outflow arises from the purchase. Similarly, cash receipts from credit customers will occur some time after the sale is made so there will be no immediate cash inflow as a result of the sale. The OCC is the period between the payment made to the supplier, for the goods concerned, and the cash received from the credit customer. Although Figure 12.7 depicts the position for a wholesaling business, the precise definition of the OCC can easily be adapted for other types of business.

The OCC is important because it has a significant influence on the financing requirements of the business. Broadly, the longer the cycle, the greater will be the financing requirements and the greater the financial risks. The business may therefore wish to reduce the OCC to the minimum period possible. A business with a short OCC is said to have 'good (or strong) cash flow'.

For businesses that buy and sell goods on credit, the OCC can be deduced from their financial statements through the use of certain ratios. The calculations required are as shown in Figure 12.8.

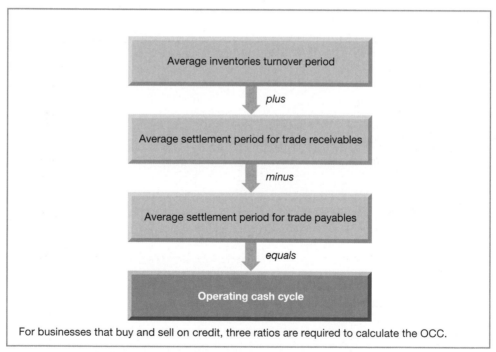

For businesses that buy and sell on credit, three ratios are required to calculate the OCC.

Figure 12.8 Calculating the operating cash cycle

The financial statements of Freezeqwik Ltd, a distributor of frozen foods, for the year ended 31 December last year are:

Income statement for the year ended 31 December last year

	£000	£000
Sales revenue		820
Cost of sales:		
Opening inventories	142	
Purchases	568	
	710	
Closing inventories	(166)	(544)
Gross profit		276
Administration expenses		(120)
Distribution expenses		(95)
Operating profit		61
Financing expenses		(32)
Profit before taxation		29
Taxation		(7)
Profit for the year		22

Statement of financial position as at 31 December last year

	£000
ASSETS	
Non-current assets	
Property, plant and equipment	364
Current assets	
Inventories	166
Trade receivables	264
Cash	24
	454
Total assets	818
EQUITY AND LIABILITIES	
Equity	
Ordinary share capital	300
Retained earnings	352
	652
Current liabilities	
Trade payables	159
Taxation	7
	166
Total equity and liabilities	818

All purchases and sales are on credit. There has been no change in the level of trade receivables or payables over the period.

Calculate the length of the OCC for the business.

The OCC may be calculated as follows:

Number of days

Average inventories turnover period:

$$\frac{\text{(Opening inventories + Closing inventories)/2}}{\text{Cost of sales}} \times 365 = \frac{(142 + 166)/2}{544} \times 365 \qquad 103$$

Average settlement period for trade receivables:

$$\frac{\text{Trade receivables}}{\text{Credit sales}} \times 365 = \frac{264}{820} \times 365 \qquad 118$$

Average settlement period for trade payables:

$$\frac{\text{Trade payables}}{\text{Credit purchases}} \times 365 = \frac{159}{568} \times 365 \qquad \underline{(102)}$$

OCC $\qquad \underline{\underline{119}}$

We can see from the formula above that, if a business wishes to reduce the OCC, it should do one or more of the following:

- reduce the average inventories turnover period;
- reduce the average settlement period for trade receivables; and/or
- increase the average settlement period for trade payables.

Activity 12.15

Assume that Freezequick Ltd (Activity 12.14) wishes to reduce its OCC by 30 days. Evaluate each of the options available to this business.

The average inventories turnover period for the business represents more than three months' sales requirements. Similarly, the average settlement period for trade receivables represents nearly four months' sales. Both periods seem quite long. It is possible that both could be reduced through greater operating efficiency. Improving inventories control and credit control procedures may achieve the required reduction in OCC without any adverse effect on future sales. If so, this may offer the best way forward.

The average settlement period for trade payables represents more than three months purchases. Any decision to extend this period, however, must be given very careful consideration. It is quite long and may already be breaching the payment terms required by suppliers.

There is no reason why the 30 days reduction in the OCC could not come from a combination of altering all three of the periods involved (inventories, trade receivables and trade payables).

Before a final decision is made, full account must be taken of current trading conditions.

It may be that a business wishes to maintain the OCC at a particular target level. However, not all days in the OCC are of equal value. In Activity 12.14, for example, the operating cycle is 119 days. If the average settlement period for both trade receivables and trade payables were increased by seven days, the OCC would remain at 119 days. The amount tied up in working capital, however, would not remain the same. Trade receivables would increase by £15,726 (that is, 7 × £820,000/365) and trade payables would increase by £10,893 (that is, 7 × £568,000/365). This means that there would be a net increase of £4,833 in working capital.

It seems that a number of businesses use the OCC, or a version of it, as a key performance indicator. **Real World 12.6** shows extracts from the annual report of Tate and Lyle, the sugar business.

REAL WORLD 12.6

Cash is sweet

Tate and Lyle plc sees the OCC as a crucial measure of management performance, so much so that it is employed as one of three measures on which senior management bonuses are based (the other two being directly profit related). It seems that many businesses base bonuses on measures of working capital management efficiency.

Tate and Lyle calls the measure the 'cash conversion cycle' (CCC), which it defines as:

The number of days between cash expenditure and collection, taking account of inventory, payables and receivables.

The report goes on to say that the purpose of the CCC is:

Measuring whether the business is managing its working capital and converting profit into cash effectively.

The report also states that the CCC was longer in 2015 than it had been the previous year. The report explains that the CCC:

. . . worsened by eight days primarily as a result of higher inventories and higher receivables.

Source: Tate and Lyle plc, Annual Report 2015, p. 73.

Real World 12.7 shows the average operating cash cycle for large European businesses.

REAL WORLD 12.7

Cycling along

The survey of working capital by Ernst and Young (see Real World 12.2, page 000) calculates the average operating cash cycle for the top 1,000 European businesses (excluding financial and auto manufacturing businesses).

→

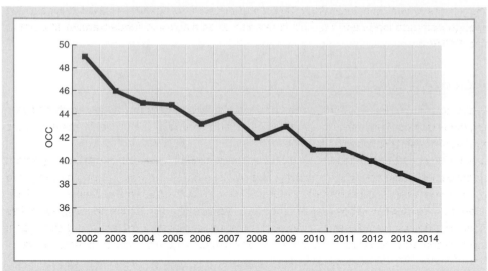

Figure 12.9 The average OCC of large European businesses for 2002 to 2014

The average operating cash cycle has reduced by 21 per cent over the 12 years between 2002 and 2014, with each element of working capital making a contribution to this. The inventories holding period fell by 3 per cent and the trade receivables settlement period fell by 11 per cent, while the trade payables settlement period increased by 7 per cent.

Source: Adapted from Table 2 in Ernst and Young (2014) *All Tied Up: Working Capital Management Report 2014*, p. 6, www.ey.com.

Cash transmission

A business will normally wish to benefit from receipts from customers at the earliest opportunity. Where cash is received, the benefit is immediate. Where payment is made by cheque, there may be a delay before it is cleared through the banking system. The business must therefore wait before it can benefit from the amount paid in. In recent years, the CHAPS (Clearing House Automated Payments) system has helped to reduce the time that cheques spend in the banking system. It is now possible for cheques to be fast tracked so that they reach the recipient's bank account on the same day. Increasingly, however, customers instruct their bank to transfer the amount owed directly to the business's bank account. The transfer is almost immediate and avoids the need to write cheques.

Another way for a business to receive money promptly is for the customer to pay by standing order or by direct debit. Both of these involve the transfer of an agreed sum from the customer's bank account to the business's bank account on an agreed date. Businesses providing services over time, such as insurance, satellite television and mobile phone services, often rely on this method of payment.

A final way in which a business may be paid promptly is through the use of a debit card. This allows the customer's bank account to be charged (debited) and the seller's bank account to be simultaneously increased (credited) with the sale price of the item.

Many types of business, including retailers and restaurants, use this method. It is operated through computerised cash tills and is referred to as electronic funds transfer at point of sale (EFTPOS).

Bank overdrafts

As we saw in Chapter 11, bank overdrafts are simply bank current accounts that have a negative balance. They are a type of bank loan and can be a useful tool in managing the business's cash flow requirements.

Real World 12.8 is based on a major analysis of business working capital management practices undertaken by REL Consulting. The survey shows how Mears Group plc managed to improve its cash flows through better working capital management. Mears is an AIM-listed business that provides maintenance and improvements to social housing, as well as other support services. Most of its work is small scale (that is, involves lots of small jobs) and outsourced to Mears by public-sector organisations. Mears' finance director, Andrew Smith, clearly believes in putting cash to work.

REAL WORLD 12.8

Dash for cash

For a support services business like Mears, which operates a low-value, high-volume business, having an efficient working capital process is absolutely imperative. According to Andrew Smith, 'The difference between success and failure is quite stark in our sector. If you don't have processes that can manage thousands of small jobs, it becomes less about competitive advantage and more of a terminal issue'.

Thankfully for Smith, Mears is one of the better performers in this area. In 2014, it was able to improve its CCC [effectively the operating cash cycle] to such an extent – a staggering 657% improvement on 2013 – that it was able to bank receivables 41 days before payables were due. How was such an improvement achieved? Having an in-house IT system that was 'written by accountants' played its part. 'The cornerstone of our system is that it is accounts-focused,' he explains. 'The business is dealing with thousands of small jobs and we are able to review costs, margins and invoices down to an individual level. The IT system is key to that.'

Many businesses introduce incentive schemes that reward individuals for enforcing strict payment terms and run efficient collection departments. But Smith at Mears says it must run deeper than that. 'If you take your eye off for a week, it can take three months to get it back in line. You have to create a cash culture that goes through every level. The job must only be seen as complete once the invoice has been paid and the cash collected,' he says. 'I work on the basis of getting in people who care about cash culture.'

Source: Extracts from Crump, R. (2015) 'Debt is king: REL working capital survey 2015', *Financial Director*, 20 August.

MANAGING TRADE PAYABLES

Most businesses buy their goods and services on credit. Trade payables are the other side of the coin from trade receivables. In a trade credit transaction, one business's trade payable is another one's trade receivable. Trade payables are an important source of finance for most businesses. They have been described as a 'spontaneous' source, as they tend to increase in line with the increase in the level of activity achieved by a business.

There are potential costs associated with taking trade credit. A business that buys supplies on credit may incur additional administration and accounting costs resulting from the scrutiny and payment of invoices, maintaining and updating payables' accounts, and so on. Furthermore, customers who take credit may not be as well treated as those who pay immediately. When goods are in short supply, they may be given lower priority. They may also be less favoured in terms of delivery dates or in gaining access to technical support. Where credit is required, customers may even have to pay more. In most industries, however, trade credit is the norm. As a result, these disadvantages do not normally apply unless, perhaps, the credit facilities are being abused.

The benefits to be gained from taking credit usually outweigh any costs involved. In effect, it is an interest-free loan from suppliers. It can also provide a more convenient way of paying for goods and services than paying by cash. Furthermore, during a period of inflation, there is an economic gain from paying later rather than sooner for goods and services supplied.

Activity 12.16

Why might a supplier prefer a customer to take a period of credit, rather than pay for the goods or services on delivery? (There are probably two reasons.)

1 Paying on delivery may not be administratively convenient for the seller. Most customers will take a period of credit, so the systems of the seller will be geared up to receive payment after a reasonable period of credit.

2 A credit period can allow any problems with the goods or service supplied to be resolved before payment is made. This might avoid the seller having to make refunds.

Delaying payment to suppliers may be a sign of financial problems. It may also, however, reflect an imbalance in bargaining power. It is not unusual for large businesses to delay payment to small suppliers, which are reliant on them for continuing trade. The UK government has encouraged large businesses to sign up to a 'Prompt Payment Code' to help small suppliers. **Real World 12.9**, however, suggests that not all signatories, including a number of 'household-name' businesses, have entered into the spirit of the Code.

Naming and shaming

The government claimed victory in its drive to name and shame big businesses that fail to commit themselves to fair treatment of suppliers after Diageo, the world's largest drinks company, backed down on a plan to lengthen payment terms. Diageo, which makes Johnnie Walker scotch and Guinness beer, said on Friday it would commit itself to a maximum 60-day term to pay small suppliers in the UK, instead of 90 days.

The commitment comes just weeks after the government strengthened the voluntary Prompt Payment Code, in an effort to crack down on extended payment terms that have provoked anguish from small suppliers that say they cannot afford them. The measures were also backed by the opposition Labour party, which has described late payments as 'a huge drag on the economy'.

Philip King, chief executive of the Chartered Institute of Credit Management, which administers the code, said: 'This is a victory for the code and a very good thing for challenging the whole late payment issue.'

Diageo had risked being the first big business to be struck off from the code, under new powers, he said. In a recent letter to suppliers, Diageo had said that: 'All our new tenders or contract agreements will request 90-day due payment terms as standard [instead of 60 days].' The company said on Friday that this letter had 'caused confusion'.

David Cutter, Diageo's president of supply and procurement, said: 'We fully recognise the importance of SMEs (small and medium-sized enterprises) to the UK economy and to the sustainability of our own business and therefore we will commit to a maximum 60-day term for all SMEs in the UK.' The group could still move to 90-day terms on new contracts with large suppliers.

Matthew Hancock, business minister, said the government was intent on 'stamping out poor payment practices'. 'This is very welcome news from Diageo. It's hugely important that large firms pay their small suppliers promptly — as late payment can create real havoc on a small firm's finances,' he said.

Other food and drinks manufacturers, including Heinz and 2 Sisters Food Group, the UK's biggest Christmas pudding maker, have sought to extend payment terms. The most controversial was Premier Foods, maker of Kipling cakes and Hovis bread, which had told suppliers last year that they could lose the chance of new contracts unless they made cash payments. It later backed down, saying it would revert 'to a more conventional type of discount negotiation'.

The relationship between Tesco and its suppliers is also under investigation. The UK's largest supermarket group could face fines if found guilty of breaches under new powers. Christine Tacon, the Groceries Code Adjudicator, launched the probe — its first — last month, after saying she had formed a 'reasonable suspicion' that the UK's largest retailer had breached the supply code of practice. The investigation is to 'consider the existence and extent of practices which have resulted in delay in payments to suppliers'.

Taking advantage of cash discounts

Where a supplier offers a discount for prompt payment, the business should give careful consideration to the possibility of paying within the discount period. The following example illustrates the cost of forgoing possible discounts.

Example 12.6

Hassan Ltd takes 70 days to pay for goods from its supplier. To encourage prompt payment, the supplier has offered the business a 2 per cent discount if payment for goods is made within 30 days. Hassan Ltd is not sure, however, whether it is worth taking the discount offered.

If the discount is taken, payment could be made on the last day of the discount period (that is, the 30th day). However, if the discount is not taken, payment will be made after 70 days. This means that, by not taking the discount, the business will receive an extra 40 days' (that is, 70 − 30) credit. The cost of this extra credit to the business will be the 2 per cent discount forgone. If we annualise the cost of this discount forgone, we have:

$$365/40 \times 2\% = 18.3\%^*$$

We can see that the annual cost of forgoing the discount is very high. It may, therefore, be profitable for the business to pay the supplier within the discount period, even if it means that it will have to borrow to enable it to do so.

* This is an approximate annual rate. For the more mathematically minded, the precise rate is:

$$\{[(1 + 2/98)^{9.125}] − 1\} \times 100\% = 20.2\%$$

The key difference is that, in this calculation, compound interest is used whereas, in the first calculation, simple interest is used, which is not strictly correct.

Controlling trade payables

To help monitor the level of trade credit taken, management can calculate the **average settlement period for trade payables ratio**. This ratio is calculated as:

$$\text{Average settlement period for trade payables} = \frac{\text{Average trade payables}}{\text{Credit purchases}} \times 365$$

Once again, this provides an average figure, which could be misleading. A more informative approach would be to produce an ageing schedule for payables. This would look much the same as the ageing schedule for receivables described earlier in Example 12.4.

As a footnote to our discussion about the management of working capital, **Real World 12.10** is an extract from an article that makes the point that many businesses do not pay as much attention to it as they should since the rewards in liberating funds tied up are often huge. The article was written by two consultants with the international management consultants, McKinsey and Company.

Uncovering cash

Managing a company's working capital isn't the sexiest task. It's often painstakingly technical. It's hard to know how well a company is doing, even relative to peers; published financial data are too high level for precise benchmarking. And because working capital doesn't appear on the income statement, it doesn't directly affect earnings or operating profit – the measures that most commonly influence compensation (salaries, bonuses and so on). Although working capital management has long been a business-school staple, our research shows that performance is surprisingly variable, even among companies in the same industry.

That's quite a missed opportunity – and it has implications beyond the finance department. Working capital can amount to as much as several months' worth of revenues, which isn't trivial. Improving its management can be a quick way to free up cash. We routinely see companies generate tens or even hundreds of millions of dollars of cash impact within 60 to 90 days, without increasing sales or cutting costs. And the rewards for persistence and dedication to continuous improvement can be lucrative.

The global aluminum company Alcoa made working capital a priority in 2009 in response to the financial crisis and global economic downturn, and it recently celebrated its 17th straight quarter of year-on-year reduction in net working capital. Over that time, the company has reduced its net working capital cycle – the amount of time it takes to turn assets and liabilities into cash – by 23 days and unlocked $1.4 billion in cash. For distressed companies, that kind of improvement can be a lifeline. For healthy companies, the windfall can often be reinvested in ways that more directly affect value creation, such as growth initiatives or increased balance-sheet flexibility. Moreover, the process of improving working capital can also highlight opportunities in other areas, such as operations, supply-chain management, procurement, sales, and finance.

Of course, not all reductions in working capital are beneficial. Too little inventory can disrupt operations. Stretching supplier payment terms can leak back in the form of higher prices, if not negotiated carefully, or unwittingly send a signal of distress to the market. But managers who are mindful of such pitfalls can still improve working capital by setting incentives that ensure visibility, collecting the right data, defining meaningful targets, and managing ongoing performance.

Working capital is often under managed simply because of lack of awareness or attention. It may not be tracked or published in a way that is transparent and relevant to employees, or it may not be communicated as a priority. In particular, working capital is often underemphasized when the performance of a business – and of its managers – is evaluated primarily on income-statement measures such as earnings before interest, taxes, depreciation, and amortization (EBITDA) or earnings per share, which don't reflect changes in working capital.

What actions should managers take, beyond communicating that working capital is important? In our experience, the selection of metrics (measurements) to manage the business and measure performance is especially important, because different metrics will lead to different outcomes. For one manufacturing company, switching from EBITDA to free cash flow as a primary measure of performance had an immediate effect; managers began to measure cash flow at the plant level and then distributed inventory metrics to frontline supervisors. As a result, inventories quickly fell as managers, for the first time, identified and debated issues such as the right level of inventories and coordination among plants.

Source: Extracted from Davies, R. and Merin, D. (2014) 'Uncovering cash and insights from working capital' McKinsey and Company, July, www.mckinsey.com.

? SELF-ASSESSMENT QUESTION 12.1

Town Mills Ltd is a wholesale business. Extracts from the business's most recent financial statements are as follows:

Income statement for the year ended 31 May

	£000
Sales	903
Cost of sales	(652)
Gross profit	251
Other operating expenses	(109)
Operating profit	142
Interest	(11)
Profit before taxation	131
Taxation	(38)
Profit for the year	93

Statement of financial position as at 31 May

	£000
ASSETS	
Non-current assets	
Property, plant and equipment at cost	714
Accumulated depreciation	(295)
	419
Current assets	
Inventories	192
Trade receivables	202
	394
Total assets	813
EQUITY AND LIABILITIES	
Equity	
Ordinary share capital	200
Retained earnings	246
	446
Current liabilities	
Trade payables	260
Borrowings (all bank overdraft)	107
	367
Total equity and liabilities	813

The levels of trade receivables and trade payables increased by 10%, by value, during the year ended 31 May. Inventories levels remained the same. The finance director believes that inventories levels are too high and should be reduced.

Required:

(a) Calculate the average operating cash cycle (in days) during the year ended 31 May and explain to what use this value can be put and what limitations it has.

(b) Discuss whether there is evidence that the company has a liquidity problem.

(c) Explain the types of risk and cost that might be reduced by following the finance director's proposal to reduce inventories levels.

The solution to this question can be found at the back of the book on page 536.

SUMMARY

The main points of this chapter may be summarised as follows.

Working capital

- Working capital is the difference between current assets and current liabilities.
- That is, working capital = inventories + trade receivables + cash − trade payables − short−term borrowings (including bank overdrafts).
- An investment in working capital cannot be avoided in practice − typically large amounts of finance are involved.

Inventories

- There are costs of holding inventories, which include:
  - lost interest;
  - storage cost;
  - insurance cost;
  - obsolescence.
- There are also costs of not holding sufficient inventories, which include:
  - loss of sales and customer goodwill;
  - production dislocation;
  - loss of flexibility − cannot take advantage of opportunities;
  - reorder costs − low inventories imply more frequent ordering.
- Practical points on inventories management include:
  - identify optimum order size − models can help with this;
  - set inventories reorder levels;
  - use budgets;
  - keep reliable inventories records;

- use accounting ratios (for example, inventories turnover period ratio);
- establish systems for security of inventories and authorisation;
- implement just-in-time (JIT) inventories management.

Trade receivables

- When assessing which customers should receive credit, the five Cs of credit can be used:
  - capital;
  - capacity;
  - collateral;
  - condition;
  - character.
- The costs of allowing credit include:
  - lost interest;
  - lost purchasing power;
  - costs of assessing customer creditworthiness;
  - administration cost;
  - bad debts;
  - cash discounts (for prompt payment).
- The costs of denying credit include:
  - loss of customer goodwill.
- Practical points on receivables management:
  - establish a policy;
  - assess and monitor customer creditworthiness;
  - establish effective administration of receivables;
  - establish a policy on bad debts;
  - consider cash discounts;
  - use financial ratios (for example, average settlement period for trade receivables ratio);
  - use ageing summaries.

Cash

- The costs of holding cash include:
  - lost interest;
  - lost purchasing power.

- The costs of holding insufficient cash include:
  - loss of supplier goodwill if unable to meet commitments on time;
  - loss of opportunities;
  - inability to claim cash discounts;
  - costs of borrowing (should an obligation need to be met at short notice).
- Practical points on cash management:
  - establish a policy;
  - plan cash flows;
  - make judicious use of bank overdraft finance – it can be cheap and flexible;
  - use short-term cash surpluses profitably;
  - bank frequently;
  - operating cash cycle (for a wholesaler) = length of time from buying inventories to receiving cash from receivables less payables' payment period (in days);
  - transmit cash promptly.
- An objective of working capital management is to limit the length of the operating cash cycle (OCC), subject to any risks that this may cause.

Trade payables

- The costs of taking credit include:
  - higher price than purchases for immediate cash settlement;
  - administrative costs;
  - restrictions imposed by seller.
- The costs of not taking credit include:
  - lost interest-free borrowing;
  - lost purchasing power;
  - inconvenience – paying at the time of purchase can be inconvenient.
- Practical points on payables management:
  - establish a policy;
  - exploit free credit as far as possible;
  - use accounting ratios (for example, average settlement period for trade payables ratio).

FURTHER READING

If you would like to explore the topics covered in this chapter in more depth, try the following books:

Arnold, G. (2012) *Corporate Financial Management,* 5th edn, Pearson, Chapter 13.

Brealey, R., Myers, S. and Allen, F. (2013) *Principles of Corporate Finance, Global edition,* 11th edn, McGraw-Hill Education, Chapter 30.

Hillier, D., Clacher I., Ross, S., Westerfield, R. and Jordan, B. (2014) *Fundamentals of Corporate Finance,* 2nd European edn, McGraw-Hill Education, Chapter 17.

McLaney E. (2014) *Business Finance: Theory and Practice*, 10th edn, Pearson, Chapters 8, 9, 11 and 12.

Pike, R., Neale, B. and Linsley, P. (2015) *Corporate Finance and Investment,* 8th edn, Pearson, Chapters 13 and 14.

? REVIEW QUESTIONS

Solutions to these questions can be found at the back of the book on pages 548–549.

12.1 Tariq is the credit manager of Heltex plc. He is concerned that the pattern of monthly cash receipts from credit sales shows that credit collection is poor compared with budget. Heltex's sales director believes that Tariq is to blame for this situation, but Tariq insists that he is not. Why might Tariq not be to blame for the deterioration in the credit collection period?

12.2 How might each of the following affect the level of inventories held by a business?

(a) An increase in the number of production bottlenecks experienced by the business.
(b) A rise in the business's cost of capital.
(c) A decision to offer customers a narrower range of products.

(d) A switch of suppliers from an overseas business to a local business.

(e) A deterioration in the quality and reliability of bought-in components.

12.3 What are the reasons for holding inventories? Are these reasons different from the reasons for holding cash?

12.4 Identify the costs of holding:

(a) too little cash; and

(b) too much cash.

 EXERCISES

*Exercises 12.1 and 12.2 are basic level. Exercise 12.3 is intermediate level and Exercises 12.4 and 12.5 are advanced level. Those with **coloured numbers** have solutions at the back of the book starting on page 575.*

12.1 The chief executive officer of Sparkrite Ltd, a trading business, has just received summary sets of financial statements for last year and this year:

Income statements for years ended 30 September

	Last year		This year	
	£000	£000	£000	£000
Sales revenue		1,800		1,920
Cost of sales				
Opening inventories	160		200	
Purchases	1,120		1,175	
	1,280		1,375	
Closing inventories	(200)	(1,080)	(250)	(1,125)
Gross profit		720		795
Expenses		(680)		(750)
Profit for the year		40		45

Statements of financial position as at 30 September

	Last year	This year
	£000	£000
ASSETS		
Non-current assets	950	930
Current assets		
Inventories	200	250
Trade receivables	375	480
Cash at bank	4	2
	579	732
Total assets	1,529	1,662
EQUITY AND LIABILITIES		
Equity		
Fully paid £1 ordinary shares	825	883
Retained earnings	509	554
	1,334	1,437
Current liabilities	195	225
Total equity and liabilities	1,529	1,662

The chief financial officer has expressed concern at the increase in inventories and trade receivables levels.

Required:

(a) Show, by using the data given, how you would calculate ratios that could be used to measure inventories and trade receivables levels during last year and this year.

(b) Discuss the ways in which the management of Sparkrite Ltd could exercise control over the levels of:

(i) inventories; and

(ii) trade receivables.

12.2 Hercules Wholesalers Ltd's managers have been particularly concerned with the business's liquidity position in recent months. The most up-to-date income statement and statement of financial position of the business are as follows:

Income statement for the year ended 31 December last year

	£000	£000
Sales revenue		452
Cost of sales:		
Opening inventories	125	
Purchases	341	
	466	
Closing inventories	(143)	(323)
Gross profit		129
Expenses		(132)
Loss for the year		(3)

Statement of financial position as at 31 December last year

	£000
ASSETS	
Non-current assets	
Property, plant and equipment	357
Current assets	
Inventories	143
Trade receivables	163
	306
Total assets	663
EQUITY AND LIABILITIES	
Equity	
Ordinary share capital	100
Retained earnings	158
	258
Non-current liabilities	
Borrowings – loans	120
Current liabilities	
Trade payables	145
Borrowings – Bank overdraft	140
	285
Total equity and liabilities	663

The trade receivables and payables were maintained at a constant level throughout the year.

Required:

(a) Explain why Hercules Wholesalers Ltd is concerned about its liquidity position.

(b) Calculate the operating cash cycle for Hercules Wholesalers Ltd.

(c) State what steps may be taken to improve the operating cash cycle of the business.

12.3 International Electric plc at present offers its customers 30 days' credit. Half of the customers, by value, pay on time. The other half takes an average of 70 days to pay. The business is considering offering a cash discount of 2 per cent to its customers for payment within 30 days.

The credit controller anticipates that half of the customers who now take an average of 70 days to pay (that is, a quarter of all customers) will pay in 30 days. The other half (the final quarter) will still take an average of 70 days to pay. The scheme will also reduce bad debts by £300,000 a year.

Annual sales revenue of £365 million is made evenly throughout the year. At present the business has a large overdraft (£60 million) with its bank at an interest cost of 10 per cent a year.

Required:

(a) Calculate the approximate equivalent annual percentage cost of a discount of 2 per cent, which reduces the time taken by credit customers to pay from 70 days to 30 days. *(Hint:* This part can be answered without reference to the narrative above.)

(b) Calculate the value of trade receivables outstanding under both the old and new schemes.

(c) How much will the scheme cost the business in discounts?

(d) Should the business go ahead with the scheme?

12.4 Mayo Computers Ltd has annual sales of £20 million. Bad debts amount to £0.1 million a year. All sales made by the business are on credit and, at present, credit terms are negotiable by the customer. On average, the settlement period for trade receivables is 60 days. Trade receivables are financed by an overdraft bearing a 10 per cent rate of interest per year. The business is currently reviewing its credit policies to see whether more efficient and profitable methods could be employed.

Only one proposal has so far been put forward concerning the management of trade credit. This is that customers should be given a $2^1/_2$ per cent discount if they pay within 30 days. For those who do not pay within this period, a maximum of 50 days' credit should be given. The credit department believes that customers who account for 60 per cent of sales will take advantage of the discount by paying at the end of the discount period. The remaining customers will pay at the end of 50 days. The credit department believes that bad debts can be effectively eliminated by adopting the proposed policies and by employing stricter credit investigation procedures, which will cost an additional £20,000 a year. The credit department is confident that these new policies will not result in any reduction in sales revenue.

Required:

Calculate the net annual cost (savings) to the business of abandoning its existing credit policies and adopting the proposals of the credit control department. *(Hint:* To answer this question you must weigh the costs of administration and cash discounts against the savings in bad debts and interest charges.)

12.5 Boswell Enterprises Ltd is reviewing its trade credit policy. The business, which sells all of its goods on credit, has estimated that sales revenue for the forthcoming year will be £3 million under the existing policy. Credit customers, representing 30 per cent of trade receivables, are expected to pay one month after being invoiced and 70 per cent are expected to pay two months after being invoiced. These estimates are in line with previous years' figures.

At present, no cash discounts are offered to customers. However, to encourage prompt payment, the business is considering giving a $2\frac{1}{2}$ per cent cash discount to credit customers who pay in one month or less. Given this incentive, the business expects that credit customers accounting for 60 per cent of trade receivables to pay one month after being invoiced and those accounting for 40 per cent of trade receivables to pay two months after being invoiced. The business believes that the introduction of a cash discount policy will prove attractive to some customers and will lead to a 5 per cent increase in total sales revenue.

Irrespective of the trade credit policy adopted, the gross profit margin of the business will be 20 per cent for the forthcoming year and three months' inventories will be held. Fixed monthly expenses of £15,000 and variable expenses (excluding discounts), equivalent to 10 per cent of sales revenue, will be incurred and will be paid one month in arrears. Trade payables will be paid in arrears and will be equal to two months' cost of sales. The business will hold a fixed cash balance of £140,000 throughout the year, whichever trade credit policy is adopted. Ignore taxation.

Required:

(a) Calculate the investment in working capital at the end of the forthcoming year under:
   (i) the existing policy; and
   (ii) the proposed policy.
(b) Calculate the expected profit for the forthcoming year under:
   (i) the existing policy; and
   (ii) the proposed policy.
(c) Advise the business as to whether it should implement the proposed policy.

(Hint: The investment in working capital will be made up of inventories, trade receivables and cash, *less* trade payables and any unpaid expenses at the year-end.)

Appendix A
GLOSSARY OF KEY TERMS

ABC system of inventories control A method of applying different levels of inventories control, based on the value of each category of inventories. *p. 470*

Absorption costing (or full costing) Deducing the total direct and indirect (overhead) costs of pursuing some activity or objective, in which an appropriate share of the total manufacturing/service provision overhead cost is included. *p. 295*

Accounting The process of identifying, measuring and communicating information to permit informed judgements and decisions by users of the information. *p. 2*

Accounting convention A generally accepted rule that accountants tend to follow when preparing financial statements. It has evolved over time to deal with practical problems rather than to reflect some theoretical ideal. *p. 50*

Accounting information system The system used within a business to identify, record, analyse and report accounting information. *p. 9*

Accounting rate of return (ARR) The average profit from an investment, expressed as a percentage of the average investment made. *p. 372*

Accruals accounting The system of accounting that follows the accruals convention. This system is followed in drawing up the statement of financial position and the income statement. *p. 89*

Accruals convention The convention of accounting that asserts that profit is the excess of revenue over expenses, not the excess of cash receipts over cash payments. *p. 89*

Accrued expenses Expenses that are outstanding at the end of a reporting period. *p. 85*

Acid test ratio A liquidity ratio that relates the liquid assets (usually defined as current assets less inventories) to the current liabilities. *p. 219*

Activity-based costing (ABC) A technique for relating overheads to specific production or provision of a service. It is based on acceptance of the fact that overheads do not just occur but are caused by activities, such as holding products in stores, which 'drive' the costs. *p. 314*

Adverse variance A difference between planned and actual performance, usually where the difference will cause the actual profit to be lower than the budgeted profit. *p. 351*

Ageing schedule of trade receivables A report analysing receivables into categories, according to the length of time outstanding. *p. 484*

Allotted share capital See Issued share capital. *p. 135*

Alternative Investment Market A stock market for the shares of smaller businesses. AIM is a junior market to the main London Stock Exchange market. It is cheaper for a business to enter and has a lighter regulatory regime. *p. 446*

Amortisation A measure of that portion of the cost (or fair value) of an intangible non-current asset that has been consumed during a reporting period. *p. 89*

Asset A resource held by a business that has certain characteristics, such as the ability to provide future benefits. *p. 34*

Asset-based finance A form of finance where assets are used as security for cash advances to the business. Factoring and invoice discounting, where the security is trade receivables, are examples of asset-based financing. *p. 435*

Auditors Independent accountants whose main duty is to make a report to shareholders as to whether, in their opinion, the financial statements of a company show a true and fair view of performance and position and comply with statutory and financial reporting standard requirements. *p. 149*

AVCO *See* Weighted average cost. *p. 99*

Average inventories turnover period ratio An efficiency ratio that measures the average period for which inventories are held by a business. *pp 210, 468*

Average settlement period for trade payables ratio An efficiency ratio that measures the average time taken for a business to pay its trade payables. *pp 212, 498*

Average settlement period for trade receivables ratio An efficiency ratio that measures the average time taken for trade receivables to pay the amounts owing. *p 211, 484*

Bad debt An amount owed to the business that is considered to be irrecoverable. *p. 105*

Balance sheet *See* Statement of financial position. *p. 000*

Bank overdraft A flexible form of borrowing that allows an individual or business to have a negative current account balance. *p. 432*

Batch costing A technique for identifying full cost, where the production of different types of goods or services involves producing a batch of identical or nearly identical units of output, but where each batch is distinctly different from other batches. *p. 309*

Bond *See* Loan note. *pp. 422*

Bonus shares Reserves that are converted into shares and issued 'free' to existing shareholders. *p. 132*

Break-even analysis The activity of deducing the break-even point of some activity by analysing the relationship between cost, volume and revenue. *p. 258*

Break-even chart A graphical representation of the cost and sales revenue of some activity, at various levels, that enables the break-even point to be identified. *p. 259*

Break-even point (BEP) A level of activity where revenue will exactly equal total cost, so there is neither profit nor loss. *p. 259*

Budget A financial plan for the short term, typically one year or less. *p. 330*

Budgetary control Using the budget as a yardstick against which the effectiveness of actual performance may be assessed. *p. 355*

Business angel An individual who supplies finance (usually equity finance) to start-up businesses or small businesses wishing to expand. Usually the amount of finance supplied falls between £10,000 and £750,000. *p. 448*

Business entity convention The convention that holds that, for accounting purposes, the business and its owner(s) are treated as quite separate and distinct. *p. 50*

Called-up share capital That part of a company's share capital for which the shareholders have been asked to pay the agreed amount. It is part of the claim of the owners against the business. *p. 135*

Capital reserves Reserves that arise from an unrealised 'capital' profits or gains, or as a result of issuing new shares at a price above their nominal value, rather than from normal realised trading activities. *p. 130*

Carrying amount The difference between the cost (or fair value) of a non-current asset and the accumulated depreciation relating to the asset. The carrying amount is also referred to as the written-down value (WDV) and the net book value (NBV). *p. 92*

Cash discount A reduction in the amount due for goods or services sold on credit in return for prompt payment. *p. 481*

Claim Obligation on the part of a business to provide cash or some other benefit to outside parties. *p. 34*

Common cost *See* Indirect cost. *p. 294*

Comparability The quality that helps users to make comparisons by treating items that are basically the same in the same way and by making accounting policies clear. It enhances the usefulness of accounting information. *p. 6*

Consistency convention The accounting convention that holds that, when a particular method of accounting is selected to deal with a transaction, this method should be applied consistently over time. *p. 104*

Consolidating Changing the nominal value of shares to a higher figure (from, say, £0.50 to £1.00) and then reducing the number of shares in issue so that each shareholder has the same total nominal value of shares as before. *p. 129*

Contribution margin ratio The contribution from an activity expressed as a percentage of the sales revenue. *p. 265*

Contribution per unit Sales revenue per unit less variable cost per unit. *p. 265*

Control Compelling events to conform to plan. *p. 334*

Convertible loan note A loan note that give investors the right to convert it into ordinary shares at a specified price and a given future date (or range of dates). *p. 424*

Corporate governance Matters concerned with directing and controlling a company. *p. 123*

Corporation tax Taxation that a limited company is liable to pay on its profits. *p. 121*

Cost Amount of resources, usually measured in monetary terms, sacrificed to achieve a particular objective. *p. 249*

Cost-plus pricing An approach to setting prices where a profit margin is added to the full cost to derive the selling price of the product or service. *p. 305*

Cost centre Some area, object, person or activity for which elements of cost are separately collected. *p. 308*

Cost driver An activity that causes cost. *p. 314*

Cost of capital The cost to a business of finance needed to fund its investments. *p. 388*

Cost of sales The cost of the goods sold during a period. Cost of sales can be derived by adding the opening inventories held to the inventories purchases for the period and then deducting the closing inventories held. *p. 77*

Cost pool The sum of the overhead costs that are seen as being caused by the same cost driver. *p. 315*

Cost unit The objective for which the cost is being deduced, usually a product or service. *p. 290*

Creative accounting Adopting accounting policies to achieve a particular view of performance and position that preparers would like users to see rather than what is a true and fair view. *p. 153*

Current asset An asset held for the short term. It includes cash itself and other assets that are held for sale or consumption in the normal course of a business's operating cycle. *p. 43*

Current liability A liability that is expected to be settled within the normal course of the business's operating cycle or within 12 months of the statement of financial position date, or which is held primarily for trading purposes, or for which the business does not have the right to defer settlement beyond 12 months of the statement of financial position date. *p. 46*

Current ratio A liquidity ratio that relates the current assets of the business to the current liabilities. *p. 218*

Debt factoring A service offered by a financial institution (a factor) that involves the factor taking over the management of the trade receivables of the business. The factor is often prepared to make an advance to the business, based on the amount of trade receivables outstanding. *p. 433*

Depreciation A measure of that portion of the cost (or fair value) of a tangible non-current asset that has been consumed during a reporting period. *p. 89*

Direct cost A cost that can be identified with a specific cost unit, to the extent that the effect of the cost can be measured in respect of that cost unit. *p. 294*

Direct method An approach to deducing the cash flows from operating activities, in a statement of cash flows, by analysing the business's cash records. *p. 175*

Directors Individuals who are appointed (normally by being elected by the shareholders) to act as the most senior level of management of a company. *p. 122*

Directors' report A report containing information of a financial and non-financial nature that the directors must produce as part of the annual financial report to shareholders. *p. 151*

Discount factor The rate applied to future cash flows to derive the present value of those cash flows. *p. 386*

Discounting Reducing the value of a cash flow expected to arise at some time in the future to reflect the time value of money. *p. 385*

Dividend The transfer of assets (usually cash) made by a company to its shareholders. *p. 128*

Dividend cover ratio An investment ratio that relates the earnings available for dividends to the dividend announced, to indicate how many times the former covers the latter. *p. 226*

Dividend payout ratio An investment ratio that relates the dividends announced for the period to the earnings available for dividends that were generated in that period. *p. 226*

Dividend yield ratio An investment ratio that relates the cash return from a share to its current market value. *p. 226*

Dual aspect convention The accounting convention that holds that each transaction has two aspects and that each aspect must be recorded in the financial statements. *p. 53*

Earnings per share (EPS) An investment ratio that relates the earnings generated by the business during a period, and available to shareholders, to the number of shares in issue. *p. 227*

Economic order quantity (EOQ) The quantity of inventories that should be bought with each order so as to minimise the sum of inventories ordering and carrying costs. *p. 472*

Efficient capital market A capital market (for example, a Stock Exchange) whose prices rapidly and accurately take account of all relevant information. *p. 443*

Equity The owners' claim on the business. In the case of a limited company, it comprises the sum of the share capital and reserves. *p. 37*

Eurobond A form of long-term borrowing where the finance is raised on an international basis. Eurobonds are issued in a currency that is not that of the country in which the bonds are issued. *p. 423*

Expense A measure of the outflow of assets (or increase in liabilities) incurred as a result of trying to generate revenue. *p. 73*

Fair value The value ascribed to an asset as an alternative to historic cost. It is usually the current market value (that is, the exchange values in an arm's-length transaction). *p. 58*

Faithful representation The ability of information to be relied on to represent what it purports to represent. This is regarded as a fundamental quality of useful accounting information. *p. 5*

Favourable variance The difference between planned and actual performance, usually where the difference will cause the actual profit to be higher than the budgeted profit. *p. 351*

Final accounts The income statement, statement of cash flows and statement of financial position taken together. *p. 33*

Finance The study of how businesses raise funds and evaluate appropriate investments. *p. 2*

Finance lease A financial arrangement where the asset title remains with the owner (the lessor), but the lease agreement transfers virtually all the rewards and risks to the business (the lessee). *p. 426*

Financial accounting The identification, measurement and communication of accounting information for external users (those users other than the managers of the business). *p. 11*

Financial derivative Any form of financial instrument, based on share capital or borrowings, which can be used by investors either to increase their returns or to decrease their exposure to risk. *p. 425*

Financial gearing The existence of fixed-payment-bearing sources of finance (for example, borrowings) in the capital structure of a business. *p. 220*

Financial management *See* Finance. *p. 2*

First in, first out (FIFO) A method of inventories costing that deals with issues of inventories as if the inventories acquired earliest are used (in production or sales) first. *p. 99*

Five Cs of credit A checklist of factors to be taken into account when assessing the creditworthiness of a customer. *p. 478*

Fixed asset *See* Non-current asset. *p. 44*

Fixed charge Where specific assets are pledged as security for a loan. *p. 419*

Fixed cost A cost that stays the same when changes occur to the volume of activity. *p. 254*

Fixed interest rate An interest rate on borrowings that will remain unchanged over the period of the loan, irrespective of rises and falls in market rates of interest. *p. 425*

Flexible budget A budget that is adjusted to reflect the actual level of output achieved. *p. 350*

Flexing the budget Revising a budget to what it would have been had the planned level of output been different. *p. 349*

Floating charge Where all a business's assets, rather than specific assets, are pledged as security for a loan. The charge will only fix on specific assets if the business defaults on its obligations. *p. 419*

Floating interest rate An interest rate on borrowings that will rise and fall with market rates of interest. *p. 425*

Forecast A prediction of future outcomes or of the future state of the environment. *p. 335*

Full cost The total amount of resources, usually measured in monetary terms, sacrificed to achieve a particular objective. *p. 290*

Full costing *See* Absorption costing. *p. 290*

Fully paid shares Shares on which the shareholders have paid the full issue price. *p. 135*

Gearing ratio A ratio that relates long-term fixed-return finance (such as borrowings) to the total long-term finance of the business. *p. 224*

Going concern convention The accounting convention that holds that a business is assumed to continue operations for the foreseeable future, unless there is reason to believe otherwise. In other words, it is assumed that there is no intention, or need, to liquidate the business. *p. 53*

Goodwill An intangible, non-current asset that lacks a clear and separate identity. The term is often used to cover various positive attributes such as the quality of products, the skill of employees and the relationship with customers. *p. 55*

Gross profit The amount remaining (if positive) after the cost of sales has been deducted from trading revenue. *p. 75*

Gross profit margin ratio A profitability ratio that expresses the gross profit as a percentage of the sales revenue for a period. *p. 208*

Hire purchase A method of acquiring an asset by paying the purchase price by instalments over a period. Normally, control of the asset will pass as soon as the hire-purchase contract is signed and the first instalment is paid, whereas ownership will pass on payment of the final instalment. *p. 429*

Historic cost What was paid for an asset when it was originally acquired *p. 249*

Historic cost convention The accounting convention that holds that assets should be recorded at their historic (acquisition) cost. *p. 51*

Impairment loss The loss to be reported following an assessment that the value of an asset has been diminished. *p. 61*

Income statement A financial statement (also known as 'profit and loss account') that measures and reports the profit (or loss) the business has generated during a period. This is derived by deducting from total revenue for a period, the total expenses associated with that revenue. *p. 29*

Indirect cost (or common cost or overheads) The element of production cost (of a product or service) that cannot be directly measured in respect of a particular cost unit – that is, all production cost except direct cost. *p. 294*

Indirect method An approach to deducing the cash flows from operating activities, in a statement of cash flows, by analysing the business's other financial statements. *p. 175*

Intangible asset An asset that does not have a physical substance (for example, patents, goodwill and trade receivables). *p. 37*

Interest cover ratio A gearing ratio that divides the operating profit (that is, profit before interest and taxation) by the interest payable for a period. *p. 224*

Internal rate of return (IRR) The discount rate for an investment that will have the effect of producing a zero NPV. *p. 389*

International Accounting Standards *See* International Financial Reporting Standards. *p. 148*

International Financial Reporting Standards Transnational accounting rules that have been adopted, or developed, by the International Accounting Standards Board and which should be followed in preparing the published financial statements of listed limited companies. *p. 148*

Inventories Products held by a business for trading purposes that are awaiting sale. *p. 62*

Invoice discounting Where a financial institution provides a loan based on a proportion of the face value of a business's credit sales outstanding. *p. 433*

Irrelevant cost A cost that is not relevant to a particular decision. *p. 250*

Issued share capital That part of the share capital that has been issued to shareholders. Also known as 'allotted share capital'. *p. 135*

Job costing A technique for identifying the full cost per cost unit, where each cost unit is not identical to other cost units produced. *p. 293*

Just-in-time (JIT) inventories management A system of inventories management that aims to have supplies delivered just in time for their required use in production or sales. *p. 475*

Last in, first out (LIFO) A method of inventories costing that deals with inventories issues as if the most recently acquired inventories are used (in production or sales) first. *p. 99*

Lead time The time lag between placing an order for goods or services and their delivery to the required location. *p. 469*

Liability A claim of an individual, or organisation, apart from the owner(s), that arises from a past transaction, or event, such as supplying goods or lending money to the business. *p. 37*

Limited company A form of business unit that is granted a separate legal existence from that of its owners. The owners of this type of business are liable for debts only up to the amount that they have agreed to invest. *p. 116*

Limited liability The restriction of the legal obligation of shareholders to meet all of the company's debts. *p. 119*

Limiting factor Some aspect of the business (for example, lack of sales demand) that will prevent it achieving its objectives to the maximum extent. *p. 336*

Loan covenant A condition contained within a loan agreement that is designed to help protect the lenders. *p. 419*

Loan note Long-term borrowing usually made by limited companies. *p. 422*

Loan stock *See* Loan note. *p. 422*

London Stock Exchange A market centred in London where new finance is raised by private businesses and public bodies and where shares and loan notes, already in issue, can be bought and sold. *p. 122*

Management accounting The identification, measurement and communication of accounting information for the managers of a business. *p. 11*

Management by exception A system of control, based on a comparison of planned and actual performance, that allows managers to focus on areas of poor performance rather than dealing with areas where performance is satisfactory. *p. 334*

Margin of safety The extent to which the planned level of output or sales lies above the break-even point. *p. 265*

Marginal analysis The activity of decision making through analysing variable cost and revenue, ignoring fixed cost. *p. 274*

Marginal cost The additional cost of producing one more unit. This is often the same as the variable cost. *p. 274*

Master budget A summary of individual budgets, usually consisting of a budgeted income statement, a budgeted statement of financial position and a cash budget. *p. 336*

Matching convention The accounting convention that holds that expenses should be matched to the revenue, which they helped generate, in the period in which the revenue is reported. *p. 84*

Materiality The quality of accounting information such that its omission or misrepresentation will alter the decisions that users make. The threshold of materiality will vary from one business to the next. *p. 5*

Materiality convention The accounting convention that states that, where the amounts involved are immaterial, only what is expedient should be considered. *p. 88*

Mission statement A brief statement setting out the essence of the business and its ambitions. *p. 330*

Mortgage A loan secured on property. *p. 425*

Net asset turnover ratio *See* Sales revenue to capital employed ratio. *p. 000*

Net book value *See* Carrying amount. *p. 92*

Net present value (NPV) A method of investment appraisal based on the present value of all relevant cash flows associated with an investment. *p. 381*

Nominal value The face value of a share in a company. Also called par value. *p. 127*

Non-current asset An asset held that does not meet the criteria of a current asset. It is held for the long-term operations of the business rather than continuously circulating within the business. It is also known as a 'fixed asset'. *p. 44*

Non-current liability A liability of the business that is not a current liability. *p. 46*

Offer for sale An issue of shares that involves a public limited company (or its shareholders) selling the shares to a financial institution that will, in turn, sell the shares to the public. *p. 442*

Operating cash cycle (OCC) The period between the outlay of cash to buy supplies and the ultimate receipt of cash from the sale of goods. *p. 489*

Operating gearing (operational gearing) The relationship between the total fixed and the total variable elements of cost for some activity. *p. 269*

Operating lease An arrangement where a business hires an asset, usually for a short time. Hiring an asset under an operating lease tends to be seen as an operating, rather than a financing, decision. *p. 426*

Operating profit The profit achieved during a period after all operating expenses have been deducted from revenues from operations. Financing expenses are deducted after the calculation of operating profit. *p. 75*

Operating profit margin ratio A profitability ratio that expresses the operating profit as a percentage of the sales revenue for the period. *p. 206*

Opportunity cost The cost incurred when one course of action prevents an opportunity to derive some benefit from another course of action. *p. 249*

Ordinary shares Portions of ownership of a company owned by those who are due the benefits of the company's activities after all other claims have been satisfied. *p. 128*

Outlay cost A cost that involves the spending of money or some other transfer of assets. *p. 250*

Outsourcing Subcontracting activities to (sourcing goods or services from) organisations outside of the business. *p. 278*

Overhead absorption (recovery) rate The rate at which overheads are charged to cost units (jobs), usually in a job costing system. *p. 299*

Overheads *See* Indirect cost. *p. 294*

Overtrading When a business is operating at a level of activity that cannot be supported by the amount of finance that has been committed. *p. 214*

Paid-up share capital That part of the share capital of a company that has been called and paid. *p. 135*

Par value *See* Nominal value. *p. 127*

Past cost A cost that has been incurred in the past. *p. 250*

Payback period (PP) The time taken for the initial outlay for an investment to be repaid from its future net cash inflows. *p. 377*

Preference shares Shares of a company that entitle their owners to the first part of any dividend that the company may pay. *p. 129*

Prepaid expenses Expenses that have been paid in advance at the end of the reporting period. *p. 87*

Price/earnings ratio An investment ratio that relates the market value of a share to the earnings per share. *p. 229*

Private limited company A limited company for which the directors can restrict the ownership of its shares. *p. 120*

Private placing An issue of shares that involves a limited company arranging for the shares to be sold to the clients of particular issuing houses or stockbrokers, rather than to the general investing public. *p. 442*

Process costing A technique for deriving the full cost per unit of output, where the units of output are exactly similar or it is reasonable to treat them as being so. *p. 293*

Profit The increase in wealth attributable to the owners of a business that arises through business operations. *p. 72*

Profit and loss account *See* Income statement. *p. 000*

Profit before taxation The result (if positive) when all appropriately matched expenses of running a business have been deducted from the revenue for the year, but before the taxation charge is deducted. *p. 140*

Profit for the period The result (if positive) when all appropriately matched expenses of running a business have been deducted from the revenue for the period. In the case of a limited company, the taxation charge for the period is also deducted. *p. 76*

Property, plant and equipment Those non-current assets that have a physical substance (for example, buildings, equipment and fittings and motor vehicles). *p. 44*

Prudence convention The accounting convention that holds that caution should be exercised when making accounting judgements. It normally involves reporting actual and expected losses immediately but reporting profits when they arise. *p. 52*

Public issue An issue of shares that involves a public limited company (plc) making a direct invitation to the public to buy shares in the company. *p. 442*

Public limited company A limited company for which the directors cannot restrict the ownership of its shares. *p. 120*

Reducing-balance method A method of calculating depreciation that applies a fixed percentage rate of depreciation to the carrying amount of an asset in each period. *p. 93*

Relevance The ability of accounting information to influence decisions. Relevance is regarded as a fundamental characteristic of useful accounting information. *p. 5*

Relevant cost A cost that is relevant to a particular decision. *p. 250*

Reporting period The timespan for which a business prepares its financial statements. *p. 41*

Reserves Part of the owners' claim (equity) of a limited company that has arisen from profits and gains and which have not been distributed to the shareholders or reduced by losses. *p. 127*

Residual value The amount for which a non-current asset is expected to be sold when the business has no further use for it. *p. 91*

Return on capital employed ratio (ROCE) A profitability ratio that expresses the operating profit (that is, profit before interest and taxation) as a percentage of the long-term funds (equity and borrowings) invested in the business. *p. 204*

Return on ordinary shareholders' funds ratio (ROSF) A profitability ratio that expresses the profit for the period available to ordinary shareholders as a percentage of the funds that they have invested. *p. 203*

Revenue A measure of the inflow of assets (for example, cash or amounts owed to a business by credit customers), or a reduction in liabilities, arising as a result of trading operations. *p. 72*

Revenue reserve Part of the owners' claim (equity) of a company that arises from realised profits and gains, including after-tax trading profits and gains from disposals of non-current assets. *p. 128*

Rights issue An issue of shares for cash to existing shareholders on the basis of the number of shares already held. *p. 439*

Risk The extent and likelihood that what is projected to occur will not actually occur. *p. 382*

Risk premium The additional return required for investing in a risky project. *p. 383*

Sale and leaseback An agreement to sell an asset (usually property) to another party and simultaneously to lease the asset back in order to continue using the asset. *p. 428*

Sales revenue per employee ratio An efficiency ratio that relates the sales revenue generated during a period to the average number of employees of the business. *p. 215*

Sales revenue to capital employed ratio An efficiency ratio that relates the sales revenue generated during a period to the capital employed. *p. 214*

Securitisation Bundling together illiquid physical or financial assets of the same type to provide backing for issuing interest-bearing securities such as bonds. *p. 430*

Security Assets pledged or guarantees given to provide lenders with some protection against default. *p. 419*

Semi-fixed (semi-variable) cost A cost that has an element of both fixed and variable cost. *p. 258*

Shares Portions of the ownership, or equity, of a company. *p. 116*

Share premium account A capital reserve reflecting any amount paid, above the nominal value of shares, that is paid when the shares are issued by a company. *p. 131*

Splitting Changing the nominal value of shares to a lower figure (from, say, £1.00 to £0.50) and then issuing sufficient shares so that each shareholder has the same total nominal value of shares as before. *p. 129*

Statement of cash flows A statement that shows a business's sources and uses of cash for a period. *p. 29*

Statement of changes in equity A financial statement, required by International Financial Reporting Standards that shows the effect of gains/losses and capital injections/withdrawals on the equity base of a company. *p. 145*

Statement of comprehensive income A financial statement that extends the conventional income statement to include other gains and losses that affect shareholders' equity. *p. 144*

Statement of financial position A statement that shows the assets of a business and the claims on those assets. It is also known as a 'balance sheet'. *p. 29*

Stepped fixed cost A fixed cost that does not remain fixed over all levels of output but which changes in steps as a threshold level of output is reached. *p. 256*

Stock Exchange A market where 'second-hand' shares may be bought and sold and new capital raised. *p. 443*

Straight-line method A method of accounting for depreciation that allocates the amount to be depreciated evenly over the useful life of the asset. *p. 91*

Strategic report A narrative report designed to provide a balanced and comprehensive analysis of financial performance for the year and financial position at the end of the year. The report must also describe the principal risks and uncertainties facing the company. *p. 151*

Tangible asset An asset that has a physical substance (for example, plant and machinery, motor vehicles). *p. 37*

Term loan Finance provided by financial institutions, for example banks and insurance companies, under a contract with the borrowing business that indicates the interest rate and date of payments of interest and repayment of the loan. The loan is not normally transferable from one lender to another. *p. 421*

Timeliness Providing accounting information in time for users to make use of it in their decision making. This quality enhances the usefulness of accounting information. *p. 6*

Trade payable An amount owed to a supplier from whom the business has received goods or services on credit. *p. 39*

Trade receivable An amount outstanding from a customer to whom the business has provided goods or services on credit. *p. 44*

UK Corporate Governance Code A code of practice for companies that are listed on the London Stock Exchange that deals with corporate governance matters. *p. 125*

Understandability The quality that enables accounting information to be understood by those for whom the information is primarily compiled. This quality enhances the usefulness of accounting information. *p. 6*

Variable cost A cost that varies according to the volume of activity. *p. 254*

Variance The financial effect, usually on the budgeted profit, of the particular factor under consideration being more or less than budgeted. *p. 351*

Variance analysis The act of examining a variance to determine the precise area in which it arose. *p. 353*

Venture capital Long-term finance provided by certain institutions to small and medium-sized businesses in order to exploit relatively high-risk opportunities. *p. 448*

Verifiability The quality that provides assurance to users that the information provided faithfully represents what it is supposed to represent. It enhances the quality of accounting information. *p. 6*

Weighted average cost (AVCO) An approach to inventories costing which assumes that inventories entering the business lose their separate identity and any issues of inventories reflect the weighted average cost of the inventories held. *p. 99*

Working capital Current assets less current liabilities. *pp. 178, 461*

Written-down value (WDV) *See* Carrying amount. *p. 92*

Appendix B
SOLUTIONS TO SELF-ASSESSMENT QUESTIONS

Chapter 2

2.1. Simonson Engineering

(a) The statement of financial position should be set out as follows:

Simonson Engineering

Statement of financial position as at 30 September 2016

	£
ASSETS	
Non-current assets	
Property, plant and equipment	
Property	72,000
Plant and machinery	25,000
Fixtures and fittings	9,000
Motor vehicles	15,000
	121,000
Current assets	
Inventories	45,000
Trade receivables	48,000
Cash in hand	1,500
	94,500
Total assets	215,500
EQUITY AND LIABILITIES	
Equity	
Closing balance	120,500
Non-current liabilities	
Long-term borrowings	51,000
Current liabilities	
Trade payables	18,000
Short-term borrowings	26,000
	44,000
Total equity and liabilities	215,500
* The equity is calculated as follows:	
Opening balance	117,500
Profit	18,000
	135,500
Drawings	(15,000)
Closing balance	120,500

(b) The statement of financial position shows:

- the biggest investment in assets is property, followed by trade receivables and inventories. These combined account for more than 76 per cent of the value of assets held;
- the investment in current assets accounts for 44 per cent of the total investment in assets;
- the total long-term finance is divided 70 per cent equity and 30 per cent long-term borrowings. There is not, therefore, excessive reliance on long-term borrowings;
- the current assets (which are cash or near cash) cover the current liabilities (which are maturing obligations) by a ratio of more than 2:1.

(c) The revised statement of position will be as follows:

Simonson Engineering
Statement of financial position as at 30 September 2016

	£
ASSETS	
Non-current assets	
Property, plant and equipment	
Property	115,000
Plant and machinery	25,000
Motor vehicles	15,000
Fixtures and fittings	9,000
	164,000
Current assets	
Inventories	38,000
Trade receivables	48,000
Cash in hand	1,500
	87,500
Total assets	251,500
EQUITY AND LIABILITIES	
Equity	
Closing balance (120,500 + 43,000 − 7,000)	156,500
Non-current liabilities	
Long-term borrowings	51,000
Current liabilities	
Trade payables	18,000
Short-term borrowings	26,000
	44,000
Total equity and liabilities	251,500

Chapter 3

3.1

TT and Co.

Statement of financial position as at 31 December 2015

	£
ASSETS	
Delivery van (12,000 − 2,500)	9,500
Inventories (143,000 + 12,000 − 74,000 − 16,000)	65,000
Trade receivables (152,000 − 132,000 − 400)	19,600
Cash at bank (50,000 − 25,000 − 500 − 1,200	750
− 12,000 − 33,500 − 1,650 − 12,000 + 35,000	
+ 132,000 − 121,000 − 9,400)	
Prepaid expenses (5,000 + 300)	5,300
Total assets	100,150
EQUITY AND LIABILITIES	
Equity (50,000 + 26,900)	76,900
Trade payables (143,000 − 121,000)	22,000
Accrued expenses (630 + 620)	1,250
Total equity and liabilities	100,150

Income statement for the year ended 31 December 2015

	£
Sales revenue (152,000 + 35,000)	187,000
Cost of goods sold (74,000 + 16,000)	(90,000)
Gross profit	97,000
Rent	(20,000)
Rates (500 + 900)	(1,400)
Wages (33,500 + 630)	(34,130)
Electricity (1,650 + 620)	(2,270)
Bad debts	(400)
Van depreciation ((12,000 − 2,000)/4)	(2,500)
Van expenses	(9,400)
Profit for the year	26,900

The statement of financial position could now be rewritten in a more stylish form as follows:

Statement of financial position as at 31 December 2015

	£
ASSETS	
Non-current assets	
Property, plant and equipment	
Delivery van at cost	12,000
Accumulated depreciation	(2,500)
	9,500
Current assets	
Inventories	65,000
Trade receivables	19,600
Prepaid expenses	5,300
Cash	750
	90,650
Total assets	100,150

EQUITY AND LIABILITIES
Equity
Closing balance   76,900
Current liabilities
Trade payables   22,000
Accrued expenses   1,250
                                                   23,250
Total equity and liabilities   100,150

Chapter 4

4.1   **Pear Ltd**
Income statement for the year ended 30 September 2016

	£000
Revenue (1,456 + 18)	1,474
Cost of sales	(768)
Gross profit	706
Salaries	(220)
Depreciation (249 + 12)	(261)
Other operating costs (131 + (2% × 200) + 2)	(137)
Operating profit	88
Interest payable (15 + 15)	(30)
Profit before taxation	58
Tax (58 × 30%)	(17)
Profit for the year	41

Statement of financial position as at 30 September 2016

	£000
Non-current assets	
Property, plant and equipment	
Cost (1,570 + 30)	1,600
Depreciation (690 + 12)	(702)
	898
Current assets	
Inventories	207
Receivables (182 + 18 − 4)	196
Cash at bank	21
	424
Total assets	1,322
Equity	
Share capital	300
Share premium account	300
Retained earnings (104 + 41 − 25)	120
	720
Non-current liabilities	
Borrowings – 10% loan (repayable 2017)	300
Current liabilities	
Trade payables	88
Other payables (20 + 30 + 15 + 2)	67
Taxation	17
Dividends approved	25
Borrowings – bank overdraft	105
	302
Total equity and liabilities	1,322

Chapter 5

5.1

Touchstone plc
Statement of cash flows for the year ended 31 December 2015

	£m
Cash flows from operating activities	
Profit before taxation (after interest) (see Note 1 below)	60
Adjustments for:	
Depreciation	16
Interest expense (Note 2)	4
	80
Increase in trade receivables (26 − 16)	(10)
Decrease in trade payables (38 − 37)	(1)
Decrease in inventories (25 − 24)	1
Cash generated from operations	70
Interest paid	(4)
Taxation paid (Note 3)	(12)
Dividend paid	(18)
Net cash from operating activities	36
Cash flows from investing activities	
Payments to acquire tangible non-current assets (Note 4)	(41)
Net cash used in investing activities	(41)
Cash flows from financing activities	
Issue of loan notes (40 − 20)	20
Net cash used in financing activities	20
Net increase in cash and cash equivalents	15
Cash and cash equivalents at 1 January 2015 Cash	4
Cash and cash equivalents at 31 December 2015 Cash	4
Treasury bills	15
	19

To see how this relates to the cash of the business at the beginning and end of the year it can be useful to provide a reconciliation as follows:

Analysis of cash and cash equivalents during the year ended 31 December 2015

	£m
Cash and cash equivalents at 1 January 2015	4
Net cash inflow	15
Cash and cash equivalents at 31 December 2015	19

Notes:

1 This is simply taken from the income statement for the year.
2 Interest payable expense must be taken out, by adding it back to the profit before taxation figure. We subsequently deduct the cash paid for interest payable during the year. In this case the two figures are identical.
3 Companies pay 50 per cent of their tax during their accounting year and the other 50 per cent in the following year. Thus the 2015 payment would have been half the tax on the 2014 profit (that is, the figure that would have appeared in the current liabilities at the end of 2014), plus half of the 2015 tax charge (that is, 4 + (1/2 × 16) = 12).

4 Since there were no disposals, the depreciation charges must be the difference between the start and end of the year's non-current asset values, adjusted by the cost of any additions:

	£m
Carrying amount at 1 January 2015	147
Additions (balancing figure)	41
	188
Depreciation (6 + 10)	(16)
Carrying amount at 31 December 2015	172

Chapter 6

6.1 Ali plc and Bhaskar plc

To answer this question, you may have used the following ratios:

	Ali plc	Bhaskar plc
Return on ordinary shareholders' funds ratio	99.9/687.6 × 100 = 14.5%	104.6/874.6 × 100 = 12.0%
Operating profit margin ratio	151.3/1,478.1 × 100 = 10.2%	166.9/1,790.4 × 100 = 9.3%
Inventories turnover period ratio	592.0/1,018.3 × 12 = 7.0 months	403.0/1,214.9 × 12 = 4.0 months
Settlement period for trade receivables ratio	176.4/1,478.1 × 12 = 1.4 months	321.9/1,790.4 × 12 = 2.2 months
Current ratio	$\dfrac{853.0}{422.4} = 2.0$	$\dfrac{816.5}{293.1} = 2.8$
Acid test ratio	$\dfrac{(853.0 - 592.0)}{422.4} = 0.6$	$\dfrac{(816.5 - 403.0)}{291.3} = 1.4$
Gearing ratio	$\dfrac{190}{(687.6 + 190)} \times 100 = 21.6\%$	$\dfrac{250}{(874.6 + 250)} \times 100 = 22.2\%$
Interest cover ratio	$\dfrac{151.3}{19.4} = 7.8$ times	$\dfrac{166.9}{27.5} = 6.1$ times
Earnings per share	$\dfrac{99.9}{320.0} = £0.31$	$\dfrac{104.6}{250.0} = £0.42$
Price earnings ratio	$\dfrac{£6.50}{£0.31} = 21.0$ times	$\dfrac{£8.20}{£0.42} = 19.5$ times

(Note: It is not possible to use any average ratios because only the end-of-year figures are provided for each business.)

Ali plc seems more effective than Bhaskar plc at generating returns for shareholders indicated by the higher ROSF ratio. This may be partly caused by Ali plc's higher operating profit margin.

Both businesses seem to have a very high inventories turnover period; this probably needs to be investigated. This ratio is particularly high for Ali plc. Both may suffer from poor inventories management.

Ali plc has a lower settlement period for trade receivables than Bhaskar plc. This may suggest that Bhaskar plc needs to exert greater control over trade receivables.

Ali plc has a much lower current ratio and acid test ratio than Bhaskar plc. The acid test ratio of Ali plc is substantially below 1.0: this may suggest a liquidity problem.

The gearing ratio of each business is quite similar. Neither business seems to have excessive borrowing. The interest cover ratio for each business is also similar. The ratios indicate that both businesses have good profit coverage for their interest charges.

Earnings per share is significantly higher for Ali plc than for Bhaskar plc. However, the P/E ratio for Ali plc is slightly higher. This latter ratio suggests that the market considers Ali plc to have slightly better prospects than Bhaskar plc.

To draw better comparisons between the two businesses, it would be useful to calculate other ratios from the financial statements. It would also be helpful to calculate ratios for both businesses over (say) five years as well as key ratios of other businesses operating in the same industry.

Chapter 7

7.1 Khan Ltd

(a) The break-even point, if only the Alpha service were provided, would be:

$$\frac{\text{Fixed costs}}{\text{Sales revenue per unit} - \text{Variable cost per unit}} = \frac{£40,000}{£30 - £(15 + 6)}$$
$$= 4,445 \text{ units (per year)}$$

(Strictly it is 4,444.44 but 4,445 is the smallest number of units of the service that must be provided to avoid a loss.)

(b)

	Alpha	Beta	Gamma
Selling price (£/unit)	30	30	20
Variable materials (£/unit)	(15)	(18)	(10)
Variable production cost (£/unit)	(6)	(10)	(5)
Contribution (£/unit)	9	11	5
Staff time (hr/unit)	2	3	1
Contribution/staff hour	£4.50	£3.67	£5.00
Order of priority	2nd	3rd	1st

(c)

	Hours		Contribution
			£
Provide:			
5,000 Gamma using	5,000	generating (that is, 5,000 × £5 =)	25,000
2,500 Alpha using	5,000	generating (that is, 2,500 × £9 =)	22,500
	10,000		47,500
		Fixed cost	(40,000)
		Profit	7,500

This leaves a demand for 500 units of Alpha and 2,000 units of Beta unsatisfied.

Chapter 8

8.1   Psilis Ltd

(a) Full cost (present basis)

	Basic		Super	
	£		£	
Direct labour (all £10/hour)	40.00	(4 hours)	60.00	(6 hours)
Direct material	15.00		20.00	
Overheads	18.20	(£4.55* × 4)	27.30	(£4.55* × 6)
	73.20		107.30	

* Total direct labour hours worked $= (40{,}000 \times 4) + (10{,}000 \times 6) = 220{,}000$ hours.
Overhead recovery rate $= £1{,}000{,}000/220{,}000 = £4.55$ per direct labour hour.

Thus the selling prices are currently:

Basic: £73.20 + 25% =   £91.50
Super: £107.30 + 25% = £134.13

(b) Full cost (activity cost basis)

Here, the cost of each cost-driving activity is apportioned between total production of the two products.

Activity	Cost £000	Basis of apportionment	Basic £000		Super £000	
Machine set-ups	280	Number of set-ups	56	(20/100)	224	(80/100)
Quality inspection	220	Number of inspections	55	(500/2,000)	165	(1,500/2,000)
Sales order processing	240	Number of orders processed	72	(1,500/5,000)	168	(3,500/5,000)
General production	260	Machine hours	182	(350/500)	78	(150/500)
Total	1,000		365		635	

The overheads per unit are:

$$\text{Basic:} \quad \frac{£365{,}000}{40{,}000} = £9.13$$

$$\text{Super:} \quad \frac{£635{,}000}{10{,}000} = £63.50$$

Thus, on an activity basis the full costs are as follows:

	Basic		Super	
	£		£	
Direct labour (all £10/hour)	40.00	(4 hours)	60.00	(6 hours)
Direct material	15.00		20.00	
Overheads	9.13		63.50	
Full cost	64.13		143.50	
Current selling price	91.50		134.13	

(c) It seems that the Supers are being sold for less than they cost to produce. If the price cannot be increased, there is a strong case for abandoning this product. At the same time, the Basics are very profitable, to the extent that it may be worth considering lowering the price to attract more sales revenue.

The fact that the overhead costs can be related to activities and, more specifically, to products does not mean that abandoning Super production would lead to immediate overhead cost savings. For example, it may not be possible or desirable to dismiss machine-setting staff overnight. It would certainly rarely be possible to release factory space occupied by machine setters and make immediate cost savings. Nevertheless, in the medium term these costs can be avoided and it may be sensible to do so.

Chapter 9

9.1 Antonio Ltd

(a) (i) Raw materials inventories budget for the six months ending 31 December (physical quantities):

	July Units	Aug Units	Sept Units	Oct Units	Nov Units	Dec Units
Opening inventories (current month's production)	500	600	600	700	750	750
Purchases (balance figure)	600	600	700	750	750	750
	1,100	1,200	1,300	1,450	1,500	1,500
Issues to production (from question)	(500)	(600)	(600)	(700)	(750)	(750)
Closing inventories (next month's production)	600	600	700	750	750	750

Raw material inventories budget for the six months ending 31 December (in financial terms), that is, the physical quantities × £8:

	July £	Aug £	Sept £	Oct £	Nov £	Dec £
Opening inventories	4,000	4,800	4,800	5,600	6,000	6,000
Purchases	4,800	4,800	5,600	6,000	6,000	6,000
	8,800	9,600	10,400	11,600	12,000	12,000
Issues to production	(4,000)	(4,800)	(4,800)	(5,600)	(6,000)	(6,000)
Closing inventories	4,800	4,800	5,600	6,000	6,000	6,000

(ii) Trade payables budget for the six months ending 31 December:

	July £	Aug £	Sept £	Oct £	Nov £	Dec £
Opening balance (current month's payment)	4,000	4,800	4,800	5,600	6,000	6,000
Purchases (from raw materials inventories budget)	4,800	4,800	5,600	6,000	6,000	6,000
	8,800	9,600	10,400	11,600	12,000	12,000
Payments	(4,000)	(4,800)	(4,800)	(5,600)	(6,000)	(6,000)
Closing balance (next month's payment)	4,800	4,800	5,600	6,000	6,000	6,000

(iii) Cash budget for the six months ending 31 December:

	July £	Aug £	Sept £	Oct £	Nov £	Dec £
Inflows						
Trade receivables (40% of sales revenue of two months previous)	2,800	3,200	3,200	4,000	4,800	5,200
Cash sales revenue (60% of current month's sales revenue)	4,800	6,000	7,200	7,800	8,400	9,600
Total inflows	7,600	9,200	10,400	11,800	13,200	14,800
Outflows						
Payables (from payables budget)	(4,000)	(4,800)	(4,800)	(5,600)	(6,000)	(6,000)
Direct costs	(3,000)	(3,600)	(3,600)	(4,200)	(4,500)	(4,500)
Advertising	(1,000)	–	–	(1,500)	–	–
Overheads: 80%	(1,280)	(1,280)	(1,280)	(1,280)	(1,600)	(1,600)
20%	(280)	(320)	(320)	(320)	(320)	(400)
New plant	–	–	(2,200)	(2,200)	(2,200)	–
Total outflows	(9,560)	(10,000)	(12,200)	(15,100)	(14,620)	(12,500)
Net inflows/(outflows)	(1,960)	(800)	(1,800)	(3,300)	(1,420)	2,300
Balance c/f	5,540	4,740	2,940	(360)	(1,780)	520

The cash balances carried forward are deduced by subtracting the deficit (net outflows) for the month from (or adding the surplus for the month to) the previous month's balance.

(iv) Budgeted income statement for May:

	£
Sales revenue (350 × £20)	7,000
Direct materials (350 × £8)	(2,800)
Direct labour (350 × £6)	(2,100)
Fixed overheads	(1,800)
Profit	300

Note how budgets are linked; in this case the inventories budget to the trade payables budget and the payables budget to the cash budget.

(b) The following are possible means of relieving the cash shortages revealed by the budget:
- Make a higher proportion of sales on a cash basis.
- Collect the money from credit customers more promptly, for example during the month following the sale.
- Hold lower inventories, both of raw materials and of finished goods.
- Increase the trade payables payment period.
- Delay the payments for advertising.
- Obtain more credit for the overhead costs; at present only 20 per cent are on credit.
- Delay the payments for the new plant.

A combination of two or more of these might be used.

(c) Income statement for May:

	Actual £	Flexed budget £
Sales revenue	7,400	7,200 (360 × £20)
Direct materials	(2,810)	(2,880) (360 × £8)
Direct labour	(2,250)	(2,160) (360 × £6)
Fixed overheads	(1,830)	(1,800)
Profit	510	360

Reconciliation

Budgeted profit (from (a)(iv))	300
Sales volume variance (£300 − £360)	60 (F)
Sales price variance (£7,400 − £7,200)	200 (F)
Direct materials variance (£2,810 − £2,880)	70 (F)
Direct labour variance (£2,250 − £2,160)	90 (A)
Fixed overheads variance (£1,830 − £1,800)	30 (A)
Actual profit	510

Chapter 10

10.1 Beacon Chemicals plc

(a) Relevant cash flows are as follows:

	Year 0 £m	Year 1 £m	Year 2 £m	Year 3 £m	Year 4 £m	Year 5 £m
Sales revenue		80	120	144	100	64
Loss of contribution		(15)	(15)	(15)	(15)	(15)
Variable cost		(40)	(50)	(48)	(30)	(32)
Fixed cost (Note 1)		(8)	(8)	(8)	(8)	(8)
Operating cash flows		17	47	73	47	9
Working capital	(30)					30
Capital cost	(100)	–	–	–	–	–
Net relevant cash flows	(130)	17	47	73	47	39

Notes:

1 Only the elements of fixed cost that are incremental to the project (only existing because of the project) are relevant. Depreciation is irrelevant because it is not a cash flow.

2 The research and development cost is irrelevant since it has been spent irrespective of the decision on X14 production.

(b) The payback period is as follows:

	Year 0 £m	Year 1 £m	Year 2 £m	Year 3 £m
Cumulative cash flows	(130)	(113)	(66)	7

Thus the equipment will have repaid the initial investment by the end of the third year of operations. The payback period is, therefore, three years.

(c) The net present value is as follows:

	Year 0 £m	Year 1 £m	Year 2 £m	Year 3 £m	Year 4 £m	Year 5 £m
Discount factor	1.00	0.926	0.857	0.794	0.735	0.681
Present value	(130)	15.74	40.28	57.96	34.55	26.56
Net present value	45.09	(that is, the sum of the present values for years 0 to 5)				

Chapter 11

11.1. Helsim Ltd

(a) The liquidity position may be assessed by using the liquidity ratios discussed in Chapter 6:

$$\text{Current ratio} = \frac{\text{Current assets}}{\text{Current liabilities}}$$

$$= \frac{£7.5 \text{ m}}{£5.4 \text{ m}}$$

$$= 1.4$$

$$\text{Acid test ratio} = \frac{\text{Current assets (excluding inventories)}}{\text{Current liabilities}}$$

$$= \frac{£3.7\text{m}}{£5.4 \text{ m}}$$

$$= 0.7$$

These ratios reveal a fairly weak liquidity position. The current ratio seems quite low and the acid test ratio very low. This latter ratio suggests that the business does not have sufficient liquid assets to meet its maturing obligations. It would be useful, however, to have details of the liquidity ratios of similar businesses in the same industry in order to make a more informed judgement. The bank overdraft represents 67 per cent of the current liabilities and 40 per cent of the total liabilities of the business. The continuing support of the bank is therefore important to the ability of the business to meet its commitments.

(b) The finance required to reduce trade payables to an average of 40 days outstanding is calculated as follows:

	£m
Trade payables at the date of the statement of financial position	1.80
Trade payables outstanding based on 40 days' credit	
40/365 × £8.4m (that is, credit purchases)	(0.92)
Finance required	0.88 (say 0.9m)

(c) The bank may not wish to provide further finance to the business. The increase in overdraft will reduce the level of trade payables but will increase the risk exposure of the bank. The additional finance invested by the bank will not generate further funds (it will not increase profit) and will not therefore be self-liquidating. The question does not make it clear whether the business has sufficient security to offer the bank for the increase in overdraft facility. The profits of the business will be reduced and the interest cover ratio, based on the profits generated last year, would reduce to about 1.6 times if the additional overdraft were granted (based on interest charged at 10 per cent each year). This is very low and means that only a small decline in profits would leave interest charges uncovered.

* Existing bank overdraft (3.6) + extension of overdraft to cover reduction in trade payables (0.9) + loan notes (3.5) = £8.0m. Assuming a 10 per cent interest rate means a yearly interest payment of £0.8m. The operating profit was £1.3m. Interest cover would be 1.63 (that is, 1.3/0.8).

(d) A number of possible sources of finance might be considered. Four possible sources are as follows:

- *Issue ordinary (equity) shares.* This option may be unattractive to investors. The return on equity is fairly low at 7.9 per cent (that is, profit for the year (0.3)/equity (3.8)) and there is no evidence that the profitability of the business will improve. If profits remain at their current level the effect of issuing more equity will be to reduce further the returns to equity.
- *Make other borrowings.* This option may prove unattractive to potential lenders. The effect of making further borrowings will have a similar effect to that of increasing the overdraft. The profits of the business will be reduced and the interest cover ratio will decrease to a low level. The gearing ratio of the business is already quite high at 48 per cent (that is, loan notes (3.5)/(loan notes + equity (3.5 + 3.8)) and it is not clear what security would be available for the loan. The gearing ratio would be much higher if the overdraft were to be included.
- *Chase trade receivables.* It may be possible to improve cash flows by reducing the level of credit outstanding from customers. At present, the average settlement period is 93 days (that is, (trade receivables (3.6)/sales revenue (14.2)) × 365), which seems quite high. A reduction in the average settlement period by approximately one-quarter would generate the funds required. However, it is not clear what effect this would have on sales.
- *Reduce inventories.* This appears to be the most attractive of the four options. At present, the average inventories holding period is 178 days (that is, (closing inventories (3.8)/cost of sales (7.8)) × 365), which seems very high. A reduction in this period by less than one-quarter would generate the funds required. However, if the business holds a large amount of slow-moving and obsolete items, it may be difficult to reduce inventories levels.

Chapter 12

12.1. Town Mills Ltd

(a) Operating cash cycle

	days
Inventories holding period	
192/652 × 365	107
Trade receivables settlement period	
202 × ((105/110)/903) × 365 (Note 1)	78
	185
Trade payables settlement period	
260 × ((105/110)/652) × 365 (Notes 1 and 2)	(139)
Operating cash cycle (days)	46

Notes:

1 Since the closing level of trade receivables/payables was 10 per cent higher at the end of the year than at the start, the average balance would be 105/110 of the end-of-year balance.

2 Since inventories were the same at both ends of the year, purchases equal cost of sales.

Knowledge of the length of the operating cash cycle (OCC) allows the business to monitor it over time, perhaps relative to other businesses or to some target. It is not possible to draw any helpful conclusions from looking at just one figure; there needs to be a basis of comparison.

A problem with using the 'bottom line' figure for the OCC is that values within it are not equivalent. In the case of Town Mills, one day's sales are worth £2,474, whereas one day's purchases or inventories holding are worth £1,786. So, while an extra day of trade receivables period coupled with an extra day of trade payables period would leave the OCC unchanged at 46 days, it would involve an additional £700 or so of investment in working capital.

(b) As mentioned in (a) above, knowing the number of days of the OCC tells us little without some basis of comparison.

The acid test ratio for this business is very low at 0.55:1. If inventories were fairly fast moving with a short trade receivables period, this might not be a worry, but this is not the case.

The current ratio is close to 1:1, which seems low. It is not possible, however, to say too much without making a comparison with similar businesses or with this business over time.

The level of the overdraft is cause for concern. It represents almost 20 per cent of the total financing of the business, according to statement of financial position values. This represents a lot of short-term finance that could be recalled instantly, or at very short notice. A term loan may be a better arrangement than an overdraft.

The level of trade payables also seems high, compared with trade receivables. This too could be a problem. It depends on the relative bargaining positions of Town Mills and its suppliers.

Overall, liquidity does not seem strong and probably needs to be reviewed. It is not possible to be too emphatic on this point, however, given such limited bases for comparison.

(c) The types of risk and cost that might be associated with high inventories levels of a wholesaler include the following:

- *Financing cost.* Inventories need to be financed. Buying on trade credit, which is free, normally covers at least some of this. In Town Mills' case, trade payables are currently greater than the value of inventories. Trade credit is linked to purchases, not to inventories levels. If inventories levels were to be reduced, the level of trade payables need not necessarily follow suit.
- *Storage costs.* These are likely to be lower where inventories are lower. How significant these costs are will depend on the nature of the inventories. Those that are high value and/or need special treatment are typically more expensive to store than other inventories.
- *Insurance cost.* This is likely to be subject to the same considerations as storage cost, of which it may be seen as forming part.
- *Obsolescence cost.* The more inventories held, the greater the risk that they will lose value through physical deterioration or obsolescence. A spare part for a machine may be in perfect condition and, in principle, capable of being used. If the machine is no longer being used, however, the spare part may be worthless.

Appendix C
SOLUTIONS TO REVIEW QUESTIONS

Chapter 1

1.1 Accounting information is provided to enable users to make more informed decisions and judgements about an organisation. Unless it fulfils this purpose, there is no point in providing it.

1.2 The main users of financial information for a university and the purposes for which they need information may be summed up as follows:

Students	Whether to enrol on a course of study. This would probably involve an assessment of the university's ability to continue to operate and to fulfil students' needs.
Other universities and colleges	How best to compete against the university. This might involve using the university's performance in various aspects as a 'benchmark' when evaluating their own performance.
Employees	Whether to take up or to continue in employment with the university. Employees might assess this by considering the ability of the university to continue to provide employment and to reward employees adequately for their labour.
Government/funding authority	How efficient and effective the university is in undertaking its various activities. Possible funding needs that the university may have.
Local community representatives	Whether to allow/encourage the university to expand its premises. To assess this, the university's ability to continue to provide employment for the community, to use community resources and to help fund environmental improvements might be considered.
Suppliers	Whether to supply the university with goods and services on credit. This would involve an assessment of the university's ability to pay for any goods and services supplied.
Lenders	Whether to lend money to the university and/or whether to require repayment of any existing loans. To assess this, the university's ability to pay interest and to repay the principal would be considered.
Board of governors and managers (faculty deans and so on)	Whether the performance of the university requires improvement. Performance to date would be compared with earlier plans or some other 'benchmark' to decide whether action needs to be taken. Whether there should be a change in the university's future direction. In making such decisions, management will need to look at the university's ability to perform and at the opportunities available to it.

We can see that the users of accounting information and their needs are similar to those of a private sector business.

1.3 Most businesses are far too large and complex for managers to be able to appreciate everything that is going on merely by personal observation. Managers need to receive information on all those aspects of the business within their control. Management accounting reports can help in providing this information. These reports can act as the 'eyes and ears' of the managers, providing insights not necessarily obvious without them.

1.4 We can never be sure what is going to happen in the future, the best we can often do is to make judgements based on past experience. Thus, information concerning past flows of cash and wealth in the recent past may well be useful in helping to form judgements about possible future outcomes.

Chapter 2

2.1 The owner seems unaware of the business entity convention in accounting. This convention requires a separation of the business from the owner(s) of the business for accounting purposes. The business is regarded as a separate entity and the statement of financial position is prepared from the perspective of the business rather than that of the owner. As a result, funds invested in the business by the owner are regarded as a claim that the owner has on the business. In the standard layout of the statement of financial position, this claim will be shown alongside other claims on the business from outsiders.

2.2 A statement of financial position does not show what a business is worth, for two major reasons:

(1) Only those items that can be measured reliably in monetary terms are shown on the statement of financial position. Thus, things of value such as the reputation for product quality, skills of employees and so on will not normally appear in the statement of financial position.
(2) The historic cost convention results in assets often being recorded at their outlay cost rather than their current value. For certain assets, the difference between historic cost and current value can be significant.

2.3 The accounting equation expresses the relationship between a business's assets, liabilities and equity. For the standard layout, it is:

Assets (current and non-current) = Equity + Liabilities (current and non-current)

For the alternative layout mentioned in the chapter, the equation is:

Assets (current and non-current) − Liabilities (current and non-current) = Equity

2.4 Some object to the idea of humans being treated as assets for inclusion on the statement of financial position. It is seen as demeaning for humans to be listed alongside inventories, plant and machinery and other assets. Others argue, however, that humans are often the most valuable resource of a business and that placing a value on this resource will help bring to the attention of managers the importance of nurturing and developing this 'asset'.

Humans are likely to meet the criterion of an asset relating to future probable benefits; otherwise there would be little point in employing them. The criterion relating to exclusive right of control is, however, more problematic. A business cannot control humans in the same way as most other assets, but it can have exclusive rights to their employment services. This makes it possible to argue that this criterion can be met.

Normally, humans sign a contract of employment and so the criterion relating to past transactions is normally met. The criterion concerning whether the value of humans (or their services) can be reliably measured poses the major difficulty. To date, none of the measurement methods proposed has achieved widespread support.

Chapter 3

3.1 When preparing the income statement, it is not always possible to determine accurately the expenses that need to be matched to the sales revenue for the period. It is perhaps only at some later point that the true position becomes clear. Nevertheless, we must try to include all relevant expenses and so estimates of the future have to be made. These estimates may include accrued expenses, depreciation charges and bad debts incurred. The income statement would lose much of its usefulness if we were to wait for all uncertainties to become clear.

3.2 Depreciation attempts to allocate the cost or fair value, less any residual value, of the asset over its useful life. Depreciation does not attempt to measure the fall in value of the asset during a particular reporting period. Thus, the carrying amount of the asset appearing on the statement of financial position normally represents the unexpired part of its cost, or fair value, rather than its current market value.

3.3 The convention of consistency aims to provide some uniformity in the application of accounting policies. In certain areas, there may be more than one method of accounting for an item, for example inventories. The convention of consistency states that, having decided on a particular accounting policy, a business should continue to apply the policy in successive periods. While this policy helps to ensure that more valid comparisons can be made of business performance *over time,* it does not ensure that valid comparisons can be made *between businesses.* Different businesses may still consistently apply different accounting policies.

3.4 An expense is that element of the cost incurred that is used up during the reporting period. An asset is that element of cost which is carried forward on the statement of financial position and which will normally be used up in future periods. Thus, both assets and expenses arise from costs being incurred. The major difference between the two is the period over which the benefits (arising from the costs incurred) accrue.

Chapter 4

4.1 Both companies and individuals are required to meet their debts to the full extent of their available assets. Thus, their liability is limited only by the extent of their assets. It is the shareholders of a limited company that enjoy greater protection. Their liability for the unsatisfied debts of a company is limited to the amount that they paid or have pledged to pay for their shares.

4.2 The key factors are as follows:

■ A private limited company may place restrictions on the transfer of its shares. (There is therefore an opportunity to control who becomes a shareholder.) A public company cannot have such restrictions.

- A public limited company must have authorised share capital of at least £50,000. There is no minimum for a private limited company.
- A public limited company may offer its shares and loan notes to the general public; a private company cannot make such an offer.

4.3 A reserve is that part of the equity (owners' claim) of a company that is not share capital. Reserves represent gains or surpluses that enhance the claim of the shareholders above the nominal value of their shares. Revenue reserves arise from realised profits and gains, such as ploughed-back trading profits. Capital reserves arise from issuing shares at a premium or from unrealised profits and gains (for example, the upward revaluation of non-current assets).

4.4 A preference share represents part of the share capital of a company. Holders of preference shares are entitled to the first part of any dividend paid by a company.

(a) Holders of preference shares are normally entitled to dividends up to a predetermined maximum value. Dividends to ordinary shareholders, meanwhile, have no predetermined maximum. The priority awarded in receiving dividends means that preference shares are seen as less risky than ordinary shares. Ordinary shareholders are the primary risk takers and are given voting rights. Preference shareholders do not normally have voting rights.

(b) Loan notes represent borrowings for the company. Loan note holders normally have a contract that specifies the rate of interest, interest payment dates and redemption date. The loan notes are often secured on the company's assets. Preference shareholders have no such contract and their claim cannot be secured. The claims of preference shareholders are ranked below those of loan note holders in the event that the company is liquidated.

Chapter 5

5.1 Cash is normally required in the settlement of claims. Employees, contractors, lenders and suppliers expect to be paid in cash. When businesses fail, it is their inability to find the cash to pay claimants that actually drives them under. These factors lead to cash being the pre-eminent business asset. It is studied carefully to assess the ability of a business to survive and/or to take advantage of commercial opportunities.

5.2 With the direct method, the business's cash records are analysed for the period concerned. The analysis reveals the amounts of cash, in total, that have been paid and received in respect of each category of the statement of cash flows. This is not difficult in principle, or in practice if it is done by computer, as a matter of routine.

The indirect method takes the approach that, while the profit (loss) for the reporting period is not equal to the net inflow (outflow) of cash from operations, they are fairly closely linked to the extent that appropriate adjustment of the profit (loss) for the period will derive the correct cash flow figure for the same period. The adjustment is concerned with depreciation charge for, and movements in relevant working capital items over, the period.

5.3 (a) *Cash flows from operating activities*. This would normally be positive, even for a business with small profits or even losses. The fact that depreciation is not a cash flow tends to lead to positive cash flows in this area in most cases.

(b) *Cash flows from investing activities.* Normally this would be negative in cash flow terms since many non-current assets wear out or become obsolete and need to be replaced in the normal course of business. This means that, typically, old non-current assets generate less cash on their disposal than must be paid to replace them.

(c) *Cash flows from financing activities.* Businesses tend either to expand or to fail. In either case, this is likely to mean that, over the years, more finance will be raised than will be redeemed.

5.4   There are several possible reasons for this, including the following:

- Changes in inventories, trade receivables and trade payables. For example, an increase In trade receivables during a reporting period would mean that the cash received from credit sales would be less than the credit sales revenue for the same period.
- Cash may have been spent on new non-current assets or received from disposals of old ones; these would not directly affect profit.
- Cash may have been spent to redeem or repay a financial claim or received as a result of the creation or the increase of a claim. These would not directly affect profit.
- Tax charged in the income statement is not normally the same as the tax paid during the same reporting period.

Chapter 6

6.1   The fact that a business operates on a low operating profit margin indicates that only a small operating profit is being produced for each £1 of sales revenue generated. However, this does not necessarily mean that the ROCE will be low. If the business is able to generate sufficient sales revenue, the operating profit may be very high even though the operating profit per £1 of sales revenue is low. If the overall operating profit is high, this can lead, in turn, to a high ROCE, since it is the total operating profit that is used as the numerator (top part of the fraction) in this ratio. Many businesses (including supermarkets) pursue a strategy of 'low margin, high sales revenue'.

6.2   The statement of financial position is drawn up at a single point in time – typically, the end of the reporting period. As a result, the figures shown on the statement represent the position at that single point in time and may not be representative of the position during the period. Wherever possible, average figures (perhaps based on monthly figures) should be used. However, an external user may have access only to the opening and closing statements of financial position for the year and so a simple average based on these figures may be all that it is possible to calculate. Where a business is seasonal in nature or is subject to cyclical changes, this simple averaging may not be sufficient.

6.3   Three possible reasons for a long inventories turnover period are:

- poor inventories controls, leading to excessive investment in inventories;
- inventories hoarding in anticipation of price rises, shortages or increased future sales;
- to be able to offer customers a wide range of products or to be able to supply promptly at all times.

A short inventories turnover period may be due to:

- tight inventories controls, reducing excessive investment in inventories and/or the amount of obsolete and slow-moving inventories;
- an inability to finance the required amount of inventories to meet sales demand;
- a difference in the mix of inventories carried by similar businesses (for example, greater investment in perishable goods which are held for a short period only).

These are not exhaustive lists; you may have thought of other reasons.

6.4 Size may well be an important factor when comparing businesses:

- Larger businesses may be able to generate economies of scale in production and distribution to an extent not available to smaller businesses.
- Larger businesses may be able to raise finance more cheaply, partly through economies of scale (for example, borrowing larger amounts) and partly through being seen as less of a risk to the lender.
- Smaller businesses may be able to be more flexible and 'lighter on their feet' than can the typical larger business.

These and other possible factors may lead to differences in performance and position between larger and smaller businesses.

Chapter 7

7.1 A *fixed cost* is one that is the same irrespective of the level of activity or output. Typical examples include rent of business accommodation, salaries of supervisory staff and insurance. A *variable cost* is one that varies with the level of activity or output. Examples include raw materials and labour, where labour is rewarded in proportion to the level of output. Note particularly that it is relative to the level of activity that costs are fixed or variable. A fixed cost will be affected by inflation and it will be greater for a longer period than for a shorter one.

For a particular product or service, knowing which element of cost is fixed and which is variable enables managers to predict the total cost for any level of activity. It also enables them to concentrate only on the variable cost in circumstances where a decision will not alter the fixed cost.

7.2 The BEP is the break-even point, that is, the level of activity, measured either in units of output or in value of sales revenue, at which the sales revenue exactly covers all of the cost, both fixed and variable elements.

Break-even point is calculated as

Fixed cost/(Sales revenue per unit − Variable cost per unit)

which may alternatively be expressed as

Fixed cost/Contribution per unit

Thus break-even will occur when the contributions for the period are sufficient to cover the fixed cost for the period.

Break-even point tends to be useful as a comparison with planned level of activity in an attempt to assess the riskiness of the activity.

7.3 Operating gearing refers to the extent of fixed cost relative to variable cost in the total cost of some activity. Where the fixed cost forms a relatively high proportion of the total (at the business's normal level of activity), we say that the activity has high operating gearing.

Typically, high operating gearing is present where there is a relatively high level of mechanisation (that is, capital-intensive environments). This is because such environments tend simultaneously to involve relatively high fixed cost of depreciation, maintenance and so on and relatively low variable cost.

High operating gearing means that the effects of increases or decreases in the level of activity have an accentuated effect on operating profit. For example, a 20 per cent decrease in output of a particular service will lead to a greater than 20 per cent decrease in operating profit, assuming no cost or price changes.

7.4 In the face of a restricting scarce resource, profit will be maximised by using the scarce resource on producing the product or service where the contribution per unit of the scarce resource is maximised.

This means that the contribution per unit of the scarce resource (for example, hour of scarce labour or unit of scarce raw material) for each competing product or service needs to be identified. It is then a question of allocating the scarce resource to the product or service that provides the highest contribution per unit of the particular scarce resource. The logic of this approach is that the scarce resource is allocated to the activity that uses it most effectively, in terms of contribution and, therefore, profit.

Chapter 8

8.1 In process costing, the total production cost for a period is divided by the number of completed units of output for the period to deduce the full cost per unit. Where there is work in progress at the beginning and/or the end of the period complications arise.

The problem is that some of the completed output incurred cost in the preceding period. Similarly, some of the cost incurred in the current period leads to completed production in the subsequent period. Account needs to be taken of these facts, if reliable full cost information is to be obtained.

8.2 The only reason for distinguishing between direct and indirect costs is to help to deduce the full cost of a unit of output in a job-costing environment. Where all units of output are identical, or near identical, a process costing approach will be taken. This avoids the need for separately identifying direct and indirect costs.

Direct cost forms that part of the total cost of pursuing some activity that can be identified with, and measured in respect of, that particular activity. Examples of direct cost items in the typical job-costing environment include direct labour and direct materials. Indirect cost is the remainder of the cost of pursuing some activity. In practice, knowledge of the direct costs tends to provide the basis used to charge overheads to jobs.

8.3 The notion of direct and indirect cost is concerned only with the extent to which the different elements of cost can be identified with, and measured in respect of, a particular cost unit, usually a product or service. The distinction between direct and indirect costs is made exclusively for the purpose of deducing the full cost of some cost unit, in an environment where each cost unit is different. Thus, it is typically in the context of job costing, or some variant of it, that the distinction between direct and indirect cost is usefully made.

The notion of variable and fixed cost is concerned entirely with how costs behave in the face of changes in the volume of output. The benefit of being able to distinguish between fixed and variable cost is that predictions can be made of what total cost will be at particular levels of volume and/or what reduction or addition to cost will occur if the volume of output is reduced or increased.

Thus the notions of direct and indirect cost, on the one hand, and that of variable and fixed cost, on the other, are not linked to one another. In most contexts, some elements of direct cost are variable, while some are fixed. Similarly, indirect cost might be fixed or variable.

8.4 ABC is a means of dealing with charging overheads to units of output to derive full cost in a multi-product (job or batch costing) environment.

The traditional approach tends to accept that once identifiable direct cost, normally labour and materials, has been taken out, all of the remaining cost (overheads) must be treated as a common cost and applied to jobs using some formula, typically on the basis of direct labour hours.

ABC takes a much more enquiring approach to overheads. It follows the philosophy that overheads occur for a reason, they must be driven by activities. For example, a particular type of product may take up a disproportionately large part of supervisors' time. If that product were not made, in the long run, the supervision cost could be cut (fewer supervisors would be needed). Whereas the traditional approach would just accept that supervisory salaries are an overhead, which needs to be apportioned along with other overheads, ABC would seek to charge that part of the supervisors' salaries which is driven by the particular type of product, to that product.

Chapter 9

9.1 A budget can be defined as a financial plan for a future period of time. Thus it sets out the intentions which management has for the period concerned. Achieving the budget plans should help to achieve the long-term plans of the business. Achievement of the long-term plans should mean, in turn, that the business is successfully working towards its strategic objectives and mission.

A budget differs from a forecast in that a forecast is a statement of what is expected to happen without the intervention of management, perhaps because they cannot intervene (as with a weather forecast). A plan is an intention to achieve.

Normally management would take account of reliable forecasts when making its plans.

9.2 1 Budgets tend to promote forward thinking and the possible identification of short-term problems. Managers must plan and the budgeting process tends to force them to do so. In doing so, they are likely to encounter potential problems. If the potential problems can be identified early enough, solutions might be easily found.

2 Budgets can be used to help co-ordination between various sections of the business. It is important that the plans of one area of the business fit in with those of other areas; a lack of co-ordination could have disastrous consequences. Having formal statements of plans for each aspect of the business enables a check to be made that plans are complementary.

3 Budgets can motivate managers to better performance. It is believed that people are motivated by having a target to aim for. Provided that the stated goals are achievable, budgets can provide an effective motivational device.

4 Budgets can provide a basis for a system of control. Having a plan against which actual performance can be measured provides a potentially useful tool of control.

5 Budgets can provide a system of authorisation. Many managers have 'spending' budgets such as research and development, staff training and so on. For these people, the size of their budget defines their authority to spend.

9.3 A variance is the effect on budgeted profit of the particular cost or revenue item being considered. It represents the difference between the budgeted profit and the actual profit assuming everything, except the item under consideration, had gone according to budget. From this, it must be the case that:

Budgeted profit + Favourable variances − Unfavourable variances = Actual profit

The purpose of analysing variances is to identify whether, and if so where, things are not going according to plan. If this can be done, it may be possible to find out the cause of things going out of control. If this can be discovered, it may then be possible to put things right for the future.

9.4 Where the budgeted and actual volumes of output do not coincide, it is impossible to make valid comparison of 'allowed' and actual costs and revenues. Flexing the original budget to reflect the actual output level enables a more informative comparison to be made.

Flexing certainly does not mean that output volume differences do not matter. Flexing will show (as the difference between flexed and original budget profits) the effect on profit of output volume differences.

Chapter 10

10.1 NPV is usually considered the best method of assessing investment opportunities because it takes account of:

- *The timing of the cash flows.* By *discounting* the various cash flows associated with each project according to when it is expected to arise, it recognises the fact that cash flows do not all occur simultaneously. Associated with this is the fact that, by discounting, using the opportunity cost of finance (that is, the return that the next best alternative opportunity would generate), the net benefit after financing costs have been met is identified (as the NPV).
- *The whole of the relevant cash flows.* NPV includes all of the relevant cash flows irrespective of when they are expected to occur. It treats them differently according to their date of occurrence, but they are all taken account of in the NPV and they all have, or can have, an influence on the decision.
- *The objectives of the business.* NPV is the only method of appraisal where the output of the analysis has a direct bearing on the wealth of the owners of the business. (Positive NPVs enhance wealth; negative ones reduce it.) Since most private-sector businesses seek to increase their owners' wealth, NPV clearly is the best approach to use.

NPV provides clear decision rules concerning acceptance/rejection of projects and the ranking of projects. It is fairly simple to use, particularly with the availability of modern computer software that takes away the need for routine calculations to be done manually.

10.2 The payback period method, in its original form, does not take account of the time value of money. However, it would be possible to modify the payback method to accommodate this requirement. Cash flows arising from a project could be discounted, using the cost of finance as the appropriate discount rate, in the same way as in the NPV and IRR methods. The discounted payback approach is used by some businesses and represents an improvement on the original approach described in the chapter. However, it still retains the other flaws of the original payback approach that were discussed. For example, it ignores relevant data after the payback period. Thus, even in its modified form, the PP method cannot be regarded as superior to NPV.

10.3 The IRR method does appear to be similar in popularity to the NPV method among practising managers. The main reasons for this appear to be as follows:

■ *A preference for a percentage return ratio rather than an absolute figure as a means of expressing the outcome of a project.* This preference for a ratio may reflect the fact that other financial goals of the business are often set in terms of ratios, for example return on capital employed.
■ *A preference for ranking projects in terms of their percentage return.* Managers feel it is easier to rank projects on the basis of percentage returns (though NPV outcomes should be just as easy for them). We saw in the chapter that the IRR method could provide misleading advice on the ranking of projects and the NPV method was preferable for this purpose.

10.4 Cash flows, rather than profit flows, are used because cash is the ultimate measure of economic wealth. Cash is used to acquire resources and for distribution to shareholders. When cash is invested in a project, an opportunity cost is incurred, as the cash cannot be used in other investment projects. Similarly, when positive cash flows are generated by the project, the cash can be used to reinvest in other projects.

Profit, on the other hand, is relevant to reporting the productive effort for a period. This measure of effort may have only a tenuous relationship to cash flows for a period. The conventions of accounting may lead to the recognition of gains and losses in one period and the relevant cash inflows and outflows occurring in another period.

Chapter 11

11.1 A sale-and-leaseback arrangement may have the following disadvantages:

■ There may be a tax liability arising on the sale of the asset.
■ The future cost of the lease payments may be difficult to predict.
■ Lease payments may become a burden over time as a result of upward reviews.
■ Where property is being used in a sale-and-leaseback arrangement, the business may have to relocate its operations at the end of the lease period if a new lease agreement cannot be reached.
■ The business will not benefit from any future increases in value of the asset.

11.2 A listed business may wish to revert to unlisted status for a number of possible reasons. These include:

- *Cost.* A Stock Exchange listing can be costly, as the business must adhere to certain administrative regulations and financial disclosures.
- *Scrutiny.* Listed companies are subject to close scrutiny by analysts and this may not be welcome if the business is engaged in sensitive negotiations or controversial business activities.
- *Takeover risk.* The shares of the business may be purchased by an unwelcome bidder and this may result in a takeover.
- *Investor profile.* If the business is dominated by a few investors who wish to retain their interest in the business and do not wish to raise further equity by public issues, the benefits of a listing are few.

11.3 An offer for sale involves an issuing house buying the shares in the business and then, in turn, selling the shares to the public. The issue will be advertised by the publication of a prospectus, which will set out details of the business and the issue price of the shares (or reserve price if a tender issue is being made). The shares issued by the issuing house may be either new shares or shares that have been purchased from existing shareholders. A public issue is where the business undertakes direct responsibility for issuing shares to the public. If an issuing house is employed it will usually be in the role of adviser and administrator of the issue. However, the issuing house may also underwrite the issue. A public issue runs the risk that the shares will not be taken up and is a less popular form of issue for businesses.

11.4 Invoice discounting is a service offered to businesses by a financial institution that is prepared to advance a sum equivalent to 80 per cent, or more, of outstanding trade receivables. The amount advanced is usually payable within 60 to 90 days. The business will retain responsibility for collecting the amounts owing from credit customers and the advance must be repaid irrespective of whether the trade receivables have been collected. Factoring is a service that is also offered to businesses by financial institutions. In this case, the factor will take over the business's sales and trade receivables records and will undertake to collect trade receivables on behalf of the client business. The factor will also be prepared to make an advance of 80 per cent, or more, of approved trade receivables which is repayable from the amounts received from customers. The service charge for invoice discounting is up to 0.5 per cent of sales revenue, whereas the service charge for factoring is up to 3 per cent of sales revenue. This difference explains, in part, why businesses have shown a preference for invoice discounting rather than factoring in recent years. However, the factor provides additional services, as explained.

Chapter 12

12.1 Although the credit manager is responsible for ensuring that credit customers pay on time, Tariq may be right in denying blame. Various factors may be responsible for the situation described which are beyond the control of the credit manager. These include:

- a downturn in the economy leading to financial difficulties among credit customers;
- decisions by other managers within the business to liberalise credit policy in order to stimulate sales;

- an increase in competition among suppliers offering credit, which is being exploited by customers;
- disputes with customers over the quality of goods or services supplied; and
- problems in the delivery of goods leading to delays.

You may have thought of others.

12.2 The level of inventories held will be affected in the following ways:

(a) An increase in production bottlenecks is likely to result in an increase in raw materials and work in progress being processed within the plant. Therefore, inventories levels should rise.

(b) A rise in the cost of capital will make holding inventories more expensive. This may, in turn, lead to a decision to reduce inventories levels.

(c) The decision to reduce the range of products should result in a lower level of inventories being held. It would no longer be necessary to hold certain items in order to meet customer demand.

(d) Switching to a local supplier may reduce the lead time between ordering an item and receiving it. This should, in turn, reduce the need to carry such high levels of the particular item.

(e) A deterioration in the quality of bought-in items may result in the purchase of higher quantities of inventories in order to take account of the defective element in inventories acquired. It may also lead to an increase in the inspection time for items received. This too would lead to a rise in inventories levels.

12.3 Inventories are held:

- to meet customer demand;
- to avoid the problems of running out of inventories; and
- to take advantage of profitable opportunities (for example, buying a product that is expected to rise steeply in price in the future).

The first reason may be described as transactionary, the second precautionary and the third speculative. They are, in essence, the same reasons why a business holds cash.

12.4 (a) The costs of holding too little cash are:
- failure to meet obligations when they fall due which can damage the reputation of the business and may, in the extreme, lead to the business being wound up;
- having to borrow and thereby incur interest charges; and
- an inability to take advantage of profitable opportunities.

(b) The costs of holding too much cash are:
- failure to use the funds available for more profitable purposes; and
- loss of value during a period of inflation.

Appendix D
SOLUTIONS TO SELECTED EXERCISES

Chapter 2

2.1

Paul
Statement of cash flows for Thursday

	£
Opening balance (from Wednesday)	59
Cash from sale of wrapping paper	47
Cash paid to purchase wrapping paper	(53)
Closing balance	53

Income statement for Thursday

	£
Sales revenue	47
Cost of goods sold	(33)
Profit	14

Statement of financial position as at Thursday evening

	£
Cash	53
Inventories of goods for resale (23 + 53 − 33)	43
Total assets	96
Equity	96

2.2

Helen
Income statement for day 1

	£
Sales revenue (70 × £0.80)	56
Cost of sales (70 × £0.50)	(35)
Profit	21

Statement of cash flows for day 1

	£
Cash introduced by Helen	40
Cash from sales	56
Cash for purchases (80 × £0.50)	(40)
Closing balance	56

Statement of financial position as at end of day 1

	£
Cash balance	56
Inventories of unsold goods (10 × £0.50)	5
Total assets	61
Equity	61

Income statement for day 2

	£
Sales revenue (65 × £0.80)	52.0
Cost of sales (65 × £0.50)	(32.5)
Profit	19.5

Statement of cash flows for day 2

	£
Opening balance	56.0
Cash from sales	52.0
Cash for purchases (60 × £0.50)	(30.0)
Closing balance	78.0

Statement of financial position as at end of day 2

	£
Cash balance	78.0
Inventories of unsold goods (5 × £0.50)	2.5
Total assets	80.5
Equity	80.5

Income statement for day 3

	£
Sales revenue (20 × £0.80) + (45 × £0.40)	34.0
Cost of sales (65 × £0.50)	(32.5)
Profit	1.5

Statement of cash flows for day 3

	£
Opening balance	78.0
Cash from sales	34.0
Cash for purchases (60 × £0.50)	(30.0)
Closing balance	82.0

Statement of financial position as at end of day 3

	£
Cash balance	82.0
Inventories of unsold goods	–
Total assets	82.0
Equity	82.0

2.4 Crafty Engineering

(a) **Statement of financial position as at 30 June last year**

	£000
ASSETS	
Non-current assets	
Property, plant and equipment	
Property	320
Equipment and tools	207
Motor vehicles	38
	565
Current assets	
Inventories	153
Trade receivables	185
	338
Total assets	903
EQUITY AND LIABILITIES	
Equity (which is the missing figure)	441
Non-current liabilities	
Long-term borrowings (loan Industrial Finance Co.)	260
Current liabilities	
Trade payables	86
Short-term borrowings	116
	202
Total equity and liabilities	903

(b) The statement of financial position reveals a large investment in non-current assets. It represents more than 60 per cent of the total investment in assets (565/903). The nature of the business may require a heavy investment in non-current assets. The current assets exceed the current liabilities by a large amount (approximately 1.7 times). Hence, there is no obvious sign of a liquidity problem. However, the statement of financial position reveals that the business has no cash balance and is therefore dependent on the continuing support of short-term borrowing to meet maturing obligations. When considering the long-term financing of the business, we can see that about 37 per cent (that is, 260/(260 + 441)) of total long-term finance is supplied by borrowings and about 63 per cent (that is, 441/(260 + 441)) by the owners. This level of long-term borrowing seems high but not excessive. However, we need to know more about the ability of the business to service the borrowing (that is, make interest payments and repayments of the amount borrowed) before a full assessment can be made.

Chapter 3

3.1 Comments

(a) Equity does increase as a result of the owners introducing more cash into the business, but it will also increase as a result of introducing other assets (for example, a motor car) and by the business generating revenue by trading. Similarly, equity decreases not only as a result of withdrawals of cash by owners but also by withdrawals of other assets (for example, inventories for the owners' personal use) and through trading expenses being incurred. Generally speaking, equity will alter more as a result of trading activities than for any other reason.

(b) An accrued expense is not one that relates to next year; it is one that needs to be matched with the revenue of the reporting period under review, but that has yet to be met in terms of cash payment. As such, it will appear on the statement of financial position as a current liability.

(c) The purpose of depreciation is not to provide for asset replacement; it is an attempt to allocate the cost, or fair value, of the asset (less any residual value) over its useful life. Depreciation provides a measure of the amount that a non-current asset has been consumed during a period. This amount is then charged as an expense for the period. Depreciation is a book entry (the outlay of cash occurs when the asset is purchased) and does not normally entail setting aside a separate amount of cash for asset replacement. Even if this were done, there would be no guarantee that sufficient funds would be available at the end of the asset's life for its replacement. Factors such as inflation and technological change may mean that the replacement cost is higher than the original cost of the asset.

(d) In the short term, the current value of a non-current asset may exceed its original cost. However, nearly all non-current assets wear out over time through being used to generate wealth. This will be the case for buildings. Thus, some measure of depreciation is needed to reflect the fact that the asset is being consumed. Some businesses revalue their buildings upwards where the current value is significantly higher than the original cost. Where this occurs, the depreciation charge should be based on the revalued amount, which will lead to higher depreciation charges.

3.3 Missing values

(a) Rent payable – expense for period	£9,000
(b) Rates and insurance – expense for period	£6,000
(c) General expenses – paid in period	£7,000
(d) Interest (on borrowings) payable – prepaid	£500
(e) Salaries – paid in period	£6,000
(f) Rent receivable – received during period	£3,000

3.5

WW Associates
Income statement for the year ended 31 December 2015

	£
Sales revenue (211,000 + 42,000)	253,000
Cost of goods sold (127,000 + 25,000)	(152,000)
Gross profit	101,000
Rent (20,000)	(20,000)
Rates (400 + 1,500)	(1,900)
Wages (−1,700 + 23,800 + 860)	(22,960)
Electricity (2,700)	(2,700)
Machinery depreciation (9,360)	(9,360)
Loss on disposal of the old machinery (13,000 − 3,900 − 9,000)	(100)
Van expenses (17,500)	(17,500)
Profit for the year	26,480

The loss on disposal of the old machinery is the carrying amount (cost less depreciation) less the disposal proceeds. Since the machinery had been owned for only one year, with a depreciation rate of 30 per cent, the depreciation on it so far is £3,900 (that is, £13,000 × 30%). The effective disposal proceeds were £9,000 because, as a result of trading it in, the business saved £9,000 on the new asset.

The depreciation expense for 2015 is based on the cost less accumulated depreciation of the assets owned at the end of 2015.

Statement of financial position as at 31 December 2015

	£
ASSETS	
Machinery (25,300 + 6,000 + 9,000 − 13,000 + 3,900 − 9,360)	21,840*
Inventories (12,200 + 143,000 + 12,000 − 127,000 − 25,000)	15,200
Trade receivables (21,300 + 211,000 − 198,000)	34,300
Cash at bank (overdraft) (8,300 − 23,000 − 25,000 − 2,000 − 6,000 − 23,800 − 2,700 − 12,000 + 42,000 + 198,000 − 156,000 − 17,500)	(19,700)
Prepaid expenses (400 − 400 + 5,000 + 500)	5,500
Total assets	57,140
EQUITY AND LIABILITIES	
Equity (owner's capital) (48,900 − 23,000 + 26,480)	52,380
Trade payables (16,900 + 143,000 − 156,000)	3,900
Accrued expenses (1,700 − 1,700 + 860)	860
Total equity and liabilities	57,140
* Cost less accumulated depreciation at 31 December 2014	25,300
Carrying amount of machine disposed of (£13,000 − £3,900)	(9,100)
Cost of new machine	15,000
Depreciation for 2015 (£31,200 × 30%)	(9,360)
Carrying amount (written-down value) of machine at 31 December 2015	21,840

The statement of financial position could now be rewritten in a more stylish form as follows:

Statement of financial position as at 31 December 2015

	£
ASSETS	
Non-current assets	
Property, plant and equipment	
Machinery at cost less depreciation	21,840
Current assets	
Inventories	15,200
Trade receivables	34,300
Prepaid expenses	5,500
	55,000
Total assets	76,840
EQUITY AND LIABILITIES	
Equity	52,380
Current liabilities	
Trade payables	3,900
Accrued expenses	860
Borrowings − bank overdraft	19,700
	24,460
Total equity and liabilities	76,840

Chapter 4

4.1 Limited companies cannot set a limit on the amount of debts they are prepared to meet. Just like individuals, they must meet their debts up to the limit of their assets. In the context of owners' claim, 'reserves' mean part of the owners' claim against the assets of the company. These assets may or may not include cash. The legal ability of the company to pay dividends is not related to the amount of cash that it has.

Preference shares do not carry a guaranteed dividend; they simply guarantee that the preference shareholders have a right to the first slice of any dividend that is paid. Shares of some companies can be bought by one investor from another through the Stock Exchange. Such a transaction has no direct effect on the company, however. These are not new shares being offered by the company but rather existing shares being sold 'second hand'.

4.3

I. Ching (Booksellers) plc
Statement of comprehensive income for the year ended 31 December 2015

	£m
Revenue	943
Cost of sales	(460)
Gross profit	483
Distribution expenses	(110)
Administrative expenses	(212)
Other expenses	(25)
Operating profit	136
Finance charges	(40)
Profit before tax	96
Taxation	(24)
Profit for the year	72
Other comprehensive income	
Revaluation of property, plant and equipment	20
Foreign currency translation differences for foreign operations	(15)
Tax on other comprehensive income	(1)
Other comprehensive income for the year, net of tax	4
Total comprehensive income for the year	76

4.4

Chips Limited
Income statement for the year ended 30 June 2016

	£000
Revenue (1,850 − 16)	1,834
Cost of sales (1,040 + 23)	(1,063)
Gross profit	771
Depreciation (220 − 2 − 5 + 8 + (94 × 20%))	(240)
Other operating costs	(375)
Operating profit	156
Interest payable (35 + 35)	(70)
Profit before taxation	86
Taxation (86 × 30%)	(26)
Profit for the year	60

Statement of financial position as at 30 June 2016

	Cost £000	Depreciation £000	£000
ASSETS			
Non-current assets			
Property, plant and equipment			
Buildings	800	(112)	688
Plant and equipment	650	(367)	283
Motor vehicles (102 − 8); (53 − 5 + 19)	94	(67)	27
	1,544	(546)	998
Current assets			
Inventories			950
Trade receivables (420 − 16)			404
Cash at bank (16 + 2)			18
			1,372
Total assets			2,370
EQUITY AND LIABILITIES			
Equity			
Ordinary shares of £1, fully paid			800
Reserves at beginning of the year			248
Retained profit for year			60
			1,108
Non-current liabilities			
Borrowings – secured 10% loan notes			700
Current liabilities			
Trade payables (361 + 23)			384
Other payables (117 + 35)			152
Taxation			26
			562
Total equity and liabilities			2,370

Chapter 5

5.1 (a) An increase in the level of inventories would, ultimately, have an adverse effect on cash.

(b) A rights issue of ordinary shares will give rise to a positive cash flow, which will be included in the 'financing' section of the statement of cash flows.

(c) A bonus issue of ordinary shares has no cash flow effect.

(d) Writing off some of the value of the inventories has no cash flow effect.

(e) A disposal for cash of a large number of shares by a major shareholder has no cash flow effect as far as the business is concerned.

(f) Depreciation does not involve cash at all. Using the indirect method of deducing cash flows from operating activities involves the depreciation expense in the calculation, but this is simply because we are trying to find out from the profit before taxation (after depreciation) figure what the profit before taxation *and* depreciation must have been.

5.3

Torrent plc

Cash flows from operating activities for the year to 31 December 2015

	£m
Profit before taxation (after interest) (see Note 1 below)	170
Adjustments for:	
Depreciation (Note 2)	78
Interest expense (Note 3)	26
	274
Decrease in inventories (41 − 35)	6
Increase in trade receivables (145 − 139)	(6)
Decrease in trade payables (54 − 41)	(13)
Cash generated from operations	261
Interest paid	(26)
Taxation paid (Note 4)	(41)
Dividend paid	(60)
Net cash from operating activities	134

Notes:

1 This is simply taken from the income statement for the year.

2 Since there were no disposals, the depreciation charges must be the difference between the start and end of the year's plant and machinery values, adjusted by the cost of any additions.

	£m
Carrying amount at 1 January 2015	325
Additions	67
Depreciation (balancing figure)	(78)
Carrying amount at 31 December 2015	314

3 Interest payable expense must be taken out by adding it back to the profit before taxation figure. We subsequently deduct the cash paid for interest payable during the year. In this case the two figures are identical.

4 Companies pay 50 per cent of their tax during their accounting year and 50 per cent in the following year. Thus the 2015 payment would have been half the tax on the 2014 profit (that is, the figure that would have appeared in the current liabilities at the end of 2014), plus half of the 2015 tax charge (that is, $23 + (^1/_2 \times 36) = 41$).

Blackstone plc
Statement of cash flows for the year ended 31 March 2016

	£m
Cash flows from operating activities	
Profit before taxation (after interest)	
(see Note 1 below)	1,853
Adjustments for:	
Depreciation (Note 2)	1,289
Interest expense (Note 3)	456
	3,598
Increase in inventories (2,410 − 1,209)	(1,201)
Increase in trade receivables (1,173 − 641)	(532)
Increase in trade payables (1,507 − 931)	576
Cash generated from operations	2,441
Interest paid	(456)
Taxation paid (Note 4)	(300)
Dividend paid	(400)
Net cash from operating activities	1,285
Cash flows from investing activities	
Proceeds of disposals	54
Payment to acquire intangible non-current asset	(700)
Payments to acquire property, plant and equipment	(4,578)
Net cash used in investing activities	(5,224)
Cash flows from financing activities	
Bank borrowings	2,000
Net cash from financing activities	2,000
Net decrease in cash and cash equivalents	(1,939)
Cash and cash equivalents at 1 April 2013	
Cash at bank	123
Cash and cash equivalents at 31 March 2014	
Bank overdraft (1,816)	(1,816)

To see how this relates to the cash of the business at the beginning and end of the year, it can be useful to provide a reconciliation as follows:

Analysis of cash and cash equivalents during the year ended 31 March 2016

	£m
Cash and cash equivalents at 1 April 2015	123
Net cash outflow	(1,939)
Cash and cash equivalents at 31 March 2016	1,816

Notes:

1 This is simply taken from the income statement for the year.

2 The full depreciation charge was that stated in Note 2 to the question (£1,251m), plus the deficit on disposal of the non-current assets. According to Note 2, these non-current assets had originally cost £581m and had been depreciated by £489m, that is, a net carrying amount of £92m. They were sold for £54m, leading to a deficit on disposal of £38m. Thus the full depreciation expense for the year was £1,289m (that is, £1,251m + £38m).

3 Interest payable expense must be taken out by adding it back to the profit before taxation figure. We subsequently deduct the cash paid for interest payable during the year. In this case the two figures are identical.

4 Companies pay tax at 50 per cent during their accounting year and the other 50 per cent in the following year. Thus the 2014 payment would have been half the tax on the 2015 profit (that is, the figure that would have appeared in the current liabilities at 31 March 2015), plus half of the 2016 tax charge (that is, $105 + (^1/_2 \times 390) = 300$).

Chapter 6

6.1 Three businesses

A plc operates a supermarket chain. The grocery business is highly competitive and to generate high sales volumes it is usually necessary to accept low operating profit margins. Thus, we can see that the operating profit margin of A plc is the lowest of the three businesses. The inventories' turnover period of supermarket chains also tends to be quite low. They are often very efficient in managing inventories and most supermarket chains have invested heavily in inventories control and logistical systems. The average settlement period for receivables is very low as most sales are for cash. A low inventories turnover period and a low average settlement period for receivables usually mean that the investment in current assets is low. Hence, the current ratio (current assets/current liabilities) is also low.

B plc is the holiday tour operator. We can see that the sales to capital employed ratio is the highest of the three businesses. This is because tour operators do not usually require a large investment of capital: they do not need a large asset base in order to conduct their operations. The inventories turnover period ratio does not apply to B plc. It is a service business that does not hold inventories for resale. We can see that the average settlement period for receivables is low. This may be because customers are invoiced near to the holiday date for any amounts outstanding and must pay before going on holiday. The lack of inventories held and low average settlement period for receivables lead to a very low current ratio.

C plc is the food manufacturing business. We can see that the sales to capital employed ratio is the lowest of the three businesses. This is because manufacturers tend to invest heavily in both current and non-current assets. The inventories turnover period is the highest of the three businesses. Three different kinds of inventories – raw materials, work in progress and finished goods – are held by manufacturers. The average receivables settlement period is also the highest of the three businesses. Manufacturers tend to sell to other businesses rather than to the public and their customers will normally demand credit. At least a one-month credit period for customers is fairly common for manufacturing businesses, although customers may receive a discount for prompt payment. The relatively high investment in inventories and receivables usually results in a high current ratio.

6.2 Amsterdam Ltd and Berlin Ltd

The ratios show that the average settlement period for trade receivables for Amsterdam Ltd is three times that for Berlin Ltd. Berlin Ltd is therefore much quicker in collecting amounts outstanding from customers. However, there is not much difference between the two businesses in the time taken to pay trade payables.

It is interesting to compare the difference in the trade receivables and payables settlement periods for each business. As Amsterdam Ltd allows an average of 63 days' credit to its customers, yet pays suppliers within 50 days, it will require greater investment in working capital than Berlin Ltd, which allows an average of only 21 days to its customers but takes 45 days to pay its suppliers.

Amsterdam Ltd has a much higher gross profit margin than Berlin Ltd. However, the operating profit margin for the two businesses is identical. This suggests that Amsterdam Ltd has much higher overheads (as a percentage of sales revenue) than Berlin Ltd. The average inventories turnover period for Amsterdam Ltd is more than twice that of Berlin Ltd. This may be due to the fact that Amsterdam Ltd maintains a wider range of inventories in an attempt to meet customer requirements. The evidence therefore suggests that Amsterdam Ltd is the one that prides itself on customer service. The higher average settlement period for trade receivables is consistent with a more relaxed attitude to credit collection (thereby maintaining customer goodwill) and the high overheads are consistent with incurring the additional costs of satisfying customers' requirements. Amsterdam Ltd's high inventories levels are consistent with maintaining a wide range of inventories, with the aim of satisfying a range of customer needs.

Berlin Ltd has the characteristics of a more price-competitive business. Its gross profit margin is much lower than that of Amsterdam Ltd, that is, a much lower gross profit for each £1 of sales revenue. However, overheads have been kept low, the effect being that the operating profit margin is the same as Amsterdam Ltd's. The low average inventories turnover period and average settlement period for trade receivables are consistent with a business that wishes to minimise investment in current assets, thereby reducing costs.

6.5 Harridges Ltd

(a)

	Year before last	Last year
ROCE	$\dfrac{310}{1,600} = 19.4\%$	$\dfrac{350}{1,700} = 20.6\%$
ROSF	$\dfrac{155}{1,100} = 14.1\%$	$\dfrac{175}{1,200} = 14.6\%$
Gross profit margin	$\dfrac{1,040}{2,600} = 40\%$	$\dfrac{1,150}{3,500} = 32.9\%$
Operating profit margin	$\dfrac{310}{2,600} = 11.9\%$	$\dfrac{350}{3,500} = 10\%$
Current ratio	$\dfrac{735}{400} = 1.8\%$	$\dfrac{660}{485} = 1.4$
Acid test ratio	$\dfrac{485}{400} = 1.2\%$	$\dfrac{260}{485} = 0.5$
Trade receivables settlement period	$\dfrac{105}{2,600} \times 365 = 15$ days	$\dfrac{145}{3,500} \times 365 = 15$ days
Trade payables settlement period	$\dfrac{300}{1,560^*} \times 365 = 70$ days	$\dfrac{375}{2,350^*} \times 365 = 58$ days
Inventories turnover period	$\dfrac{250}{1,560} \times 365 = 58$ days	$\dfrac{400}{2,350} \times 365 = 62$ days
Gearing ratio	$\dfrac{500}{1,600} = 31.3\%$	$\dfrac{500}{1,700} = 29.4\%$

* Used because the credit purchases figure is not available.

(b) There has been a considerable decline in the gross profit margin during last year. This fact, combined with the increase in sales revenue by more than one-third, suggests that a price-cutting policy has been adopted in an attempt to stimulate sales. The resulting increase in sales revenue, however, has led to only a small improvement in ROCE and ROSF.

Despite a large cut in the gross profit margin, the operating profit margin has fallen by less than 2 per cent. This suggests that overheads have been tightly controlled during last year. Certainly, overheads have not risen in proportion to sales revenue.

The current ratio has fallen and the acid test ratio has fallen by more than half. Even though liquidity ratios are lower in retailing than in manufacturing, the liquidity of the business should now be a cause for concern. However, this may be a passing problem. The business is investing heavily in non-current assets and is relying on internal funds to finance this growth. When this investment ends, the liquidity position may improve quickly.

The trade receivables period has remained unchanged over the two years, and there has been no significant change in the inventories turnover period during last year. The gearing ratio seems quite low and provides no cause for concern given the profitability of the business.

Overall, the business appears to be financially sound. Although there has been rapid growth during last year, there is no real cause for alarm provided that the liquidity of the business can be improved in the near future. In the absence of information concerning share price, it is not possible to say whether an investment should be made.

Chapter 7

7.1 Lombard Ltd

Relevant cost of undertaking the contract is:

	£
Equipment cost	200,000
Component X (20,000 × 4 × £5)	400,000
Any of these components used will need to be replaced.	
Component Y (20,000 × 3 × £8)	480,000
All of the required units will come from inventories and this will be an effective cost of the net realisable value.	
Additional cost (20,000 × £8)	160,000
	1,240,000
Revenue from the contract (20,000 × £80)	1,600,000

Thus, from a purely financial point of view the project is acceptable. (Note that there is no relevant labour cost since the staff concerned will be paid irrespective of whether the contract is undertaken.)

7.4 Products A, B and C

(a) Total time required on cutting machines is

$$(2,500 \times 1.0) + (3,400 \times 1.0) + (5,100 \times 0.5) = 8,450 \text{ hours}$$

Total time available on cutting machines is 5,000 hours. Therefore, this is a limiting factor.

Total time required on assembling machines is

$$(2,500 \times 0.5) + (3,400 \times 1.0) + (5,100 \times 0.5) = 7,200 \text{ hours}$$

Total time available on assembling machines is 8,000 hours. Therefore, this is not a limiting factor.

	A (per unit)	B (per unit)	C (per unit)
Selling price (£)	25	30	18
Variable materials (£)	(12)	(13)	(10)
Variable production cost (£)	(7)	(4)	(3)
Contribution (£)	6	13	5
Time on cutting machines	1.0 hour	1.0 hour	0.5 hour
Contribution per hour on cutting machines (£)	6	13	10
Order of priority	3rd	1st	2nd

Therefore, produce:

3,400 Product B using	3,400 hours
3,200 Product C using	1,600 hours
	5,000 hours

(b) Assuming that the business would make no saving in variable production cost by sub-contracting, it would be worth paying up to the contribution per unit (£5) for Product C, which would therefore be £5 × (5,100−3,200) = £9,500 in total.
    Similarly it would be worth paying up to £6 per unit for Product A – that is, £6 × 2,500 = £15,000 in total.

7.5 Darmor Ltd

(a) Contribution per hour of skilled labour of Product X is:

$$\frac{£(30 - 6 - 2 - 12 - 3)}{^6/_{12}} = £14$$

Given the scarcity of skilled labour, if the management is to be indifferent between the products, the contribution per skilled-labour hour must be the same. Thus for Product Y the selling price must be:

$$£((14 \times (9/12)) + 9 + 4 + 25 + 7) = £55.50$$

(that is, the contribution plus the variable cost), and for Product Z the selling price must be:

$$£((14 \times (3/12)) + 3 + 10 + 14 + 7) = £37.50$$

(b) The business could pay up to £26 an hour (£12 + £14) for additional hours of skilled labour. This is the potential contribution per hour, before taking account of the labour rate of £12 an hour.

Chapter 8

8.1 All three costing techniques are means of deducing the full cost of some activity. The distinction between them lies with the difference in the style of the production of the goods or services involved.

- *Job costing* is used where each unit of output or 'job' differs from other jobs. Because the jobs are not identical, it is not normally helpful to treat them as if they were. This means that costs need to be identified, job by job. For this purpose, costs fall into two categories: direct cost and indirect cost (or overheads).

  Direct cost can be measured directly in respect of the specific job, such as the cost of the labour that was directly applied to it. To this must be added a share of the indirect cost, usually done by taking the total overheads for the period concerned and charging part of them to the job. This is achieved using some measure of the job's size and importance, relative to the other jobs done during the period. Direct labour hours worked on the job is the most commonly used measure of size and/or importance.

  The main problem with job costing tends to be the method of charging indirect cost to jobs. Indirect cost cannot be related directly to jobs, so it must be charged on a basis that is more or less arbitrary. If indirect costs accounted for a small proportion of the total, the arbitrariness of charging them would probably not matter. However, in many cases indirect costs form the majority of total cost, so arbitrariness is a problem.

- *Process costing* is used where all output is of identical units. These can therefore be treated as having identical cost. Sometimes a process-costing approach is taken even where the units of output are not strictly identical, because process costing is much simpler and cheaper to apply than job costing. If users of the cost information are satisfied that treating units as identical when they are not strictly so is accurate enough for their decision-making purposes, the additional cost and effort of job costing are not justified. The cost per unit is found by dividing total costs for the period by the total number of units produced.

  The main problem with process costing is that at the end of any period/beginning of the next period, there will probably be partly completed units of output. An adjustment needs to be made for this work in progress if the resulting figures for cost per unit are not to be distorted.

- *Batch costing* is really an extension of job costing. Batch costing is used where production is in batches. A batch consists of more than one, perhaps many, identical units of output. The units of output differ from one batch to the next. For example, a clothing manufacturing business may produce 500 identical jackets in one batch, followed by a batch of 300 identical skirts.

  Each batch is costed as one job, using a job-costing approach. The full cost of each cost unit is then found by dividing the cost of the batch by the number of cost units in the batch.

  The main problem of batch costing is the same as that of job costing, of which it is an extension. This is the problem of dealing with overheads.

8.2 Pieman Products Ltd

Indirect costs:

	£
Indirect labour	25,000
Depreciation	8,000
Rent	10,000
Heating, lighting and power	5,000
Indirect materials	2,000
Other indirect costs	1,000
Total indirect costs	51,000

This list does not include the direct costs because we shall deal with the direct costs separately.

Probably a direct labour hour basis of charging overheads to jobs is most logical in this case (see below). The direct labour hours are given as 16,000.

Overhead recovery rate per direct labour hour:

$$£51,000/16,000 = £3.1875 \text{ per direct labour hour}$$

Full cost of the trailer:

		£
Direct materials		1,150.00
Direct labour	(250 × (£160,000/16,000))	2,500.00
Indirect costs	(250 × £3.1875)	796.88
Total cost		4,446.88

that is, about £4,450.

Direct labour hours are probably the most logical basis for charging overheads to the job. Those hours may provide the only measurable thing about the job that is a reasonable assessment of the size/complexity/importance of each job relative to the others undertaken. The business's work is probably labour intensive; it is probably difficult to introduce much machine-controlled work into making trailers to individual specifications.

8.4 Moleskin Ltd

(a) Price using absorption costing

Overhead absorption rate = total overheads/total direct labour hours = £280,000/4,000 = £70 per direct labour hour.

	JT101	GR27
	£	£
Direct materials	16.00	15.00
Direct labour	8.00	8.00
Overheads: $^1/_2$ × £70	35.00	35.00
Total cost	59.00	58.00
Mark up at 35%	20.65	20.30
Price per metre	79.65	78.30

(b) **Price using activity-based costing**
Cost driver rates:

Alpha Process	£96,000/480	=	£200 per hour
Omega Process	£44,800/1,280	=	£35 per hour
Set-ups	£42,900/260	=	£165 per set-up
Handling	£45,600/380	=	£120 per movement
Other overheads	£50,700/4,000	=	£12.68 per direct labour hour

Prices for the two products:

		JT101		GR27
		£		£
Direct materials		16.00		16.00
Direct labour		8.00		8.00
Alpha Process	(100 × £200)/1,000	20.00		–
Omega Process		–	(25 × £35)/50	17.50
Set-ups	£165/1,000	0.17	(2 × £165)/50	6.60
Ordering		–	(3 × £90)/50	5.40
Handling	£120/1,000	0.12	(5 × £120)/50	12.00
Other overheads	$\frac{1}{2}$ × £12.68	6.34	$\frac{1}{2}$ × £12.68	6.34
Total cost		50.63		71.84
35% mark-up		17.72		25.14
Price per metre		68.35		96.98

(c) **Points for the management**
- Under the traditional approach, the prices of the two products are quite similar because the direct costs are quite similar, which also leads to a similar allocation of overheads (because these are absorbed on the basis of direct labour hours).
- With ABC, the prices are quite different between the products. This is because the GR27s cause much more overhead cost than the JT101s and ABC reflects this fact.
- Management must seriously consider its pricing policy. If the traditionally-based price is, in fact, the current selling price, the GR27s are earning only a small margin on the ABC cost.
- If the market will not bear a higher price for the GR27s, management may consider dropping them and concentrating its efforts on the JT101s. Projected market demand for the two products will obviously have a major bearing on these considerations.

(d) **Practical problems of using ABC**
- Identifying the cost-driving activities and determining cost-driver rates can be difficult and expensive. It is sometimes necessary to use arbitrary approaches to certain parts of the overheads, as with 'other overheads' in the Joists/Girders example above.
- The costs of introducing ABC may outweigh the benefits.
- Changing the culture necessary to introduce ABC may pose difficulties. There may be resistance to a new approach.
- On a positive note, ABC may have benefits beyond cost determination and pricing. Careful analysis of costs and what drives them can provide a basis for exercising better control over them.

Chapter 9

9.2 Nursing home

(a) The rates per patient for the variable overheads, on the basis of experience during months 1 to 6, are as follows:

Expense	Amount for 2,700 patients £	Amount per patient £
Staffing	59,400	22
Power	27,000	10
Supplies	54,000	20
Other	8,100	3
	148,500	55

Since the expected level of activity for the full year is 6,000, the expected level of activity for the second six months is 3,300 (that is, 6,000 − 2,700).

Thus the budget for the second six months will be:

Variable element:	£	
Staffing	72,600	(3,300 × £22)
Power	33,000	(3,300 × £10)
Supplies	66,000	(3,300 × £20)
Other	9,900	(3,300 × £3)
	181,500	(3,300 × £55)
Fixed element:		
Supervision	60,000	$6/12$ of the annual figure
Depreciation/finance	93,600	ditto
Other	32,400	ditto
	186,000 (per patient = £56.36 (that is, £186,000/3,300))	
Total (second six months)	367,500 (per patient = £111.36 (that is, £56.36 + £55.00))	

(b) For the second six months the actual activity was 3,800 patients. For a valid comparison with the actual outcome, the budget will need to be revised to reflect this activity.

	Actual cost £	Budget (3,800 patients) £	Difference £
Variable element	203,300	209,000 (3,800 × £55)	5,700 (saving)
Fixed element	190,000	186,000	4,000 (overspend)
Total	393,300	395,000	1,700 (saving)

(c) Compared to the budget, there was a saving of nearly 3 per cent on the variable element and an overspend of about 2 per cent on fixed cost. Without further information, it is impossible to deduce much more than this.

The differences between the budget and the actual may be due to assumptions made in framing the budget for 3,300 patients in the second part of the year. There may be some economies of scale in the variable cost; that is, the cost may not be strictly linear. If this were the case, basing a relatively large activity budget on the experience of a relatively small activity period would tend to overstate the large activity budget. The fixed-cost budget was deduced by dividing the budget for 12 months by two. In fact, there could be seasonal factors or inflationary pressures at work that might make such a crude division of the fixed cost element unfair.

9.3 Linpet Ltd

(a) Cash budgets are extremely useful for decision-making purposes. They allow managers to see the likely effect on the cash balance of the plans that they have set in place. Cash is an important asset and it is necessary to ensure that it is properly managed. Failure to do so can have disastrous consequences for the business. Where the cash budget indicates a surplus balance, managers must decide whether this balance should be reinvested in the business or distributed to the owners. Where the cash budget indicates a deficit balance, managers must decide how this deficit should be financed or how it might be avoided.

(b) Cash budget for the six months to 30 November:

	June £	July £	Aug £	Sept £	Oct £	Nov £
Receipts						
Cash sales revenue (Note 1)	4,000	5,500	7,000	8,500	11,000	11,000
Credit sales revenue (Note 2)	–	–	4,000	5,500	7,000	8,500
	4,000	5,500	11,000	14,000	18,000	19,500
Payments						
Purchases (Note 3)	–	29,000	9,250	11,500	13,750	17,500
Overheads	500	500	500	500	650	650
Wages	900	900	900	900	900	900
Commission (Note 4)	–	320	440	560	680	880
Equipment	10,000					7,000
Motor vehicle	6,000					
Leasehold	40,000					
	57,400	30,720	11,090	13,460	15,980	26,930
Cash flow	(53,400)	(25,220)	(90)	540	2,020	(7,430)
Opening balance	60,000	6,600	(18,620)	(18,710)	(18,170)	(16,150)
Closing balance	6,600	(18,620)	(18,710)	(18,170)	(16,150)	(23,580)

Notes:

1 50 per cent of the current month's sales revenue.

2 50 per cent of sales revenue of two months previous.

3 To have sufficient inventories to meet each month's sales will require purchases of 75 per cent of the month's sales inventories figures (25 per cent is profit). In addition, each month the business will buy £1,000 more inventories than it will sell. In June, the business will also buy its initial inventories of £22,000. This will be paid for in the following month. For example, June's purchases will be (75% × £8,000) + £1,000 + £22,000 = £29,000, paid for in July.

4 This is 5 per cent of 80 per cent of the month's sales revenue, paid in the following month. For example, June's commission will be 5% × 80% × £8,000 = £320, payable in July.

9.4 Newtake Records

(a) **Inventories budget for the six months to 30 November:**

	June £000	July £000	Aug £000	Sept £000	Oct £000	Nov £000
Opening balance	112	154	104	48	39	33
Inventories purchased	180	142	94	75	66	57
	292	296	198	123	105	90
Cost of inventories sold (60% sales revenue)	(138)	(192)	(150)	(84)	(72)	(66)
Closing balance	154	104	48	39	33	24

(b) **Cash budget for the period to 30 November:**

	June £000	July £000	Aug £000	Sept £000	Oct £000	Nov £000
Cash receipts						
Sales revenue (Note 1)	227	315	246	138	118	108
Cash payments						
Administration (Note 2)	(40)	(41)	(38)	(33)	(31)	(30)
Goods purchased	(135)	(180)	(142)	(94)	(75)	(66)
Repayments of borrowings	(5)	(5)	(5)	(5)	(5)	(5)
Selling expenses	(22)	(24)	(28)	(26)	(21)	(19)
Tax paid				(22)		
Shop refurbishment	—	(14)	(18)	(6)	—	—
	(202)	(264)	(253)	(164)	(132)	(120)
Cash surplus (deficit)	25	51	(7)	(26)	(14)	(12)
Opening balance	(35)	(10)	41	34	8	(6)
Closing balance	(10)	41	34	8	(6)	(18)

Notes:

1 (50% of the current month's sales revenue) + (97% × 50% of that sales revenue). For example, the June cash receipts = (50% × £230,000) + (97% × 50% × £230,000) = £226,550.

2 The administration expenses figure for the month, *less* £15,000 for depreciation (a non-cash expense).

(c) **Budgeted income statement for the six months ending 30 November**

	£000
Sales revenue	1,170
Cost of goods sold	(702)
Gross profit (40%)	468
Selling expenses	(136)
Admin. expenses	(303)
Credit card charges	(18)
Interest charges	(6)
Profit for the period	5

(d) We are told that the business is required to eliminate the bank overdraft by the end of November. However, the cash budget suggests that this will not be achieved. There is a decline in the overdraft of nearly 50 per cent over the period, but this is not enough and ways must be found to comply with the bank's requirements. It may be possible to delay the refurbishment programme that is included in the forecasts or to obtain an injection of funds from the owners or other investors. It may also be possible to stimulate sales in some way. However, there has been a decline in the sales revenue since the end of July and the November sales revenue is approximately one-third of the July sales revenue. The reasons for this decline should be sought.

The inventories levels will fall below the preferred minimum level for each of the last three months. However, to rectify this situation it will be necessary to purchase more inventories, which will, in turn, exacerbate the cash flow problems of the business.

The budgeted income statement reveals a very low net profit for the period. For every £1 of sales revenue, the business is only managing to generate 0.4p in profit. The business should look carefully at its pricing policies and its overhead expenses. The administration expenses, for example, absorb more than one-quarter of the total sales revenue. Any reduction in overhead expenses will have a beneficial effect on cash flows.

Chapter 10

10.1 Mylo Ltd

(a) The annual depreciation of the two projects is:

$$\text{Project 1: } \frac{(£100,000 - £7,000)}{3} = £31,000$$

$$\text{Project 2: } \frac{(£60,000 - £6,000)}{3} = £18,000$$

Project 1

(i) Net present value

	Year 0 £000	Year 1 £000	Year 2 £000	Year 3 £000
Operating profit (loss)	–	29	(1)	2
Depreciation	–	31	31	31
Capital cost	(100)			
Residual value	–	–	–	7
Net cash flows	(100)	60	30	40
10% discount factor	1.000	0.909	0.826	0.751
Present value	(100.00)	54.54	24.78	30.04
Net present value	9.36	(That is, the sum of the present values for years 0 to 3.)		

(ii) Internal rate of return
   Clearly the IRR lies above 10%; try 15%:

15% discount factor	1.000	0.870	0.756	0.658
Present value	(100.00)	52.20	22.68	26.32
Net present value	1.20			

   Thus the IRR lies a little above 15%, perhaps around 16%.

(iii) Payback period
   To find the payback period, the cumulative cash flows are calculated:

Cumulative cash flows	(100)	(40)	(10)	30

   Thus the payback will occur after 3 years if we assume year-end cash flows.

Project 2

(i) Net present value

	Year 0 £000	Year 1 £000	Year 2 £000	Year 3 £000
Operating profit (loss)	–	18	(2)	4
Depreciation	–	18	18	18
Capital cost	(60)			
Residual value	–	–	–	6
Net cash flows	(60)	36	16	28
10% discount factor	1.000	0.909	0.826	0.751
Present value	(60.00)	32.72	13.22	21.03
Net present value	6.97			

(ii) Internal rate of return
   Clearly the IRR lies above 10%; try 15%:

15% discount factor	1.000	0.870	0.756	0.658
Present value	(60.00)	31.32	12.10	18.42
Net present value	1.84			

   Thus the IRR lies a little above 15%; perhaps around 17%.

(iii) Payback period
   The cumulative cash flows are:

Cumulative cash flows	(60)	(24)	(8)	20

   Thus, the payback will occur after 3 years (assuming year-end cash flows).

(b) Presuming that Mylo Ltd is pursuing a wealth-enhancement objective, Project 1 is preferable since it has the higher NPV. The difference between the two NPVs is not significant, however.

10.2 Newton Electronics Ltd

(a) **Option 1**

	Year 0 £m	Year 1 £m	Year 2 £m	Year 3 £m	Year 4 £m	Year 5 £m
Plant and equipment	(9.0)	–	–	–	–	1.0
Sales revenue	–	24.0	30.8	39.6	26.4	10.0
Variable cost	–	(11.2)	(19.6)	(25.2)	(16.8)	(7.0)
Fixed cost (excl. dep'n)	–	(0.8)	(0.8)	(0.8)	(0.8)	(0.8)
Working capital	(3.0)	–	–	–	–	3.0
Marketing cost	–	(2.0)	(2.0)	(2.0)	(2.0)	(2.0)
Opportunity cost	–	(0.1)	(0.1)	(0.1)	(0.1)	(0.1)
	(12.0)	9.9	8.3	11.5	6.7	4.1
Discount factor 10%	1.000	0.909	0.826	0.751	0.683	0.621
Present value	(12.0)	9.0	6.9	8.6	4.6	2.5
Net present value	19.6	(That is, the sum of the present values for years 0 to 5.)				

Option 2

	Year 0 £m	Year 1 £m	Year 2 £m	Year 3 £m	Year 4 £m	Year 5 £m
Royalties	–	4.4	7.7	9.9	6.6	2.8
Discount factor 10%	1.000	0.909	0.826	0.751	0.683	0.621
Present value	–	4.0	6.4	7.4	4.5	1.7
Net present value	24.0					

Option 3

	Year 0	Year 2
Instalments	12.0	12.0
Discount factor 10%	1.000	0.826
Present value	12.0	9.9
Net present value	21.9	

(b) Before making a final decision, the board should consider the following factors:
- The long-term competitiveness of the business may be affected by the sale of the patents.
- At present, the business is not involved in manufacturing and marketing products. Would a change in direction be desirable?
- The business will probably have to buy in the skills necessary to produce the product itself. This will involve costs, and problems will be incurred. Has this been taken into account?
- How accurate are the forecasts made and how valid are the assumptions on which they are based?

(c) Option 2 has the highest net present value and is, theoretically, the most attractive to shareholders. However, the points raised in (b) above need to be taken into account.

10.3 Chesterfield Wanderers

(a) Player option

Years	0 £000	1 £000	2 £000	3 £000	4 £000	5 £000
Sale of player	2,200	–	–	–	–	1,000
Purchase of Bazza	(10,000)	–	–	–	–	–
Sponsorship and so on	–	1,200	1,200	1,200	1,200	1,200
Gate receipts	–	2,500	1,300	1,300	1,300	1,300
Salaries paid	–	(800)	(800)	(800)	(800)	(1,200)
Salaries saved	–	400	400	400	400	600
	(7,800)	3,300	2,100	2,100	2,100	2,900
Discount factor 10%	1.000	0.909	0.826	0.751	0.683	0.621
Present values	(7,800)	3,000	1,735	1,577	1,434	1,801
NPV	1,747					

Ground improvement option

Years	1 £000	2 £000	3 £000	4 £000	5 £000
Ground improvements	(10,000)	–	–	–	–
Increased gate receipts	(1,800)	4,400	4,400	4,400	4,400
	(11,800)	4,400	4,400	4,400	4,400
Discount factor 10%	0.909	0.826	0.751	0.683	0.621
Present values	(10,726)	3,634	3,304	3,005	2,732
NPV	1,949				

(b) The ground improvement option provides the higher NPV and is therefore the preferable option, based on the objective of shareholder wealth maximisation.

(c) A professional football club may not wish to pursue an objective of shareholder wealth maximisation. It may prefer to invest in quality players in an attempt to enjoy future sporting success. If this is the case, the NPV approach will be less appropriate because the club is not pursuing a strict wealth-related objective.

Chapter 11

11.1 Financing issues

(a) The main benefits of leasing include ease of borrowing, reasonable cost, flexibility and avoidance of large cash outflows (which normally occurs where an asset is purchased). These points are expanded upon in the chapter.

(b) The main benefits of using retained profits include no dilution of control, no share issue costs, no delay in receiving funds and the possible tax benefits of capital appreciation over dividends. These points are expanded upon in the chapter.

(c) A business may decide to repay a loan earlier than required for various reasons including:

- A fall in interest rates may make the existing loan interest rates higher than current loan interest rates. Thus, the business may decide to repay the existing loan using finance from a cheaper loan.
- A rise in interest rates or changes in taxation policy may make loan financing more expensive than other forms of financing. This may make the business decide to repay the loan using another form of finance.
- The business may have surplus cash and may have no other profitable uses for the cash.
- The business may wish to reduce the level of financial risk by reducing the level of gearing.

11.2 H. Brown (Portsmouth) Ltd

(a) The main factors to take into account are:

- *Risk.* If a business borrows, there is a risk that at the maturity date for the repayment of the funds the business will not have sufficient funds to repay the amount owing and will be unable to find a suitable form of replacement borrowing. With short-term borrowings, the maturity dates will arrive more quickly and the type of risk outlined will occur at more frequent intervals.
- *Matching.* A business may wish to match the life of an asset with the maturity date of the borrowing. In other words, long-term assets will be purchased with long-term borrowed funds. A certain level of current assets, which form part of the long-term asset base of the business, may also be funded by long-term borrowing. Those current assets that fluctuate owing to seasonality and so on will be funded by short-term borrowing. This approach to funding assets will help reduce risks for the business.
- *Cost.* Interest rates for long-term borrowings may be higher than for short-term ones as investors may seek extra compensation for having their funds locked up for a long period. However, issue costs may be higher for short-term borrowings as there will be a need to refund at more frequent intervals.
- *Flexibility.* Short-term borrowings may be more flexible. It may be difficult to repay long-term ones before the maturity period.

(b) When deciding to grant a loan, a lender should consider the following factors:

- security;
- purpose of the loan;
- ability of the borrower to repay;
- loan period;
- availability of funds; and
- character and integrity of the senior managers.

(c) Loan conditions may include

- the need to obtain permission before issuing further loans;
- the need to maintain a certain level of liquidity during the loan period; and
- a restriction on the level of dividends and directors' pay.

11.3 Devonian plc

(a) (i) *Ex-rights price*

	£
5 original shares @ £2.10 per share	10.50
1 rights share @ £1.80	1.80
	12.30
Theoretical ex-rights price (£12.30/6)	£2.05

(ii) *Value of rights*

	£
Value of a share after the rights issue	2.05
Cost of a rights share	1.80
Value of rights	0.25
Value of rights attached to each original share = £0.25/5 =	£0.05

(b) (i) *Share price in one year's time*

(1) *Rights issue*

We must first calculate the existing P/E ratio in order to determine the share price at the end of next year. This can be done as follows:

	£m
Operating profit (this year)	40.0
Taxation (30%)	(12.0)
Profit for the year (available to shareholders)	28.0
Earnings per share (EPS) (£28.0m/200m)	= £0.14
P/E ratio	$= \dfrac{\text{Share price}}{\text{EPS}}$
	= £2.10/£0.14
	= 15 times

	£m
Operating profit (next year)	50.0
Taxation (30%)	(15.0)
Profit for the year (available to ordinary shareholders)	35.0
Earnings per share (£35m/240m)	= £0.146
Share price (end of next year)	= EPS × P/E ratio
	= £0.146 × 15
	= £2.19

(ii) Borrowing

	£m
Operating profit (next year)	50.0
Interest payable (£72m @ 10%)	(7.2)
	42.8
Taxation (30%)	(12.8)
Profit for the year (available to ordinary shareholders)	30.0
Earnings per share (£30m/200m)	= £0.15
Share price (end of next year)	= EPS × P/E ratio
	= £0.15 × 13.5
	= £2.03

These calculations reveal that, by the end of next year, the share price is expected to rise by more than 4 per cent above the current share price if a rights issue is made, whereas the share price will fall by more than 3 per cent if the business borrows the money. Given the additional financial risks attached to borrowing, it seems that a rights issue offers the better option – at least in the short term.

(c) By issuing rights shares at a discount, shareholders are encouraged to either take up the shares or to sell the right to someone that will. Failure to do one of these will lead to a loss of wealth for the shareholder. (Since the discount offered on rights shares does not represent a real bonus to the shareholders, it can be quite large.)

(d) The price at which rights issues are made is not normally critical. It should, however, be low enough to ensure that, between setting the rights price and the date of the rights issue, the market price of existing shares will not fall below the rights issue price.

Chapter 12

12.2 Hercules Wholesalers Ltd

(a) The business is probably concerned about its liquidity position because:
- it has a substantial overdraft, which together with its non-current borrowings means that it has borrowed an amount roughly equal to its equity (according to statement of financial position values);
- it has increased its investment in inventories during the past year (as shown by the income statement); and
- it has a low current ratio of 1.1:1 (that is, 306/285) and a low acid-test ratio of 0.6:1 (that is, 162/285).

(b) The operating cash cycle can be calculated as follows:

	Number of days

Average inventories turnover period:

$$\frac{[(\text{Opening inventories} + \text{Closing inventories})/2] \times 365}{\text{Cost of inventories}} = \frac{[(125 + 143/2)] \times 365}{323} = 151$$

Add Average settlement period for trade receivables:

$$\frac{\text{Trade receivables} \times 365}{\text{Credit sales revenue}} = \frac{163}{452} \times 365 \qquad\qquad = \underline{132}$$

$$283$$

Less Average settlement period for trade payables:

$$\frac{\text{Trade payables} \times 365}{\text{Credit purchases}} = \frac{145}{341} \times 365 \qquad\qquad = \underline{155}$$

Operating cash cycle (days) $\qquad\qquad \underline{128}$

(c) The business can reduce the operating cash cycle in a number of ways. The average inventories turnover period seems quite long. At present, average inventories held represent about five months' inventories usage. Reducing the level of inventories held can reduce this period. Similarly, the average settlement period for receivables seems long at more than four months' sales revenue. Imposing tighter credit control, offering discounts, charging interest on overdue accounts and so on may reduce this. However, any policy decisions concerning inventories and receivables must take account of current trading conditions.

Extending the period of credit taken to pay suppliers would also reduce the operating cash cycle. For the reasons mentioned in the chapter, however, this option must be given careful consideration.

12.4 Mayo Computers Ltd

New proposals from credit control department

	£000	£000
Current level of investment in receivables		
(£20m × (60/365))		3,288
Proposed level of investment in receivables		
((£20m × 60%) × (30/365))	(986)	
((£20m × 40%) × (50/365))	(1,096)	(2,082)
Reduction in level of investment		1,206

The reduction in overdraft interest as a result of the reduction in the level of investment will be £1,206,000 × 14% = £169,000.

	£000	£000
Cost of cash discounts offered (£20m × 60% × 2.5%)		300
Additional cost of credit administration		20
		320
Bad debt savings	(100)	
Interest charge savings (see above)	(169)	(269)
Net cost of policy each year		51

These calculations show that the business would incur additional annual cost if it implemented this proposal. It would therefore be cheaper to stay with the existing credit policy.

12.5 Boswell Enterprises Ltd

(a)

	Current policy		New policy	
	£000	£000	£000	£000
Trade receivables				
[(£3m × 1/12 × 30%) + (£3m × 2/12 × 70%)]		425.0		
[(£3.15m × 1/12 × 60%) + (£3.15m × 2/12 × 40%)]				367.5
Inventories				
{[£3m − (£3m × 20%)] × 3/12}		600.0		
{[£3.15m − (£3.15m × 20%)] × 3/12}				630.0
Cash (fixed)		140.0		140.0
		1,165.0		1,137.5
Trade payables				
[£3m − (£3m × 20%)] × 2/12]	(400.0)			
{[£3.15m − (£3.15m × 20%)] × 2/12}			(420.0)	
Accrued variable expenses				
[£3m × 1/12 × 10%]	(25.0)			
[£3.15m × 1/12 × 10%]			(26.3)	
Accrued fixed expenses	(15.0)	(440.0)	(15.0)	(461.3)
Investment in working capital		725.0		676.2

(b) The expected profit for the year

	Current policy		New policy	
	£000	£000	£000	£000
Sales revenue		3,000.0		3,150.0
Cost of goods sold		(2,400.0)		(2,520.0)
Gross profit (20%)		600.0		630.0
Variable expenses (10%)	(300.0)		(315.0)	
Fixed expenses	(180.0)		(180.0)	
Discounts (£3.15m × 60% × 2.5%)	–	(480.0)	(47.3)	(542.3)
Profit for the year		120.0		87.7

(c) Under the proposed policy we can see that the investment in working capital will be slightly lower than under the current policy. However, profits will be substantially lower as a result of offering discounts. The increase in sales revenue resulting from the discounts will not be sufficient to offset the additional cost of making the discounts to customers. It seems that the business should, therefore, stick with its current policy.

Appendix E
PRESENT VALUE TABLE

Present value of £1, that is, $1/(1 + r)^n$

where r = discount rate
n = number of periods unitl payment

	Discount rates (r)										
Periods (n)	1%	2%	3%	4%	5%	6%	7%	8%	9%	10%	
1	0.990	0.980	0.971	0.962	0.952	0.943	0.935	0.926	0.917	0.909	1
2	0.980	0.961	0.943	0.925	0.907	0.890	0.873	0.857	0.842	0.826	2
3	0.971	0.942	0.915	0.889	0.864	0.840	0.816	0.794	0.772	0.751	3
4	0.961	0.924	0.888	0.855	0.823	0.792	0.763	0.735	0.708	0.683	4
5	0.951	0.906	0.863	0.822	0.784	0.747	0.713	0.681	0.650	0.621	5
6	0.942	0.888	0.837	0.790	0.746	0.705	0.666	0.630	0.596	0.564	6
7	0.933	0.871	0.813	0.760	0.711	0.665	0.623	0.583	0.547	0.513	7
8	0.923	0.853	0.789	0.731	0.677	0.627	0.582	0.540	0.502	0.467	8
9	0.914	0.837	0.766	0.703	0.645	0.592	0.544	0.500	0.460	0.424	9
10	0.905	0.820	0.744	0.676	0.614	0.558	0.508	0.463	0.422	0.386	10
11	0.896	0.804	0.722	0.650	0.585	0.527	0.475	0.429	0.388	0.350	11
12	0.887	0.788	0.701	0.625	0.557	0.497	0.444	0.397	0.356	0.319	12
13	0.879	0.773	0.681	0.601	0.530	0.469	0.415	0.368	0.326	0.290	13
14	0.870	0.758	0.661	0.577	0.505	0.442	0.388	0.340	0.299	0.263	14
15	0.861	0.743	0.642	0.555	0.481	0.417	0.362	0.315	0.275	0.239	15

	Discount rates (r)										
Periods (n)	11%	12%	13%	14%	15%	16%	17%	18%	19%	20%	
1	0.901	0.893	0.885	0.877	0.870	0.862	0.855	0.847	0.840	0.833	1
2	0.812	0.797	0.783	0.769	0.756	0.743	0.731	0.718	0.706	0.694	2
3	0.731	0.712	0.693	0.675	0.658	0.641	0.624	0.609	0.593	0.579	3
4	0.659	0.636	0.613	0.592	0.572	0.552	0.534	0.516	0.499	0.482	4
5	0.593	0.567	0.543	0.519	0.497	0.476	0.456	0.437	0.419	0.402	5
6	0.535	0.507	0.480	0.456	0.432	0.410	0.390	0.370	0.352	0.335	6
7	0.482	0.452	0.425	0.400	0.376	0.354	0.333	0.314	0.296	0.279	7
8	0.434	0.404	0.376	0.351	0.327	0.305	0.285	0.266	0.249	0.233	8
9	0.391	0.361	0.333	0.308	0.284	0.263	0.243	0.225	0.209	0.194	9
10	0.352	0.322	0.295	0.270	0.247	0.227	0.208	0.191	0.176	0.162	10
11	0.317	0.287	0.261	0.237	0.215	0.195	0.178	0.162	0.148	0.135	11
12	0.286	0.257	0.231	0.208	0.187	0.168	0.152	0.137	0.124	0.112	12
13	0.258	0.229	0.204	0.182	0.163	0.145	0.130	0.116	0.104	0.093	13
14	0.232	0.205	0.181	0.160	0.141	0.125	0.111	0.099	0.088	0.078	14
15	0.209	0.183	0.160	0.140	0.123	0.108	0.095	0.084	0.074	0.065	15

					Discount rates (r)						
Periods (n)	21%	22%	23%	24%	25%	26%	27%	28%	29%	30%	
1	0.826	0.820	0.813	0.806	0.800	0.794	0.787	0.781	0.775	0.769	1
2	0.683	0.672	0.661	0.650	0.640	0.630	0.620	0.610	0.601	0.592	2
3	0.564	0.551	0.537	0.524	0.512	0.500	0.488	0.477	0.466	0.455	3
4	0.467	0.451	0.437	0.423	0.410	0.397	0.384	0.373	0.361	0.350	4
5	0.386	0.370	0.355	0.341	0.328	0.315	0.303	0.291	0.280	0.269	5
6	0.319	0.303	0.289	0.275	0.262	0.250	0.238	0.277	0.217	0.207	6
7	0.263	0.249	0.235	0.222	0.210	0.198	0.188	0.178	0.168	0.159	7
8	0.218	0.204	0.191	0.179	0.168	0.157	0.148	0.139	0.130	0.123	8
9	0.180	0.167	0.155	0.144	0.134	0.125	0.116	0.108	0.101	0.094	9
10	0.149	0.137	0.126	0.116	0.107	0.099	0.092	0.085	0.078	0.073	10
11	0.123	0.112	0.103	0.094	0.086	0.079	0.072	0.066	0.061	0.056	11
12	0.102	0.092	0.083	0.076	0.069	0.062	0.057	0.052	0.047	0.043	12
13	0.084	0.075	0.068	0.061	0.055	0.050	0.045	0.040	0.037	0.033	13
14	0.069	0.062	0.055	0.049	0.044	0.039	0.035	0.032	0.028	0.025	14
15	0.057	0.051	0.045	0.040	0.035	0.031	0.028	0.025	0.022	0.020	15

Index

Note: Page numbers in **bold** indicate highlighted key terms and the location of their glossary definitions.